The Trains We Rode

The Trains We Rode

Lucius Beebe & Charles Clegg

PROMONTORY
PRESS

NEW YORK

THE FRONTISPIECE

In the year 1900 which this painting by Howard Fogg depicts, Boston's South Station was only two years old, but *The Fall River Boat Train* was already the longest established run in the United States. With so heavy a consist that two of the New York, New Haven & Hartford's fine 4-4-0s are required to wheel it over the original line of the Old Colony Railroad, its cars are filled with consequential names of the great world bound for New York via the Fall River Line's historic night boat down Long Island Sound. Conductor of the train is, of course, Captain Asa Porter, most famous of his calling at that time and as much an institution as the Fall River Boat itself.

Published in 1990 by

Promontory Press
A division of LDAP, Inc.
166 Fifth Avenue
New York, NY 10010

Promontory Press is a registered trademark of LDAP, Inc.
Published by arrangement with Howell-North-Darwin-Superior.

Library of Congress Catalog Card Number: 90-61899

ISBN: 0-88394-081-7

Printed in the United States of America.

Acknowledgments

FOR GENEROUS and interested assistance in the preparation of this book the authors are indebted to a variety of custodians of the railroad past and of its legend, folklore and iconography and they, the authors, feel that the indebtedness is not theirs alone but that it extends to all readers, present and in the future, who may take pleasure or instruction in the field which has been their purview. As the trustees and custodians of whatever obligation may be felt by future students of the railroad theme, they thank Everett De Golyer of the De Golyer Foundation of Dallas, Gerald Best, Arthur D. Dubin and Alfred W. Johnson, regional directors of the Railway and Locomotive Historical Society, Mrs. Alys Freeze of the Western Collection, Denver Public Library, John H. White, Jr., Curator of Land Transport of the Smithsonian Institution, Mrs. Mary B. Gifford of the Fall River Historical Society, Grant R. Bedford of the Henry Morrison Flagler Museum of Palm Beach, Bruce Le Roy of the Washington State Historical Society, Paul A. Dowell, Station Master, The Union Terminal, Washington, D. C., Suzanne T. Cooper of the Library of Congress, Bradley Smith of the Shelburne Museum, Shelburne, Vermont, H. F. Heinkel of the architectural firm of Graham, Anderson, Probst & White of Chicago, George A. Hough, Jr. of *The Falmouth* (Mass.) *Enterprise*, Henry Beetle Hough of *The Vineyard Gazette*, Fifi Booth of *Life*, Kathleen Pierson of the State Historical Society of Colorado, James Shea and George Kraus, of the Southern Pacific Historical Collection, Mercer Sullivan of Kaufmann & Fabry, H. W. Pontin of Rail Photo Service, Ann Kuss of the New York Central Historical Collection, G. E. Payne and Craig Taylor, of the Pennsylvania Railroad Archives, Victor O. Jones of *The Boston Globe*, Amos Hewitt, The Bostonian Society, The New Bedford Historical Society, The Railway & Locomotive Historical Society of Baker Library, Harvard University, and the Valentine Museum of Richmond, Virginia. Private individuals who have opened their collections and files of their own negatives to us include Bernard Corbin, Hugh M. Comer, Douglas C. Wornom, Richard H. Kindig, Robert Le Massena, Richard Cook, W. G. Landon, Otto Perry, Fred Jukes, A. E. Brown, David Plowden, O. Winston Link, Jim Shaughnessy, Roger William McAdam, Kenneth Nims, Paul Stringham, Dr. Philip R. Hastings, Henry R. Griffiths, Jr., John Barriger, Dudley Stickles, Jim Ady, G. B. Abdill, Donald Duke, James M. Morley, Roland Petray, Herb Arey, and Oliver Jensen.

In the Golden Age of

Railroad Travel

The Steamcars Were An

Extension of the

Amenities of

De Luxe Hotel Living

Table of Contents

Introduction

THE HOLD UPON the general imagination enjoyed by the mystique of the grand hotels of the world is at once well established and authenticated by the books that have been written about them. The Paris Ritz, the Savoy in London, the once legendary Adlon in Berlin, the historic Palace in San Francisco, the New York Plaza and Ritz Carlton all enjoy bibliographies devoted to the chronicle of their wonderments ranging from monographs to full dress court portraits. An only slightly less radiant press has been enjoyed by such fabled caravansaries as Shepheard's in Cairo, the Broadmoor at Colorado Springs, the Brown Palace in Denver, Raffles in Singapore and Parker's in School Street, Boston.

Perhaps the most favored of all hotels in the field of innkeeping biography is The Savoy which has been the recipient of no fewer than three full length histories, one of them by Arnold Bennett, and a considerable multiplicity of less definitive studies, all of them perfumed with adulation and upholstered in the velvet of success. Its veriest mention, as a result, has come to reek of monocles and marahajahs, liveried house footmen, Bentley town cars and ortolans in aspic.

For some not immediately apparent reason the mystique of the great name trains of the world, while perhaps even more compulsive in its hold upon the imagination of their partisans, partakes of a more eclectic quality. Their bibliography is less extensive although often running to greater intensity of admiration and far greater expense and elaboration of format. Only two American name trains, *The Twentieth Century Limited* and *The Overland Limited* to date enjoy monographic immortality in hard covers, although more inclusive coverage has been accorded the era of Pullman and Wagner Palace Cars and the classic name trains of the age of steam.

And, yet, it will be apparent to reflective intelligence that the trains we rode in the *belle epoque* of continental surface travel in the United States were but an extension of the luxury, decor and facilities that were part of the hotels which were, in effect, their terminals or junction points. Patrons taking passage on the *Broadway Limited* might well be checking out of the Bellevue Stratford in Philadelphia en route to the Blackstone in Chicago. Regulars at the St. Regis in New York came to regard *The Century* or *Commodore Vanderbilt* as a hotel service concerned for getting them to The Palace in San Francisco with stopover privileges en route to lunch at the Pump Room in Chicago. From the Pump Room to Chasen's in Los Angeles was made acceptable through the combined agencies of the Atchison, Topeka & Santa Fe Railroad and the Fred Harvey cuisine aboard *The Chief* and *Super Chief*. A traveler bound for the St. Charles in New Orleans made the transition from the Ambassador in Chicago via the Illinois Central's incomparable *Panama Limited* and in doing so he had a gastronomic preview of dinner at Antoine's and breakfast at Brennan's.

Other runs took voyagers to destinations no less august. *The Florida Special* over the rails of the Atlantic Coast Line and Florida East Coast was, in effect, a factual and explicit extension of the Royal Poinciana Hotel at Palm Beach which was owned by the latter carrier and whose patrons were set down on its private house tracks after crossing the Flagler Trestle from West Palm Beach. Patrons of the Southern Pacific's magnificent Del Monte Hotel at Monterey got there aboard the Southern Pacific's de luxe train of the identical name. The vast resort hotels of Pasadena, Phoenix, Tucson and Los Angeles that came into emergent being in the nineties were predicated on the Pullmans of the Santa Fe whose *California Limited* paused, conveniently, under the very porte cochère of the Green Hotel at Pasadena.

Everywhere in America in the age of Pullman Standard and steam motive power the name trains of the great carriers were part of the pattern and fabric of the grand hotels which were the crowning glory of a rich and ostentatious era. They partook of the same overtones of luxury, served the same clientele and assumed the cachet of individual character that became associated with the hotels to which passengers betook themselves by omnibus, auto taxi or Parmalee Transfer on arrival.

In some instances, in an age when hotels were as famous for the personalities of their managers or owners as they were for their food or landscaping, railroad travelers patronized trains that were celebrated for their conductors or their dining car stewards. Ardent partisans of the Grand Union Hotel in New York were attracted by the wit and worldliness of its proprietor and stayed not at a Forty-second Street address but with Simeon Ford, a national celebrity in his own right. Regulars at the Waldorf Astoria regarded themselves as the guests of George Boldt, the manager, who only permitted them to pay as a matter of whim.

In much the same spirit passengers never spoke of the Fall River Line Boat Train as such because it was known all over the world as "Mr. Porter's Train" for its punctilious and bearded train captain Asa Porter. Regulars aboard the Milwaukee's *Pioneer Limited* rode it to bask in the radiant geniality of Dan Healy, a dining car steward whose fame in his time topped that of presidents and prime ministers.

In the golden noontide of their destinies the great name trains of the United States enjoyed the envy and admiration of the entire world of travel. Partisans of Cunard or North German Lloyd or P & O might claim the supremacy of ocean luxury, speed and convenience for the great maritime companies of England or Germany without fear of American contradiction. But in the realm of land transport the American railroads and the name trains that were their pride feared no competition. True, some of the amenities of sophistication were lacking that characterized the Grand European Expresses and the *voitures* of The International Sleeping Car Company of monocled George Nagelmackers. Nobody dressed for dinner even aboard the Santa Fe *de Luxe* as they did en route to Monte Carlo on *The Blue Train* or *The Orient Express,* nor was a chef from the service of the King of Spain in charge of the galley of *The Century* as was the case aboard *The St. Petersburg-Vienna-Nice-Cannes Express,* a conveyance whose very title was overwhelming. Nor was any American limited so long on the way between terminals as to make a gymnasium advisable as it was aboard the *Siberian Express* whose schedule between Western Europe and Vladivostok took rather more than a fortnight.

But the most superficial exploration of the record of Pullman travel in the United States in the period from 1890 to 1941 when its facade of luxury began to crumble under the impact of war, would demonstrate that life aboard the cars could be, for the affluent, which included the larger part of American society, very stylish indeed. Aboard the private cars of the truly rich which, for five or six decades, were the ultimate in status symbols, travel was downright sumptuous, but even a Charles Schwab or Henry Huntington, surrounded by their own servants in settings of palatial opulence and drinking vintages from their own cellars established no very great superiority over the patrons of *The Century, The Orange Blossom Special, The Sunset Limited* or *The Yankee Clipper.*

Consider briefly the qualifications for prestige of the aforementioned *de Luxe* which the Santa Fe established on a once-a-week run between Chicago and Southern California in 1911. Here was a truly limited train for the reason that its assigned equipment, which never exceeded six Pullmans, could accommodate no more than sixty patrons. Its dining car, which perhaps enjoyed the ultimate excellence of the Fred Harvey tradition, had the first air conditioning of any train and a menu replete with culinary devisings that would have credited the Ritz Carlton which opened its doors the same year in New York. An extra fare of $25 was charged, perhaps the equivalent of four or five times that sum in today's currency. While open sections were available in the observation car, only staterooms and drawing rooms rode the other three Pullman sleeping cars, and there was the full complement of services of the period including barber, valet, lady's maid, manicurist, librarian and barman. Pigskin wallets suitably engrossed with the train's name in gold were presented to gentlemen passengers, at least the first year of operation, and at the California border, westbound, uniformed pages boarded the cars with expensive corsages for each woman passenger.

Or give thought to the Great Northern's *Oriental Limited* from Chicago to Puget Sound where the lounge steward, as the cars threaded the wastelands of the Dakotas, every afternoon at five served tea from a silver service followed by a retinue of uniformed maids with small cakes and watercress sandwiches in a scene straight out of the lobby of Brown's Hotel, Dover Street, London.

Or let your attentions briefly dwell on the Florida East Coast's *Florida Special* which carried, among others, Otto Kahn, E. T. Stotesbury, Clarence Mackay and Addison Mizner to Florida resorts and was the only other train beside *The Twentieth Century Limited* to lay a red carpet down the platform at its Miami terminal. *The Special's* stationery was engrossed with the train name by Tiffany and the management, knowing that their patronage derived from the elderly well-to-do, peopled their promotional photographs with dowager types and fiduciary-looking old sirs to reassure their patrons of the train's decorum and social standing. To offset any implication of stuffiness, *The Special* also carried a Hawaiian string quartet festooned in leis which strummed behind potted palms in the lounge car at dinner hour just as the orchestra did at the Ritz Carlton in Madison Avenue.

The list of cultural luxury amenities aboard the cars of name trains is endless: free after dinner mints and chocolates with demitasse on *The Broadway*, silver finger bowls with lemon scented warm water aboard the *Golden State,* the well stocked library cars of the Santa Fe which started running in *The California Limited* in the nineties and continued until the first *Chief* in the late twenties; the executive suites with shower baths of their own aboard the *Broadway* and the Southern Railway's *Crescent Limited,* the King's Dinner featured on the *Panama Limited* with five luxury courses of Illinois Central Creole food and appropriate wines and liqueurs at a price tab of $10, the double Martinis that were featured on the Union Pacific-Southern Pacific *Forty-niner* of fragrant memory, the twenty name brands of Bourbon whisky alone available at the largest stand-up bar of all on the aforementioned *Panama Limited,* the specially assigned contact men and social arbiters who once handled all name celebrities traveling on *The Century* and *Commodore Vanderbilt* and were as well versed in the protocol of formal and professional society as any hotel receptionist at the St. Regis or Ambassador.

The list is endless but the random examples cited here are sufficient to support the thesis that the name train of the great years of railroading was, in actual fact, an extension of the de luxe hotels from which so much of its patronage derived. The whims, crotchets and eccentricities of prominent travelers were humored and their prejudices tabulated in much the same way the gastronomic preferences of its established patrons are card indexed at the Colony Restaurant or in the retentive memory of head waiters everywhere.

Crises and contretemps which are the essence of the management of grand hotels were shared in full measure by the proprietors of name trains. Forgotten silk hats were retrieved for absent minded diplomatists, birthday surprises were arranged for notables who might well have preferred to forget the occasion altogether, toilet articles were forthcoming for negligent packers without reference to the handy corner drugstore and corps of eager bellmen available to static hoteliers.

The role of the railroad as the actual proprietor and operator of conventional hotels formally emplaced at vantage points in the American landscape has been intentionally avoided in this brief enquiry into the function of the carriers as mobile hoteliers because more consideration of this aspect of their social economy will be accorded at an appropriate place. The Santa Fe, Florida East Coast, Southern Pacific, Chesapeake & Ohio, Denver & Rio Grande Western, and perhaps others, were all, at varying times and places, established in the capacity of operating resort hotels, many of them looming large in the annals of the affluent society.

The purview of this brief essay on the folklore of innkeeping on wheels has been restricted to the Pullmans that went from here to there and had no permanent address. That the name trains of a golden age were indeed one with its grand hotels is an inescapable conclusion.

Virginia City
1965

LUCIUS BEEBE
CHARLES CLEGG

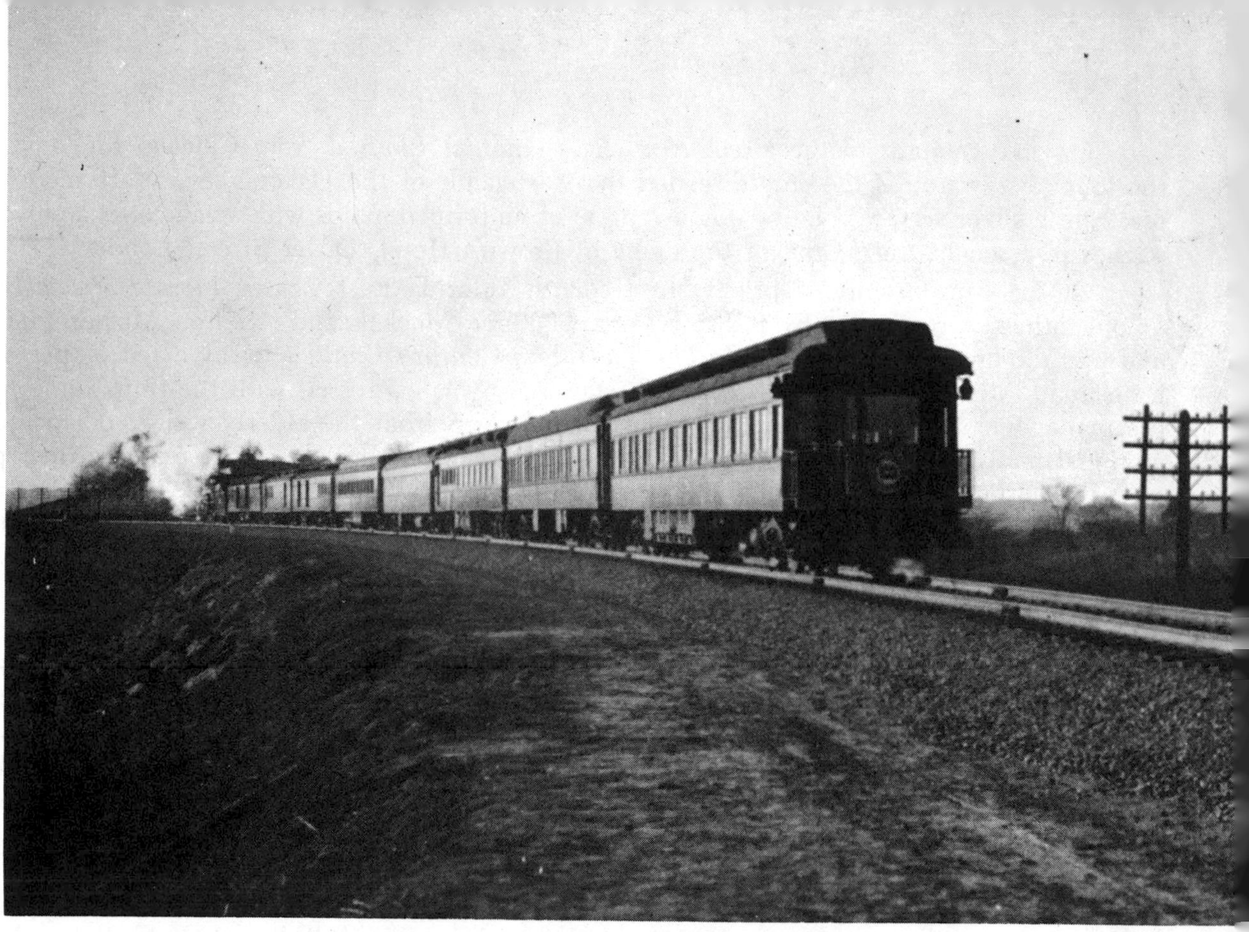

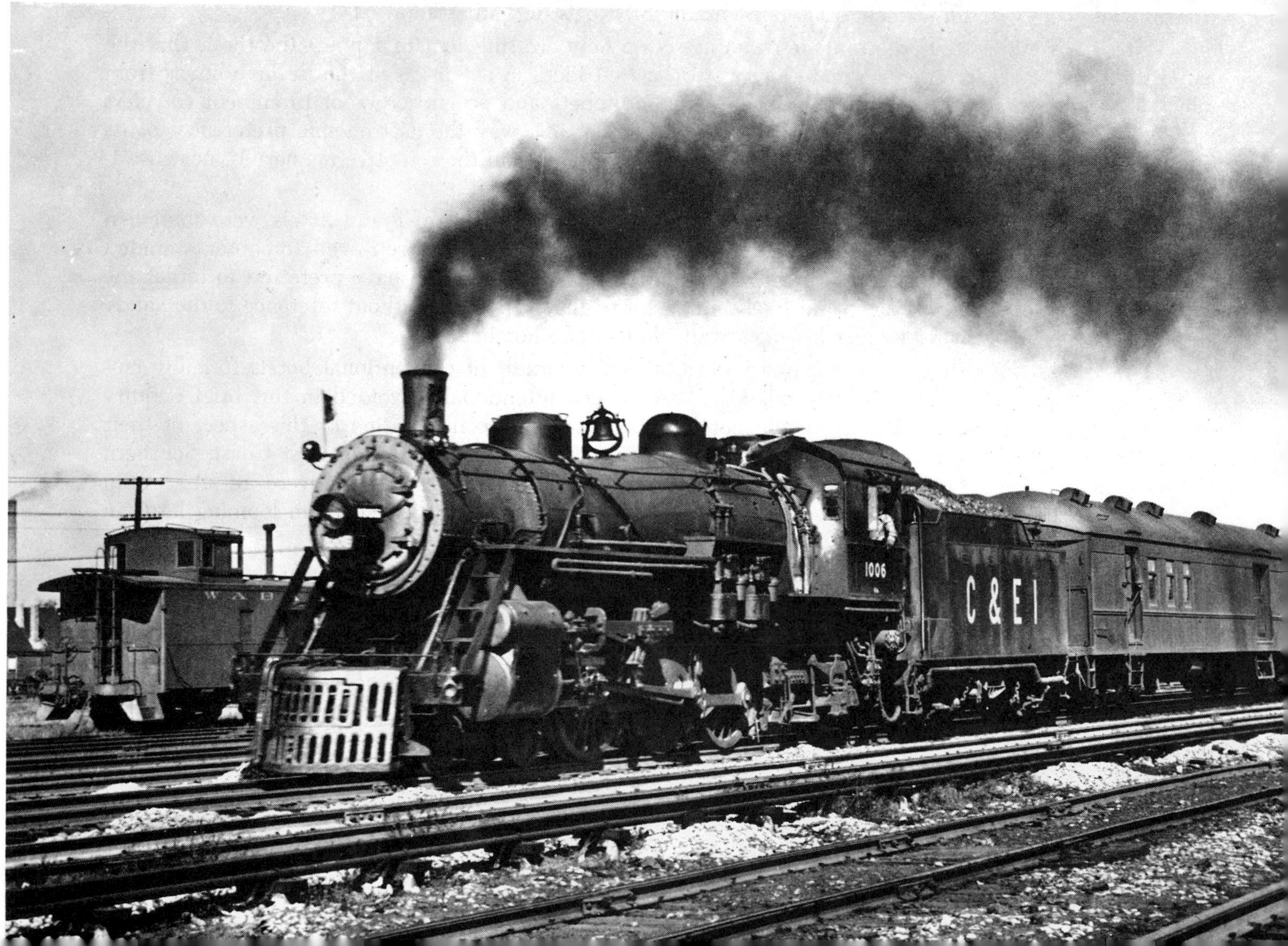
1006
C & E I

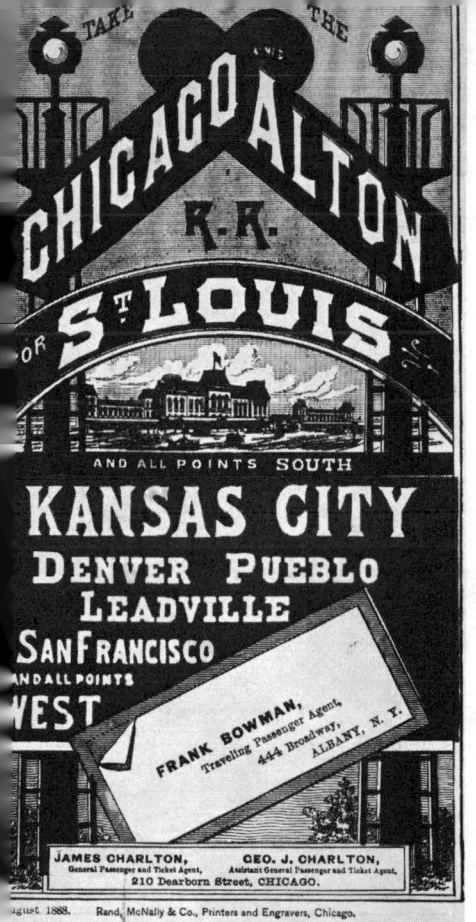

Cutthroat The Competition Through The Illinois Cornfields And Over Storied Lines

THROUGHOUT THE TWENTIES and thirties no medium length intercity run with the possible exception of the Chicago-Twin Cities traffic attracted and suffered from the direct competition of carrier services that flourished between Chicago and St. Louis. Four mainline operations, the Chicago & Alton, the Chicago & Eastern Illinois, the Wabash and the Illinois Central ran a vast competitive multiplicity of varnish trains over only slightly divergent routes, some of them all-Pullman, at all hours of the day and night and, for a time, a fifth railroad, the Mobile & Ohio, ran its *Gulf Coast Special* via St. Louis on its somewhat wayward run from Chicago to Mobile. Every type of accommodation was available; every variety of scenery within the limits of the Southern Illinois landscape was on tap with a wide range of cuisines and such amenities as valet service and midnight suppers available to travelers over routes that in no case were more than 300 miles long. Tops in elegance were probably the Alton's Trains No. 7 and 8, *The Midnight Special,* a non-stop, all-Pullman sleeping car run with a de luxe lounge car and drawing room observation car in addition to single room overnight sleepers. Equally voluptuous was the Illinois Central's sleeper hop, *The Diamond,* which provided valet service, the then new and startling radio, a shower bath and a salon-buffet where passengers could order a cold bottle and hot Welsh rarebit before retiring. Fast daylight runs at hours convenient to businessmen were scheduled by the Wabash *Blue Bird* and *Banner Blue* and the Chicago & Eastern Illinois' (at various dates) *La Salle, Century of Progress* and *Zipper.* The Illinois Central in daytime listed, over the years, the *Chicago* and *St. Louis Express, The Daylight* and, at length, the four-car streamlined and experimental *Green Diamond* with a coach and parlor car separated by a diner. Over the route where George Mortimer Pullman had scheduled his first sleepers and the original dining car, the Alton, until it was absorbed into the economy of the Gulf, Mobile & Ohio, ran *The Ann Rutledge, The Lincoln Limited* (later *The Abraham Lincoln*), and the coach-only *Prairie State Express.* Pride of this haughty and ancestral carrier was *The Alton Limited,* a six-hour de luxe consist aboard whose fine observation-parlor cars afternoon tea was served by a Japanese maiden in Oriental attire with the same ritual observance it exacted on the New Haven's equally effulgent *Yankee Clipper* and the Great Northern's *Oriental Limited.* On all the competing roads dining cars operated at substantial losses to make the trip enjoyable to the customers. The Wabash chicken pie on the *Banner Blue* became legendary and there were Creole dishes, gumbos and Gulf shellfish in profusion on the Illinois Central. Nowhere did the short-haul passenger live more handsomely or find his patronage in such request as in the spacious years of competition for the St. Louis-Chicago traffic.

THE COMPONENTS on these pages are variously the Wabash *Banner Blue* from the observation end by Roland Collons from the De Golyer Foundation, the Chicago & Eastern Illinois *St. Louis Zipper* at Englewood, Illinois, in 1943 by Charles Clegg and the Alton's main line timetable for 1888.

AS THE CARRIER over whose rails rode the first primeval sleeping cars of George Mortimer Pullman and, a few years later, the master carbuilder's first diner, the Chicago & Alton, as long as it was an independent operation, had reason to be proud of its luxury equipment and service. Train No. 1, *The Alton Limited* was for many years flagship of a fleet of varnish flyers between St. Louis and Chicago and is depicted above and at the right in its days of Pullman Standard by Paul Stringham. The standing rib roast at the right is, perhaps, being carved for a well-heeled jefe politico en route to the state capital to pocket a fat fee from the vested interests. Opposite, the *Abraham Lincoln*, when it was streamlined, carried the Presidential signature on its deep maroon nameboards. (*Douglas C. Wornom.*)

THERE IS A SCHOOL of thought among amateurs of carbuilding and Pullman design that feels that the golden age of Palace Car beauty was from 1900 to 1910 and that the observation car *Illinois* built by Pullman in 1905 represents the apogee of this Augustan age of surface transport. The car was assigned to *The Alton Limited* and measured countless thousands of miles between Chicago and St. Louis before it was again photographed in *The Limited* trainline in 1919 as it backed down into the old Union Station in Chicago for its daily run. Gone was the gaily striped awning, the arched Gothic leaded windows and much of the gold finelining that had been its pride in the glory years, but it remained a matchless product of the shops that made Pullman generic in the language. *(Right: Pullman Standard; Below: A. W. Johnson.)*

PRIDE OF The Chicago & Alton Railroad for the better part of half a century was the superbly equipped and maintained *Alton Limited* on the historic run between St. Louis and Chicago. New luxury cars had been commissioned from Pullman in 1905 as shown opposite, and in 1924 an all new *Alton Limited*, painted the Tuscan red and maroon of the company's traditional livery, was placed in service. Because the new Union Station was then building, it was placed on exhibition outdoors in Chicago where its observation car *Chicago* is depicted against the post office for background. Below is the business end of the *Limited* and here the backdrop is supplied by the soon to be finished Union Depot with the flag already flying from its structural elements. *(Two Photos: A. W. Johnson.)*

NOTHING the competition could enter in the St. Louis-Chicago run in the twenties and thirties topped the solid conservative elegance of the Alton's old established *Alton Limited* or its equally renowned *Midnight Special*. Its deep maroon and gold trimmed equipment and infallible punctuality stood for a simple standard of excellence that made it institutional. In the 1924 *Alton Limited* even the mail storage cars were named. Below an older *Limited* is seen leaving Chicago's original Union Passenger Station (*right*) over a roller-coaster track with Gothic windowed equipment and a Chicago air about its going in 1919. (*A. W. Johnson.*)

UNION PASSENGER STATION.

The Alton Limited Spanned the Years and Decades

THE BASIC UNIT of American long distance surface travel in the age of railroads was the classic devising of George Mortimer Pullman, the open sleeping section with upper and lower retractable berths. Its first crude versions were subject to immediate improvement so that the primeval Pullman sleeper *Pioneer* placed in service on the Chicago & Alton in 1858 was almost at once outmoded, but throughout most of its long and useful lifetime, the open section berth retained two durable and indeed immutable features, the heavy green baize curtains partitioning it off from the car corridor and the green net hammock wherein the passenger might place his traveling possibles. For almost a full century the open sleeping car berth was a national institution, an identifying hallmark of American travel and a staple of the national repertory of humor on a par with Brooklyn, old maids and honorary Kentucky colonels. All-room cars became a commonplace on luxury runs in the second decade of the twentieth century but time didn't really run out for the open section until the mid-thirties when all-room trains with no section accommodations at all began appearing on the New York Central, the Pennsylvania and the Santa Fe. When Pullman Standard announced that it had outshopped its last open section sleeper, the event was hailed editorially on a national scale as a turning point in the American way of life and the end of an era. As a topic of music hall humor its disappearance had no impact, for vaudeville itself had vanished before the decline of the upper berth with its seemingly limitless potentialities and variations. The last decade of rail travel which saw the open section in universal availability, although admittedly fighting a rear guard action against a rising preference for staterooms, drawing rooms, compartments and the new single bedrooms, was the 1920s when, appropriately enough, the Chicago & Alton, where it had all begun, still maintained an all-Pullman sleeping car only train on the overnight run between St. Louis and Chicago. Although following a familiar right of way through the Illinois countryside that it had first known in 1858, the lower berth had come a long way from the *Pioneer*. (*Kaufmann & Fabry*.)

IN THE YEARS of the Baltimore & Ohio's ownership and operation of The Alton, *The Abraham Lincoln* was briefly powered by one of the parent carrier's English styled 4-6-4's, the *Lord Baltimore*, with eighty-four inch drivers. No. 1 is shown above leaving Springfield, Illinois, in 1938. Opposite, in its Pullman Standard days the *Lincoln* with fifteen cars threads the maze of tracks at St. Louis Terminal. When the Alton passed into the hands of the Gulf, Mobile & Ohio, its continuity with the Lincoln legend was maintained by the streamlined *Ann Rutledge*, shown opposite, while Standard equipment survived in *The Alton Limited*, shown working the depot at Bloomington. *(Above: William Barham, Paul Stringham; Opposite, Top: Rail Photo Service; Bottom: Paul Stringham.)*

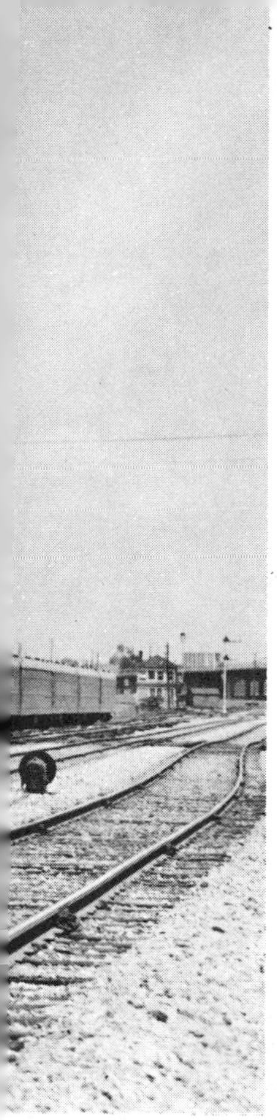

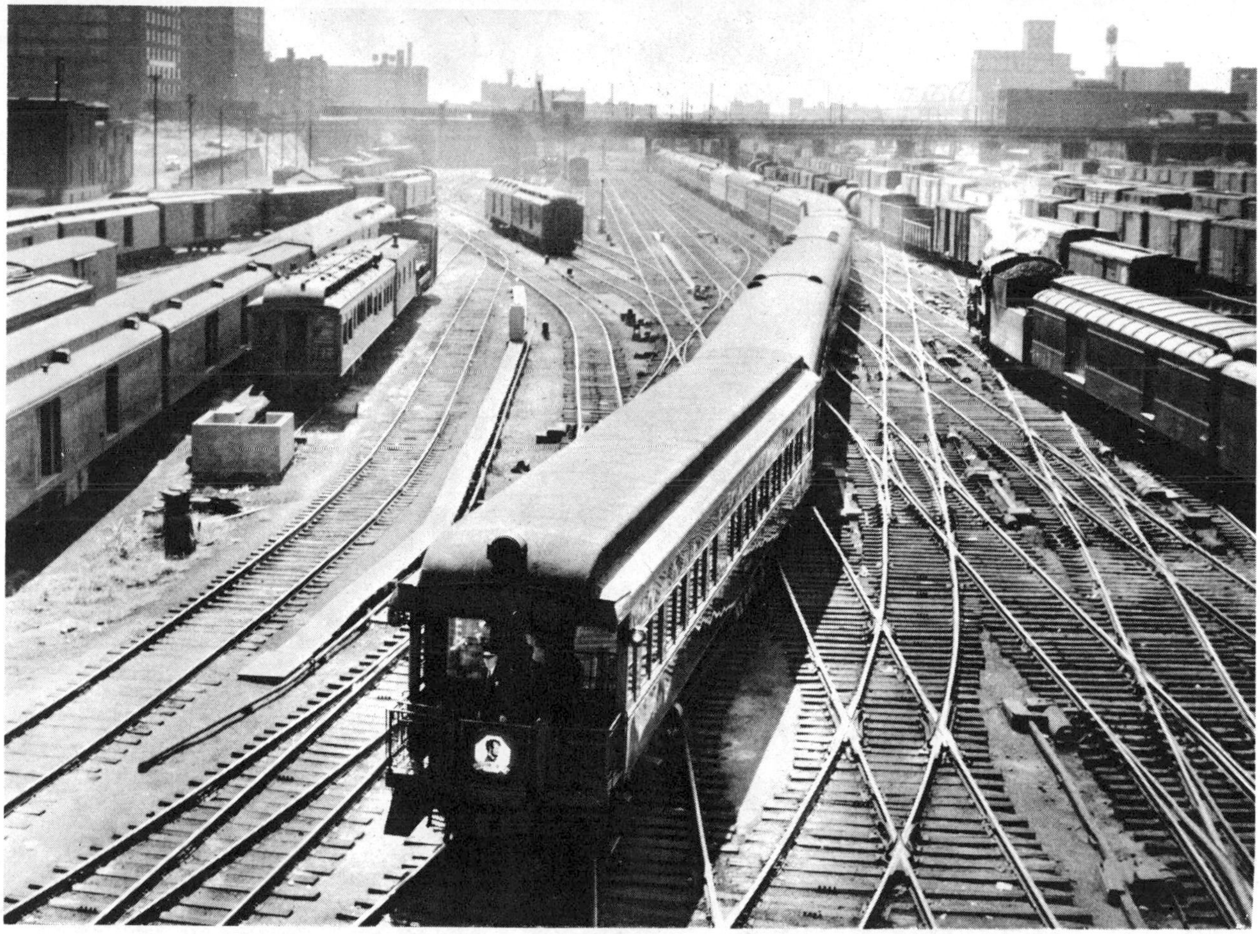

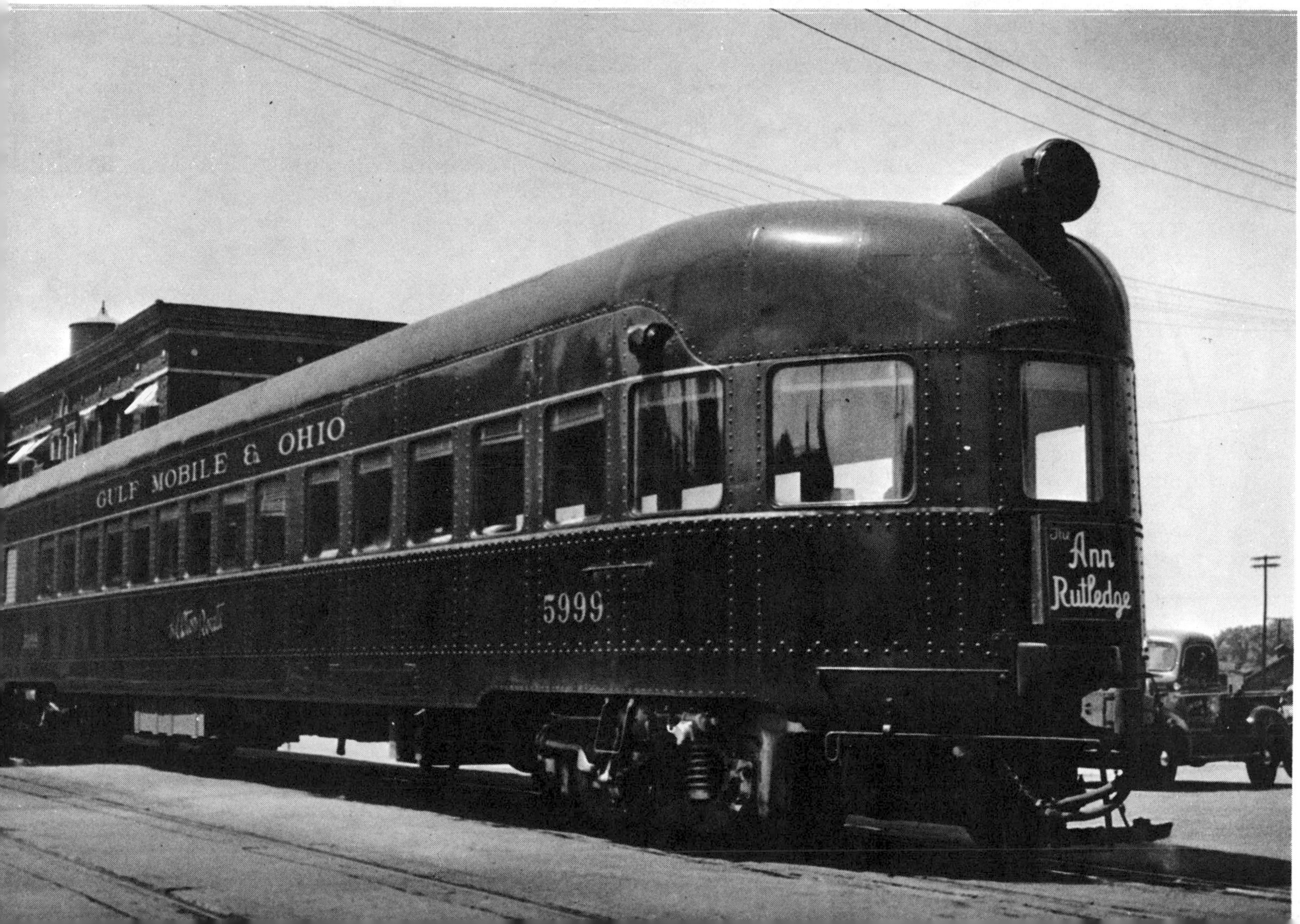
GULF MOBILE & OHIO
5999
The Ann Rutledge

THE CHICAGO & EASTERN ILLINOIS *La Salle* on the Chicago-St. Louis run before the inaugural of the *St. Louis Zipper* ironically fulfilled the suggestion made by John Barriger when he was an executive of the Pennsylvania Railroad that the name be used for the carrier's crack train between New York and Chicago rather than *The Broadway Limited*. The principal traffic of the Pennsylvania, he argued, was with ranking business executives who had their offices in La Salle Street, Chicago, and New York's Wall Street, and the designations *The La Salle* and *The Wall Street* would be more appropriate than *Broadway* whose connotations were more theatrical than financial. The Pennsylvania felt, however, that it had already so much invested in the prestige rating of *The Broadway* that it would be imprudent to make a switch, so *La Salle* went by default to the Chicago & Eastern Illinois while the Reading named their early morning Philadelphia-New York run *The Wall Streeter*. As a preview to the exquisitely stylish little *Zippers,* however, the *La Salle* with only four cars maintained the grand manner in microcosm as it bustled out of East St. Louis on its spirited dash for Lake Michigan. *(Two Photos: Lucius Beebe.)*

A TRULY *rara avis* in the litany of name trains, although it was hardly part of the Wabash-C.&E.I.-Alton-Illinois Central pattern of competition for the Chicago-St. Louis traffic, was the *Gulf Coast Special*, the wayward pride of the Mobile & Ohio Railroad on its way from Lake Michigan to Mobile. On the run from Chicago to St. Louis it shared trackage rights over the Illinois Central and from East St. Louis ran over its own iron. Meals were served aboard observation-buffet-lounge cars of non-air-conditioned vintage and the entire operation had about it an atmosphere of Civil War casualness and Deep South indifference to urgency to have bemused Bruce Catton. *The Gulf Coast Special* is shown at one of its many and leisurely stops from the collection of Everett De Golyer.

WHETHER IT WAS on view heading up *The St. Louis Zipper* out of Dearborn Depot at Chicago *(above)* or double heading *The La Salle* as seen from 47th Street Tower, the C.&E.I.'s motive power aroused the admiration of a large contingent of partisans. *(Two Photos: Rail Photo Service, W. G. Fancher and H. W. Pontin.)*

ONE DAY the Chicago & Eastern Illinois trains had to discharge their passengers in the yards while the Dearborn Street Station was burning up in December 1922, causing confusion and inconvenience not only to the Wabash, but the Monon, Santa Fe, Erie and Grand Trunk. *(Chicago Historical Society.)*

IN THE YEARS of the rainbow-hued competition between the Alton's red and maroon, the Wabash blue and the Illinois Central green on the run from Chicago to St. Louis, The I.C.'s *Daylight Limited* made a fine show against the autumn cornfields of Illinois farmlands. The Springfield, Illinois, depot that had known Abe Lincoln's congress-gaitered tread lasted the I.C. until well into the nineties.
(Above: Lucius Beebe; Right: Everett De Golyer Collection.)

28

BY THE MID-1930s the
look of *The Daylight Limited*
dining car had assumed
a comparative modernity.
An Illinois Central innovation
in lounge car decor was
the comfortable library-buffet
with rattan furniture and
individual reading lamps
under an arched roof
of typical Harriman design.
(*Two Photos: Illinois Central.*)

29

VERY MUCH IN competition with the several overnight trains of the Wabash, Alton and C.&E.I. between St. Louis and Chicago in the thirties was the Illinois Central's *Night Diamond* shown here in the half light of a summer's dawn as it approached Chicago through the tranquil Illinois countryside. *(Alfred W. Johnson.)*

Diamond

LIKE the competing Alton's all-Pullman, non-stop *Midnight Special, The Night Diamond* carried salon-buffet cars No. 4065 and No. 4066 for the benefit of patrons who wanted a highball or sandwich before they retired and where the steward could double as valet during the dark hours. *(Two Photos: Illinois Central.)*

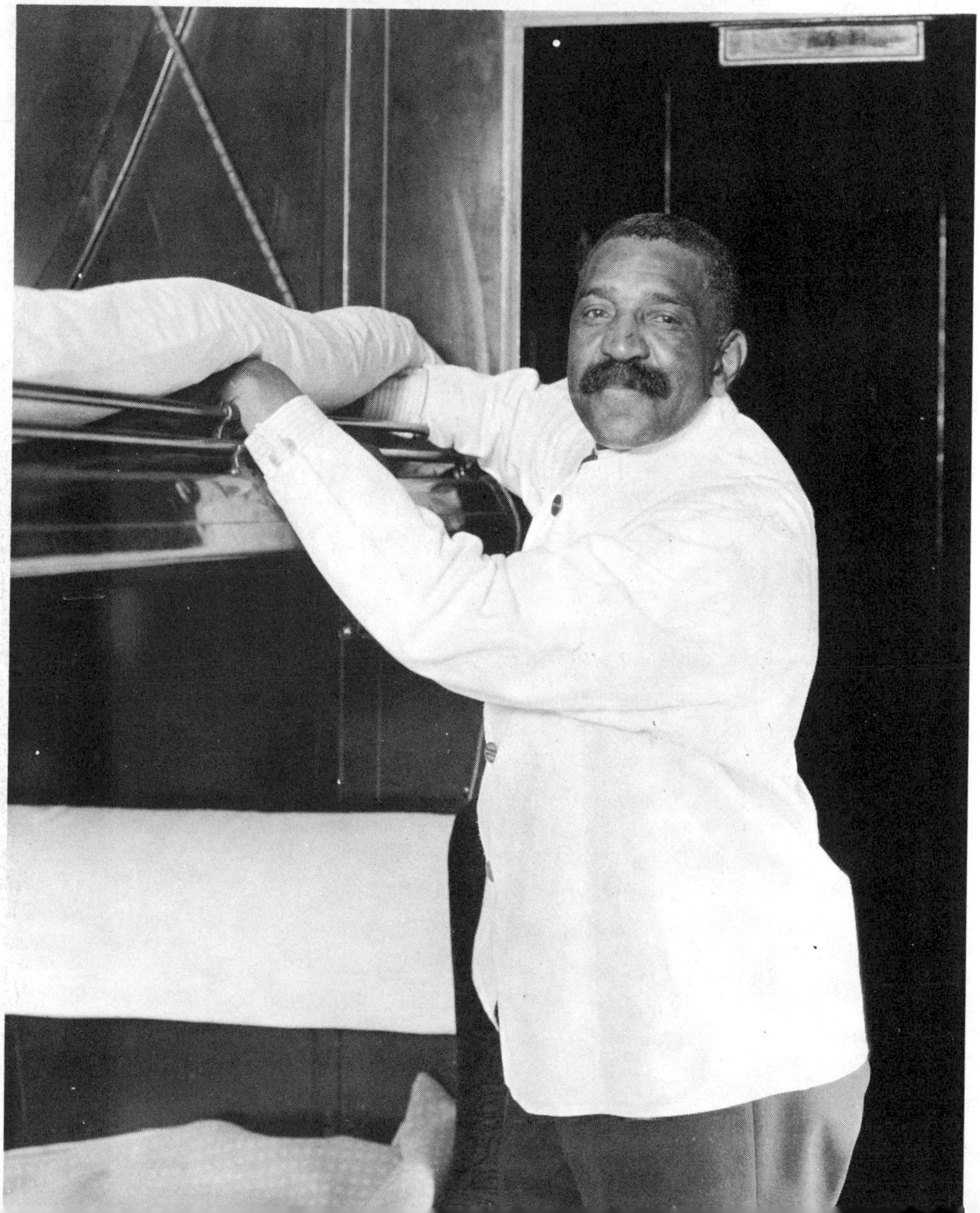

EVEN on its relatively short run between Chicago and St. Louis a meal on The I.C.'s *Daylight* in 1905 could be a pleasant venture into the realms of gastronomy. Its components derived, in large measure, from the rich farm and dairy lands that rolled past outside the windows. Steak on the luncheon menu as .45¢; the best Kentucky Bourbon: two bits, pumpkin pie baked on the cars with a slice of Wisconsin cheese was .15¢. A man could hardly afford not to eat, let alone drink. (*Right: Illinois Central; Below: Everett De Golyer Collection.*)

ALTHOUGH PATENTLY no part of the competition for passenger patronage between Chicago and St. Louis, the Chicago, Indianapolis & Louisville Railway, operating through the same American heartland of the Middle West as did the Wabash and C.&E.I., ran three name trains a day between Chicago and Indianapolis: No. 31, *The Hoosier*, No. 33, *The Tippecanoe* and No. 35, *The Midnight Special*. The two daylight runs carried Pullman diners, lounge cars and observation lounges, while *The Midnight Special*, in addition to the cafe-lounge and conventional sleepers, carried a rare and exotic Pullman observation-sleeping car, an impressive assortment of luxury equipment for a 183-mile haul. Here, in the early 1930s *The Tippecanoe*, southbound of an autumn morning, traverses a high fill that shows to its advantage a classic day train of prideful antecedents in a vintage year. *(Everett De Golyer Collection.)*

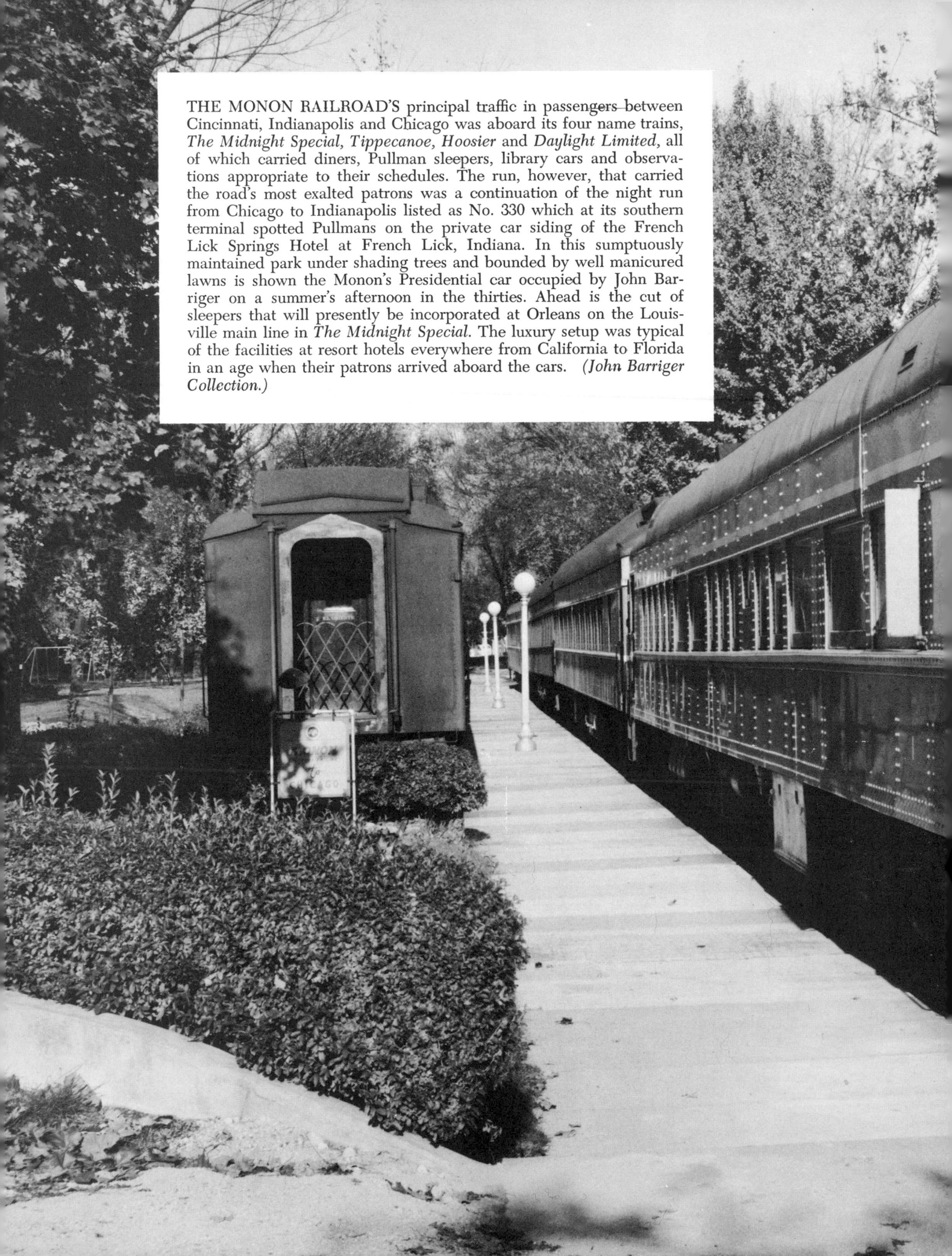

THE MONON RAILROAD'S principal traffic in passengers—between Cincinnati, Indianapolis and Chicago was aboard its four name trains, *The Midnight Special, Tippecanoe, Hoosier* and *Daylight Limited*, all of which carried diners, Pullman sleepers, library cars and observations appropriate to their schedules. The run, however, that carried the road's most exalted patrons was a continuation of the night run from Chicago to Indianapolis listed as No. 330 which at its southern terminal spotted Pullmans on the private car siding of the French Lick Springs Hotel at French Lick, Indiana. In this sumptuously maintained park under shading trees and bounded by well manicured lawns is shown the Monon's Presidential car occupied by John Barriger on a summer's afternoon in the thirties. Ahead is the cut of sleepers that will presently be incorporated at Orleans on the Louisville main line in *The Midnight Special*. The luxury setup was typical of the facilities at resort hotels everywhere from California to Florida in an age when their patrons arrived aboard the cars. (*John Barriger Collection.*)

LENDING the striking blue livery of its train exteriors and the blue theme that has dominated the nomenclature of its crack trains, the Wabash was very much a part of the competition for St. Louis-Chicago passenger traffic that embraced the Illinois Central's green and the hereditary deep maroon of the Alton and its successors. In the years of steam *The Banner Blue* and *Blue Bird* were the Wabash daylight runs on the St. Louis route and *The Blue Bird* survived with its reputation for style undiminished into the age of streamlined Diesel. Without regard, however, for changing styles of motive power and car design, one amenity of the abundant life has been celebrated on Wabash trains over the decades, and that is the chicken cream pot pie served aboard its diners. Other carriers have made a good thing, promotionally, from the service of characteristic or regional dishes, scrod on the New Haven, the Creole cuisine of the Illinois Central, *The Century's* lobster Newburg on hot corn bread and the fresh-caught Rocky Mountain trout of the Rio Grande, but chicken pie has been the hallmark of Wabash excellence, and many a traveler, remembering its succulence, has taken space on the *Banner Blue* instead of the competition. Here, long ago on a wintry morning in 1935, *The Banner Blue* at Dearborn Depot in Chicago clears its stack against the skyline of The Loop as it gets a highball on its daylight run to St. Louis. (*Lucius Beebe.*)

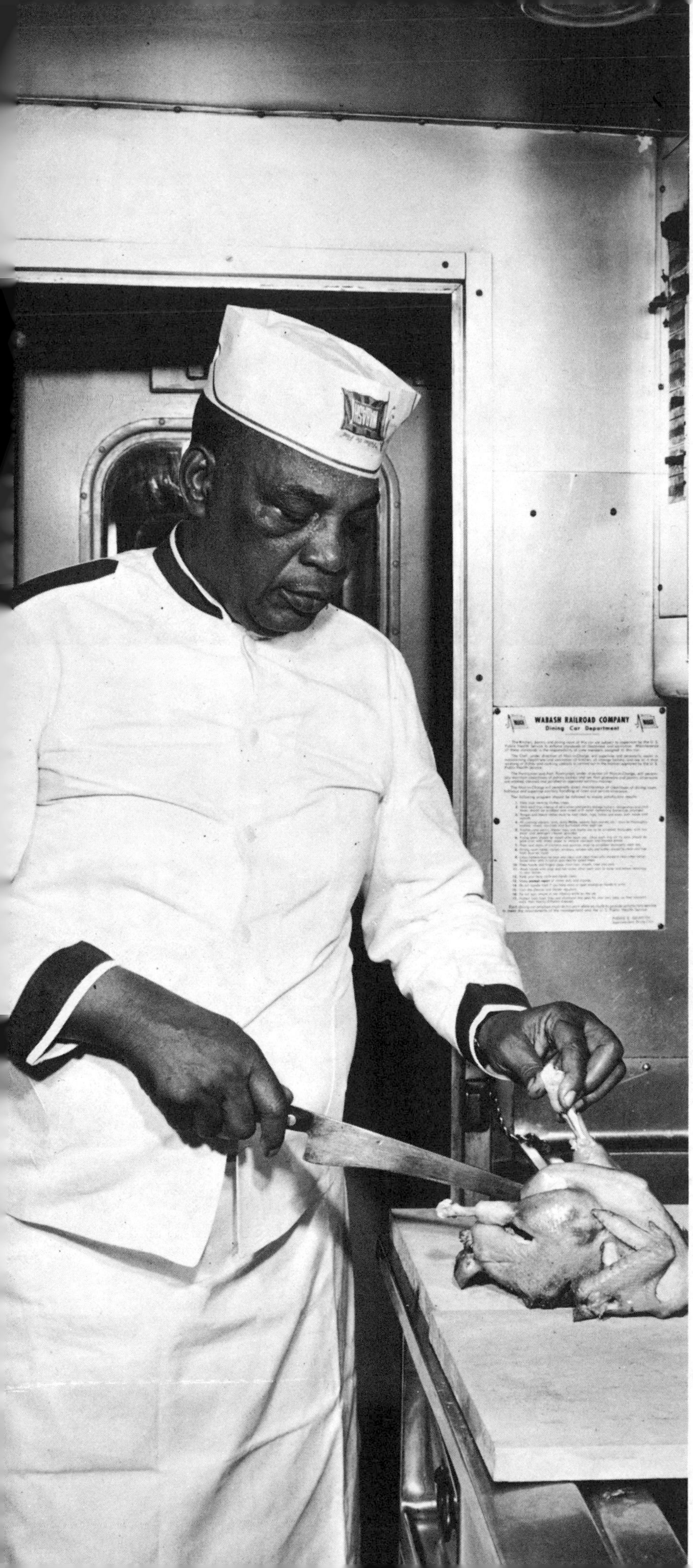

REFLECTING the *expertise* of his respected profession, a veteran Wabash dining car chef in the galley of a streamlined *Blue Bird* poses for a series of progressive photographs as he confects the cream chicken pie that for decades made Wabash diners famous. *(Four Photos: Wabash Railroad.)*

THE TRANSITION from the observation platform of the Standard Pullman parlor car *Helena Modjeska* to the streamlined solarium of *The Blue Bird* was accomplished without loss of character as one of the most admired of daylight name trains and certainly with no abatement of the blue and gold livery which had been a Wabash hallmark for so many years. *(Two Photos: Stan Repp.)*

ALMOST AS MUCH photographed by Wabash admirers as its companion train *The Banner Blue*, *The Blue Bird* on the St. Louis-Chicago late afternoon run went through the Illinois cornfields behind the identical motive power, usually the carrier's blue-painted, stubby but photogenic Pacifics. On rare occasions of conventions or summer weekend business it ran out of Chicago double headed as shown at the left with Pacific No. 662 as helper and Atlantic No. 602 as road engine. *(Top: Richard J. Cook; Left: Lucius Beebe.)*

39

TWO OF THE MOST spectacular competitors on the St. Louis run, the Wabash and the Chicago & Eastern Illinois both used the venerable Dearborn Depot as their Chicago terminal, their trains occupying adjacent slips in the train shed and passing over the same narrow throat tracks on a round-the-clock basis.

OF ALL THE COLORFUL name trains on the highly competitive run between Chicago and St. Louis, none enjoyed a more faithful following or more devoted partisans than the Wabash *Banner Limited*, whose name was later changed to *The Banner Blue*. Until the fine streamlined replacement after the 1941 war, the Wabash took a dim view of new equipment. Well worn and much loved cars such as the observation *Helena Modjeska* suited the customers right down to the ground. So did familiar train crews and a dining car personnel that was right off the Old Plantation who made *The Banner's* midday run through the golden Illinois cornfields a lyric experience to all who loved the old ways of travel best. Ordinarily the Wabash blue boilered Pacifics were sufficient for the regular five and six-car consists. When, on holiday occasions, a longer train was marked up, big time power in the form of a 4-8-4 as shown opposite was invoked. *The Banner's* open platform observation cars, finally the last in regular service anywhere, marked it, figuratively, as a train of the old school with manners of a more formal time. (*Opposite: Rail Photo Service; Left and Below: Wabash Railway.*)

ONE OF THE GLITTERING NAMES of the Western Continent, *The California Limited* was placed in service on a year-round schedule between Chicago and Los Angeles as flagship of the Santa Fe in 1892 and with the passing of time became one of the oldest of all name trains. It was photographed *(below)* in Los Angeles by William Henry Jackson of Colorado in 1894 in a view which suggests, with its splendid equipment, the regard in which the train was held by its owning carrier. Below is *The Limited* through the arcade of the Green Hotel, Pasadena, while opposite the mail and express vans met all trains. *(Three Photos: Colorado State Historical Society.)*

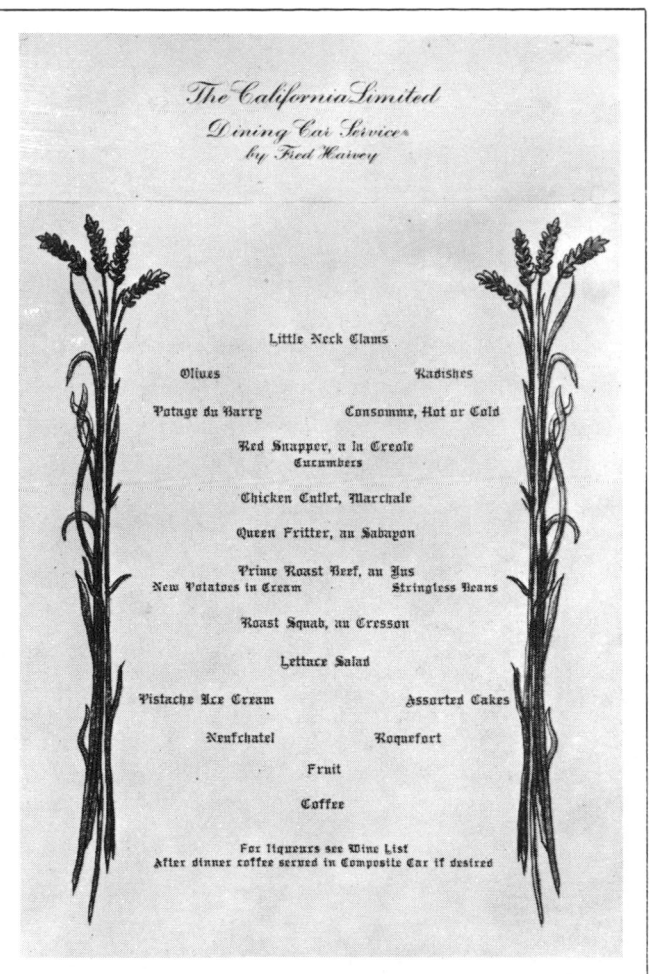

The California Limited
Dining Car Service
by Fred Harvey

Little Neck Clams

Olives   Radishes

Potage du Barry   Consomme, Hot or Cold

Red Snapper, a la Creole
Cucumbers

Chicken Cutlet, Marchale

Queen Fritter, au Sabayon

Prime Roast Beef, au Jus
New Potatoes in Cream   Stringless Beans

Roast Squab, au Cresson

Lettuce Salad

Pistache Ice Cream   Assorted Cakes

Neufchatel   Roquefort

Fruit

Coffee

For liqueurs see Wine List
After dinner coffee served in Composite Car if desired

THE CALIFORNIA LIMITED was the first of the Santa Fe's great name trains aboard which Fred Harvey was to demonstrate his culinary genius and gentle the appreciative patrons with rich fare and fastidious service. It was an age of quail and prairie chicken and other game in limitless abundance and the railroad even purchased the entire output of a famous California manufactory known as Sierra Cheese to lend distinction to its diners. *(Byron Harvey Collection.)*

IT IS EVIDENT from the magnificent equipment terminating in the plush observation Pullman *Marfa* portrayed at the right that the Santa Fe was prepared to spare no expense in competing with the Southern Pacific for the de luxe passenger traffic between Chicago and California, even though the Espee's *Sunset Limited*, which also for a time ran to Chicago, was reputedly the handsomest train in the world. Apparent, too, from the menu reproduced opposite, was the fact that tourists who entrusted themselves to the enterprising Boston firm of Raymond & Whitcomb did handsomely on *The California Limited* with the assistance of Fred Harvey. Company advertising after the turn of the century stressed Spanish senoritas, mission bells and the old way of life on the ranchos, and the lure of film stars and orange groves was still in the unguessed future. On this page the perceptive William Henry Jackson depicts a section house on the Santa Fe's main line in California characterized by a suggestion of domestic tranquility not usually associated with the hard-bitten business of keeping the railroad running. *(Above and Right: Colorado State Historical Society; Top, Opposite: Byron Harvey Collection, Arthur D. Dubin Collection.)*

44

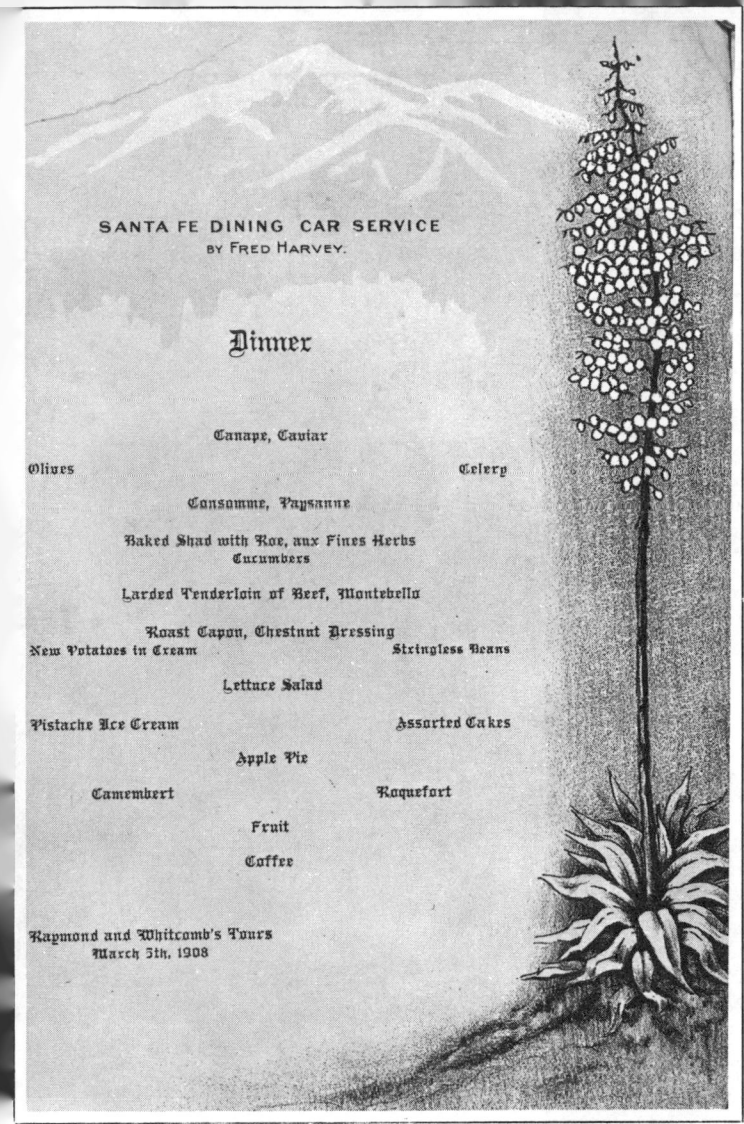

SANTA FE DINING CAR SERVICE
BY FRED HARVEY.

Dinner

Canape, Caviar

Olives   Celery

Consomme, Paysanne

Baked Shad with Roe, aux Fines Herbs
Cucumbers

Larded Tenderloin of Beef, Montebello

Roast Capon, Chestnut Dressing
New Potatoes in Cream   Stringless Beans

Lettuce Salad

Pistache Ice Cream   Assorted Cakes

Apple Pie

Camembert   Roquefort

Fruit

Coffee

Raymond and Whitcomb's Tours
March 5th, 1908

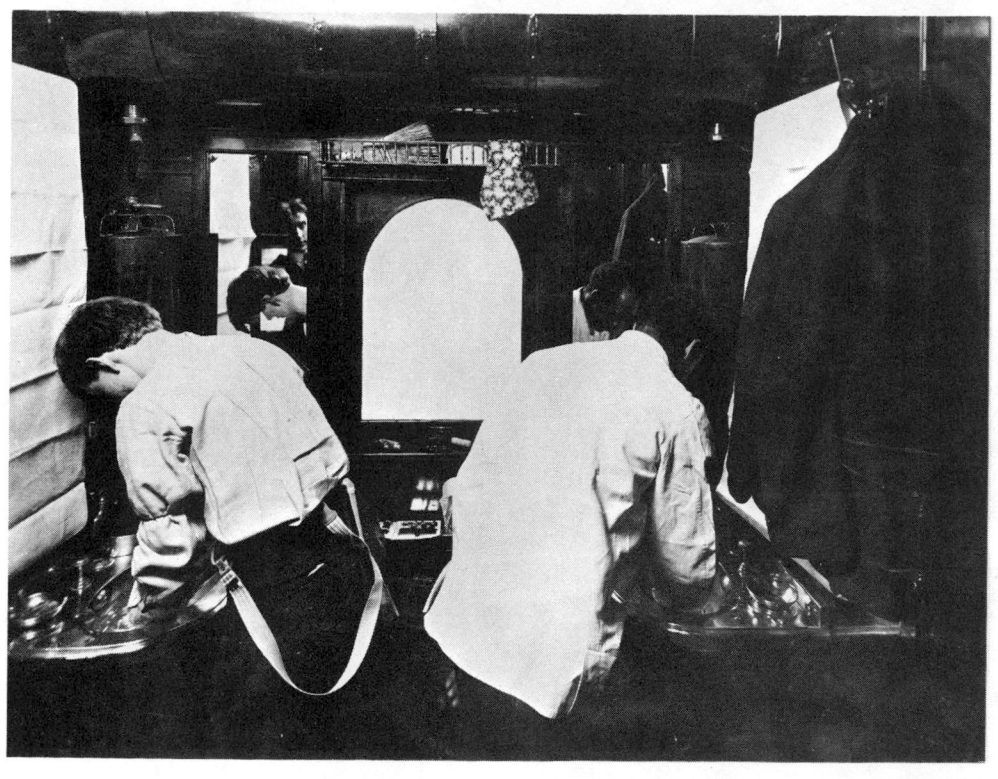

EVEN THE TOURIST class passengers on the *California Limited* in the nineties did themselves well at table if the photograph on the opposite page is to be believed and Fred Harvey's bounty was everywhere. The men's washrooms were, in those primordial times, serviced by gravity from any overhead storage tank, Ascot ties depended from the shelves and the roller towel was an honored accessory of Pullman travel. Here *The California Limited* was photographed double-headed in the desert a few miles east of Los Angeles by the celebrated William Henry Jackson of Denver while at the left, a photographer in the great tradition of Jackson himself in the person of Herb Sullivan, four decades later depicts No. 4 against the majestic backdrop of the San Bernardino Mountains as it heads into the Cajon Pass. *(Above: Colorado State Historical Society; Opposite: Two Photos, Santa Fe Railroad.)*

47

REMINISCENT of the abundant tresses of the celebrated Ogilvie Sisters, once the *beau idéal* of the American womanhood, the young lady in the primeval Santa Fe promotion photo at the right is making her toilette in a lady's retiring room aboard a Pullman dating from the nineties according to the evidence of the hand-activated plumbing. Circulating ice water was then unknown and drinking water came from the tin tank visible at the left. Below *The California Limited* pauses at the handy platform of the depot at Pasadena right by the front door of the Green Hotel, one of the vast multiplicity of California resorts built in the nineties to accommodate the newly crescent tourist trade. (*Left: Santa Fe; Below: Colorado State Historical Society.*)

ACTIVATED, PERHAPS, by the resounding *réclame* of the Lackawanna's Phoebe Snow, Santa Fe promotion photographs beginning in the nineties and continuing until the time of the *de Luxe* are notably preoccupied with women in white. They appear so frequently that it was obviously a part of considered company policy aimed at stressing the comfort and cleanliness of Pullman travel with the suggestion that even the snowiest fabric would not suffer from soot or cinders en route. While one would hesitate to assert that the carrier embarked on a policy of deliberate mendacity, those who remember the summer crossing of Kansas and the California desert aboard even such well conducted trains as *The Chief* in the years before air conditioning will take the sootless myth with a grain of salt. This publicity shot of a pre-Gibson Girl patron of *The California Limited* is also documentary evidence of the elaborate travel fashions of the year 1895. (*Santa Fe Railway.*)

AS IS SUGGESTED by the initials on the tender, the Santa Fe in the nineties entered Los Angeles under the style of The Southern California Railway Company, one of the eleven component carriers which then formed the system. *The California Limited* as photographed by William Henry Jackson behind ten wheeler No. 56 its third day out of Chicago was the company's pride. No railroad of consequence in the West of the period dreamed of neglecting the covered wagon theme in a "then and now" context in its company literature. *(Above: Colorado State Historical Society; Below: Fred Harvey.)*

THE ATMOSPHERIC natives who peopled the Santa Fe promotion and advertising of the early nineties were not the Navajos of recent times, who were largely created as a romantic symbol of the Southwest by Lee Lyles, but the proud if decayed Spanish dons of the old ranching tradition such as the picturesque hidalgos at the right who were encouraged by the railroad to lounge in photogenic poses around Capistrano depot *(below)* at train time. The mission theme of station architecture of the Santa Fe's early times included belfries with mission bells in working order which chimed romantically as *The Limited* pulled in from the east. *(Two Photos: William Henry Jackson Collection.)*

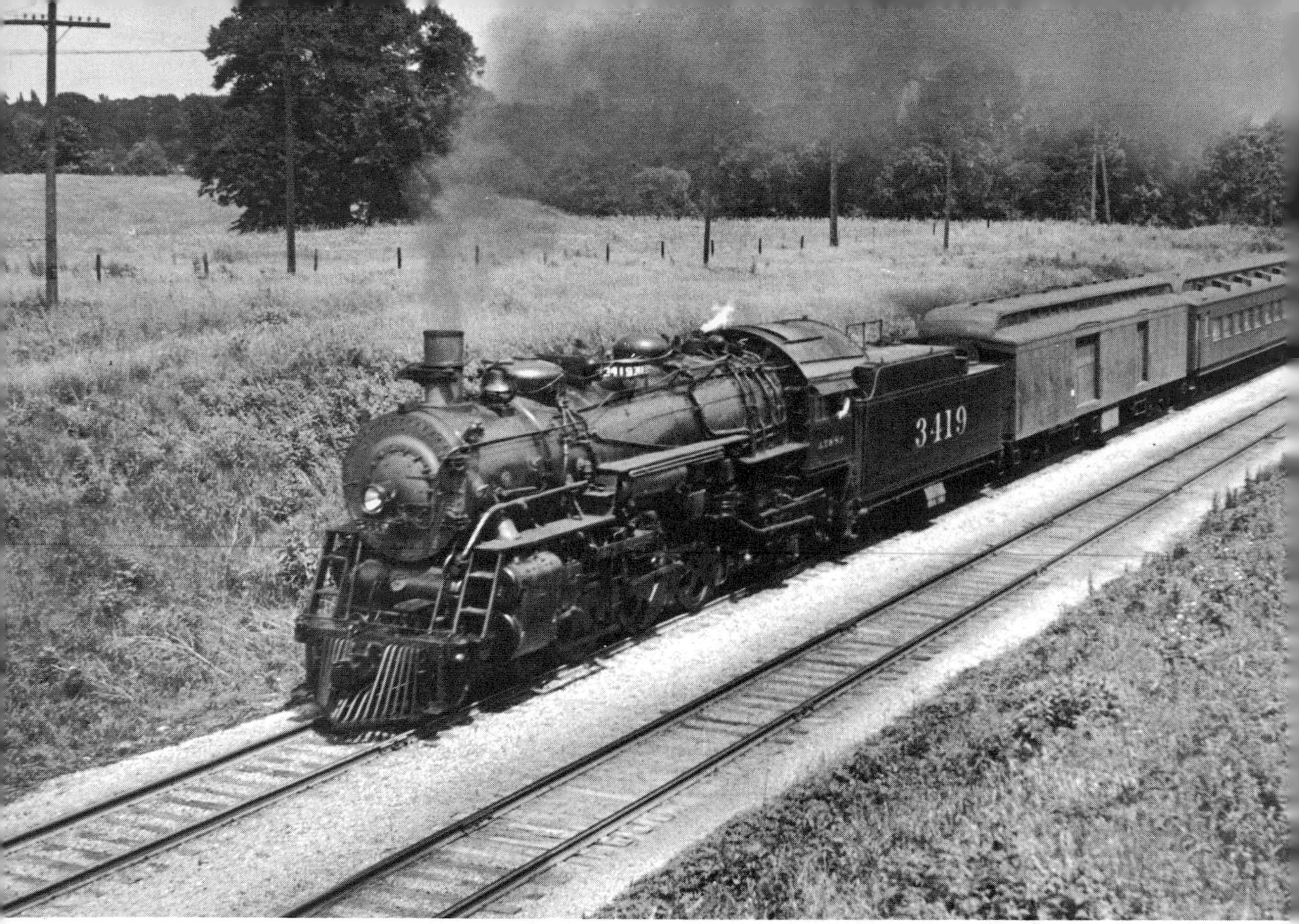
3419

California
Santa Fe
Limited

AT&SF

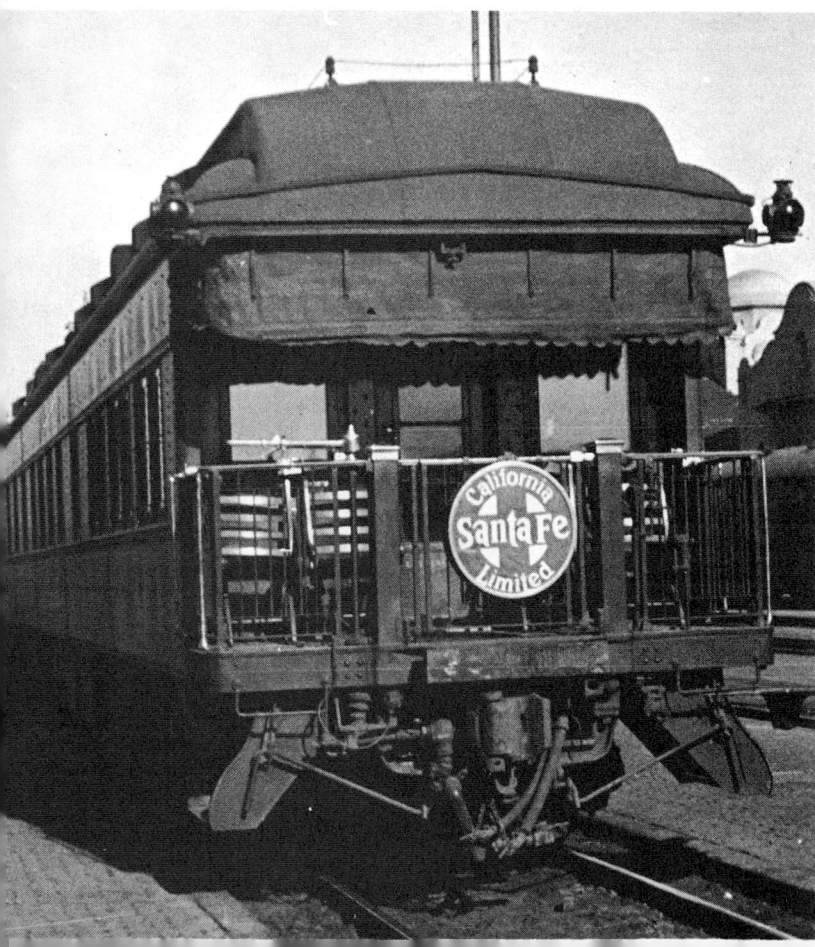

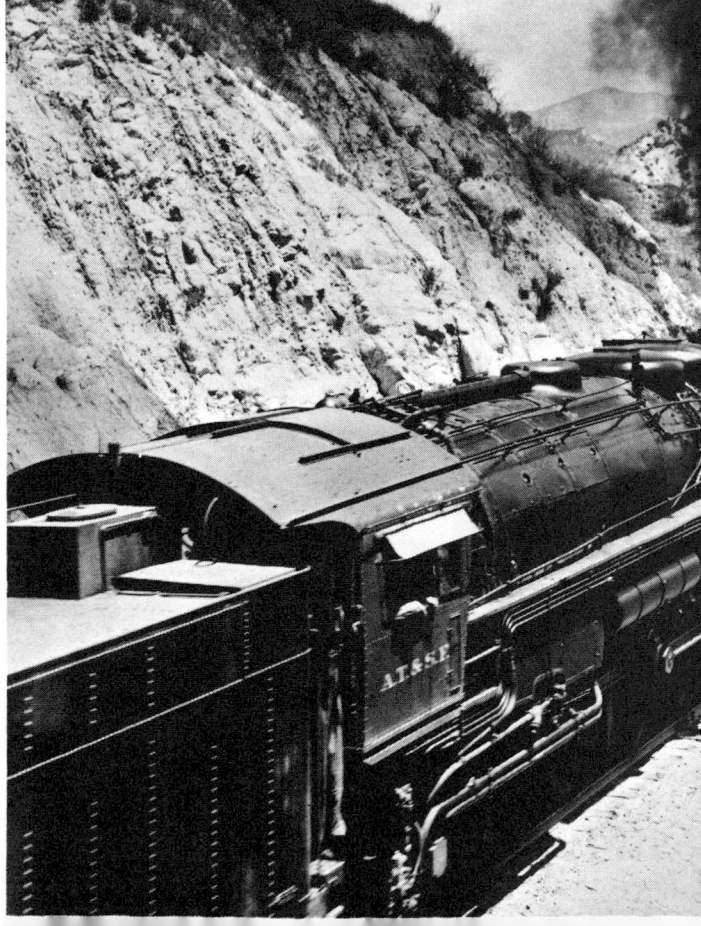

ALTHOUGH THE CUISINE aboard *The California Limited* and *The Grand Canyon* shown on the page opposite on the speedway out of East Galesburg, Illinois, and at the left double heading near the summit of the Cajon in California, was tempered to the means of passengers who preferred a non-extra fare train on a schedule somewhat abated from those of *The Chief* and *Super Chief*, it still maintained Fred Harvey standards and was generally felt to be the best between Chicago and California. Bright jewel in the Harvey diadem was, of course, the culinary elegance of *The Super Chief* whose head chef is depicted above shelling out a choice cut of beef from the ample herds of cattle bearing the Fred Harvey brand, the OIO, that grazed the ranges of the Arkansas River. *(Opposite, Top: Paul Stringham; Bottom: Jim Ady, Herb Sullivan; Above: Graphic House.)*

ALTHOUGH, in the year 1915, the once a week *de Luxe* was the pride of the Santa Fe between Chicago and Los Angeles and a premonition of splendors to come, in the fullness of time, in *The Super Chief*, the old reliable *California Limited* on a daily basis was flagship of the line and the standard of Santa Fe excellence. It was also the company's showcase and vehicle of its choicest advertising and publicity as is suggested in the period photos reproduced above and on the page opposite taken aboard the San Francisco section. In a gesture familiar to all connoisseurs of film Western, a comely maiden shades her eyes to scan far horizons, presumably in search of hostiles. In a less adventurous pose she reappears in the club car interior opposite. The handsome profile of Santa Fe power, a 4-6-4 running between Oakland and Bakersfield rounds Luzon Curve twenty years later. *(Top Opposite: David Gray Edwards, Rail Photo Service; Two Photos: Gabriel Moulin Studio.)*

Atchison, Topeka & Santa Fe The Chief
Flying Boudoir of The Western Continent

The Chief in The Cajon

(Gerald Best)

WHEN, IN MID-NOVEMBER of 1926, the Santa Fe inaugurated its new train *The Chief* as an all-Pullman, extra fare limited on a tight schedule between Chicago and Los Angeles it not only marked the date with a star in the history of railroad operations but created a durable item of social folklore. It seems probable that over the years more names that made news in the American record rode *The Chief* than comprised the sailing lists of any other long-haul varnish runs excepting only *The Twentieth Century Limited* and *The Broadway*, and in the Pullman years many of the headliners who rode the pride of the Pennsy or the Central boarded *The Chief* at Chicago to complete their transcontinental journey.

Unlike *The Broadway* and *The Century* whose clientele derived from a wide field of celebrity in finance, society, commerce, sports and the professions, *The Chief* was famous as a rolling boudoir for film celebrities and the executive hierarchies that served the studios of Hollywood in their most effulgent years. Almost no name of the entertainment era but arrived or departed from the Los Angeles terminal amidst hampers of champagne and bon voyage, long stemmed roses and the ministering attentions of studio press agents, photographers and the newspaper and magazine press. *The Chief's* arrival in Chicago was the object of similar demonstrations of a promotional nature and Greta Garbo, Myrna Loy, Douglas Fairbanks and Charlie Chaplin went their way eastbound or west amidst appropriate barrages of photo-flashes and the polite attentions of the Santa Fe's own publicity department. *The Chief* was a professional condition of life, self-contained, populous with fame and enviable ways, so that in time drawing room space in its Pullmans was a status symbol as essential to stardom as head waiter recognition at Chasen's and a Minerva town car for opening nights at Grauman's Chinese Theater. *Variety* listed the daily arrivals and departures on *The Chief* as scrupulously as *The New York Times* reported passenger lists on the *Olympic*.

Aside from the relaxed morality attributed to the train's patrons by Frederick Wakeman in "The Hucksters" but not available to precise documentation, many film stars looked forward to travel as a release from arduous training and strict diets imposed by studios while actually making films. Madeleine Carroll, a celebrated epicure when not on location or the set, was regularly served an outsize calf's liver steak for breakfast on *The Chief* and cited it as an example of Fred Harvey excellence in all things. William Randolph Hearst's explicit disapproval of Miss Marion Davies' equally emphatic fondness for an occasional restorative Martini cocktail was resolved by the maintainance at strategic points in the train consist of bottles of ready-mixed and prechilled drinks available to instant consumption when Miss Davies was able for a brief moment and on whatever pretext to elude her strong-willed patron. By these prudent logistics Miss Davies was able to make the trip with a minimum of discomfort.

The Countess Dorothy di Frasso regarded fresh Beluga caviar at $5. a spoonful as lesser *viveurs* felt about beef stew and considered a pound in the light of a reduced portion so that special provision had to be made when she booked passage. Clifton Webb's valet and his mother's two tiring maids required skilled exercise of protocol in the assignment of room space. When Lord Joseph Duveen, the princely dealer in old masters, brought a Romney or Rembrandt west for the approval of Henry Huntington, his personal staff and domestics, four Pinkertons and a locked room for the art treasures took up most of an all-drawing room Pullman. And when Vicki Baum, author of "Grand Hotel," embarked to supervise its screening in Hollywood, she remarked that *The Chief* was pretty much a sublimation of the theme of her book. This merely confirmed what the Santa Fe and Fred Harvey management had known all along, that every sailing of *The Chief* inaugurated the transcontinental landfaring of a very grand hotel indeed.

AS WAS THE CASE with many other long established name trains, *The Chief* received its streamlined, light-weight varnish from Budd, not in entire train units but piecemeal so that for a more or less extended period its diners and lounge-observation cars rode sandwiched between Standard Pullman sleepers, as is suggested below where a lightweight diner stands out in the middle of an entire train of older cars. But always, until the Santa Fe had taken over Diesel motive power to the exclusion of steam in every capacity, *The Chief* left San Bernardino early in the afternoon with a helper for the steep grade of the Cajon and until the end the pass remained a happy hunting ground for photo amateurs to whom steam was the only thinkable motive power in a properly ordered world. *(Right: Rail Photo Service, W. G. Fancher; Below: Gerald M. Best.)*

THE ERA OF THE CLOCHE HAT for women and four button suits for men found passengers aboard *The Chief* in its formative years of 1926-27 reading the novels of F. Scott Fitzgerald and Ernest Hemingway while sharing, at least in the presence of the company cameramen, boxes of Page & Shaw chocolates because of the rumored existence of prohibition. The buffet cars were not, of course, air conditioned as is attested by the double Pullman windows and electric fans and through passage was assured by a partitioned gangway which obviated the necessity of falling over the feet of patrons reading the bound files of *Collier's* and *The Literary Digest* as the cars rocked around the curves of Raton Pass. By cocktail time the decorously occupied car attendants in the photograph would be busy rushing setups to staterooms in the sleeping cars and supplying corkscrews for gentlemen who had forgotten that essential item of travel. (*Byron Harvey Collection.*)

THE PASSENGERS have scarcely reached the train gate at Dearborn Depot in Chicago before Santa Fe's yard engine No. 853 is on the rear drawbar of *The Chief's* streamlined observation lounge to snake it out of the yards for a quick turning and cleaning. The morning rush hour at Dearborn finds arrivals via the Erie, Wabash, Grand Trunk and Monon being broken up in a pattern of ordered chaos. Below: *The Chief* pauses on its inbound run at Chillicothe, Illinois, for a refill that will take it as far as Chicago yards on the last lap of its transcontinental haul. *(Two Photos: Rail Photo Service; Right: W. G. Fancher; Below: Paul Stringham.)*

DEPICTED HERE are two scenes of unusual interest as being contrary to the accepted practices of the Santa Fe management and so calculated to cheer the *aficionado* who is of good heart when routine is in the discard. Above, on a morning marked with a star in 1949, *The Chief* arrives in Dearborn station behind a Pacific, No. 3429, pressed into service east of Kansas City to bring in seventeen cars and the assigned Diesel units dead on their wheels. Below, at the same approximate date, *The Chief* docks in Chicago with an open platform observation car of antique pattern in place of regularly assigned equipment. This is not, as may at first sight be conjectured, a business car. It has no track lights and the legend on the nameboards reads "Cafe Observation." (*Two Photos: Rail Photo Service, W. G. Fancher.*)

THE FIRST two EMD road unit Diesels assigned to *The Chief* had about them an atmosphere of menace as they posed *(left)* at the head end of their by now streamlined consist at Dearborn Station, Chicago. But they rolled the cars, as shown below, at an effortless eighty in the summer of 1941 through the cornfields near Wilbern, Illinois, and sensitive observers knew that the end of the age of mainline steam motive power was at hand everywhere. Names that made news like Bing Crosby and Margaret Truman were a commonplace on *The Chief's* sailing list. The engineer at the throttle of one of the great 3700 series engines posed for his photograph at one of the terminals as is suggested by the inert speedometer. *(Opposite: Three Photos: Santa Fe Railroad; Left: Rail Photo Service, W. G. Fancher; Below: Paul Stringham.)*

IN THE THIRTIES when *The Chief* was scheduled to depart Los Angeles at 12:01 p.m., approximately an hour and fifty minutes later saw it threading the narrow clearances of the Cajon after picking up a helper in San Bernardino. Its ascent of this chaotic landscape in the full sunlight of early afternoon was a pictorial must that attracted every railroad photographer of the late twenties and the entire decade of the thirties, none more so than Herb Sullivan who took this dramatic shot of the Santa Fe's candy train of the period and the fastest thing on wheels between Chicago and the Coast with its helper engine a venerable Atlantic type that was one of the ancients of the motive power roster. On the opposite page, after the coming of lightweight trains, *The Chief* departs the Dearborn Depot in Chicago on a winter's day under a trailing pony tail of exhaust steam. The observation lounges of the 1934 *Chief* still retained the ornate window Gothic of an earlier style in carbuilding and had four sections for members of the train crew in lieu of the dormitory car of later practice. *(Above: Herb Sullivan; Opposite: Lucius Beebe, Arthur D. Dubin Collection.)*

64

Santa Fe's Ineffable de Luxe

THE IDENTIFYING HALLMARKS of a true luxury train in the *belle epoque* of railroad travel were several. They included the most sumptuous cuisine imaginable with a basic dollar dinner, a ladies' maid, baths, either tub, shower or both, periodicals and daily newspapers and stock reports put aboard at strategic points en route, a valet for gentlemen, a barber, and a buffet whose wine schedule compared favorably with the best gentlemen's clubs in New York or Boston (the wine card for the Boston & Albany's *Boston & Chicago Special* for 1893 casually lists a Chateau La Rose 1878, an item to cause swooning among oenophiles.) An all-Pullman consist harbored these amenities and brought up with a brass railed observation car whose verandah sported the train's name in ornate heraldry with electric lights. All these things and more characterized the Santa Fe's *de Luxe* which was placed in service between Chicago and Los Angeles for the winter season 1911-1912. *De Luxe* sailed once a week and space aboard its three Pullmans was limited to sixty passengers who paid a surcharge of $25., perhaps roughly the equivalent of $100. today. They slept in brass beds instead of berths. A library of choice fiction and the established classics rode a buffet car which also harbored the barber, ladies' maid and manicurist. Elegances included a pigskin wallet* tastefully engrossed with the train name in 14 carat gold for each gentleman passenger and a corsage of orchids brought aboard at the California border by uniformed messengers for each lady. Superadded to those stupifying grandeurs was Fred Harvey cuisine in the first of all air-conditioned diners where indirect lighting shone in muted splendor over rare viands and costly vintages. Patrons of this most lordly of transcontinentals were recruited from the ranks of those who not only expected the best of everything but could afford its service in the same style they might have encountered at the Waldorf-Astoria or The Savoy in London. From the time it got its first highball out of Dearborn Station in Chicago on December 11, 1911, *de Luxe* was a success of gratifying dimensions. It was immediately rescheduled for the following winter season with new and more eye-popping equipment which was rushed from Pullman during the summer months, and it continued in service until 1917 when it was a victim of wartime austerities and became the stuff of legend. As a status symbol, the high iron never knew the peer of *de Luxe*.

*The complimentary billfold, a photograph of which will be found on an adjacent page, and corsages had their origins on *The California Limited* in 1897 and appeared on *de Luxe* its initial season of operations. The practice may have continued longer, but the fact that only a single known such wallet exists argues against it.

66

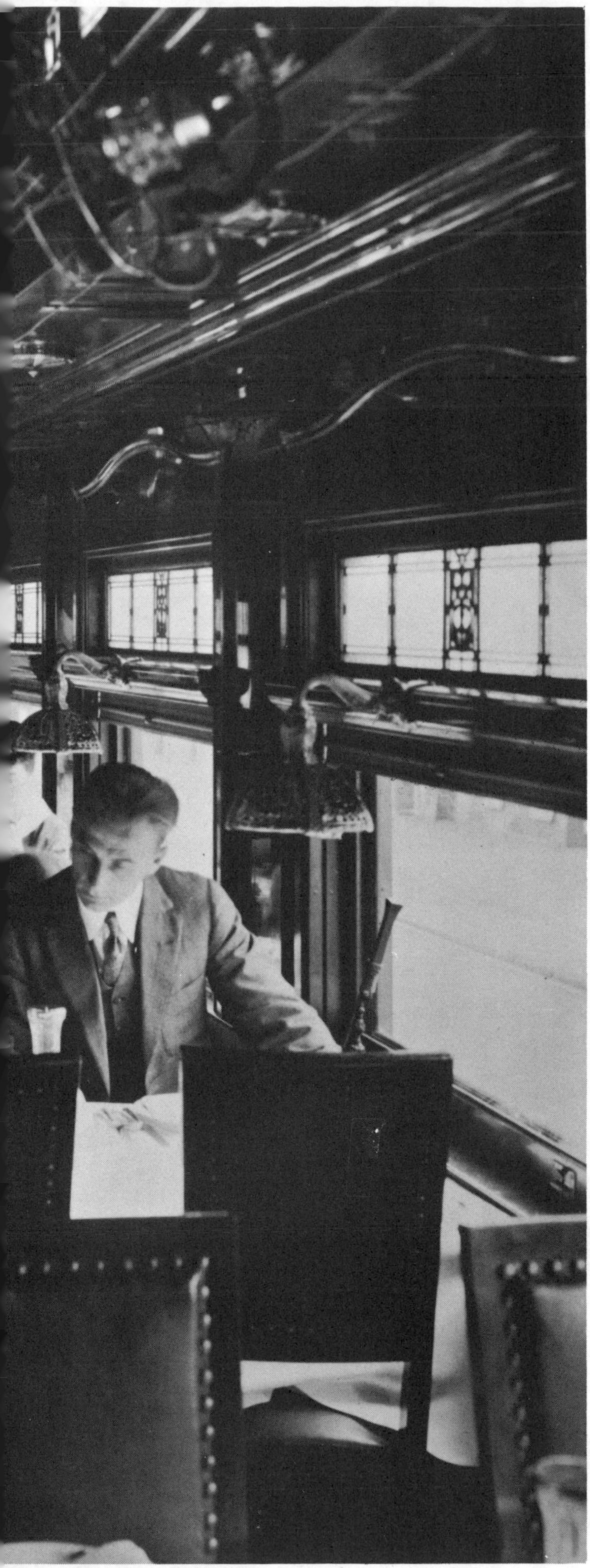

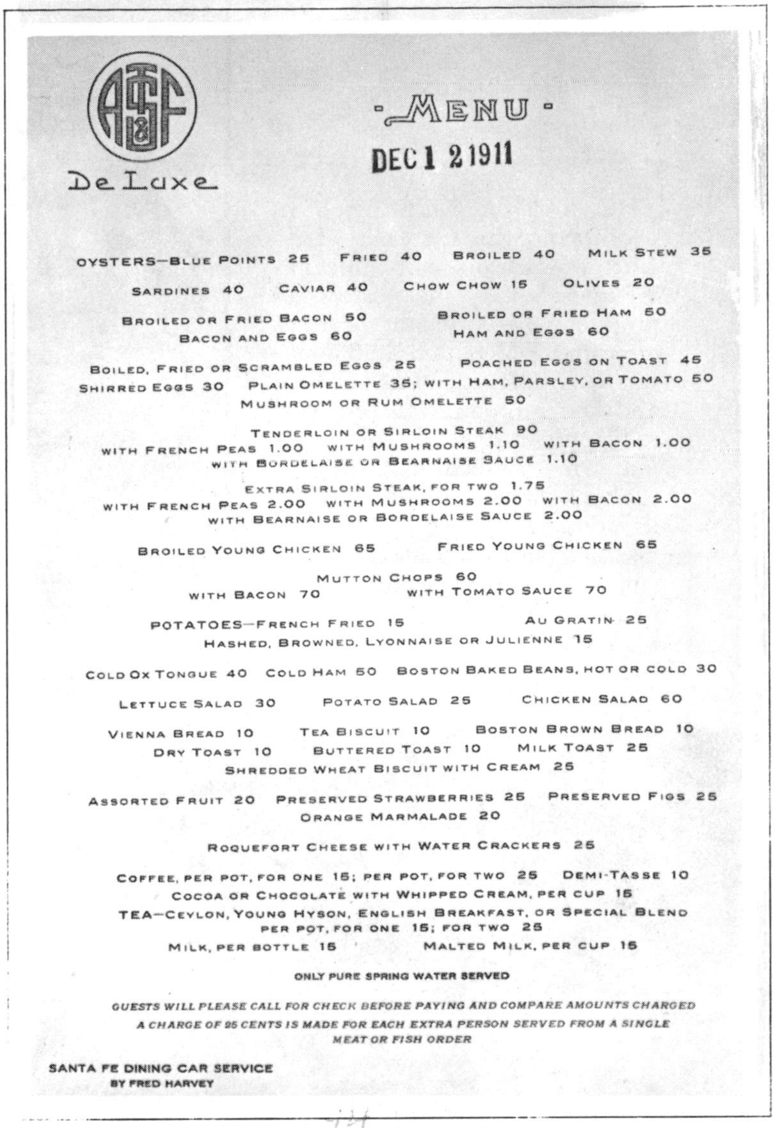

De Luxe

MENU

DEC 1 2 1911

OYSTERS—Blue Points 25 Fried 40 Broiled 40 Milk Stew 35

Sardines 40 Caviar 40 Chow Chow 15 Olives 20

Broiled or Fried Bacon 50 Broiled or Fried Ham 50
Bacon and Eggs 60 Ham and Eggs 60

Boiled, Fried or Scrambled Eggs 25 Poached Eggs on Toast 45
Shirred Eggs 30 Plain Omelette 35; with Ham, Parsley, or Tomato 50
Mushroom or Rum Omelette 50

Tenderloin or Sirloin Steak 90
with French Peas 1.00 with Mushrooms 1.10 with Bacon 1.00
with Bordelaise or Bearnaise Sauce 1.10

Extra Sirloin Steak, for two 1.75
with French Peas 2.00 with Mushrooms 2.00 with Bacon 2.00
with Bearnaise or Bordelaise Sauce 2.00

Broiled Young Chicken 65 Fried Young Chicken 65

Mutton Chops 60
with Bacon 70 with Tomato Sauce 70

POTATOES—French Fried 15 Au Gratin 25
Hashed, Browned, Lyonnaise or Julienne 15

Cold Ox Tongue 40 Cold Ham 50 Boston Baked Beans, hot or cold 30

Lettuce Salad 30 Potato Salad 25 Chicken Salad 60

Vienna Bread 10 Tea Biscuit 10 Boston Brown Bread 10
Dry Toast 10 Buttered Toast 10 Milk Toast 25
Shredded Wheat Biscuit with Cream 25

Assorted Fruit 20 Preserved Strawberries 25 Preserved Figs 25
Orange Marmalade 20

Roquefort Cheese with Water Crackers 25

Coffee, per pot, for one 15; per pot, for two 25 Demi-Tasse 10
Cocoa or Chocolate with Whipped Cream, per cup 15
TEA—Ceylon, Young Hyson, English Breakfast, or Special Blend
per pot, for one 15; for two 25
Milk, per bottle 15 Malted Milk, per cup 15

ONLY PURE SPRING WATER SERVED

GUESTS WILL PLEASE CALL FOR CHECK BEFORE PAYING AND COMPARE AMOUNTS CHARGED
A CHARGE OF 25 CENTS IS MADE FOR EACH EXTRA PERSON SERVED FROM A SINGLE MEAT OR FISH ORDER

SANTA FE DINING CAR SERVICE
BY FRED HARVEY

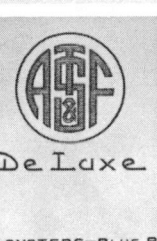

THE FIRST air cooling device on record on a railroad train was incorporated in the diner assigned to *de Luxe*, although the St. Regis Hotel in New York had already experimented with some success in air conditioning both public and private apartments. The *de Luxe* diners featured, of course, Fred Harvey meals, "the standard of excellence the world over." In addition to "the air washing device that perfectly ventilates the car, there is an 'indirect' system of lighting whereby the entire room is flooded as with sunlight, and a new style of chair that is very comfortable. The table lamps are below the level of the eye. The interior finish is mahogany." For his $25. surcharge, the passenger on this favored train, in addition to other amenities of sumptuousness, ate and drank in princely fashion. "Both chef and steward are artists in their respective lines." The use of the word chef in this context suggests the high regard in which *de Luxe* was held by the management, since almost universally until then the lexicon of railroading had preferred cook and waiter. Here in a unique photograph from the archives of the Moulin Studios, the extra fare, extra elegant patrons of *de Luxe* are shown at dinner in 1914, an age of parasols and feathered turbans and quail in aspic on the luncheon menu. *(Above: Byron Harvey Collection.)*

THE SANTA FE'S pitch in promoting the fortunes of *de Luxe* was a frank snob appeal as is suggested by the posters reproduced here. Its implications were those of butlered affluence for a strictly limited clientele and the railroad was prepared to supply just this. The depot platform at Needles, California *(below)* shown with *de Luxe* at its edge was celebrated for being the hottest of all Santa Fe stops in summer and the coldest in winter. *(Right: Arthur D. Dubin Collection; Below: Colorado State Historical Society.)*

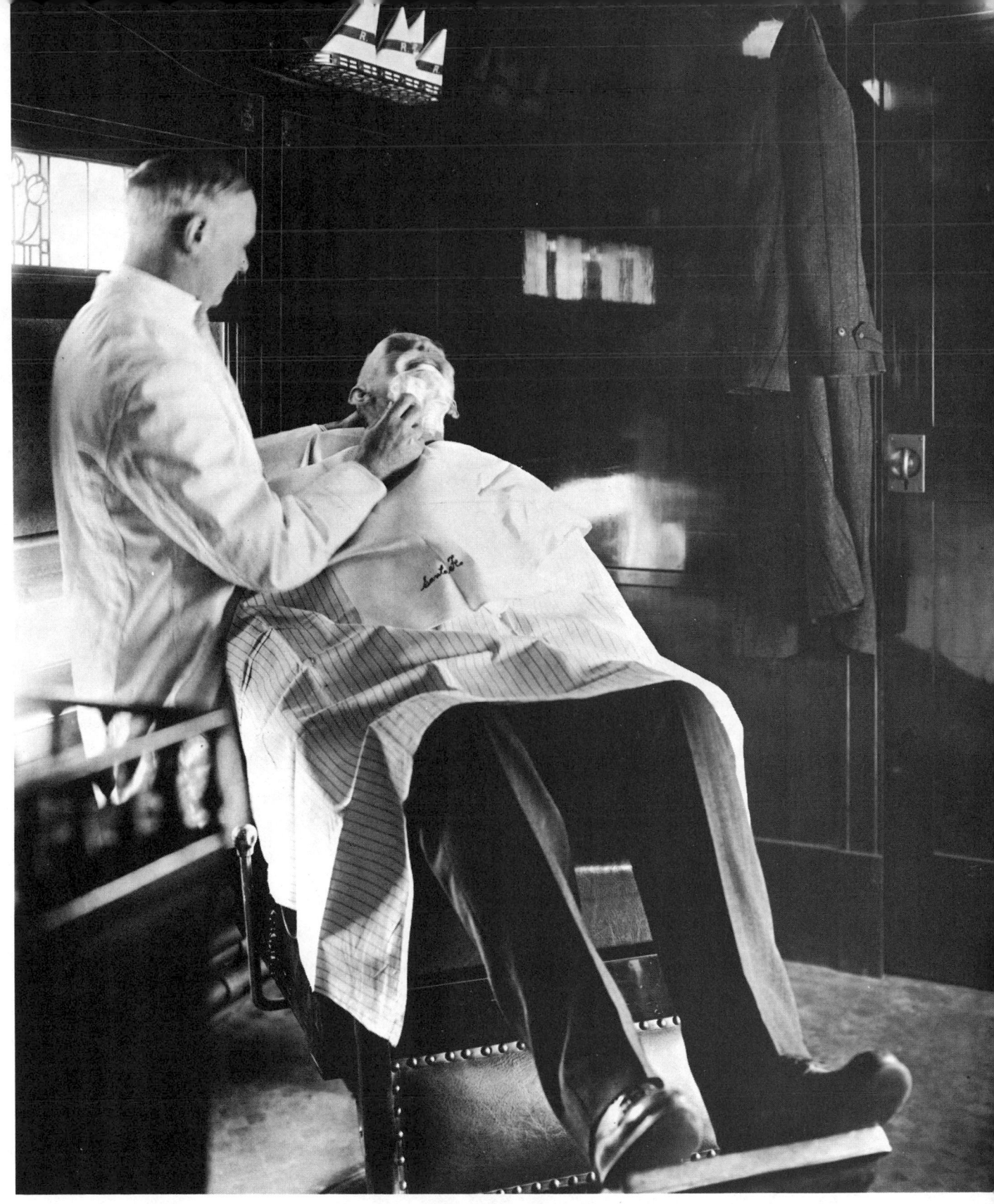

IN THE YEARS of the flowering of *de Luxe*, a train barber was as much a status symbol aboard a name train as the drumhead insigne at the observation end or game on the dining car menu. Most train barbers established confidence in their patrons with a straight razor protected by a patent guard calculated to eliminate at least some of the hazards of mischance inherent in a conventional Sheffield or Solingen blade hovering near the human carotid at seventy miles an hour. The barber aboard *de Luxe*, you may be sure, was at the top of his then honored profession. (*Moulin Studios.*)

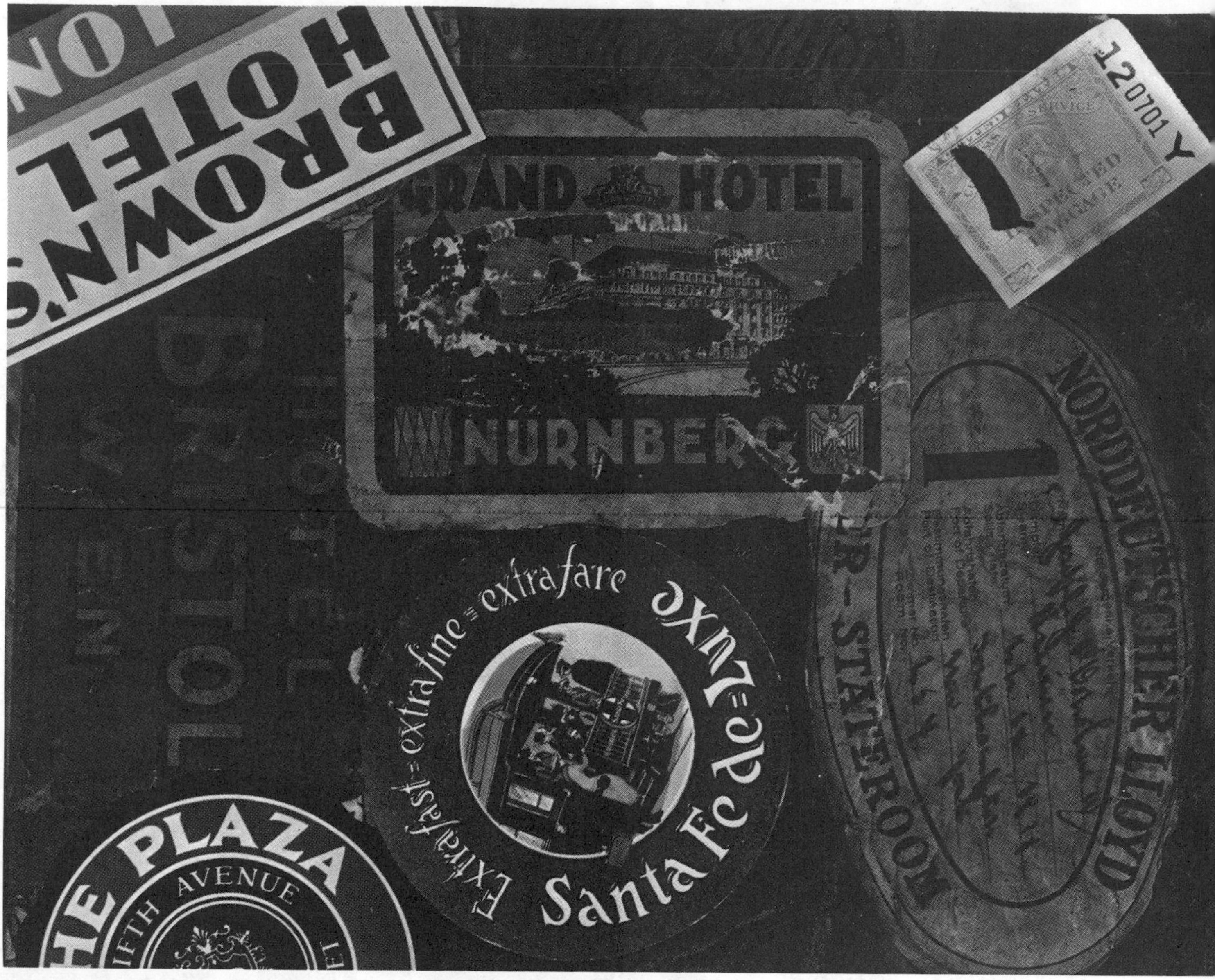
BROWN'S HOTEL
GRAND HOTEL
NÜRNBERG
Extra fast = extra fine = extra fare
Santa Fe de-Luxe
HE PLAZA
NORDDEUTSCHER LLOYD
STATEROOM

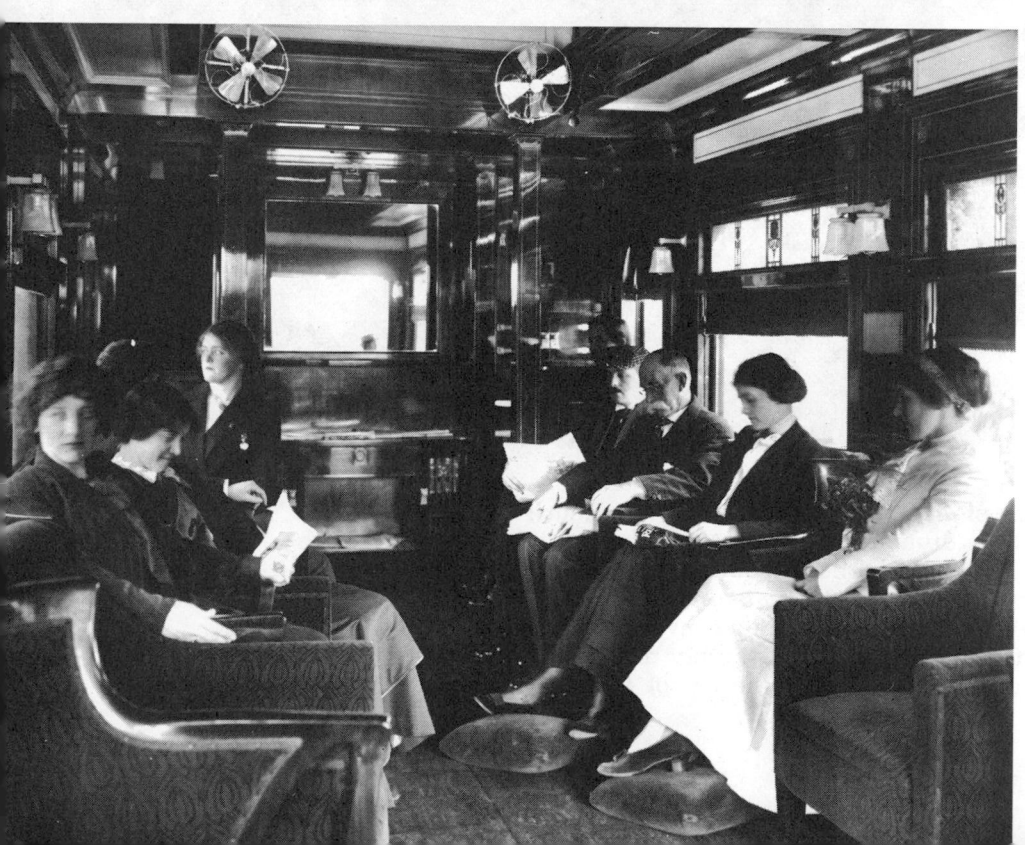

FOLLOWING THE EXAMPLE of luxury hotels and steamship companies everywhere, the Santa Fe added still another unique panache of elegance to *de Luxe* and its status symbolism when it introduced the only known such luggage sticker ever to advertise its owner's presence aboard an American name train. The three color cachet *(opposite)* was entirely at home in the company of Brown's of London, the Plaza in New York and Cunard and North German Lloyd on the North Atlantic sea lanes. Its appearance on the Louis Vuiton valises and hat boxes of the well-to-do marked them as seasoned travelers. By standards or later notions of comfort, the decor of the library car assigned to *de Luxe* shown opposite with its leaded glass transoms, hassocks and electric fans might not seem an impressive example of carbuilding. But in 1914, Honduran mahogany, bevel-edge French mirrors and wall bracket illuminations were fine indeed. Wing collars and cloth travelling caps were the accepted attire for gentlemen *en route*, and the snowy attire topped with a corsage of fresh flowers presented to lady patrons shown at the right argue an invincible optimism in an age innocent of air conditioning. Below, in one of the few known photographs of *de Luxe* at speed, it follows a ledger-ruled right of way through wintry Kansas. *(Opposite: Byron Harvey Collection, Moulin Studios; Below: Everett de Golyer Collection.)*

The Santa Fe's

De Luxe

EXTRA FINE - EXTRA FAST - EXTRA FARE

THE gold-embossed souvenir man's wallet presented by the Santa Fe to gentlemen patrons of *de Luxe* is from the Byron Harvey Collection. The travel advertisement shown here is from that of Arthur Dubin.

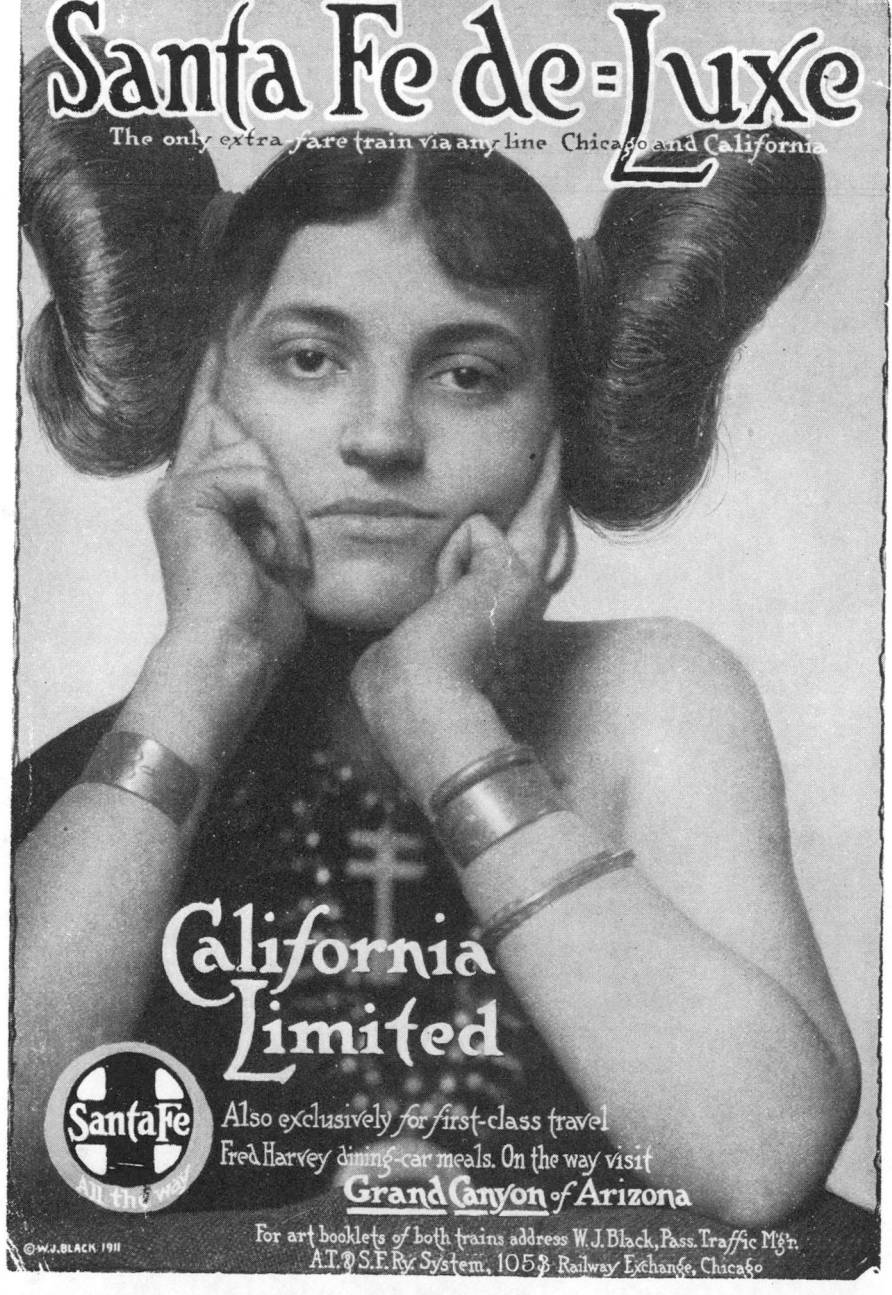

Santa Fe de=Luxe

The only extra fare train via any line Chicago and California

California Limited

Santa Fe All the way

Also exclusively for first-class travel
Fred Harvey dining-car meals. On the way visit
Grand Canyon of Arizona

For art booklets of both trains address W. J. Black, Pass. Traffic Mg'r.
A.T. & S.F. Ry. System, 1053 Railway Exchange, Chicago

© W. J. BLACK 1911

AT LA GRANDE DEPOT in Los Angeles (*left*) the approaching hour of departure of *de Luxe* scarcely appears to arouse the enraptured delight appropriate to taking passage on the world's most expensive and well-upholstered train. Junior patently doesn't want to go. The porter has begun in advance to hate his passengers, and the woman on the steps is getting ready to file complaints before the train moves out of the depot. This scene of actuality snapped about 1915 will be changed in a few years when Madison Avenue has assumed the Santa Fe's promotion and advertising. Mad delight will suffuse the faces of all concerned and Junior, from Central Casting, will be all Buster Brown smiles. In the meantime, this is how they really looked when the shutter snapped on that now distant day. (*Left: Colorado State Historical Society; Above: Moulin Studios.*)

ALTHOUGH it was owned by the rival and bitterly competitive Rio Grande Railroad, the Antlers Hotel at Colorado Springs missed no bets and sent its fine omnibus, as shown below, to meet all trains at the Santa Fe depot. Already the Santa Fe was aware of the sales and promotional potentialities of Indian artifacts, and the newsstand at The Springs a few decades later flowered with Navajo blankets, Zuni jewelry and colorful pottery ranged below copies of *Ainslee's Magazine* and toy glass pistols filled with hard candy. *(Two Photos: Western Collection, Denver Public Library.)*

THE HISTORY of the greatest railroad feud in the Old West is recapitulated in the photograph below where the Santa Fe's *Centennial State* rolls southbound out of Denver over the right of way of the Rio Grande. Once, in pioneer times in the seventies, the two emergent carriers had battled fang and claw for the passage over Raton Pass leading to the high plains of the Great Southwest, a struggle decided in favor of the Santa Fe. Later the hired gunmen of the two roads had fought pitched battles for the control of the route up the Arkansas River and the Rio Grande triumphed. In the end both carriers shared trackage rights between Pueblo and Denver as suggested here. At the bottom of the page service crews lubricate a Santa Fe Mountain type at La Junta where the Santa Fe's Pueblo extension meets the transcontinental mainline. *(Richard H. Kindig; Lucius Beebe.)*

77

IN AN AGE when the national self-consciousness decreed that Colorado should be "The Switzerland of America" and the Rocky Mountains "The American Alps," tourists had a wide and fascinating variety of things to see and do when they arrived via Denver and Colorado Springs. They demanded scenery and precious metals in that order so that a coasting party aboard a handcar on the Cripple Creek Short Line was practically a must. If they got to Leadville on the Colorado Midland's main line they invariably put up at the Vendome whose bus met all the steamcars in order to share, vicariously, in the legend of H. A. W. Tabor. (*Two Photos: Denver Public Library, Western Collection.*)

78

FOR A TIME a wholly owned subsidiary of the Santa Fe and perhaps the most beloved in remembrance of all the now vanished railroads of the Rocky Mountain region, the Colorado Midland, although a hard luck carrier from its very inception, was one of the great tourist attractions of its age, which was roughly the turn of the century. The C.M. originated at Colorado Springs and boldly assailed the ramparts of the Rockies up precipitous Ute Pass and thence to the Gunnison River at Grand Junction via the lonely reaches of South Park. At Grand Junction it disappeared in the main line of the Rio Grande so that its pretentions to a continental dimension were microscopic but its fantastic right of way through an almost inaccessible wilderness made it a tourist must throughout the nineties and the first decade of the current century. The Colorado Midland was, to be sure, only one of the railroads serving the Rocky Mountain region in the years of the great tourist bonanza. The parent Santa Fe, Union Pacific, Colorado & Southern, the Burlington, Rock Island, Fort Worth & Denver and, of course, the Denver & Rio Grande Western through its connecting Gould carriers, all benefited in greater or less degree by Colorado's celebrity for scenery, health resorts and unspoiled wilderness. Here an all-Pullman special, from its white metal marker flags on the locomotive pilot, on the Colorado Midland turns on an unidentified wye against a mountain background. It was but one of hundreds. *(The Smithsonian Institution.)*

79

COLORADO in the eighties when the Santa Fe got into the fullest stride of the tourist trade in the Rocky Mountain resort regions where it competed with the Rio Grande, the Fort Worth & Denver, the Union Pacific and the Burlington, held rich rewards for sightseers no further removed from the car windows than the railroad's own right of way. Where else, for example, save at the Santa Fe's depot at Palmer Lake, halfway between Denver and Colorado Springs, could the Palace cars expect to be met by well-dressed frontiersmen in business suits with wing collars and fresh boutonnieres, one of them wearing a bowler hat and the other carrying a Winchester express rifle and by a small boy in a goat cart? Nearly three quarters of a century later the Denver Section of *The California Limited* would leave The Springs for Denver with eleven Pullmans behind a formidable Mountain type locomotive No. 3763. *(Above: Western Collection, Denver Public Library; Right: Richard J. Cook.)*

80

FEW VISITORS in the Colorado nineties who rode into The Springs aboard the Santa Fe's Pullmans and put up at the Antlers Hotel wanted to miss seeing the Cripple Creek diggings on the far side of Pike's Peak where millions were being recovered in the last but one of the great gold rush bonanzas in the continental United States. There, on the depot platform at Victor of the Midland Terminal, which at one time was a Santa Fe subsidiary, they could see the shaggy miners waiting for the down train and Santa Fe high cars being loaded with rich ore bound for the reducing mills. They might even encounter Charlie Tutt or Spencer Penrose, many times millionaires from Cripple Creek mines and the region's most spectacular personalities. *(Two Photos: Western Collection, Denver Public Library.)*

THE FOLK-LEGENDS of the Old West maintain that civilization was imported to the roaring cow towns of Kansas and the howling wilderness of the cattle trails by the six-gun marshals of the Wyatt Earp tradition. More astute students of the social *mores* of the West and Southwest, however, assert that the greatest single prophet of urbanity and comparative decorum was an English perfectionist named Fred Harvey who, without firing a shot or kicking down the doors of a single saloon, pacified a region as vast as continental Europe through the agency of broiled quail on toast and the sternly enforced edict that customers in his restaurants wear jackets and ties while eating. The first Harvey House, operated in partnership with the then-building Santa Fe Railroad, commenced operations in 1875 at Topeka, Kansas. Good food in clean surroundings served by waitresses who were no floozies was such a success that Harvey next year opened in Florence and from there the Harvey System spread to become the universal standard of excellence in the Southwest, riding the dining cars of the railroad and having its abode at the railroads' depot hotels. Below, in a pose once familiar throughout the Southwest, *The California Limited* pauses outside the Casa del Desierto at Barstow, California, whose lobby, typical of Harvey decor is shown at the right. *(Five Photos: Byron Harvey Collection.)*

Wallace,
Kansas
1880

Somer-
ville
Texas,
1914

San
Diego,
Calif.
1930

83

TO MAINTAIN its split second schedule between Chicago and The Coast, *El Capitan*, even when running with only five cars still required a helper on the Raton grade out of Trinidad. R. H. Kindig took this revealing photograph in April 1939 near Wootton, Colorado, named for one of the last of The Mountain Men and an early benefactor of the Santa Fe. (*Right: Santa Fe.*)

THE ONLY extra-fare, all-coach train in the record when it was inaugurated as the counterpart with coaches of the sumptuously appointed *Super Chief*, the Santa Fe lavished on *El Capitan* the full grand manner treatment. Until the decline of traffic in the fifties conditioned its consolidation in a single train with *The Super Chief*, *El Capitan* was a transcontinental varnish run on an independent schedule.   *(Below: Kaufmann & Fabry.)*

IN THE THIRTIES and forties The Santa Fe maintained service between Chicago and San Francisco-Los Angeles aboard a low-cost train with coaches, Standard section-drawing room Pullmans and tourist sleepers designed primarily to solve the age-old problem of mothers with nursing infants and children of uncontrollable age who had made life a burden since the first coming of the steamcars. If special inducements such as reduced fares, budget priced meals, nursing service and tolerant porters could attract the infantile trade, the management figured it would remove a ponderable menace to the tranquility and repose of travel on its more adult trains. *The Scout,* as the rolling nursery was named, remained in service for well over a decade, a mobile nightmare of diaper changes and the inconvenient feeding habits of the very young and, although it was a sort of negative blessing, was appreciated by travelers in search of abated tumults aboard *The Chief, Super Chief* and *California Limited.* On the almost gradeless run between Oakland and Bakersfield, conventional motive power was recruited from the Santa Fe's stable of Hudsons such as No. 3454 shown above on the smoky end of *The Scout* near Richmond, California. (*Above: Rail Photo Service, David Gray Edwards; Opposite: Three Photos: Santa Fe.*)

86

BEFORE AND AFTER views
of *The San Diegan* in steam
and in Diesel were taken
in the successive years 1948 and
1949 from the identical
vantage point in San Diego
yards. They were taken
for Rail Photo Service by
Harold E. Williams
and depict the Santa Fe in its
farthest continental dimension
and greatest remove from
the views on the opposite page.

AT THE OPPOSITE end of its transcontinental main line, the affairs of the Santa Fe make an ordered chaos of the Dearborn Depot yards in Chicago as *The Chief* arrives and *The Kansas Cityan* takes its departure from the shores of Lake Michigan. The pageant of railroad vitality and animation at Dearborn embraced the arrivals and departures of varnish runs of the Monon, Chicago & Eastern Illinois, the Wabash and Erie, some of them in more than one section and represented railroading in the very grand manner. In volume of traffic the Santa Fe dominated them all as well as in the splendor of the name trains on its schedules. *(Two Photos: Rail Photo Service, W. G. Fancher.)*

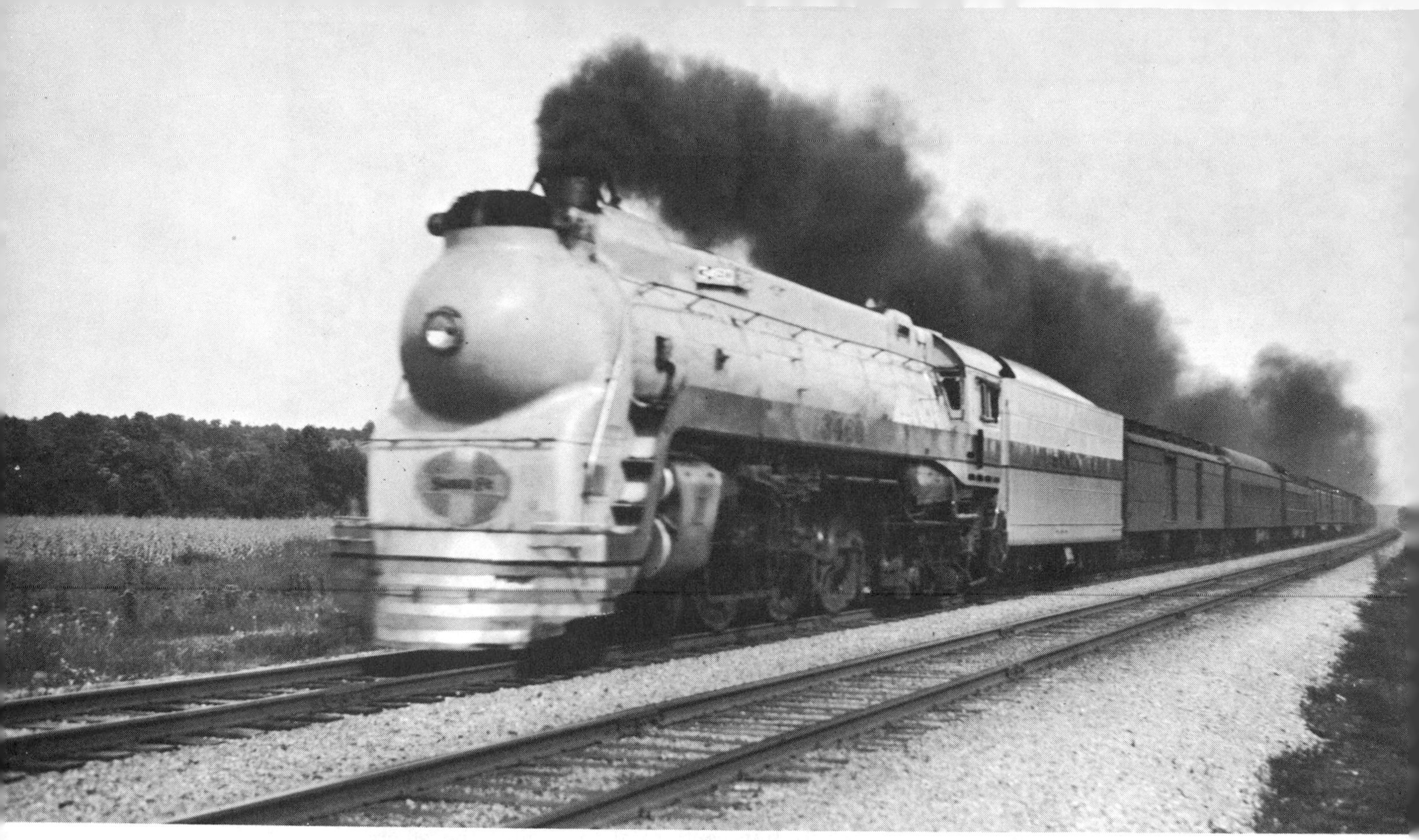

Santa Fe
MORTON
RAILWAY EXPRESS AGENCY

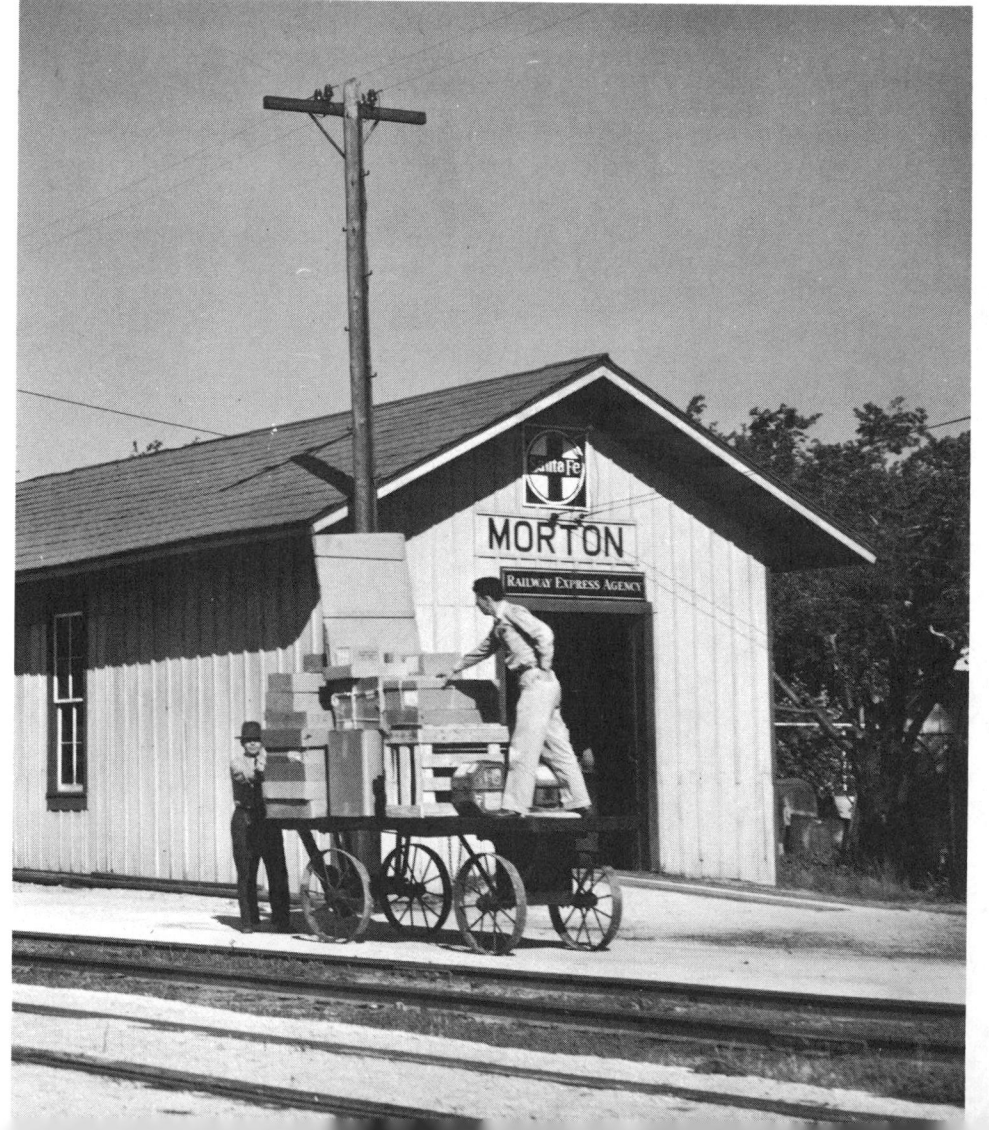

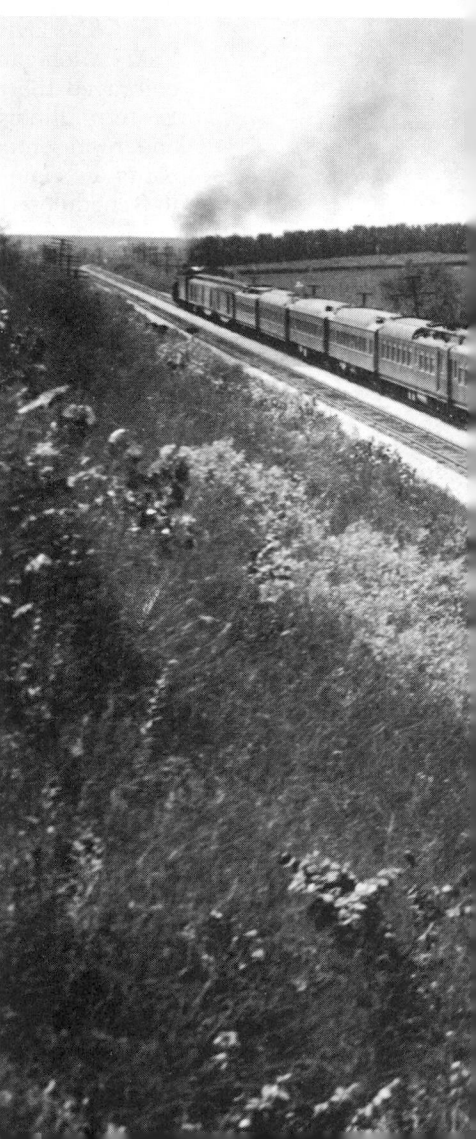

DINING SERVICE

Santa Fe / Fred Harvey

● Santa Fe dining service, managed by Fred Harvey, has been maintained on a plane of unvarying excellence for over half a century.

On the Santa Fe, all through passenger trains which do not carry dining cars, stop at attractive dining stations located about 125 miles apart.

●

At these Santa Fe dining stations, table d'hote meals are served in the Lunch Room from 50c. to $1.00; also a la carte meals at reasonable prices. Table d'hote meals only are served in the Dining-Rooms, breakfast 75c., luncheon $1.00 and dinner $1.00.

●

Santa Fe dining car meals are, in general, a la carte. There are these exceptions:

●

Dinner on The California Limited (Trains 3 and 4), and The Grand Canyon Limited (Trains 23 and 24), is either a la carte or table d'hote. as desired. Trains 23 and 24 also stop at dining stations for meals.

The Santa Fe operates the only through dining car service between Chicago and California.

●

On The Ranger, (Trains 5 and 6) between Chicago, Kansas City and Texas, table d'hote breakfasts are served at 65c. and 75c., luncheon at 90c., and dinner at $1.25. Similar table d'hote meals are served on The Navajo (Train 9) and The Missionary (Train 22) between Chicago and Kansas City.

AIR-CONDITIONED DINING CARS

● Santa Fe - Fred Harvey dining cars are AIR-CONDITIONED. In addition there are AIR-CONDITIONED cafe-observation cars on Trains 49 and 50, between Kansas City and Tulsa, and on Trains 23 and 2, between Barstow and San Francisco.

WHIMSY SELDOM raised its head in the affairs of the Santa Fe, but in the latter thirties it indulged itself in a streamlined Pacific of experimental design whose bright blue steel shroud earned for it a local celebrity as "The Blue Goose," and it is shown opposite scorching the ballast out of Chillicothe, Illinois, with *The Grand Canyon Limited* in 1941. Although the *Grand Canyon's* relaxed schedule between Chicago and Los Angeles suggests no excessive speeds, its considerable head-end business picked up at such minor stops as Morton *(opposite)* often caused it to roll like the proverbial bat out of Hell between stations and hundred mile an hour cardings in Illinois and Kansas were not infrequent. As late as 1938, when it is shown against a pastoral background near Edelstein, Illinois, in the lower frame, *The Grand Canyon* retained the grand manner and included an open platform observation car with the drumhead insigne that proclaimed it a train of pedigree. *(Three Photos: Paul Stringham.)*

TWO SANTA FE old timers of long established pedigree and a devoted following were *The Navajo* on a leisurely schedule between Chicago and Southern California with setout Pullmans for Kansas City, and *The Ranger* between Chicago and Texas points served by the Santa Fe. The handsome observation car opposite riding at the end of *Navajo* as it rolled through Chillicothe, Illinois, with its single beam underframe and roof-level markers was purest Santa Fe. Its Pullmans *(above)* even in a non-air-conditioned age held mellow memories of good times for thousands. *Ranger* as is suggested by its observation patrons, was a shirt-sleeve varnish whose dining car chefs were schooled in burning the steak for Texas tastes and which made a fine action picture on the plains with a lightweight baggage in the midst of a Standard consist of coaches and Pullmans. *(Above: Santa Fe; Opposite: Paul Stringham; Below, Two Photos: Everett De Golyer.)*

92

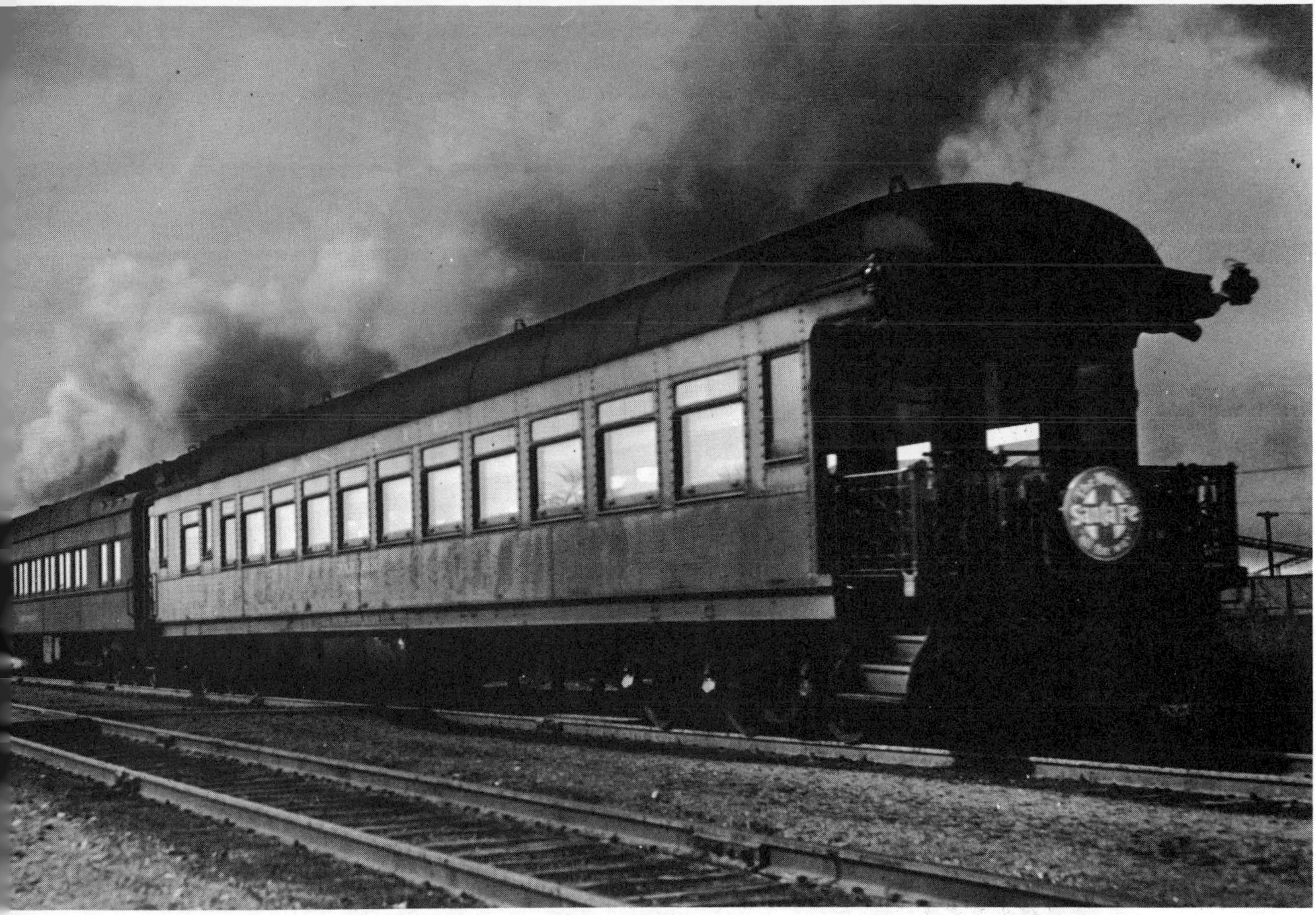

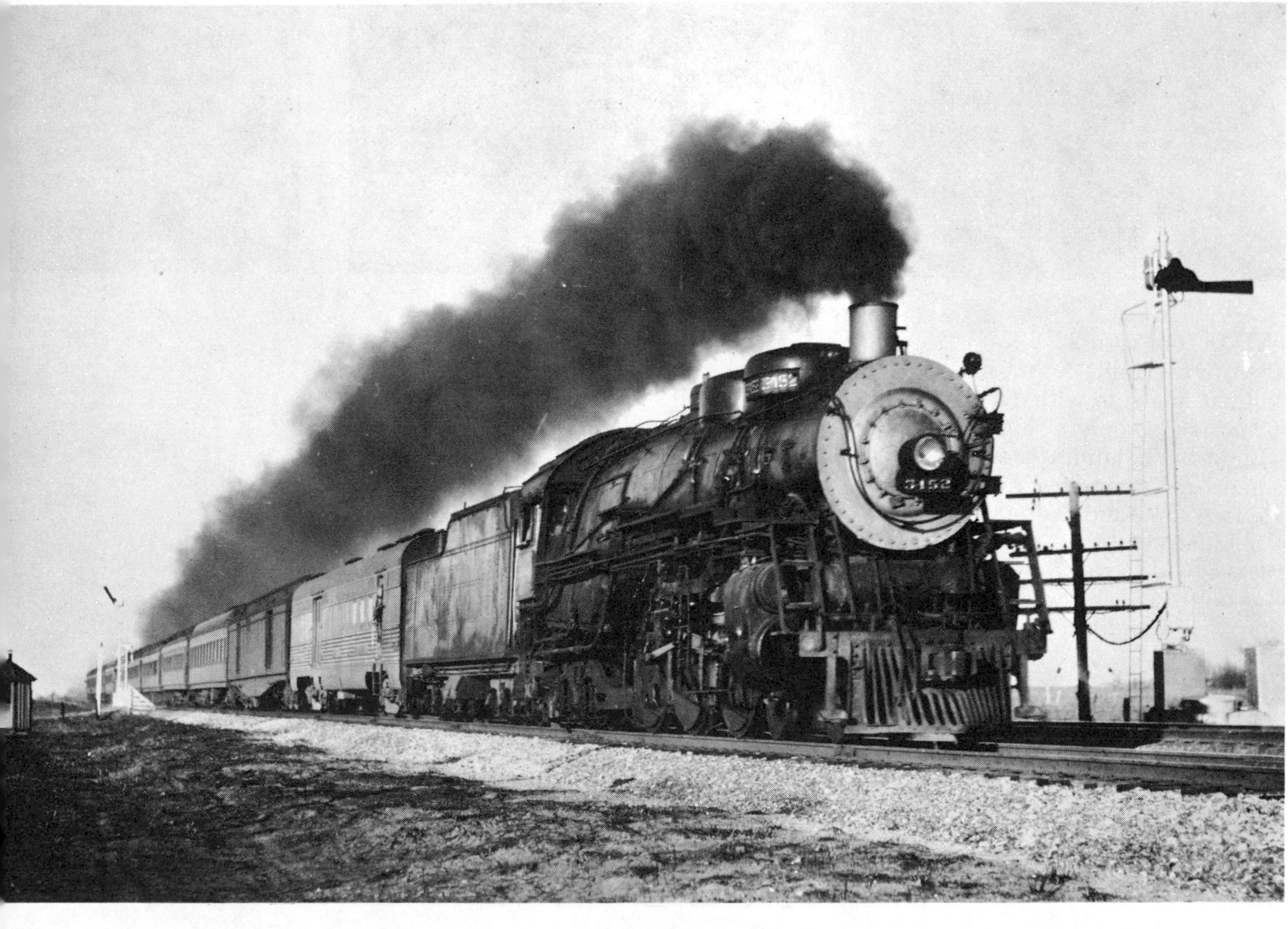

BY THE TIME, on April 22, 1937, the original units A and B made their final run with *The Super Chief (right)* only a single Budd-built stainless steel sleeper had been integrated into the train's consist and Pullman Standard still dominated equipment assigned to the flagship of the Santa Fe fleet. (*Gerald M. Best.*)

THE MAIDEN RUN of *The Super Chief* in May of 1936, depicted here in the
high desert of New Mexico, was made with all Pullman Standard equipment
behind motor units A and B. New motive power was procured in April of the
following year and streamlined equipment was integrated to the operation over
a period of several years before an all-Budd stainless steel consist was achieved.
The thirty-nine and a half hour schedule maintained in its opening months with
full weight standard equipment gave passengers such a ride as hadn't been
experienced since Death Valley Scotty's "Coyote Special," a quarter of a century
earlier. The commissary of *The Super Chief* at once became the choicest regard
of the Fred Harvey system and the most opulent showcase for its wares. Its
victualling at the Chicago yards *(opposite)* was accomplished under the watchful
eye of the steward who held fresh asparagus, Lake Primrose whitefish and Maine
lobster in a state of trust from the time they came aboard until they disappeared
off the passenger's plate. On the train's maiden sailing, May 12, 1936, calf's liver
and bacon was .70¢, larded tenderloin of beef in Madeira sauce, .95¢, and fresh
Malossol caviar, $1.75. A few years later Blue Point oysters were $1.65 for six
and double sirloin steak $7.75. Inflation notwithstanding, dinner on the Super
Chief has always been a gastronomic adventure comparable to eating at Henri
Soulé's in New York or Maxim's in Paris.   *(Above: Everett De Golyer Collection;
Opposite: Graphic House.)*

95

THE *Super* CHIEF

- DINNER -

ROMANOFF FRESH MALOSSOL CAVIAR 1.75

ANTIPASTO 75   HEARTS OF CALIFORNIA ARTICHOKES 35

Hearts of Celery 30   Salted Almonds 30   Colossal Ripe Olives 25

NEPTUNE COCKTAIL 50   AVOCADO 40

GRAPEFRUIT, ORANGE AND RAISINS 40

CHICKEN OKRA, LOUISIANNAISE IN CUP 20; TUREEN 30
Consomme, Hot or Jellied 25   Clam Broth 20

SWORDFISH STEAK SAUTE, MEUNIERE WITH CAPERS 75
POACHED TRANCHE OF SALMON, AU VIN BLANC 70

FRESH MUSHROOMS SAUTE, AU FINES HERBES, AND BACON 75
OLD FASHIONED BONELESS CHICKEN PIE, AMERICAINE 85
POACHED EGGS ON FRIED FRESH TOMATO, SAUCE HOLLANDAISE 65
SPAGHETTI WITH JULIENNE OF VIRGINIA HAM, MADAME GALLI 65
ROAST LARDED TENDERLOIN OF BEEF, SAUCE MADERE 95
Small Sirloin Steak a la Minute 1.25
Sirloin Steak for one 1.60   Sirloin Steak for two 2.75
Calf's Liver and Bacon 70   Lamb Chop, Extra Thick (1) 80
                                                                (to order—20 minutes)
Bacon 65; Half Portion 40   Ham 70; Half Portion 40
        Bacon and Eggs 70   Ham and Eggs 70

FRESH ASPARAGUS, DRAWN BUTTER 30
NEW CORN ON COB 25   NEW LIMA BEANS 20
NEW POTATOES, PERSILLADE 15   MASHED 15   COTTAGE FRIED 25

COLD

ASSORTED MEATS, POTATO SALAD 90   BRISKET OF CORNED BEEF 70
TOMATO STUFFED WITH LOBSTER SALAD 60
CHEF'S SPECIAL COMBINATION SALAD, PLATE 30
ROMAINE, COTTAGE CHEESE AND RAISIN SALAD, PLATE 30
Lettuce Salad 35   Potato 25   Chicken (White Meat) 80

Rye Bread and Dinner Rolls with Butter, per person 10   Dry or Buttered Toast 15
Melba Toast 15   Milk Toast 30 Boston Brown, Raisin or Whole Wheat 10; Toasted 15
OLD FASHIONED FRESH STRAWBERRY SHORTCAKE WITH WHIPPED CREAM 30
CANTALOUPE 20   RAISIN PIE 20   APRICOT PARFAIT 35
VANILLA ICE CREAM 25; WITH ASSORTED CAKE 35
ENGLISH CHESHIRE CHEESE WITH PRESERVED GUAVA 50
Roquefort 35   Petit Gruyere 35
Coffee, per Pot 25   Demi Tasse 15   Kaffee Hag Coffee, per Pot 25
    Cocoa or Chocolate, Whipped Cream, per Pot 20   Tea, per Pot 20

PRICES SHOWN ON THIS MENU ARE SUBJECT TO VARIOUS STATE SALES TAXES
Guests will please call for checks before paying and compare amounts charged
An extra charge of twenty-five cents each will be made for all meals served outside of Dining Car

SANTA FE DINING CAR SERVICE
    Fred Harvey

THE HALCYON AGE
of luxury living in which
The Super Chief was
inaugurated, 1937, is
reflected in the right-hand
side of the menu. Never
again was fresh caviar
to be $1.75 or larded
tenderloin of beef .95¢.
Fred Harvey's spirit must
have been gratified.

HOLLYWOOD CELEBRITIES of the late thirties accustomed to *haute cuisine* as a status symbol and able, with some degree of plausibility, to refrain from ordering three kinds of soup if the menu were in French, found the transition from Dave Chasen's, Perino's and The Vendome to the restaurant cars of *The Super Chief* an easy one. Bedsheet size menus printed in tourquoise blue and gold listed Guaymas shrimp, limestone lettuce, out of season strawberries, Cranshaw melon, Rocky Mountain trout, Westphalia hams, Mexican quail in aspic, fresh caviar and rare cheeses from France and Holland in superlative abundance. The champagne depicted in the gastronomic *trompe d'oeil* opposite is Veuve Clicquot but there was also Mumms' Extra Dry, Bollinger and, for the extra fastidious and well heeled, Dom Perignon Cuvee. The prodigal legend of Harvey hospitality found its ultimate fulfillment on the *Super Chief* where dinner jacketed maitres d'hotel confected *omelette au confitures* at table for John Ford and the Countess di Frasso and as many breakfasts were served in bed as in the diner. The only private dining room available to privileged guests on any American train was The Turquoise Room *(below)* where Cecil De Mille and Louise B. Mayer could dine in the seclusion appropriate to the storied great of the Hollywood era. On this page, with wartime westbound traffic at an all-time peak, *The Super Chief*, with two steam helpers out of Trinidad, traverses one of the infrequent tangents of the Raton Pass in the winter of 1944. *(Opposite: Graphic House, Santa Fe Railroad; Above: Charles Clegg.)*

97

SINCE THE SUPERLATIVELY AFFLUENT *de Luxe* in the years before the 1914 war and until the entry of the United States into World War II, no train on the Santa Fe timecard, not even the magnificent *Chief*, made the play for big name patronage from the worlds of communications, finance and the stage and screen implicit in the conduct of *The Super Chief*. The Fred Harvey management spread itself on menus to rival those of the great name trains of Europe, dining car stewards in morning coats and dinner jackets after six recreated the ambiance of Maxim's or the Cafe de Paris, and Hollywood press agents saw to it that the arrival and departure of their clients was covered by photographers and columnists on a national scale. The fashionable professional world of Beverly Hills regarded *The Super Chief* as the shortest distance between Dave Chasen's restaurant in Hollywood and Ernie Byfield's table at The Pump Room in Chicago, and Fred Harvey undertook to see to it that the transition was accomplished with a minimum of discomfort. At the right *The Super Chief*, inbound, passes the less august *Grand Canyon* headed west, while below the *Super Chief* for many years relied on steam to help it over the Cajon grades. *(Right: Douglas C. Wornom; Below: William Barham.)*

Dinner Aboard the Super Chief
FRED HARVEY SERVICE

Table d'Hote Dinners
(Price of Entree Determines Cost of Dinner)

Pascal Celery - Queen Olives

Chicken Broth with Noodles	Chilled Tomato Juice
Consomme en Tasse, Hot or Jellied	Marinated Herring in Sour Cream
Orange and Grapefruit Supreme	Fresh Shrimp Cocktail (50c. extra)

MOUNTAIN TROUT SAUTE MEUNIERE WITH CAPERS 4.40
  Colorado Mountain Trout, Cooked to Order, Served with Browned
  Butter Sauce, Lemon Juice, Parsley and Capers

OMELETTE WITH JULIENNE OF HAM 3.60
  Fluffy Three Egg Omelette Cooked in Butter with Tender
  Strips of Ham, Garnished with Pineapple Rings

BROILED CHICKEN REPUBLICAINE 4.30
  Half Spring Chicken Expertly Broiled, Garnished with Fresh
  Mushroom Caps and Strips of Bacon

LONDON MIXED GRILL 5.40
  Consisting of 4 oz. Prime Tenderloin Steak, One Thick French
  Lamb Chop, Mushroom Cap, Bacon and Grilled Tomato

CHARCOAL BROILED SIRLOIN STEAK 6.60
  Specially Selected and Carefully Aged for Your Pleasure

Lime Sherbet

Whipped Potatoes	Cauliflower Polonaise
French Fried Potatoes	New Peas

Chef's Combination Salad

Dinner Rolls

Vanilla Ice Cream with Cookies	Baked Apple with Cream	Layer Cake
Apple Pie Grapefruit Sections	Orange Sections	Choice of Sundae
Pumpkin Pie, Whipped Cream		"Forbidden Fruit" (Cordial)

Choice of Cheese

Beverage

SPECIAL—CALIFORNIA RED OR WHITE TABLE WINES
Bottled expressly for Fred Harvey Service—The Santa Fe Railway
Split, 6 ounces (serves two) 75
(Not Served where prohibited by State Law)

11-11-63 △ 12587

FILM actor Alan Ladd and family obviously find the luncheon menu on *The Super Chief* to their liking. Dinner will find the maitre d'hotel in evening attire. *(Two Photos: Santa Fe.)*

THE FIRST DIESEL UNITS assigned to power *The Super Chief* on the long, extra-fare, extra fast haul between Los Angeles and Chicago over the iron of "Santa Fe All The Way" were no great shakes esthetically. Flat faced with a frowning turret of air intake louvers and the proportions of an automotive shoebox, they aroused mirth or hostility in the beholder, but they delivered the trains on the tightest regular schedule, thirty-nine and a half hours, yet devised between the Great Lakes and California and *The Super Chief* tailgate insigne was a hallmark of style and sophistication. At the right one of the primal Diesels, paused at San Bernardino, depicts on its facade like a highball signal of antiquity giving it green across the continent, the shadow of a platform lamp. *(Right: Lucius Beebe; Below: Santa Fe Railway.)*

THE INTERIORS OF PUBLIC CARS on *The Super Chief*, lounges and diners were furnished in a restrained Navajo decor with pigskin furniture and broadloom carpets underfoot. The Navajo theme had long been associated with Santa Fe as a trackside asset, with Indian artifacts and pueblo atmosphere as characteristics of Harvey hotel and restaurant operations everywhere west of La Junta, but its universal acceptance in passenger equipment was in large measure attributable to the genius of Lee Lyles, who as head of Santa Fe promotion and advertising in the thirties, sold the management on Zuni and turquoise as the decorative scheme and even the names of the cars themselves. (*Two Photos: Santa Fe Railroad.*)

BEYOND the proper purview of this book, which is intended to begin in 1890, but too atmospheric to be omitted merely to conform to unity, are these two trackside views of the Baltimore & Ohio in the sixties. At the right is the stub switch and primeval switchstand where the rails diverge from the main line for Mount Savage Junction. Below, The Glades Hotel at Oakland, Maryland, offers a superb image of a depot hostel and its patrons within easy stepping distance of the lightly ballasted tracks and waiting the Palace cars of The Mother of Railroads. *(Two Photos: The Smithsonian Institution.)*

DEPICTED HERE is another period piece from the age of U. S. Grant revealing the tranquil life along the Baltimore & Ohio's main line at Annapolis Junction, Maryland where, in the right background, the Annapolis Junction Hotel awaits the not too hurried travelers of this remote era. A traveler awaiting the cars is seated comfortably on the platform in an armchair provided by the management. He is wearing Burnside whiskers, a black morning tailcoat, striped dress trousers and white top hat, the approved apparel of the well-to-do patrons of the cars at a time when Jay Gould was attempting to corner the nation's supply of gold and Commodore Vanderbilt was making his family's first $100,000,000. (*The Smithsonian Institution.*)

SOMETHING LESS than the godlike engineer poised high on the right-hand cushions with the hand of ultimate decision on the Westinghouse valve, and somewhere considerably above the cut of the baggage smasher whose duties were sometimes merged with his, the small town stationmaster was one of the well defined American characters brought into being by the railroads, even as they had created the aristocratic conductor, the breezy news butcher and the dexterous and affable waiter in the dining car. A down to earth functionary, the tank town depot master and telegraph operator knew none of the heady receptions for arriving dignitaries which brought out Big Bill Egan, the Pennsylvania's proconsul at Penn Station, New York, in cutaway coat and striped trousers. His duties were of a homelier order, his contacts more protean. His traffic was mostly in local passengers and round trip tickets to the county seat; his ambit among crated chickens and leaky Saratoga trunks rather than the aloof patrons of the Pullmans and Palace Cars. His position in the community was predicated, beside his authority as representative of the life-giving railroad, on knowing everything worth knowing before the rest of the town did. Not only did the telegraph sounder, reinforced in its wooden alcove by an empty Prince Albert tin, bring tidings of why No. 3 was late with the mail and that the general superintendent was on the warpath, but news of the great world, of wars and assassinations and elections and disasters flowed over the looping catenaries and into his secret ear to be dispensed as royal favors to the station master's confidants. Proverbially his multifarious duties reached a dimension of crisis only after the eastbound had whistled at the edge of town. This was the moment elderly female travelers chose for demanding complicated routings over connecting lines to distant destinations, that the chief dispatcher required his attention on matters of utmost urgency and that a crated hog would escape to run amok in the baggage room. Cumulative chaos followed by long periods of comparative inertia were the lot of the small town station agent. The Baltimore & Ohio proconsul shown opposite against a background of West Virginia woodland and mountain embodied at once the philosopher and the man of action. (*Valentine Museum, Richmond.*)

THE Baltimore & Ohio's one-man station at Duffields, West Virginia, where perhaps the archetypal small-town station master held dominion, gave meaning to the architecture known as modified steamboat Gothic. Under its protecting eaves the local moot discussed the perfidy of James G. Blaine. Here the town squire, venturing into the great world, wired for rooms at Barnum's Hotel in Baltimore or Willard's in Washington. Here the news of Dewey at Manila first came over the looping wires a full day before the big city newspapers came out on the local. Tidings of life and sometimes death came first to the railroad depot at Duffields as it did to a thousand similar structures everywhere in back-country America when all the world was young. (*The Smithsonian Institution.*)

MORE, PERHAPS, than was true of any other Class I carrier, antiquities and obsolescences abounded along the Baltimore & Ohio until well into the twentieth century. The railroad that was among the foremost in experimental motive power and modernity of over-all operations was still unwilling that the traces of its historic past when it was "The Mother of Railroads" should disappear from its yards and right of way, with the result that, like the Virginia & Truckee in Nevada, it became a veritable museum of vanished yesterdays. Archaisms such as stub switches, manually operated semaphores, beehive roundhouses and antiquated rolling stock were visible from the Pullman windows of *The Capitol Limited* and *Royal Blue* so that the B.&O. represented nothing more than it did continuity between times primeval and the modern here and now. The carpenter's Gothic at the right adorned the one-man depot at Brentwood on the Washington branch, while the beautiful roundhouse and shops with target switches intact remained standing at Piedmont until well into the present century. *(Two Photos: The Smithsonian Institution.)*

DOWN AROUND the depot when the trains come in had its fascinations in any century, but the B.&O. classification yards at Baltimore in 1910 still had about them much the same atmosphere as when troop trains were being made up for Gettysburg. In the same year the interior of Tower K in the yards at Washington, although possessed of the latest thing in interlocking devices, was characterized by much of the rustic flavor of a country store where the rustics assembled to discuss the relative merits of James G. Blaine and Grover Cleveland on the basis of the Mulligan Letters. *(Two Photos: The Smithsonian Institution.)*

BEFORE THE present
Union Depot in
Washington absorbed the
B.&O., its own yards
were permeated with the
flavor of yesterday.
The yard worker shown
throwing a primeval
switch to line the main
lives *(above)* in a
hutch with steamboat
Gothic trim and may well
smoke Captain Marryat
cigars. The plainest
structure in sight is RX
Tower. *(Three Photos:
The Smithsonian Institu-
tion.)*

108

the Depot

AT THE TURN OF the century if you were taking the night cars of the Baltimore & Ohio for Chicago or St. Louis or even New York which was then a short sleeper hop, you finished a leisurely dinner off diamond back terrapin in Maryland sauce and vintage Madeira at Harvey's Restaurant, climbed into a growler or hansom from the cab rank outside at the corner of Eleventh and Pennsylvania Avenue, and drove decorously through the twilight to the B.&O.'s sedate and equally leisurely conducted Washington terminal shown here. If you had been President James Garfield a short decade previous you would have driven from the White House to a rendezvous with an assassin at the same depot where the Chief Executive was walking through the waiting room with Secretary of State James G. Blaine when he was shot. Much of history rode the blue Pullmans of the B.&O. to and from this almost pastoral setting in a less urgent Washington than the Federal City was ever to be again. *(The Smithsonian Institution.)*

THE DOUBLE-HEADED
varnish run depicted in the rare
photograph reproduced
below dates from the days
when a glory rode the
Baltimore & Ohio and its
reputation for being
"The Railroad of Presidents"
was equal to that of its fame for
operational excellence
and a cuisine second to none.
(*Everett De Golyer Collection.*)

ONE OF THE CELEBRATED railroad stations of the world, ranking in renown with Euston Station, London, scene of so many of Sherlock Holmes' departures, the Gare du Nord in Paris, and the feudal fortress of the Pennsylvania at Broad Street, Philadelphia, the Baltimore & Ohio's Mount Royal Depot at Baltimore never moved out of the nineteenth century and nobody wanted it to. Its porte cochère *(opposite)* derived from an age when horse cabs were the accepted agency of local transport and its primordial steam radiators, rocking chairs and folksy atmosphere generally maintained continuity with yesterday even as Diesel power snarled in the covered train shed outside. *(Two Photos: Baltimore & Ohio.)*

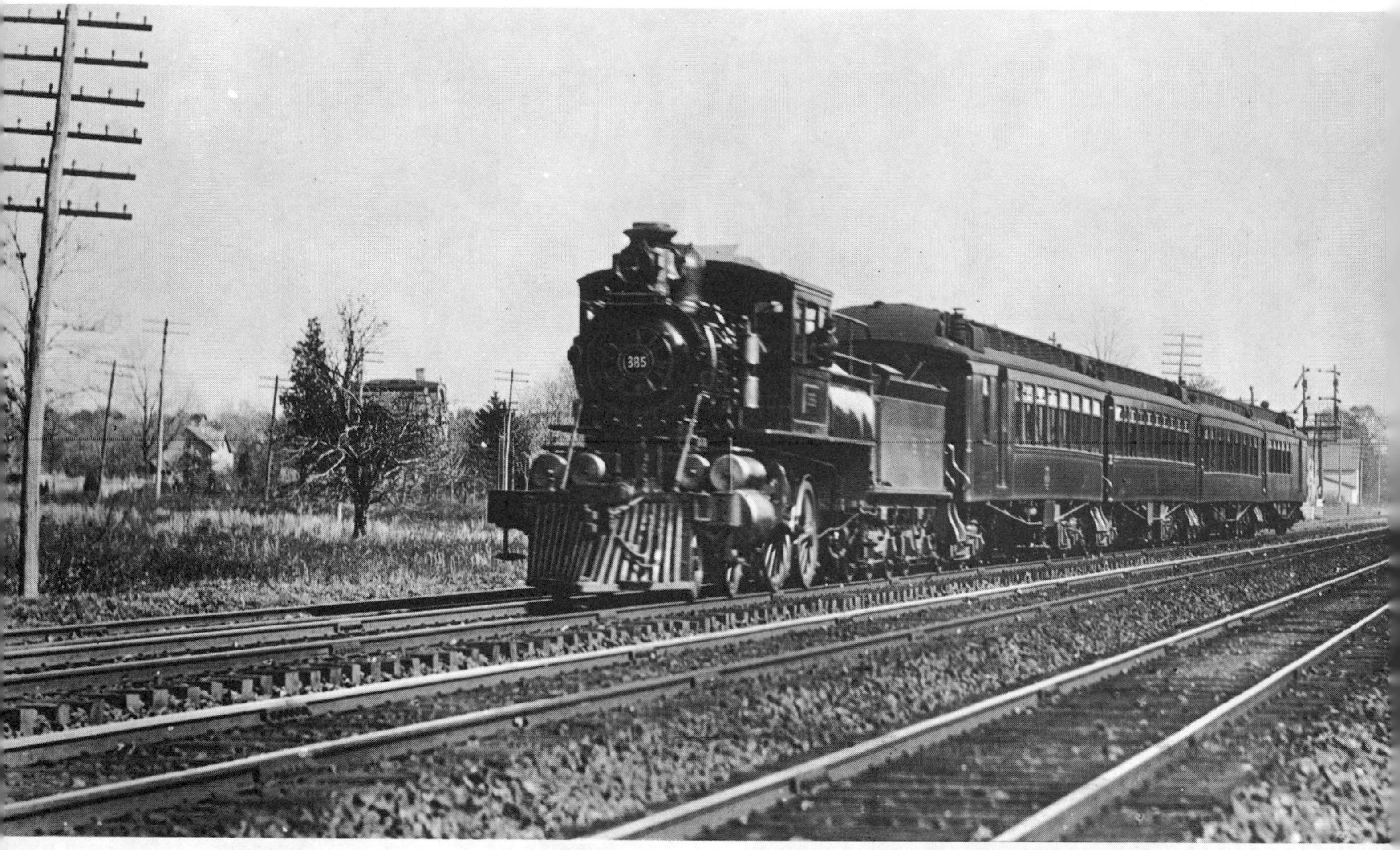
385

13
13
DEPART
3.00
BALTO. & OHIO R.R.
BALTIMORE
WILMINGTON
PHILADELPHIA
NEW YORK & POINTS EAST
PULLMAN CARS ONLY

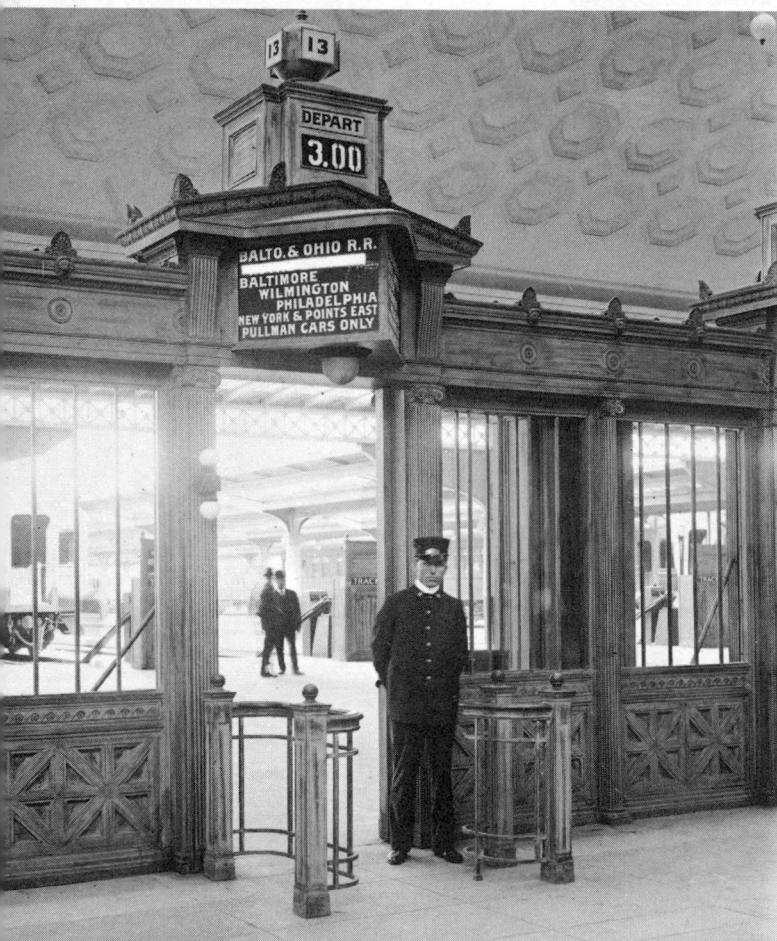

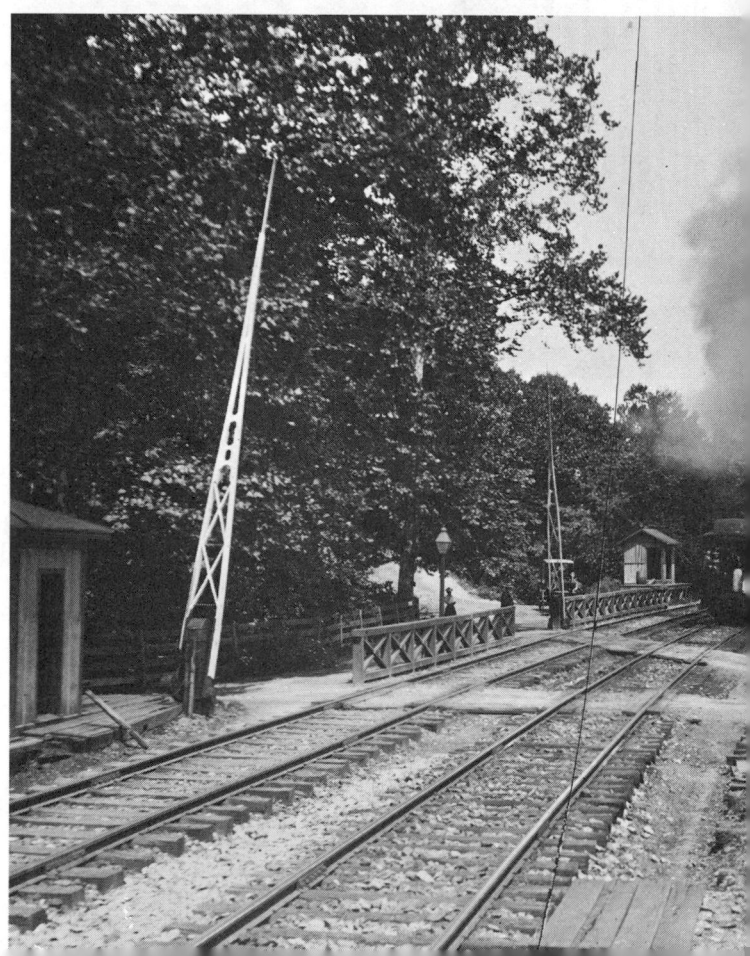

IN THE YEAR 1896 when F. W. Blauvelt took the photograph on the opposite page of the handsome train with the caption: *"The Royal Blue Line Limited* at the Speed of Fifty-five Miles an Hour" The Royal Blue Line was a combination of The Baltimore & Ohio, The Philadelphia & Reading and The Central Railroad of New Jersey running six trains a day between New York and Washington. The fastest of these was on a five-hour schedule, which was uncommonly fast for the time. Known as *The Royal Blue Trains,* the best were No. 511 and 512 which carried Pullman cars, among them the truly eye-popping *Countess* from the Chicago World's Fair, and a diner and made an irreducible number of stops en route. From Jersey City to Bound Brook they went over the Central of New Jersey and via the Reading from Bound Brook to Wayne Junction and thence to Washington on the Baltimore & Ohio's own iron. Reading engines usually took the flyers between Jersey City and Philadelphia and the high stepping camelback in the picture. No. 385 bears the initials "P.&R." on its tender. All Pullman equipment bore on its nameboards the state seal of one of the commonwealths through which it operated. At the far left is a B.&O. traingate in Washington Union Station and its guard in 1905 while at the immediate left a camera crew takes publicity photos of *The Royal Blue* against a rustic background in the same now-distant year. *(Opposite: Brown Bros., The Smithsonian Institution; Above: Fred Arone Collection.)*

AN ELECTRIC MOTOR pulled all trains through the tunnel at Mt. Royal Station at Baltimore as a precaution against engine fumes that might be generated if they were working steam as is shown opposite. Below is an early view of the Baltimore & Ohio's stately depot at Washington with a rare two-wheeled hack of pre-hansom vintage on the cab rank. The Emmet House in the background was convenient for commercial travelers and other patrons of the cars who didn't want to go as far afield as Willard's in the center of downtown Washington. Here, about 1910, the B.&O.'s *New York Express* burns up the ballast through the Maryland countryside behind a well shopped ten-wheeler. Note the hand hewn ties which even at this late date lined the right of way ready for laying. (*Three Photos: The Smithsonian Institution.*)

SPOTLESS summer whites for members of the staff characterized B.&O. diners circa 1910 and elaborately carved mahogany breakfronts concealed the steward's stock of bottled goods. *(Two Photos: The Smithsonian Institution.)*

GROUP portraits were very much in order on the rear observation platform in 1910 when the *Royal Limited* pulled out of the new Washington Union Depot. Two decades later *The Capitol Limited* showed only the rear brakeman and the club car porter on a less ornate verandah when the carrier's crack flyer to Chicago paused at venerable Relay Station. *(Two Photos: The Smithsonian Institution.)*

NOT TO BE outdone by the New York Central's *Twentieth Century Limited* or the Pennsylvania's *Broadway*, both of which boasted train secretaries as part of their operating personnel, the Baltimore & Ohio, in 1920, announced that a similar service would be among the amenities available aboard *The Capitol Limited*. A diligent youth assigned to this capacity is shown practicing his professional *expertise* at the right aboard a buffet car peopled with the three-inch stiff collars and high button boots of the period. During the great cross-word puzzle vogue of the mid-twenties, the B.&O. thoughtfully emplaced dictionaries in all its important club and lounge cars along with the *Hotel Red Book* and the *Official Guide*. Patrons were thus enabled to ascertain a four letter word for clotted blood or the name of a Spanish novelist beginning with I and ending with Z without asking the conductor. Below, *The Capitol Limited* prepares to depart its ancient Chicago terminal at a time when it was in direct and explicit competition with the Pennsylvania's scrupulously maintained *Liberty Limited*. (*Right: The Smithsonian Institution; Below: De Golyer Foundation, Collons Collection.*)

THE BAGGAGE SMASHER entered the demonology of American folklore in the era antedating steel framed trunks and valises when the comparatively vulnerable wood and canvas luggage of the period disintegrated in transit to such a degree that railroad baggage masters were universally known as "baggage smashers." Far from being a term of opprobrium, a talent for wrecking luggage was a form of celebrity among railroaders and a source of admiration in the profession. A mock-heroic account of a contest for local supremacy appeared in 1877 in *The Philadelphia Record,* a community notably on the Baltimore & Ohio main line. "Traquier (one of the contestants for the championship) humped himself over a three story Saratoga trunk with a mansard roof and, bending his muscle to the work, sent the bulky article to the very rear of the baggage car. It was admirably done and would have taken hours to collect the splinters and wearing apparel he had scattered in one brief mo-

ment. This spurred Riter, his opponent, to greater efforts. He sprang lightly to a sewing machine and raising it upon his shoulder, winked confidentially to the boys and let her go. It was a beautiful feat. Pieces of fancy cast iron and woodwork lay all over the floor. . . . The crowd enjoyed it most when the handlers gathered up an ancient valise belonging to some rural citizen. . . . When the dry goods and two dollar shoes and tinware and groceries burst their bonds, enthusiasm was unbounded. . . . It was announced that Riter would challenge for the Baggage Smashing Championship of America and a $500 side." The B.&O. baggage master posing for his official portrait below is deceptively mild of appearance while the railroad messenger boy represented a time when American youth went to work at an early age and took pride in a uniform. *(Two Photos: The Smithsonian Institution.)*

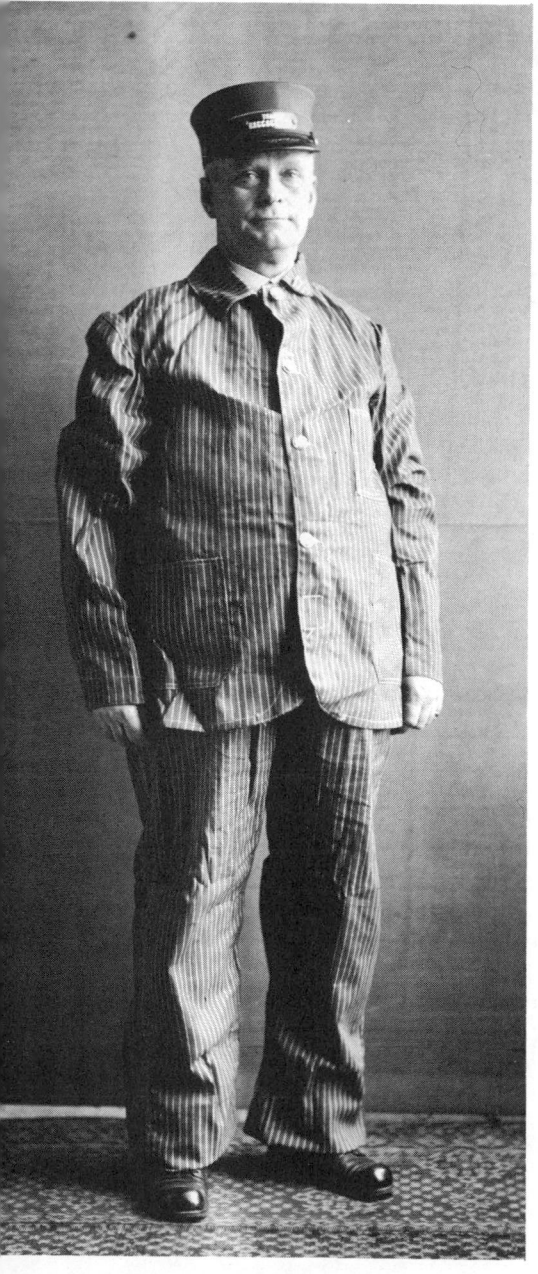

119

IN THE MID-THIRTIES the two principal Baltimore & Ohio varnish runs between St. Louis-Cincinnati and New York-Baltimore-Washington were the strictly de luxe *National Limited*, Trains No. 1 and 2 on the timecard, and *The Metropolitan Special*, a slightly less august consist, but one which boasted an exotic observation-sleeping car between St. Louis and Cincinnati and other through and set-out sleepers for Louisville, Cincinnati and New York. *The National Limited* was very much in business as a luxury run between the Atlantic seaboard and the Mississippi-Southwestern Gateway in competition with the Pennsylvania's *Spirit of St. Louis* and the New York Central's *Southwestern Limited* and made its bid for the carriage trade with a train secretary, lady's maid, valet and manicurist and the B.&O.'s dining car cuisine at its most exalted level. Veteran travelers still remember the boned planked Delaware shad in season on *The National Limited* in an era when the boning of this ambrosial fish was far from commonplace and only usually encountered in such restaurants as The Colony in New York and the perfumed ancestral precincts of Harvey's in Washington. Above, *The National Limited* posed for a formal portrait beside the Potomac for a national photo syndicate. On the page opposite, below, it heads eastbound through a Washington suburb in a Christmas card setting of snow and steam. Above, its companion train, *The Metropolitan* is double headed for the Cranberry Grade at Rodemer, West Virginia, on the climb to Terra Alta. *(Above: Ewing Galloway; Opposite: Top Rail Photo Service; Below: Everett De Golyer Collection.)*

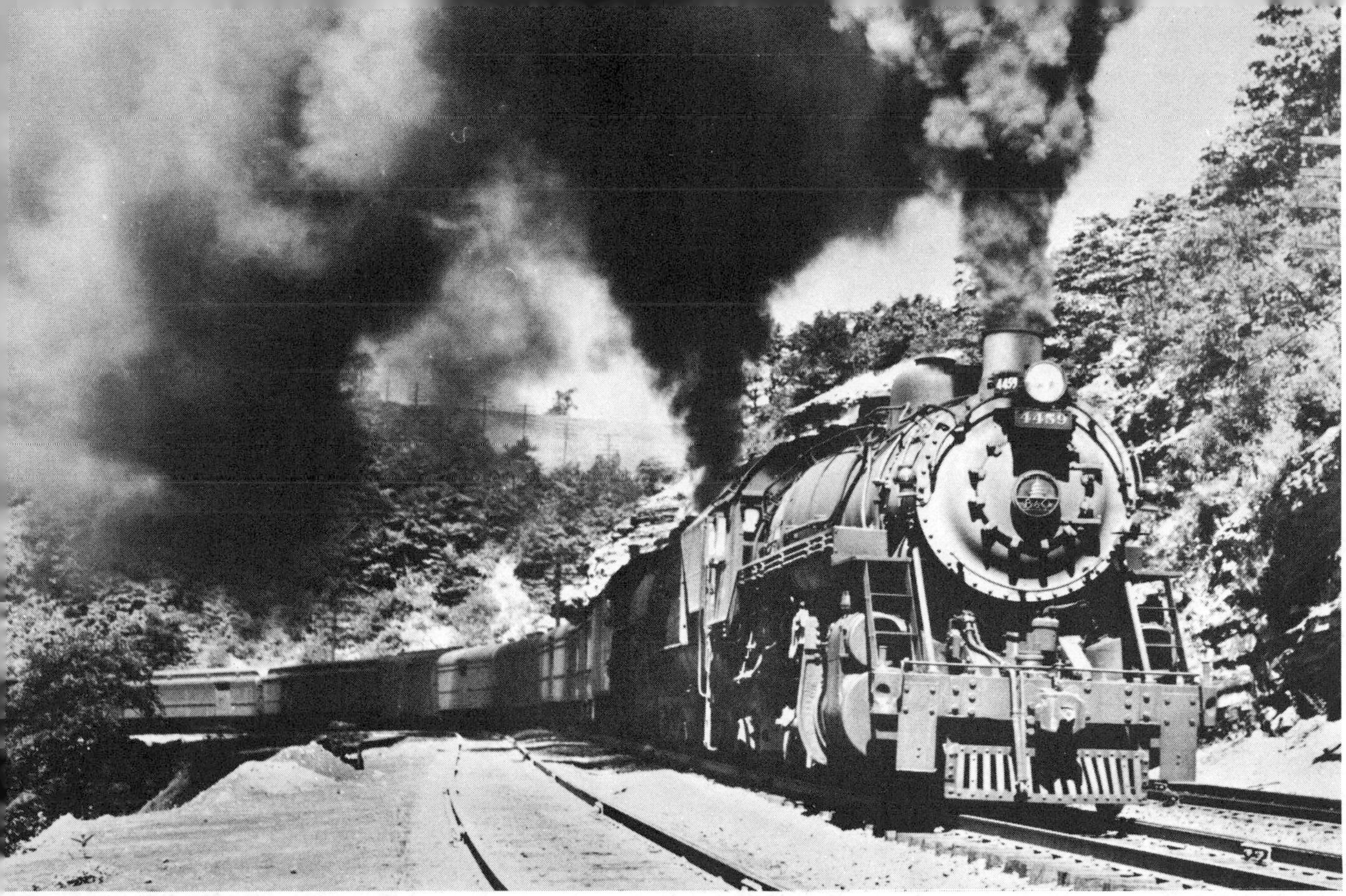
4489

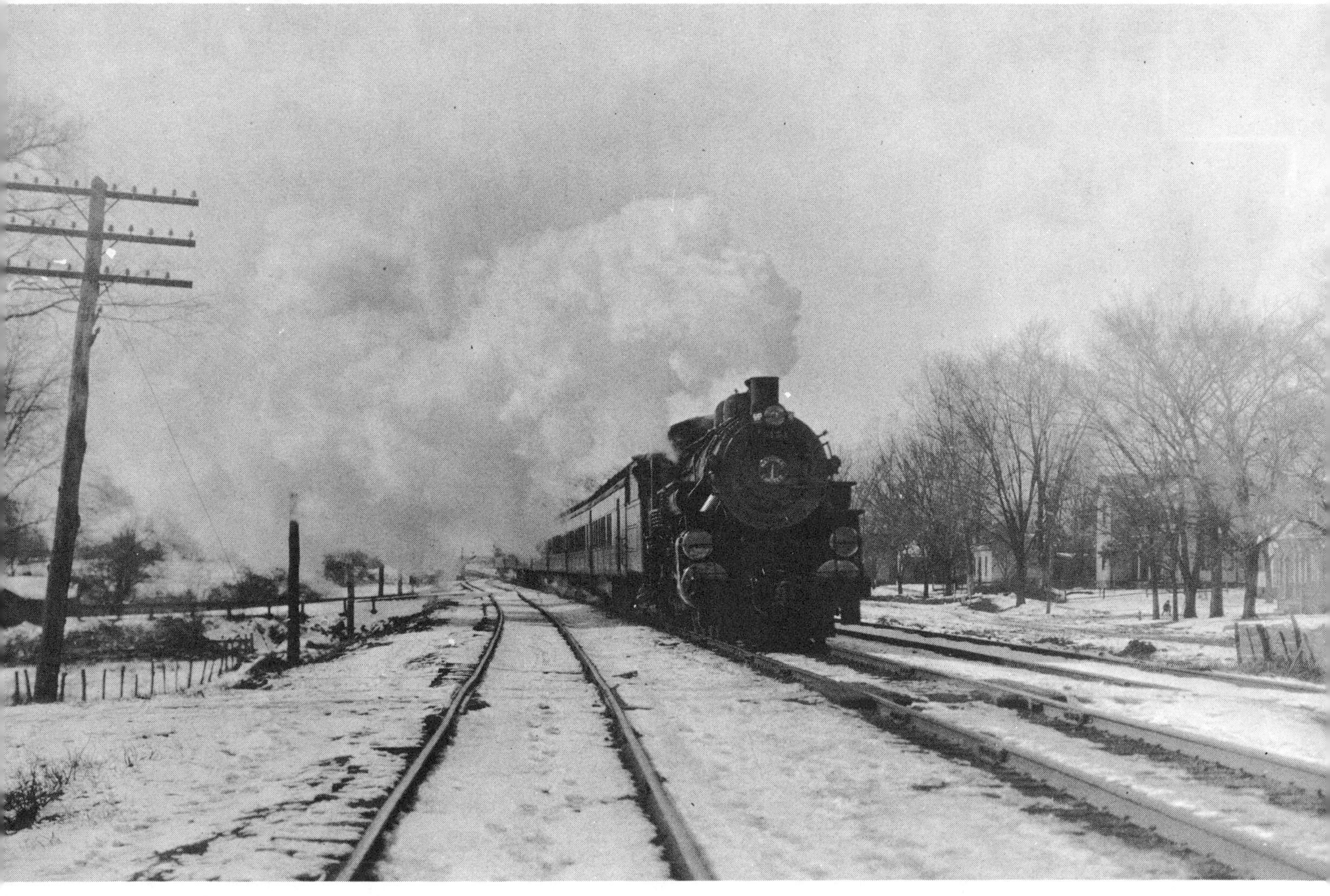

IN THE TWO VIEWS reproduced on this page, the Baltimore & Ohio's *Capitol Limited* on the Chicago-Washington run in days when it was all-Pullman is depicted front and rear as it paused under the Mount Royal Station train shed that was a Baltimore landmark for many years. Designed as a train for magnificoes, it carried its name on a miniature drumhead on the smokebox of its regularly assigned engine and again in a larger dimension on the observation platform to be sure that nobody who saw it might mistake its distinguished identity. *(Two Photos: The Smithsonian Institution.)*

OPPOSITE, against a background of one of the B.&O.'s *Royal Blue* coaches, in approximately 1910, this frock-coated conductor of the old school is notifying K Tower at Washington terminal two minutes before the departure of his train by turning his key in one of the shed post indicators handy to his train bay. The signal will be acknowledged by the towerman when he lights the upper indicator at the shed post and at the train gate, where the ticket taker will close his gate, the conductor will give the proper signal to the rear brakeman who will give the communicating whistle signal for the engineman to proceed. *(The Smithsonian Institution.)*

ALTHOUGH all railroads in the glory years of passenger travel paid lip service to the ideal of transcendental gastronomy as evoked by Brillat Savarin and advertised their resources of food and drink, the Baltimore & Ohio was one of the few carriers whose reputation in this regard actually lived up to its billing. Others were the Santa Fe, the Seaboard Air Line, the Great Northern and the New Haven. Favorably situated with one of its terminals in Tidewater Maryland, the B.&O. in the nineties featured terrapin and canvasback on its dollar dinner and when such rich opulence became impractical, it still listed Chesapeake Bay oysters and other enviable seafood. B.&O. diners in the great years ran to rich and somber decor and their staffs, recruited from the best available pools of domestic help, suggested antebellum days on the old plantation and urged corn pone and hush puppies on patrons in defiance of modern notions of caloric intake. (*Two Photos: The Smithsonian Institution.*)

AS BOLDLY LIMNED as though by a Flemish master, this cheerful Baltimore & Ohio chef in his galley was himself a notable advertisement for the carrier's cuisine. *(The Smithsonian Institution.)*

THE BALTIMORE & OHIO's all-Pullman *Fort Pitt* on the Pittsburgh-Chicago overnight run, like the New Haven's *Owl* over the Shore Line between New York and Boston and several of the competing trains between St. Louis and Chicago, ran the full distance under what amounted to slow orders in an effort to use up its carded time. Unlike *The Owl, Night Diamond* and *Silent Knight,* however, it carried a full complement of luxury equipment as is suggested by the adjacent company literature. Almost surely it was the only overnight run on an intermediate distance to boast a barber and lady's maid, showers for both sexes and a manicurist. The B.&O. had style and to spare in the twenties. The utilitarian properties of *The Fort Pitt's* lady's retiring room aboard its Pullman Standard sleepers were not sybaritic, but the travel attire of its passengers in the early 1920s make it a stunning period piece in the record of luxury transport. *(Three Photos: Baltimore & Ohio.)*

The
FORT PITT
LIMITED
All Pullman. No Extra Fare
Leaves Pittsburgh 9.30 P. M.
Arrives Chicago . 8.00 A. M.
Leaves Chicago . 8.30 P. M.
Arrives Pittsburgh 8.45 A. M.
"First Call for Breakfast!"
A RESTFUL NIGHT—a shave—a shower—and then—breakfast—one of those delightful Baltimore & Ohio meals, with an enviable reputation for quality at moderate cost.
And you arrive in Pittsburgh or Chicago ready for whatever the day may bring.
A fine train—The FORT PITT Limited—Providing Club Car, Compartment - Drawing-Room - Observation - Library - Lounge Car, with special lounge for women; Standard Sleepers. Barber; Valet; Maid; Manicure; Shower Baths for men and women; Newspapers and Magazines.
Baltimore & Ohio
SERVING THE PUBLIC SINCE 1827

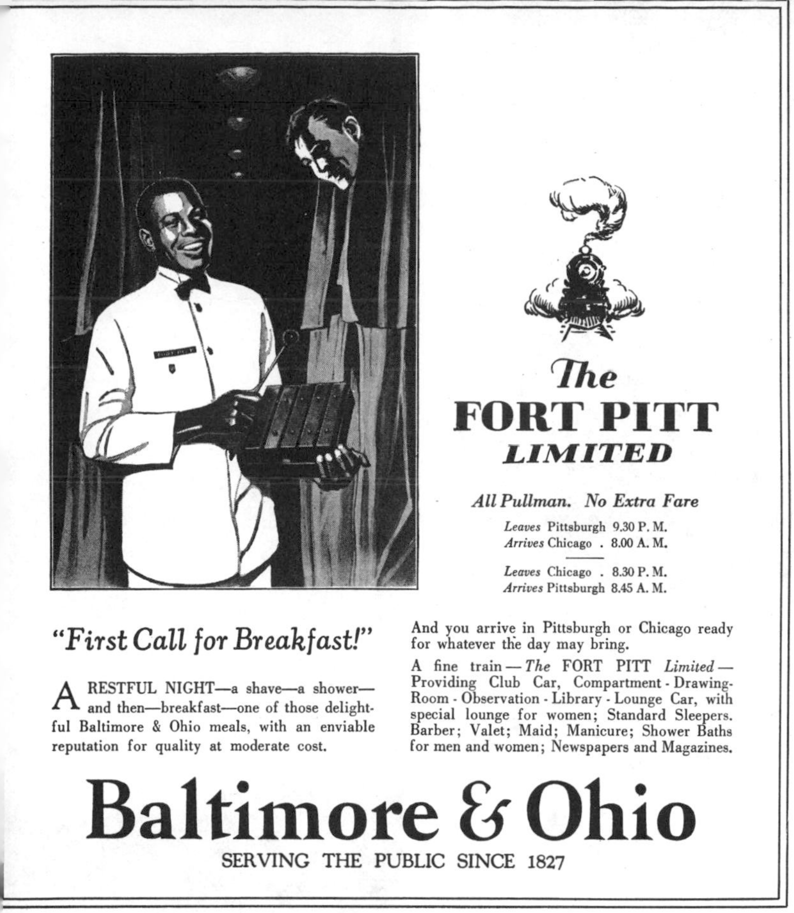

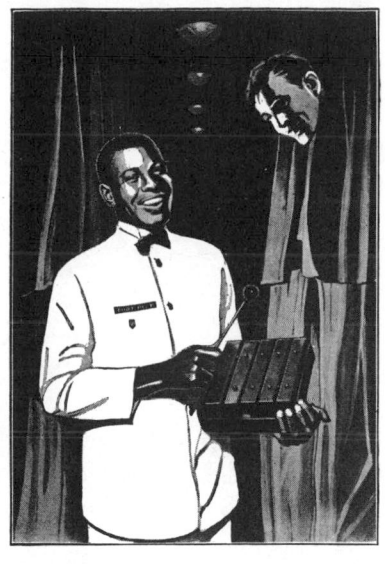

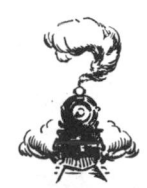

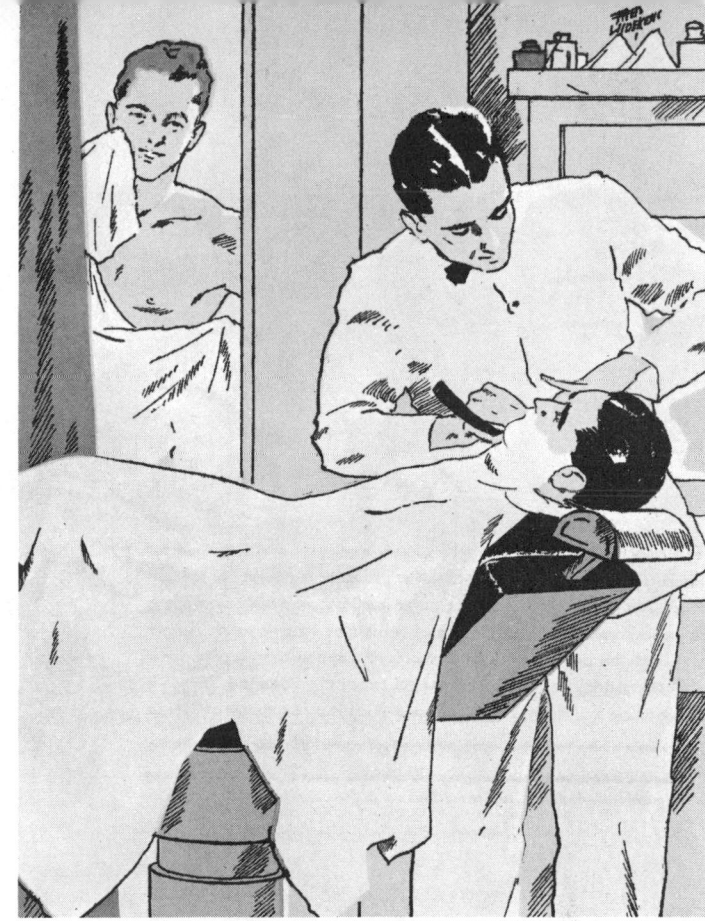

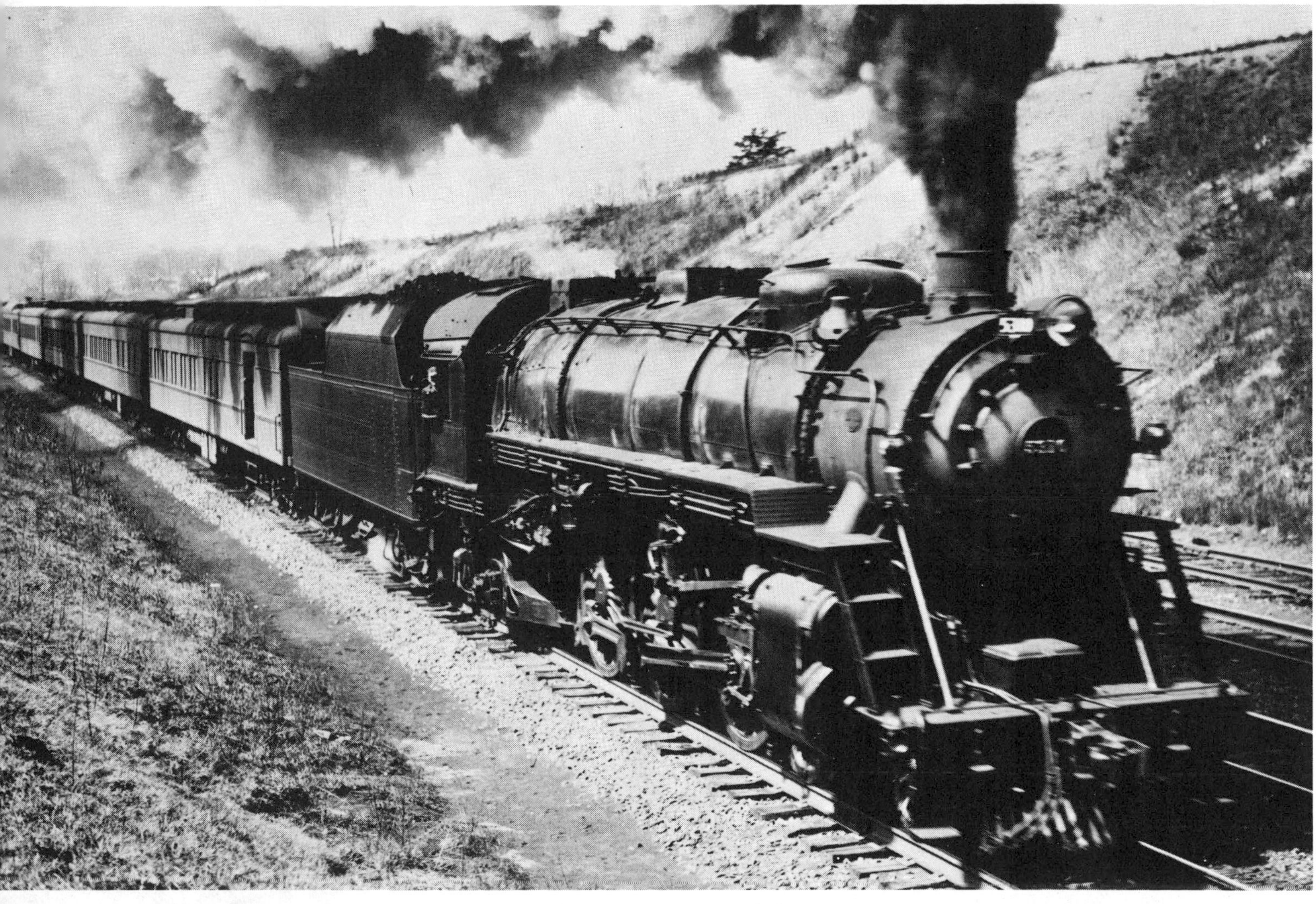

IN THE MIDDLE THIRTIES, The Baltimore & Ohio's *Capitol Limited* is shown, appropriately to its name, drawn by two name locomotives, in the upper frame by the Caprotti valve geared *President Cleveland*, and below by *President Van Buren*. It was a time of ten and twelve car trains, experimental engine types, and the B.&O. was still, as it had always been, a railroadman's railroad. (*Two Photos: Everett De Golyer Collection.*)

THE CONGEALING cold of the Lake Michigan water-front can almost be sensed, together with the sounds and very smells of Chicago railroading in mid-winter of 1930 when Alfred W. Johnson took this stunning rear-end view of *The Capitol Limited,* double headed, from Roosevelt Road bridge as it headed eastbound out of Chicago yards. Ice amidst the pilings, snow on the guard rails and the frozen calm of the Chicago River set a mood of melancholy splendor for a great train operation in the golden age of Pullman.

HERE, metaphorically, *The Columbian* gives the back of its hand to Elizabeth, New Jersey, and watchers are well advised to stand behind the white line. Below: *The Columbian* smokes up the Jersey countryside on its fast New York-Washington daylight run. *(Two Photos: Lucius Beebe)*

IN THE ROARING thirties when the national economy of boom and bust was reflected in railroad earnings and operations alike, the Baltimore & Ohio's fast daylight run between Washington and its New Jersey terminal, *The Columbian*, carried coaches, a diner and solarium lounge, all the amenities of a first class train on an intermediate run without de luxe overtones. The fast ride could be a rough one because of its numerous curves, but there were still loyal B.&O. partisans who preferred the inconvenience of a bus ride through Holland Tunnel to the impersonal Pennsylvania. The B.&O. right of way with occasional vine-clad signal towers suggested a more leisured day of transport. (*Above: Rail Photo Service; Right: The Smithsonian Institution.*)

131

SATINWOOD PANELING, fluted columns and ornate leaded window were details of the men's smoking room of observation lounge car *Lucerne*. Lunette windows in platform sidewalls were hallmark of American Car & Foundry. *(Three Photos: The Smithsonian Institution.)*

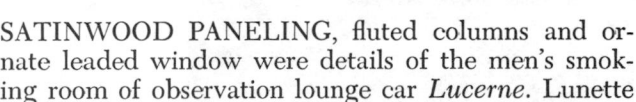

THE ULTIMATE expression of the Baltimore & Ohio's perfectionism was the conduct and appointments of its diners. Flawless service, luxurious amenities of decor and table settings and a celebrated cuisine established a Delmonico atmosphere on its great name trains.

132

IN FULLEST PANOPLY of splendor, double shotted for a heavy consist and with the train name on the sidewalls of the Pullman combine *Capitol Hill*, the Baltimore & Ohio's Train No. 6, *The Capitol Limited* with locomotives No. 5331 and 5232 on the point forms a sparkling portrait of steam varnish operations in the year 1930. The tracks here cross the Chicago River at Roosevelt Road during a river straightening project and the disused pilings and stringers of an older trestle in the foreground and ice floes in the river give the scene a Christmas card chill. (*Alfred W. Johnson.*)

THE LAST of its long line of *Royal Blue* trains which had been rolling between Jersey City and Washington since the days of Palace Cars and frock-coated conductors was inaugurated by the Baltimore & Ohio with a streamlined consist and steam motive power in 1935. Its coaches were finished with seats covered with petit point anti-macassars reminiscent of those on English Pullmans and its observation solarium car carried all the amenities of mobile elegance. With characteristic B.&O. style, professionals modeled its *Royal Blue* publicity photographs rather than the company personnel recruited for interiors by carriers less concerned for excellence in all things. *(Right: The Smithsonian Institution; Below: Everett De Golyer Collection; Two Interiors: Baltimore & Ohio.)*

FRAMED in a stately doorway of classic design and a ceiling freize of looped wreaths that would have been acceptable in the decor of any of the Adam restaurants of the world's Ritz hotels, this Baltimore & Ohio dining car steward on *The Capitol Limited* in white waistcoat of office and blue and gold livery jacket was the glass of fashion at a time when he represented the mobile amenities of life in their fullest dimension. (*Railway & Locomotive Historical Society.*)

AS LONG AS was practicable in a degenerating society and as long as how you traveled was who you were, the Baltimore & Ohio was a carrier with style in every aspect of its varnish trains. It was a railroad of fingerbowls and long-stemmed roses on its diners and heavy gauge stationery such as that on which the young lady is writing here aboard the club car of *The Royal Blue*. Like one or two other carriers in the glory years, the Florida East Coast and the New Haven in its better moments, the B.&O. saw visions of perfectionism, and style was a passenger on its varnish runs to the end. *(Baltimore & Ohio.)*

A TOUCH of style which *The Capitol Limited* shared with *The Broadway* and *Century* was a train secretary whose presence identified the B.&O. as a member of the Big Three between Chicago and the East Coast. *(Railway & Locomotive Historical Society.)*

137

IN ITS COACH TRAIN publicity and promotion, no less than in its de luxe passenger advertising, the Baltimore & Ohio went first class, and photographs to launch the *Cincinnatian* when they were taken in 1947 were posed by professional models rather than, as was standard practice elsewhere, peopling the cars with office personnel as stand-ins for authentic passengers. Amateurs of the iconography of railroading have no hesitation in asserting that in quality and atmosphere of advertising material, two carriers which were tops were the Florida East Coast and the Baltimore & Ohio. (*Four Photos: Baltimore & Ohio.*)

NO TRAIN designed for the daycoach trade was ever so carefully custom-built to carriage trade specifications of quality as *The Cincinnatian*. Its observation lounge combined *moderne* decor with every amenity of de luxe relaxation.

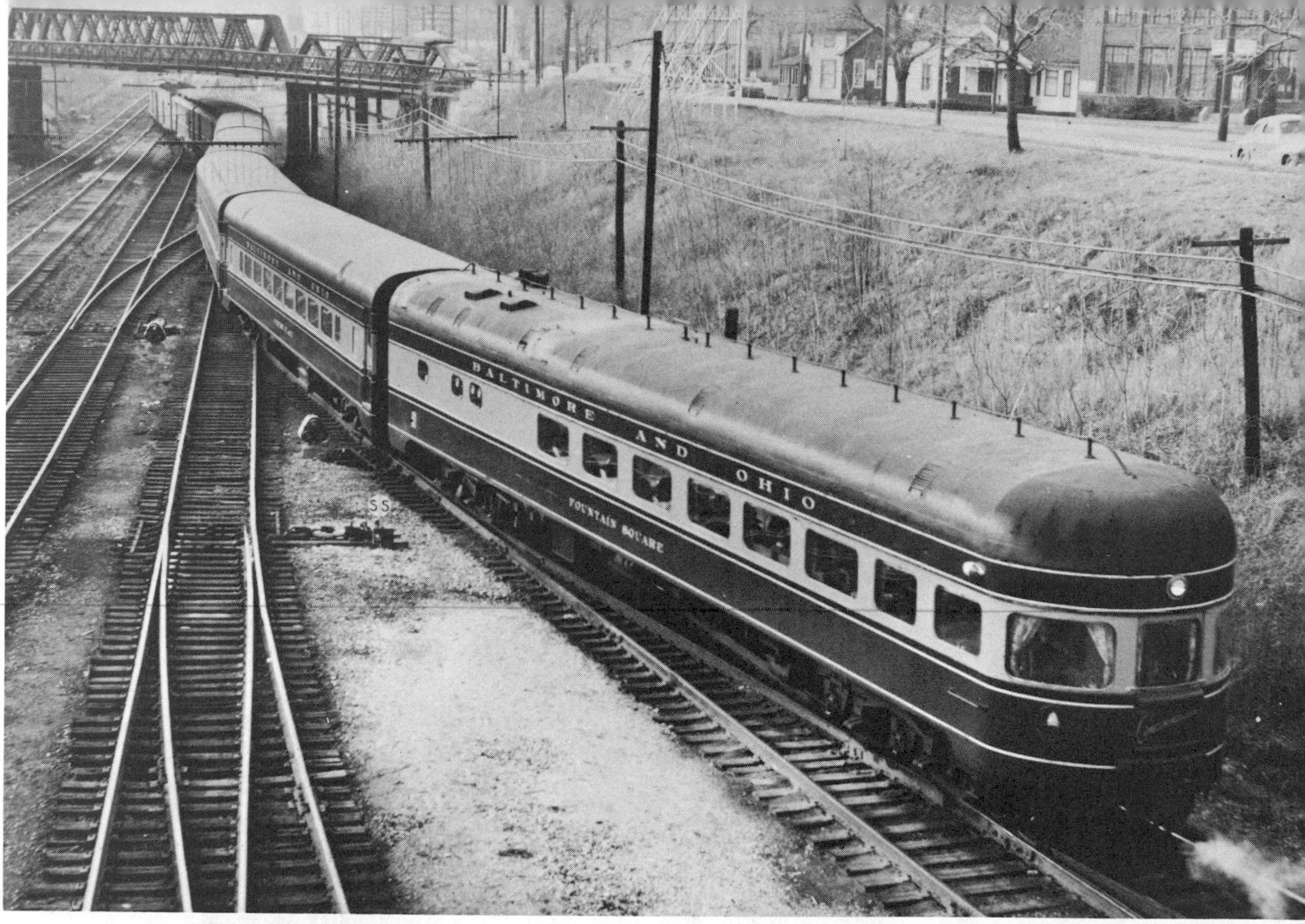
BALTIMORE AND OHIO
FOUNTAIN SQUARE

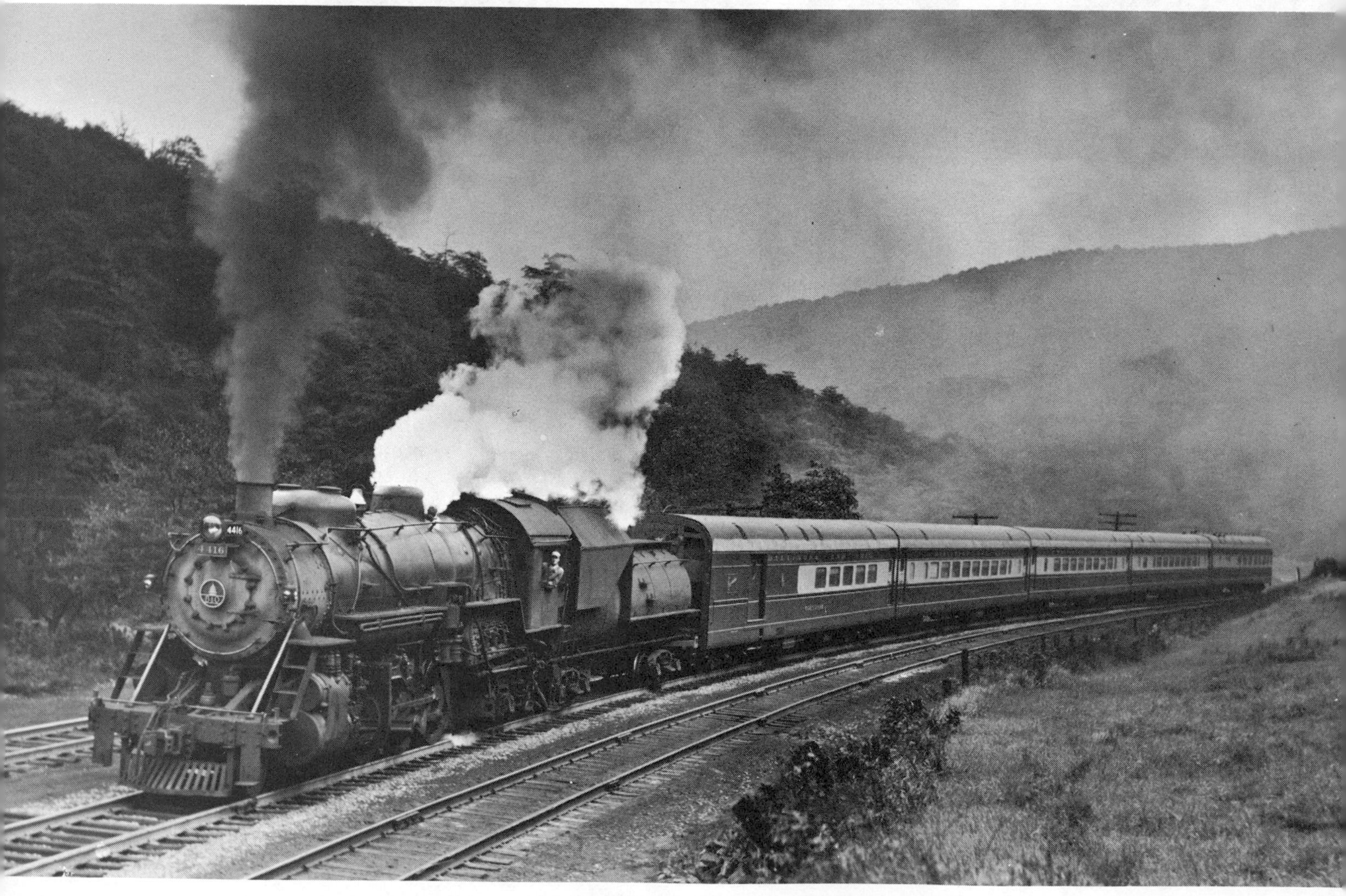
4416

THE BALTIMORE & OHIO's *Cincinnatian*, a much-photographed varnish haul because of its timing on the mountain grades in Western Maryland and the spectacular combination of steam and streamlining that characterized its consists, was a coach—only daylight train between Baltimore-Washington and the Cincinnati of its name. Placed in service immediately after the 1941 war, two President class Pacifics were streamlined for its motive power at the carrier's Mt. Clare shops, one of which is shown as assigned at the bottom of this page while opposite, *The Cincinnatian* breasts the long Seventeen Mile Grade near Swanton, Maryland, in September 1948 while its assigned locomotive was being shopped. Note the loaded mail arm that awaits its passing at trackside on the opposite page. At the right, the motive power is refreshed at Athens, Ohio, while across the margin its solarium-observation car *Fountain Square* snakes through the switches at Union Depot, Toledo, with an uncommonly heavy consist which includes four head-end revenue cars. *(Two Lower Photos: Richard H. Kindig; Above: Rail Photo Service, Robert L. Lorenz and B. F. Cutler.)*

AS BEFITTED a carrier with a long line of Boston brah-mins and Yankee grandees in its financial and operating background, the Chicago, Burlington & Quincy in the nineteenth century ran consequential varnish trains through the rich granger states that were its feudal domain, al-though for many years it forewent the panache of name limiteds so that No. 1 on the Chicago-Denver run was flag-ship of its fleet without any other designation. The library-lounge car interior of No. 1 is shown on the page opposite about 1905 in an age when the cloth traveling cap replaced more formal masculine headgear aboard the cars, while the atmospheric group boarding the Pullmans at the top of the page was taken at an unidentified depot approxi-mately five years later. The truly elegant varnish consist of fifteen Pullmans depicted at the right and terminating in the magnificent observation-lounge-compartment car *Tryphena* was a private train assembled at the whim of a railroad magnifico in 1894. On December 12 of that year the daughter of Thomas Doane, Chief Engineer of the Burlington, was married at Lincoln, Nebraska, and the train was chartered to take the happy couple and all their guests for a weekend in Chicago. (*Above, Two Photos: Burlington Route; Right: Colorado State Historical Society.*)

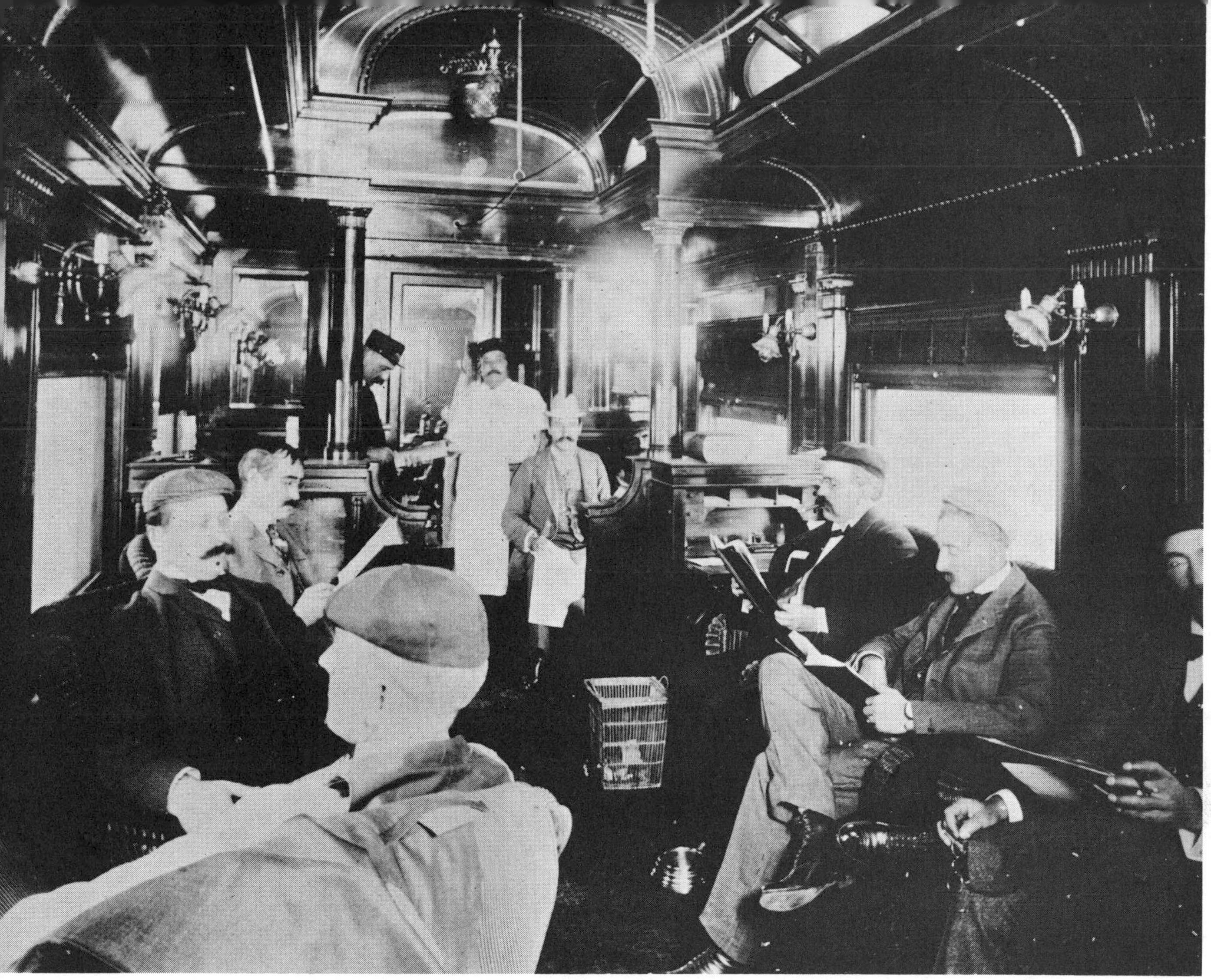

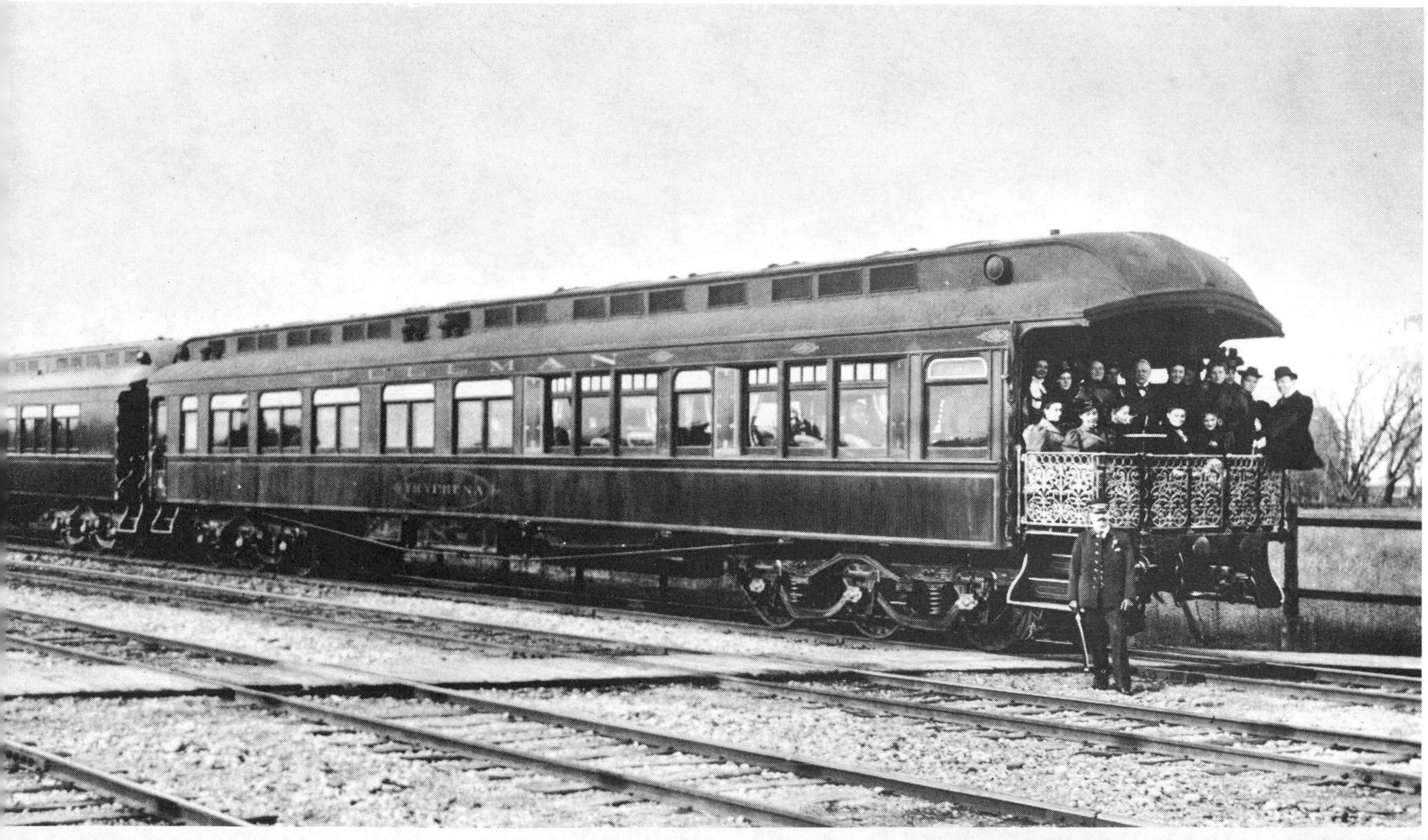

WHEN the Burlington's flagship, Train No. 1, paused at Creston, Iowa, some time just before the turn of the century, on hand to record the gleaming Pullmans and the smoking engine up ahead was the company's staff photographer, the remarkable Allen Green who had already perfected an electronic device for photographing trains at speed. By the time the observation end of *The Colorado Limited*, shown below, was photographed at Akron, Colorado, in 1910, the Burlington had gone in for name trains and their identifying tailgate signs in a big way. The *Limited* had replaced No. 1 on the Chicago-Denver run and even more splendid names were in the not too distant future. *(Right: Burlington Route; Below: Bernard Corbin Collection.)*

STEAM AND PULLMAN STANDARD were still the essential properties of de luxe long distance travel in the United States when the new Union Station in Chicago was built 1924, and Diesel motive power and streamlined equipment were in the unguessed future. Co-occupants of the fine new depot were the Alton, Pennsylvania, Milwaukee and, of course, the Burlington whose *Aristocrat* and connecting trains for such transcontinentals as *The North Coast Limited* and *Oriental Limited* berthed in its capacious train bays. Only a little more than a decade hence were the first *Denver Zephyr* and all its gleaming brood of Budd cars and Electro-Motive internal combustion motors. (*Pennsylvania Railroad.*)

145

146

SOME IDEA of the volume of traffic that converged on Lincoln, Nebraska, over the rails of the Chicago, Burlington & Quincy Railroad in the year 1905 may be gleaned from the two trackside photographs taken at the Lincoln depot sixty years gone. Here Burlington trains from St. Louis and Kansas City and from Chicago via Omaha, met, mingled, were remade, exchanged cars, passengers and head-end revenue and went their separate ways to Denver and far-off Billings, Montana. It was the high tide of the Burlington's fortunes as a granger railroad and also the heyday of the tourist car, the Saratoga trunk and the kennel size headlight on sturdy, utilitarian motive power with no frills. The Burlington brakeman shown at the immediate left antedates these busy trackside scenes by a decade or so while the depot panoramas were taken a little more than a decade before the rear-end view of *The Chicago-Nebraska Limited* with its fine open observation platform at La Vargne, Illinois, in 1916. (*Opposite, Two Photos: Burlington Lines; Left: The Smithsonian Institution; Below: Alfred W. Johnson.*)

THE BURLINGTON'S TOURIST SLEEPERS, whose rattan seats, a durable item of travel folklore, were supposed to leave a basket-weave pattern on the human anatomy for protracted periods, were populous with happy people on the Denver run in 1902, especially in summer months when Manitou and the wonders of Colorado Springs beckoned the vacation trade. Sports attire was almost unknown, even among the leisured classes, and masculine adventurers posed solemnly on donkeyback ascending Pike's Peak in brown derby hats and boiled shirts with barrel cuffs. Ladies wore hats even on the steamcars and the gentlemanly conductors of *The Denver Limited* collected fares from amidst thickets of ostrich plumes and clusters of lifelike ripe cherries which adorned the coal-scuttle bonnets of the Gaby Delys era. *(Library of Congress.)*

AT THE TURN OF THE CENTURY when action photography of trains at speed was in its infancy, the Burlington had in its employ a staff photographer named Allen Green whose speed shots of Burlington trains, notably *The Fast Mail* on the Omaha run, attracted widespread attention in photographic circles and were reproduced in the then also comparatively new halftone process in *World's Work*. Green's camera, a focal plane Graflex "equipped with an electro-mechanical device" took pictures at a speed of 1/1000 of a second and was used to take the uncommonly fine view of *The Denver Limited* shown above. Here, passengers take the air as *The Limited* pauses at an unidentified depot on the Great Plains. *(Two Photos: Burlington.)*

149

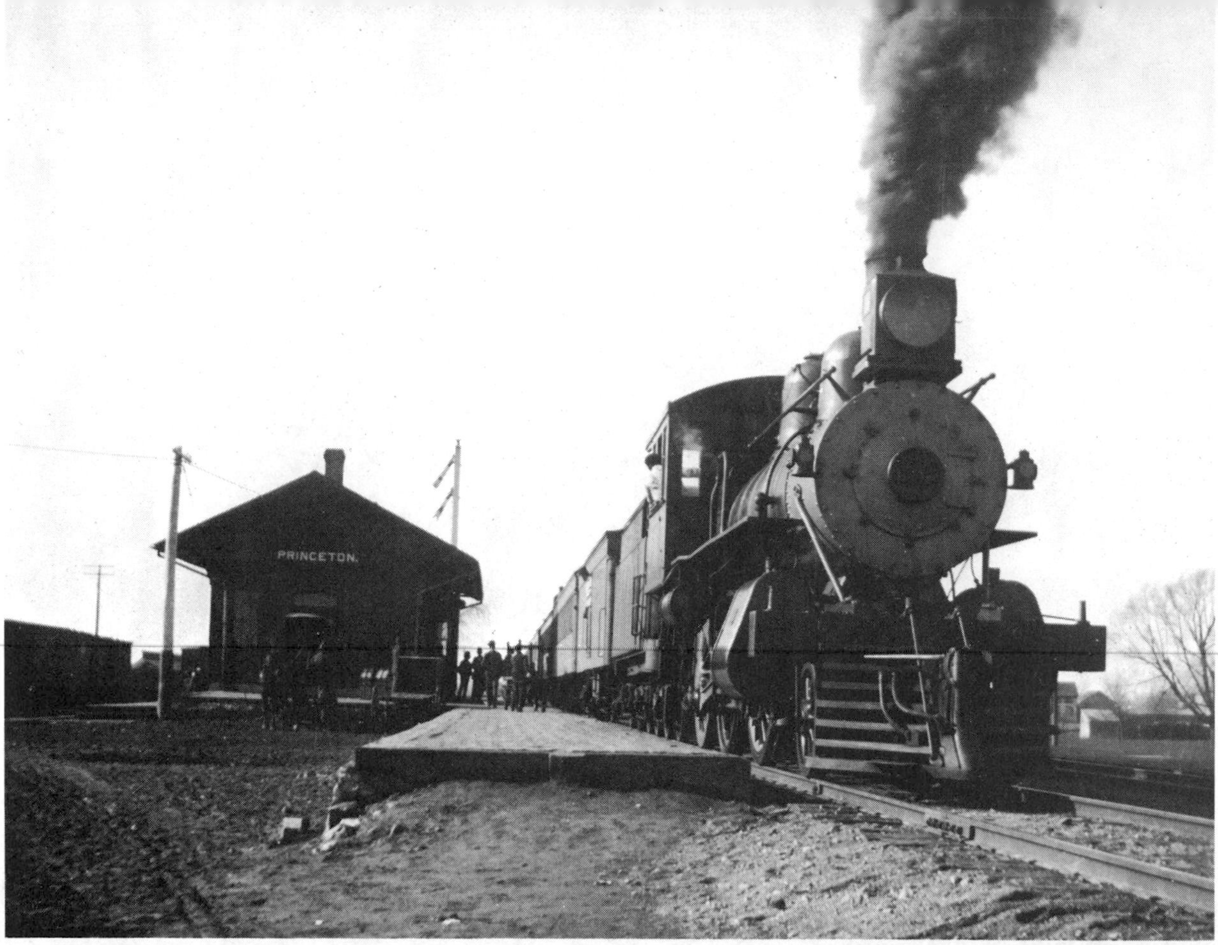
PRINCETON.

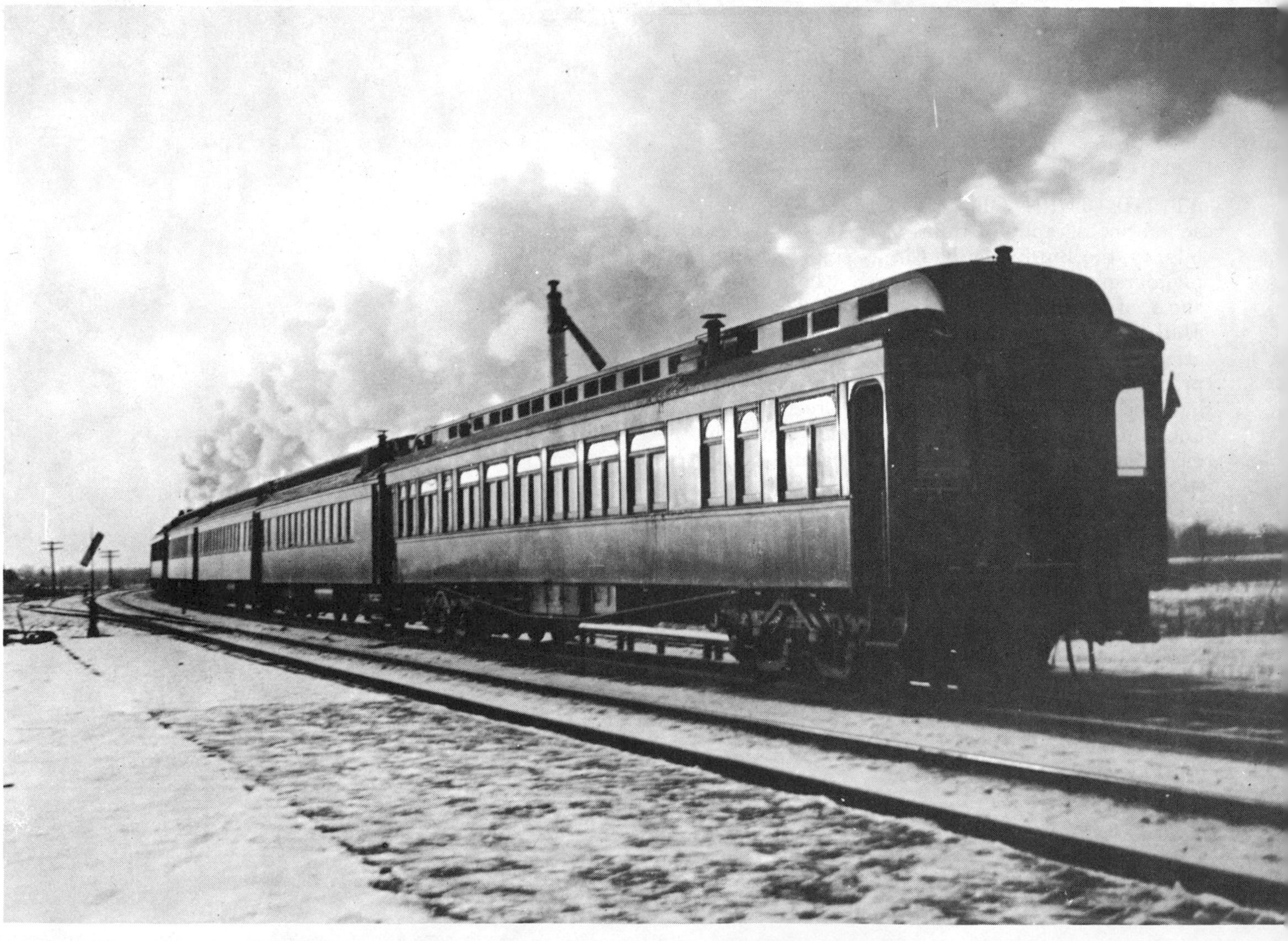

IN THE YEAR 1905 when the wonderfully atmospheric shot reproduced above was taken at the observation platform of an unidentified Burlington transcontinental, the middle aged actor it depicts named William Surrey Hart had never seen a motion picture and his first appearance in a Western was almost a decade in the future. A good guess would be that it was taken during the road tour of "The Virginian" in which he had scored one of his early Broadway successes. Wealth, adulation and fame as the originator and greatest single protagonist of the classic Western awaited "Hell's Hinges" which was not released until 1916 although he had been making two-reelers before that date. On the page opposite in 1900 the Burlington's No. 1 arrives at Princeton, Illinois, behind a representative American type and departs, trailing as its rear car a Wagner sleeper, a relic of the carbuilding firm that had gone out of business the year previous. *(Three Photos: Bernard Corbin Collection.)*

THE ARRIVAL of the dark green, sleekly maintained Pullmans, whether they were of old time wooden construction or the burnished steel of Standard, at Chicago's old Union Station carried with them the breath of romance and tidings of the far places of the continent. No stainless steel of streamlined design in times to come would be possessed of their cachet of ineffable delight. (*Two Photos: Alfred W. Johnson.*)

ELABORATELY designed, electrically illuminated tailgate insignes such as this carried by the Burlington's *Black Hawk* on its observation platform rail were manufactured in 1930 by the Crystal Manufacturing Company of Chicago for many carriers and came in a wide variety of shapes, sizes and designs. Shatterproof glass was illuminated by fifteen watt lamps and those used by the Burlington were of twenty-six gauge sheet steel approximately two feet square. *(Everett De Golyer Collection.)*

THE CHICAGO, Burlington & Quincy's *Black Hawk* on the overnight run between Chicago and the Twin Cities was part of the most fiercely competitive pattern of operations anywhere in the United States with the possible exception of the St. Louis-Chicago traffic that embraced name trains of splendor operated by the Chicago & North Western, the Milwaukee, and the Chicago Great Western. The *Black Hawk* belongs in the category of anthropology and regional history along with the *Seminole, Chief, Iroquois, Apache* and *Hawkeye* rather than in the aviary group which embraces the *Gull, Blue Bird, Owls* and *Eagles,* and was named for an Indian chieftain rather than a bird of prey. Its consist included all the accustomed devisings of luxury with bedroom sleepers and an open platform observation lounge at whose tailgate rode the train herald shown above. *(Bernard Corbin.)*

The
BUFFALO BILL
Convenient Service between
DENVER and YELLOWSTONE
AN OVERNIGHT TRAIN
Speedy tri-weekly service between Denver and Cody (eastern gateway to Yellowstone Park) during the Park season.

NORTHBOUND from Denver Mon. Wed. Fri. June 28 to Sept 1	FAST 1939 SCHEDULE	SOUTHBOUND from Cody Tue. Thu. Sat. June 29 to Sept. 2
4:00 pm Lv	Denver	Ar. 1:00 pm
4:59 pm Lv	Boulder	Ar. 11:57 am
5:19 pm Lv	Longmont	Ar. 11:33 am
5:50 pm Lv	Loveland	Ar. 11:04 am
6:13 pm Lv	Fort Collins	Ar. 10:45 am
7:35 pm Lv	Cheyenne	Ar. 9:25 am
11:00 am Ar. Cody (Yellowstone)		Lv. 7:45 pm

EXTRA VISITING HOURS
The above schedule gives Yellowstone Park passengers enroute to or from the East, several delightful hours sightseeing in and around Denver.

W. F. Cody "Buffalo Bill"

Breakfast
Aboard "The Buffalo Bill"

FISH • MEATS • AND EGGS

Broiled Fish, breakfast portion, 50
Boiled Salt Mackerel with Potatoes, 50

Ham or Breakfast Bacon and Eggs, 70
Grilled Lamb Chops with Bacon (1), 40; (2), 80
Fried Ham or Breakfast Bacon, 70;
Half Portion, 35

Corned Beef Hash with Poached Egg, 60
Shredded Ham with Scrambled Eggs, 50
Eggs: Boiled, Fried, Scrambled or Shirred, 30
Poached Eggs on Toast, 40

Plain Omelet, 35; with Jelly or Marmalade, 50

Lyonnaise, Hashed Brown or Fried Potatoes, 20

A SEASONAL vacation-land run on the Colorado & Southern in the thirties was the overnight *Buffalo Bill* which ran with Pullmans, coaches and diner between Denver and Cody at the east entrance to Yellowstone National Park. By 1939 when the above photograph was taken *The Buffalo Bill* was running so heavily patronized that double heading was necessary between Cheyenne and Denver. Forty years earlier passengers on the Burlington's Denver-Billings run had been glad to get down from the cars for breakfast at the impromptu trackside restaurant shown opposite. Aboard *The Buffalo Bill* they did better in an era when a breakfast portion of lamb chops was eighty cents with bacon. (*Above: Lucius Beebe; Below, Opposite: Wyoming State Historical Department; Company Literature: John Barriger Collection.*)

155

Abundant Glories Rode The Aristocrat

TWENTY YEARS AFTER the Santa Fe had invoked the voluptuary potential of rail travel on an almost Babylonish scale aboard its now legendary *de Luxe* with unabashed status-conscious promotion, the Burlington in 1932 placed in service between Chicago and Denver a luxury train with a name also calculated to suggest affluence and upward mobility in its patrons. The then emergent technique of Madison Avenue to create a market for ostentation where none had existed before expressed itself in the advertising of *The Aristocrat* in expensive coated paper brochures whose purple prose matched the lush upholstery of the new train's equipment. "Its matched Pullmans, decorated in dove gray, blue, maroon, gold and superbly appointed throughout, offer the quiet elegance of a town club . . . deep cushioned winged seats in pearl-green with rose undertone, lazily restful, patterned after Colonial armchairs . . . colorful runs of Oriental splendor to soften the foot-fall. The solarium-

lounge car is a symphony of color, a masterpiece of travel luxury . . . lounging rooms that whisper repose . . . cozy nooks that invite a bridge game . . . your favorite magazine . . . last minute news or a musical program by wireless . . . hourly market reports . . . a buffet whence cooling refreshments and tasty refections . . . food served as by a gracious host. . . ." The Burlington didn't explicitly suggest dressing for dinner in *The Aristocrat's* diner as was once the custom on name trains in Europe, but one got the feeling that it wouldn't have taken offense, and the hitherto prosaic business of a trip to Denver came to assume the dimension of a weekend on Cleopatra's barge or a visit to one of the more affluent Rothschilds. Above a company photograph suggests *The Aristocrat's* resources of comfort. Opposite it speeds through Red Oak, Iowa, for a court portrait by Bernard G. Corbin in 1942. Two vignettes of its motive power above are from the camera of Ivan Dimitri.

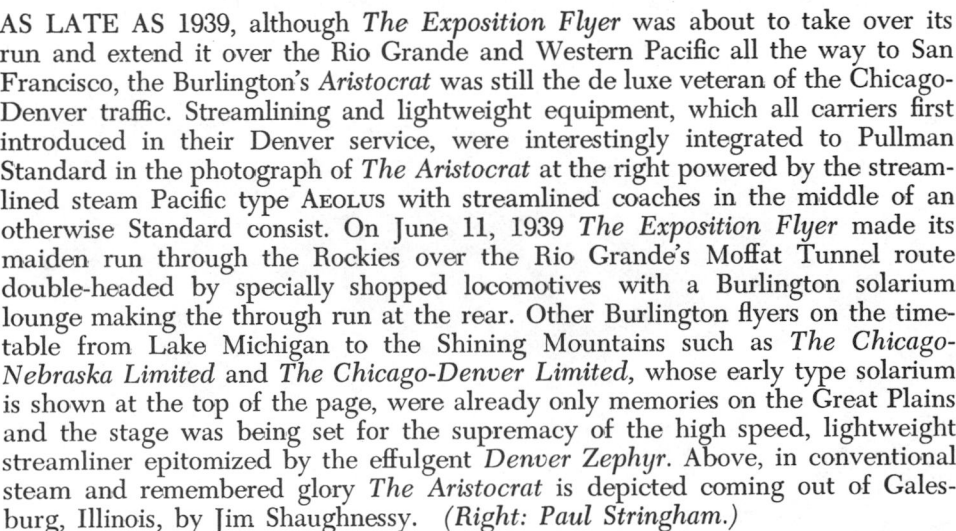

AS LATE AS 1939, although *The Exposition Flyer* was about to take over its run and extend it over the Rio Grande and Western Pacific all the way to San Francisco, the Burlington's *Aristocrat* was still the de luxe veteran of the Chicago-Denver traffic. Streamlining and lightweight equipment, which all carriers first introduced in their Denver service, were interestingly integrated to Pullman Standard in the photograph of *The Aristocrat* at the right powered by the stream-lined steam Pacific type AEOLUS with streamlined coaches in the middle of an otherwise Standard consist. On June 11, 1939 *The Exposition Flyer* made its maiden run through the Rockies over the Rio Grande's Moffat Tunnel route double-headed by specially shopped locomotives with a Burlington solarium lounge making the through run at the rear. Other Burlington flyers on the time-table from Lake Michigan to the Shining Mountains such as *The Chicago-Nebraska Limited* and *The Chicago-Denver Limited*, whose early type solarium is shown at the top of the page, were already only memories on the Great Plains and the stage was being set for the supremacy of the high speed, lightweight streamliner epitomized by the effulgent *Denver Zephyr*. Above, in conventional steam and remembered glory *The Aristocrat* is depicted coming out of Galesburg, Illinois, by Jim Shaughnessy. *(Right: Paul Stringham.)*

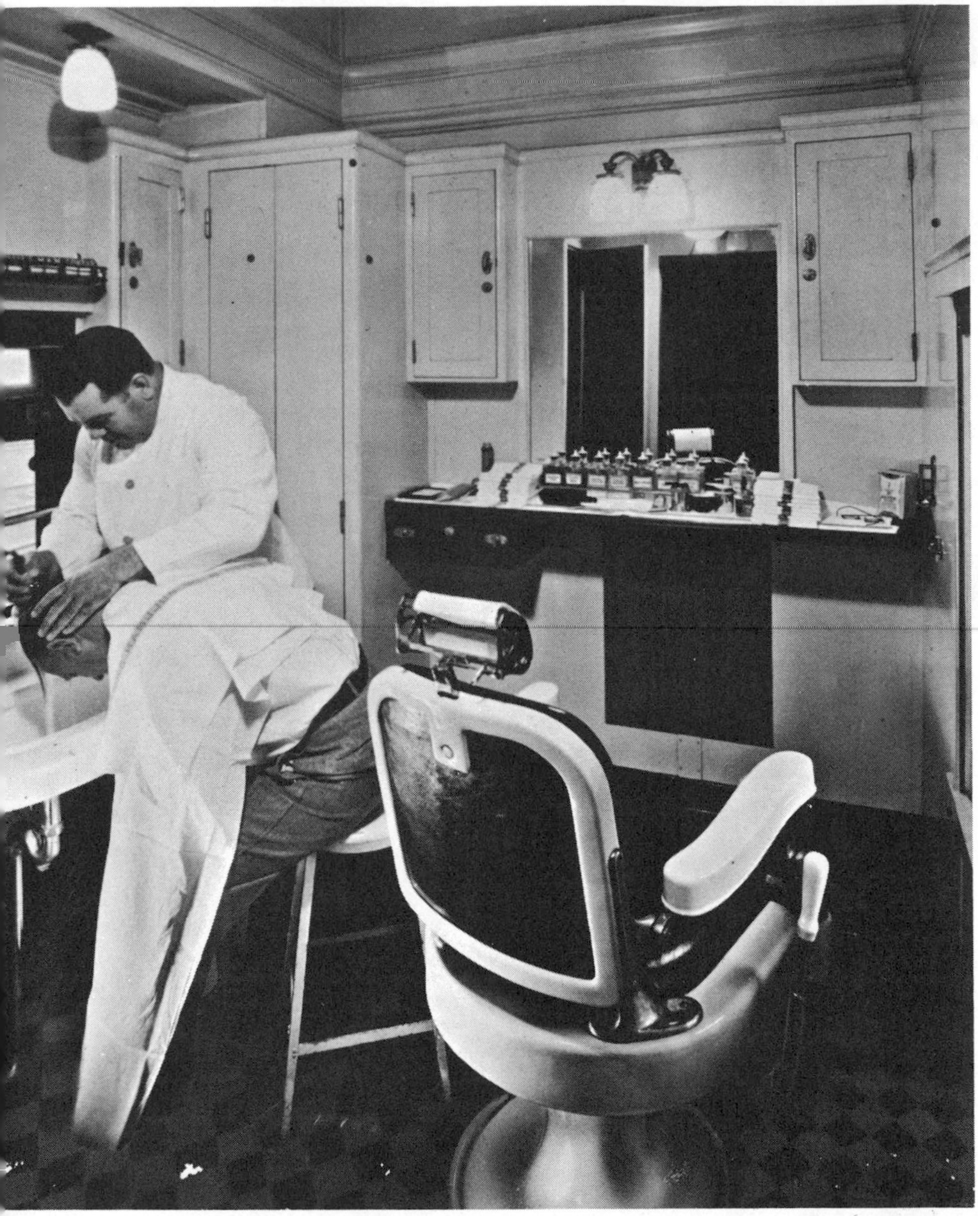

ALL THE AMENITIES of continental travel in the *belle epoque* of Pullman Standard rode behind the Burlington's finest motive power in the consist of *The Aristocrat,* a train which made no concession to hard times or depressions and in whose operation no mediocrity was thinkable. There were valets, barber and club car attendants in numerous profusion, with a radio available to women of the cloche-hatted mode of the moment. During the summers of 1939-1940, after the coming of the *Denver Zephyr* when the limited space on its cars was often sold out, the Burlington ran a sort of *Advance Zephyr* shown opposite powered by the streamlined engine AEOLUS in a portrait by Paul Stringham. Its arrestingly mixed consist included a Standard combine, two Budd lightweight sleepers, a Pullman Standard diner, sleeping car and solarium-observation at the rear. It was known as *The Overnight Denverite.* (*Three Interiors: Burlington Lines.*)

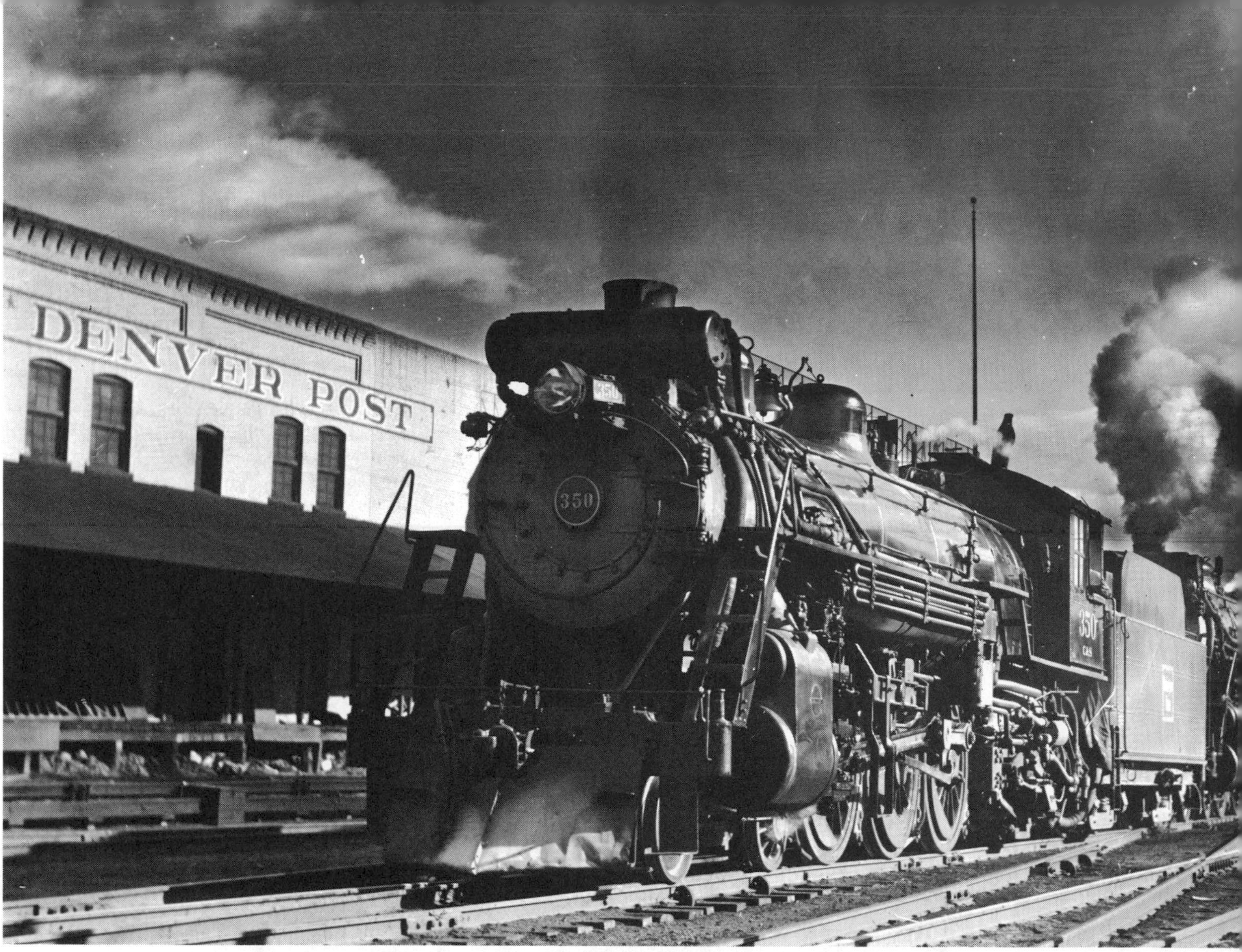
DENVER POST
350

It Shall Come to Pass
296 Still Missing
In Ocean Disaster
THE DENVER POST
750 Saved By Sea-Air Rescuers
Ruby Bond Hearing Is Recessed
EXTRA
Court Nullifies College Levy
Pope Paul Will Carry Own Cross
House Sets Battle On Aid Bill Tuesday
IN TODAY'S POST
POST DIGEST
THE WEATHER
320

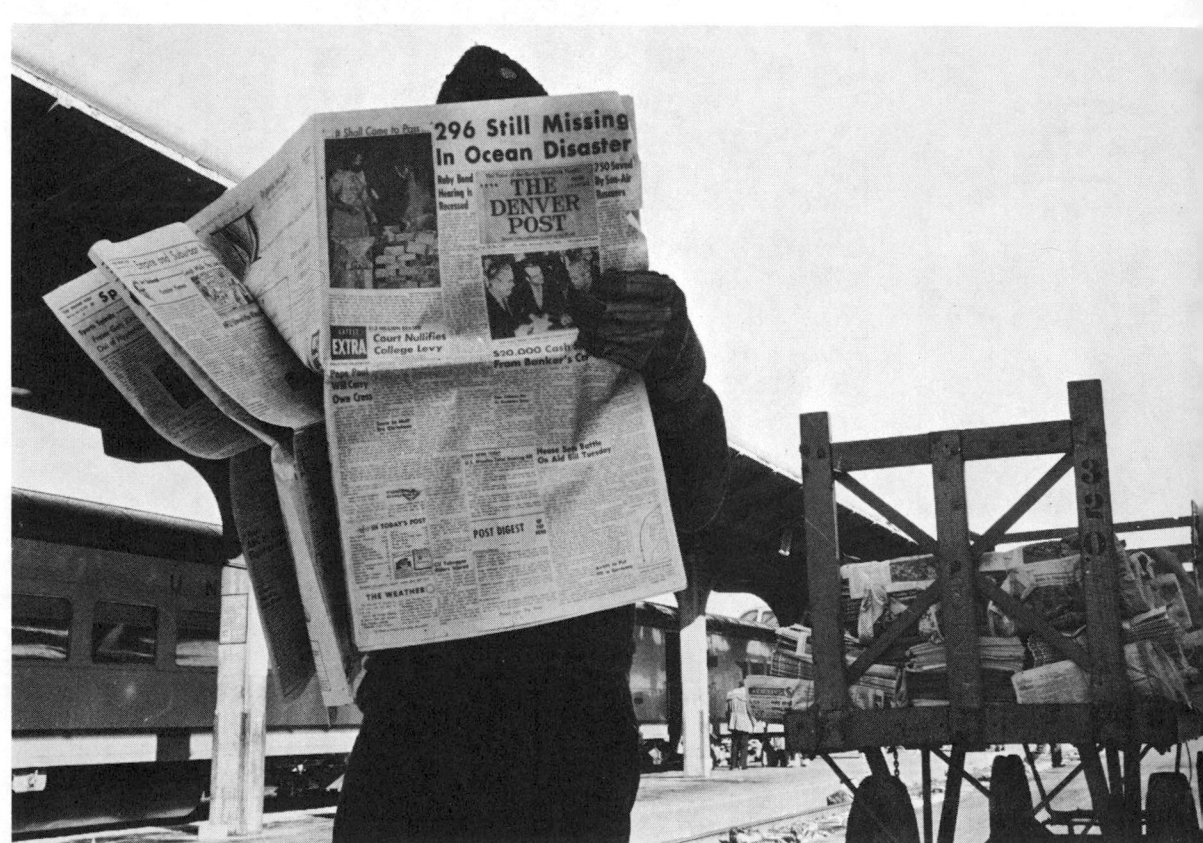

SINCE THE LEGENDARY TIMES of Fred Bonfils and Harry Tammen when *The Denver Post* was the wild eyed scandal, terror and amazement of the Cherry Creek Diggings and all the rest of Colorado, for that matter, the Colorado & Southern's trains have carried uncounted millions of copies of the Rocky Mountain region's most tumultuous newspaper to the southern parts of the state, the Panhandle and deepest Texas. Sometimes a name train as in the days when it was known as *The Gulf Coast Special*, at other times designated merely by a number, there has always been a mid-evening departure southbound out of Denver timed to pick up the early editions fresh from the presses in Champa Street and the vast Sunday supplements that made the *Post* rich. At the left the night train in 1939 is shown in Denver yards appropriately passing a warehouse where *The Denver Post* stocked its newsprint and lost no opportunity to advertise itself. Elsewhere the trucks are being unloaded and the head-end cars filled at Union Station. *(Left: Richard H. Kindig; Right: Otto Perry; Two Photos:* THE DENVER POST.)

163

NOTHING, of course, in the early days of Diesel gave partisans of steam more exquisite and unholy satisfaction than the not then infrequent spectacle of a fine new streamliner with motive power failure being taken in tow by the old reliable iron horse. Here *The Texas Zephyr*, still running with half Pullman Standard equipment, afforded Otto Perry this fine photograph at Wolhurst, Colorado, in 1943. *(Below: Ivan Dimitri.)*

AS STEAM disappeared progressively, first on the Burlington's mainline out of Omaha and then on less heavily trafficked runs, lovers of traditional motive power still found the iron horse stabled on the Colorado & Southern from Denver north to Montana and on the ancient Fort Worth & Denver City. At Dallas *(left)* a steam switcher survived into the sixties. Below, the local to Cody and Billings was caught, backlit, leaving Denver by the camera of Richard H. Kindig. *(Left: Lucius Beebe.)*

IN ITS WIDE OPEN DAYS when Denver enjoyed a reputation as the howling wilderness town of the Old West and at the same time The Queen City of The Plains with every devising of upholstered luxury on tap, its bright lights and high-stepping society were a magnet that attracted ranchers, millionaires and adventurers from every point of the compass, none more than Texas. Because it was wider open than either Kansas City or St. Louis, its gaming tables the most notorious and its bagnios the most seductive of anything west of Chicago's Everleigh Club, the Pullmans of the Fort Worth & Denver City were filled with well-heeled Texans, their pockets bursting with gold double eagles and the skirts of their frock coats covering six guns of dangerous dimensions. They

came seeking relaxation at Matty Silks' love store, roulette at Ed Chase's Navarre parlors of chance and high life in Denver's sybaritically appointed Windsor and Brown Palace Hotels. Their cowboy boots reposed in long rows outside the staterooms of the F.W.&D. and the diners stayed open all night to quench Homeric thirsts. In the thirties when *The Gulf Coast Special* between Texas and Colorado is shown above and double headed at the right, the once diamond-spangled Windsor *(lower right)* was outmoded and all Western trails led to the Ship Tavern in the Brown Palace. *(Above: Richard H. Kindig; Opposite: Otto Perry, Western Collection, Denver Public Library.)*

THE STANDUP bar in the combine of the first *Denver Zephyr* did a land office business and serious drinkers such as entertainer Shiela Barrett and Lucius Beebe sometimes found themselves still operable when the cars arrived at Denver depot after breakfast. Less dedicated patrons took their highballs sitting down in the observation lounge. *(Left and Below: Burlington Route; Right: Jerome Zerbe.)*

FEW PATRONS of the Burlington when they clamored for space aboard the sleek new *Denver Zephyr* when it was placed in service on the overnight run from Chicago in 1936 realized that the way of American life which for decades had been represented by Pullman Standard was on its way out. Rather they regarded light-weight streamlined passenger equipment powered by Diesel units as a delightful new experience and novelty and few realized it to be a revolution in the entire attitude and facade of overland travel. *The Zephyr* was indeed a beautiful train. Few who rode its inaugural units can remember without a flush of delighted nostalgia its immaculate public and private apartments, its profusion of cut flowers and the new cutlery and linen which the company provided. Its cars rode at eighty astonishing miles an hour and faster on some of the tangents as though on a bath of oil, and passengers took pleasure in filling their highball glasses to the brim and noting that none of the contents was spilled as the cars sped over switch points and crossovers. *The Denver Zephyr* began life as a streamlined unit, but integration of Pullman Standard and lightweight equipment made for interesting consists on *The Exposition Flyer*. (Left: Burlington; below: Lucius Beebe.)

THE TRANSITION from the original *Colorado Special* on the Fort Worth & Denver Railway's overnight run between the terminals of its corporate name is suggested by the photos on these two pages. At the right, in a portrait by Richard Kindig, *The Special* pants gently up the long grade out of Trinidad, Colorado, in 1939 under a summer cloud bank in steam and Pullman Standard. Below, behind Burlington's No. 554 in a mixed consist of Standard and lightweight equipment *The Texas Zephyr* soots up the skyline between Dallas and Forth Worth in 1954. Although Diesel powered north of Fort Worth, *The Zephyr,* because of inadequate Diesel servicing facilities at Dallas, ran in steam the last lap of its trip until October 1954. When *Advance Texas Zephyr* went into service in 1940, lack of streamlined equipment caused its tailgate heraldry to ride the observation-lounge *Mount Everest.* (Above: *A. E. Brown; Bottom: Everett De Golyer Photo.*)

THE END PRODUCT of the transition from steam and Pullman Standard to streamlined Diesel was represented by the original *Denver Zephyr* in its reincarnation as the *Texas Zephyr* getting out of Dallas in a hurry the day after Christmas in 1964. The drumhead rode the observation-lounge car *Silver Flash.* (*Everett De Golyer Photo.*)

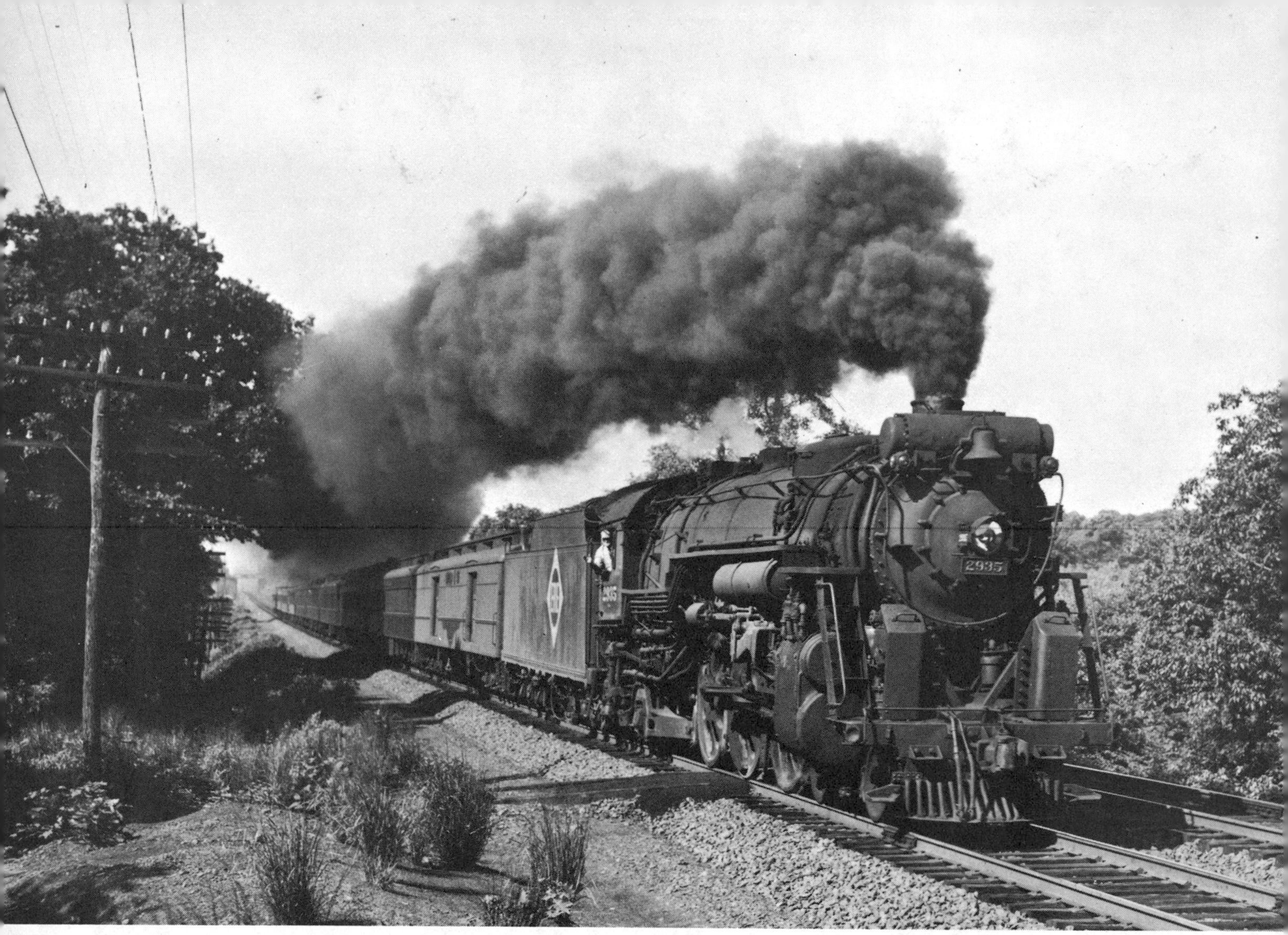
2935

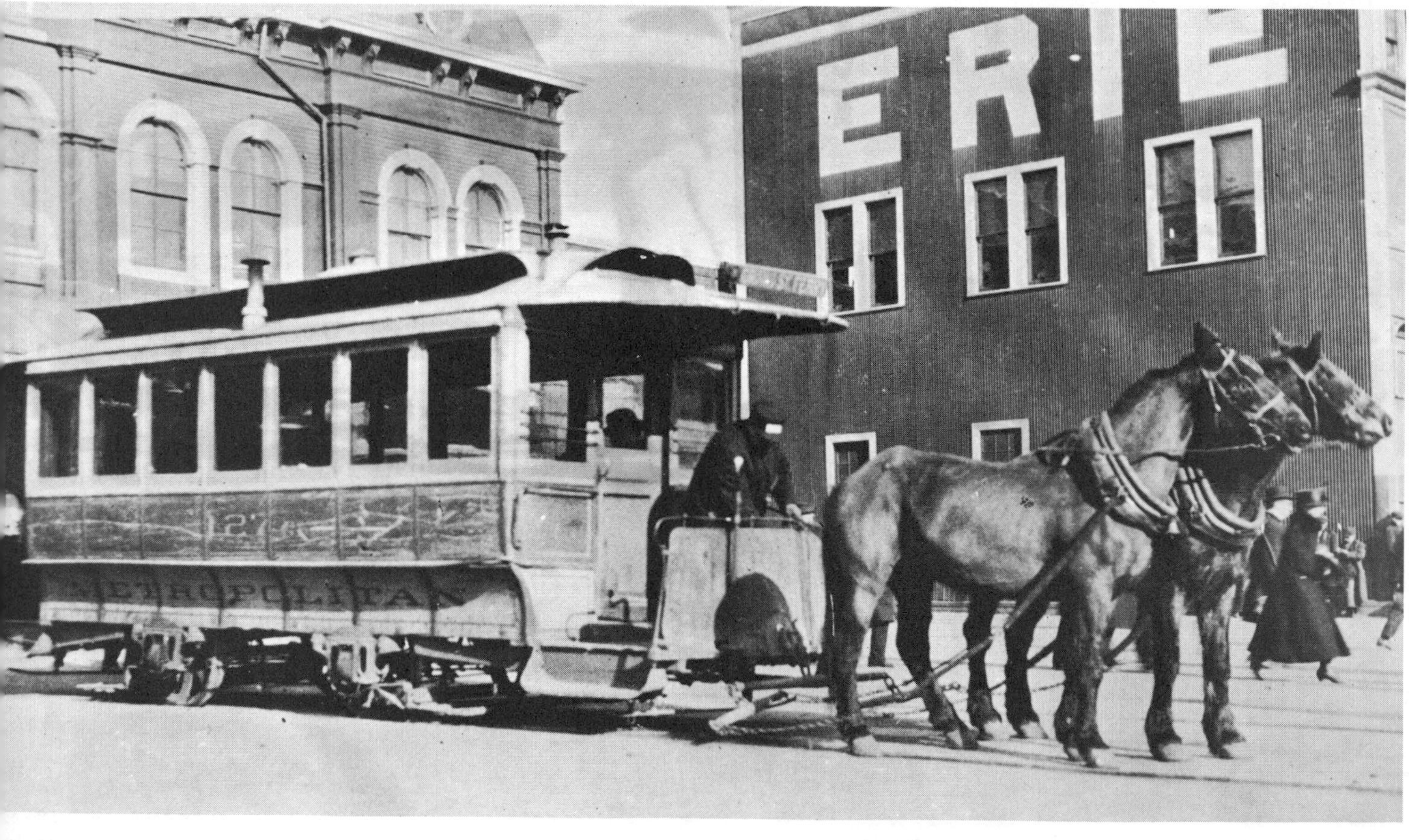
ERIE
METROPOLITAN

DESPITE its origins and eastern terminal amidst the untidy industrialization of the Jersey marshes, the Erie's mainline was essentially that of a carrier with country traffickings and rustic abode, and when it achieved the Southern Tier region of New York State, its setting was positively lyric. At the left in a characteristic portrait by Donald Furler, *The Erie Limited* rolled against the pastoral backdrop that most became it at Glen Rock, New Jersey. The Erie ferry boat *Orange* depicted here was the pride of the North River in the 1890s. It cleared its slip in lower Manhattan "on the hour by St. Paul's clock," a reference to the belfry timepiece that kept all the lower city punctual, and much of its ornate glasswork, mirrors and such came from Tiffany. Nothing imaginable could be more elegant.

FROM THE TIME of Jim Fisk and Jay Gould when it had been known as "the scarlet woman of Wall Street," the Erie had been a railroad of superlatives, good and bad. At last it enjoyed the distinction of being the last railroad in New York whose ferries from New Jersey retained a horse car connection. The Grand Street line, shown at the left at the Erie pier, was almost the last horse route in Manhattan. (*Everett De Golyer Collection.*)

NOT TOO FAR SEPARATED either in time or place are the two New Jersey country stations depicted below; Myerstown on the Reading soon after the turn of the century and Spring Valley on the Erie about 1915, if the absence of motor vehicles except for a single Model T Ford in the foreground is a reliable benchmark. The universal diamond-shaped insigne of Wells Fargo Express had not yet yielded to the closely similar monogram of Railway Express, consumers were warned that "White Bread Starvation" could be avoided by judicious use of Cerebos Salt (vitamins were as yet unborn) and for a warm breakfast on cold mornings Hecker's buckwheat flour cakes were just the thing. One could learn a lot about the local folk-habits down around the depot when the cars came in. *(Two Photos: Library of Congress.)*

174

FRAMED FOR an industrial setting in bascule girders, the Erie's train No. 606, the 5:10 p.m. local for Pittsburgh clears the Erie Terminal in Cleveland in April 1949 behind Pacific No. 2940 that could with ease have handled its tonnage several times over at eighty miles an hour. *(Richard J. Cook.)*

ALTHOUGH no identification in the Library of Congress pinpoints the stirring scene of social commotion on the Erie platfrom at Arden, New Jersey, in 1906, a shrewd guess might be that it depicts the arrival from foreign parts of the family of George Gould whose palatial estate at Georgian Court was nearby. The Goulds invariably traveled by private train with no fewer than seventy servants including the footmen who waited on the Gould butler, and could only have been accommodated by the fleet of elegant conveyances at the right. No motor car invades the scene but once at Georgian Court each Gould child had his own auto.

The *Erie Limited* Was a Country Gentleman

THOUGH ITS SCHEDULE from the New Jersey meadows to Dearborn Depot in Chicago called for twenty-five hours en route at a time when the competition was making the New York-Lake Michigan run in sixteen and a half, the Erie management suggested that Trains No. 1 and 2, *The Erie Limited* didn't take a back seat to either *The Broadway* or *The Twentieth Century Limited* and tacked a $4.80 surcharge on the fare. This heady gesture was matched by train crews in distinctive grey whipcord liveries with the train name on the jacket pocket, carpets across the buffers in the vestibules, richly embossed stationery and other amenities of a train of pedigree. Unhappily the train was placed in service in June 1929, only a matter of weeks before the stock market debacle of that fated year, and in the ensuing chaos the extra fare soon disappeared, together with some of the elegant flourishes of prosperous times. But once, if briefly, it had been a member of the extra fare club, the peer in elegant connotations of *The Cincinnati Limited, The Wolverine, The Sunset* and the New Haven's ineffable *Yankee Clipper.* The stately portrait of *The Erie Limited* was caught at Croxton, New Jersey in 1940 by Robert Le Massena. *(Smoking Stack Press.)*

BETWEEN Stirlington and Hillburn where the Erie's tracks follow closely the convolutions and reverse curves of the Ramapo River, there is a reverse curve each half of which is essentially a full quarter circle. The super elevation is eight inches and hoggers on *The Erie Limited*, as shown here headed into the spirals without abating their mile-a-minute carding. *(Everett De Golyer Collection.)*

IN THE FANTASTIC 1870s even as the manipulations of Jay Gould and Jim Fisk were making the affairs of Erie a chaos in Wall Street, the management was waging operational warfare against Commodore Vanderbilt's New York Central, advertising "The Only Route Running Cars Through From New York City to The Lakes." This was factually true at the time when at least three changes of cars were necessary on the Vanderbilt connections but the solicitation of business out of Boston was circuitous. There was, after all, The Boston & Albany. Note that at the time of this poster, train movements were being governed "by the use of an Exclusive Telegraph Line." One way or another, Erie was always a threat to the Vanderbilt peace of mind. In the photograph below, the *New York Express* heading east out of Chicago in 1923 suggests that the observation cars and tailgate heraldry was still in the Erie future. *(Left: The Smithsonian Institution; Below: Alfred W. Johnson.)*

MORE, PERHAPS, than any other part of the United States, excepting the Great Northwest empire of James Jerome Hill, it is possible and, indeed, almost mandatory to think of Florida in terms of the personality of a truly imperial railroad builder whose equally imperial whim was the organization of a vast geography as his pleasure dome and lasting monument. Henry Morrison Flagler, a partner in Standard Oil with John D. Rockefeller who retired with an immense personal fortune in vigorous middle age and full possession not only of millions but the will to spend them grandly, was able before his death to claim Florida almost in its geographical, economic and social entirety as his own creation. Call it enterprise or call it megalomania, no Roman proconsul or magnifico of medieval Italy ever brought into being so grandiose a concept as railroading and its incidental and collateral expansion in Flagler's Florida. Other railroads, the Seaboard Air Lines, Atlantic Coast Line and smaller enterprises followed the pattern of expansion of Flagler's Florida East Coast Railway. They built railroads and located cities, resorts and industries along their rights of way. They were successful, too, but not in the epic dimension of a Rockefeller partner, who with $200,000,000 in a time of hard money, undertook to make pleasure his business. Flagler's first hotel venture was The Ponce de Leon at St. Augustine, costing a then astronomical $1,250,000 and advertised as the finest resort hotel in the world. More investments followed in dizzying succession as Flagler, indifferent to considerations of profit or loss, began the realization of a vision which embraced all Florida as the playground of the nation with amenities of relaxation for every taste and purse. In 1893 he added a new dimension of splendor and costliness with the opening at Palm Beach of the incredible Royal Poinciana Hotel while the iron of the Florida East Coast was still sixty miles away at Fort Pierce. From then on resorts palatial and modest leapfrogged the railroad down the seacoast: Hobe Sound, Jupiter, Fort Lauderdale, Biscayne and Miami. At each the Florida East Coast served the resort; the resort peopled the Pullmans of the Florida East Coast. Such radiant success naturally suggested competition, most ambitious of which was that of Henry Bradley Plant whose Plant System of railroads and steamships serving the Florida west coast were to become the principal Florida elements of the Atlantic Coast Line. Florida endured cycles of recurrent boom and bust, but by the 1920s there arrived a prosperity that has hardly slackened to this day. Some of the most splendid name trains of the years of steam and steel converged from New York, Chicago, Detroit, St. Louis, Kansas City and Cincinnati, most of them funneling through Jacksonville before again diverging to their disparate destinations. Of this splendid company come to mind such names as *Miamian, Gulf Coast Limited, The Florida Special, Havana Special* and *East Coast Limited*, all-Pullman trains, never, in their golden hour, defiled by coaches. In their wake, barreling through the night along the beaches and under silhouetted palms, pass the long tally of the names of luxury on the move: *The Gulf Stream, Dixieland* and *Dixie Flyer*, the Seaboard's all-Pullman *Orange Blossom Special* beloved of Stotesburys and Wideners and names of social consequence, *The Southern States Special* and *The Southland, The Suwanee River Special, Florida Sunbeam, Royal Palm* and *Ponce de Leon, The Floridan, Seminole* and *City of Miami, The South Wind, Florida Arrow, Sunnyland, Southland Express, Pinellas Special, The Everglades, Royal Poinciana* and *Palmetto Limited* and, at long last, *The Champions* and two trains that were named for the magnifico who started it all, *The Henry M. Flagler* and *The Dixie Flagler*. In the annals of transport, only two other railroaders have had trains named for them, and Commodore Vanderbilt and James J. Hill rated but one each. If other monuments than those which still bear his name everywhere south of Jacksonville are required for Henry Flagler, one might be the memory that in the most spacious years of Florida travel, a thousand Pullman cars were in its service every night.

Florida East Coast.

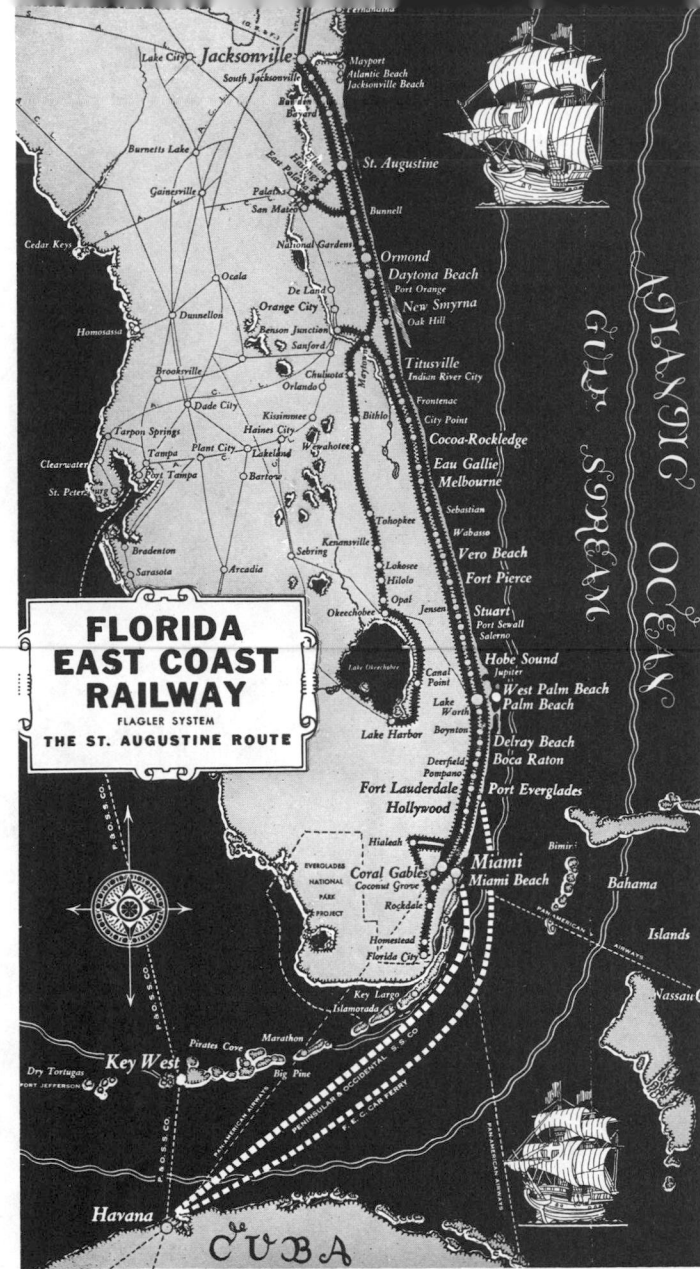

FLORIDA
EAST COAST
RAILWAY

FLAGLER SYSTEM
THE ST. AUGUSTINE ROUTE

Of the Florida East Coast's
founder, a later historian was
to remark that future
generations of Floridans would
regard Henry M. Flagler as
the human race, on an only
slightly more exalted scale, was
in the habit of regarding
patriarchal Noah.

PROUD POSSESSOR of a wonderfully atmospheric name, *The Ponce de Leon* was one of the three all year-round Florida runs originating over the rails of the Big Four in the Middle West, the others being *The Flamingo* and *Royal Palm*, shown in its streamlined livery, paused at Fort Pierce, at the left. All ran over the Big Four to Cincinnati where *The Ponce* and *The Palm* were taken over by the Southern Railway, while *The Flamingo* winged over the Louisville & Nashville on its southward flight to Jacksonville. All three carried coaches as well as luxury equipment, although for a time, a seasonal section of *The Palm,* as depicted elsewhere in these pages, ran as a Pullman-only second section known as *The Royal Palm de Luxe.* (*Left: Southern Railway; Below: Hugh M. Comer.*)

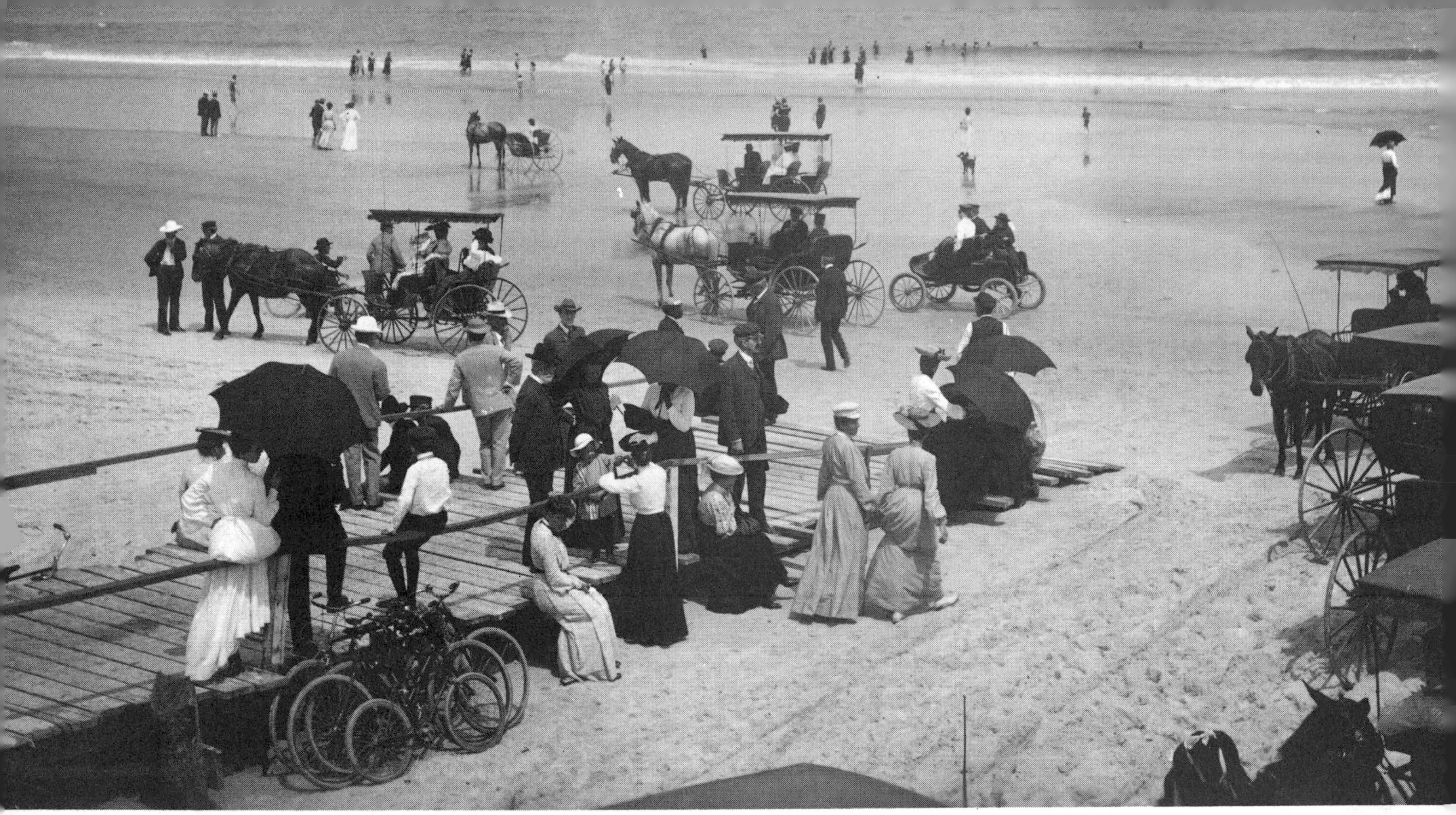

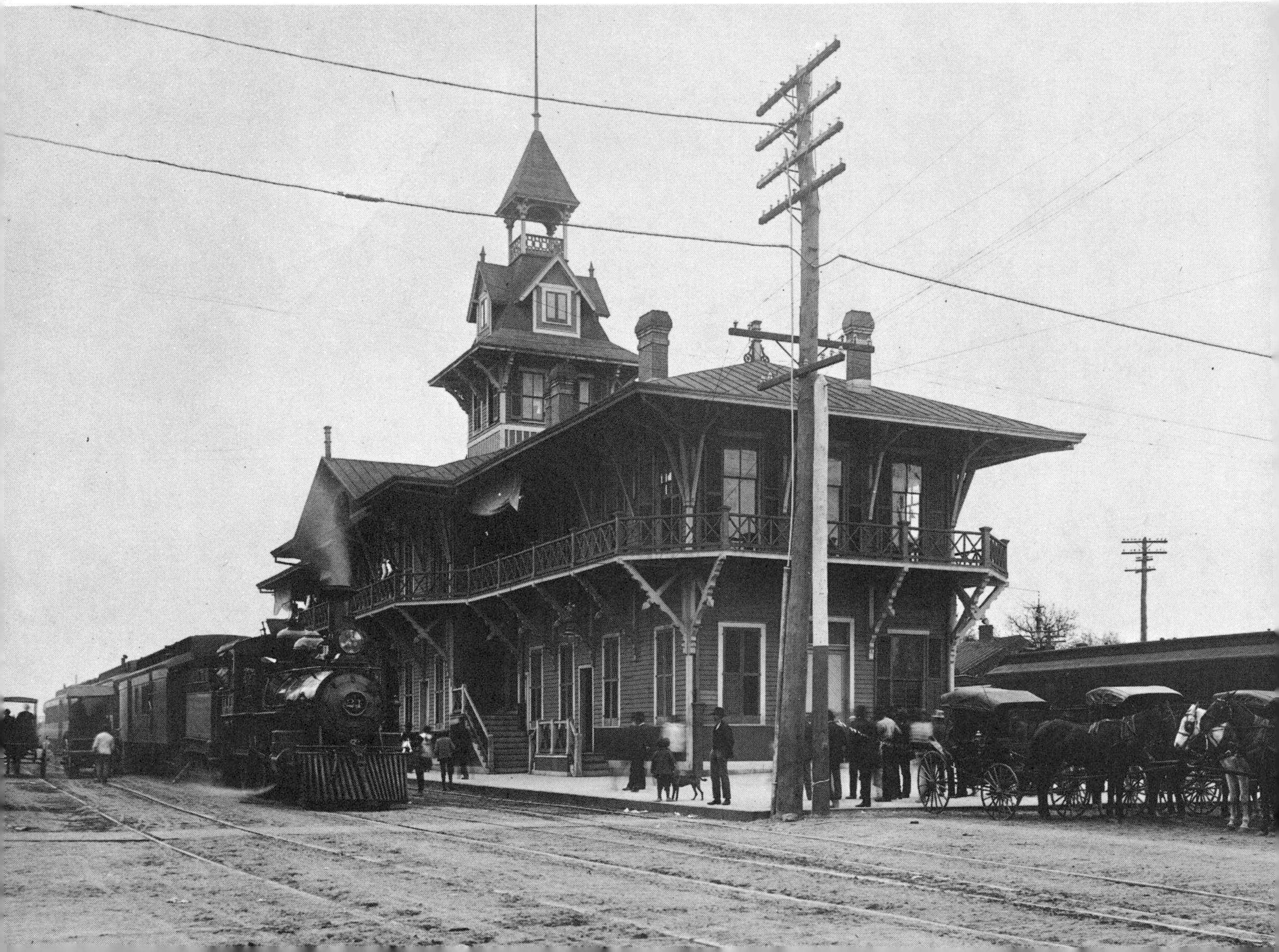

Little Neck Clams

Olives   Radishes

Potage du Barry   Consomme, Hot or Cold

Red Snapper, a la Creole
Cucumbers

Chicken Cutlet, Marchale

Queen Fritter, au Sabayon

Prime Roast Beef, au Jus
New Potatoes in Cream   Stringless Beans

Roast Squab, au Cresson

Lettuce Salad

Pistache Ice Cream   Assorted Cakes

Neufchatel   Roquefort

Fruit

Coffee

For liqueurs see Wine List
After dinner coffee served in Composite Car if desired

FLORIDA'S times primeval as a tourist resort gave scant promise of the great all-Pullman name trains that were to come and still less of the glittering age of motor transport that was eventually to abate the grandeur of the once universal iron horse. Seabreeze Beach *(above opposite)* in 1898 showed but a single curved dashboard automobile amongst its ranked bicycles and horse rigs. The Louisville & Nashville depot at Pensacola a decade later showed none. The Florida East Coast menu of the turn of the century suggests that nobody went hungry while en route to the land of sunshine and citrus fruits. *(Opposite: Library of Congress; Everett De Golyer Collection.)*

WHILE the rich and glittering feudal domain of the Florida East Coast was being gathered to the carrier of that name under the banner of Henry M. Flagler, the network of short lines serving the West Coast was being consolidated by Henry B. Plant, a sort of poor man's Flagler who bitterly resented his status which was notably inferior to that of the Standard Oil magnifico. Plant, when he encountered Flagler at Delmonico's in New York, glared menacingly at his rival, but his trains never approximated the social cachet which rode the Florida East Coast to Palm Beach. Here the Alabama Midland's No. 501, later absorbed by Plant, poses with its railroad family at Dothan, Georgia, in 1895. Baggage and first passenger car are from the Alabama Midland while the second coach is No. 53 of the Savannah, Florida & Western. Plant's properties were eventually absorbed by the Atlantic Coast Line which took over most of the West Coast as its private preserve. *(Gerald Best Collection.)*

185

The Florida Special Was a Train
for Grandees and Magnificoes

NO TRAIN in the record, not even the magnificent *Sunset Limited* of 1894 or the all-room *Century* and *Broadway* of the late 1930s, could be more aptly cited as a paradigm of the concept of the luxury train as an extension of the functions of a grand hotel than *The Florida Special* when it was placed in service in 1888. Here in every aspect and detail the parallel was fulfilled. The equipment incorporated in its structural economy every perfection both operational and in decor that was known to its age. In much the same manner that, the following year when it opened its doors in London, The Savoy Hotel enlisted the services of César Ritz to conduct its operation, the Florida East Coast prevailed upon George M. Pullman in person to ride the maiden run and lend it the enormous prestige of his name. As when any de luxe hostel was to open its doors in a later age of skilled Madison Avenue press agentry, social and civic leaders participated, on the cuff of course, at its inaugural. Communities along the right of way the train followed were encouraged to light bonfires in the night to illuminate its passing and the press, also present in the capacity of honored guests, reported breathlessly every detail of its luxurious progress. The muse of gastronomy was invoked and the palates of patrons flattered with rare viands and costly vintages whose service was personally superintended by urbane and cheerful George M. Pullman. The director of The United States Marine Band was inspired perhaps with tangible encouragement from Henry M. Flagler, to compose a "Florida Special March." Travel editors were sluiced and gentled in a manner familiar from that day until the present and Sunday supplements shortly blossomed with spreads in praise of *The Special* and the fine hotels at whose very portals it deposited fortunate seekers of Florida sunshine and relaxed attitudes generally. Nothing was neglected that could project a more than favorable image of *The Florida Special* on the general awareness, and passengers when they boarded the cars at Jersey City were made to feel as though they were already enjoying the amenities of the well-conducted Ponce de Leon Hotel and other equally sumptous caravansaries of The American Riviera. In a very real sense they were.

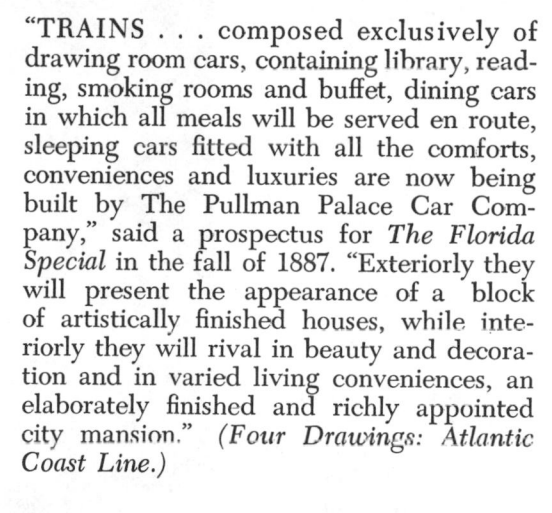

"TRAINS . . . composed exclusively of drawing room cars, containing library, reading, smoking rooms and buffet, dining cars in which all meals will be served en route, sleeping cars fitted with all the comforts, conveniences and luxuries are now being built by The Pullman Palace Car Company," said a prospectus for *The Florida Special* in the fall of 1887. "Exteriorly they will present the appearance of a block of artistically finished houses, while interiorly they will rival in beauty and decoration and in varied living conveniences, an elaborately finished and richly appointed city mansion." *(Four Drawings: Atlantic Coast Line.)*

IF DANCING to the strains of a stringed orchestra of Hawaiian youths may seem frivolous in the light of the austere and eminently solvent clientele of *The Florida Special*, it should be remembered that back in 1888 when the train was placed in service Henry Morrison Flagler himself had commissioned the circulation of the sheet music of "The Florida Special March" and that by the twenties or early Scott Fitzgerald age of New York society, the era of the great tea dance was already recognized. Largely, of course, the dancing was accomplished for the benefit of publicity photographs if only because, by the time the *Special* rolled over the Atlantic Coast Line tracks, one of the fastest roadbeds in the world, it wasn't altogether practicable. *(Three Photos: Atlantic Coast Line.)*

BETWEEN RICHMOND AND WASHINGTON, where it is depicted at the bottom of the page in 1933 in all-Pullman splendor, *The Florida Special* traversed the densely trafficked iron of the Richmond, Fredericksburg & Potomac connecting with the Pennsylvania northbound and the Atlantic Coast Line en route to Florida. The entire tone of the train's operation reflected that of a private club for gentlefolk who wanted only the best of everything without ostentation. Its porters and dining car stewards served the same patrons year after year, and Whitneys, Vanderbilts and Stotesburys were content to travel in public accommodations on *The Special* or have their private cars assigned to lesser runs. Although eminently a member of the private car set, Evalyn Walsh McLean, owner of the Hope Diamond, often rode *The Florida Special* with a large entourage of personal servants and bodyguards. She is shown under characteristic palms in one of the Royal Poinciana's "Afromobiles." In keeping with the grand manner which characterized *The Florida Special* and stemmed, of course, from the solvent perfectionism of Henry M. Flagler, even its publicity photographs *(opposite)* had a Tiffany-like cachet of elegance. Unobstrusive excellence, most expensive of all commodities, was always available to a Standard Oil partner with the tastes of a Medici. *(Left: Library of Congress; Below: Rail Photo Service, H. W. Pontin.)*

NOT ONLY was *The Florida Special* the only train of its time other than *The Century* for whose passengers a red carpet was spread, it was the first aboard which strolling bands of minstrels made music in the club car with Aloha melodies on string guitars. The feature was later copied by the competition together with personable hostesses, first run moving pictures and ballad singers, but *The Special* furnished its music unobstrusively behind potted palms like the fiddlers at the Ritz Carlton in Madison Avenue at Forty-sixth Street. Fresh pompano on the northbound menus and *The Miami Daily Herald* under every stateroom door were taken for granted. The perfectionist spirit of Henry M. Flagler gave *The Florida Special* green at every interlocking. *(Left: Florida East Coast; Below: Everett De Golyer Collection.)*

ALOOF AND CONSERVATIVE ELEGANCE was the hallmark of the all-Pullman *Florida Special* which in 1927 cut the running time between New York and Palm Beach-Miami to approximately twenty-four hours. Much of *The Special's* cachet of distinction derived from its two all-room Pullmans which came down over the New Haven from Boston in the *Colonial Express* and one of which, together with its New York counterpart, was cut out at West Palm Beach by the Florida East Coast night switcher and rolled across the Flagler Trestle to Palm Beach itself where they were spotted on the palm-fringed private car track of the Royal Poinciana Hotel. Essentially *The Florida Special* was a Florida East Coast train and showcase for that superbly aristocratic carrier, and its public cars bore the proud legend *Flagler System* on their name boards. By far the larger portion of its sailing list descended from the green cars at the Palm Beach stop where a red carpet *(vide supra)* was laid out in much the same manner, albeit in abated dimension, as was rated by *The Twentieth Century Limited* in New York. Rich but not gaudy was the livery of *The Florida Special.* (Florida East Coast.)

191

DEPARTURE from Miami of *The Gulf Stream Special* was less elegant than that of *The Florida Special* only in matter of degree.

PERFECTIONISM, inspired by the founding Henry Flagler *(left)* found expression in Florida East Coast ticket offices that might easily have been mistaken for the lobby of a luxury hotel. Company literature was printed on coated stock, tickets on banknote paper. *(Two Photos: Flagler Museum.)*

IN HIS classic treatment of surface travel in the grand manner "Some Classic Train," Arthur Dubin compares *The Florida Special* to *The Twentieth Century Limited* on the grounds that, of all the great name trains, *The Special* more often went in multiple sections than any other excepting only the Central's No. 25 and 26. He might well have extended his comparison to include other aspects of this most favored and desirable of varnish runs. It was the special pride and joy of its owning Atlantic Coast Line and Florida East Coast; its clientele was a very special classification of the elect to whom the best of everything, while entirely accustomed, was none too good; it commanded the best and newest of Pullman equipment as it came from the car shops and its sailing list, had there been one as was maintained for *The Century*, would have bristled with names that made news in every category of distinction. Like *The Century*, too, the *Florida Special* attracted members of the private car club who could easily have ridden their own varnish equipment but found the company congenial and the atmosphere of *The Special* as mannered and unobtrusive as that of a gentleman's club. There were indeed Hawaiian type guitar players in the observation lounges at dinner time, but in the diner one might encounter headliners of the conservative establishment, monocled banker Jules Bach who purchased old masters from Lord Joseph Duveen on a scale comparable to that of Andrew Mellon, Evalyn Walsh McLean, inevitably wearing the Hope Diamond and Star of the East, Cissie Patterson, publisher of the Washington *Times Herald* who demanded that her stateroom be smothered in fresh cut flowers which were renewed at strategic intervals, Bernard Baruch, Gene Tunney, Mrs. Harrison Williams or Ogden Mills. The cars that met *The Special* at West Palm Beach were the Rolls-Royces, Bentleys and Hispanos of assured privilege and when the Pullmans ground to a halt at Miami their patrons in predominant measure headed for Alfred Barton's Surf Club in Collins Avenue. Embarking or descending from *The Special*, its aloof clientele trod a crimson carpet whose only counterpart of American usage was that of *The Century*. It was that kind of train. *(Lucius Beebe.)*

THE SCENE depicts the Florida East Coast depot at West Palm Beach, entrepot to Palm Beach itself, in the golden twenties. Northbound as indicated by its tailgate insigne is *The Florida East Coast Limited*, running perhaps in two sections with the post-Washington's Birthday density of traffic out of Florida. At the right and parked next to the platform is the Rolls-Royce Mulliner two-seater convertible belonging to Reginald De B. Boardman, Boston real estate magnate, man of Commonwealth Avenue fashion and Palm Beach regular. The scene was recreated as a nostalgic souvenir of a vanished era by Howard Fogg.

FLORIDA EAST COAST LIMITED

Fogg

NO TRAIN in the Golden Age of Pullman transport enjoyed the regard of an affluent management in greater degree than did *The Florida Special* in its long run down the decades. When it was placed in service in 1887 George M. Pullman himself, no less, made the first run supervising the service of antelope steak in the dining car *Alhambra* which boasted Nile green silk plush portières at the windows and fresh cut flowers on every table. As long as it remained on the timecard of the Florida East Coast and its connecting lines it lived up to this initial elegance and its owners were pleased to advertise it as a "Train de Luxe." It was a phrase that gave the Santa Fe ideas.

FOR a stateroom passenger aboard *The Florida Special* in 1931, Frank Crowninshield's *Vanity Fair* and *Town & Country* to read en route. What else? *(Roger Sturdevant.)*

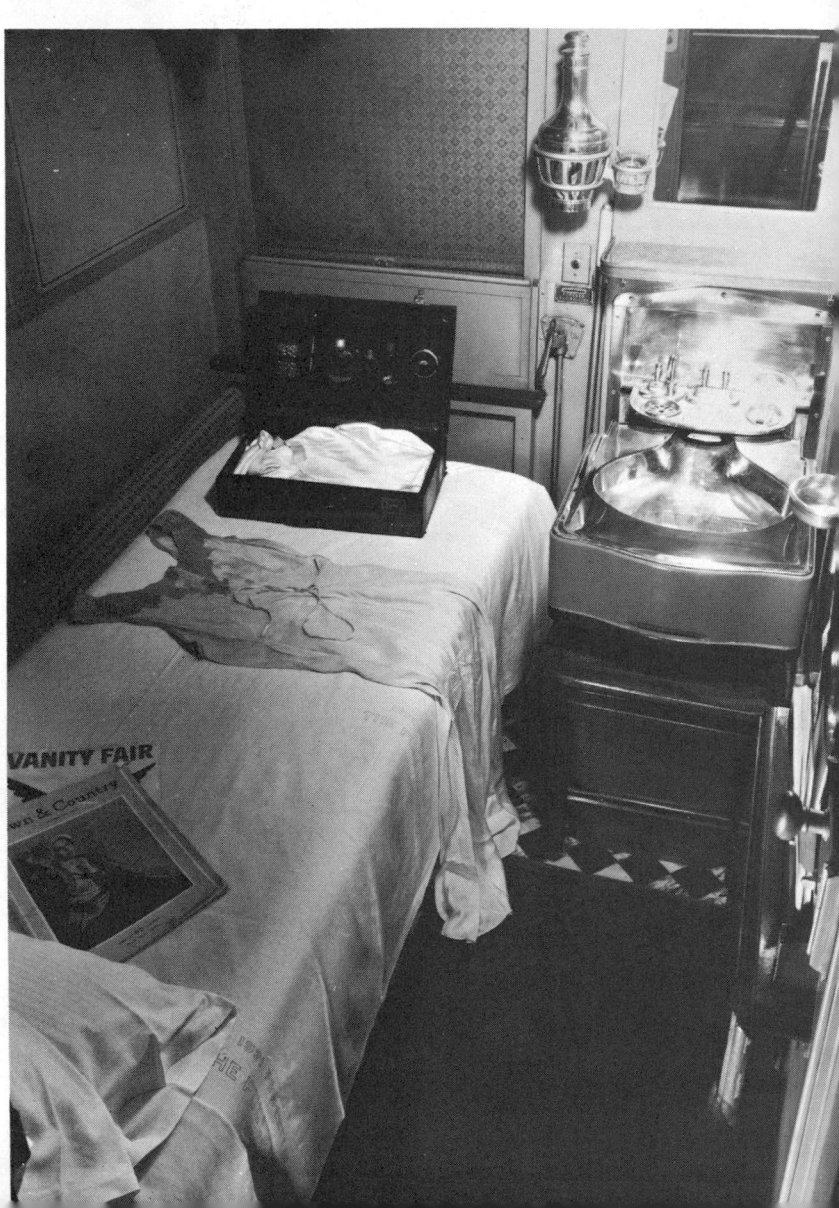

KEY WEST EXTENSION

FLORIDA EAST COAST RAILWAY

OPENED JANUARY 22ND 1912

HAVING jeweled the East Coast of Florida with a string of superb resort hotels that, in effect, turned the Palmetto State into a feudal domain of the railroad that connected them, Henry Flagler conceived the idea of one more monument to his genius for spending money profitably in the form of an extension of the Florida East Coast over the water to Key West and a foreshortened steamship connection with Cuba. It was an engineering feat that captured public imagination and the phrase "the main line that goes out to sea" had a pioneer ring about it. It also cost the lives of more than a score of construction workers and more Standard Oil money than it was ever to pay back, a matter of supreme indifference to Flagler who, when an awed secretary brought him the news that Standard had just been fined $29,000,000 in an anti-trust suit, nodded absently. "Do you happen to have those Whitehall plumbing bills handy?" he asked. The Key West extension was completed in 1912, a year before Flagler's death and lasted until it was so badly wrecked by a hurricane in 1936 that it was abandoned as a railroad right of way and a motor road laid over it. F.E.C. trains such as *The Havana Special* pulled up to pierside in Key West and discharged passengers directly aboard ferries bound for Havana itself. (*Two Photos: Flagler Museum.*)

197

TURN OF the century predecessor of *The Orange Blossom Special* was the S.A.L.'s *Atlanta Special*, known as "The Cyclone" and advertised to run "76 miles in 67 minutes." *(Fred Arone Collection.)*

A TRULY RADIANT NAME in the annals of the Florida seasonal luxury traffic was that of the Seaboard Air Line's all-Pullman *Orange Blossom Special* which, in the days when a Florida winter vacation was a prestige symbol, was in itself an index of privilege and assured social and economic status. *The Orange Blossom Special* made its maiden run November 21, 1925 directly on the heels of the Seaboard's completion of its line between Coleman and West Palm Beach and its terminus was at the latter point. Two years later *The Orange Blossom* began operating all the way through to Miami with setout Pullmans for Tampa, St. Petersburg, Sarasota, Venice and Fort Meyers. Beginning January 2, 1934, the train was completely air-conditioned and, when such improvements were in time available, it was equipped with tight-lock couplings, rubber draft gear and other luxury details. Strictly a no-nonsense varnish haul aimed at the conservative carriage trade, *The Orange Blossom* eschewed string quartets and recreation cars in favor of solid Pullman comfort with buffet-lounges, a barber, lady's maid, shower baths and open observation platforms. Its cuisine, a product of Pullman Standard dining cars, was classic and appropriate to its fastidious clientele. Train personnel was specially selected and, like the conduct of *The Twentieth Century Limited*, a complete daily report of its performance, occupancy and notable passengers was placed on the desk of the road's president every morning. The Seaboard's fine Mountain type engines assigned to *The Orange Blossom* such as No. 249 and 250 shown opposite were equipped with husky long-distance Vanderbilt tenders and ran the whole distance from Richmond to Jacksonville without change. No. 249 is an assigned engine for *The Orange Blossom*; No. 250 is shown paying its way on the business end of *The Southern States Special*. The train lasted until it was replaced by the *Silver Meteor* and *Silver Star*. (Opposite: Two Photos: Seaboard Air Lines, Fred Arone Collection; Above: Hugh M. Comer.)

IN A PUBLICITY CONSCIOUS AGE when Florida was very much in the public eye the owning carriers capitalized on *The Orange Blossom's* first run with completely air-conditioned equipment out of Pennsylvania Station in New York in 1936 with a re-christening ceremony involving a symbolic bottle of Florida orange juice in place of the usual champagne. The magnificent Penn Station, whose Roman Imperial waiting room is shown opposite, was an ideal setting as point of departure for a train as ornate in its appointments as *The Orange Blossom* and as rich in its implications of the affluent life. On the opposite page, heading the train's all-Pullman consist, is a specially assigned light Pacific-type Seaboard engine with an identifying train herald on its smokebox to proclaim its breeding and pedigree. At this remove, the significance of the white rabbit mascot has been forgotten. *(Two Photos: Seaboard Air Line; Below, Opposite: Pennsylvania Railroad.)*

ORANGE BLOSSOM SPECIAL

COMPLETELY AIR CONDITIONED

201

THE PORTRAIT OF SPLEN-
DOR shown above is that of
two Nashville, Chattanooga &
St. Louis high wheeled 4-8-4's,
the ultimate manifestation of
steam power on that historic
carrier, rolling at seventy miles
an hour up Crow Creek, at Bass,
Alabama, with the northbound
Dixie Flyer, Train No. 94. A few
miles further on at Sherwood,
the Cumberland Mountains
close in on the right of way and
the ruling grade awaits between
Tantallon and the south entrance of Cowan Tunnel and
the *Flyer's* speed will have been
cut to a scant ten miles an hour.
At the right is a turn of the century view of the old N.C.&St.L.
depot at Nashville when not a
motor car was in sight and flags
flew from every turret of a crenelated bastion of steam. *(Above:
Hugh M. Comer; Right: Everett
De Golyer Collection.)*

LEANING INTO THE SPIRALS on a curve at Vinings, Georgia, the northbound *Dixie Flyer* on its Nashville, Chattanooga & St. Louis lap of the long haul between Florida and Chicago, is shown here approximately halfway up the steep, continuous grade between the Chattahoochee River and Smyrna. No. 94 with its usual heavy consist of head-end revenue and Pullmans is headed by a Dixie type engine No. 582 over one of the really first class roadbeds of the Deep South. The time is March 1948 and the N.C.&St.L. main line between Hills Park, Atlanta and Junta, Georgia, a distance of forty-five miles to the north where the Louisville & Nashville trackage rights come to an end, was reputed at the time this photograph was taken to be the most heavily trafficked single track main line in the United States. Its heavy grades and innumerable curves could not have been adapted to the continuous flow of traffic without C.T.C. which the owning carrier had prudently installed during the 1941 war. *(Hugh M. Comer.)*

203

COVERING THE GREATER PART of its run from Chicago to Florida over its own iron or with benefit of joint trackage agreement and running with home railroad power all the way from Lake Michigan to Birmingham, the Illinois Central's *Seminole* in the fifties entered Birmingham over the tracks of the St. Louis-San Francisco from Jasper, Alabama, and was the only daily passenger train of the I.C. into the Pittsburgh of the South. Below *The Seminole* is shown in a fine attitude of steam and Pullman standard solidity on Frisco rails a mile north of Adamsville, Alabama, behind Mountain type locomotive No. 2400 in 1950. Speed is not sensational as the heavy head-end consist and trailing Pullmans slow the train's progress to twenty miles an hour on the long grade up from Warrior River. South of Jacksonville, elements of *The Seminole* which arrived from Birmingham over the Central of Georgia and Atlantic Coast Line went on to Palm Beach and Miami via the Florida East Coast whose timetables, always opulently printed, provided the ornamental map on the page opposite showing the Indian River region from which *The Seminole's* name derived. Standard diners reflected the I.C.'s reputation for Southern cooking that was a preview of the menus at Patio Lamaze when passengers had detrained at Palm Beach. The culinary tradition was not abated with the advent of streamlining as embodied in *The City of Miami* shown opposite at Fort Lauderdale depot.   *(Below: Hugh M. Comer; Opposite: Florida East Coast, Illinois Central.)*

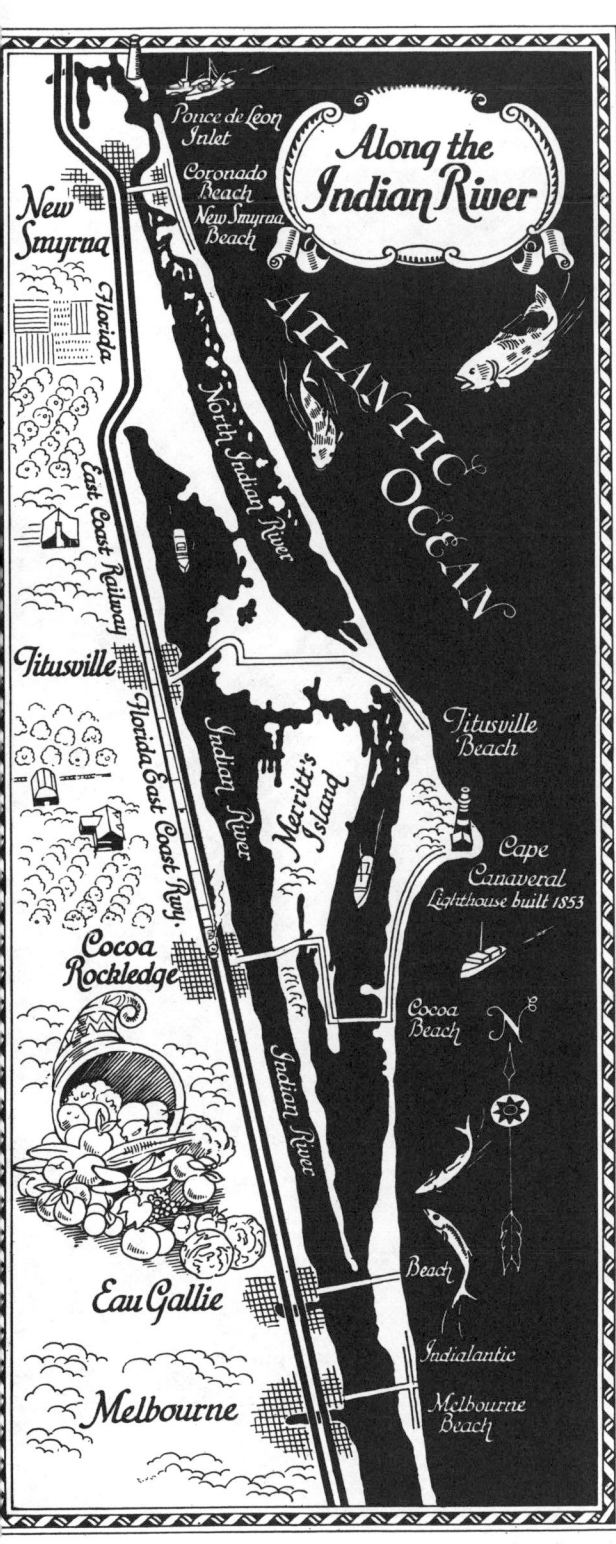

205

The Pan-American

IN THE MID-1920s, the Louisville & Nashville's pride on the Cincinnati-New Orleans overnight run was the all-Pullman *Pan American* shown here behind a resounding 4-8-2 a few miles south of Louisville, Kentucky. *(Everett De Golyer Collection.)*

THE observation car *Empress Josephine* was upholstered in gray and gold petit point and its rear platform provided a vantage point for eminently 1925 vintage period groups to view the landscape. (*Two Photos: Louisville & Nashville.*)

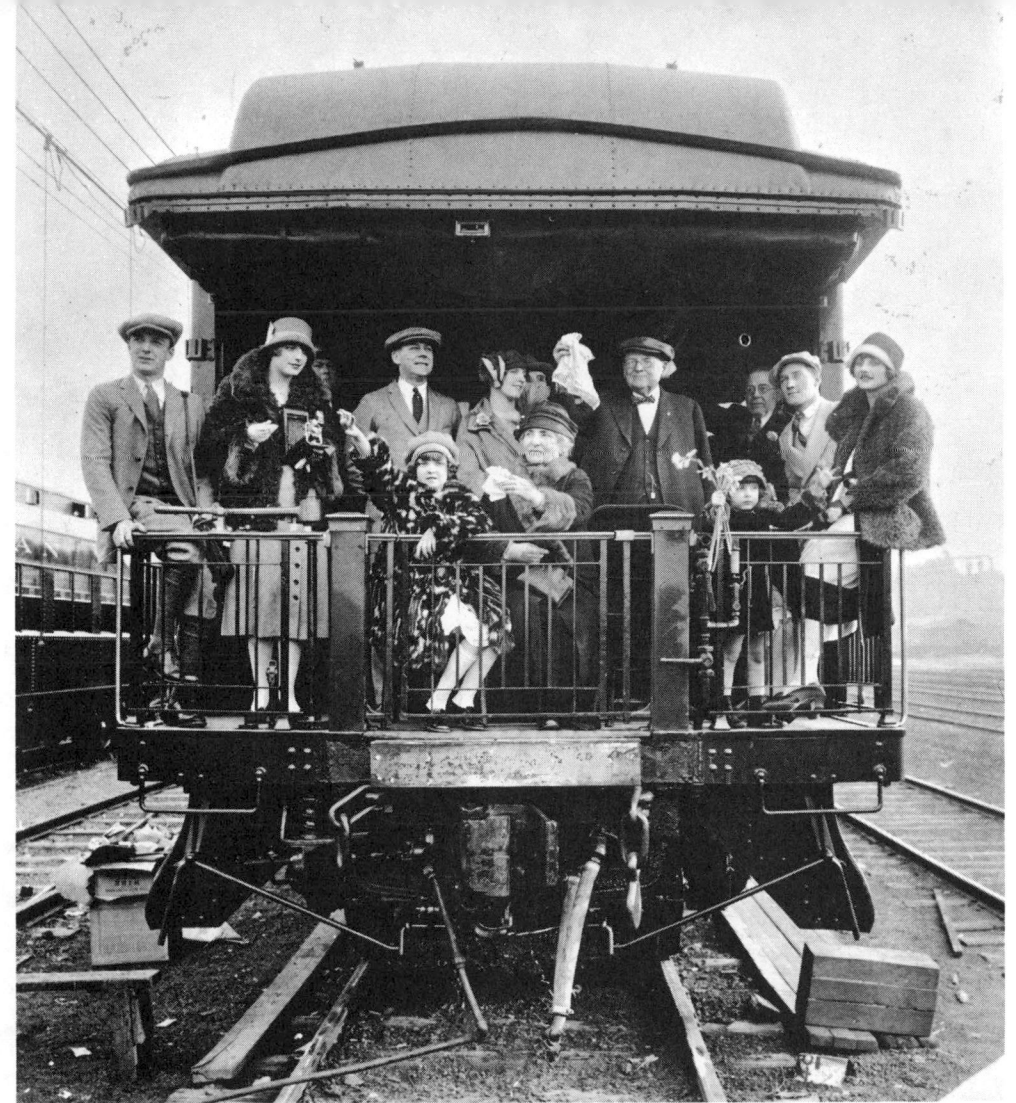

THE LOUISVILLE & Nashville's Mountain type motive power in steam times was largely assigned to the runs between Cincinnati and Atlanta. At the top of the page *The Flamingo* on an icy morning is bucking the grade at Bellwood on the outskirts of Atlanta with heavy head-end revenue cars and a long consist of Pullmans bound for the Midwest. *The Flamingo* had good company on the bird circuit, notably the K.C.S. *Flying Crow*, the S.P.'s *Lark* and *Owl*, *The Bluebird* on the Wabash, the Mopac *Texas Eagle*, the B.&M.'s *Gull* and the Louisville & Nashville's own *Humming Bird*. The interior of the ladies' retiring room on *The Pan American* dates from 1925 when the train was made all-Pullman. (*Above: Hugh M. Comer; Right: Louisville & Nashville.*)

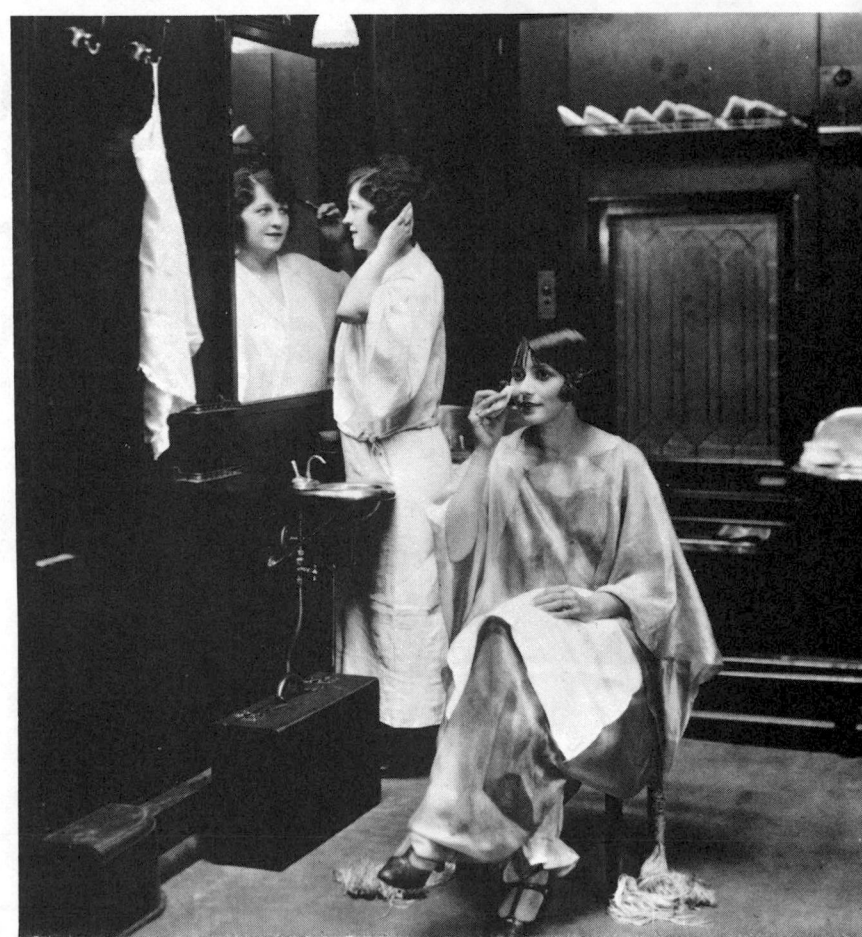

208

ALMOST EVERY MAINLINE carrier serving Chicago and the Middle West cut itself in on the winter resort travel to Florida and included the Pennsy and Big Four, the Chicago & Eastern Illinois, Illinois Central, Michigan Central, Wabash and, out of Kansas City, the St. Louis-San Francisco. The C.&E.I. rolled its *Dixie Flyer, Dixie Limited, Dixieland* and *Henry M. Flagler* which later became the *Dixie Flagler* in two and three sections in the later thirties. The same was true of the Illinois Central's *Floridan (left)* while *The Royal Poinciana* picked up through Pullmans from Chicago, St. Louis, Detroit, Cleveland and Cincinnati. Typical of the complicated routing and scheduling of setout Pullmans in the thirties was the *Flamingo*, a notable varnish haul in the railroad aviary, shown below southbound on the Atlantic Coast Line out of Albany, Georgia. The *Flamingo's* Jacksonville sleeper left Detroit over the Michigan Central, its Cleveland cars departed over The Big Four while its main section high-balled out of Chicago over the Pennsylvania. It arrived at Atlanta via the Louisville & Nashville, departed by way of the Central of Georgia and achieved Jacksonville on the Atlantic Coast Line where its elements went to East and West Coast resorts on the Florida East Coast and A.C.L. respectively. On the head end of the *Flamingo* shown below is one of the A.C.L.'s dual service Pacifics and the hogger is pouring sand on the 110-pound rail to assure adhesion for the sixty-nine inch drivers. *(Left: Illinois Central; Below: Hugh M. Comer.)*

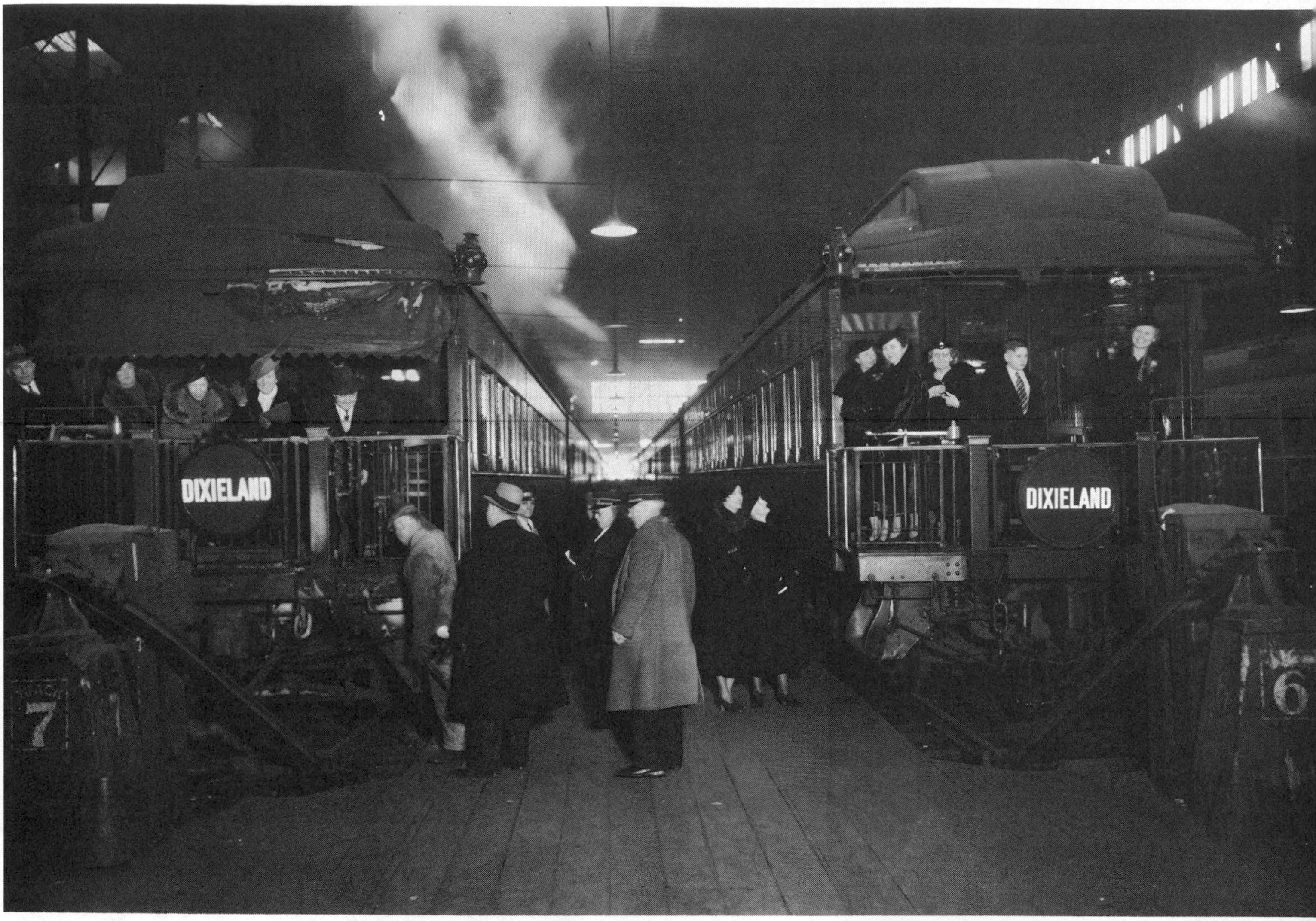
DIXIELAND
DIXIELAND
7
6

THE BOULEVARD OF STEEL
Chicago and C&EI Eastern Illinois
C&EI
JUST THAT AND BETTER!
COURTESY—SERVICE
FAST TRAINS—ALL YEAR—DAILY
between
CHICAGOLAND and DIXIELAND
and
CHICAGO, ST. LOUIS and SOUTHWEST
★
OBSERVATION, CLUB, PARLOR, CAFE-LOUNGE, DINING AND SLEEPING CARS, AND MANY COACHES
ARE AIR-CONDITIONED
THE DIXIE FLYER
THE DIXIE MAIL
★
THE CENTURY OF PROGRESS
THE SPIRIT OF PROGRESS
THE DIXIE LIMITED
Nashville, Atlanta, Birmingham, Florida, New Orleans, Gulf Coast, St. Louis, Southwest

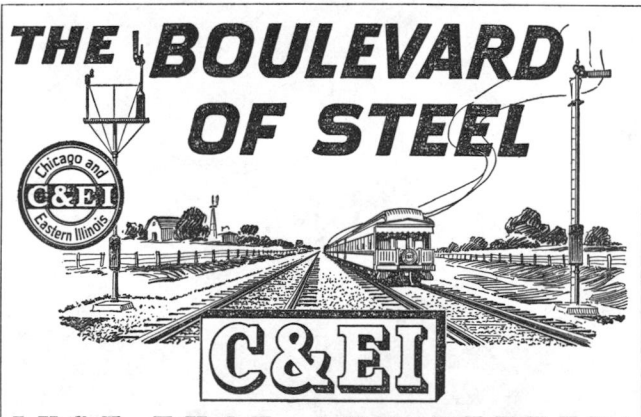

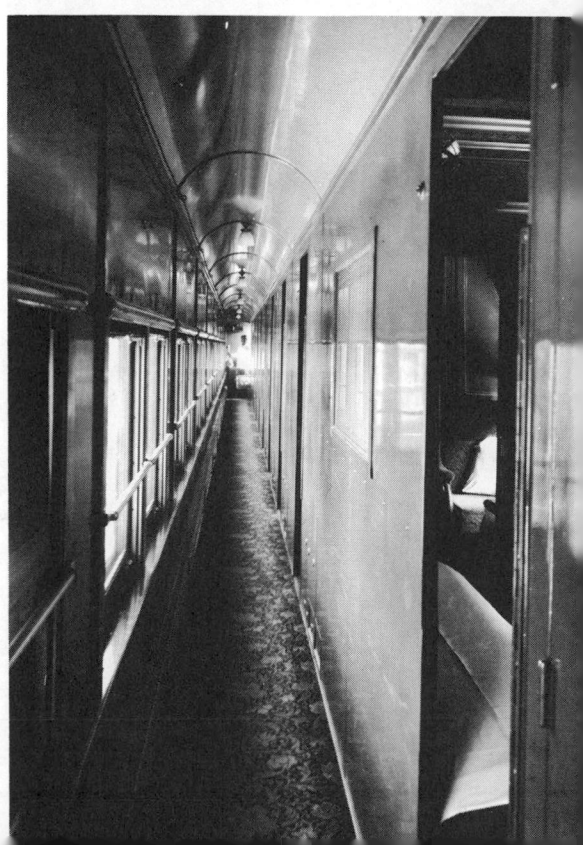

IN THE THIRTIES and forties a whole fleet of Chicago & Eastern Illinois *Dixies* rode southward out of Chicago's ancient Dearborn Station, sometimes so close on one another's rear markers as to seem like a continuous parade of name trains and their extra sections. There were *The Dixie Mail, Dixie Flyer, Dixie Limited, Dixie Express* and *Dixieland* with components destined via the routes of connecting carriers for Nashville, Atlanta, Birmingham, the Gulf Ports and Florida. The varnish runs in this long-haul category were heirs to the proud tradition of *The Chicago & Nashville Limited* which, a couple of decades earlier, had been one of the most enviable de luxe flyers between Lake Michigan and the Deep South. On the page above with a rich consist of head-end revenue cars and Pullmans adding up to fourteen cars, *The Dixie Express* passes through Englewood a few miles south of Chicago's Dearborn Station. Opposite in Dearborn's sooty depths two sections of *Dixieland* await their highball with frozen sleet on their cartops and fur-coated passengers headed for sunnier climes. Here is the archetypal study of Pullman Standard splendor when the dark green steel cars were a way of life and the open observation platform bespoke the aristocracy of surface travel. It was an era that saw the passing of the upper berth in favor of the all-room car shown below. *(Opposite: Kaufmann & Fabry; Above: Charles Clegg.)*

IN 1938 with the last great boom in passenger traffic before the 1941 war at its flood, the Chicago & Eastern Illinois kept four full trains in five regular sections and frequent extra sections smoking over the rails between Chicago and Florida and The Gulf, *The Dixieland, The Dixie Limited, The Dixie Mail* and *The Dixie Flyer,* the last of which departed Dearborn Station with one full Pullman train and a similar consist of coaches. On the page opposite *The Dixie Limited* is seen wheeling south across a desolate Illinois winter countryside behind the C.&E.I.'s compact No. 1018. Here the southbound train is shown on the Nashville, Chattanooga & St. Louis leg of the run south of Chattanooga with a full consist of head-end Pullmans and coaches behind a N.C.&St.L. "yellow striper" streamlined 4-8-4 in 1948. In the heyday of political corruption in prohibition-ridden Chicago, the C.&E.I.'s *Dixie* fleet were reportedly favored as transport between Cicero and gangland headquarters of Al Capone in Miami, but the railroad management, understandably, made no issue of it. (*Opposite: Pullman Standard; Everett De Golyer Collection; Below: Hugh M. Comer.*)

THE **DIXIE FLEET** | Chicago and C&EI Eastern Illinois

IS STILL THE

fast fleet

BETWEEN CHICAGO AND THE

SOUTH ☆ SOUTHEAST
GULF COAST ☆ FLORIDA

C & E I-DIXIE SCHEDULES

SOUTHBOUND			NORTHBOUND	
(Central Standard Time)		For Detailed	(Central Standard Time)	
LEAVE CHICAGO	TRAIN	Schedules and Equipment. See	ARRIVE CHICAGO	TRAIN
9.40 A.M.	Dixieland	Pages 3-4-5-6	6.55 P.M.	Dixieland
2.30 P.M.	Dixie Limited	and 39-40	2.00 P.M.	Dixie Limited
8.10 P.M.	Dixie Mail		7.15 A.M.	Dixie Mail
11.25 P.M.	Dixie Flyer		7.15 A.M.	Dixie Flyer (Sleepers)
			5.15 A.M.	Dixie Flyer (Coaches)

ALL C & E I-DIXIE ROUTE TRAINS depart from and arrive at DEARBORN STATION, Polk and Dearborn Streets, CHICAGO

38TH YEAR OF DIXIE SERVICE

WITH THE END in sight of the era of the classic open Pullman scction and the dawning of the age of the all or predominantly room train, Pullman added years to the life expectancy of Standard open section sleepers by redecorating them in lighter colors and more imaginative decor. Standard sleepers assigned to *The Dixie Flyer* and *Dixie Limited* had facelifting jobs in two tones of gray. Pullman green plush and mahogany bulkheads were out. *(Pullman Standard.)*

ALTHOUGH subjected over the years to the mutations of change, "improvement," "modernization" and at least one disastrous fire, Chicago's shabby old Dearborn Street Station dating from the eighties contrived to retain about its disorganized premises more of the feeling and atmosphere of railroad travel than more modern structures such as the North Western and Union depots. Its original Norman-Gothic exterior and interior decor suggestive of a Turkish hammam were updated with false ceilings and a glass-partitioned observation gallery in the thirties, but its archaic baggage facilities and crowded concourse remained right out of the period when the structure had originally been built. In the years of the great winter exodus to Florida, its Chicago & Eastern Illinois *Dixie* trains such as those depicted here often ran in two and three sections through snowstorms as shown above en route to warmer climes. Dearborn depot concourse, dramatically photographed opposite by Roland Collons, was a microcosm of railroad travel everywhere in the United States in the Pullman Standard years. (*Three Photos: De Golyer Foundation, Collons Collection.*)

214

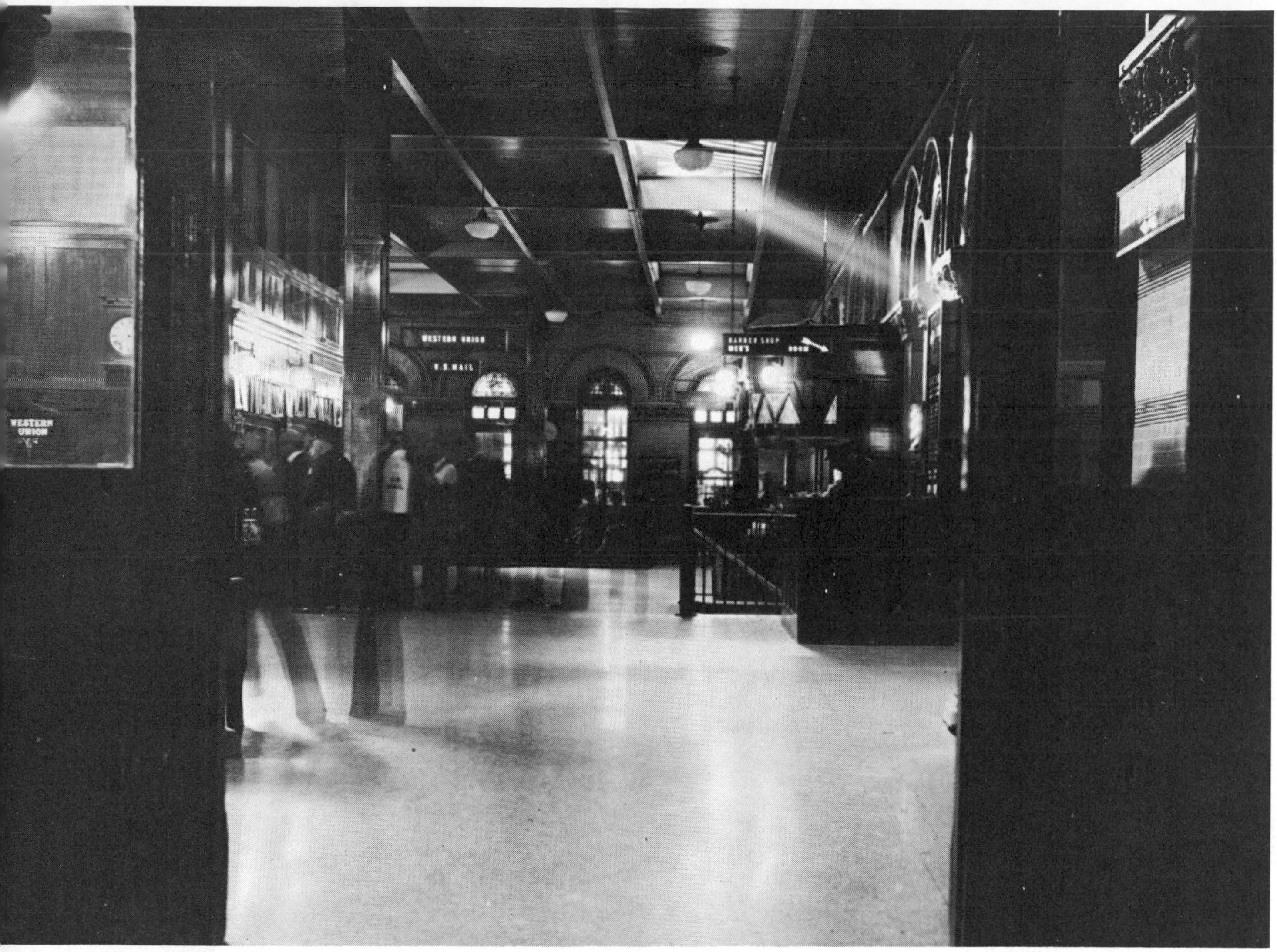
WESTERN UNION
U.S. MAIL
WESTERN UNION

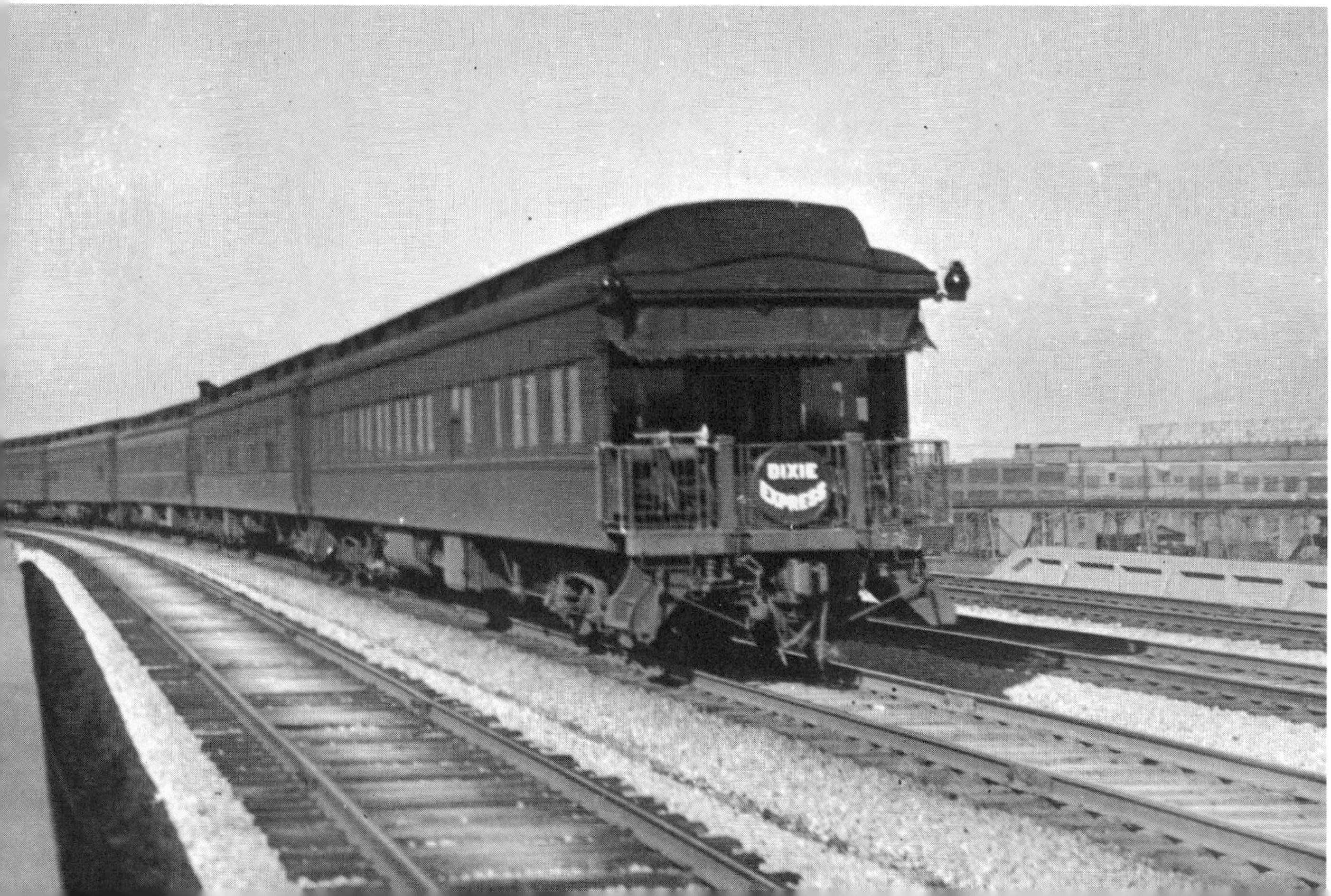
DIXIE EXPRESS

THE WEST COAST traffic of the Atlantic Coast Line in the twentieth century was largely the railroad's heritage from the efforts of Henry Bradley Plant to develop on the state's western littoral a resort and transportation empire similar to the glittering success of Flagler's Florida East Coast. Plant, consumed with jealousy of Flagler imagined himself in social competition with the superb and aloof Standard Oil partner and, once encountering Flagler at Delmonico's, enquired snidely "Friend Flagler, just where is this place you call Palm Beach?" "Just follow the crowd, Friend Plant, just follow the crowd," Flagler told him. Regardless of the less elegant status of West Coast resorts, the A.C.L. ran handsome seasonal trains to serve them, its diners continuing in their decor the theme of Spanish moss and palm trees the patrons were enjoying through the window. Below, *The Gulf Coast Limited* rolls toward St. Petersburg with seventeen cars on the drawbar of a superbly maintained Pacific whose silver cylinder heads, smokebox candlesticks and ornate bell cradle symbolize railroading in the very grand manner in its happiest hour. (*Two Photos: Atlantic Coast Line.*)

THE TRANSITION in railroad styles which saw the shift, largely accomplished in the 1920s, away from the designation of name trains as "Specials" in favor of "Limiteds" is aptly illustrated by the disappearance from the Atlantic Coast Line's timecards late in the twenties of *The Pinellas Special* and the listing in its place of *The Gulf Coast Limited. The Limited,* like *The Special* before it, was the ranking train on the West Coast run, but the steel-sheathed Pullmans and observations of the early twenties were replaced by Pullman Standard equipment. The customary assortment of sleepers out of New York was, interestingly, supplemented by a Montreal Pullman which went all the way through to St. Petersburg on Tuesday, Wednesday and Sunday during the winter months.

NAMED FOR the Pinellas Peninsula which separates Tampa Bay from the Gulf of Mexico, the "Sunshine City" of St. Petersburg was the terminal of the Atlantic Coast Line's *Pinellas Special* when this photograph was taken in 1920 at a time when Florida was enjoying one of the most spectacular of its several hysterical real estate booms which, inevitably, ended in dismal bust. St. Petersburg, The Coast Line's promotional literature was quick to point out, has sixty miles of paved city streets and the motorist of the period could "travel to any town in Pinellas County without leaving the brick highway." "St. Petersburg," it added reassuringly, "while mainly a tourist resort, is an eminently clean town hygienically, and a place where the visitor may sojourn with every comfort." The Gold Coast route from Palm Beach to Miami envisioned by Henry Flagler was barely getting under way at this time and West Coast spas such as Sarasota, Tampa, and Tarpon Springs which, like St. Petersburg were Coast Line territory, still had delusions of grandeur in the elegance sweepstakes, although the world of fashion had already indicated that the East Coast of the state would be its chosen parade in winter months.

217

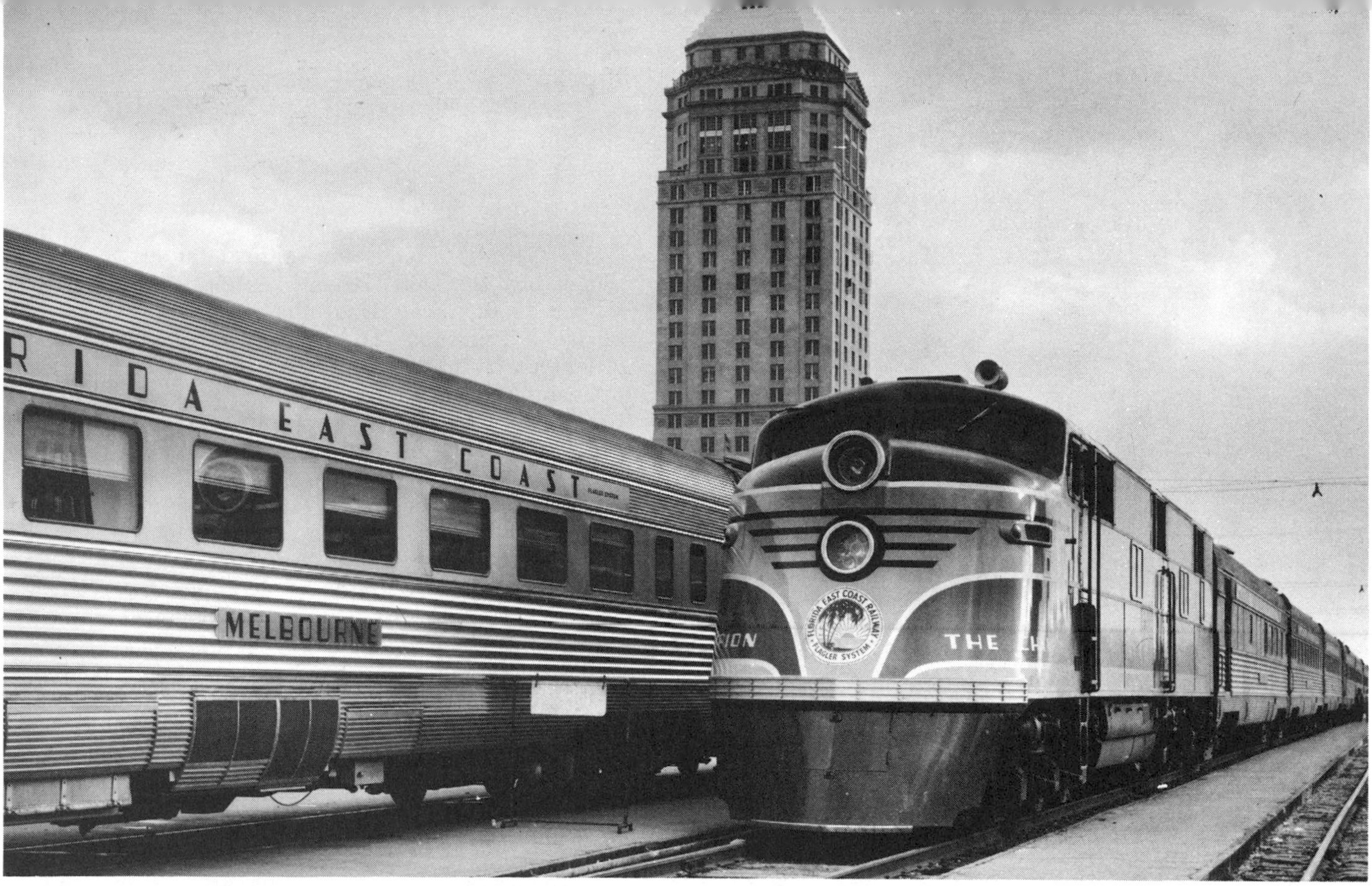
RIDA EAST COAST
MELBOURNE

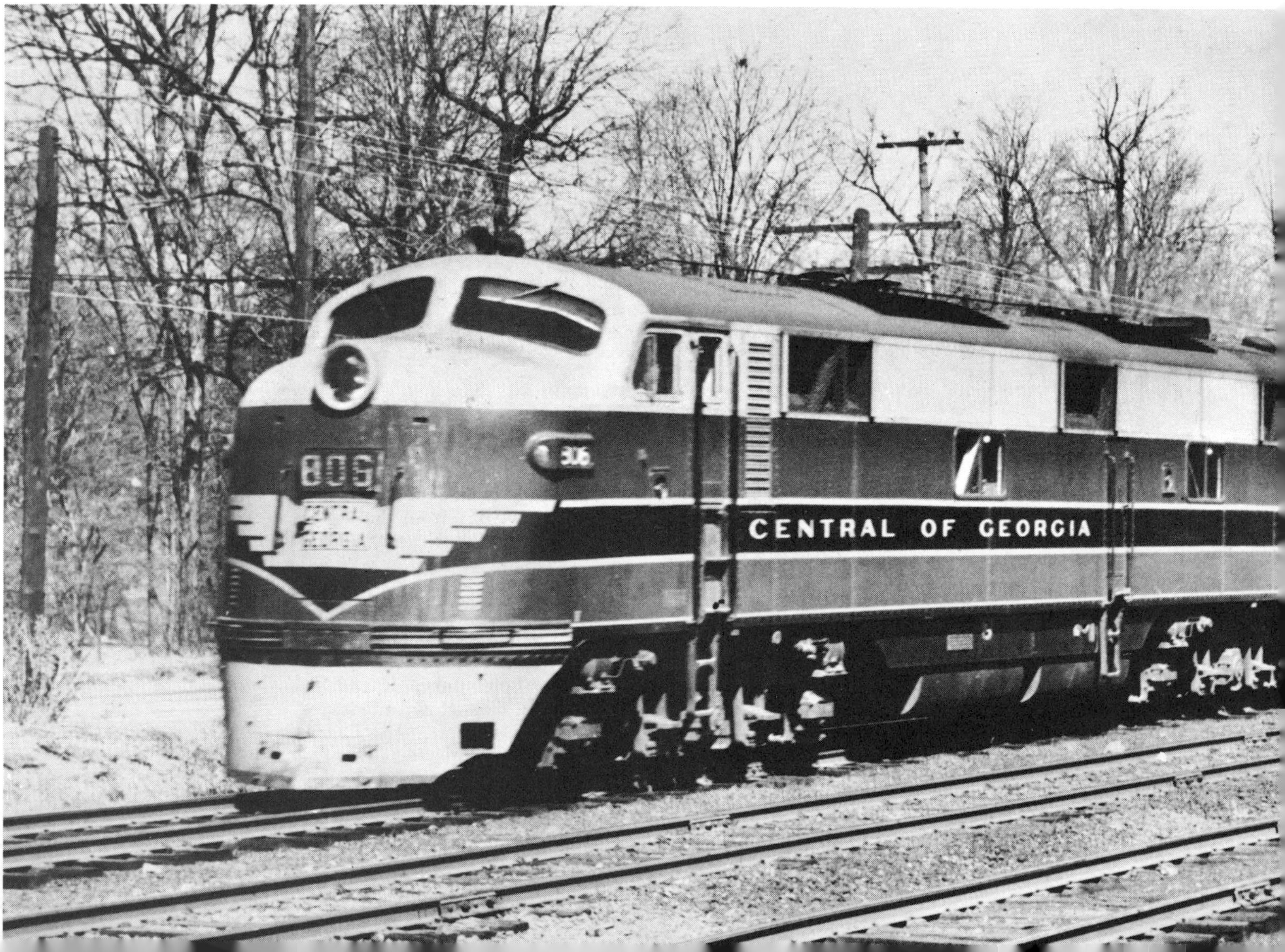
806
CENTRAL OF GEORGIA

LONG ESTABLISHED stand-by on the Detroit-Florida West Coast run was *The Southland* over the Wabash, Louisville & Nashville, Central of Georgia and Atlantic Coast Line shown in panoramic form below on the Central of Georgia in Diesel near East Point. *The Southland* carried the cream of conservative Grosse Point to equally conservative tarpon fishing resorts while flashy Miami patrons of Alfred Barton's Surf Club and those eligible for Palm Beach took the East Coast *Flamingo*. At the right *The Henry M. Flagler* preserves the memory of the grandee who started Florida on its way while opposite *The Champion* in the shadow of Dade County courthouse at Miami shows how emphatically Diesel motive power at last took over the Florida rails where once the woodburners ran. *(Opposite: Florida East Coast; Right: Lucius Beebe; Below: Rail Photo Service, Shelby F. Lowe.)*

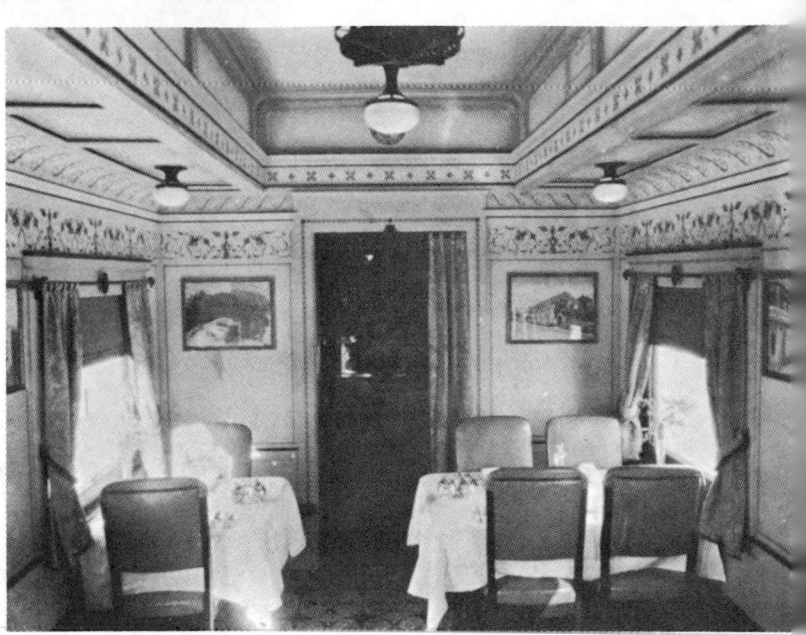

FLORIDA East Coast dining cars which were incorporated into the consists of trains such as *The Flamingo* and *The Seminole* for the run south of Jacksonville were light and cheery of decor with murals depicting scenes of historic interest to the Florida-bound vacationist. Until the new leisure and universal wealth made seasonal tourism a mass production business, diner crews knew many of the Palm Beach regulars from one year to the next and F.E.C. travel approximated a familial status. *(Florida East Coast.)*

IN THE LUSH TIMES before the 1941 war two name trains originating in the Midwest and Florida-bound operated through Georgia behind the truly dazzling motive power of the Central of Georgia, *The Seminole,* originating in Chicago on the Illinois Central and *The Flamingo* which started out from Detroit on the Michigan Central. Both converged on Jacksonville over the Atlantic Coast Line whence their components were handled to Palm Beach-Miami and Florida West Coast points by the Florida East Coast Railway and the A.C.L., respectively. For many years *The Seminole* operated on schedules competitive with other Midwestern Florida Pullman trains such as *The Dixie Flyer, The Southland* and *The Royal Palm* and is shown opposite as Central of Georgia No. 9 westbound climbing the grade at Smith's, Alabama, in March 1950, behind a fine 4-8-4 No. 455 that is just getting into its stride mounting into the Piedmont from the Chattahoochee Valley. On this page *The Flamingo* makes the grade up Byron Hill, a few miles south of Macon, behind a C. of G. Mountain type No. 483 carrying green to indicate a following section. Byron is the ruling grade westbound on the Southwestern division. *(Two Photos: Hugh M. Comer.)*

FROM THE DAY in 1893 that Henry Morrison Flagler opened the Royal Poinciana Hotel at Palm Beach that was to be the most stunning capstone to his career as hotelier and railroad builder combined, and the first full train of private cars rolled across Flagler Trestle from West Palm Beach, the Florida East Coast, it is safe to say, handled more private car movements than any other carrier in the United States. In Florida's early years as the winter resort of the nation some of the privately owned Palace cars or those rented on a per diem basis from Pullman's pool of available equipment in this category were destined for St. Augustine, Palatka, Ormond Beach or Daytona. Much later when Miami had achieved a certain, if not too conservative, vogue as a horse racing resort, the private cars of millionaire sportsmen not infrequently followed their stables to Miami, but none of this traffic was even remotely considerable in comparison to the scores and, over the years, hundreds of private car movements which terminated at the Florida East Coast's private car siding, palm shaded and manicured with greensward and rare shrubbery, in the shadow of the Poinciana. Here the private car servants of the well to do, themselves a considerable factor in the closely limited population of Palm Beach proper, passed decorously from *Japauldon* to *Doris* with invitations to cocktails, from *St. Nicholas* and *Skipaway* and *Friendship* to *Vietwood* and *Ranger* on the lordly occasions of their owners. The Private Car Age drew to its conclusion after the debacle of 1929 and closed its books save for a handful of exceptions with the 1941 war. The Flagler Trestle and the Royal Poinciana itself became memories and in 1957 when they visited Florida during the winter months, *The Virginia City (above)* owned by Charles Clegg and Lucius Beebe was spotted at West Palm Beach under the cocoa palms of the depot siding while a Florida East Coast Diesel switcher stood by to activate its facilities. *(The Miami Herald.)*

AS LATE as 1935, a dispatch of March 10 to *The New York Daily News* from its Palm Beach society correspondent, Nancy Randolph, suggested that, although the noontide of private cars was past, their sun had not yet set. *Despite a dash of rain and soupçon of wind, all the horsey folk went down to Miami today to attend the running of the Florida Derby. Joe Widener, the Pete Wideners, George D. Widener, Isabel Dodge Sloane, Col. E. R. Bradley, George Marshall and Jay F. Carlisle are only a few of the folksies-wolksies who made the trip to see the last day's racing at Hialeah this season. Lots of Palm Beachers went in a train marked "strictly private." It was composed of three private Pullmans, The Japauldon, owned by Jessie Woolworth Donahue, the Curley Hut, owned by Princess Barbara Hutton Mdivani, and now in use by her papa, Franklyn L. Hutton, and her stepmamma, Mrs. Hutton, and Vietwood, the property of Dr. and Mrs. John A. Vietor. A fourth car, just a day coach, was added to the train, but only to give it weight and ballast and make it ride more easily. No one was permitted in the coach but auxiliary members of the train crew. It really didn't cost a fortune to make this grand gesture. By chipping in $95 apiece, Mrs. Donahue, Mrs. Vietor and the Huttons were able to make the trip in pomp and privacy. In other words, the cost of the private train down and back was exactly 100 round-trip fares to Miami, and a r.t.f. to Miami is worth $2.85. This is exclusive of the light snack, sandwiches, Scotch and champagne, which the hostesses served both goin' and comin'. The train was about twenty minutes late in getting started this noontime because, when Mrs. Donahue arrived at the private train, her Pullman held the rear or caboose position. And Mrs. Donahue doesn't like to ride last. Car sways too much, she feels. So there was much switching until the Vietwood, in first position originally, right behind the empty day coach, could be switched to the rear. This delay was a lucky break for the Munn party, which arrived late and a bit breathless. In the midst of the switching, Mrs. Vincent Astor, Mary and Frances Munn and Charlie and Gurnee Munn swung aboard The Japauldon. George Marshall, his plaid racetrack coat alight with a red carnation, was a member of Mrs. Donahue's party. He almost always is these days. Frank Hutton took motion pictures of the guests as they arrived. Some bystander obliged Mrs. Vietor by cranking a movie camera of herself and her guests.*

EVEN THE MOST *blasé* Palm Beach regulars were favorably impressed in the winter season of 1910 when the Presidential Car of Daniel Willard of the lordly Baltimore & Ohio rolled across Flagler Trestle and was spotted on the private tracks of the Royal Poinciana Hotel in Palm Beach proper. Aboard this voluptuous varnish were a group of influential industrialists and favored shippers, the guests of Mr. Willard on a luxury junket to evade the rigors of northern climes amidst the palm trees and rolling chairs of the feudal domain of Henry M. Flagler. It was an age when the line demarking railroad business cars from the private Palace cars of non-railroaders was far less rigid and when, as one Florida cliff dweller remarked, "almost all railroad presidents were gentlemen." President of the B.&O. was a position beyond social reproach. (*The Smithsonian Institution.*)

223

SOMETIMES A PREY of whimsy, and always inordinately proud of its immaculately maintained green and gold motive power, the Southern Railway during one brief interlude in the carrier's long and colorful history, inaugurated the practice of naming locomotives for senior engineers who handled them on a specified run. Engineer Lee, who was usually assigned the Mountain type No. 1476, elected in the interests of modesty to have his engine named for a daughter and *Kitty Lee* accordingly rode the smokebox out of Bristol, Tennessee. The magnificently appointed diners of the Florida East Coast which were cut into the *Royal Palm De Luxe (opposite)* south of Jacksonville, were decorated with photomurals of palm trees and sandy beaches on the theory that this was what patrons were coming to Florida for and that a little more of the same could do no harm. *(Left: Ewing Galloway; Below: Florida East Coast.)*

SO GREAT was the demand for luxury space between Chicago-Cincinnati and the East Coast of Florida in the mid-twenties that in 1927 the all-year-round Big Four-Southern Railway *Royal Palm* was supplemented by a winter-only extra section running extra-fare, all-Pullman called *The Royal Palm De Luxe* on the fastest schedule to date from the Great Lakes to Palm Beach and Miami. On the same run *The Flamingo* and the legendary *Ponce de Leon* were the other Big Four all-season Florida varnish. From Cincinnati all the way to Jacksonville, *The Palms* operated over the Southern Railway and, because of light rail and cinder ballast the carrier's famed green and gold heavy Pacific and Mountain type power couldn't operate below Macon, Georgia. Here, double headed by a pair of light Pacifics and with two Pullmans deadheading on the road engine's drawbar, *The Royal Palm De Luxe* is slowing for Macon Junction and for its stunning portrait in a backlit photograph by Hugh M. Comer.

LIFE ABOARD the Florida luxury trains of the thirties offered a foretaste of the leisurely existence under the cocoa palms and tropic sunlight at Boca Raton, Palm Beach and Fort Lauderdale. These candid camera shots reflected the mood and setting aboard *The Florida East Coast Limited* in the late 1930s.

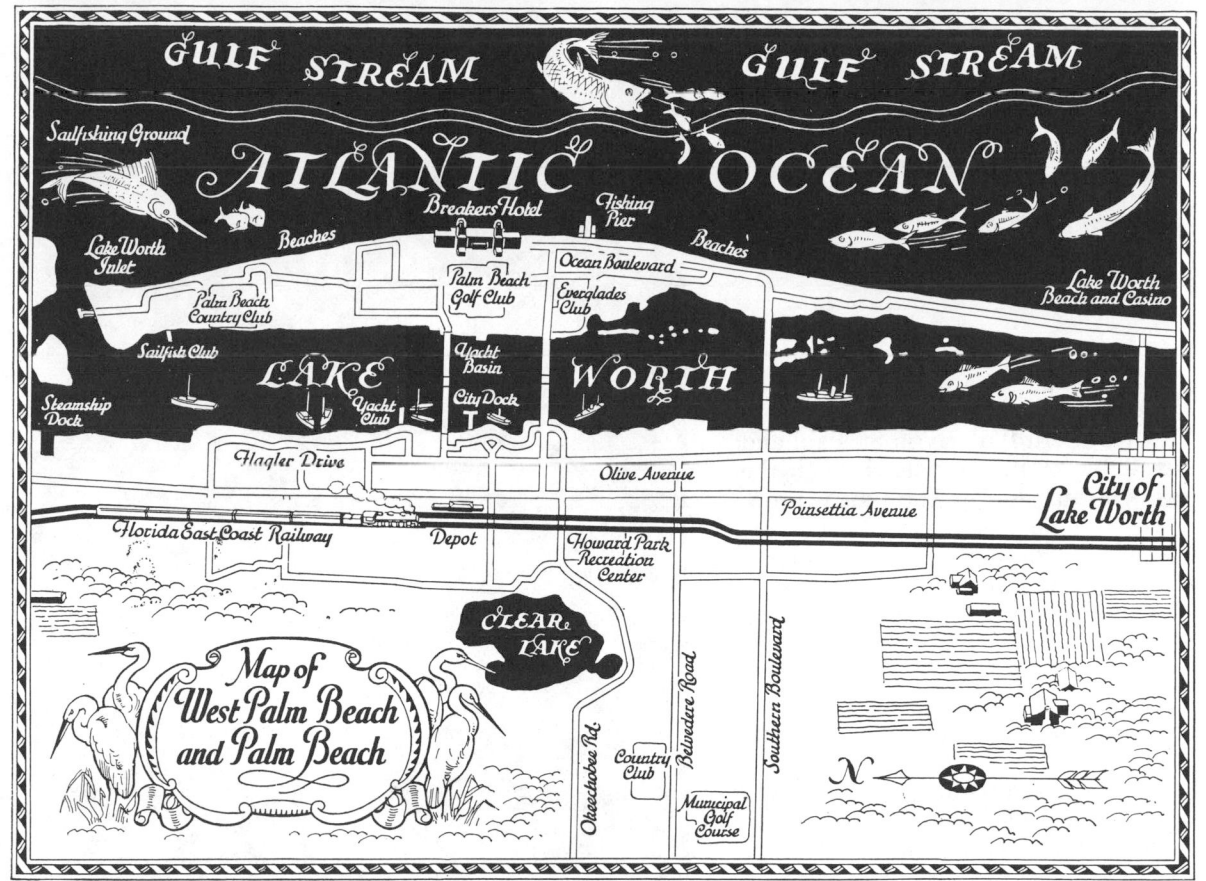

WITH EIGHTEEN Standard cars on its drawbar as it takes water at West Palm Beach to take its big 4-8-4 to Miami, the combined *Royal Palm-Dixie Flyer* has no room for head-end revenue cars, and mail and express are handled by the Florida East Coast in separate trains during the winter season. *(Everett De Golyer Collection.)*

THE VIGNETTES OF transcontinental travel on these pages are from an album recently brought to light in the archives of the Great Northern Railway in St. Paul and made available to the authors through the kindness of Frank Perrin. The year is probably 1922-23, a time of high button shoes, four-button suits and fox scarves with head and tail and claws intact. The setting is aboard *The Oriental Limited* of that year whose equipment is of no specific date but the result of a perpetual renewal and re-equipping program. Tea was served in the best *Oriental* tradition, lies were common commodity in the men's smoking room and the brass railed observation platform was still the glory and panache of stylish overland travel. *(Five Photos: Great Northern Railway.)*

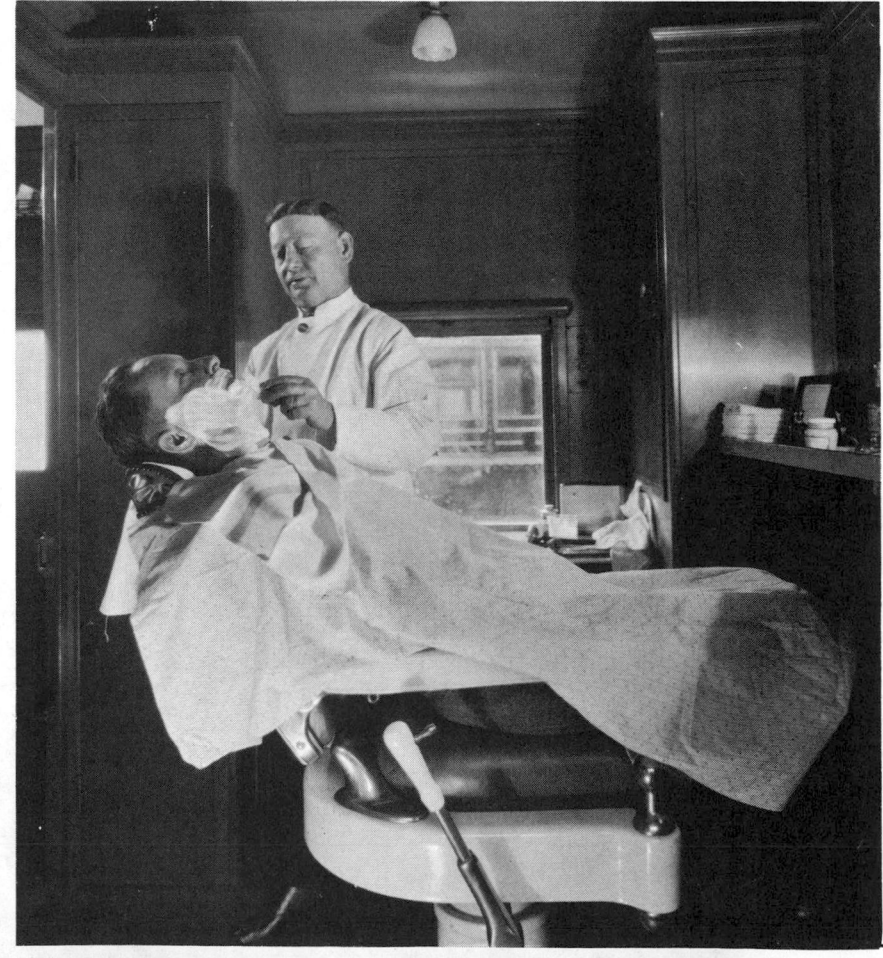

UNTIL 1929 when *The Empire Builder* was placed in service on the Twin Cities-Portland and Seattle run, the Great Northern Railway's crack transcontinental had been *The Oriental Limited* named for the Asiatic commerce which had been one of J. J. Hill's motivating objectives in building the railroad itself. Every convenience known to first class travel in its time was lavished on this splendid flyer by a management which failed to see eye to eye with the founding father's oft-quoted dictum that passenger traffic was neither useful nor ornamental. Standard weight all-steel Pullman luxury equipment was assigned to the *Oriental* and a Portland section was handled west of Spokane by the Spokane, Portland & Seattle connection. At the left *The Oriental Limited* is shown early in the twenties with its usual eight cars. A barber was conventional at the time on any long haul train with pretentions to style and the observation lounge shown is the interior of Pullman-built *Golden Peak* which later became *The Virginia City*, private car of Charles Clegg and Lucius Beebe with the Southern Pacific as its home carrier. (*Opposite, Above: Everett De Golyer Collection; Below, Two Photos: Great Northern; Here: Rail Photo Service by B. F. Cutler.*)

NO TRAIN in the record could have gratified the patriarchal James Jerome Hill in a greater dimension, not even his explicit memorial in *The Empire Builder*, than did *The Oriental Limited* when it was the Great Northern's flagship on a fifty-eight hour schedule over the 1829 miles between the Twin Cities and Puget Sound. Connecting at Seattle with the railroad's own fine 20,000-ton steamship *Minnesota*, *The Oriental* fulfilled Hill's dream of direct rail and water connection between the Middle West and Japan and the ports of the Far East. The period piece reproduced above from an early date, say 1912, possesses the abundant charm of shirtwaists and Gibson-girl hairdos for the ladies and boater hats and three-inch Arrow collars for their gentlemen. The Kodak photographs being exposed on a bellows camera by the lady in a duster will be pasted in an album embossed with the legend "Souvenirs of Happy Vacation Days." At the right *The Oriental* is shown in the glory times of Pullman Standard when the mountain goat of The Great Northern stood on a lofty peak and was monarch of all he surveyed in the Northwest. (*Two Photos: Great Northern.*)

BOTH THE CHARACTERS in these two vignettes of life aboard *The Oriental Limited* in its spacious times appear in other roles on an adjacent page. The honest barber who, in the days of which we speak, shaved passengers for two bits and cut their hair for four, also in his joint capacity as valet pressed three-piece suits by Wetzel or Brooks Brothers or perhaps Dunn of Boston for seventy-five cents and left the sleeves round if you so wished. The thirty-two volt, direct current-activated electric pressing iron was of special manufacture for railroad usage like the train's vacuum cleaners and electric toasters. The young lady using the Bell upright telephone in Seattle or Chicago where it was plugged in to a trackside connection is shown elsewhere communicating by Western Union. The date on *The World Almanac* in the book case is dated 1926 and things were in better shape than they would be three years hence, in the financial world anyway. *(Two Photos: Great Northern.)*

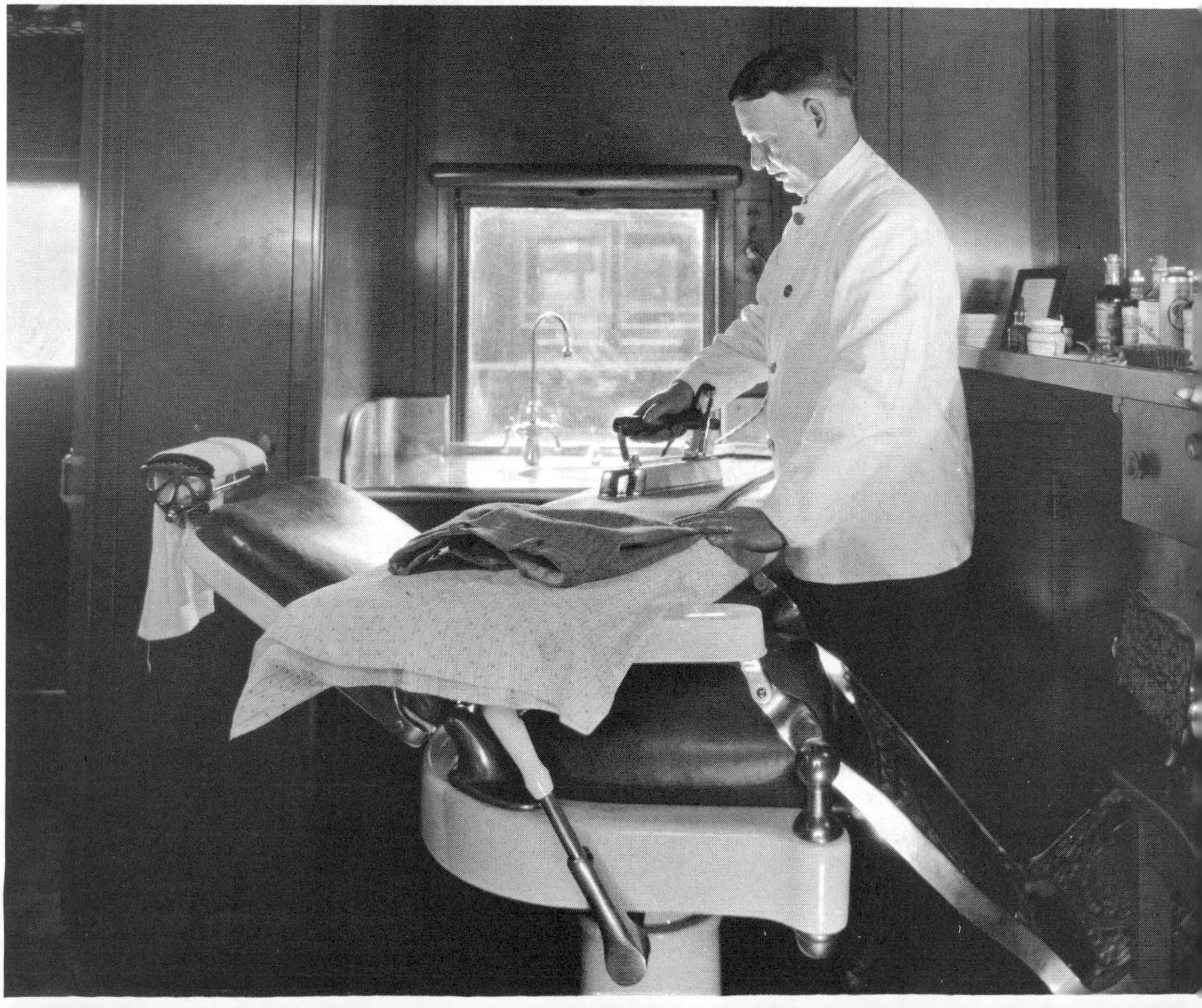

233

AS ABOARD all other trains of transcontinental consequence and many shorter runs such as *The Congressional* and *Knickerbocker* in the glory years, a lady's maid was felt to be indispensable aboard *The Oriental Limited,* and the Great Northern management stressed her presence in reassuring publicity photographs. Little could be done, even with the best intensions, however, to glamorize the men's smoking compartment in Pullman Standard. It was proverbially the scene of pre-breakfast chaos trailing galluses, lathered faces, bad tempers and untidiness generally. Occupants wearing ties, jackets and waistcoats were purely illusory. A moment of ponderous decorum is recreated above aboard *The Oriental Limited.* (*Photos: Great Northern.*)

TYPICAL OF the photography of the remarkable Azahel Curtis is the fine portrait reproduced below of *The Oriental Limited* in its days of splendor as the flagship of the Great Northern running in steam and Pullman Standard against the towering peaks that were once its Western setting and the hallmark of Curtis's railroad photography. Breakfast in bed, depicted in a company photograph, was once widely considered a symbol of practically Byzantine luxury although in actual practice its satisfactions were reported to be no more than minimal. *(Two Photos: Great Northern.)*

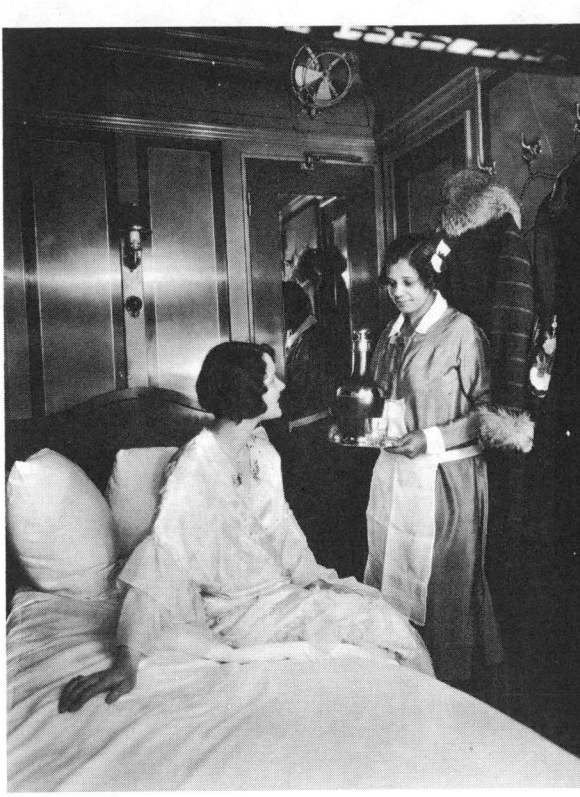

235

NOTHING COULD have been more genteel and decorous than the Great Northern's promotion literature and its accompanying photographs for *The Oriental Limited* where the joys of family togetherness were stressed rather than the sophisticated worldliness which characterized, say, the trains of the Florida East Coast or *The Broadway Limited*. Well bred moppets of both sexes reclined in mannered attitudes in its observation lounge and shared in the adult pleasures of the Great Northern way of life. Jim Hill, himself not exactly the family type, would have found it all very discouraging. *(Kaufmann & Fabry.)*

James J. Hill Rode Aboard The Oriental Limited

THE REMARKABLE picture of three piratical magnificoes of railroad operations shown at the right, depicting the Great Northern's man-eating James J. Hill in the center, arm in arm with George F. Baker at the right and Charles Steele, is a significant one in the annals of the Hill railroads and is directly related to the observation car interior shown below. Crusty, mutton-chopped George F. Baker, Morgan son-in-law, Morgan partner and patriarchal figure in Wall Street banking circles, represented the House of Morgan in the Hill-Morgan alliance against Edward Henry Harriman in the disastrous battle for control of Northern Pacific in 1901. After the dust had settled and the panic engendered by a frantic boom in N.P. had subsided, the Hill-Morgan combine was in undisputed control of Great Northern, Northern Pacific and the Burlington, which were known collectively as "The Hill Railroads," and credit for the coup was widely accorded George F. Baker. It seemed only appropriate that the splendid Pullman shown below in the consist of *The Empire Builder* should be named *George F. Baker*. Opposite *The Empire Builder* is shown in the glory days of steam and Pullman Standard. *(Right: Brown Brothers; Below and Opposite: Great Northern.)*

EMPIRE
GREAT NORTHERN
BUILDER

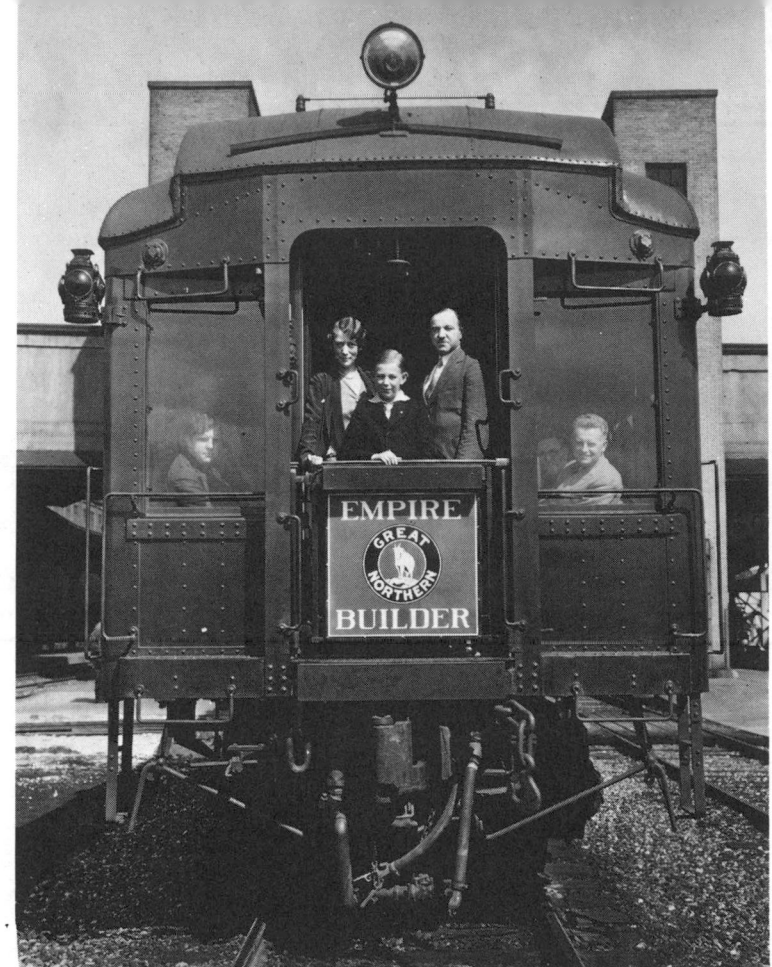

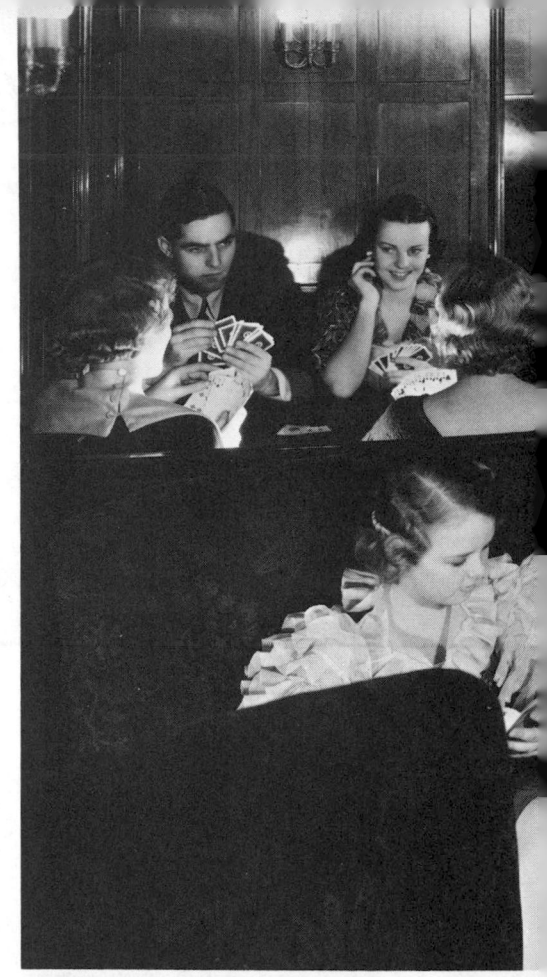

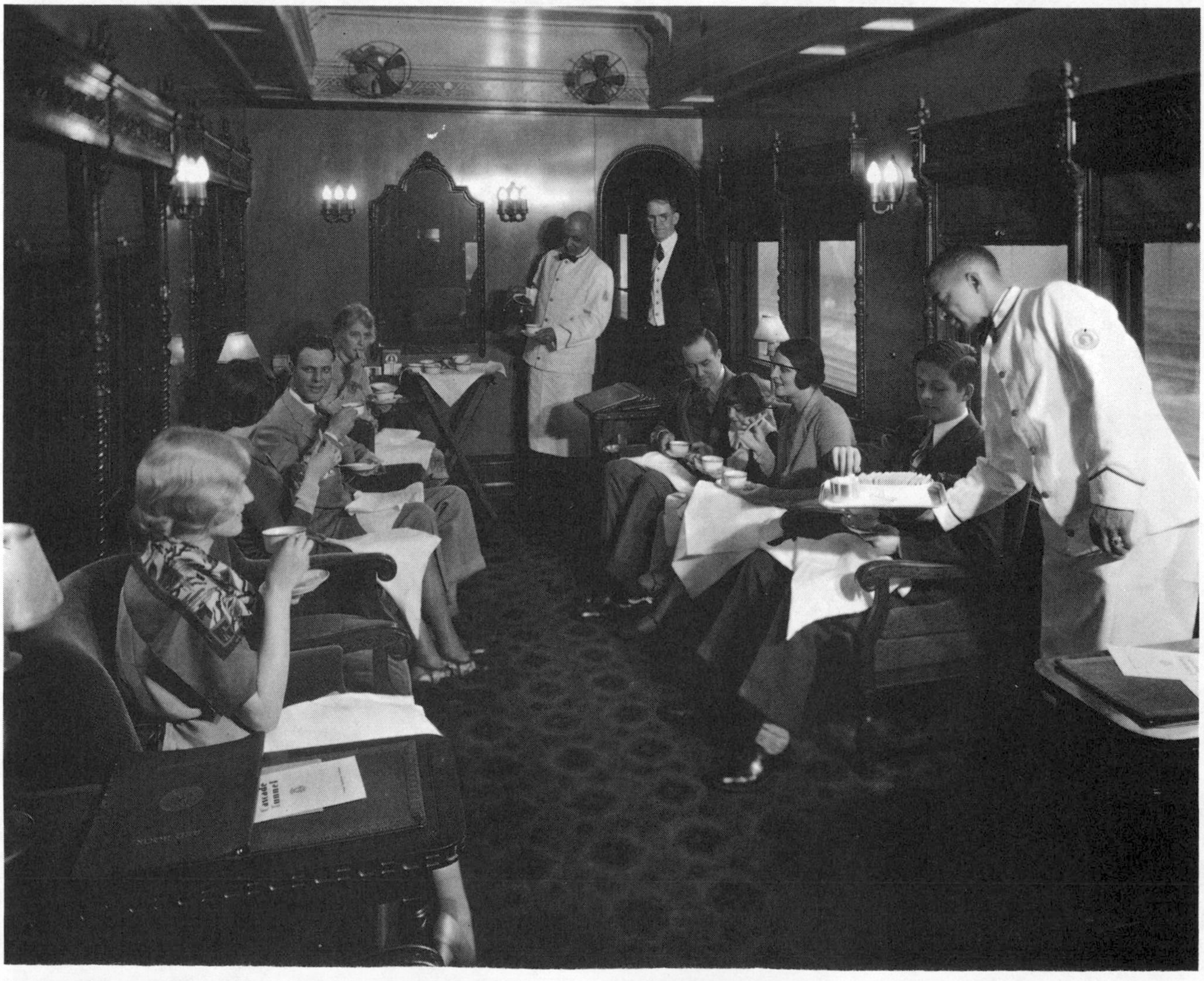

JUST AS the amenities of polite and urbane existence down to the finest detail of elegance were the concern of The Great Northern in its conduct of *The Empire Builder* in its Pullman Standard years, so the company's promotion and publicity matter achieved a degree of perfection seldom encountered elsewhere except, perhaps, on the Florida East Coast or the Santa Fe. The four interiors on these pages were the work of the distinguished photographer of the period, Sarra, and depict, on the page opposite the ritual service of afternoon tea, a rite suggested by the carrier's Oriental commerce, below, a group gathered around the radio console in the lounge, and at the left the appearance of a final nightcap at bedtime in the same opulent setting.
(Four Photos: Great Northern.)

DOUBLE THE
PLEASURE OF YOUR TRIP
By Taking the
"INTERESTING WAY"
Between
CHICAGO and SEATTLE-TACOMA-PORTLAND

Aboard the superb Empire Builder—with its air-conditioned dining and observation cars, its luxurious appointments, and its skilled and friendly service—you will gain a new conception of comfort. And along the Great Northern route—unrivalled for scenic beauty—you will experience a new travel thrill as you ride the 1600 smooth, cinderless miles behind giant oil-burning and electric locomotives—300 miles of it by day through the majestic Rockies and Cascades and 60 daylight miles along the border of Glacier Park. Great Northern's low prices for rail tickets, berths, and dining car meals are still in effect. Ask your ticket agent to show you how you may reduce travel costs via Great Northern.

A. J. Dickinson
Pass'r Traffic Manager
St. Paul, Minn.

E. H. Wilde
Gen'l Pass'r Agent
St. Paul, Minn.

C. W. Meldrum
Ass't Gen'l Pass'r Agent
Seattle, Wash.

242

ROUTE OF THE FAMOUS
EMPIRE BUILDER
AIR-CONDITIONED DINING and OBSERVATION CARS
Glacier Park . . Pacific Northwest . . California . . Alaska

GREAT NORTHERN

AS IS THE CASE in many of the other great name trains in the record, the transition from Pullman Standard, represented in *The Empire Builder* in the superb profile below where it is shown at Whitefish, Montana, in 1933, to the streamlined, Diesel powered eventuality provided some of the most atmospheric and interesting combinations of motive power and passenger equipment. Previous to the delivery of the completed streamlined units which cost the operating railroads, the Burlington and Great Northern, a cool $7,000,000 in 1947, a semi-streamlined effect was achieved by updating and repainting Standard equipment with the handsome effect shown at the left. There were partisans of this stunning limited who took a dim view of streamlining, largely because of its Diesel connotations, who maintained that this was the best *Empire Builder* of them all. The young lady at the far left, in Standard days in the thirties, is dropping off a wire at Havre to tell Ernie Byfield she will be lunching at the Pump Room two days from now. (*Far Left: Great Northern; Left: Rail Photo Service, Frank McKinlay; Below: H. H. Arey.*)

WHEN THE FIRST UNITS of five completely new streamlined *Empire Build-ers* were delivered by Pullman Standard in February 1947, at some conflict with the carbuilder's corporate name since Standard construction was now gone for-ever, even railroad amateurs who took a dim view of Diesel power were capti-vated by the beauty of these enchanting trains. The green and orange decor of their exteriors with gold finelining compelled attention and their forty-five hour schedules cut thirteen and a half hours from the best previous time between Puget Sound and the Great Lakes. So great was the impact of the new *Empire Builders*, that in 1951, after only four spectacular years in service, they were replaced by five all new trains, this time known as *The Mid-Century Empire Builder* and the original streamlined equipment reassigned to the secondary *Western Star*. Seldom in the record has downgrading been accomplished on such a scale of magnificence, even though the shakeup brought about the retirement of the long-honored *Oriental Limited*. Exclusive of motive power, the *Mid-Century Empire Builder* equipment cost a cool $12,000,000, a sum to have given pause to shaggy old one-eyed Jim Hill himself. No carrier of modern times ever presented a more glittering showcase for public approval. *(Great Northern.)*

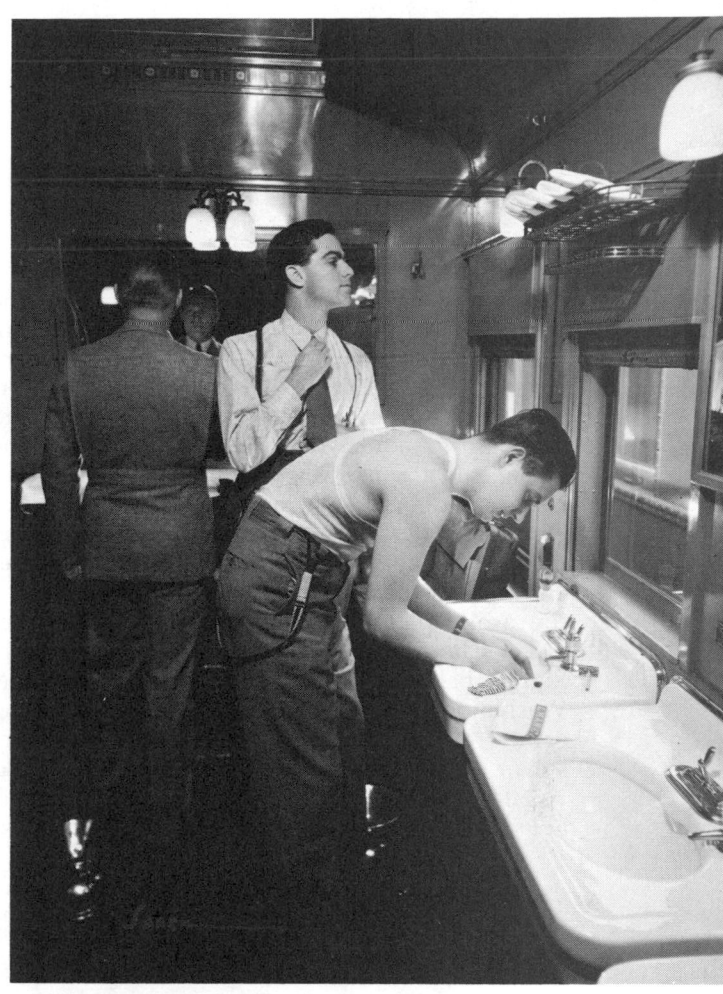

PRESIDING OVER the magnificent diners and the superlative food aboard the Diesel, streamlined version of *The Empire Builder* is the patriarchal likeness of the great dynast himself, a virile and shaggy symbol of a day in the saga of railroading before roller bearings, air conditioning and fresh cut flowers on the table. Nowhere in the transport scene does the contrast between the pioneers and the product of their vital genius find more dramatic expression. The chaos of the men's washroom in the hour before breakfast differs little, however, from that which obtained in the same premises in times primeval. (*Three Photos: Great Northern.*)

245

THE CASCADIAN, in the years before its name disappeared from the *Official Guide* and its run was downgraded to the status of a mere numbered train movement, was a stylish little varnish despite its bread-and-cheese traffickings and wayward schedule. It started out from Spokane at eight in the morning if all its head-end business was aboard, which it often was not, and didn't arrive at its Seattle terminal until seven in the evening, making every stop on the timecard. Principally its run was distinguished for the exotic place names where it paused: Soap Lake, Chumpstick, Skyskomish and Snohomish. Shown below is *The Cascadian* at Wenatchee, Washington, the apple growing and shipping capital of the universe, where it changed from steam to electric motive power for the long and usually rainy ascent to the Cascade Tunnel. *(Two Photos: Rail Photo Service, H. W. Pontin.)*

A TRAIN for all seasons, *The Cascadian,* was photographed below by Fred Jukes in a summer setting with pine trees growing to the right of way. Its lounge-observation-dining car *(left)* was austere with the relieving touch of fresh flowers and immaculate table linen.

THE S.P.&S. in more modern aspect is depicted in three vignettes opposite, photographed in 1950 by Philip Hastings. At the immediate left with Train No. 4 engine No. 700 approaches Spokane with elements of *The Empire Builder* and *North Coast Limited* framed by the Northern Pacific main line and signals at Marshall, Washington. Beyond, No. 701 drowses in the roundhouse at Yardley (Spokane) between runs, while below the same engine waits its highball out of Spokane for Portland with its pool train while on a parallel track *The Empire Builder* in Diesel is being made up for Seattle.

PORTLAND BOUND passengers on the westbound trains of the Great Northern and Northern Pacific achieved their terminal via the Spokane, Portland & Seattle Railroad between Spokane and the hills of Multnomah. Elements of *The Oriental* and later *The Empire Builder* were combined with the equivalent equipment of *The North Coast Limited*, a practice which obtains to this day, and in 1911 made up the S.P.&S. varnish run depicted below in a portrait by H. H. Arey. The daylight local in the thirties between Spokane and Portland was *The Columbia River Express*, roughly the opposite number of the Great Northern's *Cascadian* on the Seattle run. Less elegantly appointed than *The Cascadian, The Columbia River* was a coaches-only drag which belied its express billing by making every stop on the timecard and requiring thirteen hours to cover 377.8 miles. *(Below: Herb Arey Collection; Right: Rail Photo Service.)*

WHEN The Great Northern's original Cascade Tunnel, eight miles long and the longest on the American continent, was abandoned and the relocated shaft opened in 1929, the brush-grown entrance to the first shaft in a short time resembled nothing so much as a Mayan ruin in Yucatan or a Roman portico at Baalbek. Snow sheds on the abandoned right of way at Tye lasted for many years as the G.N.'s electric motors whipped into the new bore only a few miles away. (*Three Photos: Fred Jukes.*)

IN THE SPACIOUS 1920s when passenger traffic was a dominant factor in railroad economics, the G.N. maintained the sumptuous ticket office shown below in downtown Chicago. Ankle-length fur coats, beaded bags, fringed scarves and cloche hats perused richly lithographed company literature in a setting of cut flowers and expensively paneled walls. At the left, Spokane by night sees S.P.&S. 4-8-4 No. 701 waiting to depart with Great Northern No. 3 *The Western Star's* Portland connection. The G.N. Diesels will take out No. 3's first section for Seattle. (*Left: Philip R. Hastings; Below: Great Northern.*)

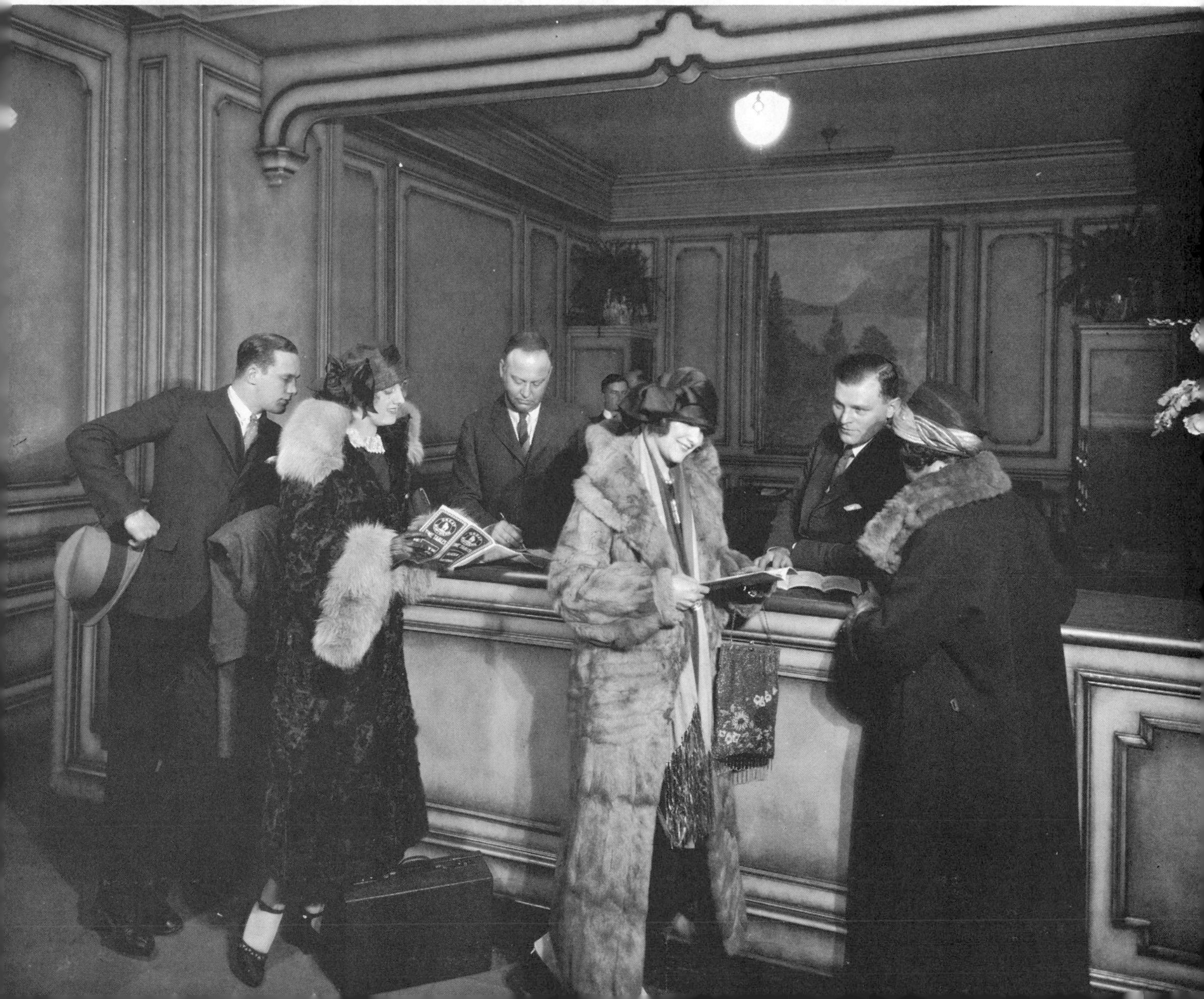

LAST of the great transcontinental carriers to invade the Northwest and in direct competition with the Great Northern and Northern Pacific in much of its territory was the Chicago, Milwaukee, St. Paul & Pacific which only in 1927 shortened its popular title to The Milwaukee Road. Flagship of its fleet of name trains was *The Olympian* between Chicago and Seattle-Tacoma, a superbly maintained varnish run which had a following of loyal partisans as devoted as those of *The North Coast Limited* and *The Oriental Limited* of the opposition. West of Harlowtown, Montana, two sections of the Milwaukee's track aggregating a total of 656 miles were electrified and meals aboard its diners were celebrated. Between Harlowtown and Avery, over the most scenic portion of its route, an open air observation rode the rear of *The Olympian*. In the two photographs above *The Olympian* is depicted by two of the most notable of all railroad photographers, in steam by Roland Collons and in electric motor by Azahel Curtis. The Milwaukee's passenger operations with their distinctive orange-painted equipment and wide variety of observation cars were picturesque in the extreme and, even in an age innocent of air conditioning, its lounge and observation car *City of Everett*, shown below, boasted roller bearing trucks and other refinements of an advanced order. (*Above and Right: De Golyer Foundation; Top Opposite: Washington State Historical Society.*)

NO RAILROAD was ever more prodigal in its assignment of observation cars than the Milwaukee and few achieved the range and variety of design of those which rode not only the carrier's name trains but, in many instances, secondary runs only known by a number on the timetable. The solarium-lounge car *Waukoma* of the combined *Southwest Limited-Arrow* on the largely Pullman overnight run between Chicago and Omaha-Sioux City was a luxury bonus in a consist that already included what the company was pleased to call a "limousine lounge car" with three double bedrooms. Designated "beavertail lounges," the observations of *Hiawatha* were a sensational innovation when they first appeared. A later elaboration of the solarium theme on *The Twin Cities Hiawatha* had windows on all sides and in the roof, too. *(The De Golyer Foundation, Collons Collection; Below: The Perry* DAILY CHIEF.*)*

NAME TRAINS by the score illustrated the Milwaukee's company literature in the spacious days when its passenger operations ran from Chicago to Puget Sound and provided a network of transport throughout Nebraska, the Dakotas, Minnesota, Wisconsin and Iowa. Many ran to the theme of Indian names, *Hiawatha, Arrow, Tomahawk* and *Sioux*. Pride of the line was *The Olympian* and later *The Olympian Hiawatha* all the way to the Great Northwest. *The Day Express* was a prime contender in the Chicago-Twin Cities daylight competition while *The Pioneer Limited* was its aristocratic nighttime opposite number. There was the resounding *Copper Country Limited*, the academic *Varsity* to the college town of Madison and something brightly designated "*On Wisconsin.*" Shown above in electric motor power in Idaho in a portrait by Asahel Curtis is *The Columbian* on the secondary run to Puget Sound. Roland Collons snapped *The Day Express* at the left.

255

PREDECESSOR OF *The Panama Limited* on the pre-1911 Illinois Central timecards was the *Chicago & New Orleans Limited* on the run suggested by its stately, old-fashioned name. In a period when the almost universal practice was to cut dining cars in and out at mealtimes at appropriate stops on a leisurely schedule, it is shown below with only four Pullmans in its consist, one of which may well have been *Crescent City*, an eight-section buffet-library-observation car of beautiful lines built by Pullman for the run in 1901. *(Bottom: Library of Congress; Below: Illinois Central.)*

ELECTRIC FANS WHIRRED deliciously, fresh cut flowers were on all the tables and young ladies in the plumed bonnets and sensible shirtwaists of the period ordered shrimp Remoulade from a mustached steward at dinner time aboard *The Chicago & New Orleans Limited* when it was the pride of the Illinois Central's long-run fleet. *(Illinois Central.)*

Patriarchal and Patrician, The Illinois

Central Was a Carrier of The Grandees

ALWAYS a railroad that encouraged fastidious habits and well groomed patrons, the Illinois Central maintained a barber shop aboard the *Panama Limited* in Pullman Standard times and only abandoned this amenity when the streamlined consist went into service during the 1941 war. Strictly a prestige convenience, barbers never paid their way but, like tailgate signs on the observation car, were a hallmark of aloof operation and marked a train as possessing the most elevated imaginable *ton*. Below, *The Panama Limited* in the closing years of steam presented a fine appearance in the I.C. depot at Chicago against a background of Coca-Cola and Seagram's whisky, neither of which, it may be imagined, were big sellers in its magnificently resourceful bars. *(Right: Illinois Central; Below: De Golyer Foundation, Collons Collection.)*

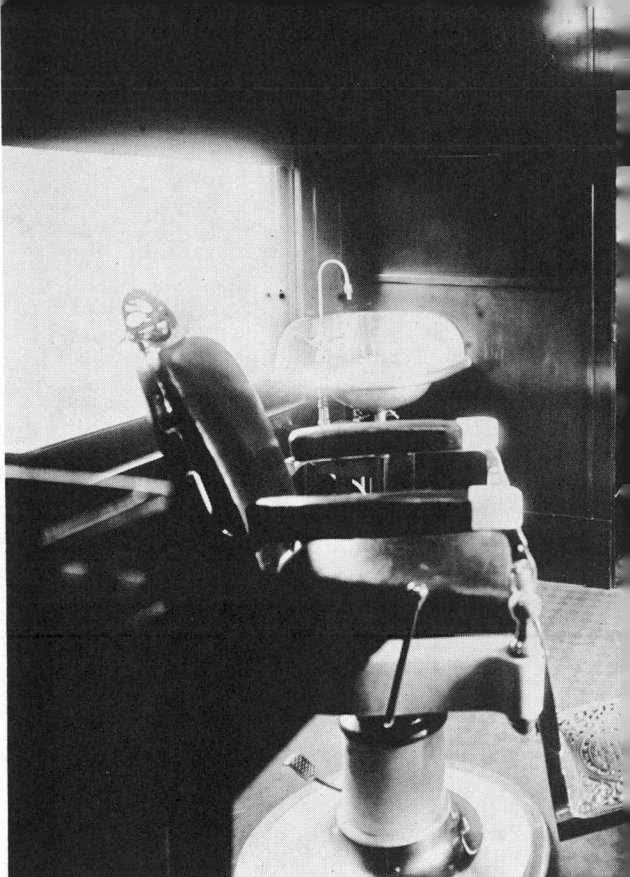

A CARRIER whose patrician antecedents and venerable age allowed its indulgence in mild eccentricities, the Illinois Central, until it was eliminated as part of the Lake Front Improvement Program, maintained in its Van Buren Street suburban depot in Chicago what may well have been the only octagon railroad station in the record. The structure was built in 1879 and looked like this in 1896, a matchless tribute to architectural whimsy and defiance of conformity. Below: the I.C.'s trains at Browns, Illinois, all stopped at the Southern Railway crossover to open a gate before crossing the right of way of the competition. *(Two Photos: Everett De Golyer Collection.)*

259

WHILE THE INSPIRATION for the operation of many long-haul luxury runs in the extra fare, all-Pullman years was a well appointed hotel, the Illinois Central thought of its *Panama Limited* in the image of a gentleman's club to which women, with some reservations on the part of the management, were admitted. An entire generation of travelers in the Deep South felt the same way about *The Panama Limited*. Its overstuffed leather armchairs *(opposite)* a staff with long memories for the preferences and persons of patrons, and the most opulent resources of Bourbon whisky (forty-two name brands and blends at one count) all contributed to the illusion that one had stepped into The Travellers Club in Paris, The Carlton in London or The Century in Manhattan. It was a train with an air, and on "The Mainline of Mid-America" it glittered in its going. *(Illinois Central.)*

ALTHOUGH it remained for an airflow, Dieselized *Panama Limited* to keep the faith as one of the last all-Pullman runs and shaming rival dining car managements with a $10 "Kings Dinner" when carriers elsewhere were insulting guests with frozen steaks, an older *Panama Limited* was secure in the affections of another generation. Its Standard diners such as that shown here, its luxurious lounges and a less impetuous carding suggested "Dinner At Antoine's" and the Creole gentility of Francis Parkinson Keyes. *The Panama* went by "The River Road" all the way. *(Three Photos: Illinois Central.)*

AT A TIME when gentlemen wore wing collars with street attire and sensible woolen traveling skirts were indicated for women, *The Panama's* patrons read *Munsey's Magazine* and *The Outlook* in a substantial mahogany paneled library-lounge car. Diners carried Hydrox mineral water on every table to reassure patrons who had heard unfavorable comment on the drinking water in the Deep South. (*Two Photos: Illinois Central.*)

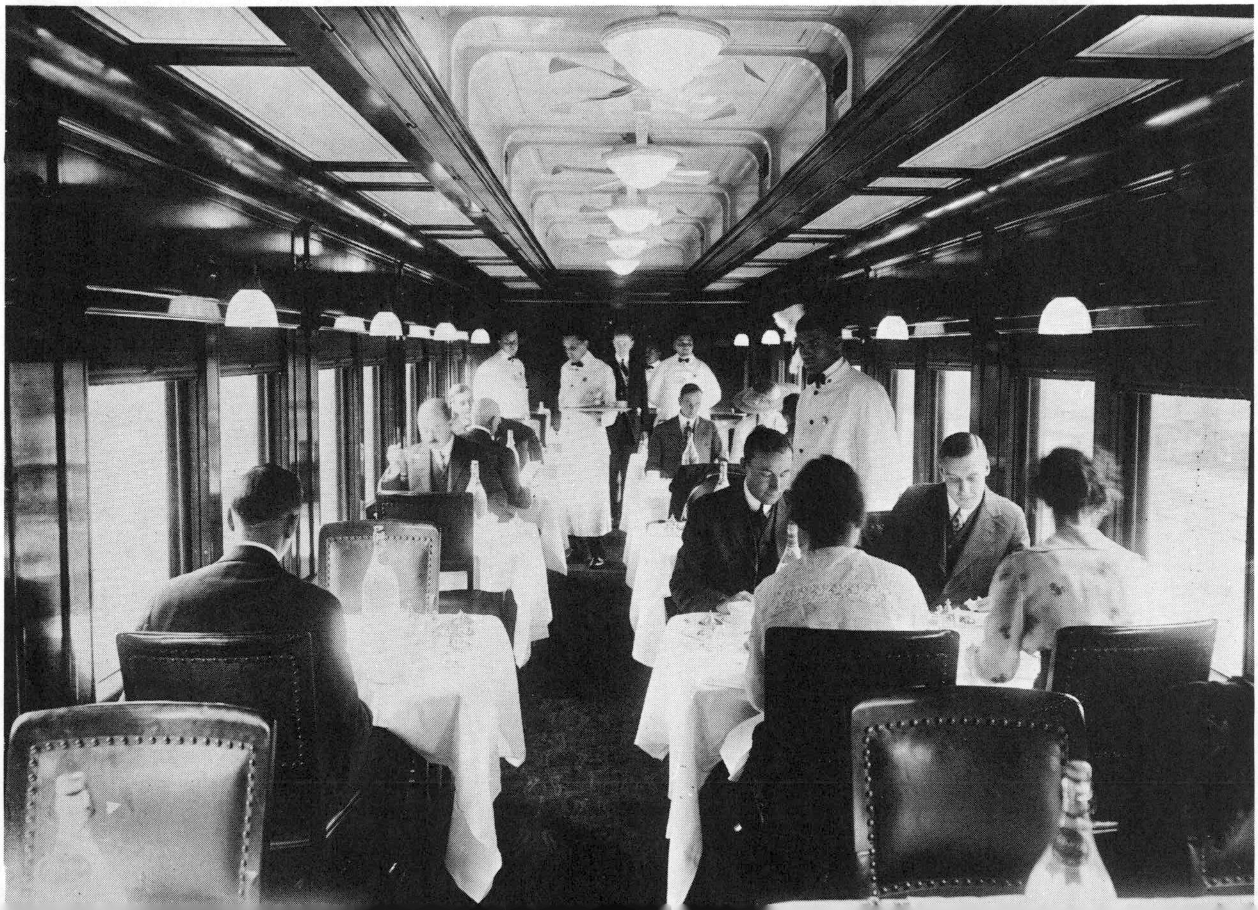

IN 1911, when the Illinois Central renamed its *Chicago & New Orleans Limited*, the Panama Canal, like the Erie Canal before it, was still "The Work of the Age" and the railroad was quick to cash in on its prestige by naming its new train for it. In 1916 *The Panama Limited* became all-Pullman with a surcharge that was refunded if it was more than an hour late. So venerated was this varnish run that in Vaiden, Mississippi, court was recessed daily so everyone could see its passage through town. The New Orleans decor in the bar shown at the left is, of course, from the streamlined *Panama*. Below, in one of its rare operations double-headed, it approaches Chicago over the I.C.'s electrified suburban trackage in 1937. *(Left: Illinois Central; Below: De Golyer Foundation, Collons Collection.)*

THE STREAMLINED *Panama Limited,* placed in service in 1942 in the midst of the war effort was the last new train to be built until the conclusion of hostilities, but in every way consistent with its radically new construction and operation on an eighteen-hour schedule, it maintained continuity with its institutional predecessor. The train name appeared on the assigned motor units, a nicety that soon disappeared elsewhere as Diesel took over, and the decor recreated the atmosphere of the Vieux Carré in New Orleans, the town's principal tourist attraction. The Mardi Gras theme of its parlor car *(right)* was continued in the most capacious of all stand-up bars on any American train in its diner unit. Lyle Saxon, the great New Orleans man of letters who was sure, before he rode it, that it would be "all crummy chromium" declared that its food and personnel shamed the Boston Club. *(Above: Lucius Beebe; Right: Illinois Central.)*

264

SCORNING the shabby devisings of frugality and re-trenchments adopted by less prideful carriers, the Illinois Central inaugurated aboard *The Panama* a "King's Dinner" rivalling in its plenitude of good things the menus of Brennan's and the legendary Count Arnaud in New Orleans. *(Three Photos: Illinois Central.)*

HOW TO LIVE LIKE ROYALTY?
EASY!
ENJOY THE "KING'S DINNER"!!
9.85

Manhattan or Martini Cocktail
(Swirler Service or On-The-Rocks)

Appetizers

Fresh Gulf Shrimp Cocktail
or
Crab Fingers
(special sauce)

A 13-Ounce Bottle of Imported Bertoli Vinrosa

The Fish Course

CHARCOAL BROILED BONELESS SIRLOIN STEAK
Buttered Mushroom Slices

Your Choice of Potato and Vegetable
A Special Salad Created by Your Waiter

Dinner Bread

A Heady Cheese with Fresh Apple Wedges
Toasted Saltines

I.C. Coffee

Liqueur
(Creme de Cacao, Creme de Menthe or
Blackberry Liqueur)

RARE, INDEED, was the occasion for double heading in the Kansas City Southern's varnish category, but when in 1941 a troop extra out of Camp Polk, Louisiiana, ran as part of *The Flying Crow* for a scene of smoky splendor seldom equalled on the line, A. E. Brown was there to record the event. Brown, who was in time to become the dean of Louisiana and East Texas railroad iconographers and official historian of the K.C.S., is represented on adjacent pages by his equally devoted coverage of the Louisiana & Arkansas, a subsidiary of the K.C.S., of country wayfarings and photogenic charm.

EVEN IN A CALLING noted for its enduring loyalties, The Kansas City Southern's *Flying Crow* was distinguished for two members of its train staff, Passenger Conductor W. E. (Wade) Hampton who never missed a run in twenty years and never was seen on duty without a large red rose in the lapel of his uniform jacket, while Pullman Conductor Thomas A. Chapman rode *The Crow* for twenty-two years and then went to the *Southern Belle*. (*Everett De Golyer Collection.*)

267

ALTHOUGH PATENTLY NAMED FROM THE AVIARY, The Kansas City Southern's *Flying Crow* out of Kansas City for the Gulf ports of Lake Charles-Port Arthur was more down-to-earth in the available nomenclature of flight names than those scheduled by carriers elsewhere in the land. The straight-as-the-crow-flies routing suggested by its name was also largely fictitious since the Kansas City Southern's right of way through the Ozarks embraced degrees of curvature that made a fast schedule illusory. The Kaysee Southern, however, was Kansas City's own railroad, the dream child of the exotic Arthur E. Stilwell whose financial operations were based on advice from the spirit world and for whom Port Arthur is named, and *The Flying Crow* was cherished on that account and as a local institution. Here its raven form, relieved by silver smokebox and cylinder heads on No. 803, nears its northern terminal on a fine morning in 1935. Opposite and even more spectacularly, it rolls south out of Shreveport double headed for an uncommonly heavy consist. (*Above: Lucius Beebe; Opposite: A. E. Brown.*)

WHEN THE Kansas City Southern
replaced the steam powered
Flying Crow with the streamlined
Diesel motivated *Southern Belle*, it
still felt that the displaced
iron horse was more photogenic, and
the lounge murals of *The Belle*
had for their principal theme
the carrier's fine steam motive power
that was even then fast
becoming a memory. *(Kansas
City Southern.)*

L&A
THE HUSTLER
RAILWAY
L&A
RAILWAY
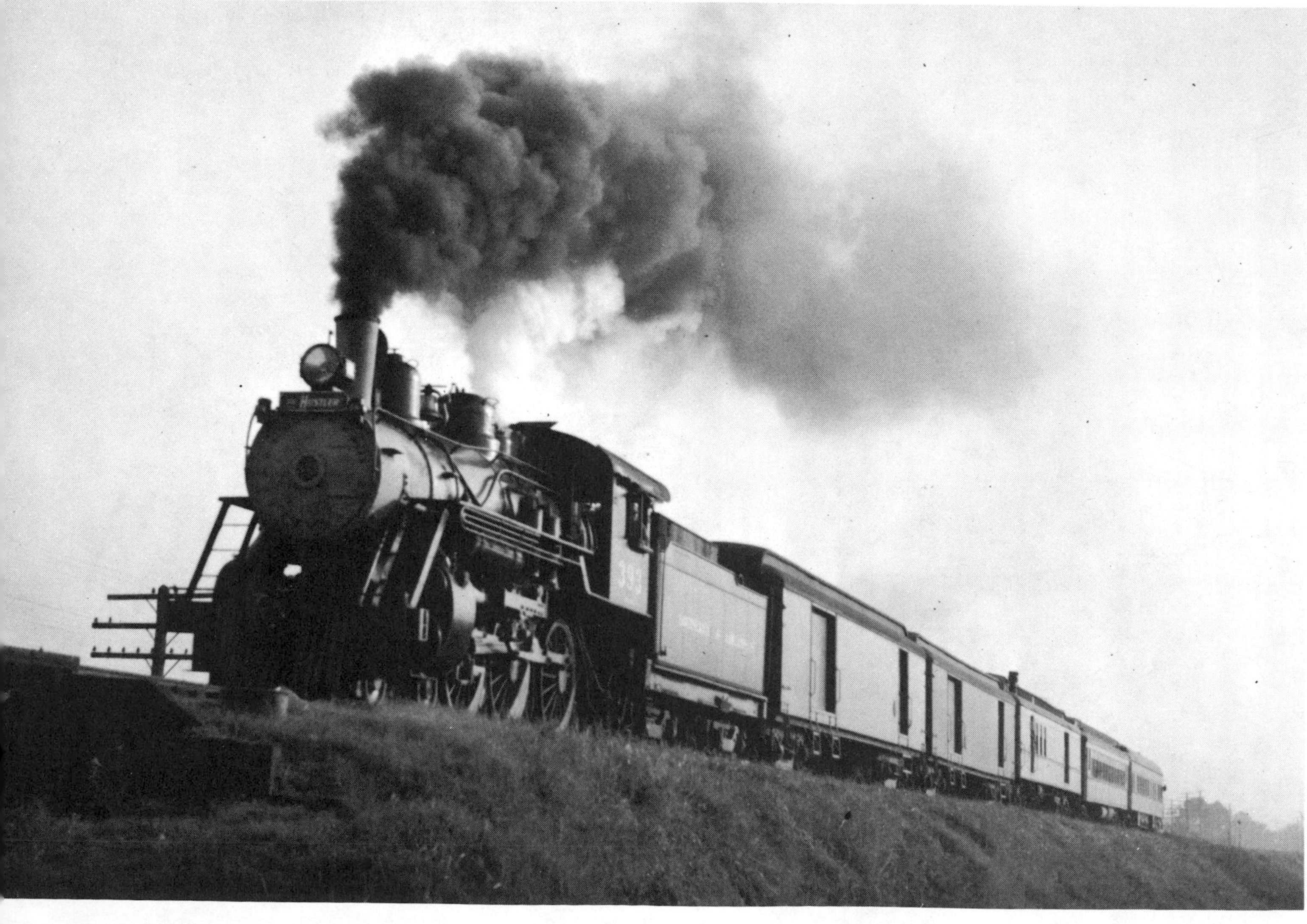

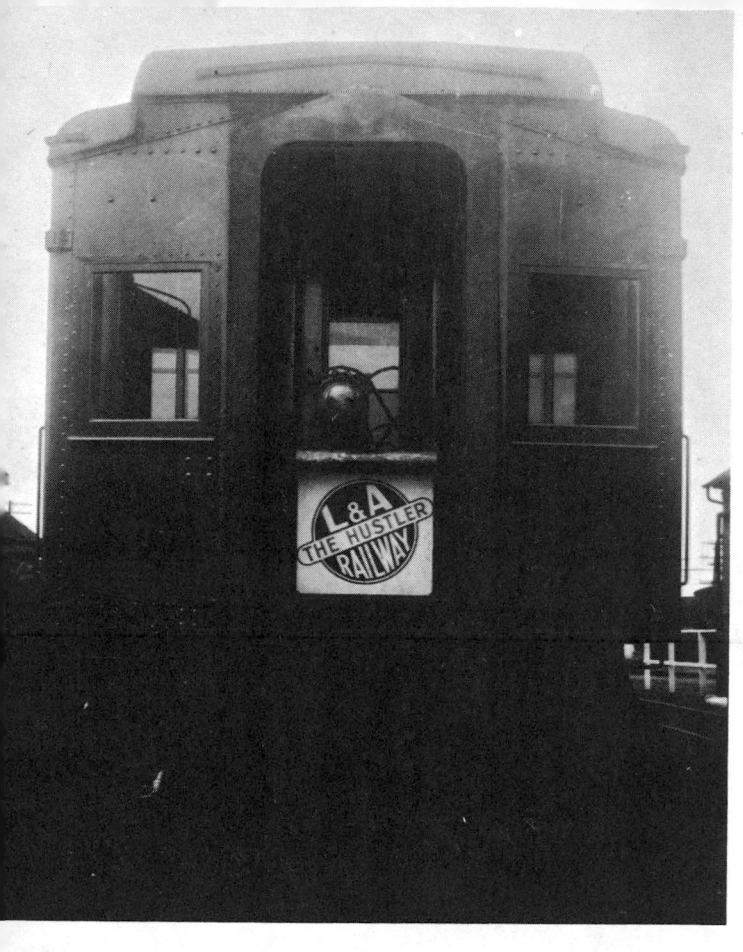

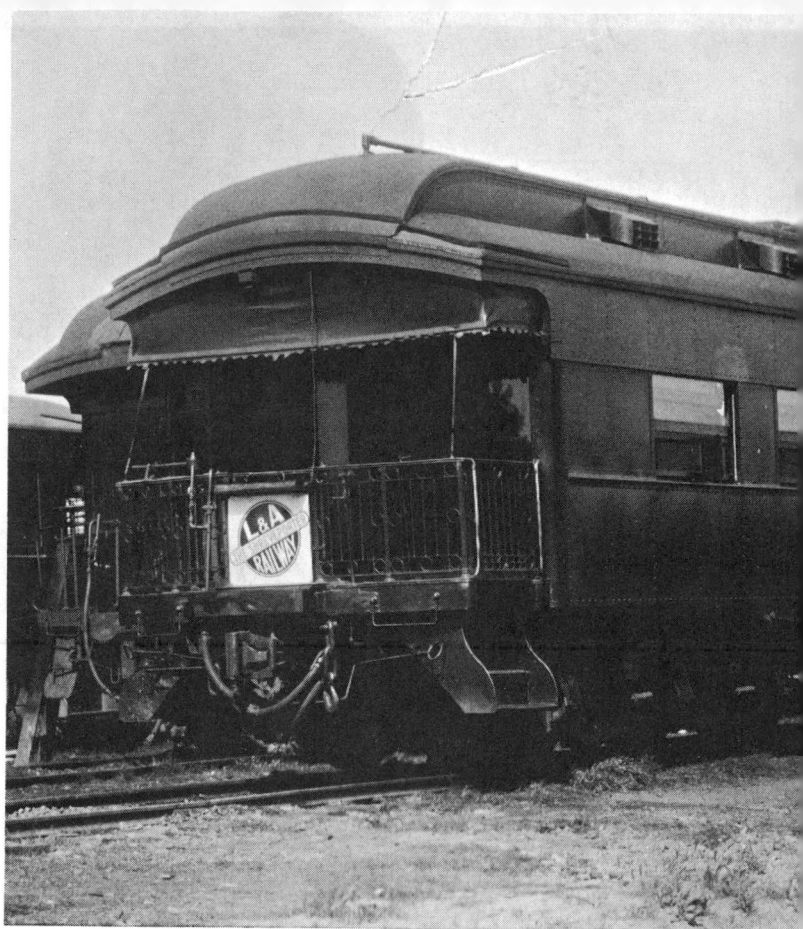

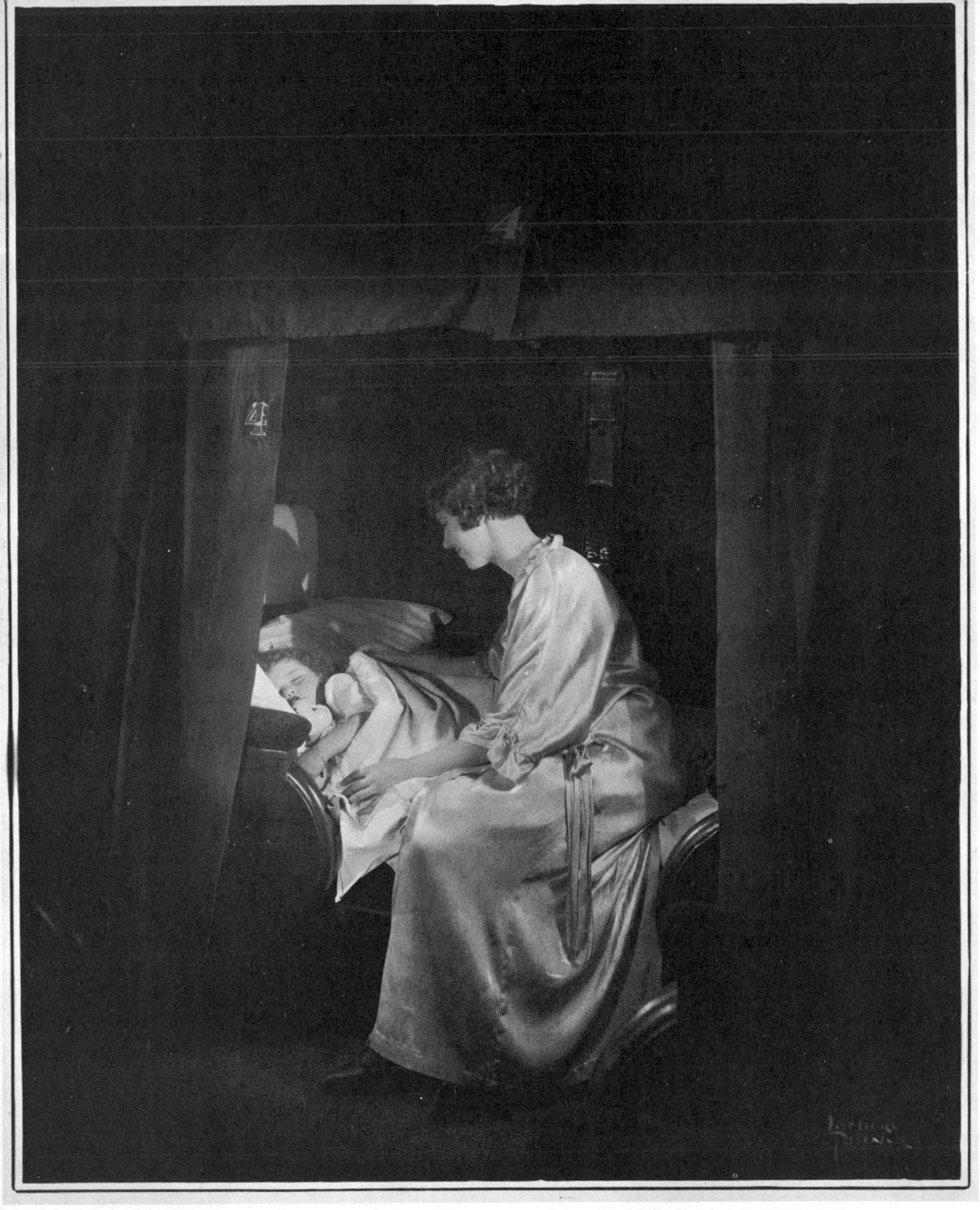

AS THOUGH a single name train were not sufficient panache of elegance for a carrier of the dimensions of the Louisiana & Arkansas, a second prestige varnish run designated *The Hustler* was added to the timecard and is shown opposite behind assigned engine No. 393 with its name on the smokebox as it races across Bossier Parish in 1939. It was usual for the two trains, *The Hustler* and *The Shreveporter* to combine at Minden for the remaining thirty miles into Shreveport as Train No. 1, but when A. E. Brown took the photograph reproduced here, *The Hustler* was operating independently as Second No. 1 with three head-end cars, a coach and the Shreveport Pullman making a fine show of smalltime railroading in the grand manner. Both trains carried tailgate insignes on whatever cars terminated their consists, while another bond with the big time, as is suggested above, was promotion that would have done credit to any Class I carrier. The L.&A. called the scene "Bedtime on *The Shreveporter*."

A SUBSIDIARY of the Kansas City Southern, the Louisiana & Arkansas ran in the 1930s between Shreveport, Louisiana, and New Orleans, a scant 331 miles as the New Orleans section of *The Flying Crow* flew. Yet over its lightly-ballasted and well-worn iron the L.&A. maintained an overnight varnish run called *The Hustler* with amenities of comfort to do credit to a more richly-endowed carrier, while on its 108-mile branch from Hope to Shreveport, it ran *The Shreveporter* shown above at Shreveport depot. *The Shreveporter* carried a setout Pullman from the Missouri Pacific connection at Hope and served meals from a charcoal grill in observation-buffet cars which carried an illuminated train herald on its tailgate. (*Above: Harold K. Vollrath Collection; Below: A. E. Brown.*)

TAKING A BACK SEAT TO NOBODY including the Pennsylvania, Texas & Pacific and other consequential carriers who made a practice of identifying their proudest name trains with nameplates on the smokebox of their locomotives, the Louisiana & Arkansas had designated engines assigned to both *The Hustler* and *The Shreveporter*. L.&A. No. 240 shown here with *The Shreveporter's* plate, although at other times it ran in *The Hustler* as well, was a former Missouri-Kansas-Texas ten-wheeler via the Louisiana, Arkansas & Texas whose life span of glory lasted until the carrier came by some more modern motive power for its passenger runs. Clearly attesting its Katy ancestry is the hooded stack light which, when running at night, assisted the fireman in determining what sort of a fire he was maintaining. Below in a misty panorama of early morning splendor *The Shreveporter* en route from Hope with its Pullman from *The Sunshine Special* was blood brother in the knighthood of railroad chivalry with *The Broadway* or *The Overland Limited*. (Two Photos: A. E. Brown.)

A TRULY patrician indifference to mere appearances is suggested by the Louisiana & Arkansas depot at Dry Prong, Louisiana, where paint is infrequently applied and a raffish informality contributes to the pervading atmosphere of seedy grandeur. (*A. E. Brown.*)

THE PRIDE of the Louisiana & Arkansas, *The Shreveporter* was maintained with all the stylish accessories of bigtime railroading and was cherished by its owning carrier with all the pride that attended the operation of *The Aristocrat* or *The Overland Limited*. Creole entrees were served with a New Orleans flourish in the observation-cafe-parlor car depicted here whose brass railed verandah carried an electrically illuminated train herald as it pursued its homely occasions. On the page opposite *The Shreveporter* is powered by No. 309 as it crosses the river at the city of its name in 1935. *(Two Photos: A. E. Brown.)*

SAINT LOUIS — COTTON BELT ROUTE — SOUTHWESTERN

ANOTHER little varnish run whose memory is wistful in the Louisiana bayous where the Spanish moss hangs above lightly ballasted rails was the stub end of the St. Louis-Southwestern's *Lone Star Limited* which for many years shuttled in the night between Shreveport and Lewisville, Arkansas. The train tied up at Shreveport, going up at nine every evening and taking two hours for the sixty mile run to connect with the northbound *Lone Star Limited* out of Dallas at Lewisville. Soon after five in the morning it cut the Shreveport Pullman out of the southbound *Lone Star*, arriving with it and a coach at Shreveport at seven a.m. Here coming off the same long bridge at Shreveport used by the name trains of the Louisiana & Arkansas *The Lone Star* stub connection rolls in the morning mists of a long time ago. The main line section of No. 5 is shown opposite picking up speed out of Texarkana en route to Mt. Pleasant, Texas, the next stop of consequence. *(Above and Bottom Opposite: A. E. Brown; Top Opposite, Two Photos: Everett De Golyer.)*

LONE STAR
COTTON BELT ROUTE
TRAINS
COTTON BELT
LONE STAR
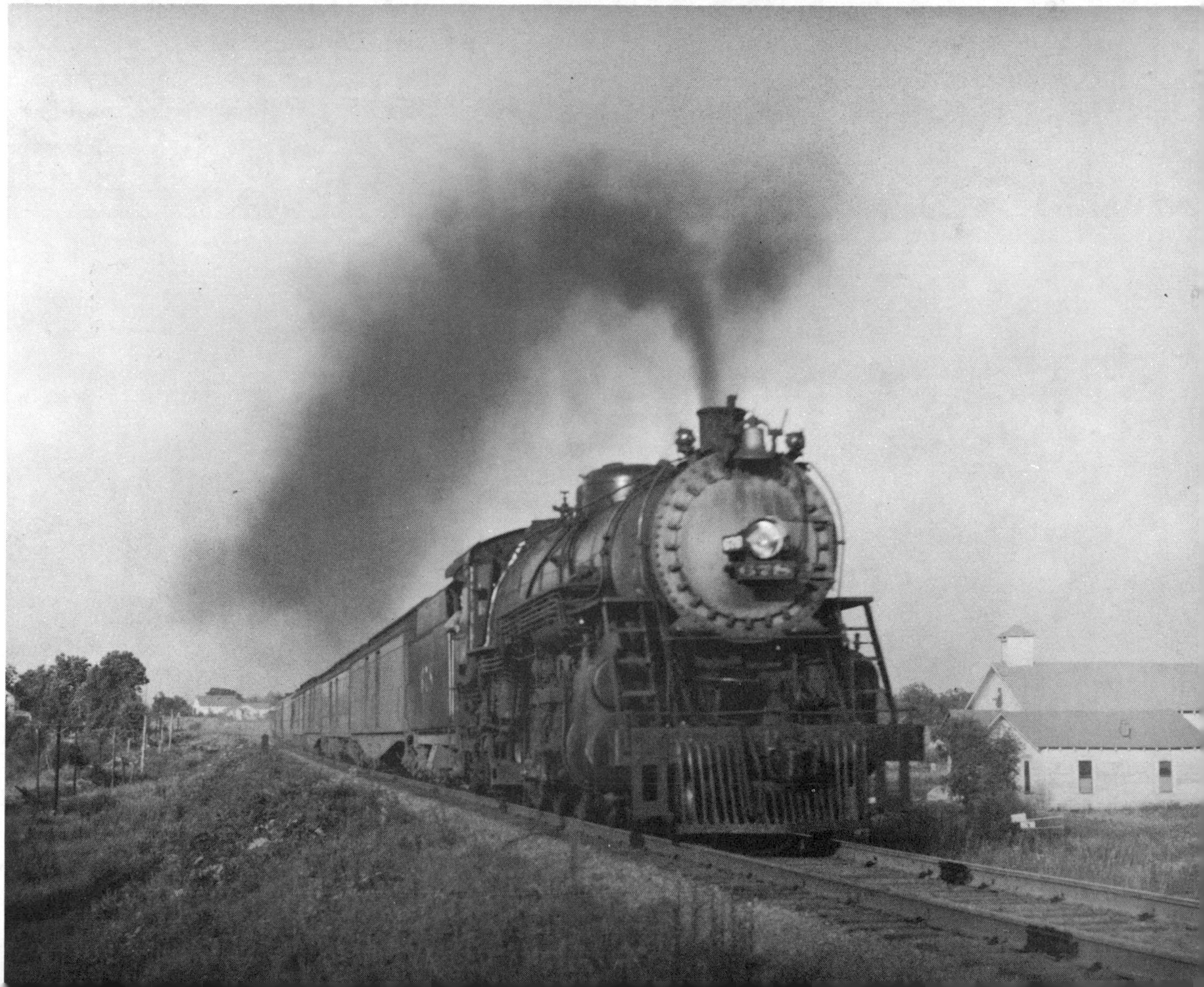

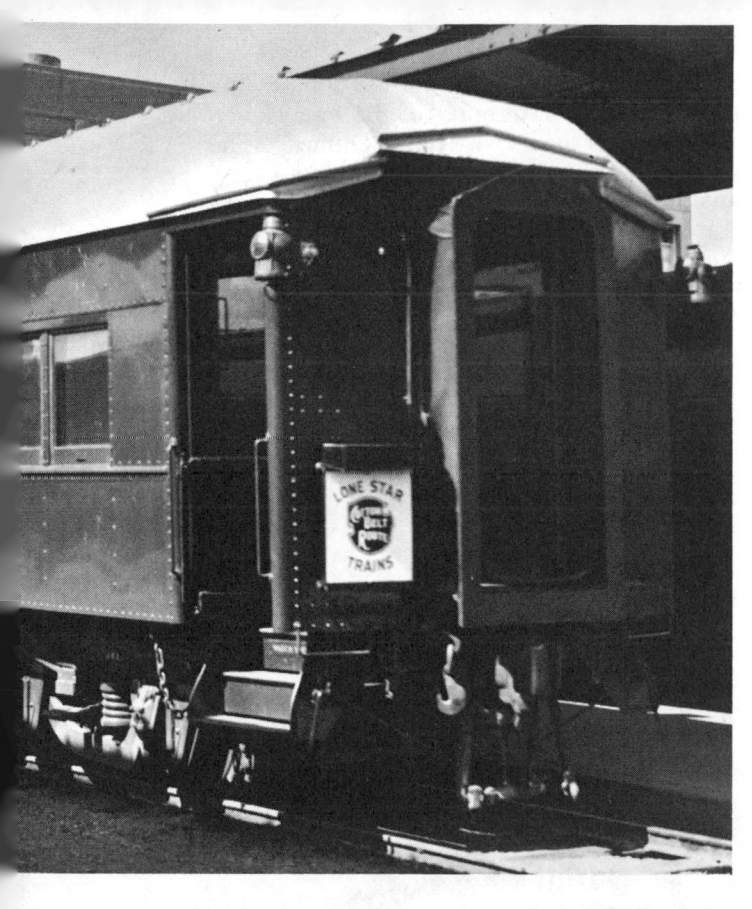

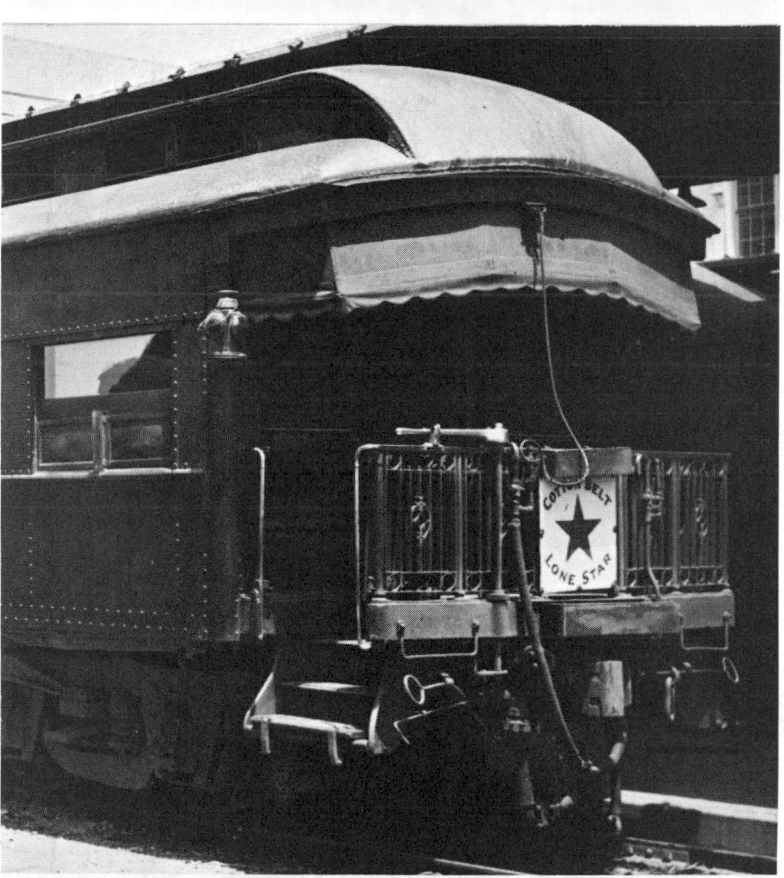

A NOTABLE PARTISAN of the camelback locomotive in the heyday of this atmospheric motive power, the Lehigh Valley assigned Mother Hubbards to its crack *Black Diamond* for many useful years. Immediately below it appears in a classic action shot taken by F. W. Blauvelt in a lush New Jersey setting in 1895 "at 65 miles an hour." At the bottom of the page No. 2410 powers a five-car *Black Diamond* about 1910. On the opposite page in a fine period pose a camelback-headed local storms out of the depot at Fair Haven, terminal of the Fair Haven branch on the shores of Lake Ontario. The splendid American type 4-4-0 vignetted below in another Blauvelt likeness was the JAMES DONNELLY which lent splendor to the first run of *The Black Diamond* in 1895. (*Below and Bottom Opposite: Brown Bros.; Others: Everett De Golyer Collection.*)

Many Anthracite Carriers Favored Camelbacks

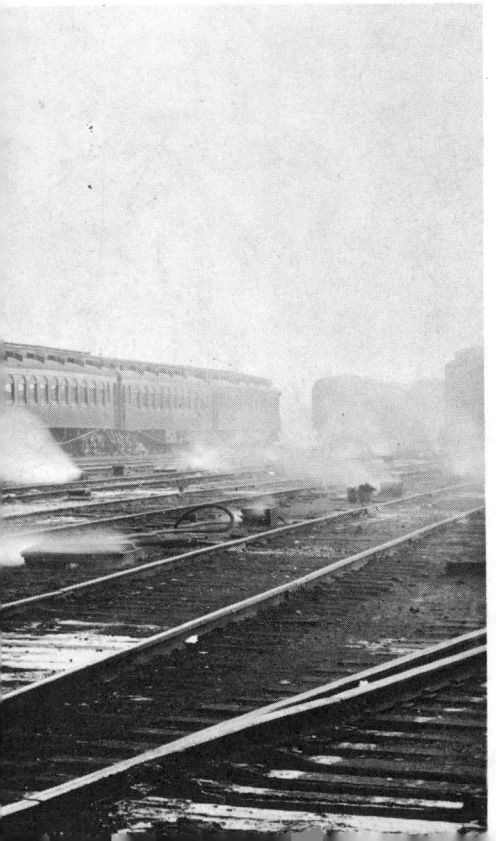

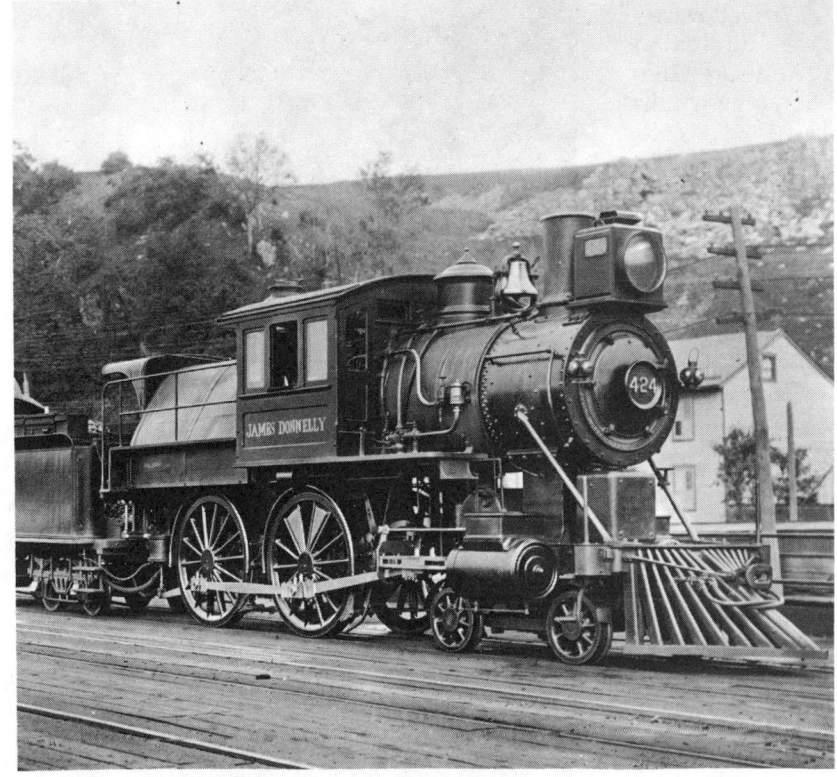

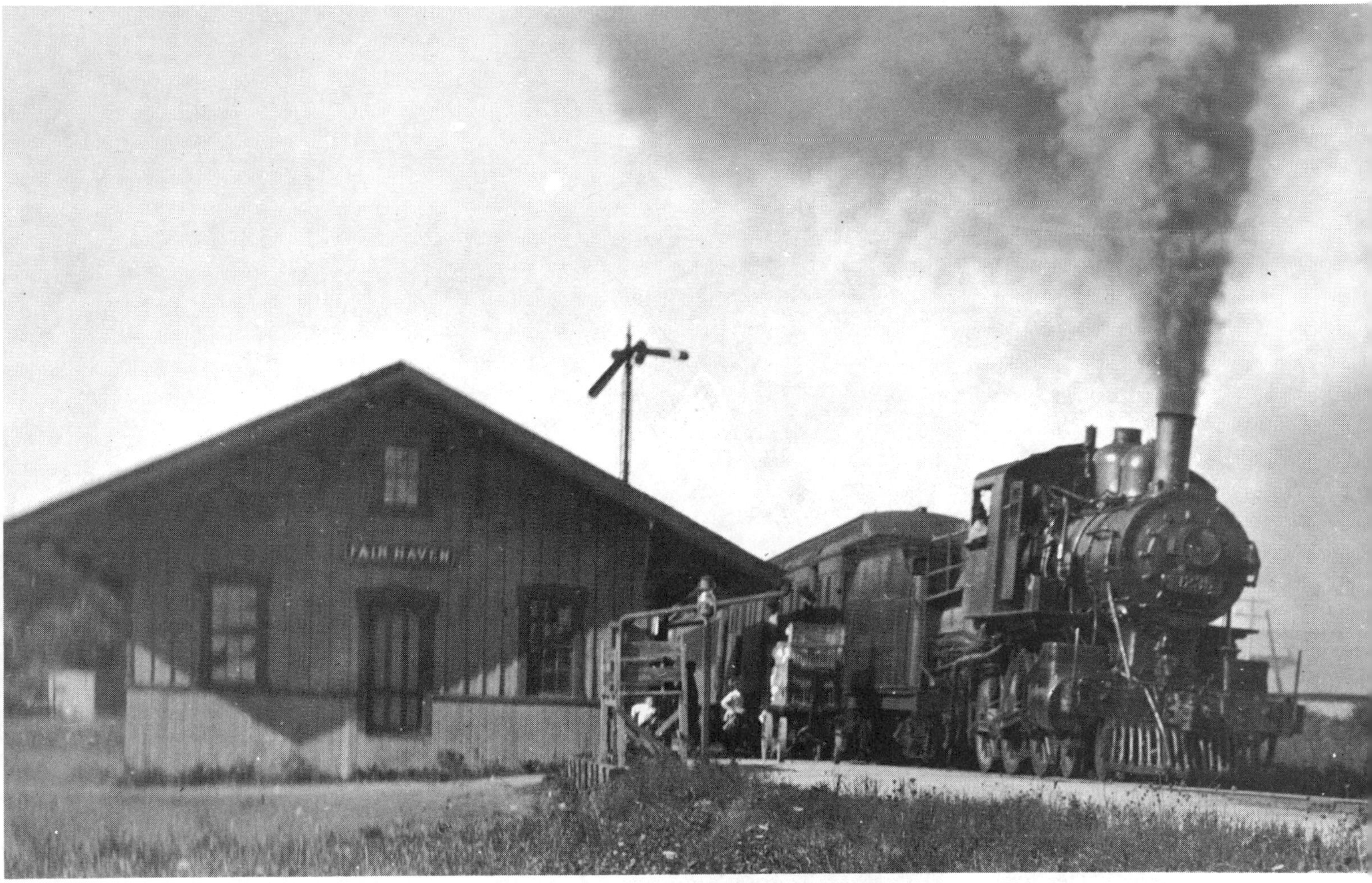

ANOTHER CARRIER hopefully built in the latter nineteenth century to serve "The Southern Tier" of New York State was the New York, Ontario & Western, whose varnish run, circa 1910, is shown below as it pauses at Woodridge, New York, Milepost 106. *(Library of Congress.)*

EQUALLY evocative of period atmosphere along "The Southern Tier" was the depot platform of the Ulster & Delaware's Pine Hill Station in 1900 where zinc-bound Saratoga trunks and widows' weeds form a background to the vacation life of the Catskills at this remote era. *(Library of Congress.)*

ALTHOUGH a number of American trains were named to honor historic figures in the national record, *Buffalo Bill, James Whitcomb Riley, The Jeffersonian, Sam Houston Zephyr, George Washington* and *Abraham Lincoln* among them, only a handful, *The Commodore Vanderbilt, Empire Builder, Henry M. Flagler* and *Dixie Flagler* were named to commemorate practicing railroaders. One of these was the Lehigh Valley's *Asa Packer,* shown here amongst the hedgerows of the New Jersey countryside near South Plainfield, named for the shrewd Yankee who brought the Lehigh Valley Railroad into being, became the richest Pennsylvanian of his time and founded Lehigh College. Specially-assigned equipment bore the train name of golden script and its high-wheeled Pacific such as No. 2138 were scrupulously maintained. *(Lucius Beebe.)*

AS LONG AS the passenger business maintained
a possible operational level the
Lehigh Valley's varnish runs carried on in
the great tradition of excellence of
*The Black Diamond, The Lehigh Limited,
The Wyoming Valley Express* and *The Toronto*
with through sleeping cars out of New York
for Canada. The historic *Black Diamond*
itself rolled down the decades, its
consists and motive power modified to meet
changing times. In the nineties it had run all the
way to Buffalo with camelback motive
power. In 1939 it shared two streamlined Pacifics
designed by Otto Kuhler with the
John Wilkes, but in more familiar mechanical
garb it is shown above behind a Pacific
with gleaming cylinder heads against an
appropriately pastoral backdrop. By the thirties,
the once proud observation *Seneca* had
yielded to two enclosed solarium-observation
lounges, *Black Diamond* and *White Diamond*.
*(Top Opposite, Two Photos:
Lehigh Valley; Above: Everett De Golyer
Collection; Left: Smithsonian Institution.)*

The Lehigh Valley's daylight run between New York and Wilkes Barre in 1939 was accomplished by a coach, diner and parlor car consist called *The John Wilkes* whose semi-streamlined equipment and spectacularly streamlined motive power sooted up the countryside while contented patrons lunched off braised beef and corn fritters. The peculiar conformation of the smoke lifters built into the engine cowling produced a symmetrical blossom of smoke or steam exhaust that was a hallmark of the train's identity as it traversed a right of way with knife edge ballast that might have come from Tiffany. (*Lucius Beebe.*)

SHARING TERMINAL RIGHTS at Pennsylvania Station with the New Haven and Long Island, the Lehigh Valley's *John Wilkes* started its run behind a Pennsy GG-1 electric, changing to streamlined steam in New Jersey. Although primarily an industrial carrier, the L.V. until well into the thirties rolled through rural grade crossings as rustic as that below. (*Below: Everett De Golyer Collection; Bottom: Library of Congress; Right: Ewing Galloway.*)

OF THE THREE major carriers sharing the passenger business out of St. Louis for the Texas Southwest, the Missouri Pacific, the St. Louis-San Francisco and the Missouri-Kansas-Texas, the last of these, universally known as The Katy, maintained the most lasting hold upon the loyalties both of railroad *aficionados* and on-line communities which benefitted from its traffickings. Its usually light-weight motive power was radiantly maintained with the red and white M.K.T. ensign on tenders drawn by engines with burnished rod assemblies and white-tired drivers. On its fast passenger runs to Texas it was a frequent M.K.T. practice to include among the head-end revenue cars a reefer fitted with roller bearing trucks for such perishables as the first strawberry pack of the season. Opposite: framed by the Texas sky and needled cactus plants at San Antonio yard limits, the Katy's northbound *Bluebonnet* rolls behind burnished Pacific No. 401. Here, in an enduring vignette suggesting the scrupulous dimension of its passenger operations, Pacific type locomotive No. 380 is reflected together with Texas clouds in the window of the dining car *Dallas* waiting at San Antonio to go north in the road's crack *Bluebonnet* in 1948. *(Two Photos: Philip R. Hastings.)*

FOR REASONS not superficially apparent, the Katy in its years of teem enjoyed an acceptance and regional affection in the Southwest not in the same measure accorded competing carriers. It may be that despite its vested management in far-off New York, its facade was more folksy and its ear attuned to the needs and mores of the countryside it served. Certainly that is the way Chairman of the Board Matthew S. Sloan wanted it. At the right *The Katy Special* is shown westbound with a streamlined consist in a panoramic view by Philip Hastings, and in more conventional Pullman Standard dress in 1949 by R. S. Plummer.

HANSEL AND GRETEL might very well have lived in the gingerbread house that served as the Katy depot and freight shed at Point, Texas, on the branch from Greenville to Mineola. Built before Dewey took Manila, it served a freight line only, which seems a pity. *(A. E. Brown.)*

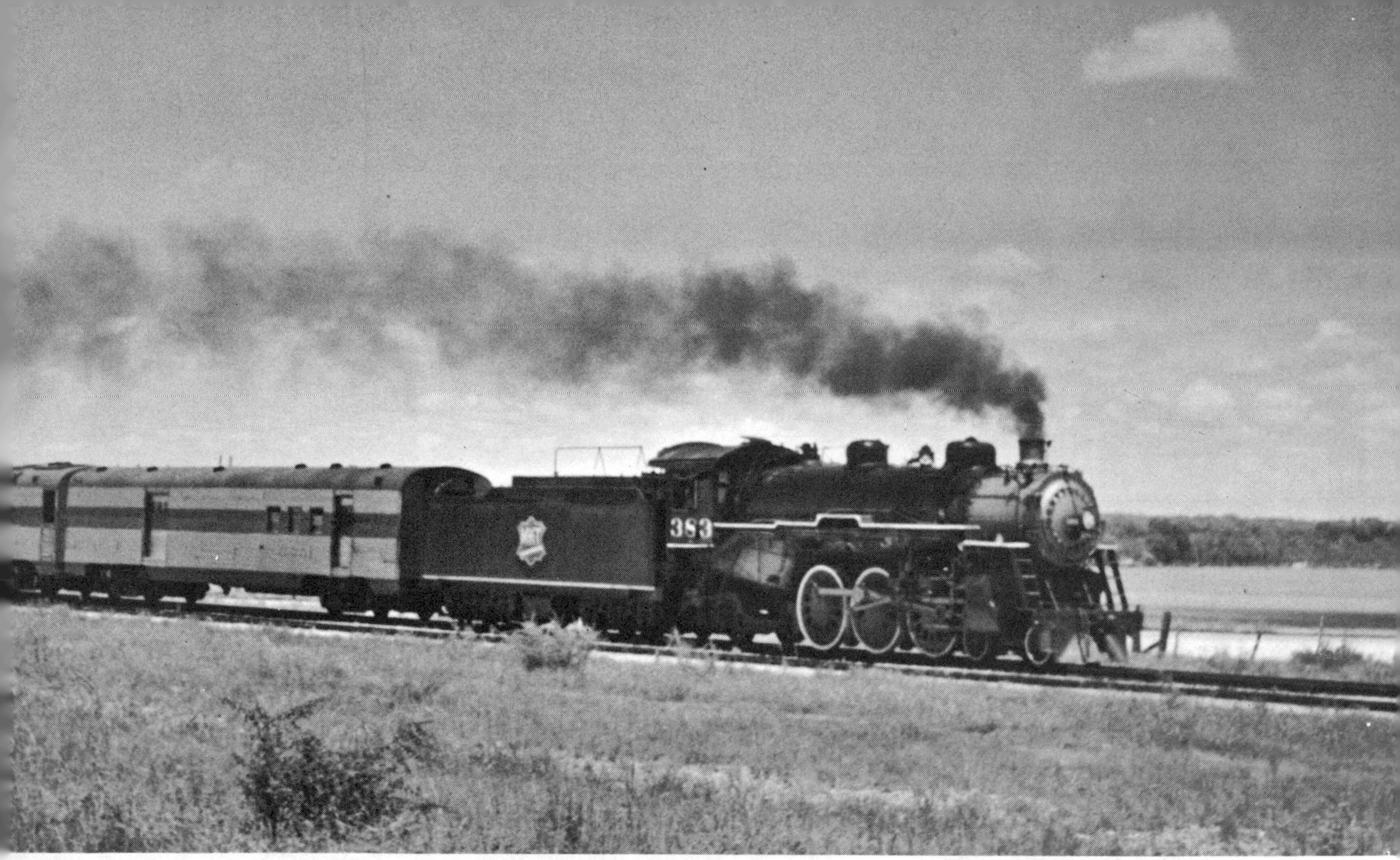
383

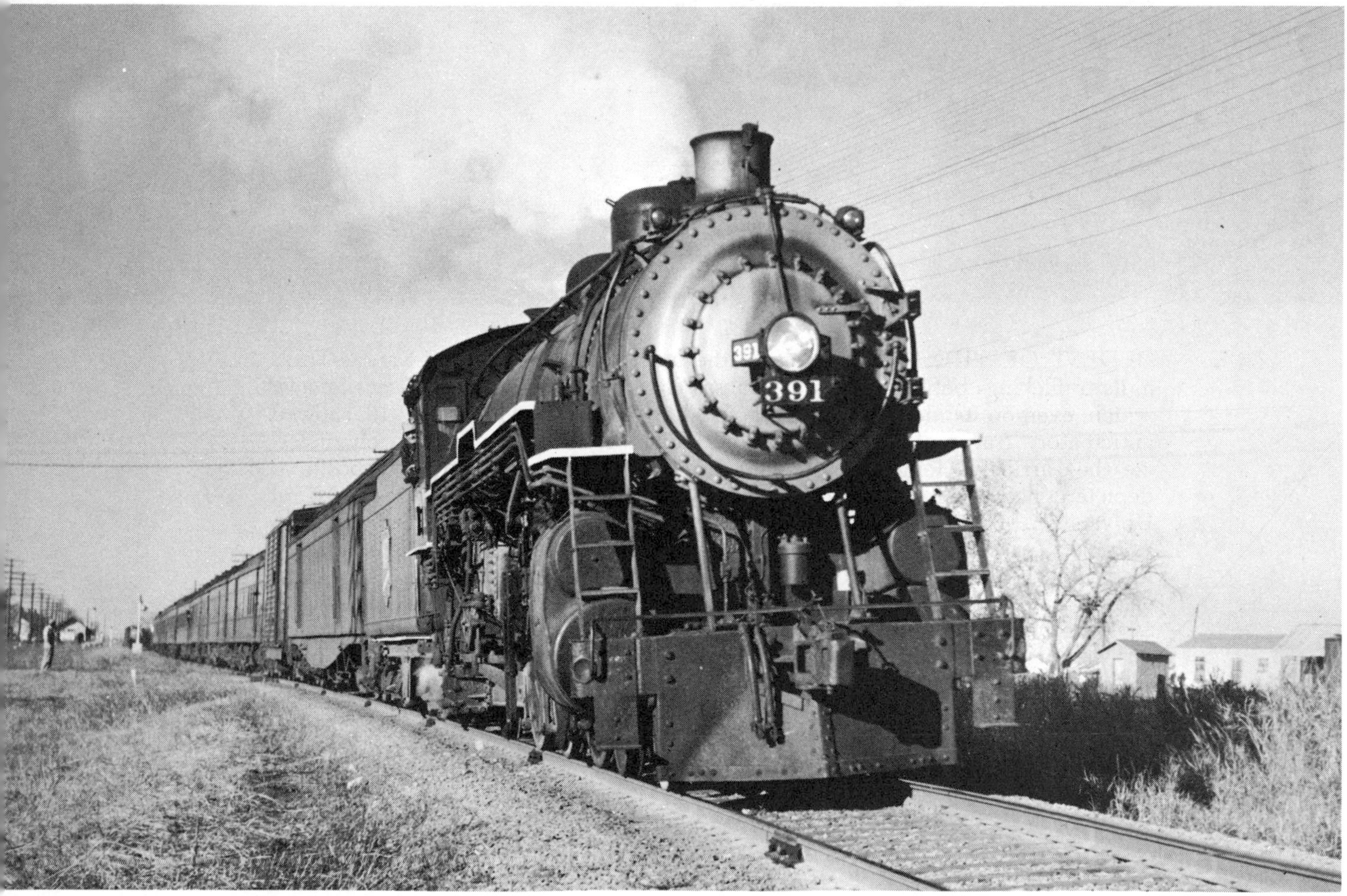
391
391

OLDEST OF THE NAME trains in the annals of The Missouri-Kansas-Texas in its traffickings between St. Louis-Kansas City and Texas was *The Texas Special* which, even on its maiden voyage depicted above, on December 5, 1916, showed anticipatory traces of the elegance and superb style which were to characterize the carrier as long as passengers were a major consideration. Opposite is depicted, not the refectory of one of the more venerable colleges of Oxford University, but the cathedral-like waiting room of the Katy's depot at San Antonio, Texas. Seated in one of the pews is Mrs. S. A. Agnew who went to work in 1917 when the structure was opened as one of the then numerous corps of Katy matrons whose function was directing passengers to connecting trains, assisting invalids and being otherwise motherly and helpful. It was a unique service on a railroad entirely unique in many other aspects of its conduct. (*Above: Everett De Golyer Collection; Opposite: Philip R. Hastings.*)

INTERESTING for its combination of conventional equipment with what passed for progress in the field of motive power is the portrait of *The Texas Special* shown below in June 1947 entering Dallas en route from Waco. Standard Pullmans ride serenely behind a Diesel road engine with the train's name in the grand manner on its forward unit. With the demise of the original *Texas Special,* the jointly maintained Frisco-Katy train from Texas to St. Louis continued under the same name with a mixed consist of streamlined and Standard equipment. (*A. E. Brown.*)

EVERYTHING about the M.K.T. operation in the regime of Matthew Sloan, a perfectionist in the great tradition of Henry M. Flagler, reflected a well-ordered administration that had no compromise with mediocrity. Appropriately, even the yard office at Sloan Yard, San Antonio (*opposite*) occupied a country club setting of flawless lawns and well-watered shrubbery while the yard goats were as gleamingly maintained as the high stepping road engines of *The Texas Special* and *Bluebonnet*. Part of an immaculate operation was the icing of the dining car *Sam Houston* at Sloan for its northbound run in *The Texas Special*. When *The Bluebonnet* as shown below carried a business car, the train herald still rode grandly on its observation platform. (*Both at Left: Philip R. Hastings; Below: De Golyer Foundation, Collons Collection.*)

ON AN IMMACULATE stub track in the Katy's San Antonio depot *The Bluebonnet*, northbound awaits a highball behind gleaming Pacific No. 380. Typical of many of the carrier's passenger operations is the roller bearing fitted reefer between the tender and head-end cars where such perishables as Gulf pompano or the first of the Texas melon crop rode north on passenger carding. At the right Mrs. S. A. Agnew, veteran San Antonio depot matron, chats with a crewman before the departure of *The Texas Special* in its years of lightweight equipment. After the end of the 1941 war with its capacity passenger traffic, Mrs. Agnew had fewer duties, but still regarded both the stately depot and the entire railroad operation with a possessive eye. (*Two Photos: Philip R. Hastings.*)

IT IS IMPROBABLE that, during the period when Matthew S. Sloan was President and Chairman of the Board of the Missouri-Kansas-Texas, any railroad operation in the world was conducted with greater regard for precision, detail of operation and over-all style. Its depot lawns were the greenest, its tracks and sidings were ballasted in crushed stone that would have ornamented the private driveway of a millionaire, its passenger equipment gleamed from constant and unremitting washing. Here the observation car of *The Texas Special* gets a sluicing at San Antonio before being turned for its return trip north. *(Philip R. Hastings.)*

The New Haven Was
A Carrier for Blue Bloods

The Bay State Limited, 1911

W. G. Landon

No railroad in the record, not even the aristocratic Vanderbilt lines or the Illinois Central in whose history high finance, social eminence and political distinction are dominant bloodlines, was more familiar with the great and well born of the world than the New York, New Haven & Hartford in the years of its most golden destinies. Oliver Wendell Holmes, the elder, complained about the tumults and poor accommodations of its old New Haven depot. The senior John Pierpont Morgan regarded it for many years as his favorite railroad property until its finances were debauched by reckless over-expansion. General Grant and his military staff evacuated his private car when a female patron who had mistaken it for an uncommonly ornate public accommodation complained about his smoking and use of spitting tobacco. Its multiplicity of wrecks became a standard of regional humor. Three generations of conservative Bostonians led the abundant life on its dividends and aboard its cars on the Shore Line, a German royal princess insisted that luncheon be served off her own gold plate by her own crimson liveried butlers and footmen. Its football specials in the spacious time of Harvard and Yale supremacy were covered by society reporters from the New York papers as assiduously as they covered openings at the Metropolitan Opera, and throughout its long life of opulence the names that rode *The Merchants Limited, The Senator, The Owl* and *The Gilt Edge* were the consequential names of the great world everywhere.

Until well into the twentieth century, the social, financial, political and economic interests which dominated Boston and comprised what may be termed The Establishment were well defined and their components recognized for their essentially New England character. One of them was The New York, New Haven & Hartford Railroad which bridged the distance both factually and metaphorically that separated Boston's social and economic interests from those of New York and served as the principal agency of communications between State Street and Wall Street, the Back Bay and Murray Hill. In many of its aspects, excepting, of course, that of its dimension of geographic and industrial importance, the New Haven had the same relationship to Boston as the Pennsylvania bore to Philadelphia. Its management and financing had originally derived largely from Boston, its flavor was primarily that of a New England-dominated enterprise, and in Beacon Street and Bay State Road it was a household institution comparable to *The Boston Evening Transcript*, Harvard University and fishballs for Sunday breakfast.

The New Haven was variously viewed with admiration, in its years of teem, as a gilt edge investment, and with tolerance, humor and affection for its sometime vagrant character and many operational excellences. Its established position in regional folklore was attested when in the Broadway production of Clarence Day's "Life With Father" one of the characters opens his morning paper to read aloud from the news of that day: "Not much news; it's going to rain and, oh, another wreck on the New Haven!" Unhappily there was a period along 1910 when wrecks on the New Haven were all too frequent.

As in Boston itself, travel on the New Haven retained the formal amenities of other years longer than they survived elsewhere. Passengers of conspicuously solvent estate continued to bring shoebox lunches aboard *The Merchants Limited* and *Knickerbocker* long after it had become common

297

knowledge that dining cars were entirely respectable and no longer under the management of members of the Borgia family. Even after the advent of air-conditioning when such precautions were no longer necessary or advised, gentlemen hung up their derbies and donned cloth traveling caps and gloves as protection against the hazards of soot that didn't exist. If Miss Amy Lowell wished to smoke a cigar, which she did often, nobody in the club car looked twice and gentlemen with single eyeglasses reading the *Journal de Debats* attracted no more attention than snowy bearded Professor George Lyman Kittredge of Harvard reading *The Boston Herald*.

The New Haven's name trains had great character, *The Knickerbocker Limited* and later the *Yankee Clipper* on the noon run were all-parlor car, extra fare whose dining and club cars had about them a breath of the Somerset Club and whose cuisine was above reproach. The broiled Maine lobster was generally considered the par of its equivalent in Lock Ober's Winter Place Wine Rooms, which was very good indeed. Maitre d'hotels knew all the right people which, since practically nobody else rode *The Knickerbocker*, meant the entire passenger list. The ship's clock in the diner of *The Clipper* kept ship's time which confused everyone in a pleasant sort of way. One of the most accurate indexes of the status of travelers, their luggage, would have indicated a very conservative, well bred clientele indeed. The age of light weight luggage had yet to dawn and ponderous valises, Gladstones and portmanteaux bearing the hallmarks of Louis Vuiton in Paris and John Pound of London mingled with wicker hampers in the Continental style and the improvised containers, corded and strapped, of people so assured they needed no ostentations of modernity to establish their social standing.

The Merchants Limited was almost wholly masculine in tone and, if *The Knickerbocker* recruited its patrons from The Chilton and Somerset Clubs, its clientele derived from the Union Club in Park Street and the board rooms of Lee Higginson and Stone & Webster. The resources of cigars and spirits from S. S. Pierce and Cobb, Bates & Yerxa were expensive and choice. Prohibition made hardly a dent in the consumption of liquor on *The Merchants* and if anything increased individual consumption to a point where patrons in wine sometimes had to be helped off at either

terminal. *The Wall Street Journal* and *Boston News Bureau* were almost the only reading matter aboard the train. The market debacle of the early thirties at times diminished the number of passengers on the extra-fare runs to fewer than fifty persons but the New Haven simply cut the number of parlor cars and in no way compromised elsewhere with hard times.

Some of the most elaborately upholstered special trains in the railroad record were those of the early years of the century over the New Haven to New Haven itself or Boston on alternate years when the Harvard-Yale football game climaxed the fall social season. A lesser occasion but still stylish was the Yale-Princeton game at New Haven, it being the time when only Ivy League colleges were mentioned in polite conversation and the New York and Boston newspapers didn't even report the score of ballgames west of the Hudson River. Sixteen car coach trains carried *hoi polloi* to these events, but really spectacular arrivals were the all-parlor car specials aboard which the elite rolled in comfort, their every want supplied by armies of menials and to which were attached, as often as not, the beautiful private cars of such sporting enthusiasts as Harry Payne Whitney or William K. Vanderbilt.

For the 1905 Yale-Princeton game no fewer than fifty privately chartered Pullman parlor cars were carried to New Haven in five specials with white flags at their locomotive smokebox. Aboard most of these lunch was privately catered not by the railroad but by Louis Sherry whose liveried waiters passed *huitres a la Camilé* and terrapin Maryland along with Krug's Private Cuvee '98 which was then in its prime. Tea, lady fingers and more Krug was served on the return trip and a crowd of several thousand people jammed Grand Central just to see their arrival. The ladies, of course, drank Apollinaris or Poland water, but aboard E. S. Auchincloss's parlor car, where the Yale victory 23-4 was uncommonly popular, four cases of champagne were served, according to Sherry's bill, or better than two bottles per masculine occupant.

Less mannered were the sleepers carried in *The Owl* to Yale-Harvard games at Boston during prohibition, often in eight extra sections filled with alcoholic tumults in which sleeping was a secondary consideration. Their occupants, groggy

298

and battered, streaming into South Station at breakfast time had the appearance of a defeated army in retreat. Confidence was restored in the stricken at the bars of the Harvard Club or the Porcellian in Cambridge and late that night the same extra sections carried the celebrants back to New York.

Beside the self-contained New Haven name trains operating only over the Shore Line, the railroad carried an appropriate number of varnish runs and Pullmans for interchange with the Pennsylvania for Washington, Florida and other distant terminals. Trains Nos. 172 and 173, *The Federal* carried the bulk of the overnight Boston-Washington traffic with all-bedroom Pullmans and a buffet car for late snacks out of either terminal. It picked up and set out a sleeping car at New Haven *en route* and southbound carried a Providence-Philadelphia sleeper. *The Colonial* and *The Senator* were daylight de luxe hauls between The Hub and the Federal City with parlor, lounge and observation cars usually supplemented by Pennsylvania diners over the entire route. In 1917 and for a brief time thereafter there was a full train of through Pullmans out of Boston called *The Boston-Pittsburgh-St. Louis Express* with St. Louis, Cin-

cinnati and Pittsburgh sleepers, and in 1934 there were through Boston sleepers for Pittsburgh set out and Chicago in the *Iron City Express* westbound, and eastbound from Pittsburgh to Boston in *The New Englander* and from Chicago in *The Manhattan Limited*. The Pennsylvania advertised this service smugly: "Stay in Your Own Pullman, Boston to Chicago" and obviously scheduled its New Haven connection with Boston in direct competition with *The Minute Man* on the Boston & Maine and the several Boston & Albany name train connections which included *The Twentieth Century Limited, The Lake Shore* and *The Boston Wolverine.*

The good years of the New Haven Railroad were also the good years of Boston's most ample destinies, years when the geneological columns of *The Boston Evening Transcript* were devotional reading on Beacon Hill, when splendid dinners at the Algonquin Club terminated with the house specialty, diminutive cheese croquettes with hot mustard sauce, and when strollers in Commonwealth Avenue invariably paused to admire the rare orchids that bloomed in the conservatory of the Phineas Sprague residence.

They were the years of the ortolans in Boston.

ALTHOUGH LOCATED AT greater remove from the fashionable residential faubourgs of the Back Bay than the Boston & Providence passenger station in Park Square, no tangible reminder of any railroad in New England was closer to the hearts of the Boston Establishment than the Old Colony & Newport Depot at the corner of South and Kneeland Streets. Through some managerial whim or perhaps mere accident of timing, when this atmospheric photograph was taken the Old Colony legend of its identification had been newly gilded while the lettering of the Fall River Line below it is dingy and neglected, but make no mistake about it, the Fall River steamboat connections were what kept the Old Colony's quarterly dividend checks as regular in Commonwealth Avenue as clockwork. From these sedate and conservative premises, until the opening of the South Station in the closing years of the century only two blocks away, there departed daily the Fall River Boat Train in charge of Conductor Asa R. Porter freighted with the names that made news in the worlds of politics, finance and society. The South Street horsecar, shown here turning out of Kneeland Street, ran past the business offices where three generations of forebears of the senior collaborator in this book earned their living in leather and hides. A block further on was the United States Hotel, generally acknowledged to be *the* railroad hotel of town where drummers of the gray derby and ratcatcher suit age foregathered. The Old Colony Depot was at the center of practically everything. (*The Bostonian Society.*)

SOME IDEA of the close proximity of railroading to the residential district of Boston in the nineteenth century, a proximity which in the case of the Providence Railroad was symbolic of the carrier's role in the social and economic structure of the town, may be suggested by the below photograph which depicts the original Providence depot only a stone's throw from the fine mansion of a Yankee grandee. The depot looms in the background, a vaguely classical facade completely dominated by the residence at the corner of Boylston and Carver Streets of Winslow Lewis, Captain of the Boston Sea Fencibles and a notable of the first chop in the community affairs of his time. In the circular view the Providence belfry is shown again framed by the Bullfinch fronts of private houses in Boylston Street which was still an unpaved thoroughfare. Boston merchant princes admired to live within view of the sources of their tangible wealth. *(Two Photos: The Bostonian Society.)*

IN AN ERA when nothing gave an American community greater status than a railroad, the crowning panache of glory was a railroad depot disguised as a Norman castle, Greek classic temple, a French chateau from the banks of the Loire or an Egyptian temple such as the Old Colony's terminal at New Bedford, Massachusetts, shown here. The Old Colony Railroad was chartered in 1838 to build from Taunton to New Bedford and in eighteen months trains were in operation and the fetching structure shown here was opened with civic ceremony on July 1, 1840. "The car house and ticket office is built in the Egyptian style of architecture," said a somewhat redundant contemporary account, "with ends in imitation of the entrance of the catacombs, or the arches of gates. The appearance of the building is singularly odd and appropriate." There were originally four columns supporting the facade but two were removed in mid-century to accommodate the passage of patrons and baggage. The photograph here reproduced with a three-horse open horsecar was taken fifty years later when, to a day, the structure was razed "and the foundations were laid on the same site for the present commodious and imposing freight depot." When this photograph was taken the Old Colony was still an independent and celebratedly profitable New England institution, but in the mid-nineties the foundations were laid for its absorption by the New Haven, a merger that was finally concluded in 1898, coinciding with the completion of the great South Station shown above. (*Right: New Bedford Historical Society.*)

THE EAGLE-CROWNED FACADE shown opposite in a photograph of Boston's splendid South Station, after the emplacement of the Dewey Memorial pylon in the foreground but before the construction of the elevated railroad tracks, depicts the structure in an aspect of beauty it was never to know again. The date would be about 1900 and another view, taken from the same spot some years later, is shown elsewhere in this volume when the elevated and the surge of heavy commercial traffic had engulfed its noble dimensions. *(The Bostonian Society.)*

STILL ANOTHER aspect of boarding the steamcars in Southern New England was this pastoral vignette of rural life at Grants, Connecticut, a depot built for the Connecticut Western in 1872. Its split-rail-fenced pasture in the foreground and array of milk cans on a platform open to the elements, passed to the Central New England in 1897 and remained on the company timetables until as late as 1937. *(Dudley Stickels Collection.)*

303

The Old Fall River Line Boat Train
"Mr. Porter's Train" Met The Steamers for Ninety Years

AN INSTITUTION of national dimension and international celebrity, the Fall River Line Steamboat Company and the train of its parent Old Colony Railroad, later the New York, New Haven & Hartford, engaged the attention of travelers of two centuries. The combined agencies of *The Boat Train* out of Boston and the long succession of palatial steamers out of Fall River for New York linked the financial, cultural and economic centers of the United States for nine full decades and became a household legend which lingers in New England to this day. Above, in one of Bishop's superb photographs *The Boat Train* approaches Fall River behind Old Colony No. 43 while opposite passengers on the boat deck of *Bristol* listen to the band playing "On The Old Fall River Line." *(Everett De Golyer Collection; Opposite: Fall River Historical Society.)*

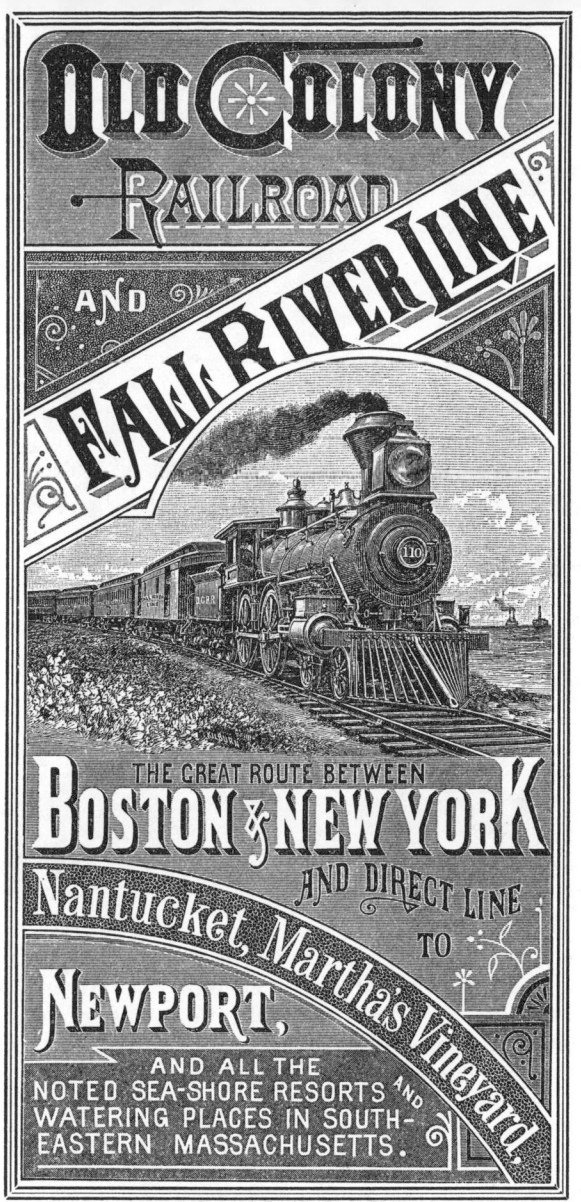

OLD COLONY RAILROAD AND FALL RIVER LINE

THE GREAT ROUTE BETWEEN

BOSTON & NEW YORK

AND DIRECT LINE TO

Nantucket, Martha's Vineyard, NEWPORT,

AND ALL THE NOTED SEA-SHORE RESORTS AND WATERING PLACES IN SOUTH-EASTERN MASSACHUSETTS.

GEO. H. ELLIS, 141 Franklin Street, Boston.

INCOMPARABLY the most celebrated boat-train service in the annals of transportation, The Fall River Line steamers and the Old Colony *Fall River Boat Trains* between Boston and dockside were national institutions spanning nine decades of superbly operated and luxuriously upholstered surface travel. *(Above: Everett De Golyer Collection; Below: Oliver Jensen Collection.)*

IT IS DIFFICULT in chronicling even briefly the great days of steamer travel on Long Island Sound and the *Fall River Boat Train* not to resort to superlatives that have become cliches from overuse. It was indeed a wonderful time and way to travel. The steamers that ran in the New York-Boston passenger trade were indeed beautiful and they were much loved. The men who captained them and the courtly generation of passengers who rode them were of a stature that has not since been seen. The whole scheme of things and way of travel were a pattern of wonder and delight that will not come again. These have been established beyond doubting by sober and veracious annalists who were sentimental only in recognizing excellence when they encountered it. That they encountered it in full measure and the most ample dimension aboard *Priscilla, Commonwealth, Bay State, Bristol, Providence* and the trains that served them cannot be gainsaid.

When, full of years and honors in 1937, the *Fall River Boat Train* over the New Haven closed its books forever, it was the oldest passenger run in continuous operation in the United States. It had met the steamers for ninety years. Its origin in 1847 had been long before continuous train passage between Boston and New York either via the Shore Line or over the older New York & New England Air Line through central Connecticut. *The Boat Train* left Boston from the beginning to the end in the late afternoon, set down its passengers at the Fall River Line Pier at Fall River where they embarked for New York and picked up its return loading from the up boat early the next morning. The completion of the New Haven's far faster Shore Line with its five-hour limited trains only dented its faithful patronage.

When finally an end came for the mannered way of life it represented The Fall River Line and *The Boat Train* were already enshrined in the Pantheon of New England institutions, one with the bedsheet pages of *The Boston Evening Transcript*, tripe on the menu at Young's Hotel, Friday afternoon at Symphony Hall, and, of course *The White Train* and *The Dude Flyer* it outlived. It had taken Union soldiers toward the battles of the Civil War, it had known the tread of Jim Fisk and President Grant, its patrons had spanned the gap of years and decades from the stovepipe hat and Inverness traveling cloak to the attache case of the air age. And it had been as regular as sidereal time or an Eddy clock.

The Fall River Route between Boston and New York had its origins when competition flourished in a variety of alternate train and steamboat operations on Long Island Sound. There were boat trains to Newport, Providence, Bristol and even as far afield as Stonington in Connecticut, and for a time it appeared that the dominant route to New York would be via a connection at Greenport with the Long Island Railroad and a steamer from Norwich or Stonington.

The triumph over all competition of the Fall River Line was widely and probably correctly attributed to a single man in the person of its legendary Conductor Asa R. Porter who for thirty-two years was captain of *The Fall River Boat Train* and one of the most famous railroaders in America. A man of grave courtesy and commanding dignity, he was on good terms with the great of the world, presidents, senators, bankers and merchant princes who rode under his care. Invariably attired in the blue frock coat of his office and with a pink in his buttonhole, his "May I please see your transportation?" instead of the more usual "Tickets, please" and his memory for names soon made him a celebrity in his own right. Inevitably *The Boat Train* was known as "Mr. Porter's train."

The Boat Train ran over the rails of The Old Colony as far as South Braintree and from there on The Fall River Railroad to its terminal. A feature of its service was a company clerk who would today be known as a purser who rode the train itself and conned the passenger list with the conductor and then boarded the steamer and rode through to its destination as a continual contact between the carrier and its patrons. Keys to staterooms on the steamer were distributed by him on the train which was met at the pier by a large corps of porters all wearing white cotton gloves. The Fall River Line was a stickler for style.

Many volumes have been devoted to the fine steamers of the Fall River Line which made the New York run for nine profitable decades, *Bristol, Providence, Pilgrim, Puritan, Commonwealth* and most beloved of all, *Priscilla*. Each in succession was more princely of appointments than its predecessor with splendid public halls, majestic grand staircases and comfortable staterooms whose occupancy averaged a cost of $3. The menu on board *Priscilla* covered four pages of fine type and service was of the order expected by patrons of Parker's Hotel in School Street. Waiter captains were largely recruited from the best Boston and New York hotels and knew the social status and protocol to be accorded their passengers in a reassuring degree.

The Boat Train consist varied as little as its schedule and usually comprised a baggage car, two Pullman parlor cars and a number of coaches appropriate to the seasonal traffic. The original parlor cars were named *Pansy* and *Violet* and were followed by *Pilgrim* and *Puritan*, names which occasioned less embarrassment among their riders. Air conditioning came to coaches and parlor cars alike the same year it appeared on the crack *Merchants Limited* on the Shore Line run.

Newspaper editorialists and feature writers are, perhaps, too prone to attribute "the end of an era" to the passing of long established persons or institutions. The last run of the Fall River Line, however, did indeed terminate an era, for with it there ended the age of inland water travel in the United States. On a handful of other routes steamer service continued briefly, the Albany Night Boats, the Eastern Steamship run through Cape Cod Canal and a trickle of traffic on the Norfolk run out of New York and Philadelphia. But the Fall River Line was the handwriting on the wall and when *Priscilla* was towed away to be scrapped the end was in sight.

Well might they have tolled the Lutine Bell at Lloyd's, for her loss was as tragic as any more spectacular disaster in deeper water.

The OLD COLONY RAILROAD

"MY RECOLLECTIONS of Mr. Porter," writes Mary B. Gifford of The Fall River Historical Society, "were necessarily those of a small child, but I remember most clearly two things: his unfailing interest whenever we took his train in what we had been doing since our last trip, and the fact that his whiskers were just like my own grandfather's. He used to tell us children's jokes as he punched our tickets and let the tiny pieces fall into our hands so we could see what shape they were in. A bit of the pleasure of the trip was lost when he no longer rode the train."

POPULAR LEGEND in New England credited Conductor Asa Porter with a major portion of the success of *The Fall River Boat Train* which was in his charge for a record term of thirty-two years from 1864 to 1896. Like his contemporary and opposite number, Conductor Augustus Messer of *The Dude Flyer*, Porter was institutional in a time and place that set great store by continuity of office and where an employee's value to his principals was in direct proportion to his length of service. Known to newspaper readers as "the man who made *The Fall River Train*," Porter was famous far beyond the parochial activities of his calling and his conduct of the cars was proprietary so that, with the passing of time, patrons of the Old Colony found themselves to be less customers of its services than they were the personal guests of Captain Porter and *The Boat Train* was known as "Mr. Porter's Train." His blue frock coat of office with its fresh pink daily in its buttonhole was familiar to the great and powerful of the world as well as every President during his time in office. Like Conductor Messer, Captain Porter died in harness and his memory, still green in New England, is the measure of the good old gentleman who made the run his own.

IT WAS FROM the Old Colony's Kneeland Street depot in Boston, for many years one of the landmarks in the older part of the city, that *The Fall River Boat Train* departed every afternoon for many prosperous decades. The New Haven, eventual repository of so many New England carriers, absorbed the Old Colony in 1893 but Kneeland Street remained its terminal until the opening of the capacious new South Station five years later. The woodcut above shows Kneeland Street in 1885. Below is the grand staircase of *Pilgrim* one of the much loved steamers of the Fall River Line whose appointments of luxury and convenience bugged the eyes of travelers in the age of the Saratoga trunk. Bostonians felt that *Pilgrim* was fully as elegant as the fine new Vendome Hotel in Commonwealth Avenue and there was no more superlative tribute. (*Two woodcuts: Kenneth Nims Collection.*)

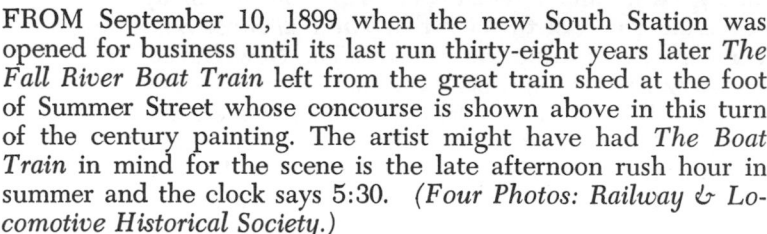

FROM September 10, 1899 when the new South Station was opened for business until its last run thirty-eight years later *The Fall River Boat Train* left from the great train shed at the foot of Summer Street whose concourse is shown above in this turn of the century painting. The artist might have had *The Boat Train* in mind for the scene is the late afternoon rush hour in summer and the clock says 5:30. *(Four Photos: Railway & Locomotive Historical Society.)*

HAD YOU BEEN a Boston boy in 1889 embarking on the great adventure of a trip to New York aboard the Fall River steamer with your bearded and derby-hatted father, you would have worn the knee pants, cotton stockings and Windsor tie of the young man shown above as you waited in the New Bedford depot to board the magnificent *Pilgrim* or perhaps the new all-steel *Puritan.* You might have arrived from Boston in the deep velour chairs of the Old Colony parlor car *Plymouth Rock* and you would have marvelled at the solid woodwork of the depot interior which suggested the railroad's lease might run till doomsday.

311

THE PHOTOGRAPH by George W. Rigby reproduced above shows *Commonwealth,* largest and perhaps finest of all the Fall River fleet, at its pier at Fall River. *The Boat Train* cars arrived and departed from the shed at the left. A freight *Boat Train* such as that under the stone train shed at the right left Boston with merchandise for the steamers every afternoon at three. At the right is the grand stairway of *Commonwealth;* below the Old Colony drawing room car *Pilgrim,* a familiar property of the *Boat Train* in the eighties. (*Above, Below: Roger William McAdam Collection; Right: Fall River Historical Society.*)

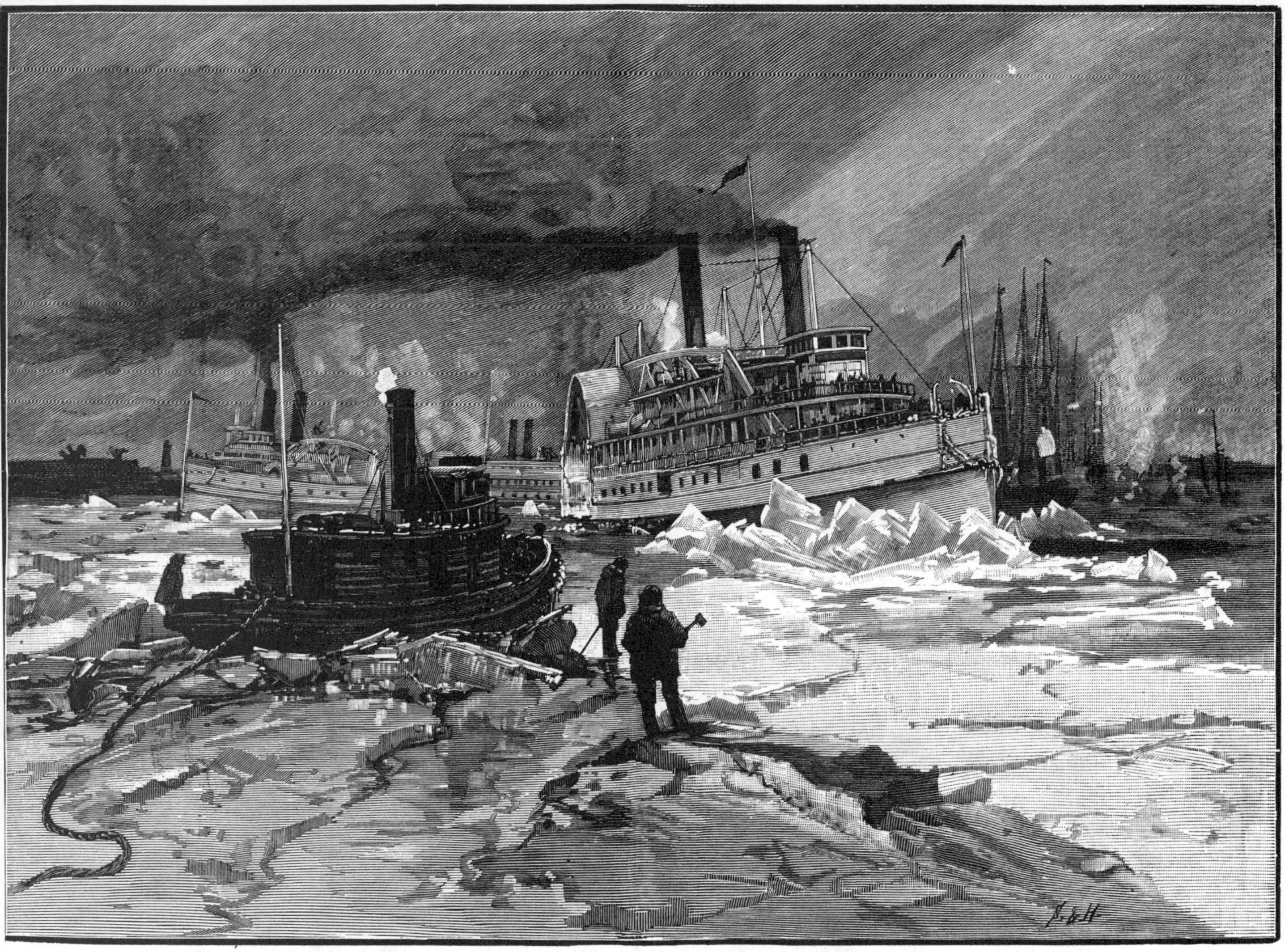

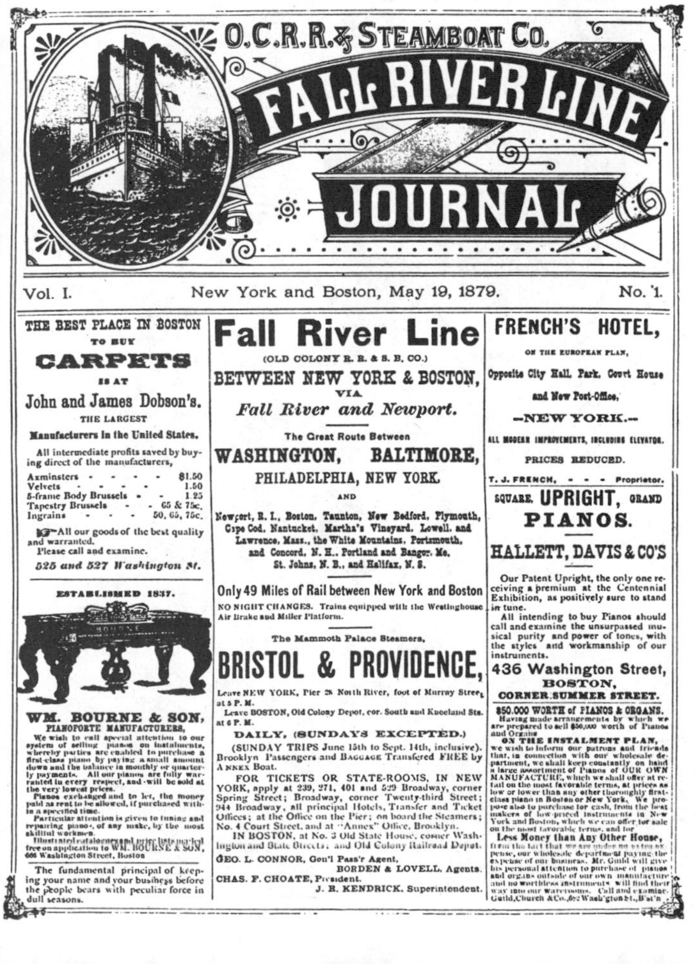

O.C.R.R. & STEAMBOAT CO.

FALL RIVER LINE JOURNAL

Vol. I. New York and Boston, May 19, 1879. No. 1.

THE BEST PLACE IN BOSTON TO BUY

CARPETS

IS AT

John and James Dobson's.

THE LARGEST

Manufacturers in the United States.

All intermediate profits saved by buying direct of the manufacturers,

Axminsters	$1.50
Velvets	1.50
5-frame Body Brussels	1.25
Tapestry Brussels	65 & 75c.
Ingrains	50, 65, 75c.

☞All our goods of the best quality and warranted.

Please call and examine.

525 and 527 Washington St.

ESTABLISHED 1837.

WM. BOURNE & SON, PIANOFORTE MANUFACTURERS,

We wish to call special attention to our system of selling pianos on instalments, whereby parties are enabled to purchase a first-class piano by paying a small amount down and the balance in monthly or quarterly payments. All our pianos are fully warranted in every respect, and will be sold at the very lowest prices.

Pianos exchanged and to let, the money paid as rent to be allowed, if purchased within a specified time.

Particular attention is given to tuning and repairing pianos, of any make, by the most skillful workmen.

Illustrated catalogues and price lists mailed free on application to WM. BOURNE & SON, 666 Washington Street, Boston

The fundamental principal of keeping your name and your business before the people bears with peculiar force in dull seasons.

Fall River Line

(OLD COLONY R. R. & S. B. CO.)

BETWEEN NEW YORK & BOSTON, VIA *Fall River and Newport.*

The Great Route Between

WASHINGTON, BALTIMORE, PHILADELPHIA, NEW YORK

AND

Newport, R. I., Boston, Taunton, New Bedford, Plymouth, Cape Cod, Nantucket, Martha's Vineyard, Lowell, and Lawrence, Mass., the White Mountains, Portsmouth, and Concord, N. H., Portland and Bangor, Me. St. Johns, N. B., and Halifax, N. S.

Only 49 Miles of Rail between New York and Boston

NO NIGHT CHANGES. Trains equipped with the Westinghouse Air Brake and Miller Platform.

The Mammoth Palace Steamers,

BRISTOL & PROVIDENCE,

Leave NEW YORK, Pier 28 North River, foot of Murray Street, at 5 P. M.

Leave BOSTON, Old Colony Depot, cor. South and Kneeland Sts. at 6 P. M.

DAILY, (SUNDAYS EXCEPTED.)

(SUNDAY TRIPS June 15th to Sept. 14th, inclusive). Brooklyn Passengers and BAGGAGE Transfered FREE by ANNEX Boat.

FOR TICKETS OR STATE-ROOMS, IN NEW YORK, apply at 239, 271, 401 and 529 Broadway, corner Spring Street; Broadway, corner Twenty-third Street; 944 Broadway, all principal Hotels, Transfer and Ticket Offices; at the Office on the Pier; on board the Steamers; No. 4 Court Street, and at "Annex" Office, Brooklyn.

IN BOSTON, at No. 3 Old State House, corner Washington and State Streets; and Old Colony Railroad Depot.

GEO. L. CONNOR, Gen'l Pass'r Agent,

BORDEN & LOVELL, Agents.

CHAS. F. CHOATE, President.

J. R. KENDRICK, Superintendent.

FRENCH'S HOTEL,

ON THE EUROPEAN PLAN,

Opposite City Hall, Park, Court House and New Post-Office,

—NEW YORK.—

ALL MODERN IMPROVEMENTS, INCLUDING ELEVATOR.

PRICES REDUCED.

T. J. FRENCH, - - - Proprietor.

SQUARE, UPRIGHT, GRAND PIANOS.

HALLETT, DAVIS & CO'S

Our Patent Upright, the only one receiving a premium at the Centennial Exhibition, as positively sure to stand in tune.

All intending to buy Pianos should call and examine the unsurpassed musical purity and power of tones, with the styles and workmanship of our instruments.

436 Washington Street, BOSTON, CORNER SUMMER STREET.

$50.000 WORTH of PIANOS & ORGANS.

Having made arrangements by which we are prepared to sell $50,000 worth of Pianos and Organs

ON THE INSTALMENT PLAN,

we wish to inform our patrons and friends that, in connection with our wholesale department, we shall keep constantly on hand a large assortment of Pianos of OUR OWN MANUFACTURE, which we shall offer at retail on the most favorable terms, at prices as low or lower than any other thoroughly first-class piano in Boston or New York. We propose also to purchase for cash, from the best makers of low-priced instruments in New York and Boston, which we can offer for sale on the most favorable terms, and for

Less Money than Any Other House,

from the fact that we are under no extra expense, our wholesale department paying the expense of our business. Mr. Guild will give his personal attention to purchase of pianos and organs outside of our own manufacture and no worthless instruments will find their way into our warerooms. Call and examine. Guild, Church & Co., 682 Wash'gton St., B'st'n

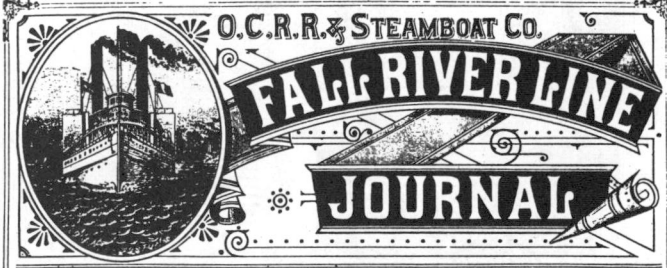

AN ALMOST legendary New England property, The Old Colony Railroad & Steamboat Company and its most famous and affluent subsidiary the Fall River Line for many years paid dividends that paid for mansions on Beacon Hill and carriages by Brewster for the proper Bostonians and was widely regarded as one of the blue chip properties of its time and place. When in 1885 its stock hit 154, the *Boston Post* remarked smugly that "The Old Colony is the most firmly based railroad system on the continent." It is notable that The Old Colony was the key property for control of which the Reading's audacious A. A. McLeod dared battle J. P. Morgan and retired in irretrievable ruin. Its association with the Borden family of Fall River lent it a whiff of the most famous of all nineteenth century murders. Among other superlatives and firsts, The Fall River Line published the first house organ in the record of American commerce *(left)*. One of the worst hazards of its operation in Long Island Sound next to fog was winter ice as depicted above in *Harper's Magazine* for February 1885. When the Fall River Boat was late it was front page news in every New York afternoon paper, but with rare exceptions its arrivals were on the dot and it remained the most reliable communication between Boston and New York until the completion of the New Haven Railroad's Shore Line.

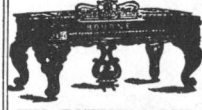

BRIDAL CHAMBER

GRAND SALOON

DINING SALOON.

GRAND STAIR CASE

PILGRIM

IN THE PUBLIC IMAGINATION the *Fall River Boat Train* and the long succession of splendid steamers it served were a single continuous operation, the one as inseparable from the other as the boat trains that met Cunarders at Liverpool and Southampton or the trains that were and still are part of the Channel crossing between London and Paris. With the passing of time, the continuity came to be two dimensional: it joined not only the land and water elements of surface travel, but also the past and present so that a passenger aboard *Commonwealth* or *Priscilla*, was, in a manner of speaking, taking passage with Jim Fisk and President Grant aboard *Bristol*, a vicarious participant in history and in great moments of the nation's past. The Fall River Line and the steamcars of the Old Colony were not only parochial as part of the New England way of life, but came to assume a national dimension, so that when *Pilgrim* was building *(opposite)* it achieved full page space in *Harper's Weekly,* "The Journal of Civilization" and financial writers quoted gossip heard among its influential passengers in much the same way they sought news in the men's bars at the Windsor and the Waldorf. The fine wood engraving of *Pilgrim* under a full moon on its appointed occasions on Long Island Sound was part of a company brochure that sold in thousands at the newsstand of the Old Colony Depot in Boston and aboard the steamer itself.

WHEN it was built in 1890, *Pilgrim*, shown above on the stocks in a drawing for *Harper's Weekly* by Theodore R. Davis, one of the noted news artists of his day, was the largest coastwise vessel in the world and its over-all length of 390 feet was ten feet longer than its companion ship *Bristol*. Its forty-one foot paddle wheels turned on the largest drive shaft ever forged and its thirty-five ton cylinder with its fourteen-foot stroke, shown being hoisted aboard, was the talk of the shipping industry. Comparable to its fabulous statistics was the luxury of its public apartments whose electric lighting was as sensational as its cost which was a staggering million and a half dollars in an era of gold currency. The Fall River Line's pier at the foot of Murray Street in Manhattan was a citadel of water-borne commerce. (*Two Drawings: Kenneth Nims Collection.*)

316

THE TWO Fall River Line steamers most closely associated with Jubilee Jim Fisk were first *Providence* and *Bristol*. It was aboard *Providence* that Fisk, in full nautical regalia as "Admiral" of the Fall River Fleet, entertained President Grant en route to the Peace Jubilee at Boston and, after a superb dinner, approached the Chief Executive with his shady proposal for cornering the gold market. Aboard both *Bristol* and *Providence* eye-popping luxury greeted the customers. Brass bands played far into the night and more than 200 canaries in gold cages sang in *Providence'* public rooms. Four bartenders at a magnificent mahogany bar served oceans of the best of everything. A ship of superlatives to the end, when *Bristol* was destroyed by fire at Newport in 1888 it was the biggest blaze in the history of the seaport. *(Two Pictures: Oliver Jensen Collection.)*

All the Year Round Service.

Throughout the year, other than the midsummer season, the Fall River Line schedule is as follows:

STEAMERS LEAVE NEW YORK

at 5.00 p. m., touching at Newport at 3.15 a. m.; due Fall River, 5.00 a. m. Pullman Vestibuled Express trains leave steamboat wharf, Fall River, at 5.30 and 7.40 a. m., being due at Park Square Station, Boston (New York, New Haven & Hartford Railroad—Old Colony System), at 6.50 and 9.00 a. m. respectively.

FROM THE EAST

Pullman Vestibuled trains leave Park Square Station week-days at 6.00 p. m., connecting with steamers leaving Fall River at 7.40 p. m., touching at Newport an hour later; due in New York 7.00 a. m.

THROUGHOUT the entire latter half of the nineteenth century, *The Fall River Boat Train* and its connecting steamers were institutions of national magnitude. Their princely traffic involved names of universal celebrity so that the least episodes in their operation automatically made headlines. Their regularity, too, without regard to tide or season, was wonderful and an object of great admiration. *(Roger William McAdam Collection.)*

317

"NO VANISHED RAILROAD in all New England seems to dwell quite so sweetly in the memories of those who knew it as The Old Colony," wrote Alvin F. Harlow, dean of Down East railroad historians. "Its very name was a happy conception, a phrase hallowed by centuries of history and harking back to one of the most celebrated events in the chronicles of America: it invited the clustering about it of pleasant associations." From the time of its inception in 1844 until long after it had become part of the operational and financial economy of the New York, New Haven & Hartford, The Old Colony was a railroad that attracted superlatives. Its 600 miles of track, microscopic in comparison with the great transcontinental trunk lines building in the years of its finest flowering, carried such density of traffic and at such rewarding rates that generations of well-placed Bostonians lived in affluence on its dividends. In the nineteenth century it was the superlatively gilt edged railroad property of the continent. Fragrant auspices were present at its inception, for no less notables than Daniel Webster and John Quincy Adams made the dedicatory speeches when it opened. If a panache of sensationalism were needed to lend spice to the Old Colony's well bred aloofness and generally patrician facade, the Fall River Railroad, which soon connected with it, was the private property of the Borden family of Fall River which furnished the folklore of American violence with Lizzie Borden and her axe. By long odds, however, the greatest contribution to the legend of transport of the Old Colony was the Fall River Line Boat Train, a varnish run hallowed by long accustomed usage which, when the end came in 1937, was the oldest name train in the record of American railroading. *The Fall River Boat Train* had run over The Old Colony and its Fall River Railroad connection for ninety years. It had come a far piece in the national epic.

318

THE FIRST SECTION of the Boat Train, carried in later years on the New Haven's schedules as the *Fall River Line Special* which left the wharfside at Fall River at the unearthly hour of 5:30 in the morning, carried neither the parlor cars nor the cachet of splendor that surrounded the later or *real* Boat Train. Below it is depicted with but two coaches paused early of a summer morning on its way to The Hub with early risers, probably about 1910. (*Above: Roger Williams McAdam Collection; Below: Everett De Golyer Collection.*)

DAY EXPRESS TRAIN,

WITH

Pullman Buffet Parlor Cars,

BOSTON, MASS., TO HARRISBURG, PA.

WITHOUT CHANGE.

Poughkeepsie Bridge Route.

Miles.	STATIONS.	Runs week days only.
0	Boston, Mass., { Boston & Maine R. R. / Boston & Lowell Sta'n } lv.	8.00 A. M.
28	Hudson, Mass., B.&M.R.R. "	8 48 "
42	Oakdale, " " "	9.11 "
75	Ware, " " "	10.10 "
97	Amherst, " " "	10 47 "
105	Northampton, " " arr.	11.00 "
	Northampton, " N.Y.,N.H.& H.R.R. lv.	11.00 "
110	Easthampton, " " "	11.18 "
	Holyoke, " " "	10.38 "
121	Westfield, " " "	11.32 "
	Hartford, Conn , C.N.E. & W.R.R. "	11.25 "
139	Simsbury, " " "	12.10 P. M.
159	Winsted, " " "	12.51 "
169	Norfolk, " " "	1.11 "
179	Canaan, " " "	1.32 "
188	Lakeville, " " "	1.54 "
198	Boston Cor's, N.Y., " "	2.10 "
240	Poughkeepsie, " " "	3.25 "
267	Maybrook Jc., " " arr.	4.25 "
	Maybrook Jc., " O.C.R.R. lv.	4.35 "
280	Greycourt, " " "	5.15 "
290	Warwick, " L. & H.R.R. "	5.40 "
343	Belvidere, N. J., " "	7.23 "
357	Phillipsburg, " Penn.R.R. arr.	7.50 "
	Phillipsburg, " C.R.R.of N.J. lv.	8.11 "
358	Easton, Pa., " "	8.17 "
369	Bethlehem, " " "	8.39 "
374	Allentown, " " arr.	8.52 "
	Allentown, " P. & R.R.R. lv.	9.05 "
410	Reading, " " "	10.25 "
438	Lebanon, " " "	11.20 "
464	Harrisburg, " " arr.	12.10 night.

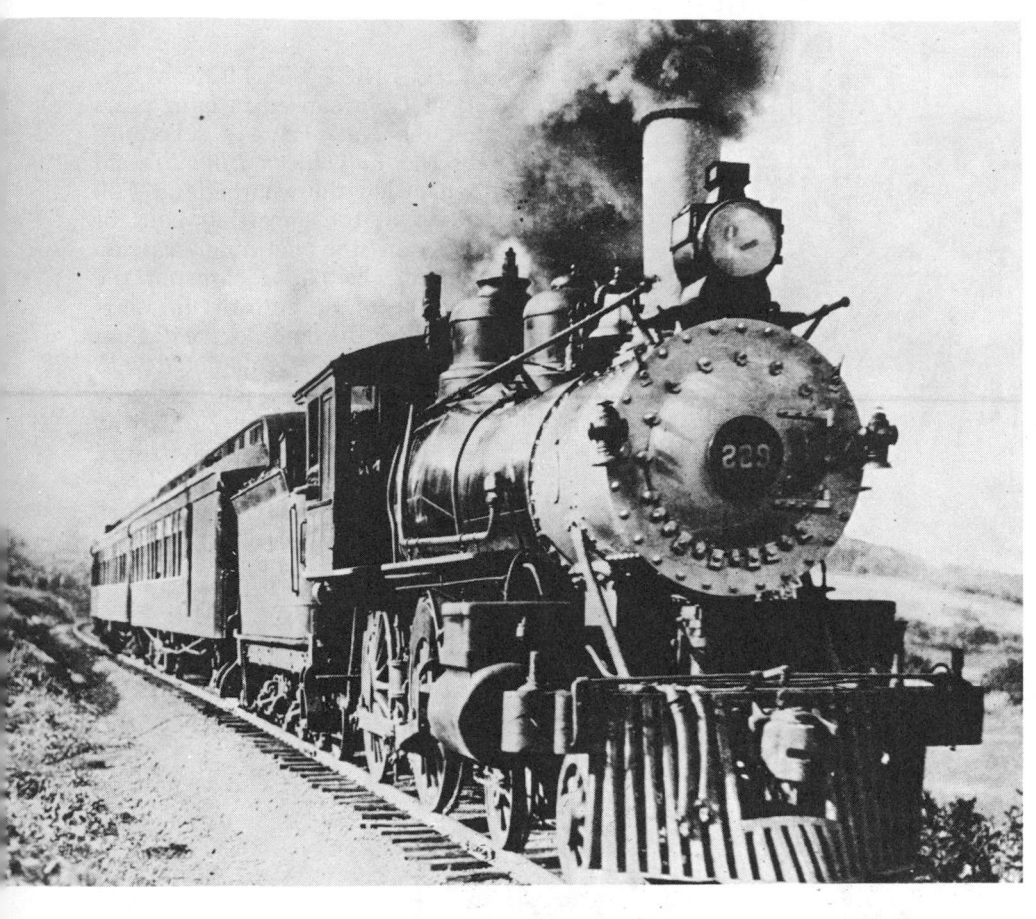

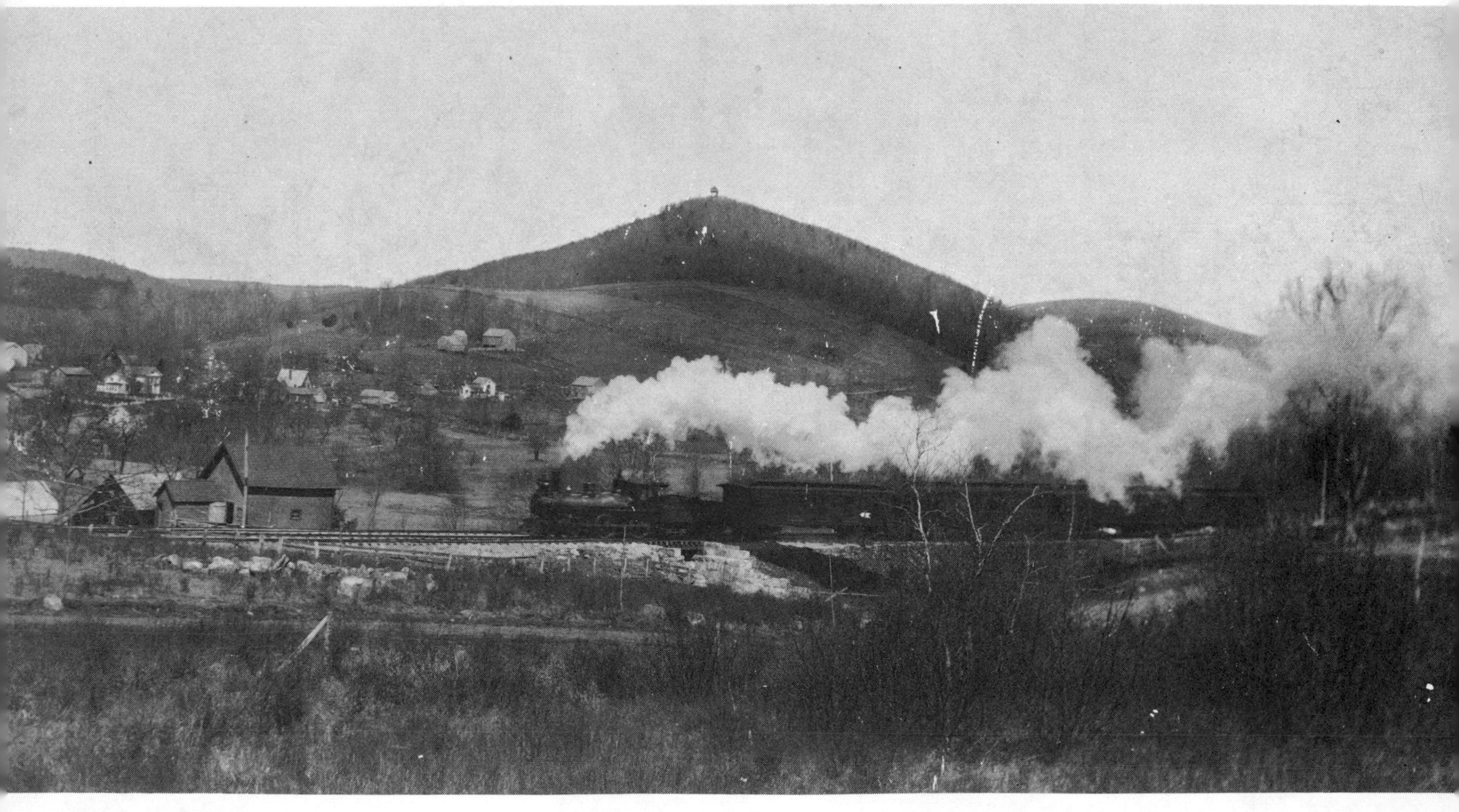

CLOSELY ALLIED to the Central New England & Western Railroad whose *Day Express* between Boston and Harrisburg in 1890 is portrayed on the page opposite, was the Newburgh, Dutchess & Connecticut which connected with the C.N.E. to form a patchwork of little carriers between the Hudson River and Hartford, elements of which were eventually absorbed by the New Haven as part of its Air Line across Connecticut to Boston. Depicted in this pastoral by Howard Fogg is a two-car varnish of the N.D.&C., as it pounded past Briercliffe Farms in 1890 under the proud title of *The Millbrook Special,* a stop only made to take aboard shipments of pheasants raised locally and destined for the tables of the elite of Boston and New York. Crowning glory of *The Millbrook Special* were its weekend runs when its consist included a richly mirrored parlor car with guests bound for

Halcyon Hall, a hilltop resort hotel on its mainline, "the luxury of whose appointments cajoled New Yorkers sufficiently locuplete to meet its tariff," in the words of a contemporary. "How inspiring to watch the eager locomotive leading *The Special* out from Dutchess Junction at five in the afternoon. The watcher could rest assured that No. 10 would land those dainty commuters at Halcyon Hall in season to don their dinner gowns." On the opposite page The Central New England's *Day Express* is depicted with two cars behind C.N.E. No. 229 about 1907 and below, with a four-car consist including the Pullman buffet-parlor car mentioned in the timetable as it passes Haystack Mountain at Norfolk, Connecticut. *(Above, Opposite: Dudley Stickels Collection; Bottom: Everett De Golyer Collection.)*

321

BOSTON'S MASSIVE and historic South Station, shown in the below photograph about 1910, was completed in 1897 and occupied the following year by the New York, New Haven & Hartford and the Boston & Albany Railroads, the latter of which removed from its nearby Kneeland Street station. By 1899, according to the Massachusetts Railroad Commission, the astounding number of 728 trains a day were moving in and out of its vast train shed. The area in the immediate foreground was named Dewey Square in honor of the hero of Manila Bay shortly after the South Station opened and the pylon in front of its main entrance, shown on an adjacent page, was known as The Dewey Memorial. In 1901 the tracks of the Boston Elevated Railway, shown here with a passing train, were built along Atlantic Avenue, connecting directly with the Boston & Maine's North Station on the far side of town, and extending deep into Roxbury to the south. The view to the right depicts the roof of South Station and the back of the great clock tower surmounted by its massive eagle which dominated traffic through the three main doorways to the depot. Through the door admission was gained to the works of the timepiece which for sixty years kept the time of day for a million Bostonians. *(Below: Boston Globe; Right: Herbert H. Harwood Collection.)*

ENTIRE GENERATIONS of Bostonians were accustomed to entrain for social or business occasions in New York or football games at New Haven in South Station's vast and drafty train shed. They took the *Bay State Limited,* shown below, *The Merchants, Knickerbocker* or *The Colonial,* but they never again saw South Station as neat and tidy as at the bottom of the page the week it opened. *(Above: Everett De Golyer Collection; Below: Herbert H. Harwood Collection.)*

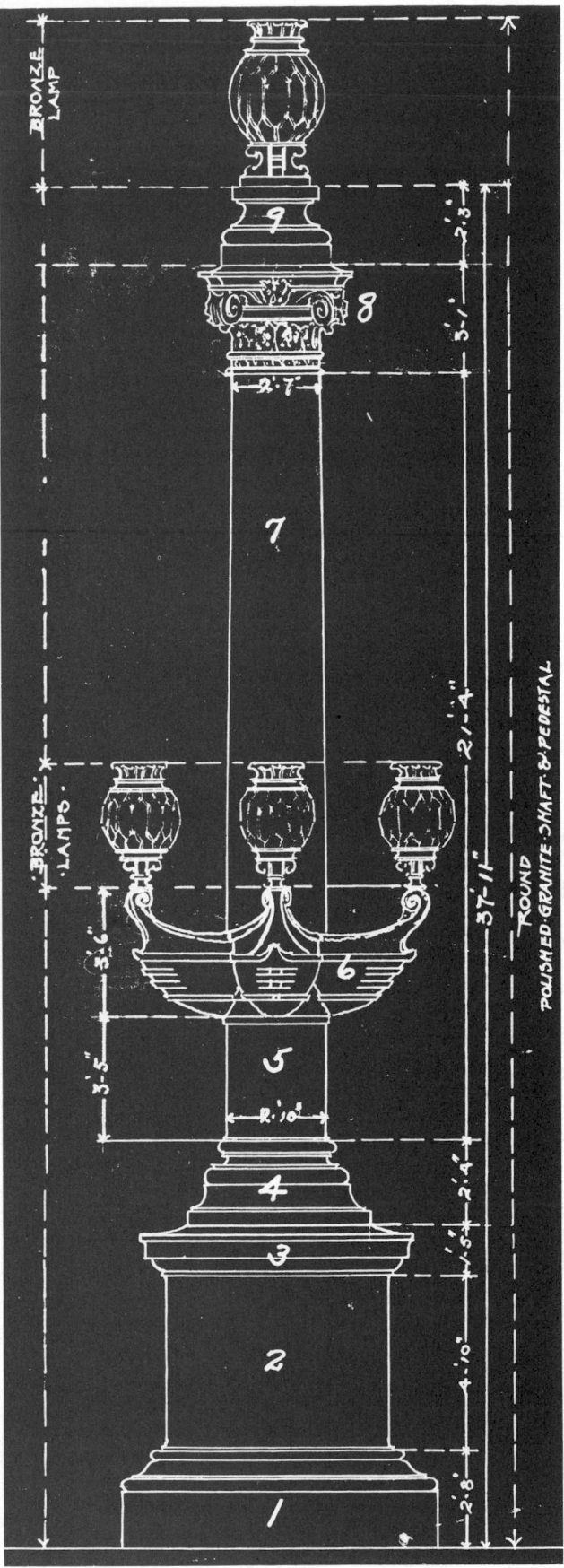

PAST THE ELECTRICALLY LIT PYLON facing on Dewey Square and through the noble portals in the curved facade of Boston's massive South Station millions of persons passed every year upon their occasions with the New Haven Railroad or the Boston & Albany. Built in 1893, the South Station was a Boston landmark and institution comparable to the gilded dome of the State House on Beacon Hill or Deacon Shem Drowne's grasshopper weather vane on Faneuil Hall. For many years the tracks of the elevated giving direct connection to the Boston & Maine's North Station ran directly in front of South Station marring, as some felt, its beauty, but providing rail transport to the rest of a vast metropolitan area. Reproduced here are original blueprint elevations of South Station as designed by the architectural firm of Shepley, Rutan & Coolidge from the files of its successor, Shepley, Bullfinch, Richardson & Abbott.

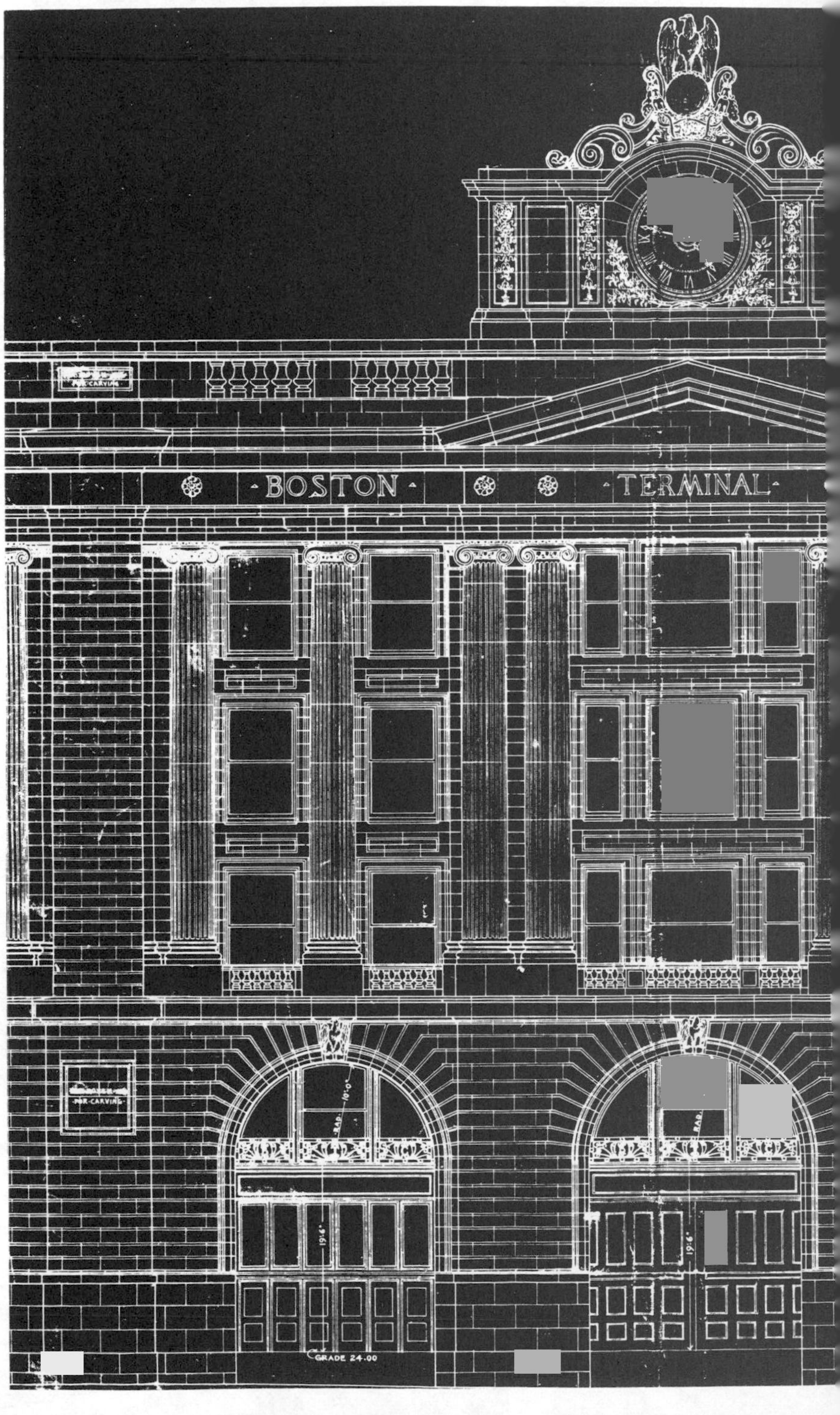

Clock and Balustrade Revised.
See No. 209 and 226.
222. 226.

COMPANY

MUCH RAILROAD HISTORY arrived and departed from the vast arched train shed of the South Station. Until its discontinuance in the thirties it saw the daily cars of *The Fall River Boat Train,* a tangible link with the dawn years of steam transport in New England. Here, too, originated successive generations of the New York, New Haven & Hartford's commuter trains and locals for Boston's South Shore and over the Old Colony route to Cape Cod. The New Haven's name trains on the Shore Line to New York, *The Gilt Edge (above), Knickerbocker Limited, Merchants* and *Yankee Clipper* originated here as did through trains via the Pennsylvania for Pittsburgh, Washington, the Deep South and Florida. Here was the terminal of the Boston & Albany whose train bays knew the Boston sections of *The Century, Wolverine, North Shore Limited* and finally *The New England States.* Life and death, the record of a nation perpetually in movement rode the tides of traffic that made the South Station one of the great railroad depots of the world. *(Everett De Golyer Collection.)*

A TRAIN whose regional connotations of aristocratic aloofness still find occasional echoes around Buzzard's Bay and Falmouth, Massachusetts, was the *Flying Dude* which in the closing decades of the nineteenth century and until the 1914 war whisked affluent passengers from Boston to the resort areas of Western Cape Cod in all the privacy of a gentleman's club and with many of a club's amenities of comfort.

In 1884 the word dude was possessed of a somewhat less parochial significance than it came later to achieve as a synonym for fastidious dress and embraced men of Corinthian tastes and the means for their gratification on a broader scale than merely sartorially.

"The New Haven's *Dude Train's* passengers were hardly dudes in the narrow sense of the word," read a feature on this celebrated flyer in *The Falmouth Enterprise* for October 19, 1945, "but they were folks whose money put them in a class by themselves in the eyes of people who didn't get to ride on the crack train.

"They were dudes in the sense that they could afford a train club and a chartered string of pullmans to take them back and forth between city offices and country homes. They were dudes in that they could enjoy the luxury of great estates along the Falmouth shore. Their names were Beebe, Fay, Weld, Minot, and Emmons and all others remembered as belonging to the Falmouth estates just before and after the turn of the century. Regular passengers were Richard Olney, President Cleveland's secretary of state; John Parkinson, State street banker; the Forbes family of Naushon island.

"In 1884 these men of wealth who summered along the Old Colony railroad line between Falmouth and Wareham arranged to charter a train to make the regular weekday trip between Falmouth and Boston. The private train was given the name *Dude* by its first conductor, Harry Meyers of North Easton, and the name clung. As its speed became matter of public knowledge it was soon called *The Flying Dude.*

"*The Flying Dude* left Boston weekdays at 3:10 p.m. and reached Woods Hole at 4:50 p.m. Returning, it left Woods Hole at 7:40 a.m. and was due in Boston at 9:25 a.m. Its first stop on the Boston to Woods Hole run was Tempest Knob, just below Wareham, where many wealthy families maintained summer homes. Its stops were only where passengers requested. Its passengers were only subscribers. Guests of subscribers were allowed to ride only by presenting a guest card, signed by the subscriber extending the invitation.

"This train streaked through the countryside between Holbrook and Middleboro, attaining a speed of a mile a minute along this stretch. No train since has brought country and city so close together in time. It had the advantage of the best equipment of its day and no stops for commuters along most of its route. In 1892, a Fairhaven *Dude* was added between Boston and Fairhaven. This train was consolidated with the Woods Hole *Dude* in 1896.

"*The Flying Dude* was a First World War casualty. It made its last run on October 2, 1916. There was no *Dude* for the war summer of 1917.

"An investigation by the public service commission in 1914 gave the public an inside picture of the *Dude's* service. The *Enterprise* reported:

"'After considering all the circumstances under which the *Dude Train* is operated by the New York, New Haven & Hartford railroad, the public service commission has decided the arrangements for the summer are in conformity to law and the train will be allowed to run. The railroad has filed its tariff schedule to go into effect June 5 for the private train between Boston and Woods Hole. This service is for the exclusive use of the members of the train club, who have guaranteed the company a minimum income of $22,185 for the season between June 5 and October 5. The passengers will pay the regular local fares, trip rates, excursion or commutation fares obtained on the general service, and will have the privilege of transportation of family supplies, at their own risk, in packages not exceeding 60 pounds. Baggage, dogs, and other articles are to be handled in accordance with the regular tariff. The commission finds there is no discrimination in the arrangement.'

"First equipment of the Woods Hole *Dude* comprised an Old Colony combination (#168), Old Colony Drawing Room Cars *Naushon* and *Mayflower*, which later gave way to Old Colony Drawing Room cars *King Philip* and *Cottage City*. The first locomotive assigned to the *Dude* was FOXBORO No. 100. Equipment was always two parlor cars and a combination baggage-smoker.

"The *Dude's* original train crew included Conductor Harry Meyers, Engineer James Davis, Fireman Edward Proud, Baggagemaster Wyman Lincoln, and Brakeman Walter Pierce. A few years later Augustus S. Messer became the conductor. He served for 14 years.

"When Messer died in May, 1904, he was the oldest conductor in point of service in employ of the New Haven. He had been a conductor for 32 years and all of that time on the Woods Hole and Boston run. Messer was the first conductor to bring a train to Woods Hole when the Old Colony line was extended from Monument Beach in July, 1872."

THE VENERABLE and dignified gentleman on the opposite page was Augustus S. Messer, captain, in the honored parlance of an older time, of the New Haven Railroad's *Flying Dude* over the fourteen-year span from 1890 to 1904. Known, of course, to the elect who rode with him as Mr. Messer, he in turn knew all the subscribers and deferred to their whims as to those of royalty which, after a fashion, they were. He died, quite literally, in harness. The excitement of working the first *Flying Dude* of the summer season of 1904 brought on a fatal stroke, and his obituaries in the New England press were of the sort usually accorded the bankers and merchant princes with whom he was on terms of easy social equality. (*Falmouth (Mass.) Enterprise; George Hough, Jr. Collection.*)

IN SUMMERTIME as was the pleasant custom at many New England resorts of the era, a band was housed in an ornate pavilion at the pierhead to play for the arrival and departure of *Monohansett*. Those not bound for The Sea View Hotel just above the landing, continued across the island on the narrow gauge for Edgartown which met the boats at Oak Bluffs.

"THE PERIOD from about 1870 to 1890 was one of great glory here on The Vineyard," writes Mrs. Henry Beetle Hough, editor of *The Vineyard Gazette* and herself a notable repository of Vineyard erudition and folklore. "There was never such service on the New Haven as when *The Flying Dude* brought us the *old* people of *old* wealth who wouldn't have thanked you for mention of upstart places like Newport." Best remembered of the side-wheel steamers which met *The Flying Dude* at Wood's Hole was *Monohansett* which had been a dispatch boat for General Grant in the Civil War and whose arrival and departure were the social events of the Vineyard day when crowds gathered on the pier and bands played. *Monohansett* was later sold into river service and, sadly, sunk. It was supplanted on the Island run by *Sankaty* and *Gay Head*. (*Two Photos: Elizabeth Bowie Hough Collection.*)

FROM 1884 until its demise in the universal chaos of the Federal government's administration of the railroads during the 1914 war, *The Dude Flyer* was institutional in New England. Its existence was predicated, according to Alvin Harlow, the New Haven's historian, on the whim of the merchant princes of State Street sometimes to have dinner as early as six o'clock on the wide porches of the Sea View Hotel at Martha's Vineyard where, in the solid Boston tradition of conservative money and well bred affluence, they wanted their fresh lobsters boiled with drawn butter and no nonsense about Thermidor or Newburg. Some kept their own *Flying Cloud* Madeira at the Sea View from year to year. The Vineyard's narrow gauge ran through the hotel's front yard and its verandahs afforded a fine view of the steamer landing. Above, in an appropriate setting of tidewater, lobster pots and the summer mansions of the nabobs, *The Dude* is shown on the outskirts of Falmouth. The Sea View is at the left. *(Two Photos: Elizabeth Bowie Hough Collection.)*

329

New York & New England RAILROAD.

DINING CAR SERVICE.

Meals & Beverages

ABOARD THE

New England Limited.

WINE LIST.

CHAMPAGNES.

	QTS.	PTS.
Pommery & Greno (Sec)	$3.50	$2.00
G. H. Mumm's (Extra Dry)	3.50	2.00
Perrier, Jouet & Co., Extra Dry, Special	3.50	2.00
Moet & Chandon	3.50	2.00
Jules Mumm & Co., "Grand Sec" (½ pints)		1.00

WHITE WINES.

Brandenberg Frere's Latour Blanche, 1874	2.50	1.50
" " Haut Sauternes	1.25	.75

CLARET WINES.

Brandenberg Frere's St. Julien, 1873	1.00	.50
" " Pontet Canet, 1878	2.00	1.00
" " Chateau La Rose	3.50	1.75

HOCK.

Ruedesheimer, 1868	2.00	1.00
Niersteiner, C. Lauteren, 1876	1.50	.75

CORDIALS, WINES, LIQUORS, Etc.

Bass' Pale Ale and Guinness' Dublin Porter	.30
Belfast Ginger Ale	.25
Hygeia Club Soda	.25
Apollinaris Water	.25
Hathorn Water	.25
St. Louis Lager Beer	.20
Pierce's Cider	.25
Bergner and Engle Tannhaeuser Beer	.20

	GLASS.
Lemonade	.15
Amontillado Sherry	.20
Old Sour Mash Whiskey	.20
Fine Old Monongahela Whiskey	.20
Vieux Cognac (Pony, 25 cents), 1842	.40
Old Tom Gin	.20
Cream de Minte	.20
Benedictine	.20
Chartreuse, Yellow	.20
Maraschino	.20
Vermouth	.20

Imported Cigars, selected, 10, 15, 20, and 25 cents
Cigarettes, 25 cents.

Playing Cards, 50 Cents per Pack.

11-3-'91.

THE WHITE TRAIN made operational stops at Middletown, shown here in 1895, not so much to pick up and set down passengers as to get a clearance for crossing the tracks of the Hartford & Connecticut River Railroad between Saybrook and Hartford and shown on the far side of the depot. *(Kaufmann & Fabry.)*

WILLIMANTIC platform was a scene of great activity as the arrival of *The White Train* impended.

DURING the brief interlude when its cream and gold livery, the uniforms of its personnel and even the whitewashed coal in its tender got for it the name of "The White Train," *The New England Limited* over the tracks of the New York & New England and the New Haven between Boston and New York in six hours was one of the most famous trains in the world. The wine card shown opposite so closely duplicated that of the Boston & Albany's *Boston & Chicago Special*, then the crack train between New England and Lake Michigan, that it is reasonable to suppose it was composed by the same wine merchants. This could have been either the patriarchal Boston firm of S. S. Pierce or the equally respected Cobb, Bates & Yerxa. *(Three Photos: Everett De Golyer Collection.)*

331

THE New York & New England's
Air Line Limited, although
it never achieved the celebrity which
caused Rudyard Kipling, then a
Vermont visitor, to pen a short story about
"The White Train," was very much
a run of breeding and pedigree.
Its clientele alone saw to that. Five o'clock
tea for the brahmins of Beacon Hill,
as well as beverages featuring
Lawrence's Medford Rum, equally in
favor with the Boston carriage trade, had
their origins in the buffet galley
shown at the right.
The Air Line Limited itself, posed
below behind one of the twin
headlight Rogers locomotives specially
built for the run, lasted until 1902
when it was supplanted by *The Knickerbocker Limited.* (Two Photos:
Smithsonian Institution.)

A DECADE before the New Haven's Shore Line Route between Boston and New York along the margins of Long Island Sound was made an all-rail connection by the elimination of two ferries across the Thames and the Connecticut Rivers, the favored route between the two cities was the New York & New England-New Haven connection via the so-called Air Line through Central Connecticut. Over this speedy right of way the crack daylight varnish was *The New England Limited* with a six-hour carding between its terminals and which, for a brief interlude in the nineties, achieved world celebrity when its short-lived cream and gold livery got it the name of "The White Train." When operation of "The White Train" proved impracticable and it was suspended in 1895, its successor was *The Air Line Limited* which now made the run in five hours with only a single operational stop at Middletown, Connecticut. This carding so enraged New Haven that it was shortly found prudent to include a pause for passengers at the Elm City. Hallmark of *The Air Line Limited* were twin headlight engines which were assigned power on the New Haven as well as the New England end of the run. In its later years venturesome patrons of *The Air Line Limited* might view the speeding countryside from wicker armchairs on the ornately railed observation platform shown above. (*The Smithsonian Institution.*)

333

BY THE YEAR 1911 when this atmospheric photograph was taken by W. G. Landon, a New York Central locomotive driver, the New Haven had added *The Bankers Express*, shown here, and *The Gilt Edge* to its fleet of Shore Line flyers. The cream of the Boston-Washington traffic, carried by *The Colonial Express* and *The Federal*, no longer went around New York City aboard a car ferry as shown on the timetable opposite. They went under Manhattan Island and the East and North Rivers via the tunnels of Alexander Cassatt's Pennsylvania connection. *(W. G. Landon.)*

THE NEW HAVEN's Shore Line service between Boston and New York entered the realm of modern luxury travel with the inaugural in 1903 of the all-Pullman, extra-fare *Merchants Limited,* the interior of one of whose first parlor cars, shown here, was still lit by Pintsch gas as a concession to Boston's inbred conservatism. In 1905, the company timetable listed three extra-fare trains, *The Bay State, The Merchants* and *The Knickerbocker.* A fourth, *The Mayflower,* was added the following year. The newspaper account of the inaugural of *The Merchants Limited* is from *The Boston Globe,* December 15, 1903. *(Pullman Standard: Kenneth Nims Collection.)*

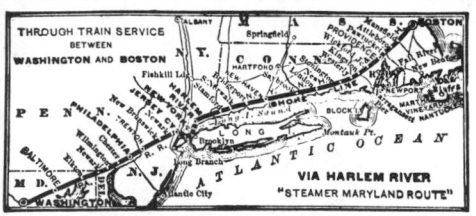

THROUGH TRAIN SERVICE
BETWEEN
WASHINGTON AND BOSTON

VIA HARLEM RIVER
"STEAMER MARYLAND ROUTE"

Colonial Express	Federal Express
Pullman Vestibuled Day Train Daily, Sundays Excepted	Pullman Vestibuled Night Train Daily, Sundays Included

Through Washington, Baltimore, from Philadelphia and Boston

Through Service via Pennsylvania Railroad, Steamer Maryland Transfer and Shore Line

Colonial Express (Daily Sundays excepted)	Federal Express Daily	Miles	STATIONS.	Colonial Express (Daily Sundays excepted)	Federal Express Daily
AM	PM		READ DOWN. READ UP.	PM	AM
7.40	5 35	-	Lv.... WASHINGTON .... Ar	9.44	9.45
8.40	6.35	43	"......Baltimore..... "	8.43	8.41
		78	"...Havre-de-Grace.. "	7.51	
		79	"......Perryville.... "	7.47	
		94	"......Elkton....... "	7.25	
g10.02	8.06	112	"....Wilmington..... "	g7.00	7.15
		126	"......Chester...... "	g6.41	
10 50	8.55	139	"..Philadel phia, Broad St.. "	6.10	6.15
g10 54	g8 59		"..West Philadelphia.. "	g6.06	g6.11
g11.01	g9 07	145	"..North Philadelphia.. "	g5.58	g6.02
g11.33	g9 42	173	"......Trenton...... "	g5 21	g5.26
g12.34	g10.48	221	"......Newark...... "	g4 28	g4 33
	1 43	268	Ar .....Stamford.... Lv		1.07
3.24	1.57	276	"....South Norwalk.. "	1 40	12.53
3.46	2.19	290	"......Bridgeport.... "	k1.24	12.30
4 15	2.46	308	"......New Haven.... "	1 00	12.00
5 28	3.59	359	"......New London.... "	11.40	10.43
		373	"......Stonington.... "		
06 07	04.40	379	"......Westerly..... "	11.10	10 08
6 31		396	"......Kingston..... "		r9145
	75.16	403	"....Wickford Junction.. "		r9133
		403	"....East Greenwich.. "		
7.13	6.50	423	"......Providence.... "	10.07	9.07
	6.11	427	"......Pawtucket.... "		
	6 36	442	"......Mansfield..... "		
8 15	7.13		"......Boston, Back Bay.. "	9.04	8.04
8.20	7.18	467	Ar. BOSTON SO. STATION. Lv	9.00	8.00
PM	AM			AM	PM

g Stops only to take passengers for or leave passengers from points East of Harlem River
/ Stop on signal only.
k Stops only on signal to take passengers for points west of Jersey City.
l Stops to leave passengers from or take passengers for New Haven and beyond.
§ Sundays only.
o Stops only to leave passengers from south of Jersey City.
v Stops only to take passengers for New London and beyond, until Nov. 1.

EQUIPMENT OF TRAINS.

The ' Colonial Express" consisting of Parlor Buffet Smoking Car, Parlor Cars and Day Coaches, all vestibuled, Washington and Boston. Dining Car South Norwalk and Boston.
Food will not be served from Buffet while Dining Car is attached.

The * Federal Express" has Pullman Vestibuled Sleeping Car, Washington and Boston; Pullman Vestibuled Sleeping Car, Philadelphia and Boston; Passenger Coach, Washington and Boston; and Dining Car, Washington and Philadelphia.

THROUGH TICKETS AND PULLMAN ACCOMMODATIONS.

In Washington: Northeast corner 15th and G Streets, N. W., and Station corner 6th and B Streets.
In Baltimore: Northeast corner Baltimore and Calvert Streets, and Union Station.
In Philadelphia: No. 838 Chestnut Street, No. 1411 Chestnut Street, No. 4 Chelton Avenue, Germantown, and Broad Street Station.

Three Splendid Trains

Between New York and Boston

The Bay State
The Knickerbocker
The Merchants

These are limited trains---but it costs only a little more to travel on them than on the regular trains.

You pay extra for luxury and magnificence.

The hours of departure are the same in either direction--- very convenient.

FIVE-HOUR TRAINS

From New York and from Boston at the same hour

10:00 A.M.   The Bay State Limited. Compartment and Buffet Smoker. Dining Car.

1:00 P.M.   The Knickerbocker Limited. Compartment and Buffet Smoking Car. Dining Car.

5:00 P.M.   The Merchants Limited. Dining Car and Buffet Smoking Car.

A special form of ticket will be required for passage on these trains

Telephone N. J. Lee, General Agent, Grand Central Station, 3600— 38th Street, for information

New York, New Haven & Hartford Railroad

ANOTHER FLYER STARTS.

New Five-Hour Train to New York Leaves on First Trip—Inauguration Very Successful.

With wreaths of steam curling triumphantly around her cylinders, locomotive 609 of the New York, New Haven & Hartford railroad last evening slowly drew from the chilly train shed of the South station the "Merchants' Limited" for New York, and the new five-hour 5 p m train put on by Pres C. S. Mellen for the special benefit of Boston business men was on its first journey.

Success of a pronounced kind attended the inauguration of the new train, for not only were all the seats in the four parlor cars originally assigned to the train purchased in advance, but every seat in an additional parlor car was taken.

In addition to parlor cars 2173, 2183, 2172 and 2179, all handsomely upholstered in blue silk plush, the train included drawing room car 2239, having baggage compartment in the forward end, and the dining car Bronx.

The equipment is much the same as that which has been used in connection with the Bay State limited, the diner being a beautiful new car finished in dark oak.

The train was in charge of conductor Oliver H. Ingalls, who for a long time ran on the Knickerbocker limited, and who six months ago took charge of the Colonial express.

The parlor car conductor is J. A. Morse, another veteran employe, who has latterly been on the Gilt Edge train, and who for 13 years previous to that ran the Shore line express.

The dining car carries a staff of nine, in charge of C. E. Foley, the chef being Martin Moore. For the engine crew two of the best men in the entire system have been detailed, engineer Henry L. Stearns and fireman J. H. Flynn.

The entire train crew is to run through to New Haven, except those in charge of the dining car, which goes no farther than New London on the run to New York.

The new train is to run every week day, leaving both Boston and New York at 5 p m and running through in five hours. Stops are made only at Back Bay station, Providence, New London and New Haven. The train staff will include a maid, who will look after the comfort of women passengers.

CITADEL AND STRONGHOLD of the entrenched power of the Vanderbilt lines and command post from which orders went out to all points on the New York Central and its allied, interdependent and subsidiary carriers, Grand Central Terminal was very much one of the sights of New York in the year 1900 when the above photograph was taken showing the east portion of the Forty-second Street facade housing the public rooms and offices of the New York, New Haven & Hartford Railroad. Hansoms and growlers lined what is now the intersection of Forty-second Street and Park Avenue South, while, at the extreme right, summer awnings shade the windows of Simeon Ford's Grand Union Hotel. At the right is the stairway leading to the freight annex offices off the New Haven waiting room and to the elevated station in the street. On the page opposite is the dead-end carriage entry where drivers awaited the arrival of New Haven trains in 1900. In the background is the train shed itself. *(Above: New Haven Railroad; Right: Smithsonian Institution; Opposite, Two Photos: Everett De Golyer Collection.)*

On the Shore Line run east of New Haven, the *Mail & Express* in 1910 was headed by a classic 4-4-0 on a winter's day near Madison. *(Everett De Golyer Collection.)*

NEW-YORK & HARLEM R.R.
N. YORK & NEW-HAVEN R.R.
TRAL & HUDSON R.R.R.
RESTAURANT.
TAURANT

A. F. BISHOP'S action shot of *The Shore Line Express* taken in 1895 at North Haven, Connecticut, when that now populous suburb was largely unbuilt countryside, despite the dazzling maintenance of the New Haven's capped-stack No. 128 with its brass candlesticks and polished cylinder heads, shows a remarkable lack of uniformity in the cars on its drawbar. Ancient flat roof coaches alternate with more recent mail and baggage cars with ventilated clerestories while a solitary parlor car brings up at the rear.   *(Everett De Golyer Collection.)*

THE TWO VIEWS opposite of the New Haven's or eastern end of Grand Central taken in the nineties depict the famous New York landmark in its most ornate aspect before the Forty-second Street facade with its fine marble trim was sheathed in brownstone and its Mansard turrets altered to resemble Mooresque domes. The corner of Park Avenue occupied in the lower view by the Park Avenue Oyster Bar was shortly, in 1907, to be the site of the swaggering Belmont Hotel. The cab rank, filled with growlers in this photograph, was in that year to be occupied by one of the first fleets of the new French-built auto-taxis of the New York Taxicab Company, "bright red with green panels and equipped with odometers." Other stands were soon established at The Plaza, St. Regis, the Netherlands hotels and at Rector's Restaurant. *(Two Photos: Everett De Golyer Collection.)*

339

THE VIEW OF GRAND CENTRAL reproduced at the right and showing the north facade and train shed can be dated with some accuracy by the presence of the Belmont Hotel rising in the background, which was completed in 1908, and the circumstance that the original Vanderbilt train shed was torn down to make way for the present structure in 1910. The Belmont Hotel, built by August Belmont II, the Rothschilds' American representative and also the builder of Belmont Park, was closely connected with the destinies of the New Haven Railroad from which a large portion of its patronage derived. Bostonians on their business and social occasions favored the hotel because it was connected by a private passageway under Forty-second Street with the traingate area from which departed the *Merchants Limited, The Gilt Edge* and other Shore Line extra fare flyers. The Belmont was a victim, in the thirties, of predatory progress and when it was torn down, ironically, to make way for an air line office, its fishball breakfasts for Bostonians just off *The Owl* became only a memory. Another hotel of more than regional celebrity, the Manhattan, a block west on Forty-second Street rises above the train shed at the right. Below is shown *The Merchants Limited* southbound in the early years of the road's electrification west of Stamford. (*Three Photos: Everett De Golyer Collection.*)

The Merchants Limited Over The Shore Line

"The Best Thing About Boston Is The Five O'Clock Train to New York"

FOR NEARLY THREE DECADES beginning shortly after the turn of the century the New Haven's two candy trains between Boston and New York were the *Knickerbocker Limited* and *The Merchants Limited* regionally known as The One O'Clock and The Five O'Clock, respectively. Both were all-Pullman, extra fare prestige runs and generally regarded as flagships of the New Haven fleet. Elsewhere on the Shore Line timecard were *The Gilt Edge, The Shore Line Express, The Bankers, The 42nd Street Express, The Owl* at midnight and *The Senator* and *Colonial* on the through Boston-Washington run, at first via car ferry across the North River and later over Hell Gate Bridge. On the sumptuously maintained *Knickerbocker* and *Merchants* rode, in consideration of a $2.50 surcharge, the Brahmins of Beacon Hill and bankers of State Street. George Santayana could be encountered in the club car drinking Scotch purveyed by S. S. Pierce, and in the diner might be Hooper Hooper, the aristocratic Commonwealth Avenue wine merchant whose morning coats and tilted tile hats were Boston landmarks. New Haven diners were famous for their scrodded haddock, boiled Maine lobster, Cotuit oysters and for dessert, a special brand of figs in syrup. Patronage of *The Merchants* was masculine in a proportion of nearly ten to one, filling its two diners, two club cars and parlor cars suited to the season with satraps of Lee Higginson and viceroys of Stone & Webster. The bar stewards were busy serving Heublein's martinis and Upmann Specials to Robert Lincoln O'Brien of *The Boston Herald* and Serge Kousevitsky of the Boston Symphony. Excepting only *The Century* and perhaps *The Overland Limited,* no trains in America carried more celebrities than the New Haven's showpieces and none at all such a density of Boston *bon ton,* grandees and economic royalty. Conductors on the two trains were among the last to wear blue frock coats of office and a pink in their buttonholes, dining cars stewards wore morning coats and striped trousers, and Fred Wright, senior colored porter on *The Merchants* observation lounge, was popularly believed to be second only to the revered Charles Alexander, society editor of *The Boston Evening Transcript,* as an authority on the first families of the Back Bay and Brookline. Both trains enjoyed a radiant contemporary press at their two terminals and once, when a well mannered mouse was discovered to be riding back and forth as occupant of a parlor car (what else?) an editorial campaign was waged at both ends of the run to prevent his eviction. *The Merchants* is shown opposite in 1911 under the catenaries of the electrified end of the run by W. G. Landon.

ABOARD THE NEW HAVEN'S parlor cars of
the ball-fringe era and later assigned to
extra fare trains tea was served at an
appropriate hour in the afternoon accompanied
by Huntley & Palmer's English sweet biscuit
from the firm of S. S. Pierce, the
patriarchal grocery firm of Copley Square.
To smoke the cigars for which she
was celebrated Miss Amy Lowell was usually
asked please to step into the club car of
The Merchants or *Knickerbocker*
in an age when these premises were conventionally reserved for masculine passengers.
It was felt by the New Haven's
management that the sister of the President
of Harvard University was sufficiently
worldly to associate on terms of equality with
patrons who carried with them overtones
of the Somerset Club in Beacon Street
even when they traveled. *(Houghton Mifflin.)*

"THE BEST THING ABOUT BOSTON," declared Arnold Bennett, the celebrated English novelist who found everything about The Hub too British for endurance, "is the five o'clock train that takes you away from there to New York." Bennett's approval, even though ambiguously bestowed, was not ungratifying to the New Haven Railroad, for Bennett was one of the foremost of all admirers of the grand manner and his novel "Hotel Imperial" centering about the Savoy in London was already a classic. *The Merchants* at five o'clock and its opposite number, *The Knickerbocker* at one o'clock also figured largely in "They Told Barron," the reminiscences of conversations with tycoons of banking and industry by the owner of *The Wall Street Journal* and *The Boston News Bureau*. Clarence Barron was a regular aboard the New Haven cars where his aggressive whiskers, braided edge morning coats and benevolent regard for dining car stewards and waiters who fed him good things were recognized properties of the New England twenties and thirties. At times so great was the demand for parlor car space on the all-Pullman *Merchants*, shown at speed south of Boston on the page opposite, that, as was the practice with *The Century*, an *Advance Merchants* ran fifteen minutes ahead of the regular section. At the bottom of the page opposite, *The Merchants* companion train *The Knickerbocker Limited*, four hours ahead of it, pulls out of New Haven depot behind an electric motor. To counteract the reputation of *The Merchants* for being a gentleman's club to the virtual exclusion of women, the carrier, as depicted at the right, at one time circulated specially posed promotion photos to encourage feminine patronage. *(Opposite, Two Photos: Rail Photo Service; Right, Above: Douglas Wornom Collection; Below: New Haven Railroad.)*

344

345

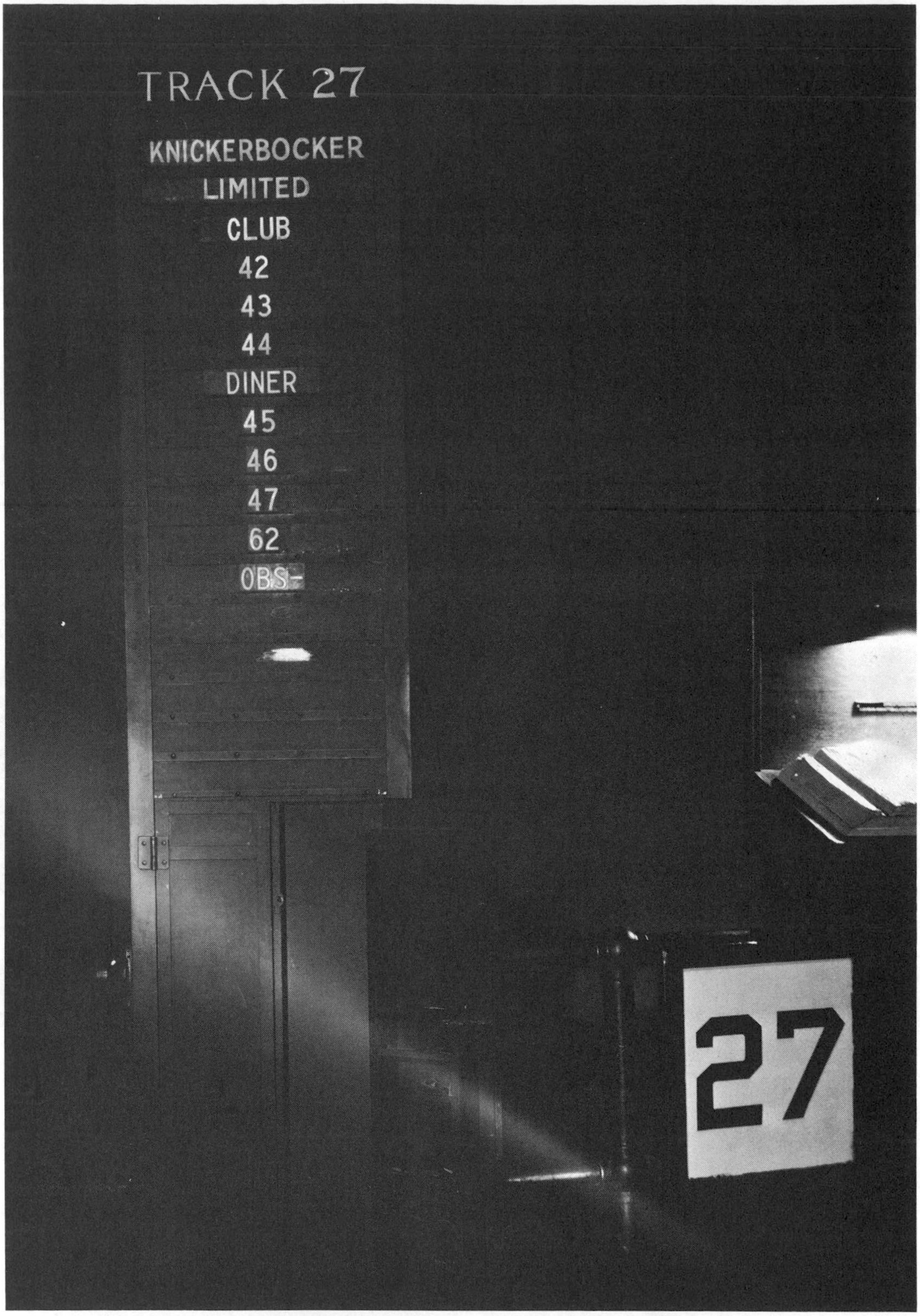

TRACK 27

KNICKERBOCKER
LIMITED
CLUB
42
43
44
DINER
45
46
47
62
OBS-

27

THE TRAIN of Boston's bankers, brokers and financial power structure usually was the *Merchants Limited* because of its five o'clock departure from South Station and Grand Central, but the town's literary and communications establishment as represented at the right took the *Knickerbocker* whose one o'clock sailing got them to their destinations in time for dinner. The New Haven itself figured largely in the novels of John Marquand *(left)* notably "Wickford Point" whose protagonist was a regular and commented at length on the folkways of its nocturnal Pullmans. President Abbott Lawrence Lowell of Harvard, a towering magnifico *(center)* admired the scrod in the New Haven diners, while Robert Lincoln O'Brien, editor of the *Boston Herald,* was hatchet man and aristocratic fixer for Boston's complicated interlocking directorates. *(Little Brown: Harvard University; The Boston Herald.)*

IN THE YEAR 1911, as depicted above in a dramatic panorama by W. G. Landon, himself a New York Central engineer and pioneer action photographer, *The Knickerbocker Limited* is the center of three trains preparing to highball from Boston's South Station behind a light Pacific with neatly silvered smokebox. New Haven trains often left South Station only half filled but picked up a capacity load at Back Bay which was more convenient to the social faubourgs that supplied their Pullman clientele.

SECOND ONLY to the enduring celebrity of Stamford as an enclave of well upholstered commuters to Madison Avenue and Wall Street, Westport on the New Haven and Saugatuck, which held joint tenure on the carrier's depot, were synonymous with the upper income brackets of the impressive concentration of writers, artists, advertising nabobs, magazine editors and playwrights whose persons haunted its platform in the morning and whose chauffeured station wagons met the up-cars at night. Here under the postered gaze of participants in current Broadway productions and the whiskies and cigarets favored by men of distinction, brief-cased and Brooks suited, the executives plotted advertising campaigns with their peers or sought privacy behind the *Wall Street Journal* as temperament or degree of hangover decreed. In Grand Central, the New Haven's glittering *Knickerbocker Limited,* until it was replaced with *The Yankee Clipper,* in the thirties shared train gates and loading platforms with the Central's *Exposition Flyer.* (Right: New York Central; Below: Everett De Golyer Collection.)

AGAINST a background of looming summer thunder clouds and under the New Haven's symmetry of electric catenaries and signal bridges, the road's crack *Knickerbocker Limited* over the Shore Line from Boston rolls toward Grand Central on its appointed schedule in all-Pullman, extra-fare splendor. (*Ewing Galloway.*)

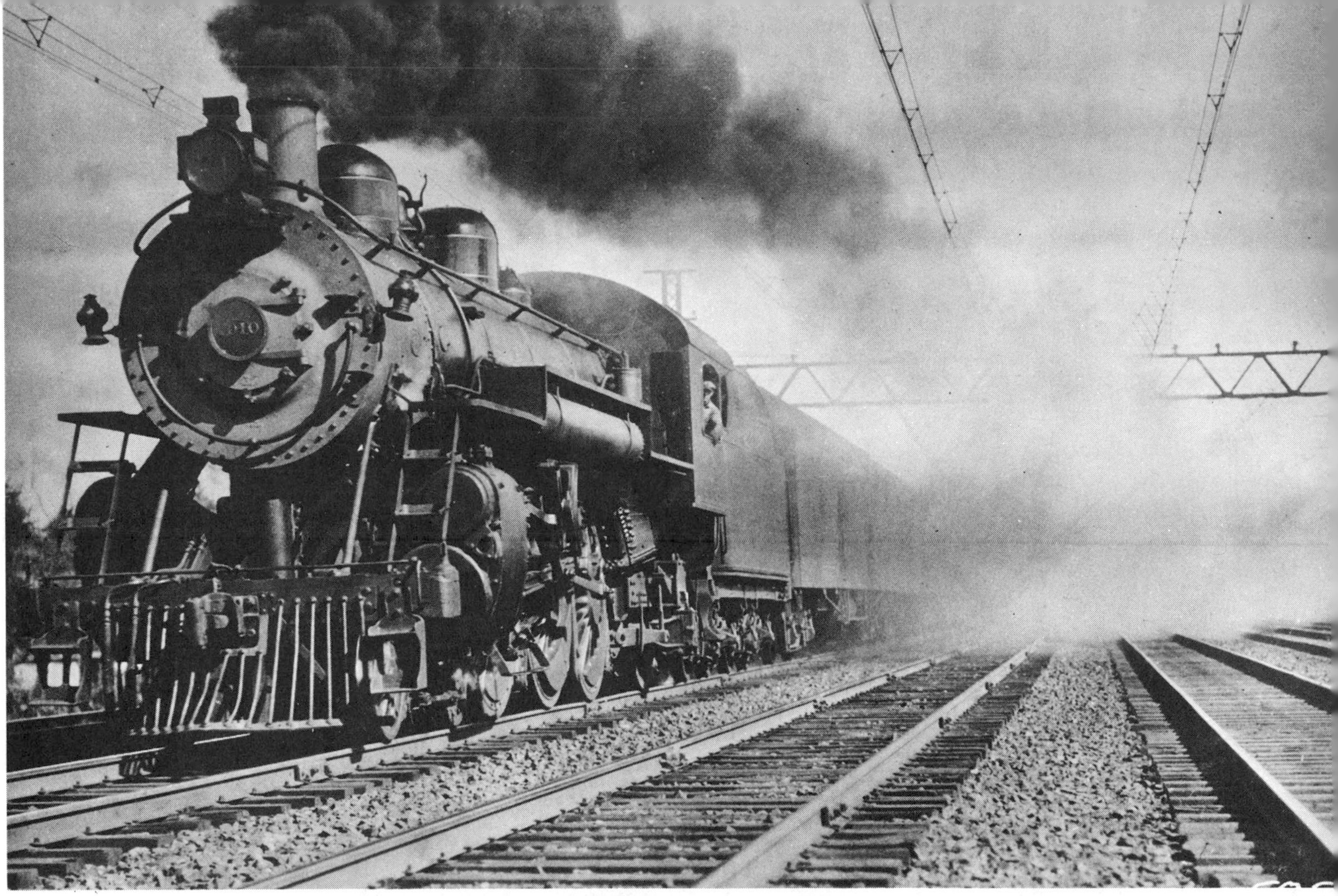

CKETS AT THE GATES
ALL PASSENGERS W
TRACK 27
TRACK 26
PULLMAN
CAR
NUMBERS
CLUB
45
44
216
168
46
DINER
72
43
85
42
OBS-
20TH CENTURY
LIMITED
2·45 P. M.
CHICAGO
12·00 NOON
KNICKERBOCKER
LIMITED
PARLOR CARS ONLY
NEW HAVEN
NEW LONDON
PROVIDENCE
BOSTON
PULLMAN
CAR
NUMBERS
40
41
42
DINER
43
44
49
OBS-

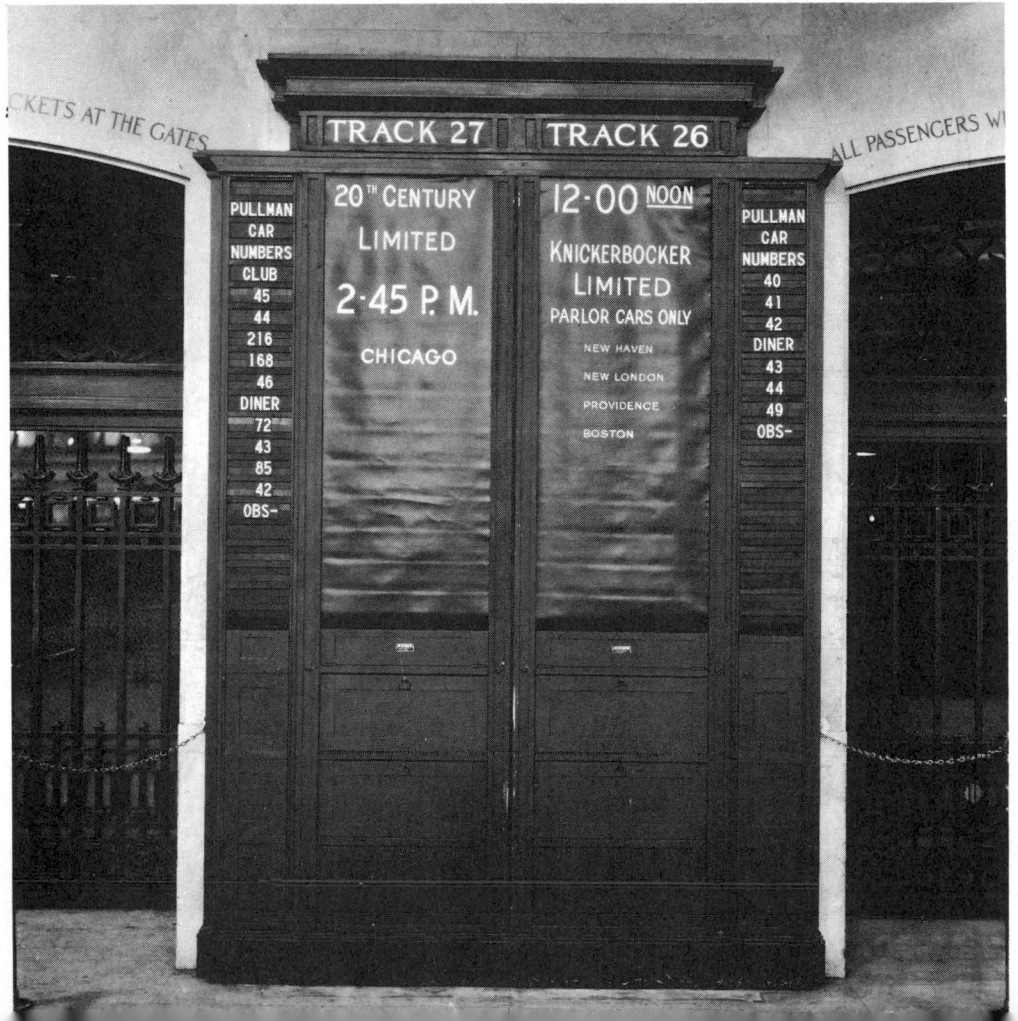

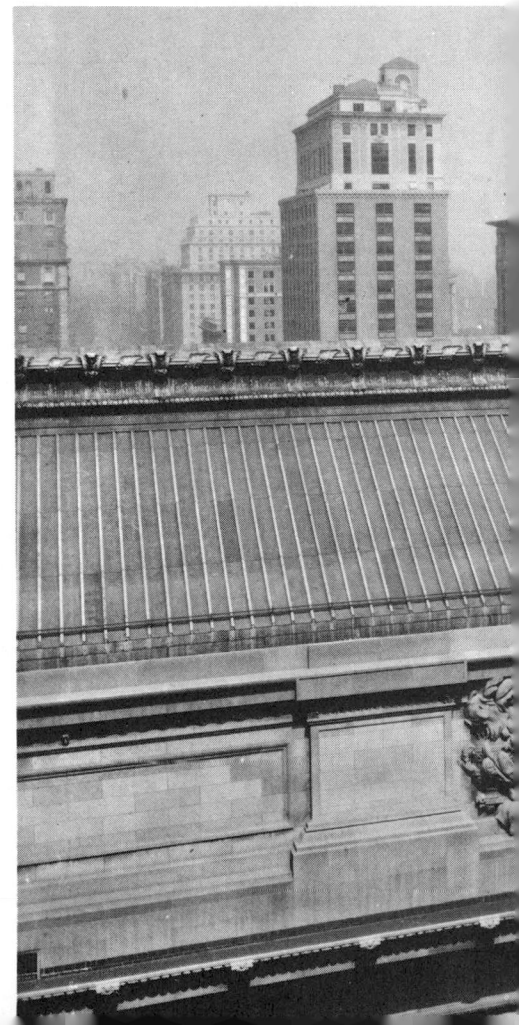

IN THE NEW HAVEN's glory years, circa 1910, *The Gilt Edge* is shown on the page opposite running in steam under the catenaries which then carried electrification as far as Stamford. Happily named (for the New Haven was even then a blue chip investment) it was the peer on the Shore Line run with *The Bay State, The Bankers, Puritan* and, of course, the aloof and extra fare *Merchants* and *Knickerbocker*. It was no accident of chance that the last of these should be scheduled to depart *(below)* from a track at Grand Central adjacent to that of *The Century*. Each was the flagship of a fleet of magnificent name trains that enjoyed at once the regard of their own management, the envy of the competition and the admiration of the great world which comprised their sailing lists. Here a venerable New Haven porter assists a patron aboard the cars at approximately the same period, a respected functionary and, in many cases a personal friend of the regulars who rode with him. *(Opposite: The Smithsonian Institution, The New York Central; Left: Everett De Golyer Collection.)*

WHETHER the group atop the south facade of Grand Central Terminal represents, as some say, The Glory of Commerce or, as another school maintains, The Spirit of Transportation, no one has arisen to deny its place as one of the landmarks of New York in the twentieth century. Devised by the French sculptor Jules Coutan, the figure of Mercury alone is twenty-eight feet high, the dial of the clock thirteen feet in diameter and the width of the entire group fifty feet. From beneath it, the New York Central's trains depart under potent auspices. *(New York Central.)*

351

NEW HAVEN TRAINS such as *The Senator* shown below on the long curve at North Haven, Connecticut, crossed the East River on Hell Gate Bridge, plunged under it through the Long Island tunnel, paused briefly in the stone and steel grottos of Penn Station and emerged behind Pennsylvania motive power from the Hudson River tunnel as shown at the right. Its subterranean progress unhindered by geography or the elements was one of the wonders of the engineering age. *(Two Photos: Everett De Golyer Collection.)*

OF THE FOUR MAJOR CARRIERS with direct access to Manhattan Island only one, The New Haven, could claim availability at both of the great terminal depots which confronted each other as symbols of the unceasing hostility of the New York Central and the Pennsylvania. Direct connections to and from over the Shore Line and via Hell Gate Bridge were made with the Pennsylvania at Penn Station where New Haven electric motive power took over name trains from the south and west and where passengers from Florida, Washington, Pittsburgh and St. Louis slept in their staterooms or dined or dozed without conscious awareness of the interchange between one great mainline carrier and another. Here a dry point etching suggests the relaxed atmosphere of Penn Station in the dawn hours while far below the sleepers rumble through on their comfortable occasions. (*Pennsylvania Railroad.*)

353

DESPITE the circumstance that *The Owl* was institutional and needed no more advertising than the circus, the New Haven maintained a brisk campaign for its promotion in the thirties both with house ads and photographic handouts. *(New Haven Railroad.)*

THE NARRAGANSETT, as suggested by the train boards in the photograph opposite was the all-coach companion overnight run between Boston and New York to *The Owl.* Sometimes it carried the Providence sleeper and usually, as in the photograph at the left behind one of the streamlined Hudsons, lots of head end as it rolled toward Boston on a summer's morning in the late 1930s. *(Everett De Golyer Collection.)*

THE NEW HAVEN's *Owl*, which ran on a leisurely schedule and often in several sections over the Shore Line between Boston and New York with a midnight departure at either end, was for many years a Pullman only train and carried only as many passengers as held sleeping space. An extremely decelerated carding used up six and a half hours against *The Clipper's* four and a half and its late departure made evening engagements at either terminal possible. Single bedroom cars restfully named *Night Sky, Night Haven* and *Night Cove* were in great request even in the depths of the depression of the 1930s. Above *The Owl* heads into the home stretch for Manhattan somewhere west of Stamford on a summer's morning in the early years of electrification. Its departure *(left)* was a Grand Central ritual second only to that of *The Century.* (Above: Everett De Golyer Collection; Left: New Haven Railroad.)

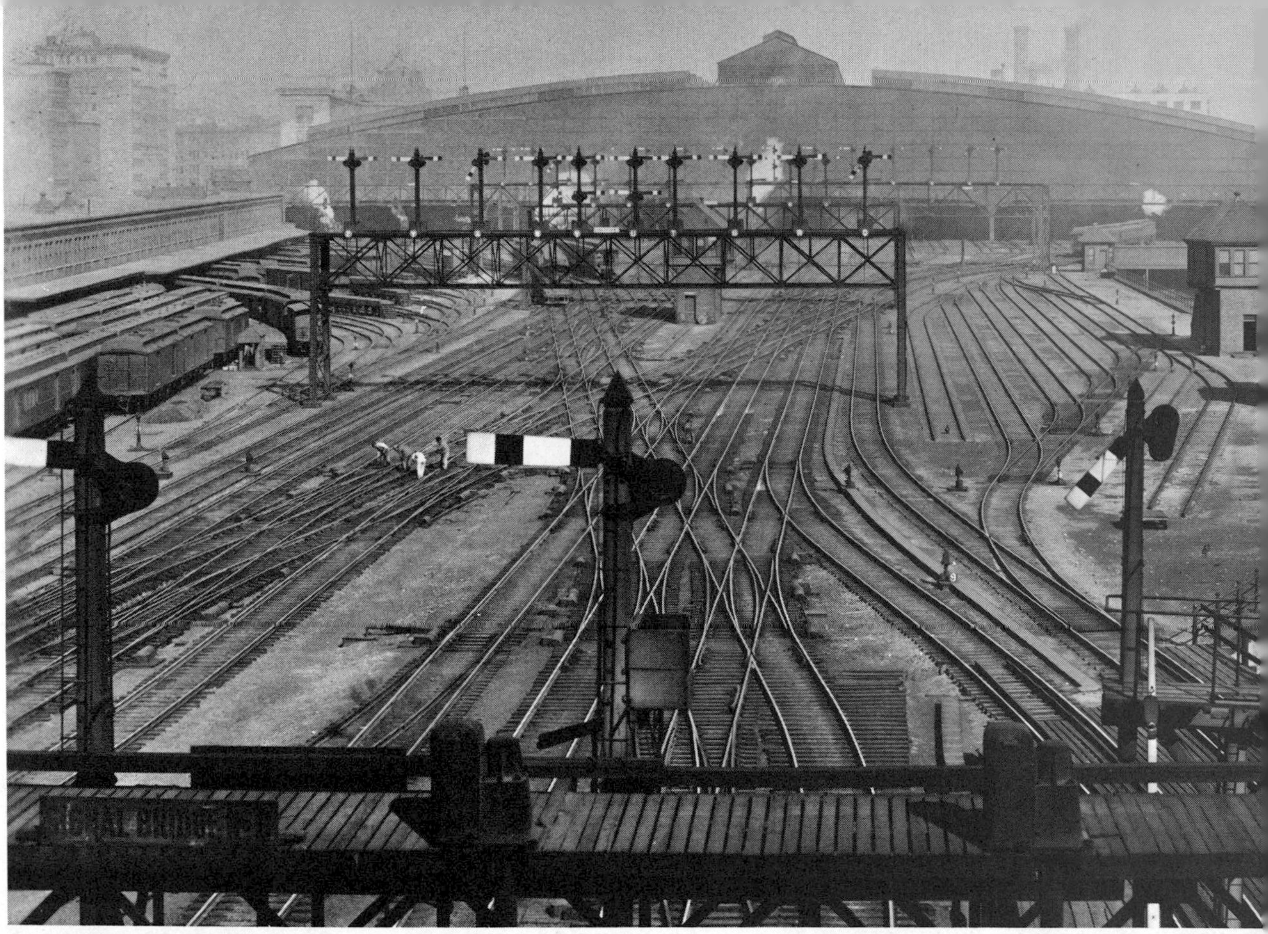

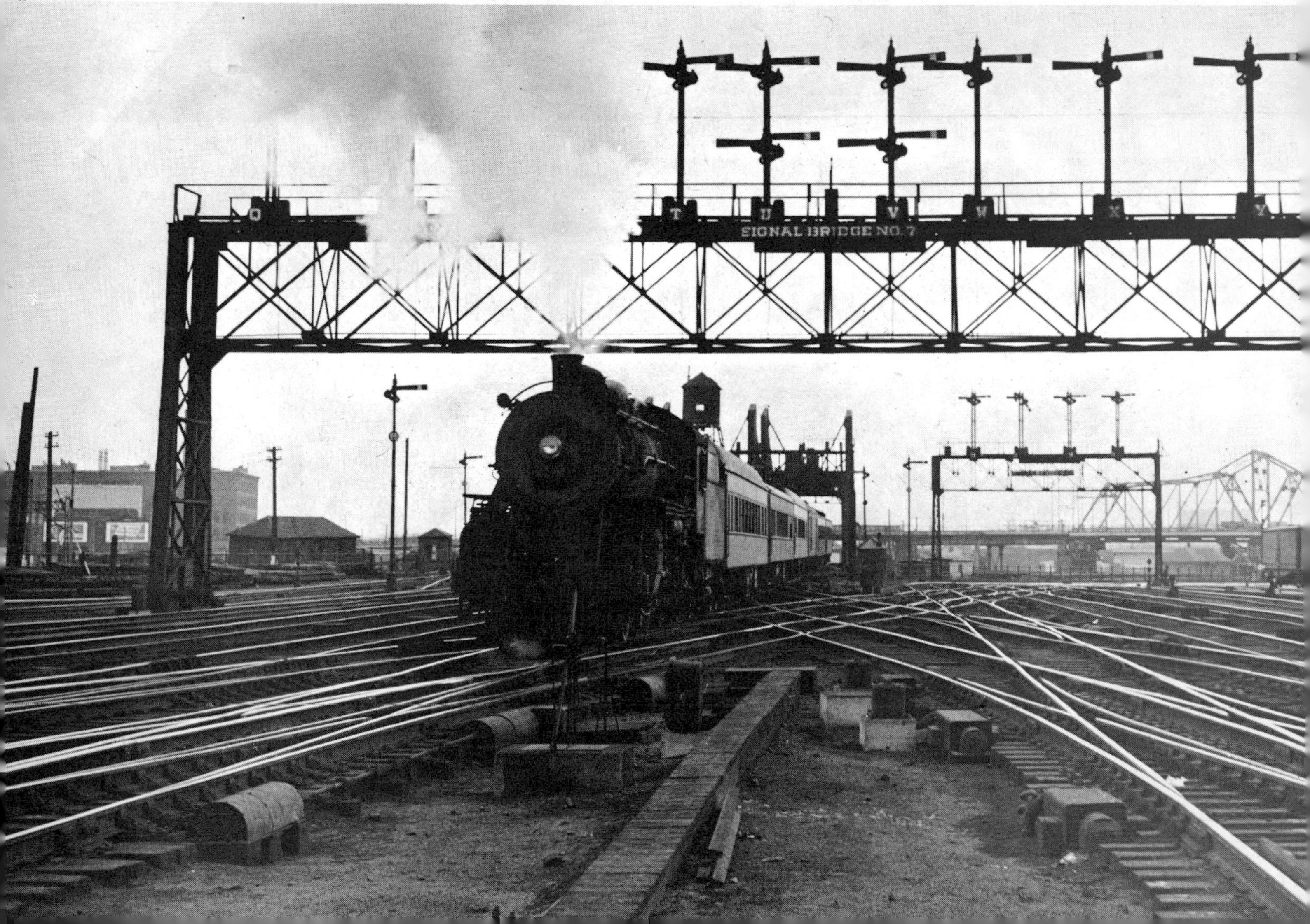
SIGNAL BRIDGE NO. 7

FEW TERMINAL YARDS in the United States equalled, none topped the dramatic sweep of trackage at the South Station in Boston although the switching layout at St. Louis was, perhaps, more complicated. At the bottom of the page opposite a second section of *The Owl* with pickup sleepers from New Haven and miscellaneous extra cars out of New York approaches its bay at South Station on a summer morning in the age of steam. Here, *The Senator* Washington-bound crosses The Hutchinson River in the Bronx on its way to Hell Gate Bridge to Long Island and Penn Station with seven Pullmans behind the latest thing in New Haven electric motors. *(Opposite: Library of Congress, top; Everett De Golyer Collection; Below: Ewing Galloway.)*

ONE OF THE FEW TRAINS in the United States where the service of afternoon tea was a ritual in every car comparable to the same sacramental observance in the main lounge of *The Queen Mary* or in Brown's Hotel, Dover Street, London, the New York, New Haven & Hartford's *Yankee Clipper* was the last of the long line of splendid name trains to be placed in service on the Shore Line between Boston and New York. Making a noon departure from its either terminal and covering its run in four hours and forty-five minutes, *The Clipper* was all-Pullman parlor cars, extra fare and its clientele was, if possible, even more genteel and perfumed with Commonwealth Avenue names than its companion in elegance, the venerable *Merchants Limited*. There was a colored maid, as well as the conventional bar steward in the solarium-observation lounge. Upmann Specials in the buffet and scrod on the menu offered by an impeccable maitre d'hotel in morning dress. Ladies on *The Clipper* addressed each other in Chilton Club accents and wore Queen Mary bonnets from R. H. Stearns & Co. in Tremont Street, and altogether it was as quintessential Boston as Faneuil Hall market or curling on the ice at The Country Club. *The Yankee Clipper* is shown here in the noontide of its prideful going under the electric catenaries eastbound at New Haven. The long established *Knickerbocker Limited* which it displaced on the afternoon run via the Shore Line found a continuum in *The Clipper*. (Above: New Haven Railroad; Opposite, Top: Pullman Standard; Bottom: New Haven.)

The New Haven's *Yankee Clipper*
Five O'Clock Tea for Beacon Hill Brahmins

MUCH OF THE GENTLEMAN'S CLUB atmosphere that the New Haven was fond of suggesting in its promotion and advertising did in fact obtain aboard the lounges and public cars of *The Yankee Clipper* and even more aboard *The Merchants Limited* at five o'clock after the business day was over and executives were free to relax over *The Wall Street Journal* and a highball before the porters began getting down hats and topcoats for Back Bay Station. Both were pre-eminently trains of cigar smokers as is suggested by the company promotional photograph reproduced above and Harvard's Professor George Lyman Kittredge, a regular patron, shown on the opposite page. The smoke that was wafted through the ventilators was that of Principe de Galles, Hoyo de Monterey, Corona Corona and Upmann Special, while the entire tone of the train was one of big business tempered by the amenities of well-bred society accustomed to the best of everything and ready to pay for it. Aboard the club car *Dudley*, named for an early Governor of Massachusetts, vice presidents of Farmer's Loan felt free to exchange Belinda Fancy Tales with trust officers of the Fourth Atlantic Bank of Boston secure in the knowledge that the social and financial rating of passengers was at least that of the Algonquin Club in Commonwealth Avenue. *(Opposite: Harvard University, Everett De Golyer Collection; Above: New Haven Railroad.)*

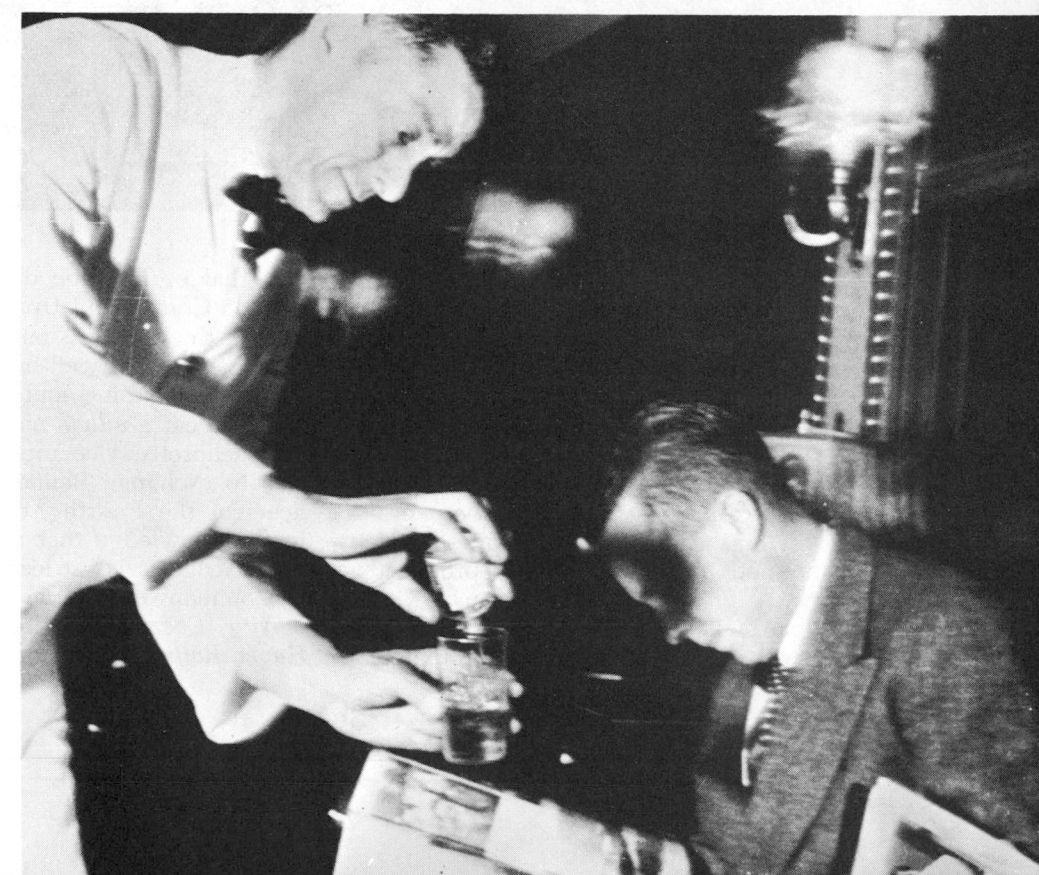

REVENUE deriving from the various club cars and buffets which kept the New Haven's Shore Line patrons happy between Boston and New York was a not inconsiderable factor in the carrier's over-all finances in the great years of the passenger traffic.

362

THE PHOTOGRAPH reproduced here was taken at East Haven, Connecticut, by Ronald Patry in 1939 and depicts the New Haven's august *Yankee Clipper* in unaccustomed pose with a baggage car on the head end, violating all the operating proprieties which usually governed the conduct of this aloof consist. The occupant of the baggage car was a prize Hereford bull being transported to the North Shore estate of a Boston magnifico at a fee sufficient to warrant his riding an extra fare train, although a dim view of the matter was taken by Elmer Bacon, the conductor on the run. "A hell of a way to run a railroad," was Bacon's comment when apprised of the fact that livestock was being added to his usually select sailing list of Morgan partners and grandees with Bay State Road addresses. The South Station train board of the *Gilt Edge* indicates a run of no such elegance with but a single parlor car and every thinkable stop along the way. *(Left: Amos Hewitt Collection; Below: The Bostonian Society.)*

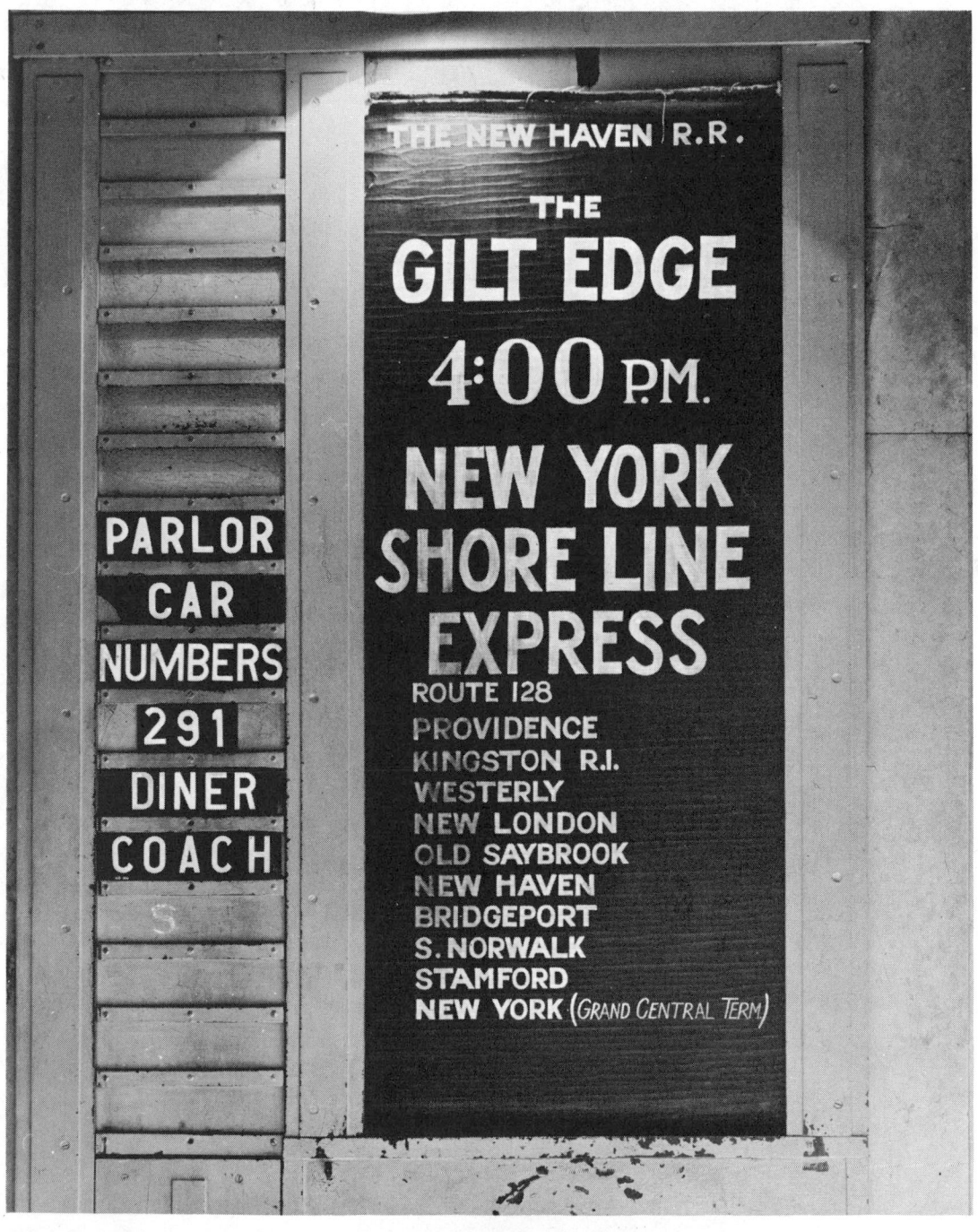

PARLOR CAR NUMBERS 291 DINER COACH

THE NEW HAVEN R.R.

THE GILT EDGE 4:00 P.M. NEW YORK SHORE LINE EXPRESS

ROUTE 128
PROVIDENCE
KINGSTON R.I.
WESTERLY
NEW LONDON
OLD SAYBROOK
NEW HAVEN
BRIDGEPORT
S. NORWALK
STAMFORD
NEW YORK (GRAND CENTRAL TERM.)

0305
NEW HAVEN
0306

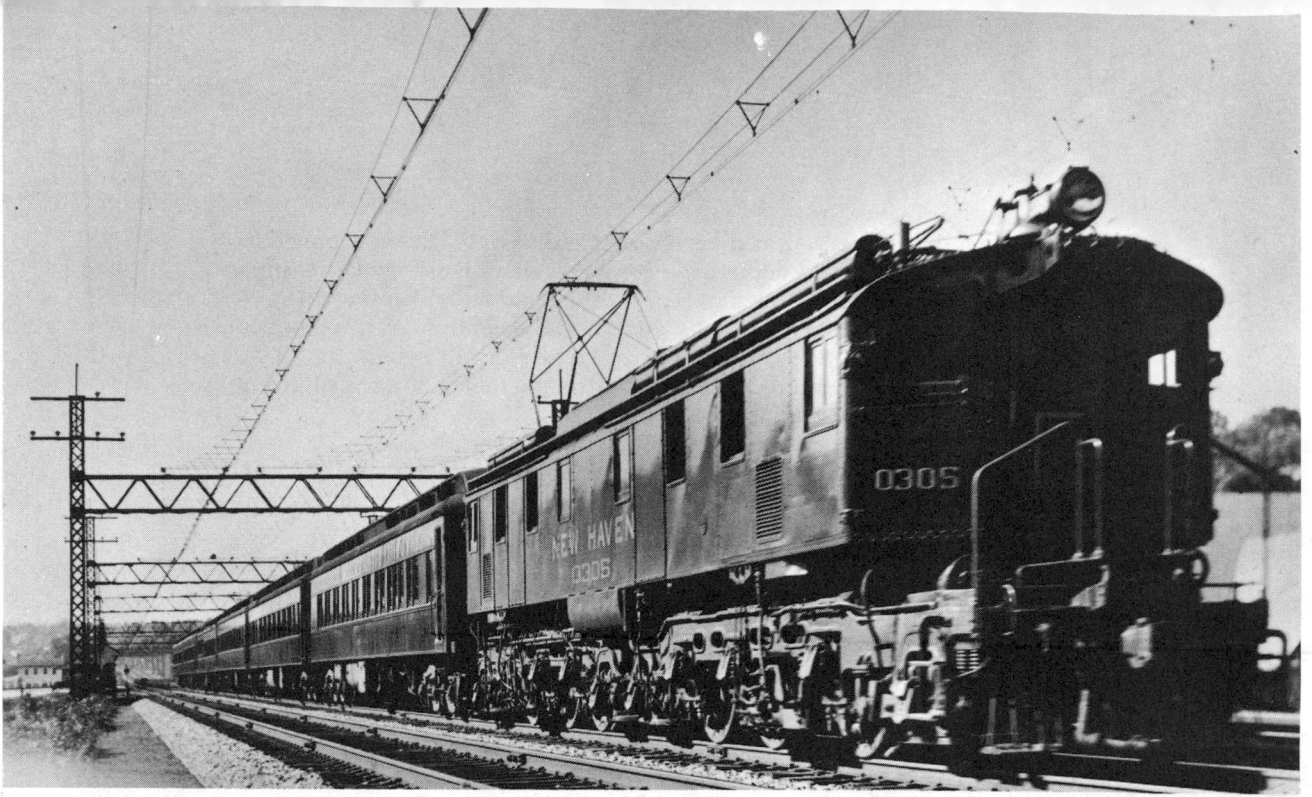

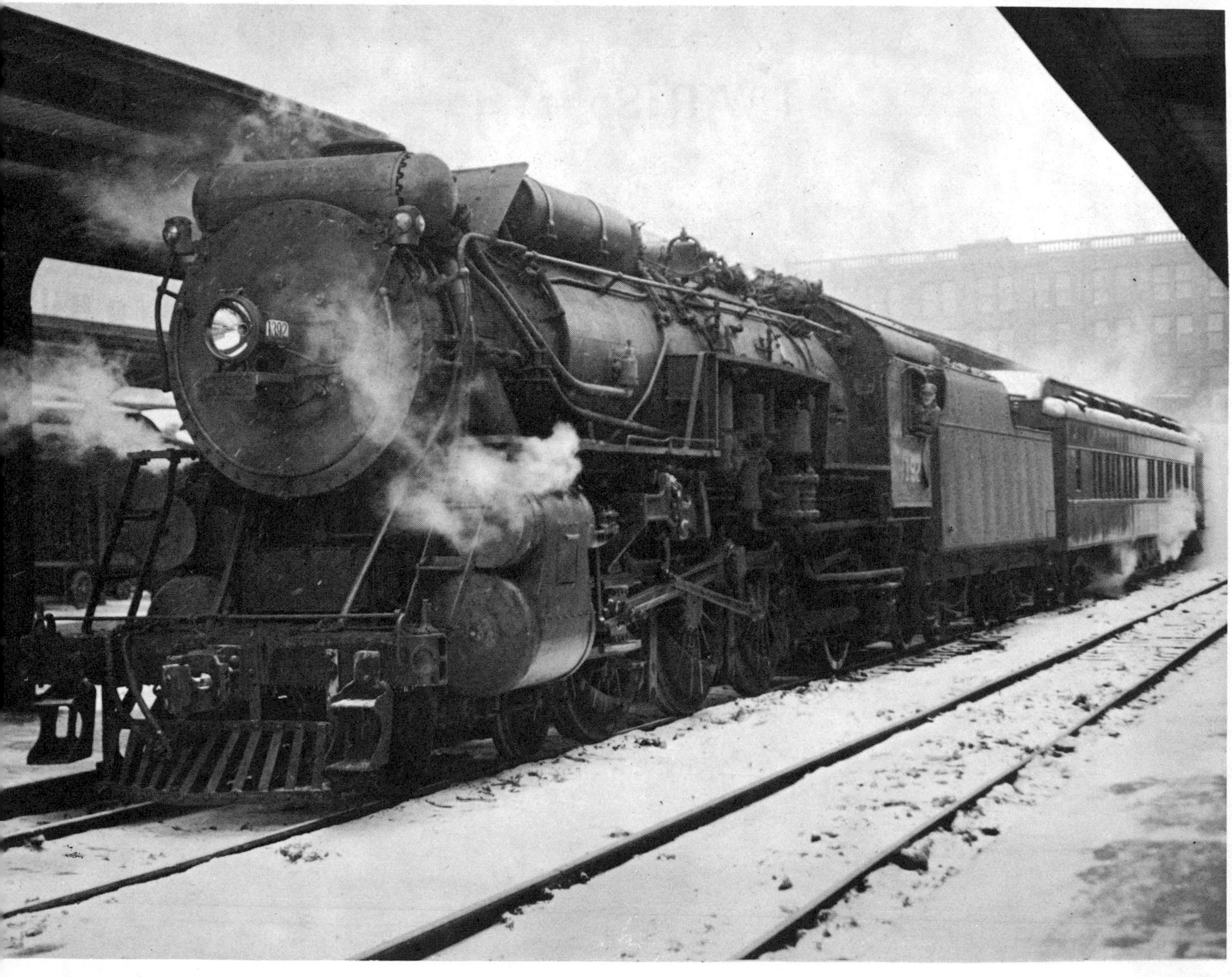
1302

SOMETIME in the now distant year 1901 when both South Station and the twentieth century were new together the photograph reproduced above was taken in the main waiting room of Boston's enviable, capacious and architecturally admired South Station. The news and refreshment kiosks with their domes of many colored glass and their remembered and pervading scent of chocolate lasted until well into the 1920s dispensing Necco Wafers, Lowney's chocolates and Page & Shaw for the affluent, all of them sweets of local origin and celebrity. Hard candies were sold from heavily stoppered glass containers and the 7-20-4 cigar, also a regional favorite, was a staple of commerce. Passengers purchased space from the ticket windows at the extreme left before venturing into the drafty train shed to board *The Knickerbocker, Owl* or *Twentieth Century Limited* as their destinations and dispositions might suggest. The South Station was institutional. *(Herbert H. Harwood Collection.)*

ON THE PAGE OPPOSITE and approximately three decades after the photograph of the South Station reproduced above, the New Haven's crack *Yankee Clipper* is shown in two attitudes of action and alert repose.
At the top of the page it races west out of New Haven behind electric motive power while below, on a snowy winter's afternoon behind a classic New Haven Pacific, *The Clipper* awaits a highball at South Station. The absence of head-end revenue cars in both views marks it as a train of almost unearthly elegance. *(Above: Rail Photo Service; Below: Everett De Golyer Collection.)*

365

FIRST NAME TRAIN of the New Haven's working day to chuff out of South Station, pause at Back Bay and then head out into the long tangent through Roxbury where it is shown above was *The Colonial* at nine o'clock for Washington via Hell Gate Bridge and the Pennsylvania connection at New York. On the drawbar is one of the last series of steam locomotives ordered for the New Haven, a streamlined Hudson with disk wheels and fine, fast, dependable motive power that raised abundant hell with the New Haven's track and showed daylight between tire and rails when the drivers lifted to some of the curves. At the right is a house ad for *The Montrealer* the overnight Pennsylvania connection from Washington to Canada over the New Haven's Springfield route. *(Above: Lucius Beebe; Right: Henry Mercur Collection.)*

366

A SPECIALLY assigned New Haven Pacific No. 1358 with silver cylinder heads and catwalks backs the all-Pullman parlor car *Yankee Clipper* over the complex network of switches into its appropriate train bay at South Station, Boston, for the extra-fare run of the Shore Line day. *(Lucius Beebe.)*

FOR SERVICE in *The Senator* and other connecting trains of the New Haven on the Boston-Washington run, the Pennsylvania commissioned from Pullman in 1930 a number of luxuriously upholstered observation-lounge and parlor cars whose cream decor and lively carpets were an abrupt departure from the mahogany painted panels and traditional Pullman green upholstery of established tradition. Vineleaf iron tracery pattern charmed passengers in the lounge car *Broadway*. *(Pullman Standard.)*

367

Rich Heritage of The Vanderbilts

Name trains of splendor and resounding title were not new to the New York Central & Hudson River Railroad when George Henry Daniels became General Passenger Agent and *ex officio* chief of promotion and publicity in the early nineties. But the *Lake Shore Limited*, all-Wagner de luxe varnish on the Chicago-New York run with a Boston section, was about as expansive as nomenclature went and the *Lake Shore* was flagship of the Vanderbilt fleet. There was also *The Empire State Express* which Chauncey Depew, then President of the road, considered a flight into almost pure poetry but which was presently, in Daniels' hands, to assume a radiance and world celebrity that may well have astonished its owners. For it was on May 10, 1893, with the immortal Charlie Hogan on the engineer's cushions that a Buchanan locomotive, the No. 999 rolled *The Empire State Express* for a measured speed near Batavia, New York, of 112.5 miles an hour, the fastest a human being had ever yet moved and lived to tell. Overnight *The Empire State* became the most celebrated train in the world. It went to the World's Columbian Exposition at Chicago where it eclipsed the sensational success of a dancer named Little Egypt and even the regal presence of Mrs. Potter Palmer. When Daniels was able to persuade the Postmaster General to emplace an image of *The Empire State Express* with No. 999 in full color on a two-cent stamp that is now a *rara avis* of the collector's world, he was firmly committed to the belief that the right name could do wonders for a New York Central train. Nine years later he went on to prove his thesis when, in a moment of transcendent genius, he came up with the name *The Twentieth Century Limited* for the Central's new, all-Pullman, extra fare New York-Chicago flyer that was to amaze the world by maintaining a regular, sustained daily carded speed of twenty hours. From then on the New York Central management had no doubts at all about the value of a memorable name to give a train a cachet of elegance and fix it in the public mind. Not all of the subsequent name trains on the time-tables and in the pages of *The Official Guide* lived up to the implications of *The Empire State* and *The Century*. *The Detroit Night Express* and *The Motor City Special* quickened few pulses, but the overall tally of the New York Central's name trains is an immortal component of the legend of great railroading. Few can transcend the majestic syllables of *The Southwestern Limited*, *The Knickerbocker*, *The Iroquois*, *The De Witt Clinton*, *The Twilight Limited*, *The Wolverine* and *The Niagara*. And, although they came long after his departure from the scene, *The Fifth Avenue Special* and *The Commodore Vanderbilt* would have done credit to the genius of stout, white goateed and inventive George Henry Daniels. Other railroads, notably the Pennsylvania, obviously saw merit in a fleet of resounding names for, in the years and decades that followed the acclaim achieved by *The Empire State Express* and *The Twentieth Century Limited*, the carriers of the land pillaged the Postal Guide, ravished their rights of way and exhausted the special lexicons of folklore and Indian tribes, regional celebrities of ancient and contemporary times, horticulture, geography and the aviary for names with which to enoble their most regarded varnish hauls. The point may be argued, but there is much evidence to suggest that Daniels and the Vanderbilt lines kindled the torch and lit the way. *(Peter Stackpole.)*

POWERED BY ONE OF WILLIAM BUCHANAN'S celebrated 4-4-0 engines, *The Saratoga Limited,* as depicted by Blauvelt, passes between a venerable bearded ancient attending the crossing gates at the left and a cache of beer barrels at the right of the Central's four-track right of way. The Central shared the High Bridge depot with the New York & Putnam Rail Road out of the picture at the right. A lone pedestrian looks down from High Bridge upon the atmospheric scene of railroading in the golden nineties. The Putnam Division was celebrated at the turn of the century and for many years afterward as a museum piece of period railroading and the recipient of the parent carrier's oldest and most decrepit equipment. On the page opposite a Putnam capped stacker is shown approaching the platform of an unidentified rustic stopping place while below, a Harlem Railroad coach that must have dated from the times of the Commodore himself is sheltered in a single stall coach house somewhere in the suburbs. *(Above: Brown Bros.; Opposite: Two Photos Everett De Golyer Collection.)*

371

UNTIL THE INAUGURAL in the spring of 1902 of *The Twentieth Century Limited* the new York Central's candy train on the New York-Chicago run was the magnificently appointed *Lake Shore Limited* whose Wagner Palace Car consist at the turn of the century is shown below at High Bridge on the Harlem River in a classic study by Blauvelt. Even after it had been displaced in the affections of the management by *The Century*, the *Lake Shore* continued to be a favorite with many conservative travelers who regarded the extra fare splendors of No. 25 and 26 as ostentatious and its company of bankers, playactresses and barbed wire salesmen as being as fast, in the slang of the period, as its scheduling. *(Right: New York Central; Below: Brown Brothers.)*

DRAWING-ROOM AND LIBRARY CARS.

OVER THE

New York Central

AND

Hudson River Railroad,

AND THE

Lake Shore

AND

Michigan Southern R'y.

THE VESTIBULE.

THE VESTIBULE SLEEPING CAR.

THE VESTIBULE DINING CAR.

One of these unsurpassed trains of Palaces on Wheels leaves Grand Central Station, New York, every day in the year at 9.50 A. M. arriving at Lake Shore and Michigan Southern Railway Station in Chicago the following morning at 9.50.

Another leaves Lake Shore and Michigan Southern Railway Station, Chicago, every day in the year at 5.30 P. M.; arriving at Grand Central Station, New York, the following day at 7.30 P. M.

The new Sleeping Cars now in regular service on the Limited and Fast Express Trains on the NEW YORK CENTRAL and LAKE SHORE were built by the Wagner Palace Car Company, the controlling . in construction being to secure absolute comfort to the occupants he cars, and no expense has been spared to attain that end. In nce of finish and luxurious appointments the new sleeping cars unsurpassed.

IN THE DINING CAR PASSING THE PALISADES OF THE HUDSON
SUPERIOR CUISINE.   ELEGANT SERVICE.

THE VESTIBULE
BUFFET SMOKING AND LIBRARY CAR.

Entirely unique and original in design are the New Wagner Compartment or Saloon Sleeping Cars, a comprehensive sectional view of which we present herewith. The interior of the car is divided into ten inclosed compartments, each intended for the accommodation of two persons, affording the utmost privacy and seclusion to occupants, and with the most artistic, costly and elaborate interior furnishings and decorations. Complete toilet accessories; lavatory, hot and cold running water, and closets; also electric call-bells, brass chandeliers arranged for the Pintsch system of gas lighting, and other convenient devices are provided in each compartment. Folding doors between the rooms permit of their being arranged en suite, if desired, for the accommodation of families or large parties. A handsome buffet from which is dispensed light refreshments, and a well-filled bookcase for the free use of passengers, are popular innovations.

THE BLOOD LINES AND ARMORIAL QUARTERINGS OF *The Lake Shore Limited* were among the purest of any name train in *The Official Guide*, the "Burke's Peerage" of American railroading aristocracy. It had its beginnings on the timecards of the New York Central & Hudson River Railroad and the Lake Shore & Michigan Southern, for the latter of which it was, of course, named in the nineties when the Vanderbilt Lines, as is suggested in the company literature reproduced above, were still the best customers of the Wagner Palace Carbuilding Company of which Dr. William Seward Webb, a Vanderbilt in-law was president. Some of the finest products of the Wagner shops were built to the special order of the owners of *The Lake Shore Limited* and carried the train's title on their nameboards until the great switch to Pullman in 1899. The steel engravings, produced by the American Bank Note Company, and reproduced here will supply ample testimony that the equipment of the *Limited* was termed palatial with complete propriety.   (*New York Central.*)

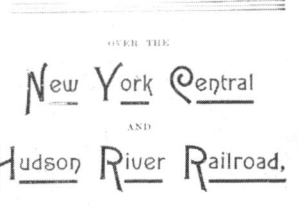

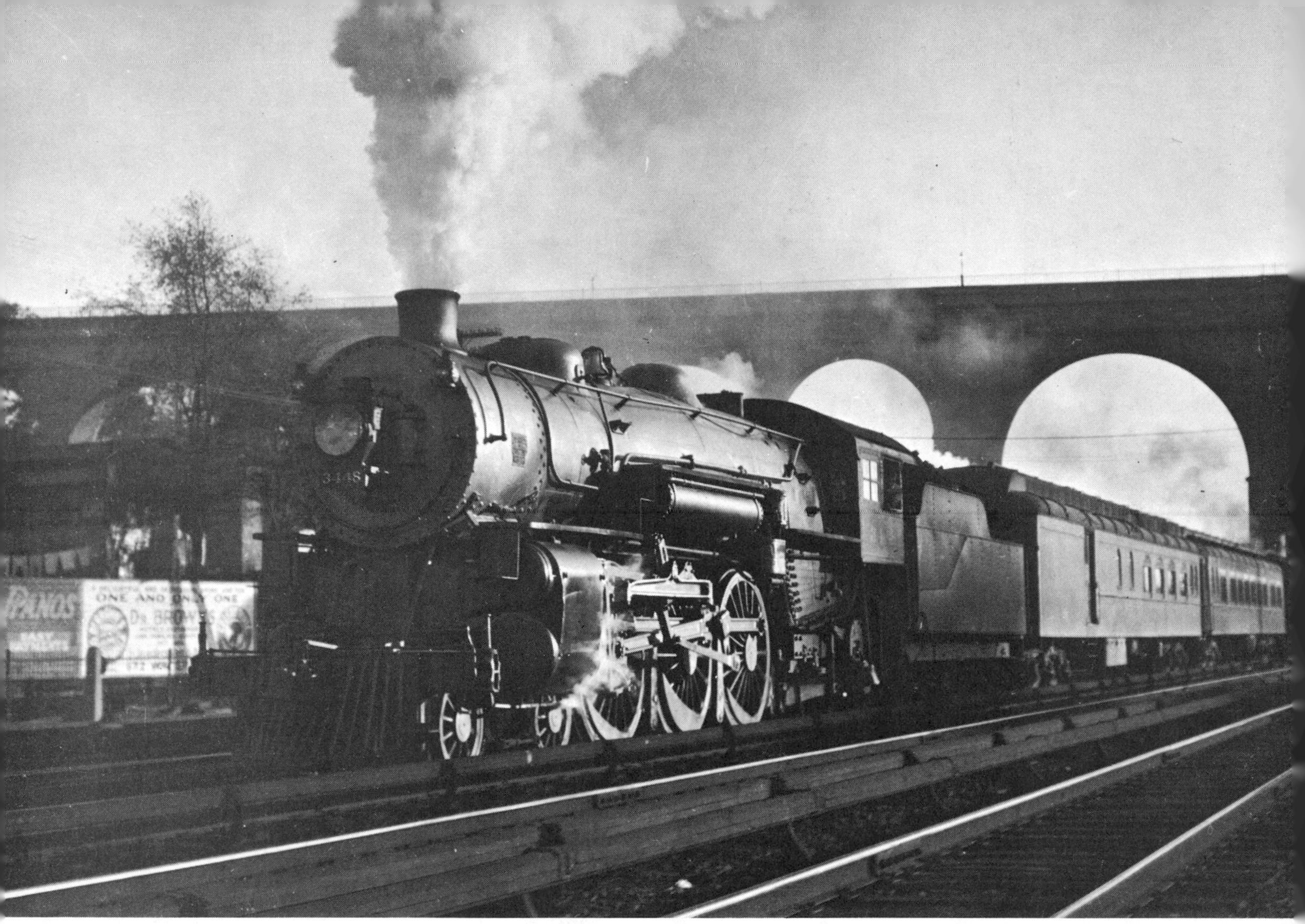
ONE AND ONLY ONE

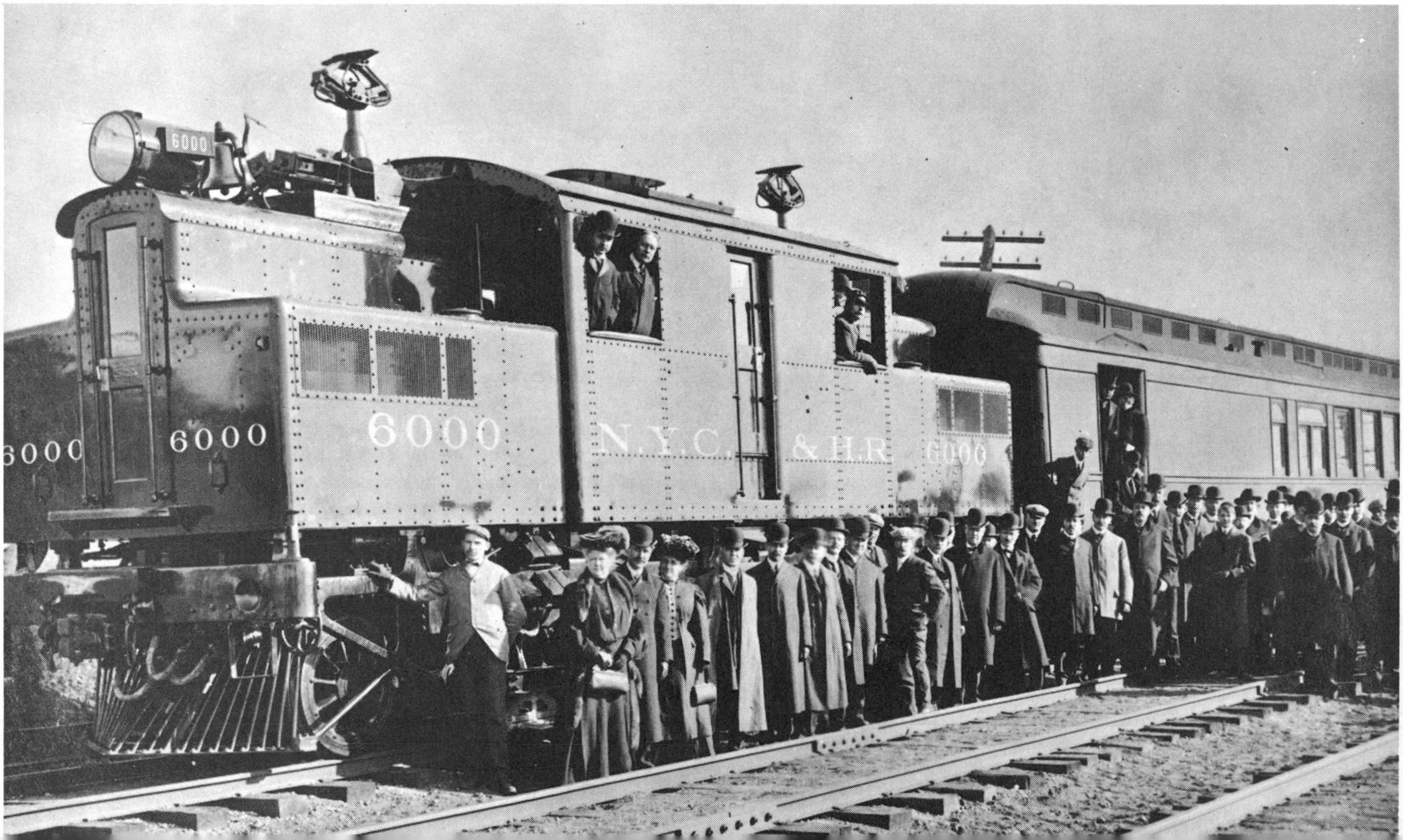
6000
6000
6000
6000
N.Y.C. & H.R. 6000

SECOND ONLY to *The Twentieth Century Limited* and, perhaps, *The Empire State Express, The Southwestern Limited* on the New York-St. Louis run enjoyed the favorable regard of the New York Central management. A Boston section made the connection with the New York train at Albany and its all-Pullman progress in the year 1910 when it was photographed *(above)* by F. W. Blauvelt at High Bridge, The Bronx, was accorded green all the way on the Central's longest single run. Below, opposite, the first run of the *Southwestern* between Grand Central and Harmon in electric power was an event which called for special rejoicing and a posed photograph of invited guests. The buffet car in this photograph is of Wagner construction indicating the early date of the event itself. Above, on this page, *The Southwestern* poses at Terre Haute while at the right, a recent train gate at Grand Central indicated a ratio of eight Pullmans to one coach in the train consist. *(Top Opposite: The Smithsonian Institution; Three Photos: New York Central.)*

375

AN ATMOSPHERE of implicit hooray pervades this embarcation scene at Grand Central Station in 1898 recorded by the celebrated New York theatrical photographer Joseph Byron. It depicts a group of friends and well wishers saying bon voyage to Alice Nielsen, a popular actress of the time, as she boards the cars for Toronto. Miss Nielsen grips the brake wheel firmly and the legend "Wagner" on the vestibule frame evidences the loyalty of Vanderbilt lines to the carbuilder who, only a year later, was to be absorbed by Pullman. Below, at approximately the year 1910, the New York Central's ticket office at 275 Columbus Avenue, New York City, was opulent with period atmosphere. *(Right: Museum of the City of New York; Below: Everett De Golyer Collection.)*

SO EARLY on a summer's morning in the now distant year 1911 that no
diner is included in its all-Pullman consist and arriving passengers
will breakfast at Grand Central or the equally handy Belmont Hotel,
The New York Central Limited meets its schedule along the banks
of the lordly Hudson River which brought the Vanderbilt lines into being.
Its passing is mirrored in placid waters while affluence and power
dominate the scene from hilltop mansions. *(W. G. Landon.)*

377

TYPICAL OF The Central's extra fare, all-Pullman de luxe varnish runs of the period but unusual as an example of action photography in 1913 is this portrait of *The Detroiter* taken south of Albany by W. G. Landon, himself a New York Central fireman with a taste for amateur picture taking. The head-end Gothic-windowed combination buffet-baggage car with a long line of sleepers on its drawbar might equally plausibly have been *The Century, The Lake Shore* or *The New York Central Limited* of the period. Twenty years later it was inevitable that Kaye Don of speedboat racing fame should have taken *The Detroiter* en route for the world capital of internal combustion for which it was named. (*Above: W. G. Landon; Left: New York Central.*)

378

THE SEDATE and well-appointed dining car whose interior is depicted above together with its smartly turned-out staff and white waist-coated steward, is typical of the New York Central restaurants in the 1920s. As a rule new diners when they came from Pullman found themselves assigned to *The Twentieth Century Limited, The Lake Shore, Southwestern, Detroiter* or one of the other all-Pullman runs, after which, like business cars and other luxury equipment generally, they were downgraded as new equipment was delivered. Track pans such as those shown here at Poughkeepsie were a railroad property of the age of speed and steam that never failed in their fascination for photographers. (*Two Photos: New York Central.*)

379

TRACK 34

PARLOR	**9-00 A.M.**
A	N.Y.C.R.R.
B	
DINER	**STREAMLINED**
COACH	**EMPIRE STATE**
NUMBERS	**EXPRESS**
E 1	
E 2	ALL SEATS RESERVED
E 3	VISITORS NOT PERMITTED
E 4	THROUGH GATE
E 5	
DINER	ALBANY
E 7	SCHENECTADY
E 8	UTICA
E 9	SYRACUSE
CLUB-LOUNGE	ROCHESTER
	BUFFALO
	WESTFIELD
	ERIE
	CLEVELAND
	ELYRIA
	SUNDUSKY
	TOLEDO
	ST. THOMAS
	DETROIT

From its very beginnings in 1891 down to the time when its streamlined version was hailed as one of the world's most beautiful trains, *The Empire State Express* was a showpiece for the New York Central & Hudson River Railroad. Antedating the venerable *Century* by eleven years, *The Empire State,* as recounted on an adjacent page was also the prime vehicle for the genius of the carrier's most adroit practitioner of publicity, George Henry Daniels whose achievements with its image blazed a pathway for other publicists to follow. Here in its days of splendor with No. 999 on its drawbar, *The Empire State Express,* pride of the Vanderbilt Lines and fastest train in the world, is painted by the eminent railroad artist, Howard Fogg. *(Above: John Barriger Collection; Left and Opposite: New York Central.)*

WHEN, IN THE FALL OF 1941, the New York Central commissioned two new super-streamlined *Empire State Express* trains, hailed by the management as "the world's finest day trains" it was just in time to honor the fiftieth anniversary of the *Empire State's* maiden run in 1891. It also kept a date with history when the new units made their first run on December 7 when events shaping up on the other side of the world took the edge off its publicity. It was the last luxury train to be placed in service before the 1941 war and barely made it. Thirty-two cars comprised the consists of the two trains and the carbuilder's bill had been a cool $2,500,000. Statistical minded observers remarked that in its half century of service *The Empire State* had covered 17,000,000 rail miles in 40,000 one way trips between New York City and its upstate terminals without serious injury to a single passenger. That the new train was given the benefit of superb interior decor is testified by the photographs on these pages. Interiors were by Paul Cret and historical paintings in lounges and diners portrayed such themes as "Rip Van Winkle," "The Legend of Sleepy Hollow," "Burgoyne's Surrender" and "Dutch Fur Buyers at Manhattan Island." Below is shown the dining car whose restraint and opulence would have done credit to any of New York's top flight luxury restaurants. *(Three Photos: New York Central.)*

MURALS depicting
early day scenes
of transport and sail-
ing ship romance
on The Hudson
adorned the bulk-
head behind the club
car service bar.

PIGSKIN
upholstered ban-
quettes that would
have found favor in
any gentleman's
club afforded solid
comfort to tarriers in
the *Empire State's*
lounge.

383

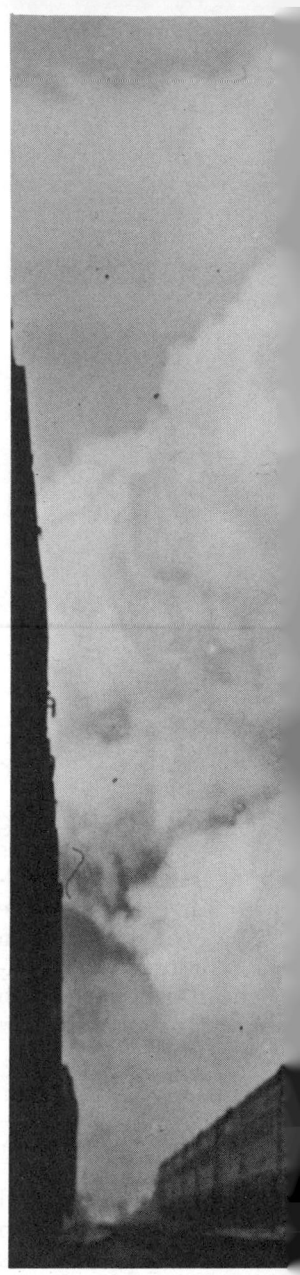

ALTHOUGH when it was first inaugurated along with the all-room *Twentieth Century Limited* styled by Henry Dreyfuss in 1938, the streamlined *Empire State Express* was powered with a specially designed two tone Hudson with silver pie-plate wheels and the train's name proudly engrossed under the cat-walk, another bullet nose was on the head end when the fine action shot above taken by Richard J. Cook, Jr., at Euclid, Ohio. With a consist of two parlor cars, two diners, eight coaches and an observation lounge, *The Empire State* was not only heir to a legacy of long ago triumphs, but the most imaginably luxurious paradigm of a daylight train in the grand manner. It is shown opposite through the catenaries of the Jamestown, Westfield & Northwestern interurban at Westfield, New York, in the heart of the grape-growing region. The car at the right is the inter-urban's No. 301 and the time, Easter Morning, 1946. *(Above and Below Opposite: Richard J. Cook, Jr.; Other Photos: New York Central.)*

ALL ALONG ITS ROUTE, the coming of *The Empire State Express* was the event of the daylight hours in a railroading world where many of the great name trains passed in the night. Here, against one of the handsome murals depicting the New York past that adorned the bulkheads in both coaches and luxury public cars, *The Empire State* hostess checks her routine with the train captain. Below, the train's observation end is silhoutted against a sunset sky as it traverses Sandusky Bay Causeway. On the opposite page, *The Empire State*, running behind its originally assigned two-tone locomotive, makes an atmospheric vignette for the camera of Richard J. Cook through the window of B. R. Tower at the east end of Collinwood Yards, Cleveland. The date is July 30, 1944. *(Two Photos: New York Central.)*

Although by 1935 the barber, maid and valet service that were still part of the panache of *The Twentieth Century Limited* had disappeared from the available amenities of *The Southwestern Limited*, it still was Number 2 Train in the affections of its owning carrier, running in direct competition to the Pennsylvania's splendid *Spirit of St. Louis*. In addition to the conventional public and sleeping cars of a classic train in the great tradition, *The Southwestern* was distinguished for its drawing-room-and-single-stateroom observation sleeper shown here at Grand Central with its telephone jack plugged in prior to its 6 p.m. departure. The crew, in attitude and physiognomy were, of course, right out of Central Casting. *(New York Central.)*

ABOUT 1935 when the photographs on this page were taken, *The Southwestern Limited* shared the New York-St. Louis run, for some now obscure reason, with an undistinguished train No. 37, *The Missourian* on the westbound run and with No. 24, the strictly first class *Knickerbocker* eastbound. Above: *The Southwestern* heads out of East St. Louis over the rails of the Big Four behind Hudson No. 5336, while at the left, a companion engine of the Central's classic breed waits for green on the same train outside the long train shed of the once teeming St. Louis Terminal. *(Two Photos: Lucius Beebe.)*

IN MARCH 1947 before spring had come to Ohio and while the trees were still bare with snow on the ground, *The Southwestern Limited* pounded past the steamboat Gothic depot at Berea, a few miles west of Cleveland for a portrait of big time railroading as the age of steam drew to a close. On its head end were New York Central 4-6-2 No. 4952 as helper and 4-6-4 No. 5382 as road engine and *The Southwestern* was still king of the road over the Big Four lines into the gateway to the region whose name it carried. *(Richard J. Cook.)*

390

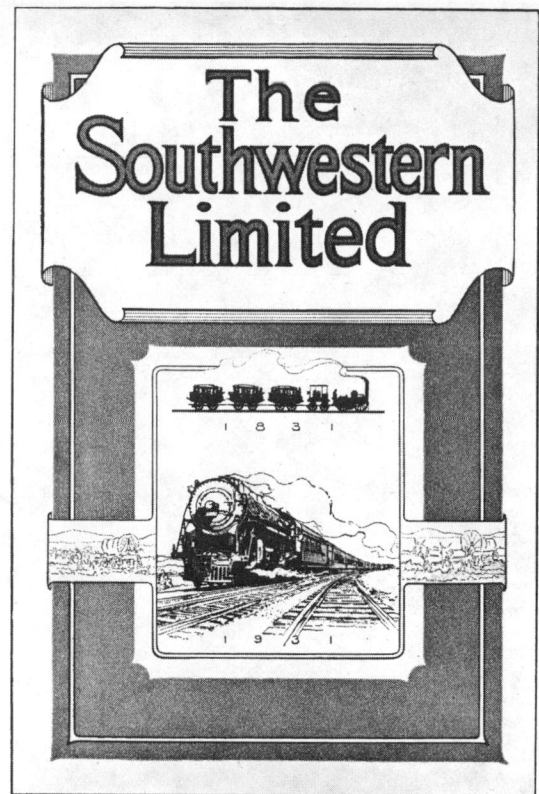

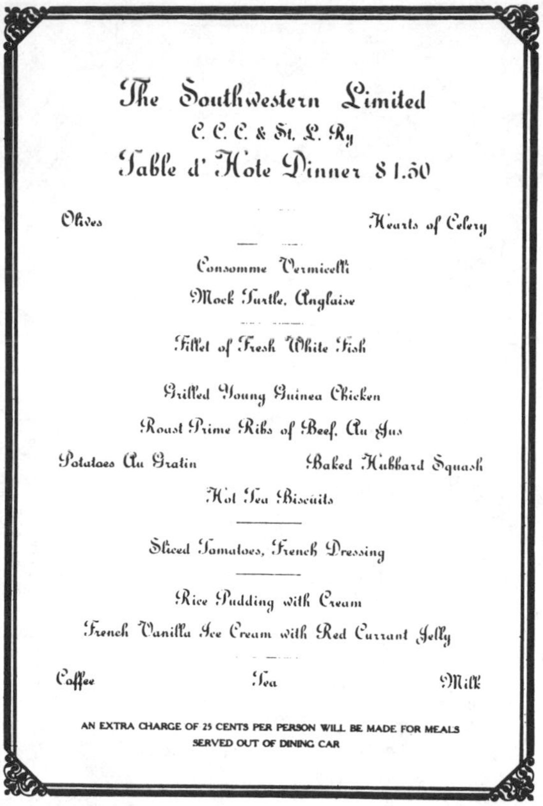

The Southwestern Limited

The Southwestern Limited
C. C. C. & St. L. Ry
Table d' Hote Dinner $1.50

Olives   Hearts of Celery

Consomme Vermicelli
Mock Turtle, Anglaise

Fillet of Fresh White Fish

Grilled Young Guinea Chicken
Roast Prime Ribs of Beef, Au Jus
Potatoes Au Gratin   Baked Hubbard Squash
Hot Tea Biscuits

Sliced Tomatoes, French Dressing

Rice Pudding with Cream
French Vanilla Ice Cream with Red Currant Jelly

Coffee   Tea   Milk

AN EXTRA CHARGE OF 25 CENTS PER PERSON WILL BE MADE FOR MEALS
SERVED OUT OF DINING CAR

SOME IDEA of the regard in which *The Southwestern Limited* was held by the New York Central may be suggested by the special menu reproduced above that graced its diners rather than a mere system bill of fare. *The Southwestern's* departure from Grand Central Station was an event of the day second only in magnitude to that of *The Twentieth Century Limited*. *(Three Photos: New York Central.)*

TRACK 29

12-25 A.M.

FORT ORANGE

PULLMAN
CAR
NUMBERS
COACH
55
59
52
53
54

YONKERS
TARRYTOWN
OSSINING
HARMON
MONTROSE
PEEKSKILL
GARRISON
COLD SPRING
BEACON
NEW HAMBURG
POUGHKEEPSIE
HUDSON
ALBANY
SCHENECTADY
AMSTERDAM
FONDA
PALATINE BRIDGE
FORT PLAIN
ST. JOHNSVILLE
LITTLE FALLS
HERKIMER
NORTH ILION
UTICA

TRACK 28

8-00 P.M.

SOUTHWESTERN
LIMITED

CLEVELAND
BELLEFONTAINE
MUNCIE
ANDERSON
INDIANAPOLIS
TERRE HAUTE
MATTOON
ST. LOUIS

PULLMAN
NUMBERS
COACH
150
151
187
152
DINER-LOUNGE
37
46
47
OBS

TRACK 28

ALL PASSENGERS WILL BE REQUIRED TO SHOW THEIR TICKETS AT THE GATES

BECAUSE *The Southwestern Limited* had to meet the direct competition of the Pennsylvania's equally well maintained *Spirit of St. Louis* on the New York-St. Louis run, it received preferential treatment and when the second streamlined *Century* was placed in service *The Southwestern* got the first train's airflow equipment. Its departure from Grand Central was accorded every honor that marked the sailing of No. 25 with the single exception of the red carpet, an imperial accolade reserved for *The Century* alone. The Grand Central news vendor was on hand with his portable newsrack, Western Union boys prowled in the gloom of the upper level, car porters in uniforms suitable to the season stood at attention at every Pullman door and the maitre d'hotel waited on name passengers in their staterooms with menu and winecard in hand. Except for the missing red carpet and the presence of the identifying tailgate insigne, it might have been the sailing of *The Twenieth Century Limited.* (*Above: New York Central; Right: Rail Photo Service.*)

392

TO MEET the competition of the rival
Pennsylvania which, in the postwar flood tide
of passenger business placed on the New York-
St. Louis run an entire train designated
as the *Sunshine Special* and which
connected in the late afternoon at The Gateway
with the Missouri Pacific's Texas-bound
run of that name, the Central
countered with a Texas-Oklahoma section of
the *Southwestern*. Sleepers continued
through to the impressive list of
destinations on the trainboard shown here
and the equipment, such as the lounge interior
depicted below included hand-me-down
de luxe streamlined cars that had
originally been assigned to No. 25 and 26.
(Two Photos: New York Central.)

393

BOSTON & ALBANY R. R. . . . . . .

DINING · CAR · SERVICE

— BETWEEN —

BOSTON AND UTICA

— ON THE —

BOSTON AND CHICAGO SPECIAL.

Patrons will confer a favor by reporting any cause for
dissatisfaction to A. S. Hanson, General
Passenger Agent, Boston, Mass.

BOSTON & ALBANY RAILROAD
····· DINNER. ·····

SOUP.
Fish Chowder.   Consomme Spaghetti.

FISH.
Baked Bluefish, Stuffed, Tomato Sauce.

ROAST.
English Ribs of Beef with Browned Potatoes.
Ribs of Beef.   Young Turkey with Dressing, Giblet Sauce.

ENTREES.
Filet of Beef, Larded, with Mushrooms.
Orange Fritters, Wine Sauce.   Small Oyster Patties.

RASPBERRY ICE.

SALADS.
Fresh Lobster.   Potato.   Lettuce.

RELISHES.
Pickled Onions.   Gherkins.   Queen Olives.
Chow Chow.   Celery.

VEGETABLES.
Mashed Potatoes.   Boiled Potatoes.   French Peas.
Boiled Potatoes with Cream.   String Beans.
Succotash.   Boiled Rice.   Stewed Tomatoes.

PASTRY, ETC.
Tapioca Custard Pudding, Wine Sauce.
Green Apple Pie.   Ice Cream.   Assorted Cake.
Oranges.   Grapes.   Bananas.   Apples.
Edam and Roquefort Cheese.   Marmalade.
Bent's Water Crackers.   French Coffee.

MEALS, ONE DOLLAR.

D.C. 4-200.

PATRONS of the diner of *The Boston & Chicago Special*, 1891 predecessor of the Boston *Century* might admire the Boston & Albany's Worcester depot of the period while enjoying four course dinners for a dollar. *(Above: Fred Arone Collection.)*

R·R·Depot.

EVERY DAY an hour before the scheduled departure of the Boston section of *The Twentieth Century Limited* the Boston & Albany's *Fast Mail & Express (top)* departed South Station behind an American 4-4-0 type locomotive whose tapered boiler and spidery-spoked drivers represented the last word in speed in 1911. *The Century* itself in that now distant year awaited its highball behind Pacific No. 3543 whose centered headlight on the smokebox alone betrays the date of this impressive scene. *(Top: Herbert H. Harwood Collection; Below: W. G. Landon.)*

THE FINE new Union Station at Worcester, Massachusetts, depicted on the opposite page in 1910, the year of its completion, was jointly occupied by the Boston & Albany and the Boston & Maine and gleams as a backdrop for an equally resplendent through train, probably *The Southwestern Limited.* As yet only two tracks have been elevated above the street level, supported by temporary cribbing. The stone tower of the original depot, now relegated to the status of a freight shed, shows at the right while the Boston & Maine tracks for the east curve away at the left. The depot trolley is depicted below at its terminal stop under the stone clocktower of the first Worcester station. The auto taxi had not yet come to Worcester and Fritz the venerable cabman waited in the rain for fares. *(Two Photos: Herbert H. Harwood Collection.)*

WHEN this photograph
was taken on the
Boston & Albany at
Palmer, Massachusetts,
in 1910, the year the
new Worcester
depot opened, accidents
involving trains and
autos were usually fatal
to the latter.
Grade crossings were
largely unguarded
and daredevils knew
they could beat
the engines to the other
side. (*Herbert H.
Harwood Collection.*)

ON THE PAGE OPPOSITE, three photographs from the collection of Herbert H. Harwood suggest the essentially rustic nature of even such an important main line as The Boston & Albany at its Boston terminal. They were taken in 1898 just before the B.&A. moved into the fine new South Station and depict scenes at the carrier's old Kneeland Street Station deep in the Hub's hide and leather district. At the top the well-maintained vans of United States mail are spotted at the express loading platform before making their shuttle trips to Postoffice Square in the financial center of town. Below, against a timeless highball signal mast governing the yard movements and the train shed on the Utica Street side of the depot, the B.&M. yardmaster and his staff pose for their portrait. The ornate gazebo and counterweighted semaphores control the flow of traffic as it merges from the passenger train shed and the team and express tracks at the extreme right. On this page and some four decades after the pastoral simplicities suggested opposite, the Boston & Albany's big, square-domed Hudsons were impressive motive power that evoked the admiration of New England buffs and professional railroaders alike. (*Philip R. Hastings.*)

398

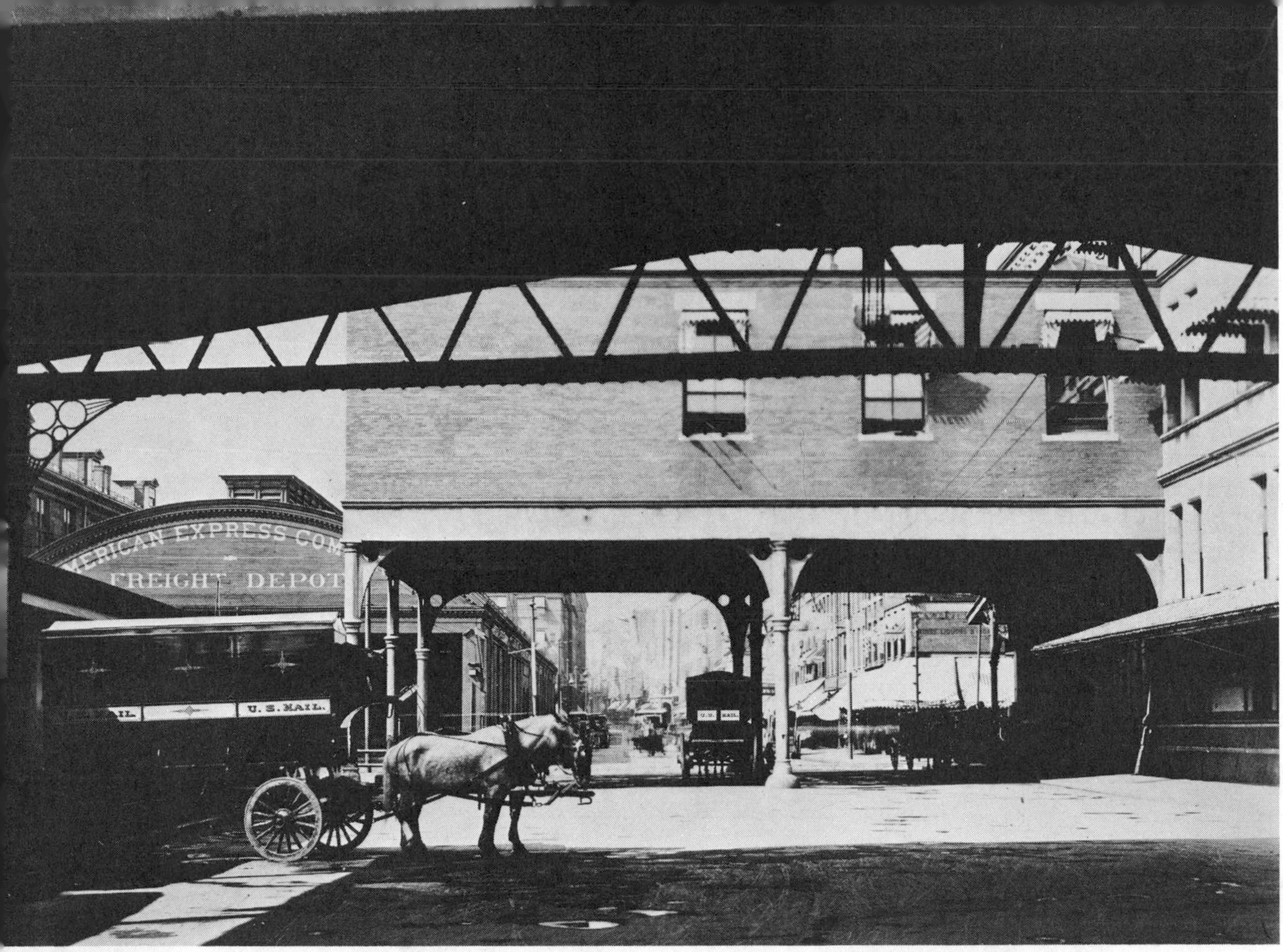
MERICAN EXPRESS COM
FREIGHT DEPOT
U.S. MAIL

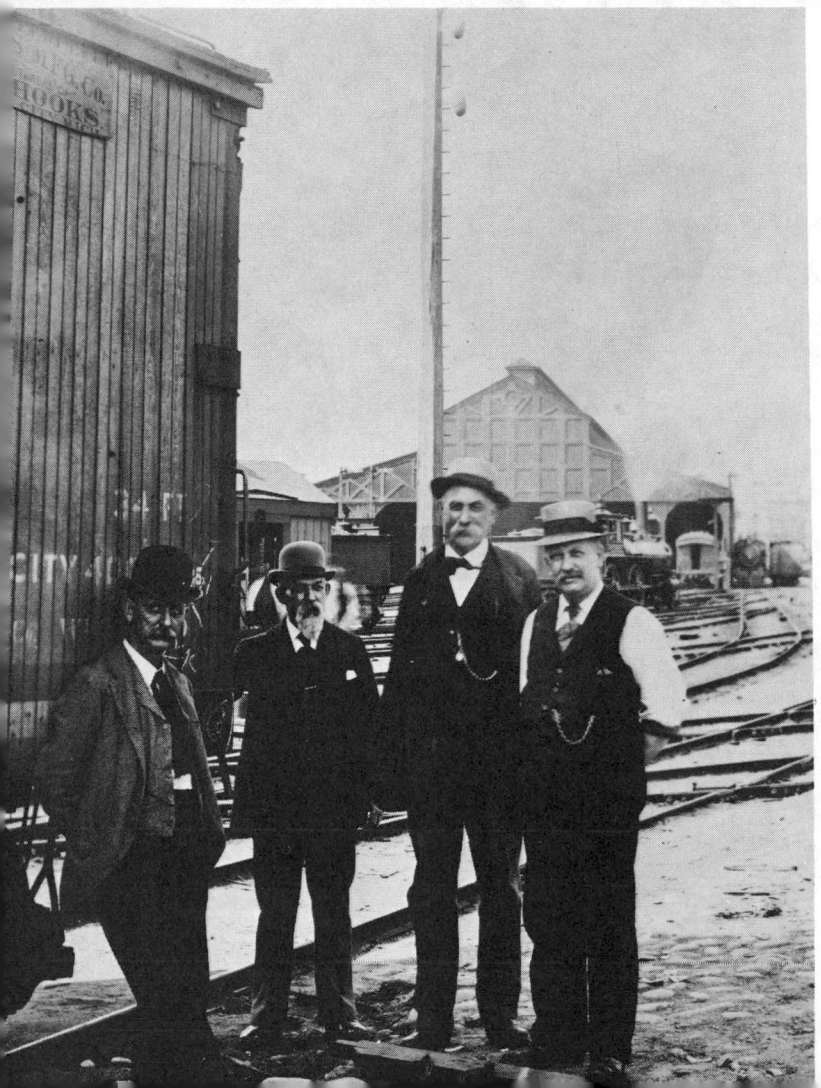

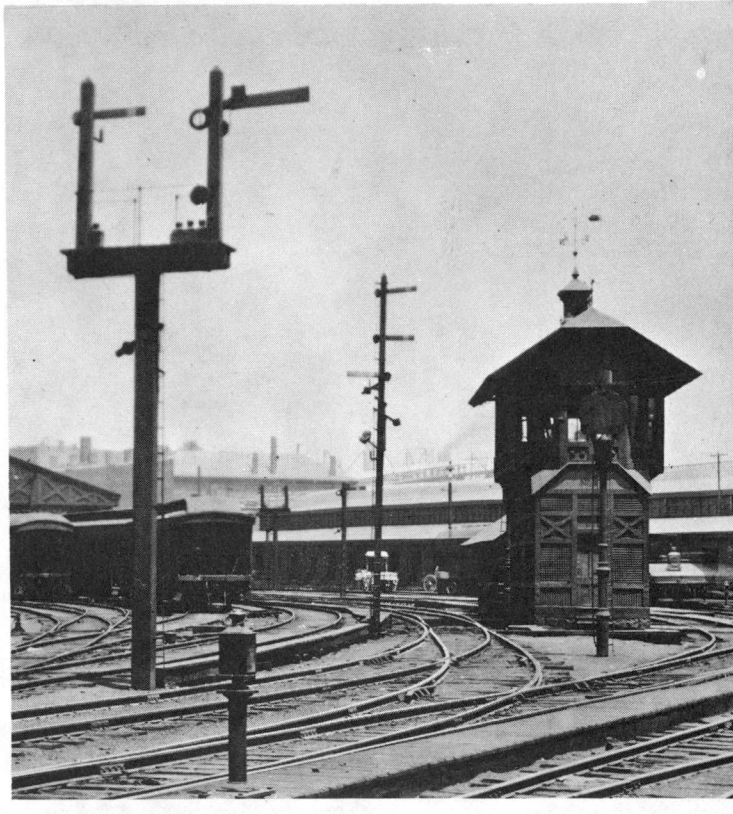

THE BOSTON SECTION of *The Century* makes a fine picture of classic railroading *(below)* in the years of steam and Pullman Standard as it tops Charlton Summit in the Berkshire Hills of Western Massachusetts amidst a summer thunderstorm. State Line, where the B.&A. passed from Massachusetts to New York in 1905 presented a tranquil background for young ladies in straw bonnets and long white skirts, but the brick enclosed water tower at the end of the platform testifies to the sub-zero temperatures of a mountain winter. *(Right: Herbert H. Harwood Collection; Below: Rail Photo Service, H. W. Pontin.)*

WELLESLEY, Massachusetts, seat of Wellesley College, is an enclave of female erudition on the Boston & Albany main line fifteen miles west of Boston Stone where, in the ordinary course of things, through trains never stopped. At Christmas and Easter vacation time, however, the Boston section of *The Century* paused briefly there and in the photograph the assembled bluestockings cheer its arrival in the cloche hat era. *(Everett De Golyer Collection.)*

DINING car patrons of *The Century* at approximately the same period as the vignette of student life shown above reflected the fashions of the John Held and early Scott Fitzgerald era. *(New York Central.)*

IN THE LAST YEAR of its long and enviable run over the Boston & Albany *The Twentieth Century Limited* was still a patrician among name trains on the New England scene. The streamlining of No. 25 and 26 out of New York and the delays incidental to cutting in the Boston cars at Albany made the inaugural of a new through train with a single consist Boston to Chicago expedient and *The New England States* came into being. Here *The Century* in its last months retained the massive assurance of steam and Pullman Standard as it rounds the long curve at South Station yards in Boston and heads down the murky tangent to Trinity Place. *(Lucius Beebe.)*

WHEN *The New England States* replaced the historic Boston Section of *The Century* passengers could still eat before leaving at the South Station dining room whose stately portals are shown below in the original architect's elevation from which they were built in 1897. Informed travelers, however, reserved their appetites for the chicken pot pie for which *The States* achieved a celebrity comparable to that of the same dish on the Wabash. *(Left: Rail Photo Service; Below: Shepley, Bullfinch, Richardson & Abbott.)*

HAVE YOU TRIED OUR CHICKEN PIE?

Lucius Beebe, writing in Gourmet Magazine, July, 1963, says:

". . . a beautifully confected individual serving with every justification of the menu's advertisement of its 'rich, flaky crust.'"

". . . plenty of white meat, and the lovely 'goozly' Southern type of gravy. And no green peas. Green peas have no place in a chicken pie . . ."

Thank you, Mr. Beebe.

If you agree, our dining car department at 466 Lexington Avenue, New York 17, will be happy to send you the recipe upon request.

403

A NAME TRAIN whose legend and excellences have exhausted the superlative, the New York Central's *Twentieth Century Limited* on the New York-Chicago run was, for decades on end, the most celebrated train in the world, one of its fastest and certainly among the three or four best conducted varnish runs of all time. Placed in service in 1902 as an all-Pullman, extra fare, de luxe convenience for the affluent and powerful of a well-ordered world, it became with time, a national institution, a way of life and its owning carrier's most radiant showcase and advertisement. It also became the stuff of folklore, the central theme of plays and motion pictures and possessed of perhaps the most ample bibliography* of any train in the record of surface transportation. Great drama and momentous

decisions of state and finance rode its luxuriously upholstered cars and it was and is the only train to arouse so fierce and enduring a loyalty that a club of gentlemen was organized for the sole purpose of riding aboard it and holding their annual dinner en route. On the pages immediately following are reproduced a necessarily limited sampling of the ample iconography of "The Greatest Train in The World." Below, it skirts the lordly Hudson that is its most appropriate backdrop in 1913 for a panoramic likeness by W. G. Landon.

A more detailed study of The Century than is practicable in the space available will be found in "20TH CENTURY, THE GREATEST TRAIN IN THE WORLD," by Lucius Beebe, Howell-North Books, Berkeley, 1962.

Elkhart, 1929   *Alfred W. Johnson*

The 20th Century Limited
"My Gentleman's Club in The United States"

Flagship of The Fleet, Clark & 16th St.

A. W. Johnson

A highly articulate group of partisans actively believed that the company's claim to maintaining "the greatest train in the world" partook of understatement. That an equally biased contingent of regular travelers favored the competing Pennsylvania's *Broadway Limited* was the basis for a running feud that, in some cases, divided brother against brother and provided conversation in drawing rooms in the Chicago Gold Coast and along the Main Line in Philadelphia that endured over entire generations. *The Century* and *The Broadway* began their long runs in the American legend on the same day in 1902 and for a full half century paced each other through the night and down the corridors of time. They were superbly matched. Each management had standing orders with Pullman for the most improved passenger equipment as it came off the transfer table. Each maintained a culinary standard whose variety and opulence staggered foreign visitors accustomed to the regimented dining car service of England and the Continent. *The Broadway* and *The Century* had rights over everything that moved on their respective tracks and, in an age when motive power failure was not unthinkable, relief engines stood by at strategic points all through the night with pressure on the gauge and a crew handy. For many years a report on *The Century's* performance the night before was on the desk of the Central's president each morning including the on-time record, gross revenue to a penny, a chart of occupied space, a list of name celebrities on the secretary's sailing list and remarks they may have made to the dining car steward or Pullman conductor. When the Central's President Alfred H. Smith traveled abroad, *The Century's* statistics for the day before were cabled in full to him every night and when he hunted in Africa they were brought into the jungle by native runners in a forked stick. So celebrated was, and is, the crimson carpet laid for the train's departure at Grand Central that it entered the national lexicon in the phrase "red carpet treatment." In the light of this sort of thing it isn't difficult to see how *The Century* became part of the American legend, approximating the glory of the Concord coach and the drinking exploits of John L. Sullivan. In the above group William K. Vanderbilt, Mayor and Mrs. James J. Walker of New York and President F. E. Williamson pose in April 1932 on the occasion of the reduction in schedule of *The Century* from twenty to eighteen hours. (*New York Central.*)

407

THE PHOTOGRAPHS on these two pages, all of them dating from the year 1912, are of special interest to students of *The Century* legend because they each represent a departure from the conventional properties and iconography of the train itself. On this page No. 25 is shown in a wintry pastoral passing under High Bridge, The Bronx, from the camera of Charles B. Chaney, a dedicated partisan and photographer of the competing Pennsylvania Railroad who seldom ventured into the domains of the Vanderbilts. At the bottom of the page opposite is shown the switching in of the Boston cars at Albany, leaving the Boston & Albany diner spotted at the extreme right. It also shows what is believed to have been the first tailgate train herald carried on *The Century* all the way between New York and Chicago. On an adjacent page is shown a similar nameboard identifying No. 25 within the confines of Grand Central and which is conjectured to have been removed, along with the service connections, at sailing time. Whether or not this train herald was illuminated cannot be determined from the available likenesses. (*Above: The Smithsonian Institution; Opposite, Two Photos: New York Central.*)

THE TWENTIETH
CENTURY LIMITED

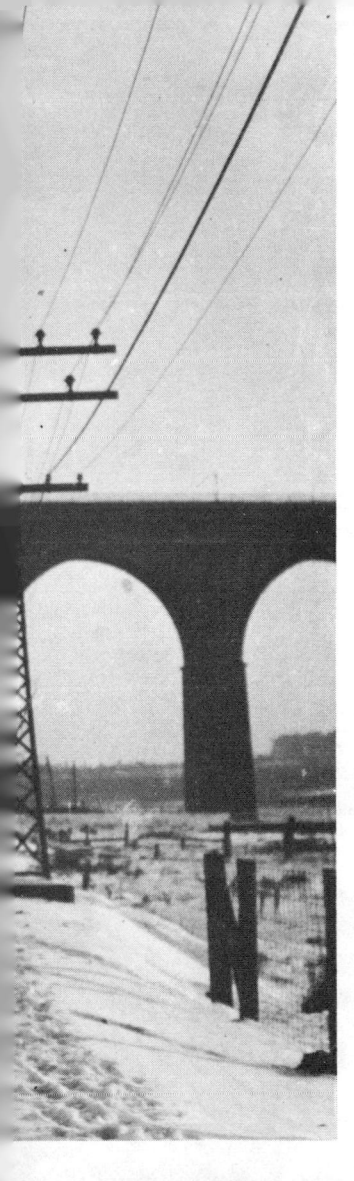

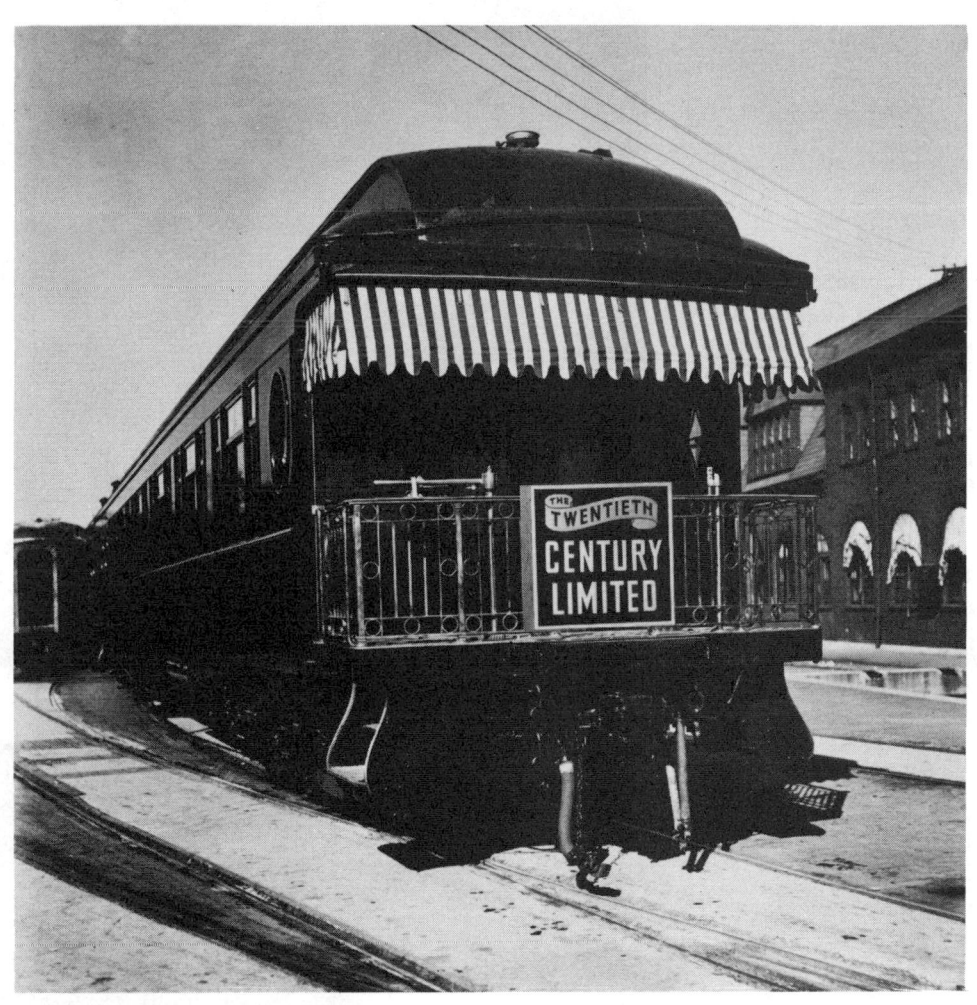

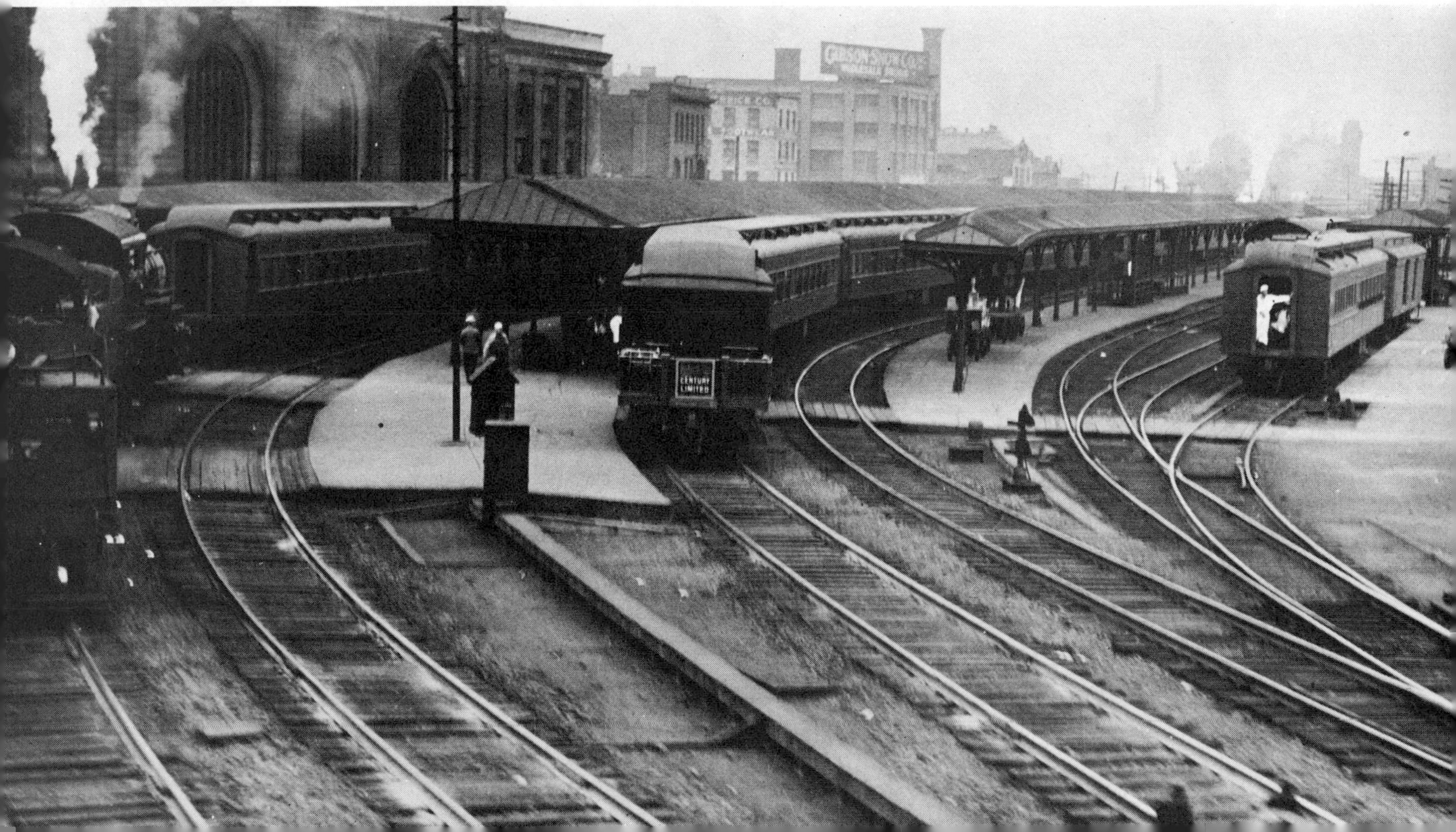
CENTURY LIMITED

EVEN in its early years, probably about 1912, as is suggested by the Gothic-windowed Pullmans, delaying the progress of No. 25 was a lapse to congeal the marrow of New York Central operating personnel. When, therefore, *The Century* was unaccountably stabbed in the shadow of Harlem River High Bridge at Spuyten Duyvil, the obvious consternation of crew members was understandable. *(Everett De Golyer Collection.)*

THIS STUNNING period piece is as precisely dated by the internal evidence of its principals as by any record in the New York Central archives and is beyond all peradventure from the period between 1922 and 1925. Students of masculine fashion will readily identify the soft roll, notched lapel jacket and twenty-two inch trouser bottoms on the young man at the right as coming from the cutting rooms of J. Press or Arthur Rosenberg at New Haven, arbiters of men's fashions of the era, while the plus fours and Glenargyll golf stockings of his younger brother are archetypal of the moment's style at Hotchkiss. The confirmation of the women's attire is superfluous. (*New York Central.*)

411

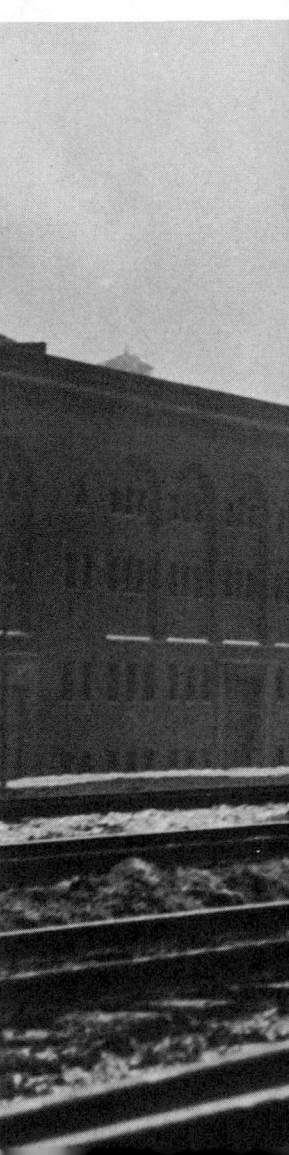

ALMOST as familiar an item in the
folk-iconography of the American
People as Custer's Last Stand, over the
years has been the image of
The Twentieth Century Limited
speeding, with flags at its smokebox
across calendars and lithographs
in countless millions of copies.
A less dramatic presentation depicts it
here arriving at Chicago of a misty
morning behind a classic
New York Central Hudson in the
Pullman Standard years.
Opposite, No. 26 leaves Englewood
on a snowy afternoon of the same period
for a Christmas card vignette by
Alfred W. Johnson.
The two services depicted are among
the essential amenities of the good
life on "The Greatest Train in The World."
(Above: Everett De Golyer
Collection; Two Photos: New York
Central.)

412

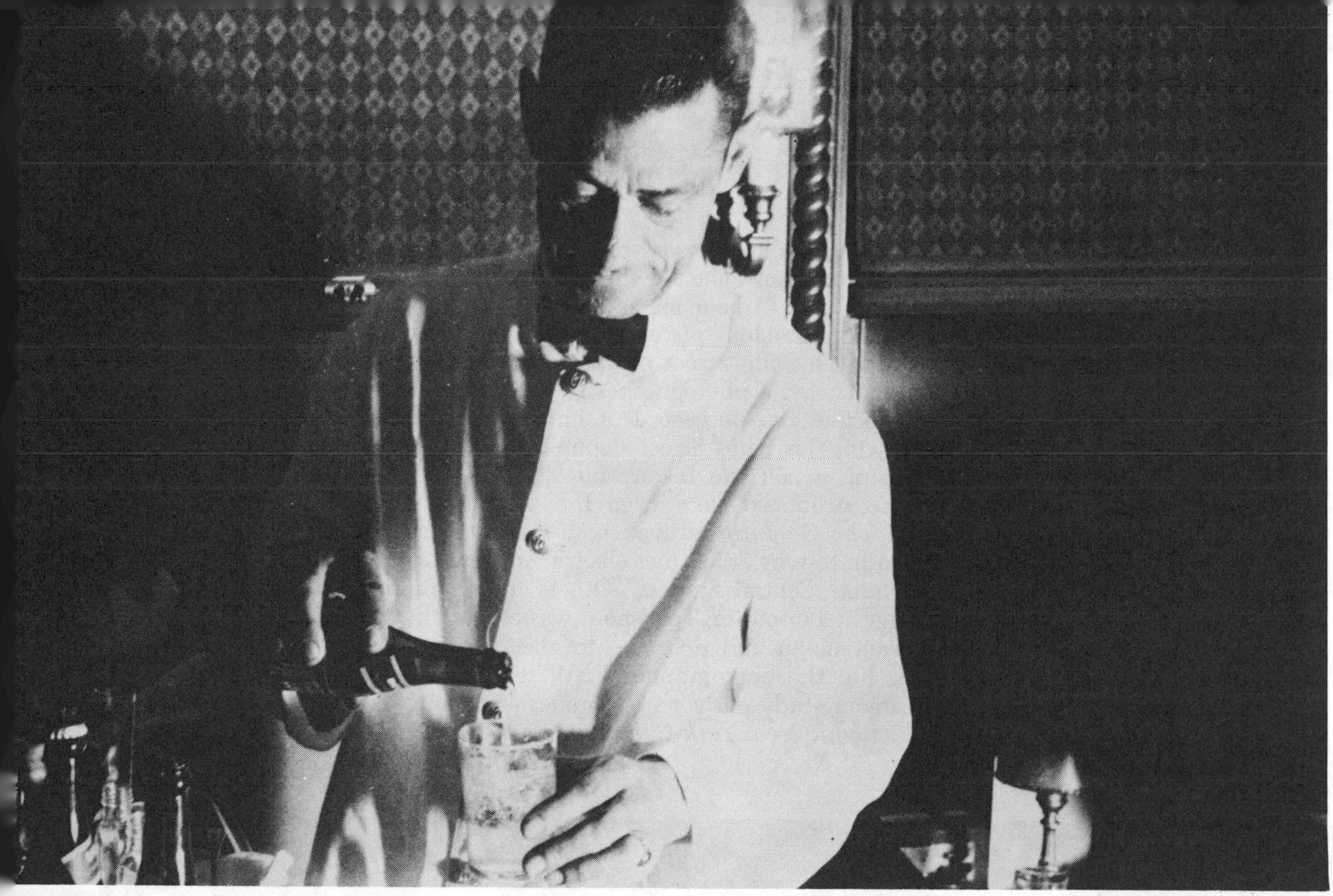

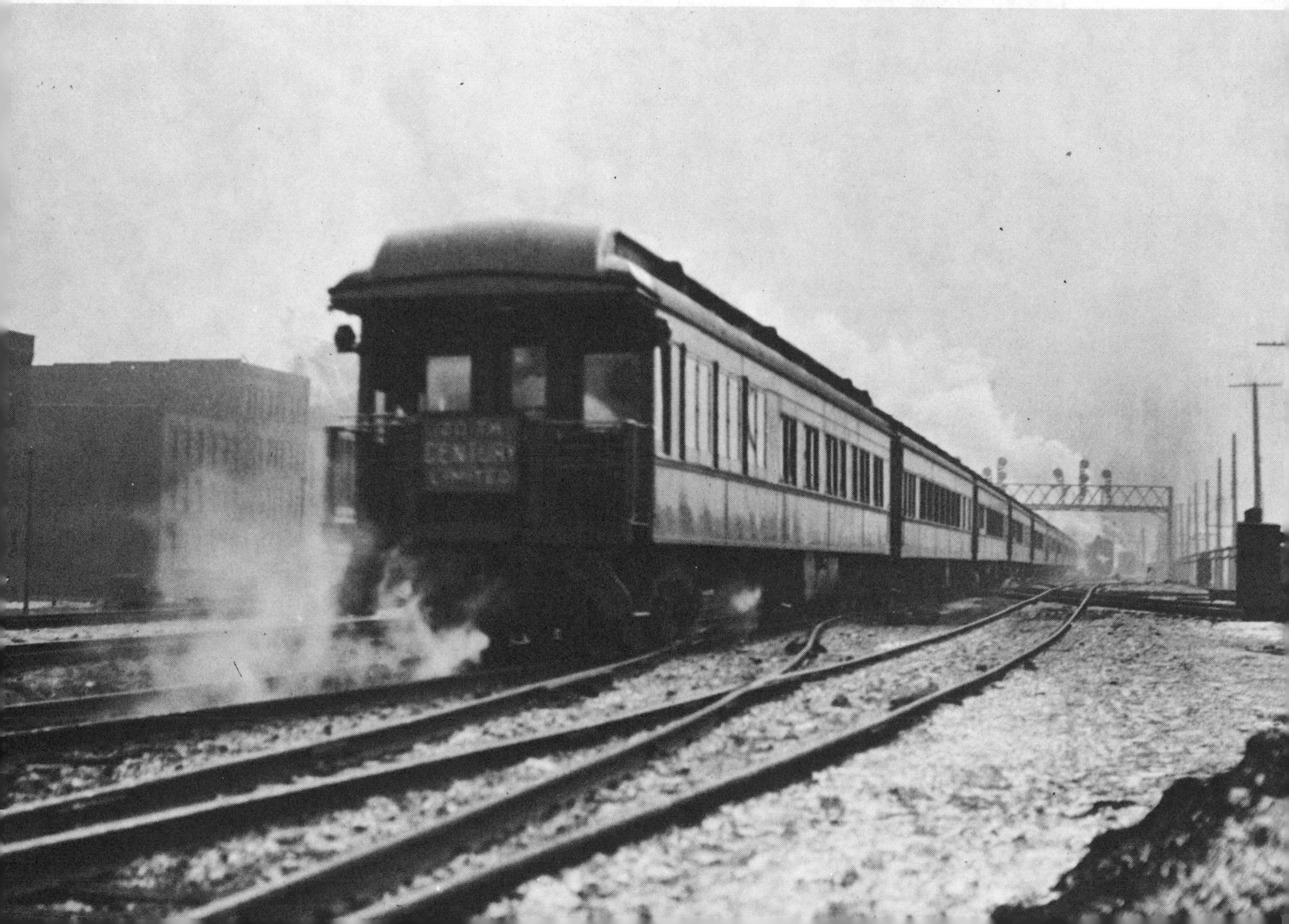

"The Century celebrates its twenty-fifth anniversary this spring," wrote the much-loved Christopher Morley in his column, "The Bowling Green" in *The Saturday Review of Literature* for April 2, 1927. "I hear much of King Ganaway, the Chicago photographer who has done marvelous pictures of engines. I hope he'll do *The Century* as she pulls out of La Salle Street on the morning of June 15th." As a matter of record, King Ganaway, a photographer so elusive at this remove that the Chicago Historical Society has no record of him, had already photographed *The Century* not leaving La Salle Street depot but arriving six years earlier. He called his photograph which was taken March 31, 1921, "The Spirit of Transportation" and it is reproduced here from the private collection of Everett De Golyer of Dallas. *The Century* outlived both Ganaway and Morley who has long since been taken in tow by "the quiet electric engine, Peace, which brings him at last into his Grand Central Station." Others took a more earthy view of *The Century* as is suggested opposite. To some it was essentially a private club with a spacious restaurant menu and doorman to check the members in and out over the red carpet. For the photographer F. W. Blauvelt (*bottom*) it was the subject for a fine camera study early on a summer's morning as it left Albany in September 1914.   (*Right: New York Central; Below: Everett De Golyer Collection; Opposite Top: Ed Nowak.*)

TWENTIETH CENTURY LIMITED

DINNER SPECIALS

CHICKEN OKRA SOUP *with Rice*.......................in Cup 25; Tureen 35
COLD TOMATO BOUILLON..in Cup 25
CONSOMME *Hot or Cold*..in Cup 25

FRIED FILLET OF FLOUNDER *with Tartar Sauce* 70
BROILED FRESH MACKEREL, *Boiled Potato*................ 75
BROILED SCROD *with Bacon*............................. 75
MIXED FRUIT OMELETTE... 65
FRESH VEGETABLE DINNER... 70
ROAST BEEF HASH, *Browned in Pan*................................. 65
LAMB CHOP *en Casserole with Vegetables*........................ 90
FRICASSEE OF CHICKEN *with Rice Curry* 90
ROAST PRIME RIBS OF BEEF, *with Mashed or Boiled Potato* 90
COLD BAKED HAM ⎫
COLD ROAST BEEF ⎬ *with Potato Salad*........................... 85
COLD ROAST PORK ⎭
SALMON OR SHRIMP SALAD *with Mayonnaise*...................... 60
LETTUCE WITH TOMATOES OR CUCUMBERS........................ 40
PINEAPPLE SALAD *with Cream Cheese*............................. 50

FRESH SPINACH.. 25
NEW CABBAGE.................................... 20
BAKED WHITE ONIONS............................ 25
MASHED OR BOILED POTATO................... 20
NEW POTATO *in Cream* 25

BANANA CREAM CUSTARD............................. 25
COFFEE JELL, *Whipped Cream* 25
ICED WATERMELON................................. 25
CANTALOUPE *a la mode*..................... 50
FRESH BLUEBERRY PIE.................... 25
ORIENTAL FRUIT CAKE.................... 20
VANILLA ICE CREAM OR FROZEN PUDDING 30
BLUEBERRIES WITH BOWL OF CRACKERS AND MILK ... 55

Special Combination No. 1 — $1.25

FRIED FILLET OF FLOUNDER *with Tartar Sauce* or
BROILED FRESH MACKEREL, *Maitre d'Hotel*
FRESH SPINACH   POTATO *in Cream*
ASSORTED BREAD *or* ROLLS
COFFEE JELL, *Whipped Cream*   BANANA CREAM CUSTARD
TEA, COFFEE, MILK

Special Combination No. 2 — $1.50

CHOICE OF COLD MEATS *with Potato Salad* or
FRICASSEE *of* CHICKEN *with Rice Curry* or
ROAST PRIME RIBS OF BEEF *au Jus*
BAKED WHITE ONIONS   MASHED POTATO
ASSORTED BREAD *or* ROLLS
PIE   BANANA CREAM CUSTARD   ICE CREAM
TEA   COFFEE   MILK

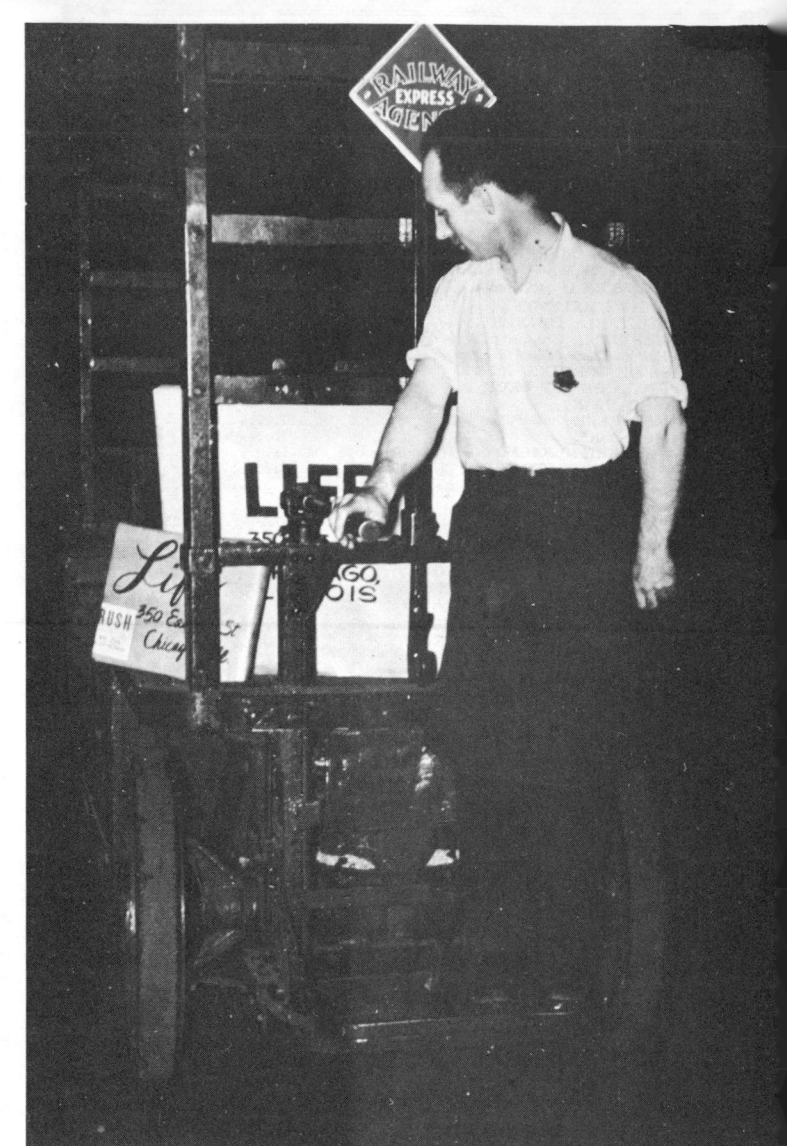

416

MANY AS WERE the regular patrons to whom *The Twentieth Century Limited* was a way of life and frequent experience, none was so constant a rider every night for years on end as Henry R. Luce represented by *Life* magazine. Luce *in propria persona* might well be installed in Car 250 but the pictures, layouts and editorial matter of Luce publications received even more preferential treatment in the Railway Post Office up ahead. The grand manner usually accompanied the arrival at Track 27 of the dispatch cases and ostentatiously identified layouts of Time Inc. Like Mrs. Vanderbilt making an entry at the Metropolitan Opera, the messenger from Rockefeller Center was often the last man through the train gate and if he didn't have time to sprint the sixteen car lengths before No. 25 high-balled out of its slip, he handed his pouch up to a Pullman conductor as the train was moving. At Englewood, because it was nearer the printing plant of R. R. Donnelley where *Life* was run, an equally swift messenger with a motorcycle retrieved the copy next morning and sped it to 350 East Twenty-second Street. Like the train it rode, the routing of *Life* was accomplished with a panache and awareness of drama. *(Left: Everett De Golyer Collection; Four Photos:* Life.)

417

A VIEW of the observation section of the Dreyfuss streamlined *Century* on Track 29 at Grand Central Station suggests a continuity with the lush days when the train's florist bills alone ran to better than $1,000 a month in the hard gold currency of the times. Although the barbers, manicurists, and many of the other once essential amenities of first class travel had gone with the wind, *The Twentieth Century Limited,* when well into its seventh decade of almost continuous operation, was still a train in the very grand manner and a name to conjure with in the lexicon of American institutions. The vignette of luxury reproduced here was taken especially for this book by the New York Central.

TO IMPLY THAT, at least in recent years, the cuisine of *The Century* would shame the management of Maxim's in Paris or arouse envy in the heart of Henri Soulé would be to trifle with veracity, but in the years when the best food in America was being served and eaten on rails, its dining car service ranked second to none. In the train's formative years all its butter came from the celebrated Vermont dairy farm of Dr. William Seward Webb, a Vanderbilt in-law whose groceries afforded passengers a vicarious acquaintance with the aristocracy. When *The Century* raised the price of the until then almost universal dollar dinner to $1.50 it elevated its status to that of Sherry's and Delmonico's. In good times, the dining car management of the Central felt that if its food took in fifty cents for every dollar it cost the showing was highly creditable. Fine food and service maintained at a loss were the pride of all railroads which, quite correctly, regarded their passenger service as their best advertising and their diners as their best showcase for it. *Century* specialties were planked shad in season and a special variety of uncommonly succulent watermelon pickle. Here the fish cook practices his art on a mess of fresh brooktrout. Below, the streamlined *Century* in steam leaves Englewood, Illinois, eastbound. *(Left: New York Central; Below: Everett De Golyer Collection.)*

THE MOST COMPULSIVE DYNASTY of builders in the
American record, the Vanderbilt family provided
New York City with its most notable landmarks in the closing
years of the nineteenth century.
They ranged from the formidable array of Vanderbilt chateaux
in upper Fifth Avenue to the equally massive St. Johns Park
freight station and first Grand Central Terminal.
It was built in 1871 at the command of Commodore Vanderbilt
by Isaac C. Buckout, chief engineer of the
New York & Harlem Railroad over whose tracks the other
Vanderbilt lines entered New York. The huge covered
train shed was the largest such structure in the United States
and no locomotive smoke ever soiled its soaring arches.
Trains made a running start in the yards, the engines
were uncoupled at speed and ran on ahead to be switched out in
an operation that would curl the hair of today's railroaders,
while the cars were hand-braked to a halt in their
appropriate bays. No accident was ever known
to result from the practice. First Grand Central survived as
shown here with few alterations until 1903.
Cards advertising Simeon Ford's Grand Union Hotel
(see opposite) like that at the right were passed out by
New York Central trainmen for many years.
(Two Drawings: Museum of the City of New York.)

ALTHOUGH A GREAT NUMBER of hotels arose in the vicinity of Grand Central both in the nineteenth and twentieth centuries, the Belmont, Biltmore, Manhattan, Commodore, Barclay and Murray Hill, one in particular, the Grand Union was notable for its close bonds with the terminal. Occupying the entire half of the block bounded by Park Avenue, Forty-second and Forty-first Streets, the Grand Union, until its demise in 1914, was so closely associated in the public mind with Grand Central as to constitute an actual extension of its facilities. In an era when hotels were far less impersonal than they were to become, and when many derived their celebrity from their host or proprietor, the Grand Union was inseparably identified with its owner, Simeon Ford, a wit, raconteur and after-dinner speaker whose *bon mots* were fully as notable as those of the great Joseph Choate or Chauncey M. Depew, President of the New York Central, whose office was just across the street. Ford made a calculated bid for the transient trade deriving from the Central's Palace Cars just as the Belmont, on the opposite corner, was later to cater specially to patrons arriving from Boston via the New Haven. Ford advertised the Grand Union widely in Upstate New York, stressing its handy location, dollar rooms and free porter service to and from the train gates. Its several restaurants carried condensed timetables on the reverse side of their menus and the lobby bristled with railroad maps, travel literature and other conveniences for mobile patrons. There was also a transportation porter, something new at the time, who was reputedly able to procure hard-to-get space on the Vanderbilt lines. The Grand Union was, in fact, the small town depot hotel of Railroad Street sublimated on a vast scale so as to rank as a national institution. Its advertised amenities included "hair curlers, hot house roses and hand-painted pianos" but its cluttered and sprawling public apartments were designed to set at ease rustic patrons who might feel self-conscious among the French *maitres d'hotel* and evening dressed patrons of the Windsor or Waldorf. In its final years the Grand Union enjoyed an extremely shady reputation as a place where marriage certificates were never asked. The view shown here depicts its facade on Park Avenue South with, in the foreground, the original Harlem Railroad tunnel that is today a vehicular underpass. *(Museum of the City of New York.)*

421

IN THE YEAR 1905, a date proclaimed in the window card showing reduced rates to the St. Louis Fair, The New York Central maintained a ticket office at No. 338 Fulton Street in darkest Brooklyn, where a lady typist, derby hats and a sheet iron stove endorse the date. Evidence, too, that Brooklyn was then of more account than it was later to be is in the presence next door of Knox the princely hatter who did no business in rundown communities. Note the bonnet of a primordial motor truck obtruding at the left. *(Two Photos: Everett De Golyer Collection.)*

THE NEW GRAND CENTRAL had recently been opened with its high level platforms and subterranean trackage when the photograph reproduced below was taken of an unidentified New York Central train which is fascinating to the student of railroad lore for two special reasons. Seated on the observation rail was Yale's rising young Professor William Lyon Phelps who was then attracting national attention by his advanced literary views while, visible on his car and those in the background were examples of the then-emergent rear-end train herald. On Professor Phelps' train, with its richly bonneted and perhaps literary ladies, was an electrically illuminated oval insigne with merely the name of the owning carrier visible. On the track beyond is *The Twentieth Century Limited* with a square but otherwise similar identification containing in its legend the hour of the train's departure suggesting that this may have been hung from the observation railing only while the train was in Grand Central and then removed with the service connections at sailing time. In the dim background and visible under a reading glass a similar arrangement prevails on *The Southwestern Limited*. (Brown Brothers.)

423

TRAINS emerging from the train shed at Grand Central headed north along Park Avenue in a three-mile skirmish with grade crossings and an improbable pattern of switches. Forty-second Street traffic *(right)* in the horsecab era rolled up to the New Haven's own entrance to the depot and was less of a problem. *(Two Photos: Everett De Golyer Collection.)*

424

LESS THAN a decade before it was to be torn down and replaced by the present Grand Central the Forty-second Street facade was denuded of its original red brick and white marble trim and refaced with brown sandstone. Scaffolding from this operation was still in place when the photo at left was taken about 1905. In the background is the structure of the fine new Manhattan Hotel, celebrated as the birthplace of Manhattan cocktails. Returning from an alarm, as is suggested by its leisurely pace, is a steam fire pumper headed east through Forty-second Street traffic. *(Everett De Golyer Collection.)*

THE FORTY-SECOND STREET horsecars ran directly under the office windows of William Henry Vanderbilt. In the background is the Grand Central stub end and station of the Lexington Avenue elevated, demolished when the Times Square shuttle subway was built. (*Two Steel Engravings:* HARPER'S WEEKLY.)

ONE OF THE SEVERAL massive monuments to the Vanderbilt family genius
for acquisition and passion for architecture that dotted Manhattan Island, the
first Grand Central Station in the horsecab and gaslamp era was one of the
ranking showplaces of New York. Its fine mansarded towers, ornate window trim
and striped awnings in summer were symbolic of Vanderbilt solidity although
its internal arrangements were somewhat inept. Entirely separate waiting rooms
were provided for each of its three tenants, the Central, the Harlem and the New
Haven, the most commodious of these, curiously enough, being that of the New
Haven at the east end of the structure nearest Lexington Avenue. At Grand
Central until the time of his death, William Henry Vanderbilt occupied handsome offices and patronized the barber shop in the basement next Vanderbilt
Avenue. The turn of the century face lifting, shown on this page, which was a
stopgap until the new depot should be opening in 1913, was dimly regarded by
New Yorkers. Its sandstone sheathing was felt to be commonplace, the vanished
mansard roofs were mourned. Its detractors felt it an example of the futility of
progress and said the Commodore was made restless by it in his mausoleum at
New Dorp. Perhaps he was. *(Above: New York Central; Opposite: Library of
Congress.)*

427

New York Central

Manhattan Cathedral

FOLKLORE GATHERS thickly around Grand Central Terminal and the dedicated student of the railroad legend is often hard put to separate the warp of fancy from the woof of reality. It was to its antecedent structure whose likeness is amply recorded on adjacent pages, that wags of the gay nineties admired to address letters to the august President of the New York Central & Hudson River Railroad as "Hon. Chauncey M. Depot, Care: The Grand Central Depew." There was a well-publicized mouse with a nice taste for the better things who rode back and forth to Boston on the New Haven's *Merchants Limited*, spending a night at South Station or a week at Grand Central as fancy dictated. The Belmont Hotel, handily available through a passage under Forty-second Street was designed by its architect in the outline of a barrel, widest at its mid-elevation and tapering slightly at the top and bottom, to remind train-bound tarriers to stop at its wonderful square bar en route to the appropriate train gate for the *Bay State Express* or *Lake Shore Limited*. Chief of Redcaps James H. Williams was never tipped by Presidents of the United States; protocol required instead an autographed photograph. The pearls reportedly found by patrons of Grand Central's celebrated oyster bar would, collectively, have supplied Tiffany for a year. The verifiable facts of Grand Central had about them an Arabian nights cachet of mystery and splendor. By the end of the nineteenth century it had become apparent that first Grand Central designed by Isaac C. Buckout and the pride and joy of Commodore Cornelius Vanderbilt, was outmoded and its demolition began in 1903. The transition from the old terminal facilities to the new, without interruption of service in any appreciable degree, took just a decade and the incredibly handsome structure of today was opened in 1913.

Overnight Grand Central became institutional, one of the sights of the city and its vast sunlit concourse hailed as "the most beautiful room in the world." Artists and photographers, fascinated by its dimension and patterns of light and dark, glorified in silver bromide and dry point etchings the sunlight that streamed through its immensely tall windows. Outside on the ramp that was a continuation of Park Avenue South, The Commodore himself, in immemorial bronze and rescued from the pediment of the St. Johns Park freight house where he had been emplaced with oratory by Mayor A. Oakey Hall, surveyed the city vista with a regard of benevolent rapacity.

Other people than photographers and artists were passionate partisans of Grand Central, including the editors of *The New Yorker* who waged a vitriolic campaign to prevent commercials from being broadcast on its loud speaker system at rush hours. Booklovers browsed in its four excellent bookshops. Others patronized its newsreel theater and ate Cotuits and Lynnhavens in uncounted millions at its oyster bar without ever passing through a train gate. Thousands used its miles of ramps, tunnels and passageways as short cuts to the Biltmore, the Yale Club, the Belmont, Roosevelt and Commodore hotels, not to mention the New York subway. To the confirmed New Yorker, Grand Central was a condition of life in the metropolis, from trainboards to taxis and the arrival and departure of the great aboard such name trains as *The Century, The Southwestern, The Empire State* and the New Haven's *Yankee Clipper* and *Merchants Limited*.

EXCEPT IN MINOR DETAILS, the appearance
of Grand Central changed little from its opening in 1871 as the most massive of Vanderbilt
landmarks in New York City, until 1899 when
a temporary over-all facelifting was attempted
as a stopgap until the erection of the entire new
structure of 1913. Some of the improvements of
the 1899 renovation were high level platforms
in the old train shed *(right)* and a false front at
the southern bulkhead *(below)* with individual
track gates and consequently enlarged waiting
room and office space. Because the new false-
work partially obstructed the original clock, a
second or supplementary clock was emplaced,
but victims of progress, many New Yorkers felt,
were the fine bronze battle lanterns which had
illuminated the concourse at every track gate
in the old days. The changes were only intended
as temporary conveniences for when they were
inaugurated at the end of the century, plans
were already being made for the present structure and the demolition of adjacent properties
for its accommodation started in 1903. *(Two
Photos: The Smithsonian Institution.)*

GRAND CENTRAL's Information Bureau, which was relocated in the center of the great concourse in the new structure where it is to this day a New York landmark, in the original Grand Central was located adjacent to the train shed whose monumental arch can be seen through the transom in this rare photograph from about 1900. In addition to the information desk personnel a corps of uniformed ushers was maintained (as distinct from the redcaps) whose duties were those of couriers and liason generally, much like those of the passenger agents of a later organization. (*New York Central.*)

NEW YORK CENTRAL SYSTEM

TIME SHOWN IS EASTERN STANDARD

SPECIAL NOTICE

TRAIN NO	NAME	DUE	WILL ARRIVE ABOUT	TRACK
54	Albany Express	4.31		
72	The Henry Hudson	4.40		
102	Chatham	5.02		
	...ghkeepsie	5.50		
	...rth Shore Ltd.	6.00		
	...th Adams-Pittsfield	6.56		
	The Missourian	7.00		
	...cal	1.03	on time	40
	...K	1.15	1.10	29
	...wk	1.15	on time	27	Made up at Syracuse Western Train.

COMING TRAIN
...ACK NUMBERS
...OSTED ABOUT
...MINUTES BEFORE
...RRIVAL

THE NEW

TRAIN NO	NAME	DUE
75	Spring...	
11	The ...	
105	Day...	

ELECTRONICS and a public address system had supplanted the leather-lunged stentor of arriving trains when this photograph was taken in Grand Central's west waiting room in the thirties. Experienced travelers and regulars in Grand Central knew that from the west waiting room direct access via underground passageways led to the Biltmore Hotel lobby and the Yale Club, but that the cab service, indicated in the photograph opposite, which functioned in a subterranean branch of hell, was ineffectual in fair weather and worse when it rained. Chances for taxis were much better up the Biltmore staircase and out into Forty-third Street. *(Two Photos: New York Central.)*

432

NOT candidates for space on *The Century,* but perhaps to be routed to their destination via *The Pacemaker* are these clients of the Traveler's Aid desk in Grand Central concourse. *(New York Central.)*

NAMED FOR THE REMARKABLE old pirate who was the primal architect of the fortunes of the New York Central & Hudson River Railroad and whose family, as long as they remained in control of its destinies, maintained one of the finest agencies of passenger transport in the world, *The Commodore Vanderbilt* was placed in service on the New York-Chicago run to absorb the traffic which overflowed from *The Century* into *The Advance Century*. Its hour of departure from each terminal anticipated *The Century* by an hour and its arrival was usually half an hour before No. 25 and 26 and there was no extra fare. Otherwise *The Commodore* was practically indistinguishable from *The Twentieth Century Limited* and, much of the time, operated with the same equipment. Lacking were some of the haughtier amenities of elegance such as the train secretary and the red carpet which accompanied the sailing of *The Century* from Grand Central but the speed and assurance of *The Commodore's* operation made it to all but the most informed intelligence, the counterpart of its more sumptuous sister run on the Water Level Route. Here the first section of *The Commodore*, Train 67 rolls past Manitou in 1940 at a time when streamlined equipment, handed down from *The Century* was being integrated to its consist. (*Edward L. May.*)

AT THE TIME of his death
when the likeness reproduced
above occupied the entire
front page of *Harper's Weekly*,
Commodore Vanderbilt was
the most wealthy of all
Americans and the master railroad builder and operator
of a generation of brass
knuckles in Wall Street and
along the high iron.
When the train named for the
old gentleman supplanted
The Advance Century,
all the amenities of Pullman
travel were available aboard all-
room cars of latest design
and superlative riding qualities.
(New York Central.)

EVEN AS THE *COMMODORE VANDERBILT* had been designed by the New York Central to supplant *The Advance Twentieth Century Limited* and had largely assumed the traffic of that train, so the great surge of postwar passenger business in the middle forties found *The Commodore* itself unable to take care of all the early afternoon patronage between Chicago and New York and was in turn supplemented by *The Advance Commodore Vanderbilt.* For a time, as is suggested by the accompanying timecards, *The Advance Commodore* carried the through car from San Francisco on its eastbound run and, since it shared the car pool with its parent train its appearance was identical with *The Commodore Vanderbilt* proper. It is shown below running beside the Hudson behind Niagara type locomotive No. 6008 whose elephant ear smoke deflectors became for a time the identifying hallmark of the Central's steam superpower. *(Edward L. May.)*

No. 65—Advance Commodore Vanderbilt—Daily

Lounge Sleeping Car
  New York to Chicago (6 Double Bedroom-Buffet)
Sleeping Cars
  New York to Chicago (4 Comp.-4 Bedroom-2 D.R.)
  New York to Chicago (13 Double Bedroom)
  New York to Chicago (18 Roomette)
  New York to Chicago (10 Sec.-2 Double Bedroom-1 Comp.)
  New York to Chicago (8 Sec.-D.R.-2 Comp.)
  Albany to Chicago (8 Sec.-5 Double Bedroom)
  Albany to Chicago (12 Sec.-D.R.)
  Syracuse to Chicago (12 Sec.-D.R.)
  Buffalo to Chicago (12 Sec.-D.R.)—*Open 9.00 p.m.*
Dining Service
Coach
  New York to Chicago

No. 66—Advance Commodore Vanderbilt—Daily

Lounge Sleeping Car
  Chicago to New York (6 Double Bedroom-Buffet)
Sleeping Cars
  San Francisco to New York (10 Sec.-D.R.-2 Comp.)— *From W. P.-D. & R. G. W.-C. B. & Q. No. 40 at Chicago —Leaves San Francisco August 3, 5 and every other day thereafter*
  Chicago to New York (4 Comp.-4 Bedroom-2 D.R.)
  Chicago to New York (13 Double Bedroom)
  Chicago to New York (18 Roomette)
  Chicago to New York (10 Sec.-2 Double Bedroom-1 Comp.)
  Chicago to New York (8 Sec.-D.R.-2 Comp.)
Dining Service
Reclining Seat Coaches—All seats reserved and assigned in advance. No extra charge.
  Chicago to New York

INAUGURATED as an all-Pullman luxury run, *The Commodore,* in addition to its Chicago sleepers, carried a Pittsburgh section which ran over the Pittsburgh & Lake Erie from Cleveland as an explicit invasion of Pennsylvania territory in the ceaseless warfare between the two carriers. In the infrequent event that space couldn't be found on No. 25 by Reginald Rose who had charge of gentling celebrities at the New York end, notables such as Douglas Fairbanks, Jr., and his wife found *The Commodore* equally satisfactory in every aspect save that of status and prestige. *(Three Photos: New York Central.)*

COMMODORE VANDERBILT—
CITY OF SAN FRANCISCO
(Westbound and Eastbound)

Leave New York EVEN days during July, Sept. and Oct.; ODD days during Aug., Nov. and Dec.

Leave San Francisco ODD days during July, Sept. and Oct.; EVEN days during Aug., Nov. and Dec.

Westbound Example READ DOWN		EVERY OTHER DAY	Eastbound Example READ UP	
Fri.	■5 30 P M	lv. New York (Gd. Cent. Term.) . (NYC) (EDT) ar.	9 00 A M	Mon.
»	■6 16 P M	lv. Harmon .... » » ar.	8 02 A M	»
Sat.	8 30 A M	ar. Chicago (LaSalle St. Sta.) .... » (CDT) lv.	■4 00 P M	Sun.
»	*7 30* A M	ar. *Chicago* .... » (CST) lv.	*3 00* P M	»
»	6 30 P M	lv. Chicago (Union Sta.)..... (Milw.) » ar.	11 15 A M	»
Sun.	2 45 A M	ar. Omaha, Neb.............. » » lv.	3 00 A M	»
»	9 15 A M	ar. Cheyenne, Wyo.......... (UP)(MST) lv.	6 40 P M	Sat.
»	6 30 P M	ar. Ogden, Utah............. » » lv.	9 40 A M	»
Mon.	2 50 A M	ar. Reno, Nev................ (SP)(PST) lv.	11 14 P M	Fri.
»	7 30 A M	ar. Sacramento, Calif........ » » lv.	6 43 P M	»
»	9 32 A M	ar. Oakland, Calif. (16th St.)... » » lv.	4 40 P M	»
Mon.	10 20 A M	ar. San Francisco, Calif...... » » lv.	4 00 P M	Fri.

NEW YORK-SAN FRANCISCO (10 Roomette, 6 Double Bedroom) Car 6710.

SAN FRANCISCO-NEW YORK (10 Roomette, 6 Double Bedroom) Car 1022.

■On Saturdays and July 3, 4, 5 and September 1 leaves New York 6 00 p.m., Harmon 6 46 p.m. (E.D.T.) westbound, and leaves Chicago 4 30 p.m. (C.D.T.) eastbound.

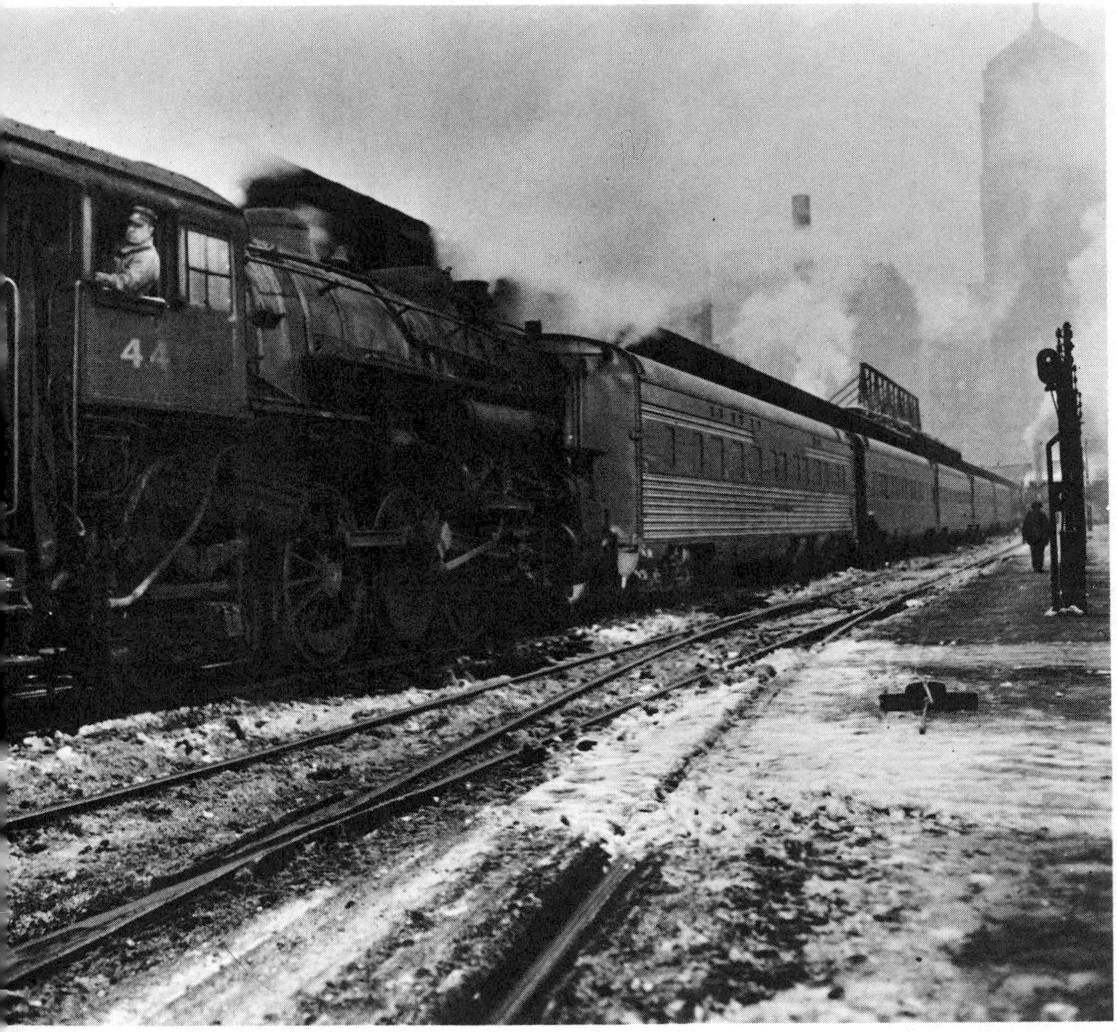

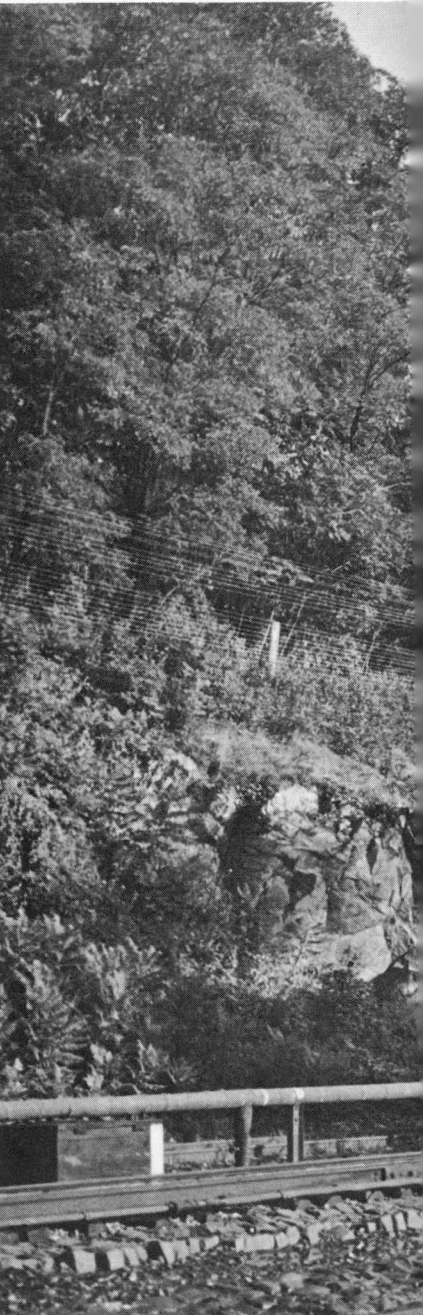

FOLLOWING THE LONG and acidulous campaigns of Robert R. Young featuring the pig who could travel coast-to-coast without changing cars, both the New York Central and the Pennsylvania instituted through Pullman car service through an involved complex of connections at Chicago for California as well as to Texas through the St. Louis Gateway. On the Central, cars were carried on *The Century, The Wolverine* and *The Commodore Vanderbilt* for Los Angeles via *The Super Chief* and *The City of Los Angeles* and for San Francisco via *The City of San Francisco* and *The California Zephyr*. The circumstance that the connections at Chicago rotated on an every other day basis with the connecting carriers, excepting *The Century-Super Chief* which was daily, made a chaos of ticketing routines and induced dementia in the minds of the traveling public. The entire California-New York setup was scrapped with few regrets following the great decline of business in 1957.

ON THE OPPOSITE PAGE the sleeper destined for *The City of San Francisco* is being cut out of *The Commodore* at La Salle Street Station. Here *The Commodore* takes water on the fly as its ten cars barrel past the track pans at Tivoli, New York. (*Opposite: Courtesy* HOLIDAY *Magazine; Above: Edward L. May.*)

THE NOTORIOUSLY HOSTILE elements of the Great Lakes had slowed *The Advance Commodore Vanderbilt* down to where it was an hour off schedule when it arrived, in the above photograph, at Indiana Harbor, Indiana, in pre-streamlined times. Although the density of names that made news on *The Commodores* never approximated that of *The Century*, many a celebrity such as Al Jolson *(right)* recognized it as the peer of No. 25 in everything but status symbolism. *The Commodore's* enclosed solarium is shown opposite bearing a generally assigned New York Central Lines train herald and below with its own proper designation after the streamlined equipment had been delivered. *(Above: Ravenswood Photos; Right: New York Central; Opposite, Two Photos: Rail Photo Service.)*

440

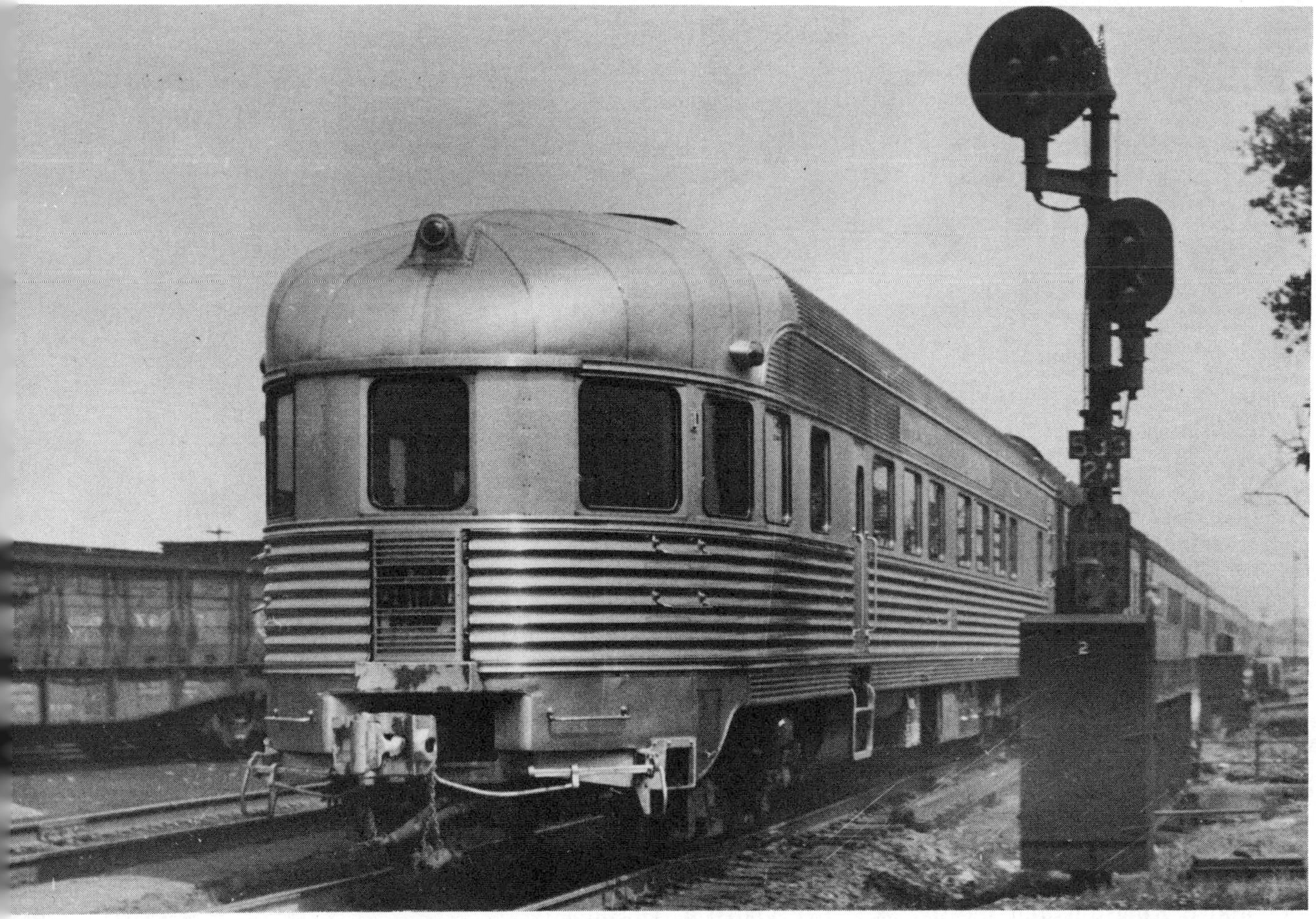

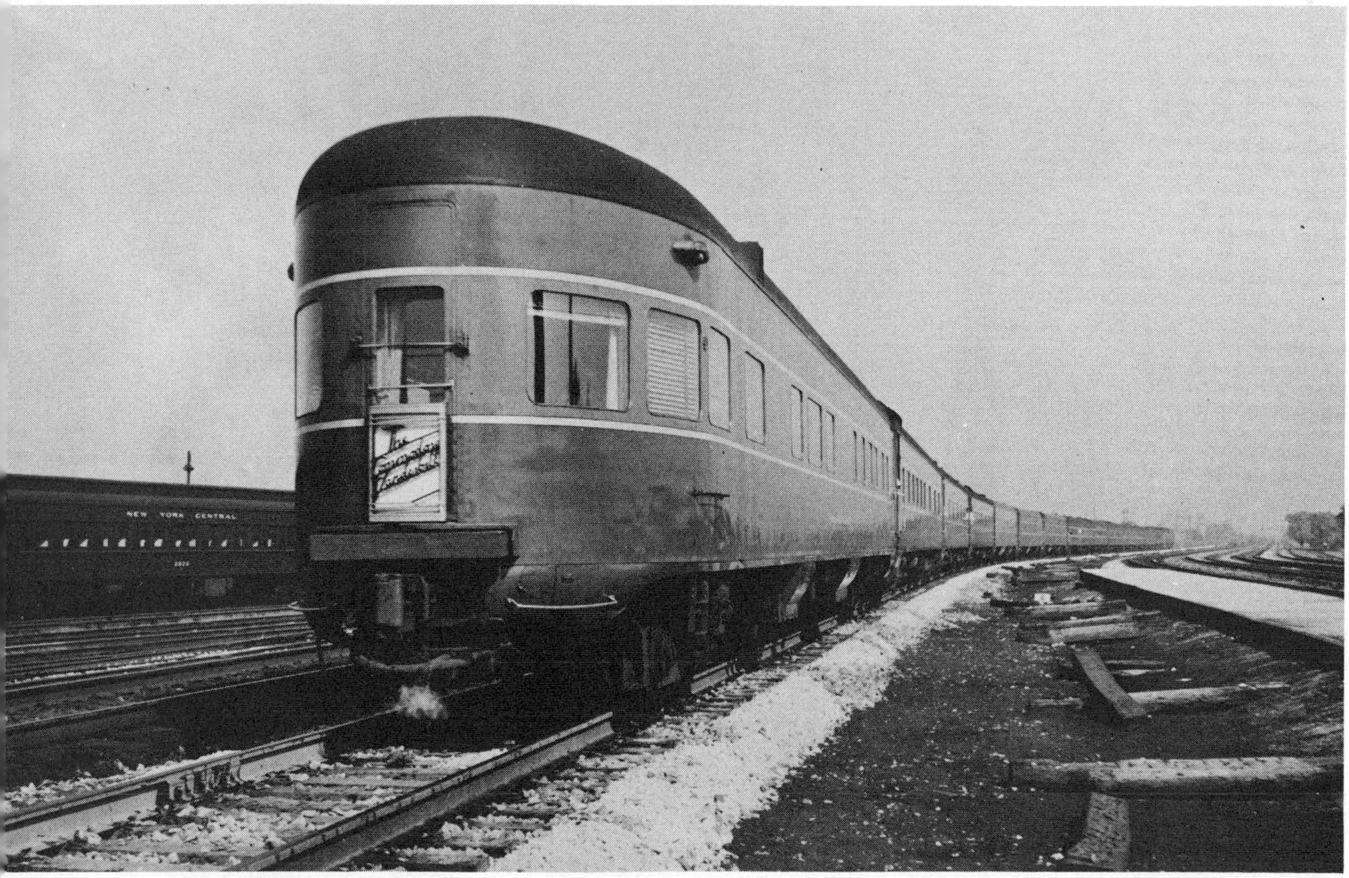
NEW YORK CENTRAL

WHEN TRAFFIC was extra heavy, *The Rip Van Winkle* ran triple headed on the steep grades above Kingston, but mostly, as shown above at Oneonta in 1900 behind a big boilered U.&D. 4-4-0. *(Two Photos: New York Central.)*

THE HAUNTS OF RIP VAN WINKLE.

THE ULSTER & DELAWARE Railroad, originally built to connect with the West Shore Route of the New York Central at Kingston and later absorbed into the N.Y.C. System as its Catskill Division, ran westward from the Hudson Valley into the superbly mountainous Washington Irving country which, in the nineties and first two decades of the twentieth century, was populous with vast wooden summer resort hotels which derived a substantial seasonal patronage from the steamcars. Name trains ran in florid profusion out of Weehawken even as early as 1896 when the Ulster & Delaware ended at Bloomville, eighty-seven miles west of Kingston. Name trains included the *Saratoga & Mohawk Valley Express* with a drawing room-parlor car to Bloomville, the *Saratoga Limited* with a buffet-drawing room car, and the ambiguously named *Rip Van Winkle Flyer* which was inaugurated in the early nineties and still running in 1935 and carried a buffet-drawing room car from Washington via the Pennsylvania, West Shore and U.&D. These sumptuous little resort varnish trains wrote an almost forgotten chapter in railroad travel, carrying their traffic to such sprawling resorts as the Catskill Mountain House, the Grand Hotel and Hotel Kaaterskill in an age of innocent pleasures. With delightful incongruity, the Ulster & Delaware had no hesitation in trading on Washington Irving's "Legend of Sleepy Hollow" and other regional folklore and saw nothing paradoxical in naming *The Rip Van Winkle Flyer*. Below is Big Indian Station long ago on the U.&D. with passengers awaiting the down train and at the extreme right an elderly party in stovepipe hat and sidewhiskers wondering if he may, with propriety, be in the picture. (*Two Photos: New York Central.*)

CATSKILL ROUTE
PROMPT
CONNECTIONS BY BOAT OR RAIL
FOR ALL POINTS NORTH AND SOUTH
HAINES CORNERS STATION.

THE SEASONAL passenger traffic over the Ulster & Delaware and its connecting West Shore division of the New York Central was almost in its entirety in vacationists bound for the great resort hotels of the Washington Irving country such as the mountaintop Kaaterskill shown here. In an age when the one night tourist was unknown, vacationing New Yorkers arrived with mountains of Saratoga trunks, hatboxes and Gladstones and moved in for the season. The New York, West Shore & Buffalo Railway, to give the route its full formal title, also maintained through and connecting Pullman services between Washington, Philadelphia and New York to Canada and the West eliminating the change of cars between Manhattan and the South required to take the Central's mainline. Opposite: West Shore depots such as that at Highland Falls had a drowsy atmosphere of their own that was a fitting prelude to the haunts of Rip Van Winkle. The Catskill & Tannerville Railroad's narrow gauge No. 2 ran from Tannerville to the Catskill Mountain House, a distance of five miles from the Otis Elevating Railway which brought passengers up from Catskill Landing. *(Above and Opposite Below: Library of Congress; Right: Fred Arone Collection; Opposite Above: Everett De Golyer Collection.)*

"Hudson River Route"

New York, West Shore, & Buffalo R'y.

CHICAGO.
BUFFALO.
SYRACUSE.
MONTREAL.
SARATOGA.
ALBANY.
CATSKILLS.
THE HUDSON.

FOR FURTHER INFORMATION CALL ON NEAREST AGENT, OR ADDRESS

HENRY MONETT, GENERAL PASSENGER AGENT.

No. 24 STATE STREET, NEW YORK.

THE TWO CRACK TRAINS on the Ulster & Delaware-New York Central West Shore service to the Catskills in 1911 were *The West Shore Express (above)* and the *Catskill Mountain Limited,* both long since vanished from the company's timetables and photographed in that distant year at Kingston, New York, by W. G. Landon. The main salon of the Central's ferry *Weehawken* depicted opposite with its graceful balustrades and stately stairs was not without some of the dignity that had characterized the long run river steamers of an earlier era. *(Two Photos: W. G. Landon; Opposite: New York Central.)*

WEST SHORE RAILROAD
NIAGARA FALLS ROUTE
N.Y.C.& H.R.R.R. Co. LESSEE

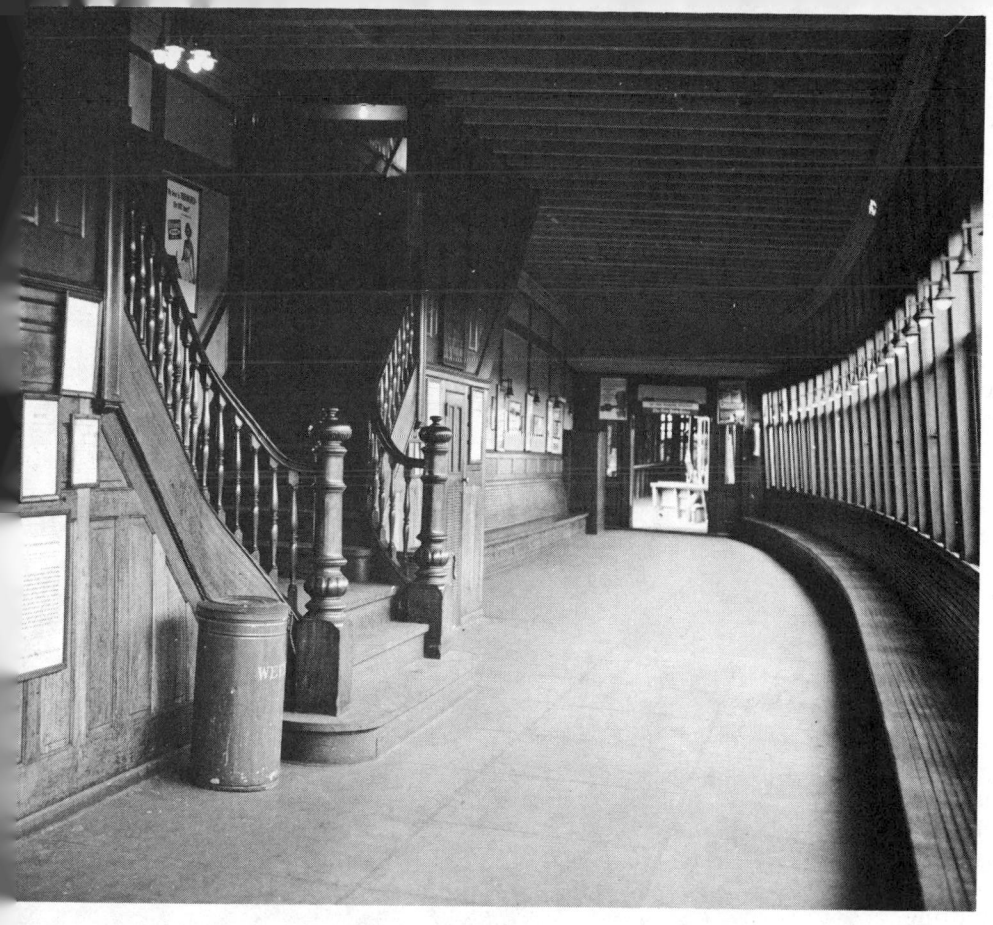

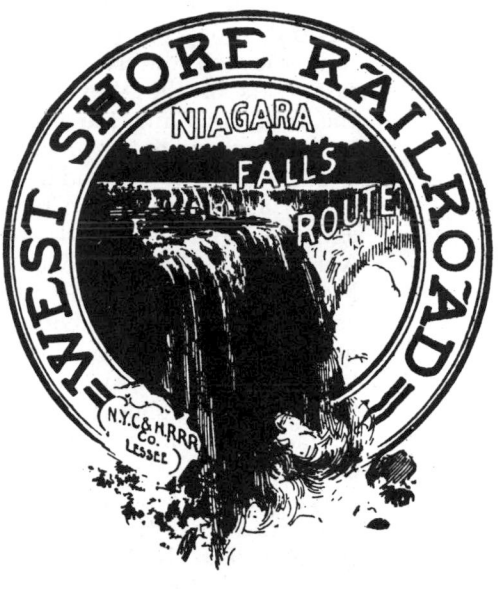

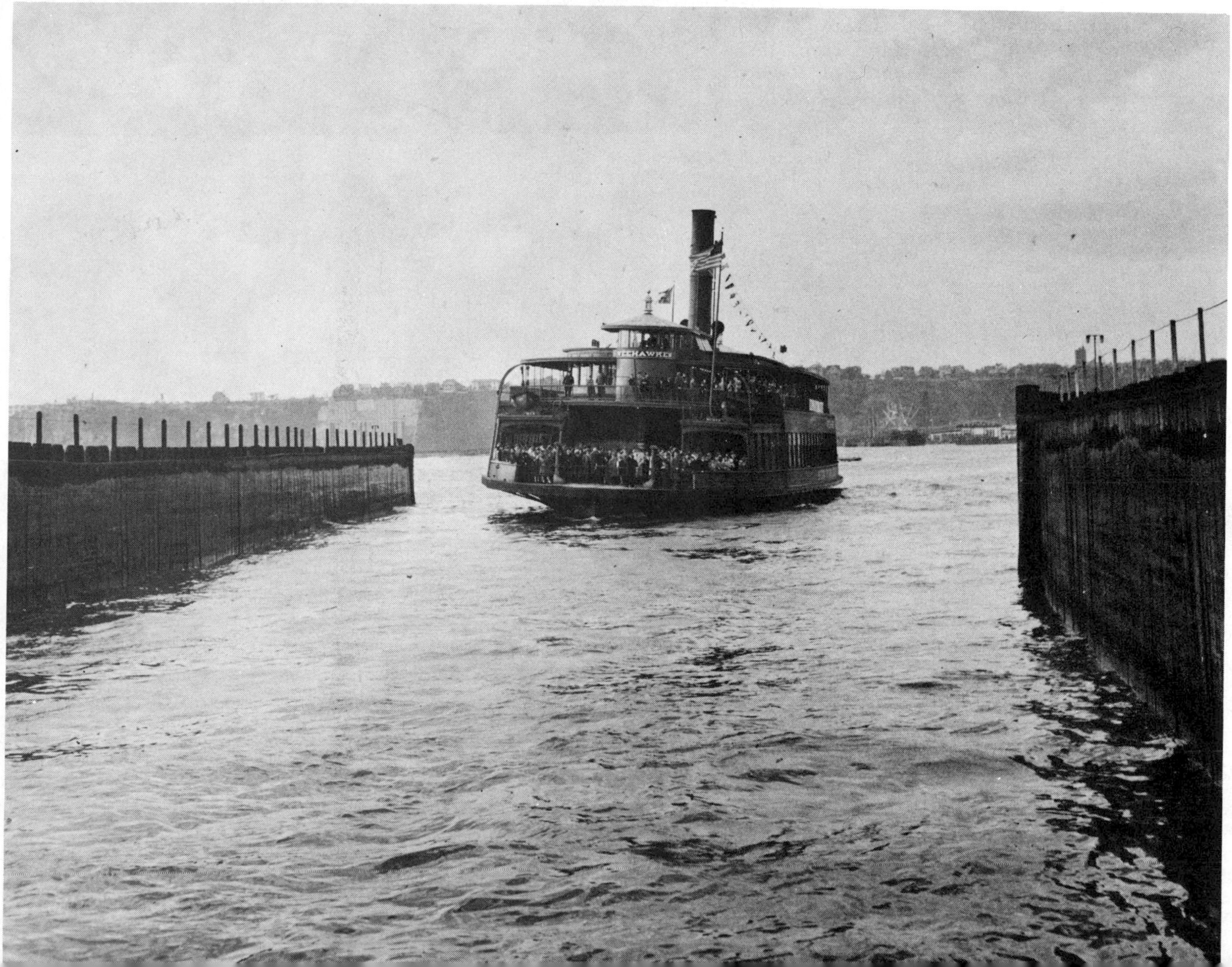

JUST AS the ferries of the Southern Pacific Railroad to Oakland and Sausalito, beautiful and almost as numerous as sea birds, had been the glory of San Francisco Bay, so the ferries serving the railroads of the Jersey shore, the Erie, Lackawanna, Pennsylvania, Central of New Jersey, the Reading, and New York Central in happier times were splendidly numerous on the North River. In the last years of the West Shore Railroad the ferries serving the New York Central's Weehawken terminal were *Weehawken* and *Albany* and like all steamers of any age they came to be institutional and, by some, beloved. Some ferries were famous for their views of Lower Manhattan, some for the speed of their crossing, others for the coffee and doughnuts which served commuters as breakfast; the Weehawken boats were celebrated for their shoeshine boys. Familiar characters of a familiar service, they cleaned the boots of generations of West Shore patrons who remember over the years the cheerful performance of a homely office. In 1963 the *Albany*, last of "the long ferries" that for thirty-four years had plied the North River between Courtland Street in lower Manhattan and Weehawken, whistled a parting salute *(opposite)* to the Singer Building in a portrait by David Plowden just before the West Shore Line suspended passenger service. *(Right and Below: New York Central; Opposite: Courtesy* AMERICAN HERITAGE.*)*

THE CENTRAL's Train No. 8, *The Wolverine*, east-bound out of Chicago over the six-track right of way of the Illinois Central with its Michigan Central connection to Detroit was, in the twenties when it is shown above, primarily a train of big business. Its traffic was in executives of general motors, Henry Ford's hatchet men and bankers for the Dodge brothers competitive empire on wheels and, although much of its consist ran through between New York and Chicago, it was primarily a Motor City train. What can be speculated about the character of the power elite of an industrial hierarchy a cross section of which is portrayed opposite in the mid-twenties? Monolithic uniformity of attire, character and attitudes of menace was the keynote of an oligarchy of arrogant togetherness which was doomed in the debacle of 1929 and much of it rode *The Wolverine*. (*Above: Everett De Golyer Collection; Opposite: New York Central, De Golyer Foundation, Collons Collection.*)

No. 8—The Wolverine-Detroiter. Daily.

Lounge Cars ...Chicago to New York—6 Double Bedrooms, Buffet.
                  Chicago to Boston—8-Section Buffet (in N Y. C. No. 14 from Buffalo, B. & A. No. 8 from Albany).
Sleeping Cars ..Chicago to New York—8-Section Drawing-room, 2-Compartment.
                  Chicago to New York—12-Section Drawing-room.
                  Chicago to Boston—8-Section Drawing-room, 2-Compartment (in N. Y. C. No. 14 from Buffalo, B. & A. No. 8 from Albany).
                  Chicago to Boston—10-Section Drawing-room, 2-Compartment (in N. Y. C. No. 14 from Buffalo, B. & A. No. 8 from Albany).
                  Detroit to Boston—12-Section Drawing-room (in N. Y. C. No. 14 from Buffalo, B. & A. No. 8 from Albany).
                  Detroit to New York—6-Compartment, 3-Drawing-room.
                  Detroit to New York—14-Section (2).
                  Detroit to New York—8-Section, 5 Single Bedrooms.
                  Detroit to New York—8-Section, 4 Double Bedrooms.
                  Detroit to New York—8 Single Bedrooms.
Parlor Car .....Chicago to Detroit.
Dining Car.....Serving all meals.
Coaches........Chicago to New York.

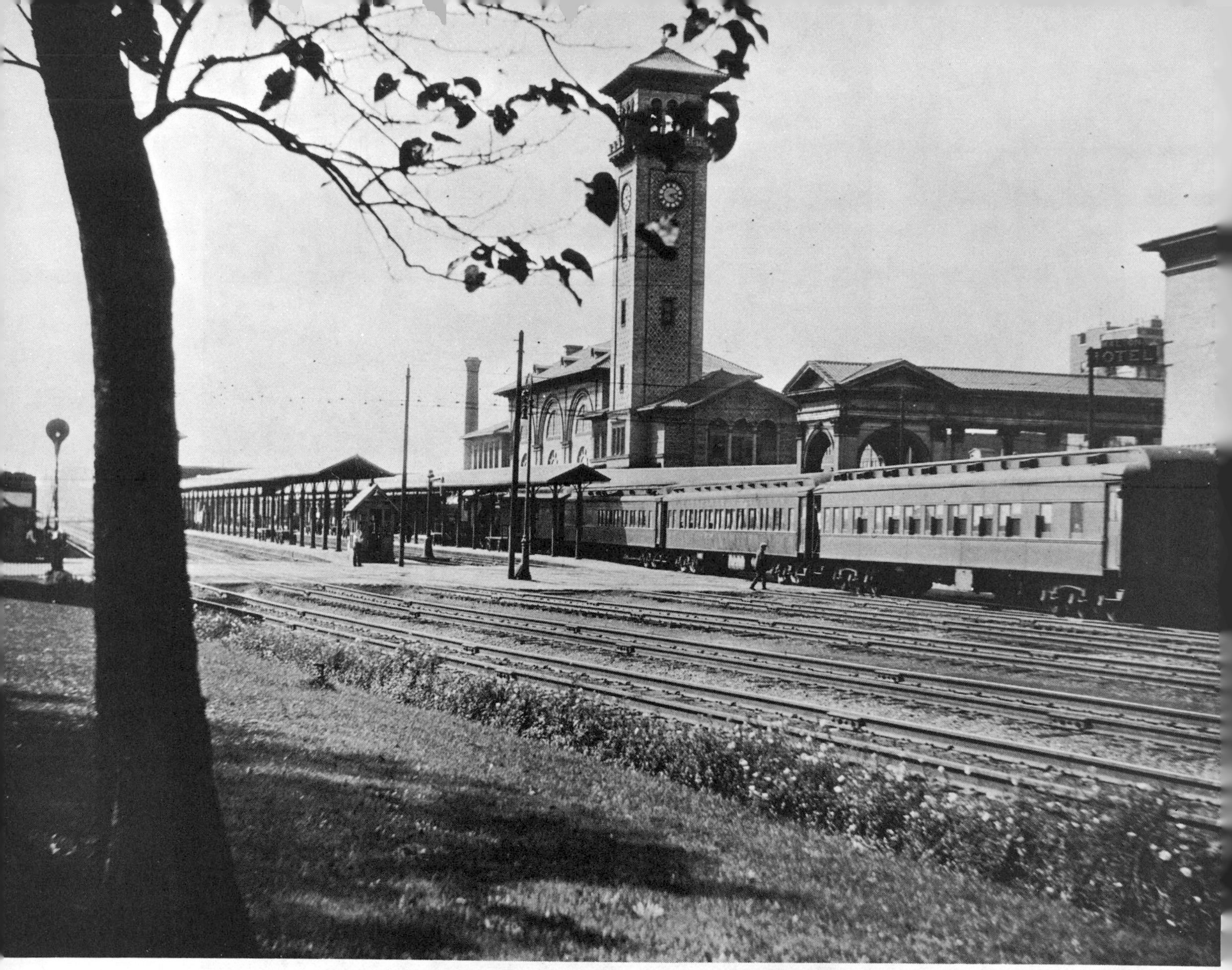
HOTEL

TRACK 34
PULLMAN
CAR
NUMBERS
COACH
150
151
LOUNGE
152
82
153
154
1502
4·00 P.M.
OHIO STATE
LIMITED
VISITORS NOT PERMITTED
THROUGH GATE
ALBANY
SCHENECTADY
SYRACUSE
BUFFALO
COLUMBUS
SPRINGFIELD, OHIO
DAYTON
MIDDLETOWN, OHIO
CINCINNATI
VIA DELAWARE & HUDSON R.R.
SARATOGA SPRINGS EX. SUN.
K 34

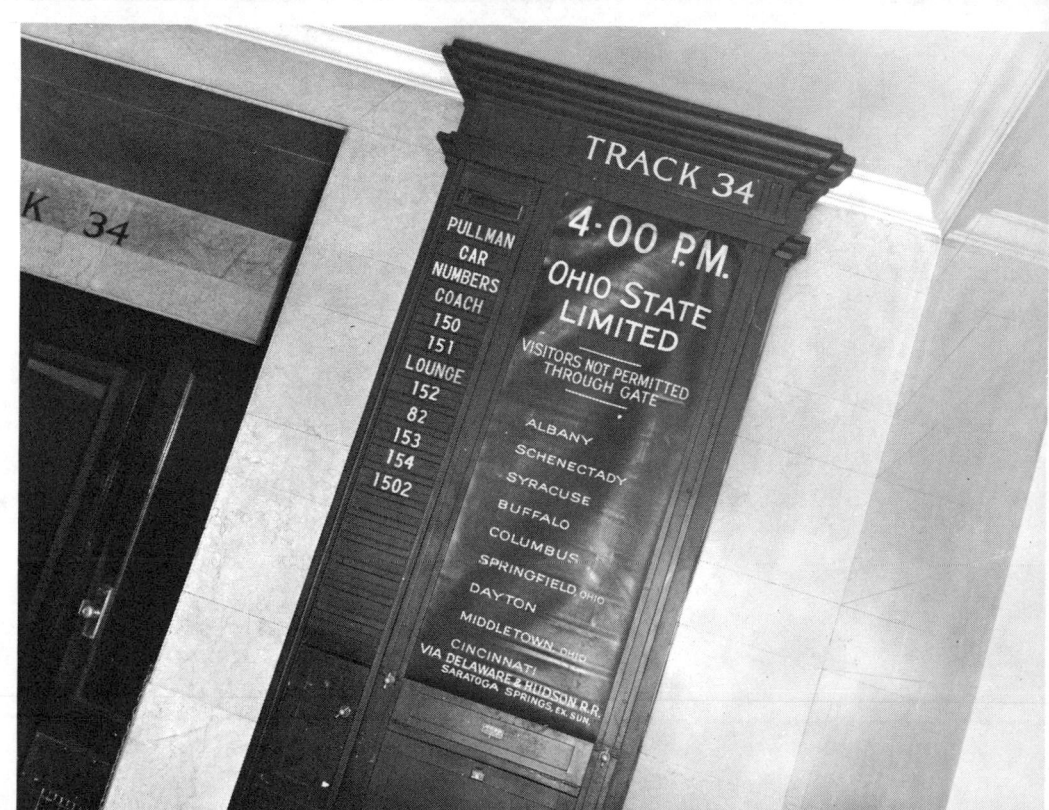

ONE OF THE FAST intermediate or intrastate runs in the Midwest once was the New York Central's Train No. 445, *The Capital City Special*, a late afternoon ballast scorcher between Cleveland and Columbus and a great favorite with businessmen and politicians with affairs at the State House early next morning. On July 30, 1944 it is shown pounding down the Big Four main line just west of Berea, Ohio, whose Gothic station tower is shown through the foliage in the background. On the page opposite, another Midwestern name to conjure with was *The Ohio State Limited*, elements of whose progress from Manhattan to Cincinnati are the train board indicating its departure from Track 34 at Grand Central and the atmospheric scene as its Pullmans are being switched in the shadow of the campanile at Dayton. *(Above: Richard J. Cook; Opposite: Ewing Galloway, New York Central.)*

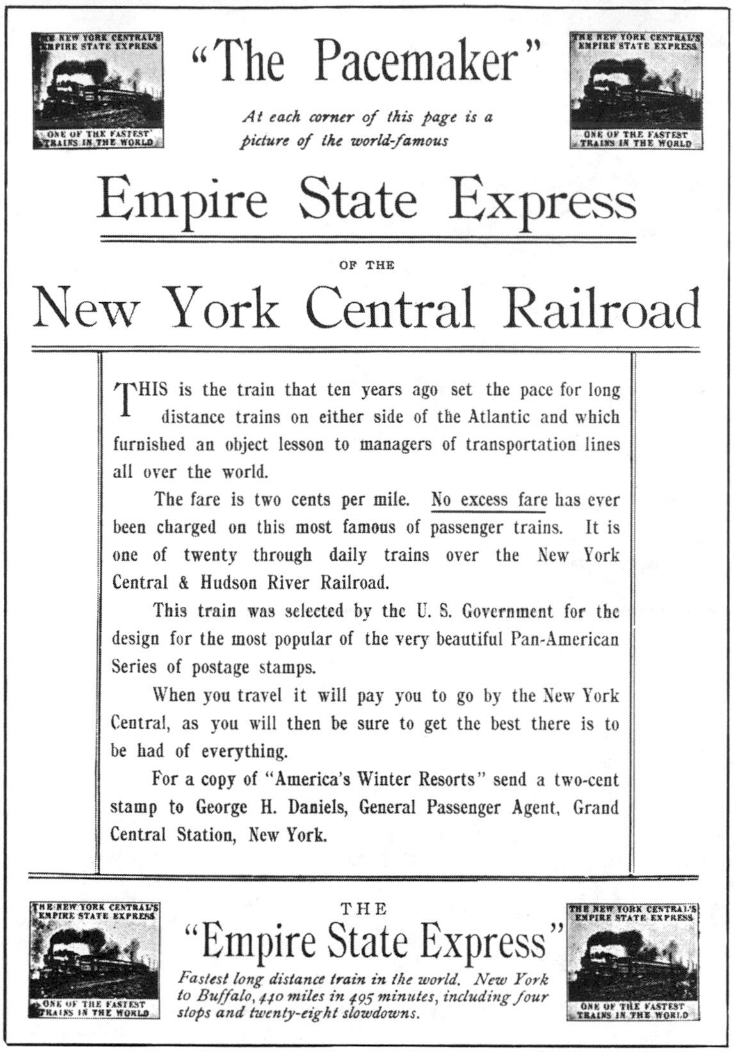

"The Pacemaker"

At each corner of this page is a
picture of the world-famous

Empire State Express

OF THE

New York Central Railroad

THIS is the train that ten years ago set the pace for long distance trains on either side of the Atlantic and which furnished an object lesson to managers of transportation lines all over the world.

The fare is two cents per mile. No excess fare has ever been charged on this most famous of passenger trains. It is one of twenty through daily trains over the New York Central & Hudson River Railroad.

This train was selected by the U. S. Government for the design for the most popular of the very beautiful Pan-American Series of postage stamps.

When you travel it will pay you to go by the New York Central, as you will then be sure to get the best there is to be had of everything.

For a copy of "America's Winter Resorts" send a two-cent stamp to George H. Daniels, General Passenger Agent, Grand Central Station, New York.

THE

"Empire State Express"

Fastest long distance train in the world. New York to Buffalo, 440 miles in 495 minutes, including four stops and twenty-eight slowdowns.

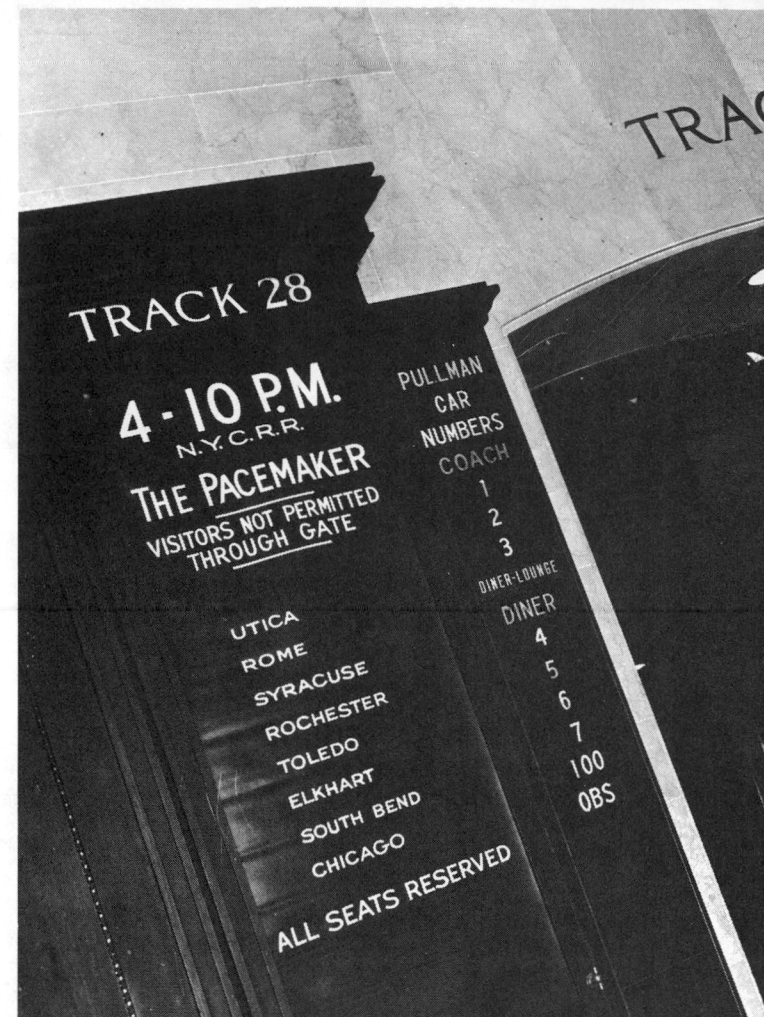

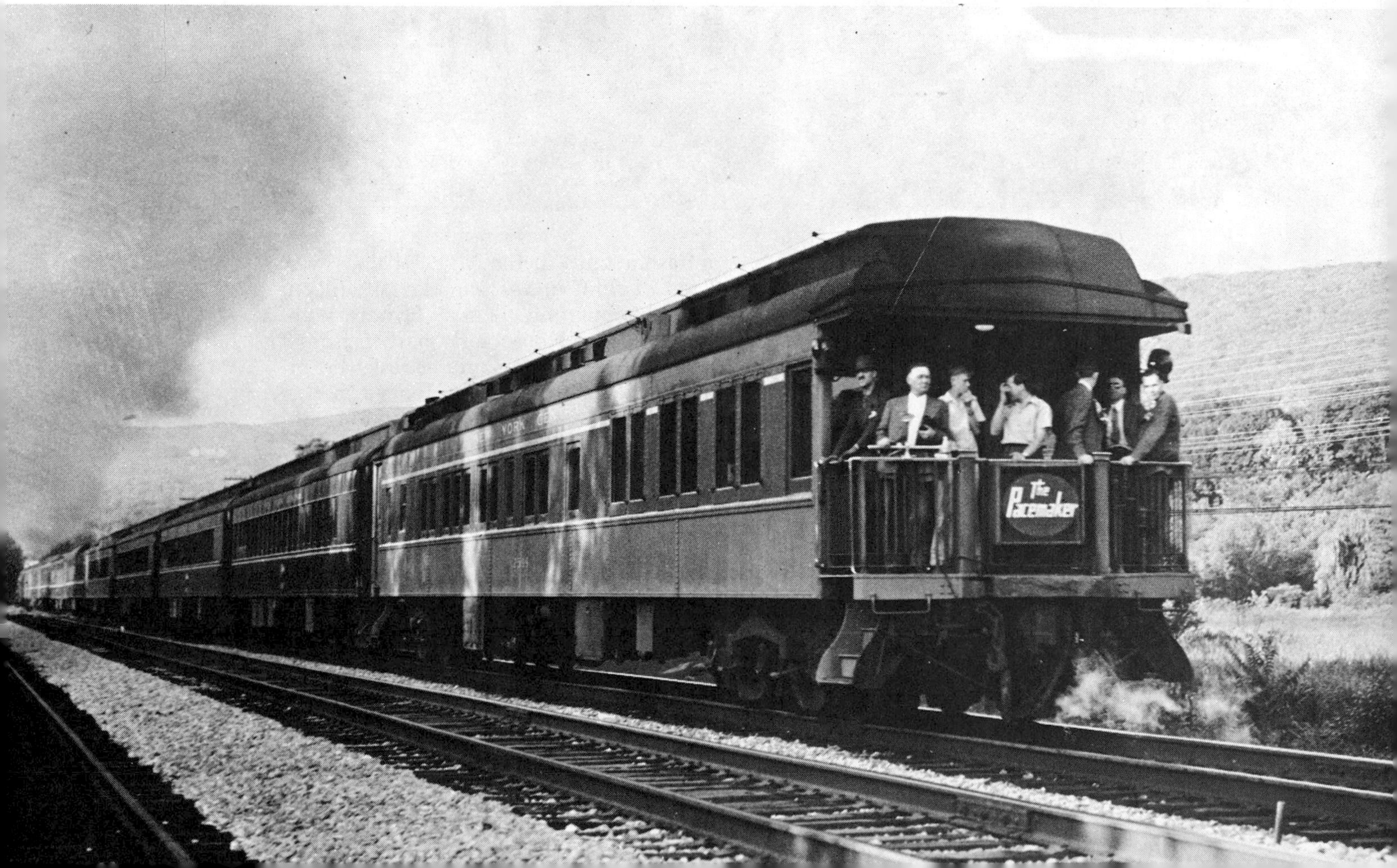

LONG AFTER GEORGE HENRY DANIELS, whose promotional genius had evolved *The Empire State Express* and *The Twentieth Century Limited* had departed, his influential shade shaped the naming of the Central's all-coach train on the New York-Chicago run designed to offer competition to the Pennsylvania's *Trail Blazer*. Central traffic officials searching for a name came upon Daniels' promotional material dating from the nineties *(page opposite)* in which he designated *The Empire State* as "The Pacemaker" and their problem was solved. The original *Pacemaker*, as is suggested by the view of its observation end on the opposite page, was hastily run up from available Standard equipment and hardly attracted *Century* type patronage. But it made up in comfort what it lacked in elegance and maintained the New York Central-Pennsylvania record for cutthroat competition unblemished. A postwar *Pacemaker (above)* gave the Pennsylvania's Custom-built *Trail Blazer* with its luxury overtones a better run for its money. *(Below, opposite: Edward L. May; Three Photos: New York Central.)*

455

THE SLATE-SHEATHED GOTHIC tower and pointed cathedral windows of Berea depot made it for many decades a landmark on the Big Four main line a few miles west of Cleveland. Despite its factually utilitarian function as a railroad station in a college town of ivied overtones, the structure with its dimension of gloom suggested secret chambers in its turrets peopled with spectral characters from the novels of William Harrison Ainsworth or replete with Gothic horror from "The Castle of Otranto." *(Richard J. Cook.)*

AGAINST THE MASSIVE industrial background of downtown Cleveland, the second section of the New York Central's Train No. 407, *The Missourian,* with eleven cars of mail and a rider coach rolls ponderously west in June 1953. Motive power is the utilitarian Hudson type that became the hallmark of Central high speed operations and long consists everywhere from Manhattan to the Mississippi. The steam-activated jackknife bridge framing the train has long since been replaced by a vertical lift span. *(Richard J. Cook.)*

457

AT AN unidentified depot along the Michigan Central right of way on a summer's evening a straw hatted group of passengers await the coming of *The Twilight* en route to Chicago. The quiet scene is dated by the six-wheel pickup truck parked in the background. *(Below: Everett De Golyer Collection; Left: New York Central; Bottom: Rail Photo Service, G. Grabill, Jr.)*

THE TWILIGHT LIMITED

ALMOST PRECISELY the counterpart of the New Haven's five o'clock *Merchants Limited* as a gentleman's club for businessmen in the more exalted echelons, the New York Central's *Twilight Limited* between Detroit and Chicago over its Michigan Central connection was, in the beginning, an all-Pullman run with terminals, at least metaphorically, in the Chicago Club and Book Cadillac Hotel at Detroit. In direct competition for the tycoon trade with the Pennsylvania-Wabash high speed *Detroit Arrow*, the *Twilight* was perfumed with folding money and its atmosphere suggestive of Dow-Jones Averages. The head end seen at the angle reproduced here from the discerning camera of Alfred W. Johnson as it gathered speed out of Chicago in the early thirties, *The Twilight Limited* so closely resembled *The Century* which left from an adjacent track at La Salle Depot that an onlooker would have been well advised to await the passing of its tailgate insigne before identifying it.

THE SOLARIUM END of The Mercury's observation lounge was like nothing else that rode the rails and reminded riders of the gunners' blister on a bombing plane. It afforded clear visibility for 180 degrees and rode as on a bath of oil. Below, it is shown on a windy day crossing Sandusky Bay bridge in 1946. *(Two Photos: New York Central.)*

ONE OF THE FASTEST THINGS on wheels in 1945, the New York Central's *Mercury* sped, like the gods' messenger, on winged feet between Detroit and Cleveland and was the favored means of travel between them until air travel and turnpike killed it completely. Here the eastbound No. 76 enters Toledo city limits with a big wave from the engineer on a warm July evening in 1945. Original *Mercury* equipment, as shown in the first car, was supplemented by newer coaches as business flourished. Heavier, huskier Hudsons took over from the original steamlined Pacifics. Passengers on *The Mercury* were mostly businessmen a cut above the commonality of Midwestern travelers and ate accordingly. Genuine Russian caviar was sixty-five cents a portion, royal mushrooms on toast, forty-five cents and Martini cocktails, thirty-five cents. Where else could you get roast ribs of prime heavy Kansas City beef for $1.40 while rolling at eighty miles an hour? *(Richard J. Cook.)*

NO LUXURY EQUIPMENT rode the drawbar of the Peoria & Eastern's jaunty *Peorian* behind N.Y.C. light Pacific No. 63 running between Indianapolis and Peoria in 1947. Operational practice was to change motive power for a fresh engine at Urbana, halfway between terminals, and *The Peorian* looked very stylish indeed when it was photographed on a long tangent between cornfields near Farmer City on a summer morning. After Dieselization the run's name was changed to *Corn Belt Limited.* *(Paul Stringham.)*

NOT ALL the glamor of the New York Central's fleet of name trains derived from such long-haul limiteds as *The Century, The Southwestern* and *The Empire State.* The observation lounge of *Mercury (left)* watched the miles roll out from under high speed trucks without the inconvenience (or quite the thrill either) of the open observation platform of an older tradition. The inaugural menu of *The James Whitcomb Riley* on the Cincinnati-Chicago run in 1941 treated the company's guests to both breakfast and luncheon and included a special on toasted cornbread reminiscent of the more celebrated lobster Newburg on corn bread associated with dining on *The Century. (Left: Richard J. Cook; Below: New York Central.)*

The James Whitcomb Riley

Souvenir Menus . . . Special Preview Run, Chicago to Cincinnati . . . Friday, April 18, 1941

Breakfast

Grape Fruit Juice   Orange Juice   Pineapple Juice
Tomato Juice
Half Grape Fruit   Prunes in Cream
Fresh Strawberries with Cream

———

Cereal with Cream

———

Eggs, any·style
Ham or Bacon with Eggs
Wheat Cakes with Bacon, Maple Syrup
French Toast, Wild Cherry Jelly
Salt Mackerel, Drawn Butter

———

Toast, Dry or Buttered   Corn Muffins
Rolls
Orange Marmalade   Guava Jelly

———

Tea   Coffee   Cocoa
Individual Milk

Enroute April 18, 1941

Luncheon

Spiced Apricots   Celery Hearts Farcie   Radishes Rosette
Mixed Olives

Creme Longchamps
Consomme Duchesse   Tomato Juice Cocktail
Crab Flake and Shrimp Cocktail
Fresh Fruit Cup, Grenadine

———

Fresh Boneless Shad with Roe Saute, Lemon Butter
Fresh Asparagus Omelette
Fricassee of Chicken with Fresh Mushrooms on Toasted Corn Bread
Roast Baby Spring Lamb (1941), Mint Jelly

Fresh Asparagus Tips Hollandaise   Baked Idaho Potato
New Peas in Butter   New Bermuda Potatoes

———

N.Y.C. Salad Bowl, Cheese Dressing

Ginger Sticks   Assorted Rolls   Cocoanut Muffins

Apricot and Almond Custard
Individual Rhubarb Pie   Strawberry Shortcake a la Mode
Pears in Syrup
or
Camembert Cheese with Toasted Biscuits
Cream Cheese with Toasted Cinnamon Raisin Bread, Wild Plum Jelly

Tea   Coffee   Individual Milk

Enroute April 18, 1941

NAMED FOR the folksy Hoosier poet and so a direct affront to President John Barriger of the Monon who liked to claim James Whitcomb Riley as patron poet of his railroad and printed his homey verses on menus of *The Tippecanoe* and other company literature, the New York Central's *James Whitcomb Riley* made its inaugural daylight run between Chicago and Cincinnati on April 18, 1941. Miffed by this affrontery, President Barriger retained a private poet laureate of his own who penned a deathless ode with words *and music* beginning "Down along the Monon, everything is fine" which he printed conspicuously on his menus while relegating to an inferior position on the back page the treacherously purloined Hoosier homilies of Riley. *The James Whitcomb Riley* did yeoman service on the 600-mile round trip daily with coaches only but adequate luxury touches in a lounge car with a fine circular bar *(right)* and dinner serving the meals appropriate to the time of day. Encouraged by its patronage of *belles lettres*, the Central placed *The Booth Tarkington* on the alternative run between Chicago and Cincinnati, thus placing itself one-up on the Burlington whose *Mark Twain Zephyr* is the only other salute to American letters in *The Official Guide*. *(Two Photos: New York Central.)*

ON ITS MAIDEN run, April 18, 1941, where it is shown above carrying the white flags of a special at its smokebox, *The James Whitcomb Riley* had an assigned Hudson type engine of singularly unappealing design. By the time, however, in August 1944 when it was photographed *(below)* by Richard J. Cook, running down the Illinois Central's multi-tracked main line at 47th Street, Chicago, the unsightly and inconvenient cowling was gone and the train rolled behind a conventional and utilitarian engine without contrivings of modernity. *(Top: New York Central; Below: Richard J. Cook.)*

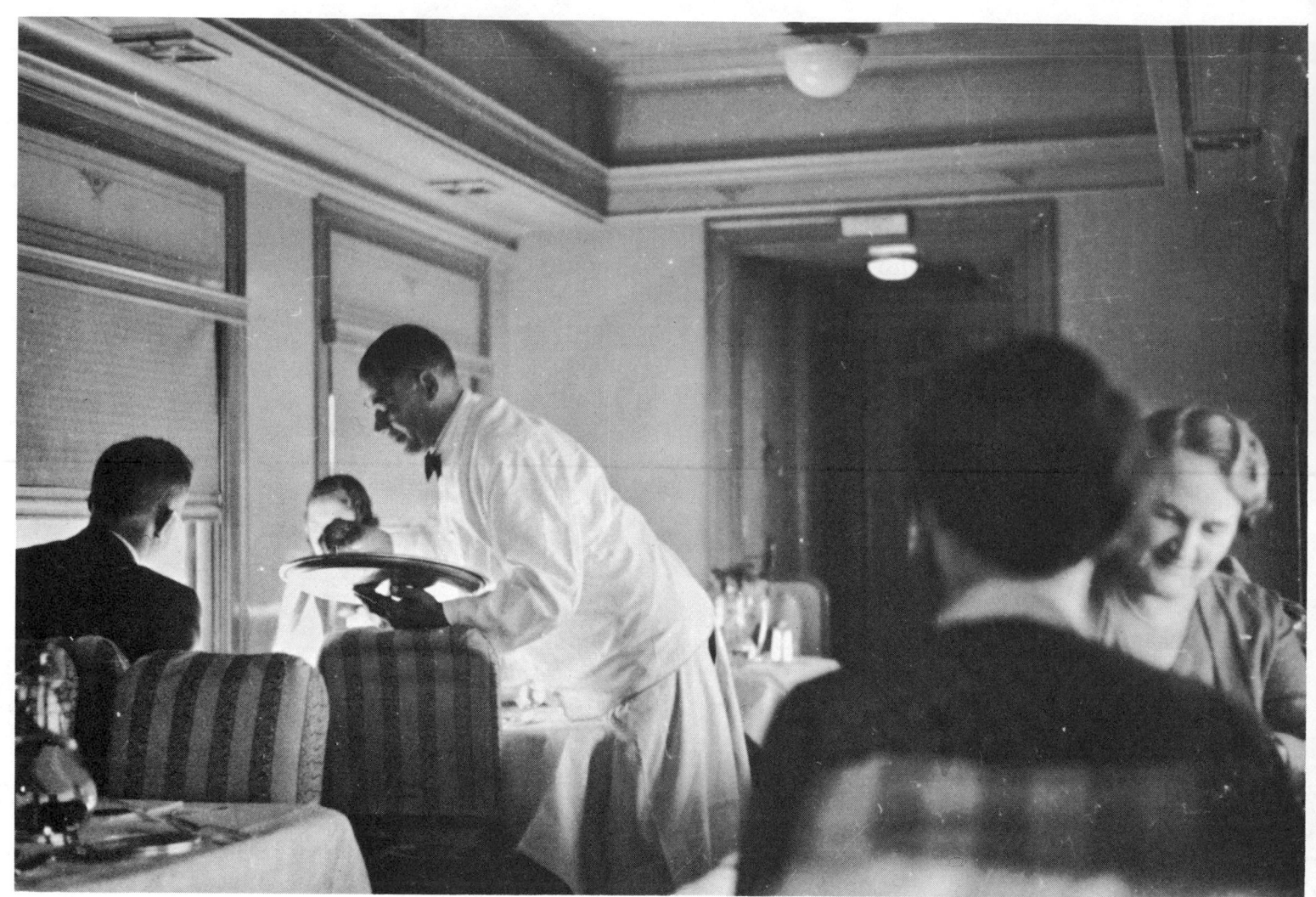

SOUTHERN PACIFIC

The real charm of a train is self-contained and has very little to do with its destination . . .
The real joy to be had from riding them begins where their usefulness ends.

John Mason Brown

AT NO TIME in its long and sometimes glamorous history was *The North Coast Limited* freighted with great financial destinies comparable to those that rode its staterooms during the years 1905-1907 when the fearful war of the copper kings raged between F. Augustus Heinze and the representatives of Standard Oil and John D. Rockefeller for the control of Montana copper. Beginning in the sixties as a gold and silver camp, Butte by the turn of the century had exhausted its precious metals but was found to be sitting atop the world's greatest single deposit of almost pure copper. Previous contenders for this truly colossal bonanza had been Marcus Daly and William A. Clark, but Daly died in 1900 and Clark, having achieved his life's ambition of election to the United States Senate, had sold his vast holdings to H. H. Rogers and William Rockefeller. Heinze, strictly an adventurer collected the better part of Daly's holdings and in the ensuing decade Butte was the scene of warfare, treachery and legal chaos that attracted international attention to Montana. *The North Coast Limited,* throughout these skirmishes and alarms, operated as an extension of Wall Street and Boston's State Street. Titans of finance and their general staffs, the highest paid legal talent in the land and financial writers from as far afield as London foregathered nightly in its diners and lounges and held secret conclave in private drawing rooms. On one occasion the Rockefeller interests, speaking through Thomas W. Lawson, the publicity broker of the age, claimed Heinze had sold his Butte holdings to a New York stock jobber and was claiming mines in which he held no equity. $5,000,000 in stock certificates were hastily jammed into a suitcase by a Heinze lieutenant and rushed aboard *The North Coast* to be displayed in a Butte bank next day to refute the story. At length, when the smoke of battle cleared, Heinze was found to be a ruined man and the copper wealth of Montana became a Rockefeller barony under the name of Anaconda. But while it lasted the Pullmans of *The North Coast Limited* had been the setting for as much concentrated melodrama as ever, in an E. Phillips Oppenheim novel, rode the *Simplon-Orient Express* or *The Blue Train* en route to Monte Carlo.

NO TRAIN was more abundantly heir to the tradition of the Old West and
its immense distances of time and space than *The North Coast Limited*.
When it went into service toward the end of 1900, at first as a
summer-only vacation run and soon thereafter as an all-year round
name train of continental consequence, the Western frontier had only been
officially declared closed for a decade and evidences of the cattle trade
that was still its most romantic preoccupation were on every hand.
On the page opposite the scene at the top antedates *The North Coast
Limited* by nearly a decade and was taken in 1891 at Gardiner,
Montana, by the great William Henry Jackson as the spring wagon from
the O K Ranch came down to meet the cars. Below: *The Limited* was
twenty years old and institutional when it paused at Garrison, Montana, on
a summer's day in 1920 while the Butte connection waited on the
depot track across the platform. *(Above: Southern Pacific; Opposite:
Everett De Golyer Collection; Northern Pacific.)*

468

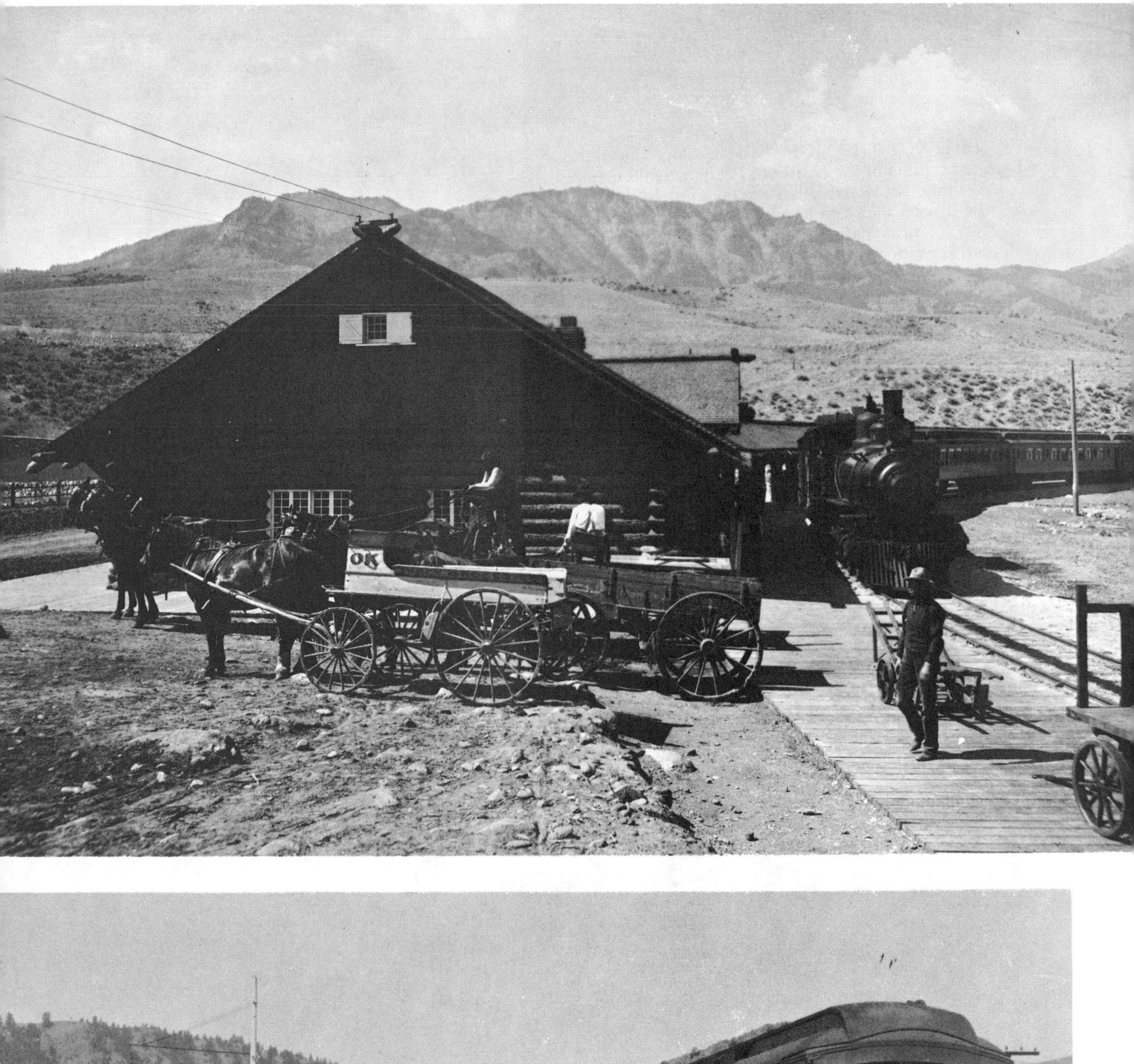
OK

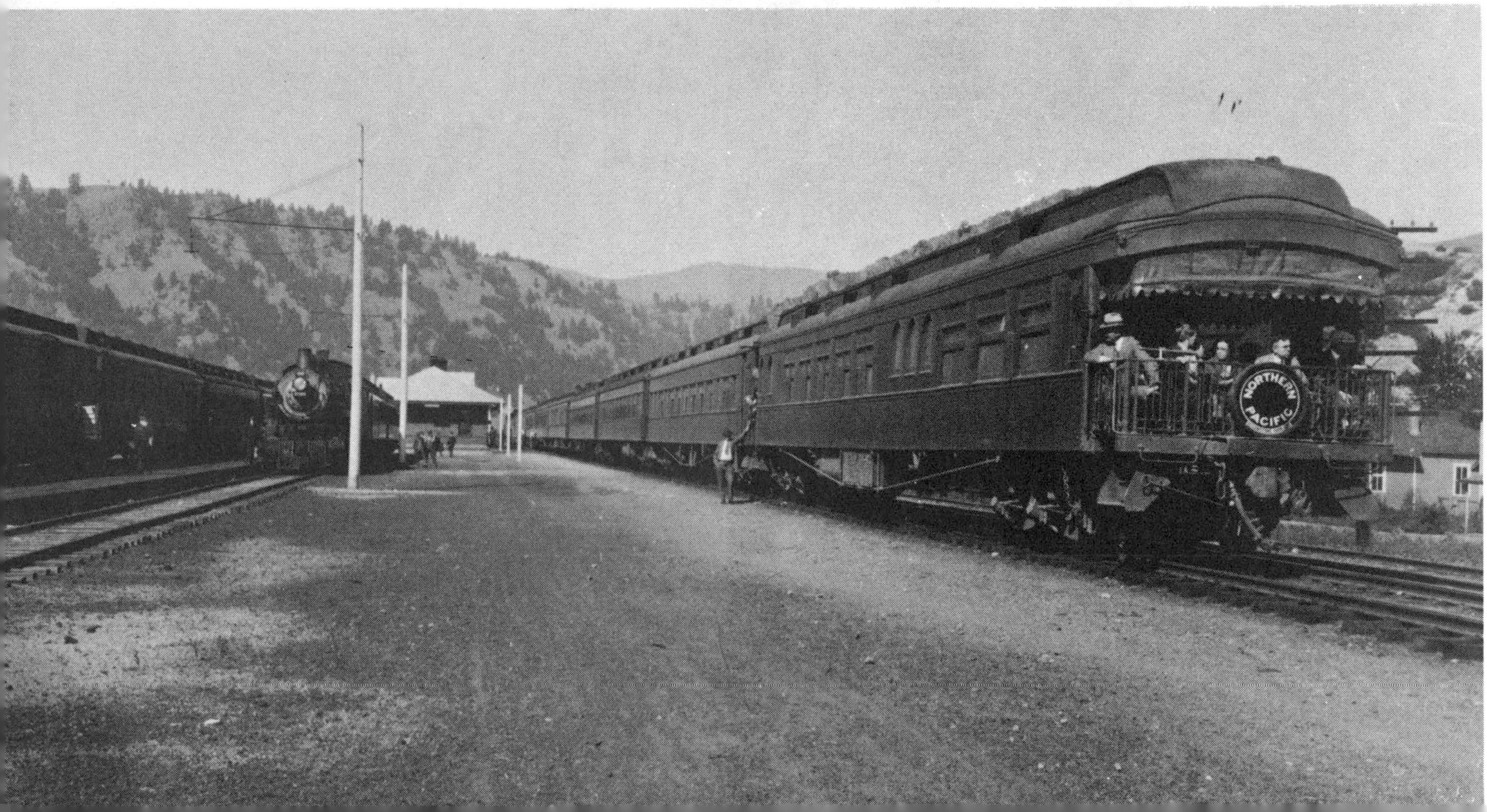
NORTHERN PACIFIC

HAD NOT THE MONAD been adopted as the heraldic symbol of the Northern Pacific, an alternate might reasonably have been a fine bushy set of whiskers such as adorned many of the carrier's principals and patrons in the years of its greatest excitements during the wars of the copper kings. Most celebrated of these, beyond all peradventure, was the Visigothic facade of Senator William Andrews Clark (*opposite*) archboodler of Montana's epic scuffles for fortune and preferment around the copper smelters of Butte.

Almost as magnificent was the beard of Thomas F. Oakes, President of the Northern Pacific (*right*) who, in a generation of railroad executives who looked the part, guided its destinies at a time when, as shown below, *The North Coast Limited* headed out of Missoula, Montana, shortly after the turn of the century behind two primordial locomotives with steam chests big enough to serve as kennels for St. Bernards. (*Everett De Golyer Collection.*)

AT THE CENTURY'S turn, when the Pullmans of the *North Coast Limited* were awash with financial notables ranking from Tom Lawson to William Rockefeller and representatives of the Rothschilds, the most celebrated patron of its ample buffet was fiercely acquisitive and boundlessly ambitious William A. Clark *(left)* who began life selling tobacco and mining tools and ended as one of the wealthiest of United States senators when that body was known as the most exclusive rich man's club in the world. In a time when silver and gold were the preoccupation of the mining world, Clark foresaw the day when the immense copper resources underlying Butte would dominate the world market for the red metal.

His smelting works, shown below in a contemporary engraving by the celebrated team of Western artists, Tavernier & Frenziny, made him incalculably wealthy so that, not without scandal, he was able to become senator and the greatest single figure in copper until the coming, many years later, of Daniel Jackling of Utah.   *(Brown Bros.)*

THE SUPERBLY matched and polished Circassian walnut, the marquetry and blue velvet of *The North Coast Limited* library-lounge-buffet car shown at the immediate left (another elevation of the same interior is depicted on an adjacent page) knew the aggressive whiskers of Senator William A. Clark and the other battle-scarred veterans of the wars of the copper kings. Its brocaded velvet valances and tulip-shaded electroliers lent it a beauty remarkable even in a period of splendid Palace Cars from Pullman. The restrained delight of the patrons on the observation platform of *The North Coast Limited* shown opposite dates from the 1930s, while below *The Limited* is shown running against a background of wilderness beside the Green River in the Cascades where, between Seattle and Stampede Pass it crosses the river eleven times. *(Above, Two Photos: Northern Pacific; Below: Everett De Golyer Collection.)*

AT THE FAR MARGIN of the opposite page a Northern Pacific travel ad for the summer of 1912 lists three name trains, *The North Coast Limited, The Northern Pacific Express* and *The Puget Sound Limited*. It is worth noting that while the flagship of the N.P. fleet left Chicago over the connecting iron of the Chicago & North Western, the two secondary trains departed via the Burlington. The last line of type at the bottom looks forward three years hence to the Panama Pacific Exposition at San Francisco, while "the BIG Baked Potato" is a capitalized feature on the diner.
(Arthur D. Dubin Collection.)

473

AMONG THE IDENTIFYING hallmarks of a train of pedigree in the great years of luxury travel one of the foremost status symbols was, of course, the barbershop, usually located in the forward combination baggage buffet car and attended by a talented tonsor whose professional expertise included not only the use of a straight razor at accelerated speeds over dubious roadbeds with an acceptable average of casualties, but a wide range of conversational versatility. It was a time when politics dominated the barbershop colloquies of the land and the man of lather and lilac water who aimed to please became adept at sizing up the political complexions buried under the hot towels and adapting himself to them. On a railroad train the maintenance of a barbershop was the ultimate in elegance because the economic facts of patronage of a one-man operation were precarious and the owning carrier usually ran the establishment at a loss. On the other hand, the company was apt to be better than average and the tips on a flyer such as *The North Coast Limited* more rewarding than elsewhere. Thus when, after his defeat in the Presidential campaign of 1916 by Woodrow Wilson, Charles Evans Hughes and Mrs. Hughes took a nice vacation at Yellowstone to recoup from the fatigues of campaigning, the *North Coast* barber was assured of at least one singe and trim job on the most exalted imaginable plane. American police still wore helmets at the time and Spokane (*opposite*) was no exception. (*Opposite: Arthur D. Dubin Collection; Left: Northern Pacific.*)

474

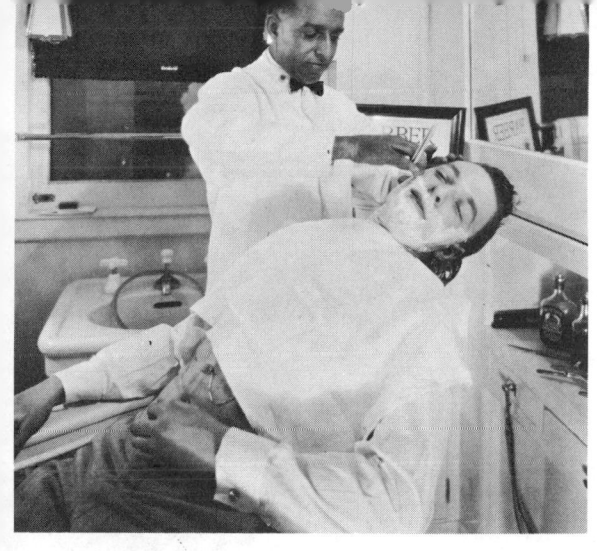

A LATER, and presumably more degenerate age saw
The Limited's barbershop shorn of its plush and finely grained
and polished woodwork in favor of devisings of sanitation
that could have been encountered in any good hospital.
Senator Clark and his contemporaries would not, it is safe to say,
have approved.   *(Northern Pacific.)*

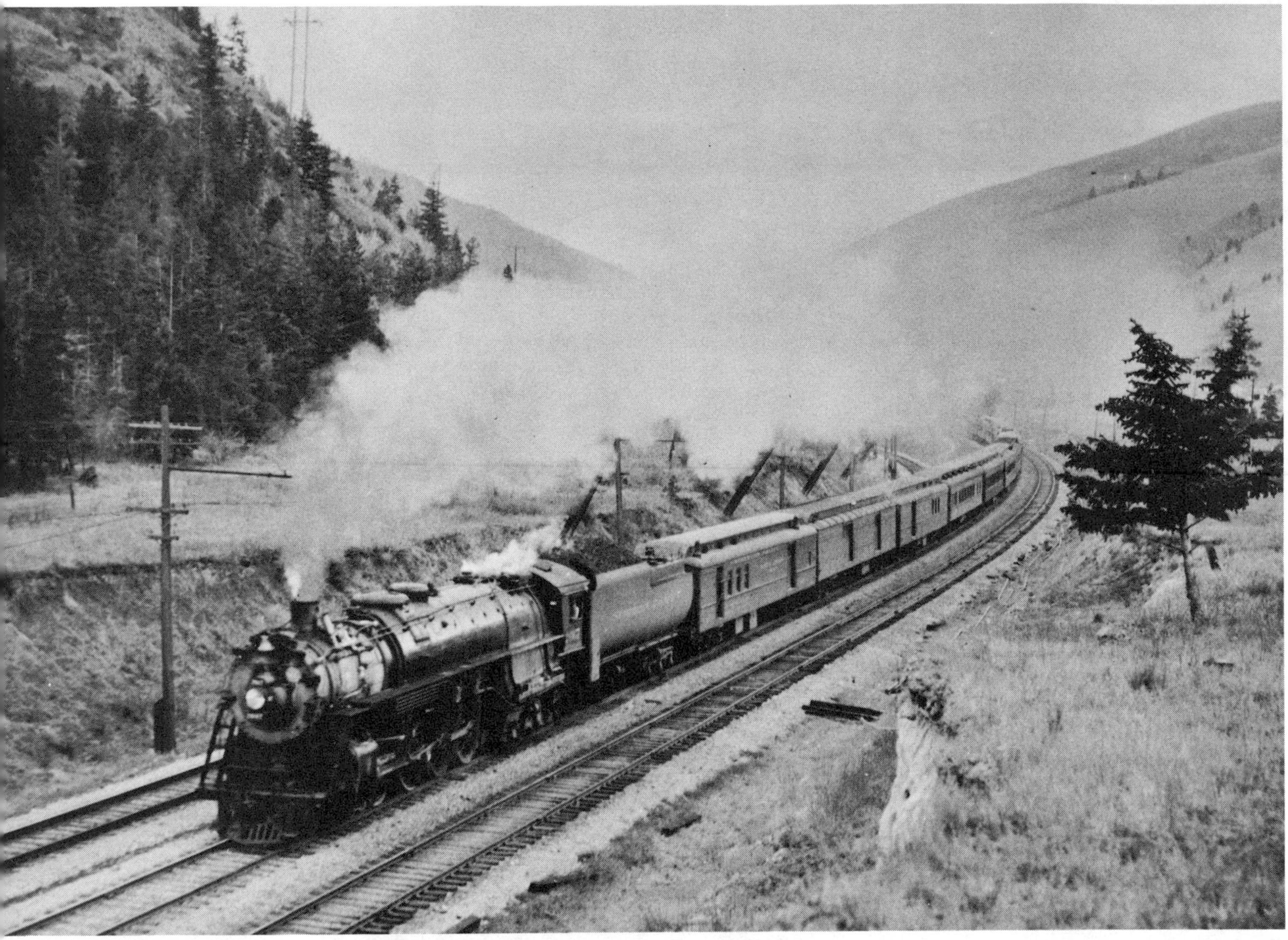

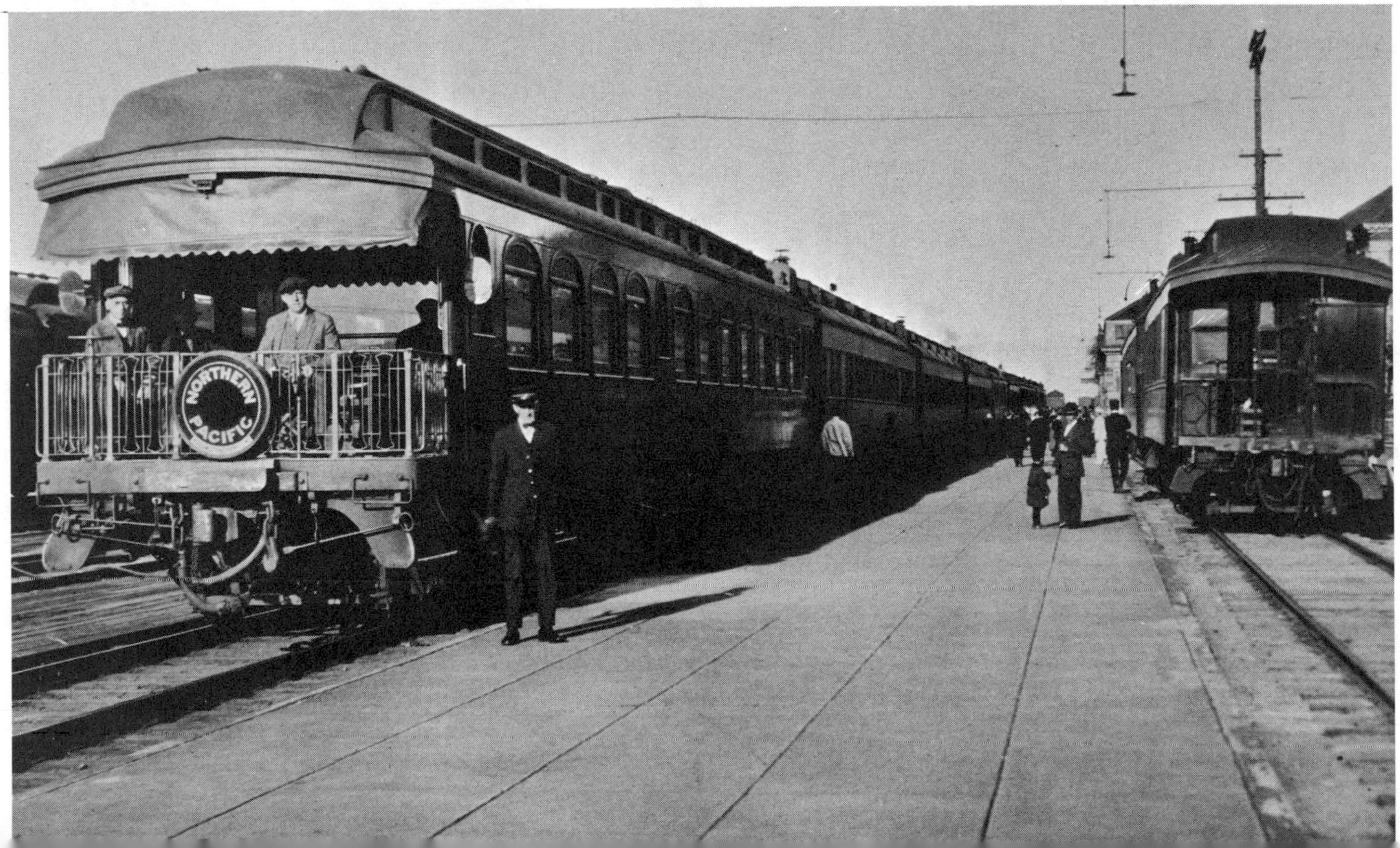
NORTHERN
PACIFIC

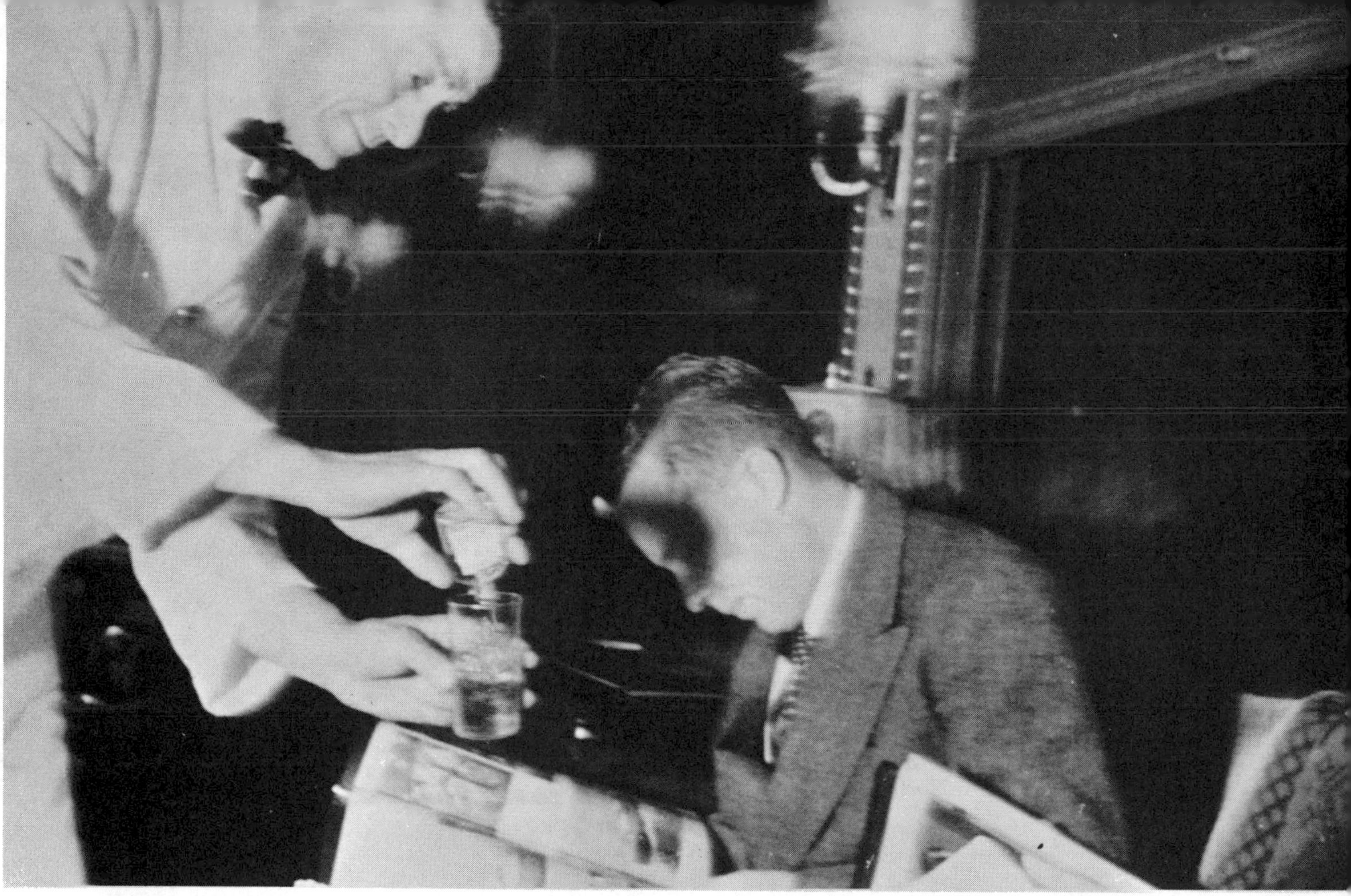

COCKTAIL TIME, "The Hour" of
the immortal Bernard De Voto,
on the lounge cars of
The North Coast Limited was an
unhurried sacrament. Time was on
the side of the Martinis. Wherever
the cars were at six in the
evening, they wouldn't get there
until tomorrow and the diner crew
had nothing to do but await the
convenience of the patrons.
The radio console in the club car
was a hallmark of opulence in the
1930s. From earliest times the image
of the Northern Pacific *(opposite)*
was that of big time railroading
reflected in the vast distance it
traversed and the big sky above its
right of way. Its rear end, posed
at Livingston, Montana, in 1924 was
the profile of luxury in the age
of Pullman Standard.
(Four Photos: Northern Pacific.)

ACCORDING TO Sinologists as well as on the word of Arthur D. Dubin, foremost student of American train heraldry and railroad insignia, the black and white figure which is the Northern Pacific's heraldic device, the monad, was created in 1017 A.D., by Chinese philosopher Chow Lien Ki to represent the eternal forces of light and darkness, life and death, good and evil. Who adapted it to the Northern Pacific's use is not known but Dubin maintains that its first appearance in company literature was in 1900 in connection with the inaugural of *The North Coast Limited.* Since then, the monad has been associated with the N.P. the way the legendary mountain goat symbolized the Great Northern and the keystone the Pennsylvania. On some runs the monad was incorporated with the train name on drumhead heralds as on the *Yellowstone Comet* opposite. On the streamlined *North Coast Limited* solarium it was subordinated to the Mars light which, *faute de mieux*, rode the drawbar. *(Three Photos: Northern Pacific.)*

AS THE IRON of the Northern Pacific was laid ever westward to become the second transcontinental carrier, its architect Henry Villard made a practice of taking trainloads of notables out to the end of track where they lived sumptuously aboard specially appointed Palace Cars and were sluiced with rare vintages while witnessing the tribal dances and other ceremonies of the Crows and other relatively tame Indians. In lesser degree, perhaps, than they figured in the promotional advertising of the Santa Fe, Indians still were one of the picturesque assets of the Northern Pacific until well into the twentieth century and, at appropriate stops along the way, gathered around *The Yellowstone Comet* in an age of Brownie cameras and high button boots as suggested here and on the opposite page. (*Two Photos: Northern Pacific.*)

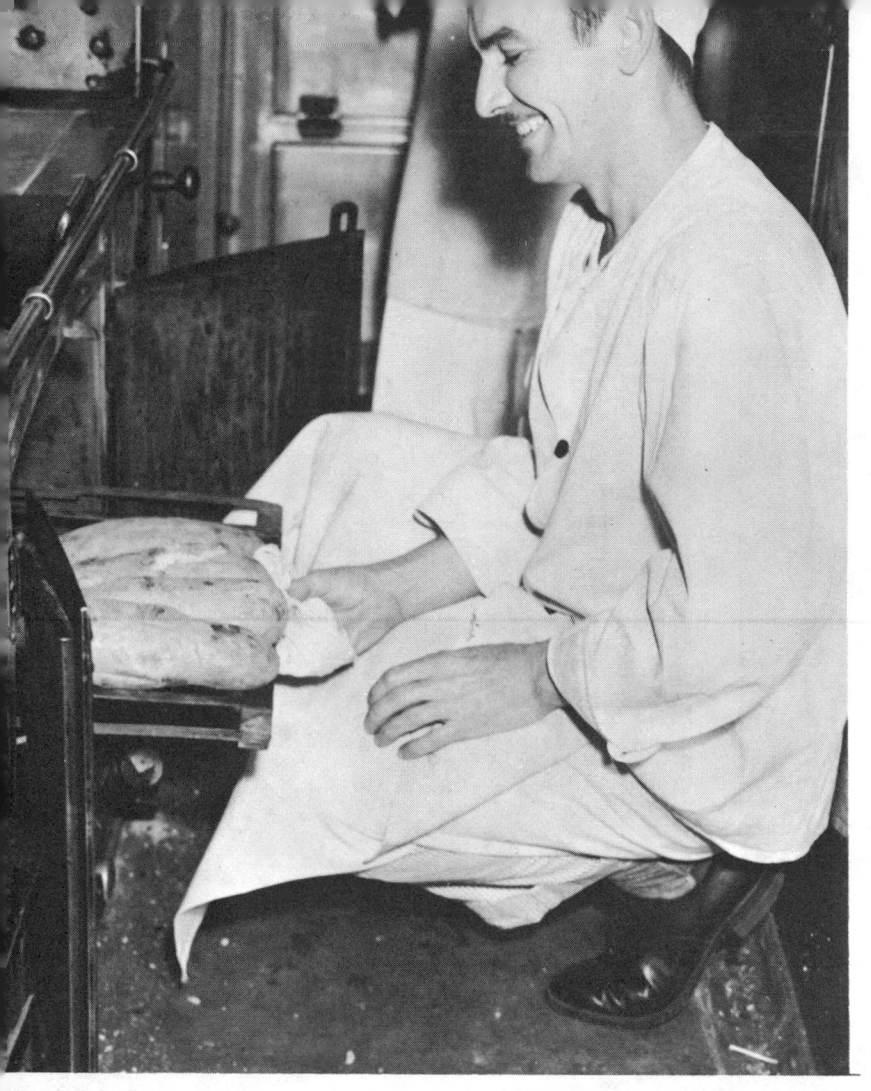

IN THE YEAR 1930 when the photographs on these two pages were taken, no varnish run in the pages of *The Official Guide* more dazzlingly lived up to the concept of what a classic transcontinental should be. From the pilot of its long barreled 4-8-4 locomotives to the illuminated heraldry that rode the tailgate of its observation, it was Pullman Standard, the finest construction the world of car-building has ever known, and, as of the year mentioned, fitted entirely with roller bearing trucks. Its pedigree was without reproach, reaching back to the days when the Northern Pacific was truly a pioneer carrier and the Old West a remembered reality. Its patrons had been the overlords of feudal estates, mines, ranches and timberlands and its amenities were tailored to those who wanted the best and nothing else. Just as its competing Great Northern made a symbol of the huge Wenatchee apple and promoted the Red Delicious of Lake Chelan on its menus, so the Northern Pacific featured "great big Idaho baked potaoes" as evidenced in the photograph opposite. At one time in the regime of William Jeffers the Union Pacific undertook to appropriate the symbolism of the Idaho potato but without notable success. It was too well established in the public awareness as a Northern Pacific property. The train's beaming chefs did nothing to dispel the illusion of good things to come at mealtimes. Above, *The North Coast Limited* threads its way along the Yakima River in Washington State. *(Four Photos: Northern Pacific.)*

THROUGHOUT its long and honored annals, *The North Coast Limited,* like flagship runs on other mainline carriers, was assigned the newest and finest equipment as it came from the drawing boards of Budd, Pullman and A.C.F., while earlier equipment was handed down to secondary trains. Thirty-seven new sleepers and public cars ordered from Pullman just before the market debacle of 1929 was the last large order for Standard equipment before the advent of streamlining. After the 1941 war a streamlined, Diesel-powered *North Coast* carried the North Coast fleet pennon first hoisted before the century's turn. Wall-to-wall carpeting, cheerful murals and private banquettes characterized the diner *(opposite)* while, as portrayed on this page the buffet lounge car *Traveller's Rest* was decorated with portraits of Meriwether Lewis and William Clark from originals by Wilson Peale. Below the great Northwestern pathfinders are shown with Sacajawea in the style of the artists of the period. *(Four Photos: Northern Pacific.)*

AT the top of the page, the stream-lined *North Coast Limited* gets a window-wash during its long run across the continent. *(Rail Photo Service.)*

Like the Erie, The Nickel Plate-Lackawanna
Provided an Alternate Route to Chicago

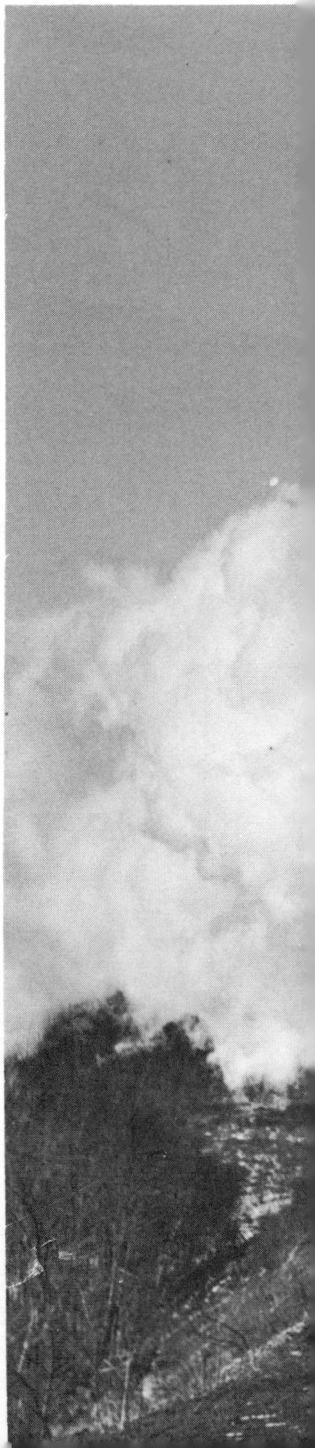

WHILE, in the great years of passenger transport by rail which climaxed in 1922 and again reached all-time highs during the necessitous times of the 1941 war, the vast majority of travelers between New York and Chicago took passage on one of the big three, the Pennsylvania, the New York Central or the Baltimore & Ohio, an agreeable alternative routing was available on slower cardings and at differential rates over the Erie and the Nickel Plate-Delaware, Lackawanna & Western. Through coaches and Pullmans were exchanged, usually during the night, at the Lackawanna's western terminal at Buffalo with the Nickel Plate where the components of the Lackawanna's flagship, *The Lackawanna Limited,* were integrated to the *Nickel Plate Limited* for the run terminating at La Salle Depot beside Lake Michigan. The Nickel Plate's unnamed No. 7 absorbed the Lackawanna's sun par-

lor-buffet-lounge-sleeper and conventional Pullman from Newark from *The Chicago Limited* while through elements of *The Western Special* were routed over the Michigan Central in the consist of *The Wolverine* west of Buffalo. Sleepers from the Lackawanna's other consequential name train, *The Whitelight Limited,* terminated at Buffalo, as did Pullmans in *The Buffalo Mail.* In the mid-thirties *The Lackawanna Limited* was a fine thing to see as is suggested in its likeness taken on a winter day near Summit, New Jersey. Opposite, one of the Lackawanna's Hoboken ferry boats operating out of Barclay Street in lower Manhattan is depicted in the North River through the rigging of a passing vessel of greater tonnage. *(Below: Lucius Beebe; Opposite: Everett De Golyer Collection.)*

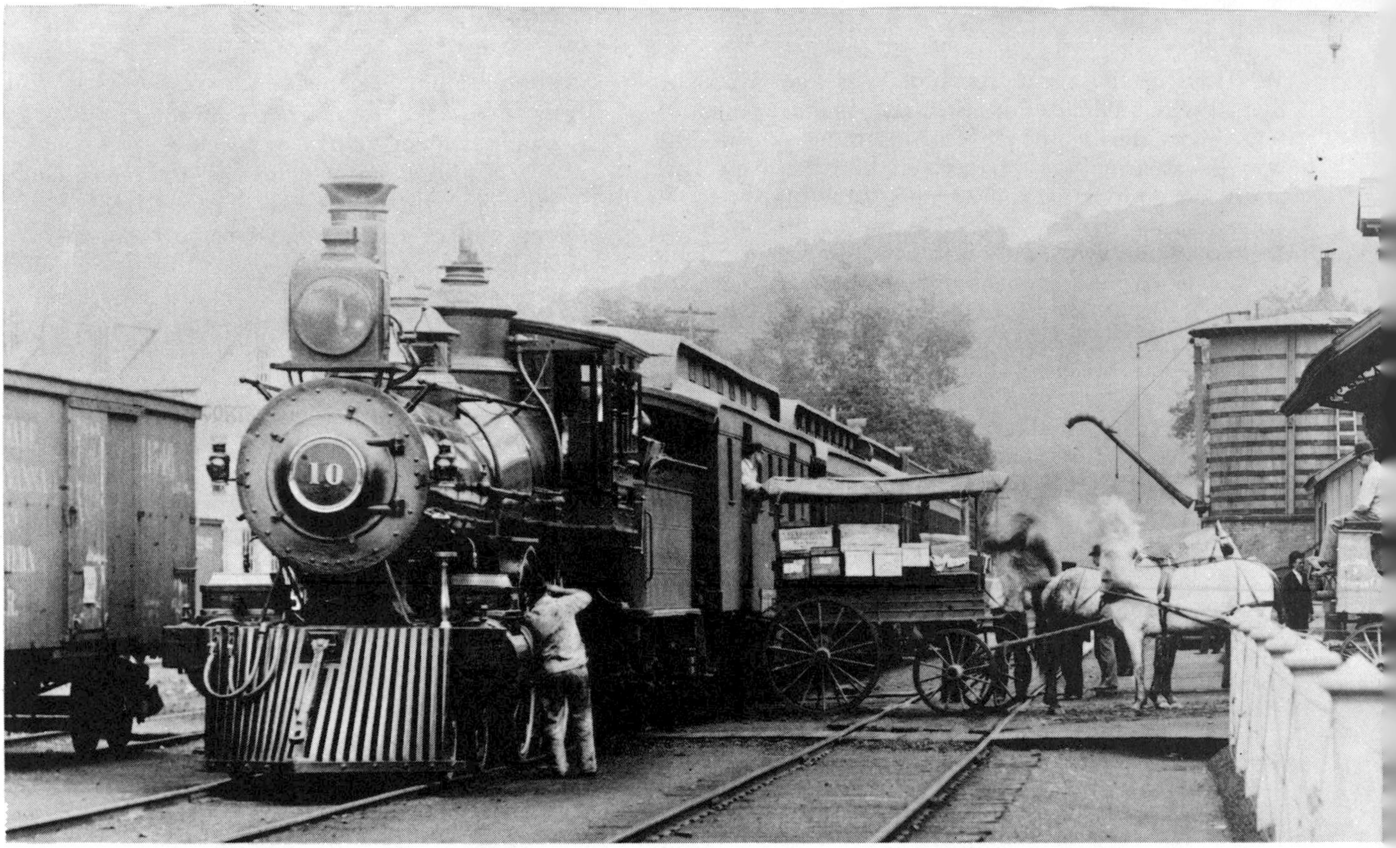
10

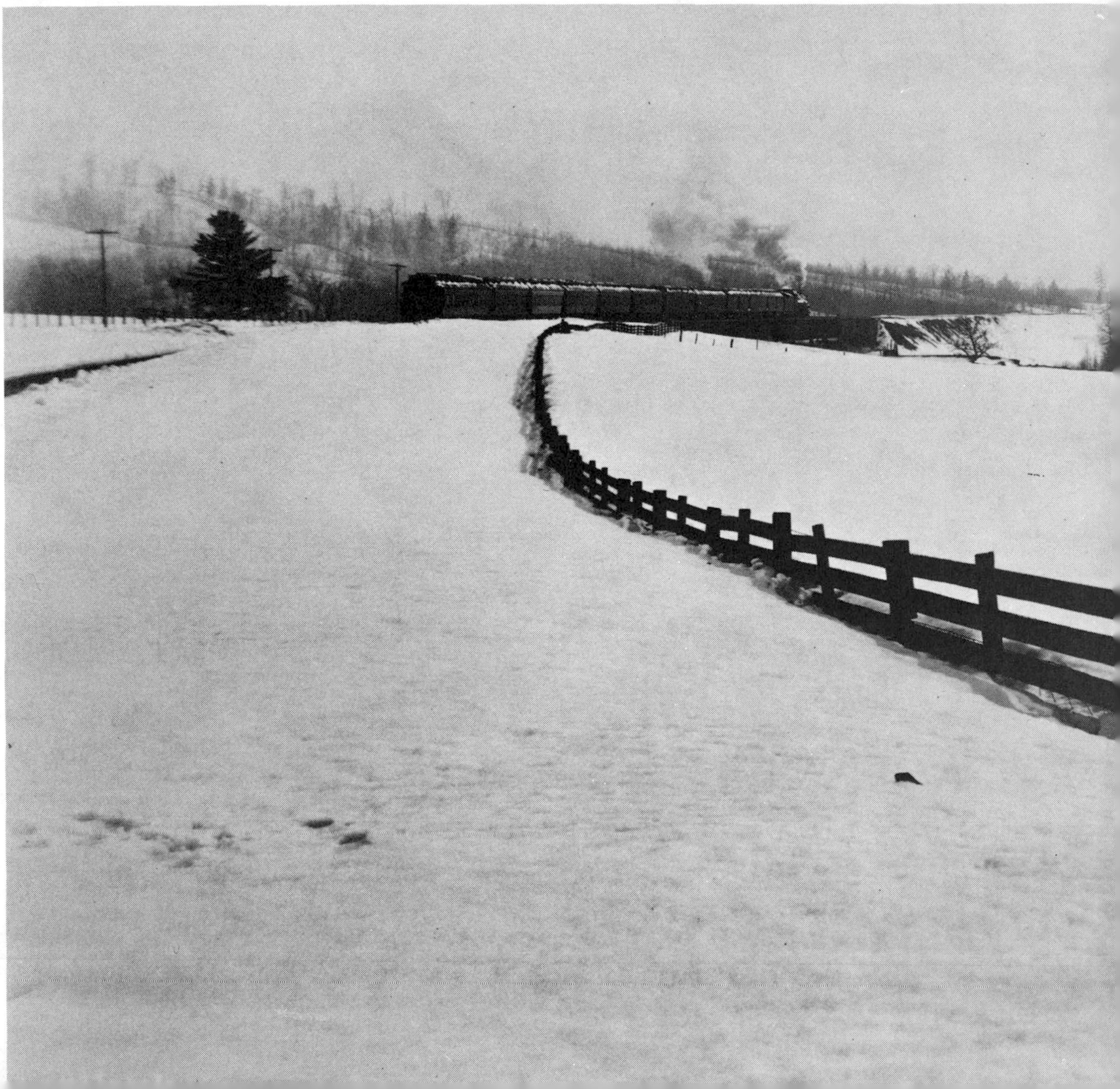

LIKE THE OTHER coal-haul carriers, the Reading, Lehigh Valley, Central of New Jersey and the New York, Ontario & Western, the Delaware, Lackawanna & Western, running from Hoboken, New Jersey, to Buffalo where it made through connections for Chicago with the Nickel Plate and the Michigan Central, burned anthracite in a vast fleet of both camelback and conventional locomotives in freight and passenger service. Opposite in an atmospheric scene of 1900, the Lackawanna local discharges mail and express at Stroudsburg, Pennsylvania, while the town hack waits at the depot platform for business. Below, in a winter pastoral of snowy fields and split-rail fences, *The Buffalo Mail* snakes across the gelid countryside of the Southern Tier. Stone coal, the anthracite of the Lehigh, was the basis of the Lackawanna's century-long prosperity as it had been for the Reading and as was attested by the folk-ballad of sootless Phoebe Snow. Shown in this homely old-time scene, anthracite was delivered in a thousand communities in the East in half-ton tipcarts drawn by gentle draft horses over the cobblestone pavements of the turn of the century. *(Three Photos: Everett De Golyer Collection.)*

(Via Michigan Cent. R.R.)	
Lv. **Chicago** (*C.T.*)	*9 00 P M
Lv. **Kalamazoo** (*C.T.*)	11 54 P M
Lv. **Detroit** (*E.T.*)	— —
Ar. **Buffalo** (*E.T.*)	9 18 A M
......See **Note** ⊡	....
(*Via Nickel Plate.*)	....
Lv. **Chicago**	*7 30 P M
Lv. **Fort Wayne**..	10 58 P M
Lv **East Cleveland**..	4 13 A M
Lv. **Erie**.............	6 22 A M
Ar. **Buffalo**........	8 10 A M
......See **Note** ⊡	....
Lv. **Buffalo**	*9 30 A M
Ar. **Elmira**........	12 45 P M
Lv. **Ithaca**........	12 25 P M
Lv. **Oswego**.......	10 45 A M
Lv. **Syracuse**	12 00 Noon
Ar. **Binghamton** ..	2 05 P M
Ar. **Scranton**.....	3 30 P M
Ar. **Philadelphia**.	8 34 P M
(*30th Street Sta.*)	....
Ar. **Newark**	6 40 P M
Ar. **New York**	7 12 P M

No. 6—LACKAWANNA LIMITED.
Daily

Runs via Blairstown and Newark.
Observation Parlor Lounge Car.. Buffalo to New York.
Sleeping Car...Chicago to New York— Drawing-room, via M.C. No. 40.
Club Lounge....Chicago to Buffalo.
Parlor Car......Oswego to N.Y.—D.R.
Individual Seat Coaches, Buffalo to New York.
Oswego to New York.
Dining Car.....St. Thomas to Buffalo.
Buffalo to New York.
Coaches........Chicago to Buffalo.
Syracuse to Binghamton.
Ithaca to Owego.
(Lackawanna Limited train No. 6 will be held not to exceed 40 minutes for connection with Michigan Central No. 40 at Buffalo).

(*Via Nickel Plate No. 4.*)
Last trip from Chicago Sept. 8th.
Sleeping Car...Chicago to New York— Compartment, D.R.

Dining Car for meal service on Nickel Plate No. 4.
Coaches........Chicago to Buffalo

Note ⊡—Nickel Plate connection discontinued September 8th.

BY 1935 *The Lackawanna Limited* had cut two hours from the schedule of *The Chicago Limited* as shown opposite and made the connection west of Buffalo via the Nickel Plate instead of the Michigan Central. A train of distinctive character if not overwhelming style, it was favored by loyal partisans to whom a split second schedule was less of a consideration than an old fashioned daylight ride through the superlative setting of the Poconos and the countryside of the Southern Tier. (*Everett De Golyer Collection.*)

IN THE YEAR 1913 when the young lady in the long skirts and picture hat was being solicited as a patron of the Lackawanna's *Chicago Limited*, twenty-seven hours between New York and Lake Michigan via the Michigan Central connection west of Buffalo was not as long a schedule as it might have been thought a decade or so later. *The Broadway* and *The Century* were then twenty hour trains and the Lackawanna made no pretense of being in direct competition with them. After all, it was less than ten years since Lackawanna passengers on the way to its New Jersey terminal via the company ferry who did not wish to incur the expense of a growler or hansom cab had taken the horse cars, one of the last remaining lines in Manhattan, down Twenty-third Street to the ferry slip as shown below. *(Everett De Golyer Collection.)*

ERIE-LACKAWANNA'S Train No. 10 stands in snowy Binghamton, New York in December 1963 with nine head-end cars and a rider coach for a portrait of silent midnight. *(Richard Allen.)*

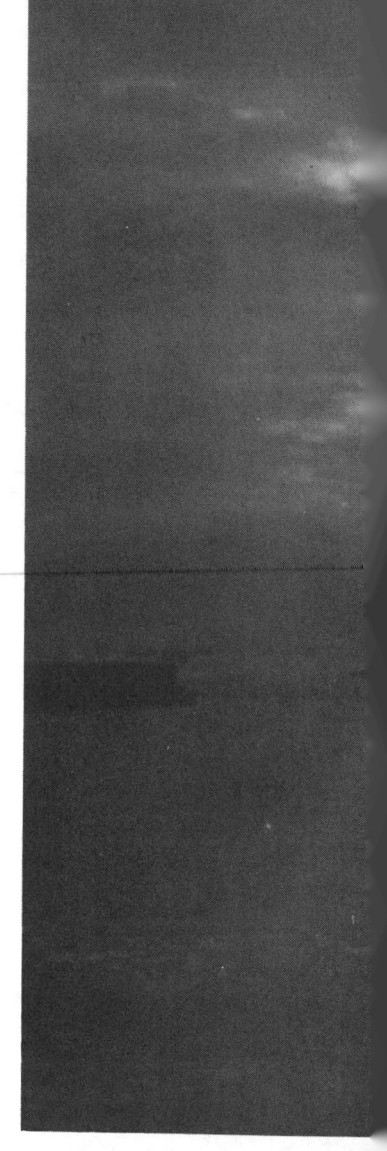

LOOKING down-harbor toward The Narrows and the Statue of Liberty, a Lackawanna ferry in its slip on the Jersey shore of the North River forms a twilight vignette of marine tranquility. At the left Erie-Lackawanna Train No. 43 ends its run for the day at Binghamton, while on the page opposite Charles B. Chaney photographed *The Lackawanna Express* in the Jersey Meadows in 1921. *(Above: Everett De Golyer Collection; Right: Richard Allen; Opposite: The Smithsonian Institution.)*

PHOTOGRAPHED AT EAST ORANGE, New Jersey, at Christmas 1939, *The Lackawanna Limited* is heading westbound behind 4-6-4 No. 1106 and 4-8-4 No. 1504 running tandem to carry the holiday tonnage. Ordinarily a ten car consist, the Lackawanna's pride was conventionally handled between Hoboken and Scranton by a single high wheeled 4-8-4, but for the occasion shown here, the carrier's candy run required a helper. Pullman sleepers, a sun-lounge cafe car, two coaches, a diner and head-end revenue were all present and accounted for. On the page opposite: like all consequential railroads at the time, the Lackawanna maintained ticket agencies and travel bureaus at strategic points around New York and its suburbs where prospective patrons could be gentled amidst opulent surroundings by the subdued rustle of coated paper brochures advertising the rich resources of watering places at distant remove. This ticket desk was at the Lackawanna's Travel Bureau at 500 Fifth Avenue in the mid-thirties, a location calculated to skim the cream of the mid-town carriage trade with a minimum of inconvenience. In the below vignette, *The Pocono Express* nears the New York end of its run behind an identifying camelback at approximately the same period. *(Below: Robert Le Massena; Opposite: Lackawanna Railroad, Everett De Golyer Collection.)*

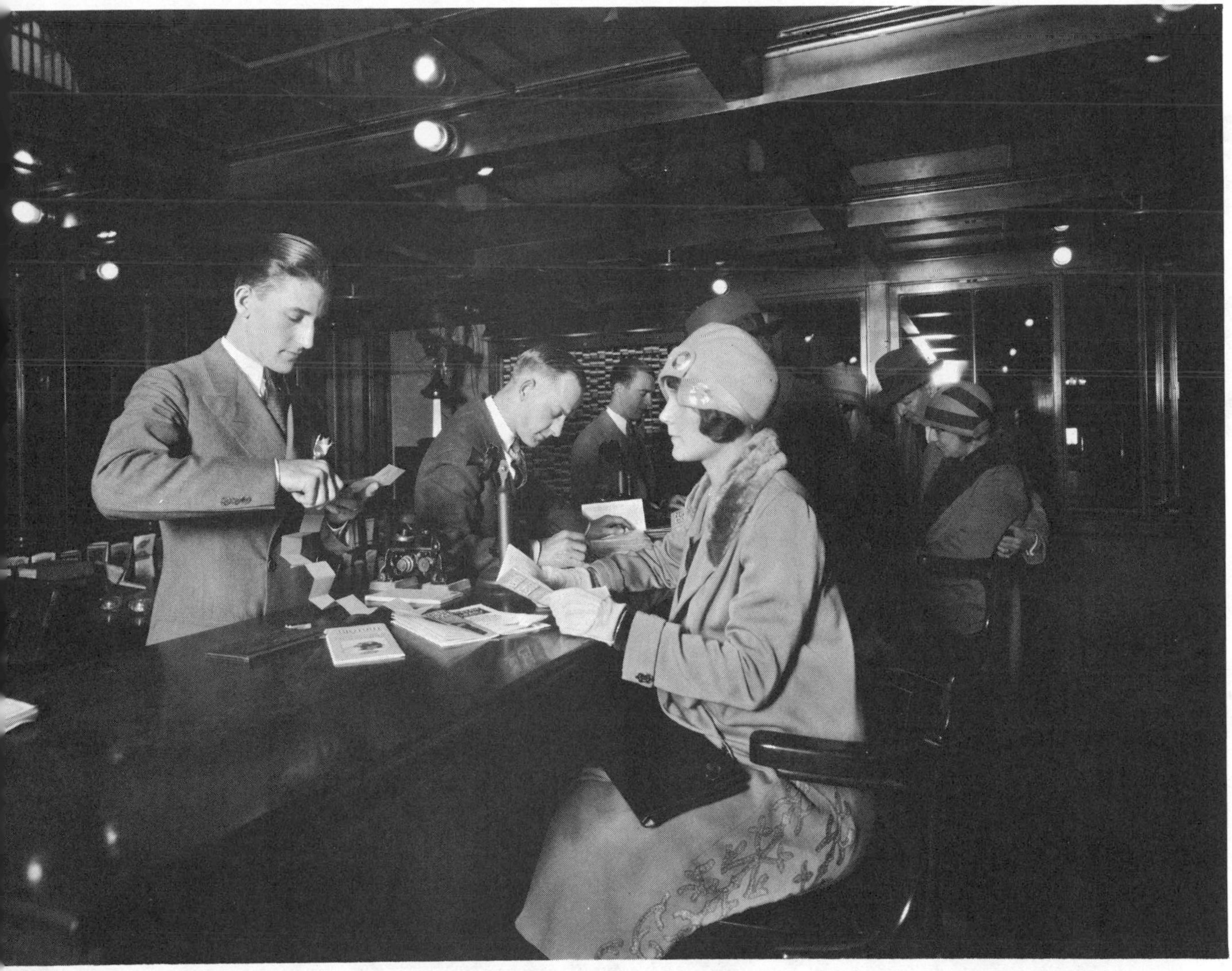

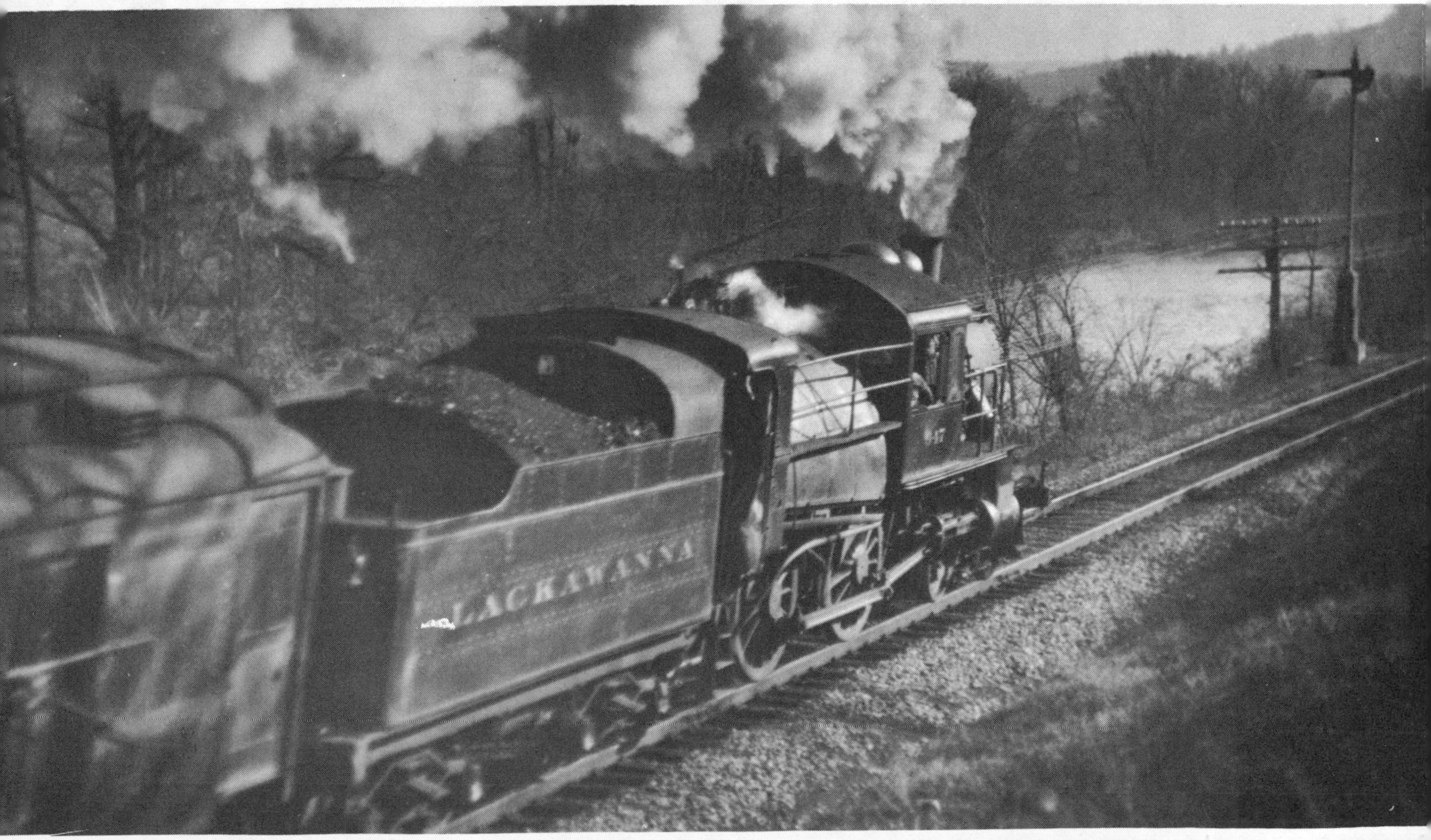
LACKAWANNA

NO COMPETITION IN THE FIELD OF SPEED to the *Broadway* or *Century*, but characterized by solid comfort on an unpretentious schedule was the Chicago-New York run on The Nickel Plate Railroad's *Nickel Plate Limited* with connecting sleepers east of Buffalo in The Delaware, Lackawanna & Western's *Lackawanna Limited*. Twenty-three hours between La Salle Street and downtown New York was required aboard the *Limited's* eight section-solarium-lounge cars, the western end of the haul through the industrial heartland of the Midwest and the eastern leg through the Poconos which unhurried travelers felt were as rewarding as the scenery along the Central's Water Level Route. Here *The Nickel Plate Limited*, eastbound at Hammond, Indiana, in 1944 rolls against the background of summer thunderclouds piling in an August sky for a court portrait of minor royalty by Richard J. Cook.

THE NICKEL PLATE'S passenger operations embodied in the *Nickel Plate Limited* represented, in microcosm, the grand manner that was implied by its name. On its Train No. 9, too, the Cleveland-St. Louis overnight, a stylish company herald rode the tailgate of the observation-sleeper, *Kitchi-Gammi Club* and its companion car, *The Carlton Club,* with the same assurance more august insignes marked the goings of *The Super Chief* or *Liberty Limited.* Its Pullman-built diners were among the earliest with high-speed trucks and waiters filled coffee cups to the brim to demonstrate their effectiveness. *(Left: Richard J. Cook; Below: Timken Roller Bearings.)*

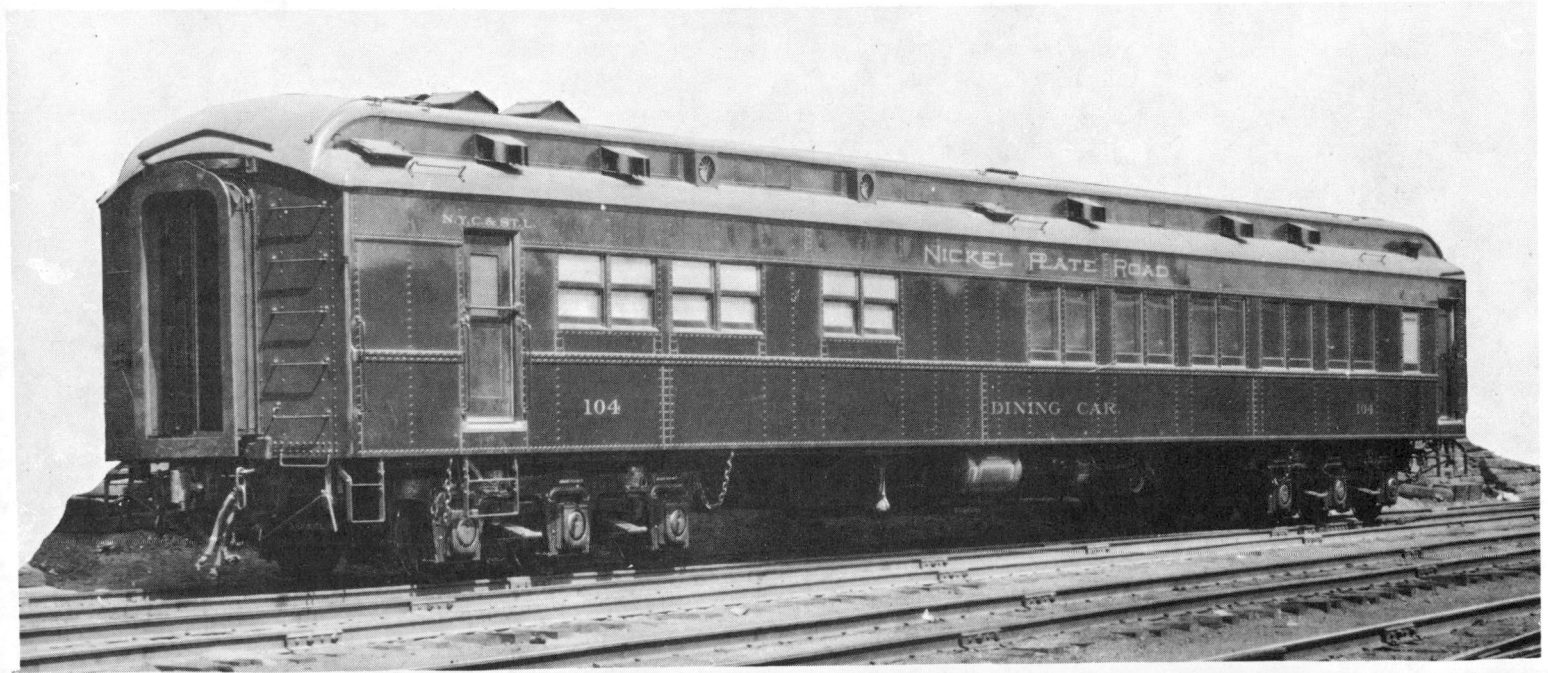

WARMED by the traditional cannonball stove of railway legend, the Nickel Plate operator at Angola, New York, gets his lineup from the dispatcher in the year 1958. Ninety-one years earlier another pot-bellied stove had made melancholy history at Angola when it fired the wreckage of the Lake Shore & Michigan Southern's *New York Express* with the loss of fifty lives in what came to be known to history as "The Angola Horror." Below, *The Nickel Plate Limited* departs Englewood, Illinois, with through Pullmans for the Lackawanna interchange at Buffalo against the identifying background of the Englewood gas works in the mid-thirties. *(Right: Philip R. Hastings; Below: De Golyer Foundation, Collons Collection.)*

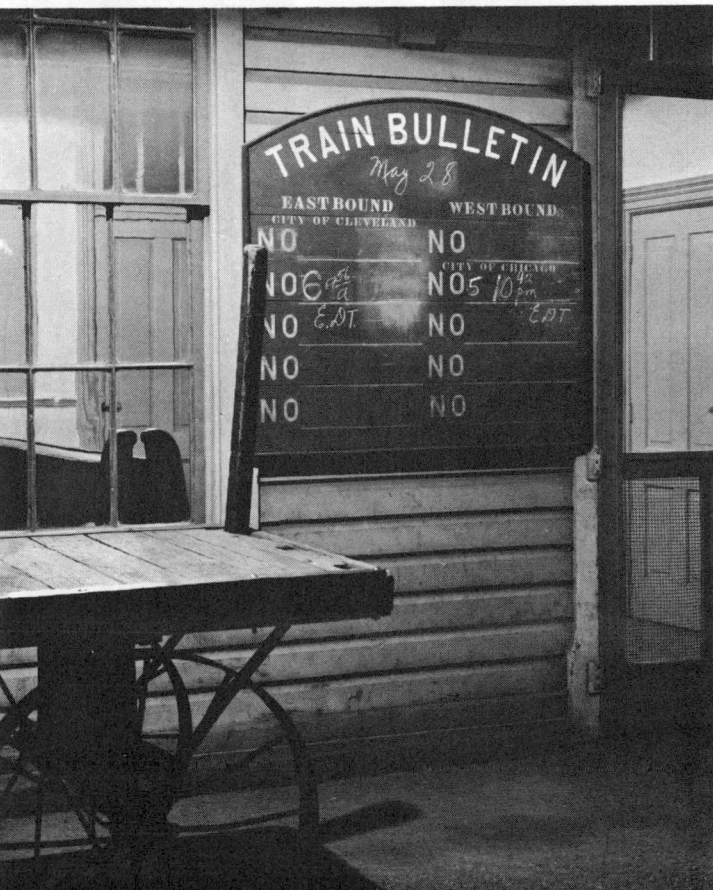

THE THROUGH Pullmans between Hoboken and Chicago via the *Lackawanna Limited* and the Nickel Plate was not the only through run over these connecting carriers in the mid-thirties. A sleeper went west in the Lackawanna's *Western Special* to be picked up at Buffalo by the Nickel Plate's No. 7 and returned in *The Lackawanna Special*, shown here double heading through Summit, New Jersey, in the early morning hours for a pre-breakfast arrival at its Hoboken terminal. At the left the Nickel Plate depot at Conneaut, Ohio, in May of 1965 listed only two through passenger trains that paused at this once important stop, mute testimony to the carrier's ensmalled traffic and a desolate time. *(Above: Everett De Golyer Collection; Left: Richard J. Cook.)*

Devoid of fear
With roadbed clear
Miss Phoebe with
The Engineer
Notes green and white
Of signal light
'Tis the safe Road
Of Anthracite.

Lackawanna
Railroad

ONE OF THE FEW trains in *The Official Guide* to be named for a woman, the Erie-Lackawanna *Phoebe Snow* was a postdated tribute to the imaginary heroine of the Lackawanna's earliest skirmishes with promotion and publicity long before its merger with Erie. To focus attention on the carrier's antiseptic aspects as an anthracite burning railroad, a now forgotten genius, shortly after the turn of the century, confected no fewer than sixty four-line jingles about a mythical Miss Phoebe Snow whose garments remained stainless although exposed to all known vicissitudes of travel in the age of steam. No friend of the dry cleaning industry, where rival soft coal burning roads were felt to have a vested interest, the Lackawanna made abundant capital of Miss Phoebe until she at length entered the national lexicon of popular awareness along with Buster Brown and the Flora Dora Girls. Years later, after the merger with Erie, the name seemed a natural for the carrier's new, stylish streamliner on the Buffalo-Hoboken daylight run, and the sleeping princess of advertising was re-animated fifty years after her first incarnation. At the right *The Phoebe Snow* is shown at Binghamton, New York, running six hours off schedule with the Christmas mails in 1956. *(Above & Right: Lackawanna Railroad; Photograph: Richard Allen.)*

miss phoebe
again welcomes you to the

E ERIE LACKAWANNA
The Friendly Service Route

The Folk-legend Became Reality

PRIMARILY a de luxe run between New York and Cincinnati with through cars from Washington via the Big Four to Louisville, St. Louis and Chicago, The Chesapeake & Ohio's *George Washington* was one of the great name trains of the Tidewater lexicon of railroading. The C & O owned both The Homestead at Hot Springs, Virginia, and The Greenbrier sixty odd miles away at White Sulphur and its candy trains, like those of the Florida East Coast, gave patrons a foretaste of the excellence they might expect at company hotels. In a pre-diner age, mammy types had sold Southern delicacies at depots where the cars paused. (*Lucius Beebe.*)

500

THE CAREFULLY CULTIVATED atmosphere of the Old South in ante-bellum times with which the Chesapeake & Ohio invested its hotel properties was also part of the facade of its three crack name trains, *The George Washington, The F.F.V.* and *The Sportsman.* The food aboard the dining cars and hand picked crews of cheerful and personable Pullman porters suggested old days on the plantation in the best Gone With the Wind tradition. The railroad never committed itself as to whether F.F.V. stood for Fast Flying Virginian or First Families of Virginia. It was agreeable to either interpretation and the aristocratic ways it suggested.

DURING A brief skirmish with airflow design, *F.F.V.* in the summer of 1947 poses at Hinton, West Virginia, for a profile photograph by Gene Huddleston for Rail Photo Service.

NO more effective tailgate insigne was ever devised for a crack varnish run than the simple portrait of the Founding Father which rode without further remark or identification at the end of *The George Washington's* observation lounge. *(Rail Photo Service.)*

LIKE MANY MEN of small stature, Robert R. Young had Napoleonic ideas and admired to surround himself with the great names of the world. Among them were the Duke and Duchess of Windsor at White Sulphur, and also many other headliners to add to the resort's century old and well established luster. Here the Windsors arrive aboard his private car No. 28 which, after his death, became the property of Mrs. Joan Payson, sister of John Hay Whitney, thus maintaining continuity with names that made news. *(Two Photos: Chesapeake & Ohio.)*

502

NO RAILROAD, not even the Southern Pacific and Del Monte or the Santa Fe and its Harvey Houses, was ever more closely associated with the hotel business than was the Chesapeake & Ohio through the agency of The Greenbrier at White Sulphur Springs. General Robert E. Lee had arrived aboard the cars in 1867 and from then until the time of Robert R. Young both its financial and social rating were beyond reproach. The only thinkable way to achieve The Greenbrier was *The George Washington*, while patrons of its rival, The Homestead came on *The F.F.V.* Snobbism rode the C.&O. stylishly and unabated. "You can see it on the train," a stately dowager told Cleveland Amory. "The people you want to be with are all going to The Hotel." The spring house is an ancient symbol of the allegedly therapeutic quality of the waters. *(Two Photos: Chesapeake & Ohio.)*

COMPANION TRAIN to the Chesapeake & Ohio's *George Washington* and *The Fast Flying Virginian* was *The Sportsman* with sleepers from Tidewater and Washington for Pittsburgh, Cincinnati and Detroit, the last of which terminals was reached over the iron of the subsidiary Pere Marquette. Above, its Pullman sleeper lounge is shown leaving Alexandria, just across the Potomoc from Washington and below is its Detroit section shortened to a mere five-car consist at the end of the run.   (*Above: Lucius Beebe; Below: Rail Photo Service.*)

THE EXTENT to which the Chesapeake & Ohio Railroad was involved in the business of innkeeping represented by the Greenbrier Hotel at White Sulphur Springs, West Virginia, was the precise parallel of the commitment of the Southern Pacific in Del Monte on Monterey Peninsula or of Henry M. Flagler's Florida East Coast in the Flagler hotels at St. Augustine, Palm Beach or other resorts of the Florida littoral. Their affairs were interdependent, the *George Washington* providing the means of transport for arriving guests and departing patrons of the Greenbrier taking passage on *The Fast Flying Virginian*. It was a pattern of partnership of lodging and transport common to California, Florida, Colorado, New Jersey and wherever resorts were available via the cars in the age of Pullman. (*Two Photos: Chesapeake & Ohio.*)

505

THE CAFE-CHAIR CAR depicted below, a rare and exotic product of Pullman, was outshopped in June 1905 for the Great Central Route, a brief lived consolidation of the Cincinnati, Hamilton & Dayton, the Pere Marquette (to which No. 1008 was assigned and initialled) and the Chicago, Cincinnati & Louisville, a pattern of transport reaching from Cincinnati to Northern Michigan and from Buffalo west to Springfield, Illinois. No. 1008 ran in its *East Coast Flyer* between Chicago and Grand Rapids until the venture ended ingloriously in 1907. (*Arthur D. Dubin Collection.*)

SUNSET ON A SUMMER'S EVENING in the early thirties illuminates the smokebox *(opposite)* of the engine assigned to the Pere Marquette's Train No. 9, *The Resort Special* as it loads at the Fort Street Station in Detroit for the overnight run to Bay View with sleepers and a diner-lounge from Chicago it will pick up at Grand Rapids. Near its Bay View, Michigan, terminal, hard by the Straits of Mackinac, it will pass through the town of Petoskey, in the thirties a junction point of less consequence than it had been in 1908 when the photograph was taken that is reproduced above. Petoskey was then also on line of the Grand Rapids & Indiana and very much of a railroad community. *(Opposite: Ewing Galloway; Above: Smithsonian Institution.)*

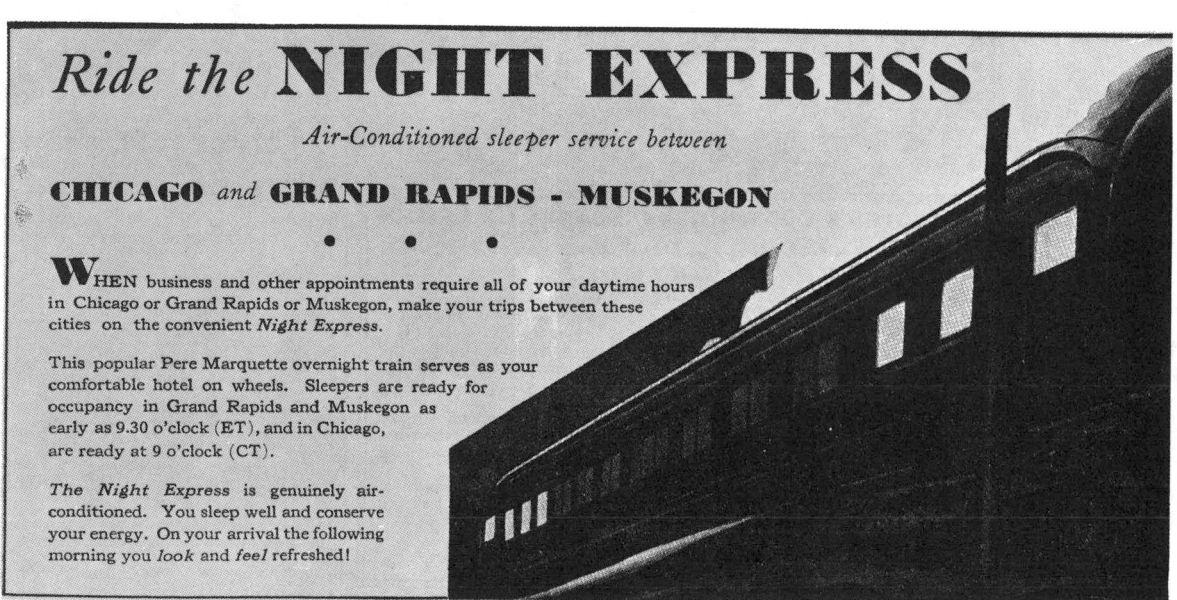

SPECIAL ASPECTS of fascination in the character or operations of a single railroad have sometimes so fetched the imagination of individual photographers that their work has become specifically associated with one carrier almost to the exclusion of all others. O. Winston Link, a New York commercial photographer of great distinction, happily while steam still ruled this essentially Tidewater and coal haul road, fell in love with the Norfolk & Western, and tokens of his devotion are the two photographs appearing here and on the opposite page. Opposite, behind a bullet-nosed 4-8-4 the Norfolk & Western's *Powhatan Arrow* on the all day long run between Norfolk and Cincinnati with coaches only emerges westbound from Montgomery Tunnel twenty-seven miles west of Roanoke. Here Trains No. 1 and 2 with New York Pullmans from the Pennsylvania connection via the Shenandoah Valley route for Roanoke, Virginia, meet at Hager Tower, Hagerstown, Maryland. The time is January 1948. *(Two Photos: O. Winston Link.)*

DINERS, on the Norfolk & Western's two crack trains of the thirties, *The Pocahontas* and *The Cavalier* were informal and their cuisine Southern rather than Lucullan but could be entirely satisfying eaten against the incomparable backdrop of the N & W's scenic runs. Below: at Hagerstown, Maryland, the head-end crew of No. 129 climb down from the dual service streamlined engine cab preparatory to turning it over to the night crew who will take it south with Pullmans from the Pennsylvania interchange. *(Right: Norfolk & Western; Below: Jim Shaughnessy.)*

HERE, in pre-streamlined times, The Norfolk & Western's pride and companion train to *The Cavalier*, *The Pocahontas* provides an impressionist vignette of speed and power in a great name train in action. (*Norfolk & Western Magazine.*)

THE CHICAGO & NORTH WESTERN'S second passenger depot in Chicago, photographed in the opposite reproduction at the time of the 1893 Chicago World's Columbian Exposition is remarkable not only for its institutional architecture which made it as familiar a landmark as The Rookery, Potter Palmer's magnificent hotel or Marshall Field's store, but for the variety of surface transport in the picture. Visible are the ubiquitous stages of the Parmelee Transfer which shuttled between all Chicago railroad terminals then as today, an electric street car, a private brougham just coming off the bridge and at the extreme left, the public hack rank of coupes and hansoms. Not identifiable in the press of traffic, but unquestionably present in this, Chicago's year marked with a star, were the scrupulously maintained fleet of private hansoms kept on duty at the North Western Depot to meet incoming transcontinental trains by the enterprising Marshall Field. They were there to meet arriving Western millionaires from the Comstock or from Texas and to transport them directly to Field's world famous store before they could be induced to patronize the competition and, in many cases, before they even registered at their hotels. (Library of Congress.)

SHOWN immediately above on the fine summer morning of July 8, 1898, in a photograph from the archives of the State Historical Society of Wisconsin is the Chicago, St. Paul, Minneapolis & Omaha Railroad's Train No. 1 at an unidentified water stop. Notable are the two women at trackside attired in sunbonnets and the prudent country skirts of that now remote day. At the bottom of the page opposite the North Western's *Duluth-Superior Limited* approaches its Chicago terminal near Grand Avenue with a wooden diner next to the observation car with its identifying drumhead. (*The De Golyer Foundation, Roland Collons Collection.*)

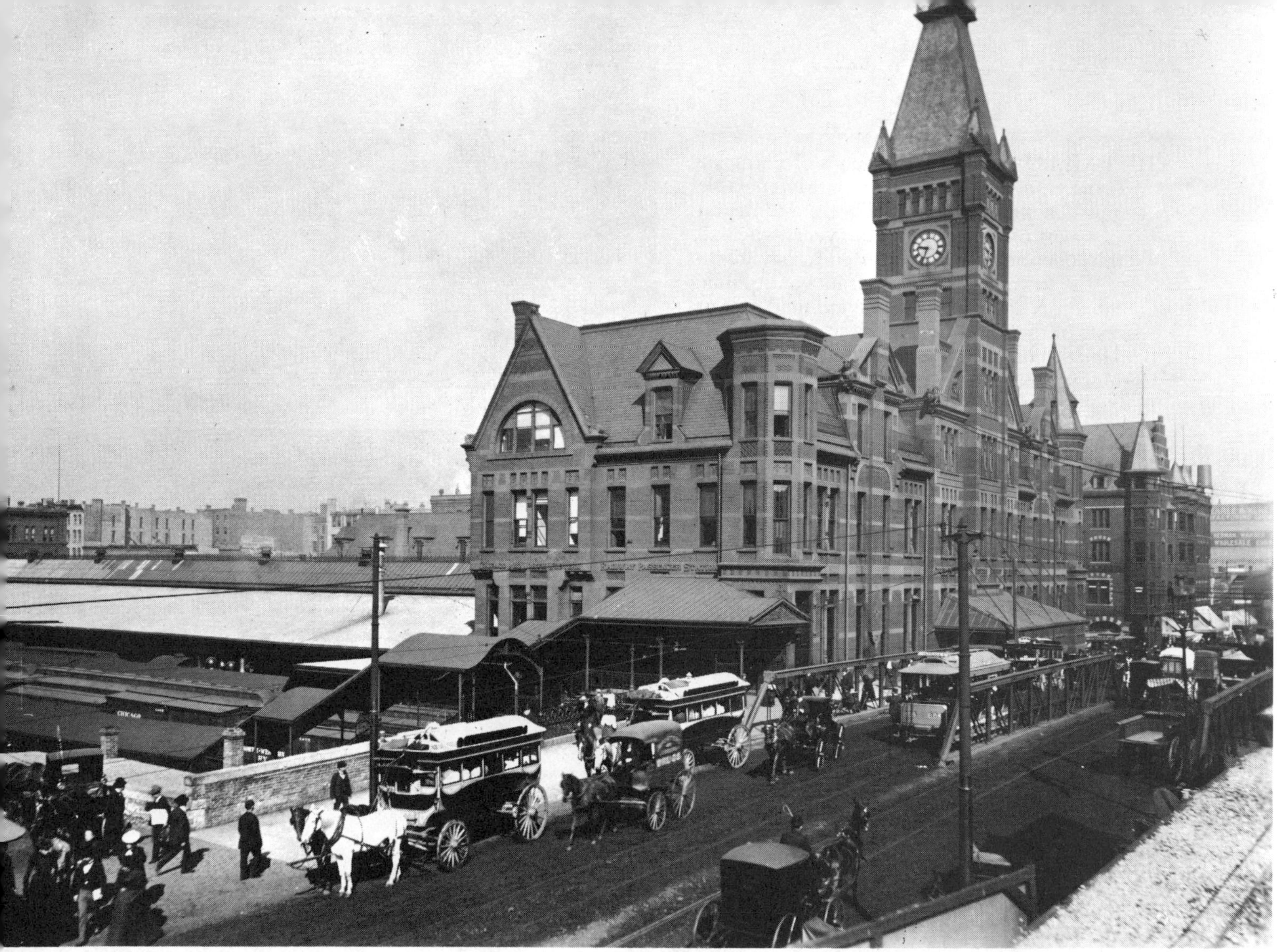

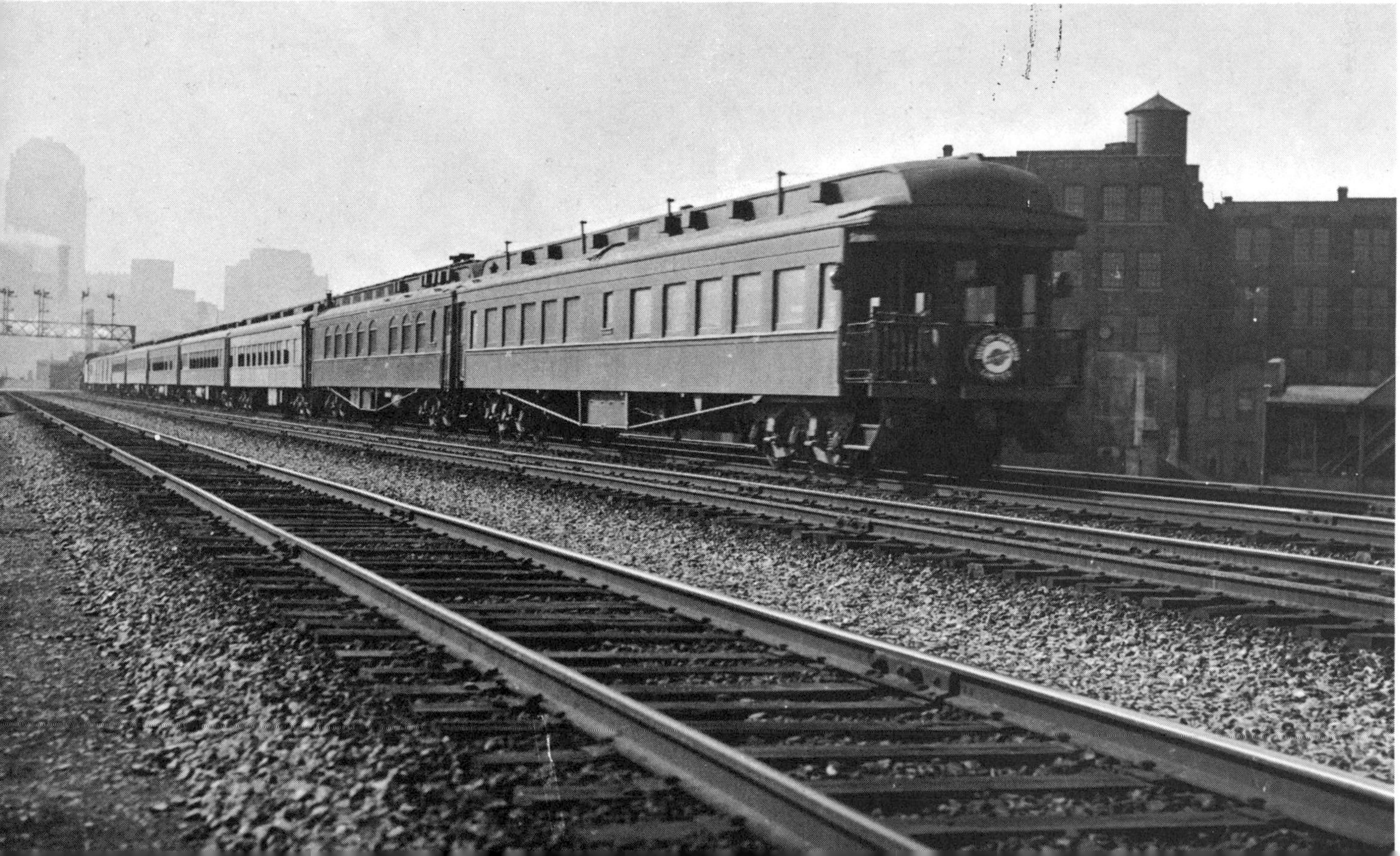

THE RAILROAD DEPOT coaches of Parmelee Transfer, a Chicago institution as venerable as the water works, were an integral part of city travel in the years when all transcontinental traffic paused to pay toll to the town's hotels, restaurants and public facilities before it continued east or west. In the mid-twenties inter-station traffic rode aboard an opera-coach type omnibus entered from the rear end. *(John Barriger.)*

IN THE YEARS of Vanderbilt domination of the Chicago & North Western, the antecedent trains to *The North Western Limited, The Short Line Limited* and *The Vestibuled Limited* had, of course, carried luxury equipment from the shops of Webster Wagner, reflecting the Vanderbilt alliance with the great rival and competitor of George M. Pullman. By the year 1898 when *The North Western Limited* had come to be known by the name it was to carry as flagship of the *North Western* fleet for five full decades to come, equipment was still by Wagner but the following year Wagner was absorbed by Pullman and from then on Pullman sleepers, diners and buffets rode in the train that its owning carrier was pleased to call "The Best in The West." By the late thirties when the photographs of and aboard *The North Western Limited* were taken, it was an all-Pullman run of truly continental dimension with the bulk of its equipment assigned to the through run between Chicago and the Twin Cities with set-out Pullmans from Milwaukee and Fond du Lac and a connecting sleeper for Duluth. What the management was pleased to call "limousine solarium" lounges *(right)* had replaced the open observation platform of tradition and motive power was sometimes the handsome green shrouded streamlined 4-8-4s usually reserved for the Omaha run. *(Above: Everett De Golyer Collection; Right: The De Golyer Foundation, Roland Collons.)*

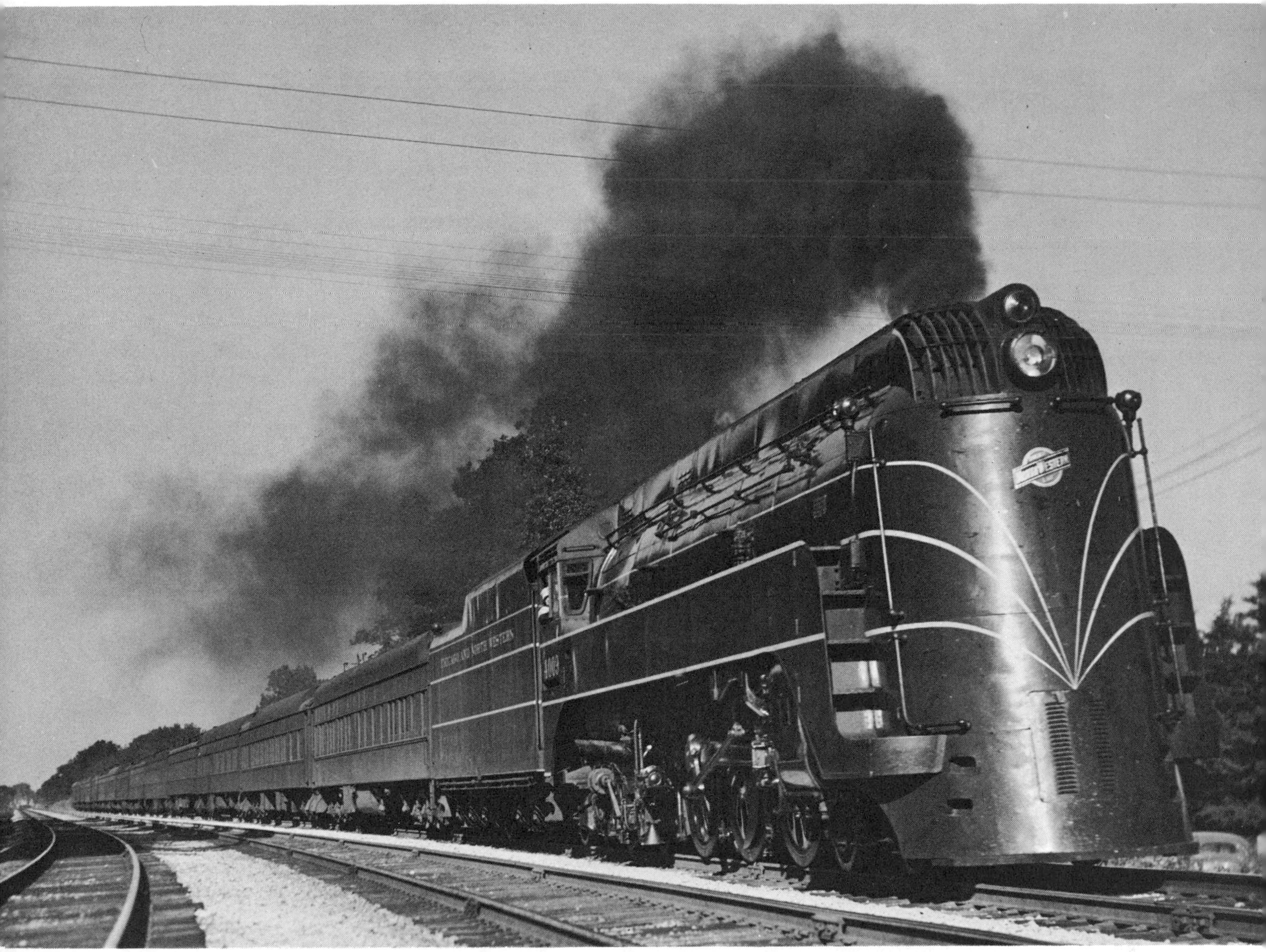
CHICAGO AND NORTH WESTERN

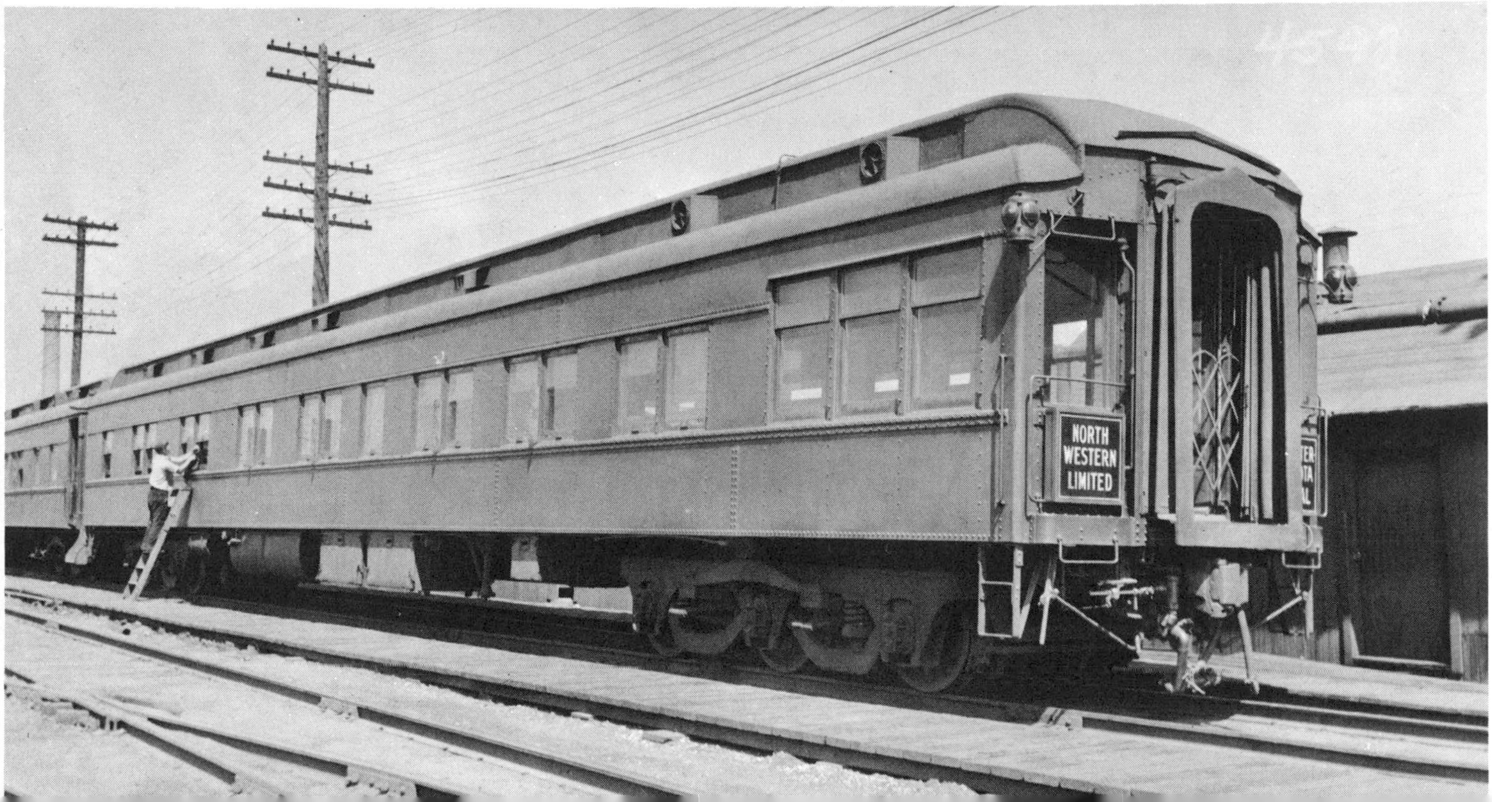
NORTH
WESTERN
LIMITED

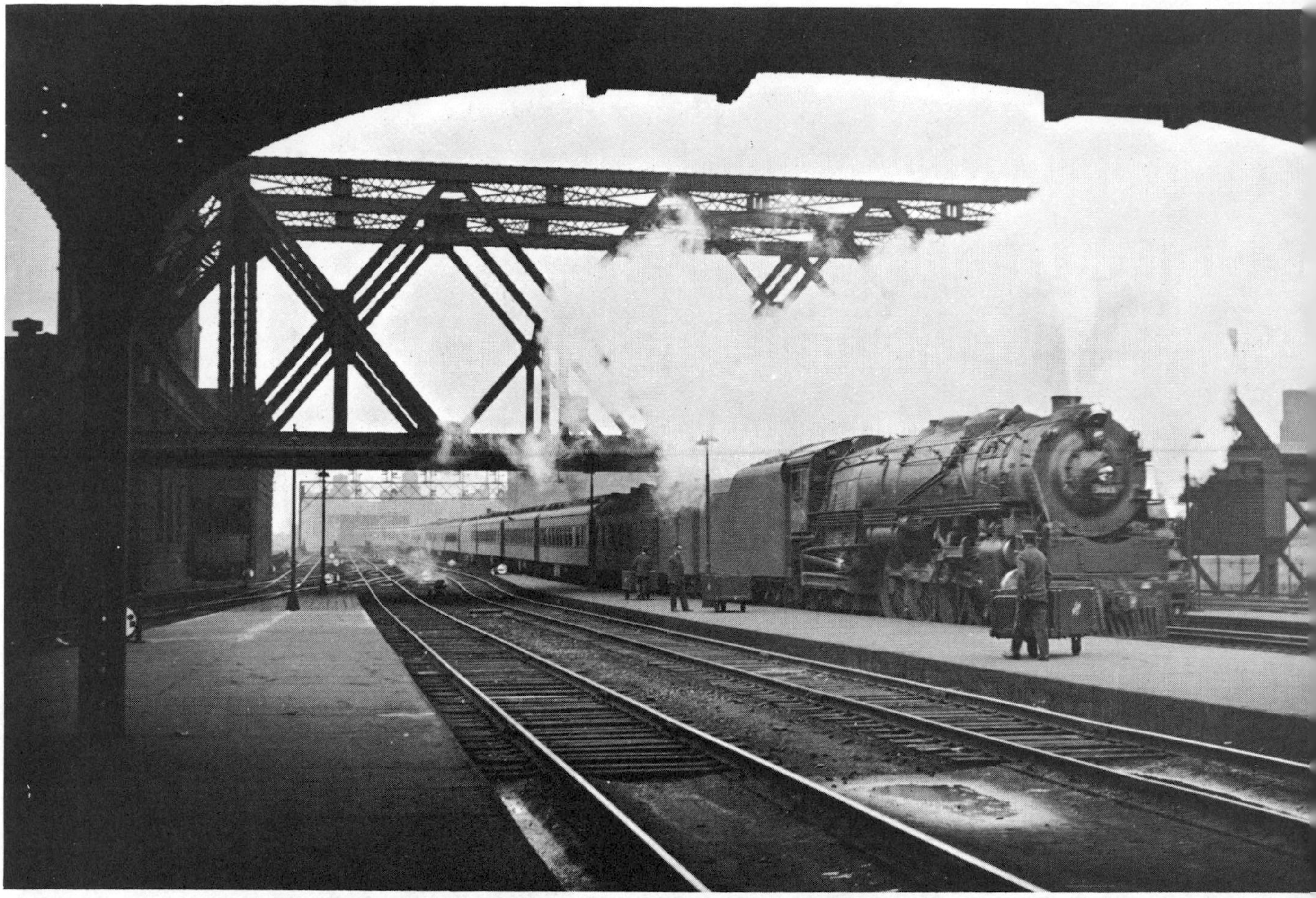

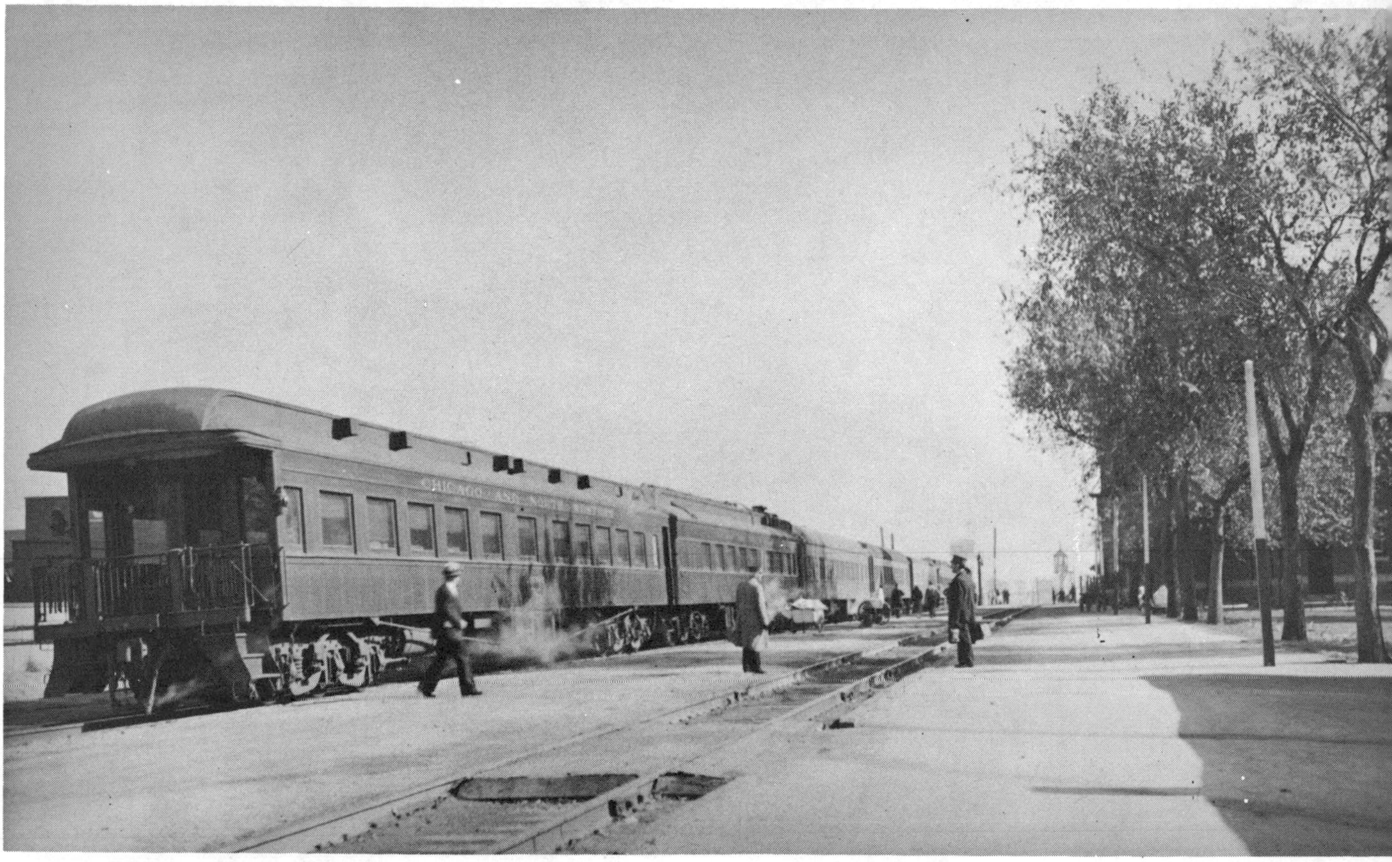

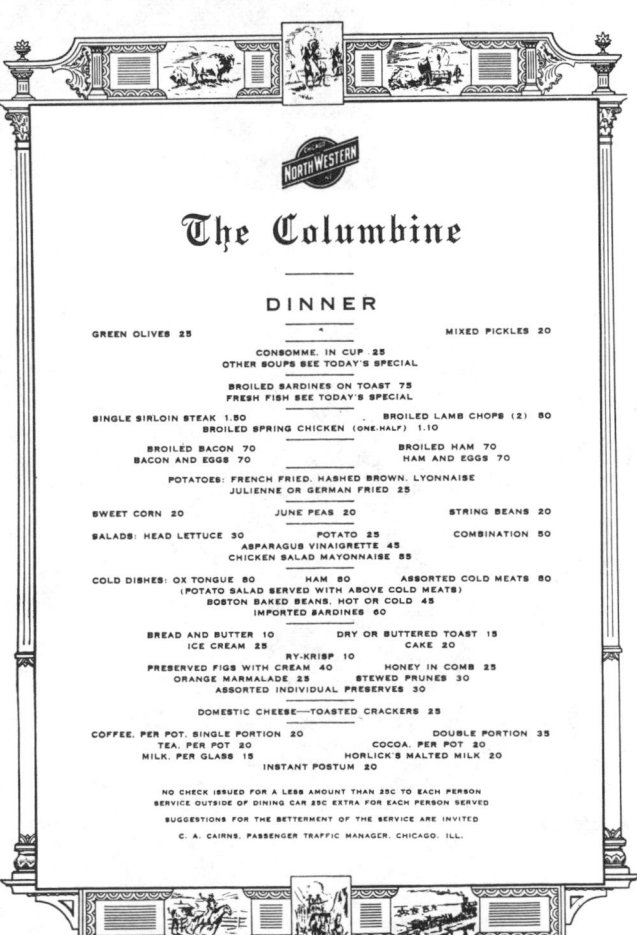

The Columbine

DINNER

GREEN OLIVES 25   MIXED PICKLES 20

CONSOMME, IN CUP 25
OTHER SOUPS SEE TODAY'S SPECIAL

BROILED SARDINES ON TOAST 75
FRESH FISH SEE TODAY'S SPECIAL

SINGLE SIRLOIN STEAK 1.50   BROILED LAMB CHOPS (2) 80
BROILED SPRING CHICKEN (ONE-HALF) 1.10

BROILED BACON 70   BROILED HAM 70
BACON AND EGGS 70   HAM AND EGGS 70

POTATOES: FRENCH FRIED, HASHED BROWN, LYONNAISE
JULIENNE OR GERMAN FRIED 25

SWEET CORN 20   JUNE PEAS 20   STRING BEANS 20

SALADS: HEAD LETTUCE 30   POTATO 25   COMBINATION 50
ASPARAGUS VINAIGRETTE 45
CHICKEN SALAD MAYONNAISE 85

COLD DISHES: OX TONGUE 80   HAM 80   ASSORTED COLD MEATS 80
(POTATO SALAD SERVED WITH ABOVE COLD MEATS)
BOSTON BAKED BEANS, HOT OR COLD 45
IMPORTED SARDINES 60

BREAD AND BUTTER 10   DRY OR BUTTERED TOAST 15
ICE CREAM 25   CAKE 20
RY-KRISP 10
PRESERVED FIGS WITH CREAM 40   HONEY IN COMB 25
ORANGE MARMALADE 25   STEWED PRUNES 30
ASSORTED INDIVIDUAL PRESERVES 30

DOMESTIC CHEESE—TOASTED CRACKERS 25

COFFEE, PER POT, SINGLE PORTION 20   DOUBLE PORTION 35
TEA, PER POT 20   COCOA, PER POT 20
MILK, PER GLASS 15   HORLICK'S MALTED MILK 20
INSTANT POSTUM 20

NO CHECK ISSUED FOR A LESS AMOUNT THAN 25C TO EACH PERSON
SERVICE OUTSIDE OF DINING CAR 25C EXTRA FOR EACH PERSON SERVED

SUGGESTIONS FOR THE BETTERMENT OF THE SERVICE ARE INVITED

C. A. CAIRNS, PASSENGER TRAFFIC MANAGER, CHICAGO, ILL.

AT THE APOGEE of its vast and diffused passenger operations when, in the mid-1930s, there was still a Vanderbilt on the board of directors to maintain continuity with its once proud estate as a Vanderbilt line, the Chicago & North Western operated a roster of name trains at least comparable to the fleet of varnish flyers of the Southern Pacific and the Pennsylvania. Excepting *The North Western Limited*, few of the name trains running exclusively over the North Western's left hand iron, *The Corn King, The Iron & Copper Country Express, The Iron Range Express, The Victory, The Rochester-Minnesota Special, The Viking* or *The Mondamin* could be termed de luxe runs. Luxury rode, rather, on its connecting trains via Union Pacific out of Omaha, *The Overland Limited, The Portland Rose, The Columbine, The Los Angeles Limited, The Mountain Bluebird* and, later *The City* streamliners until they were diverted to the Milwaukee. At the top opposite *The Corn King* arrives at Chicago behind one of the North Western's massive Class H, 4-8-4s. Below, *The Columbine* before the days of its elaborate Union Pacific solarium lounges, whose menu is shown adjacent, pauses at Boone, Iowa, on its Denver run. *The Continental Limited*, shown above through the arches of Mannheim Road viaduct at Bellwood, Illinois, in 1926 was an accommodation train to Portland and the northwest. *(Opposite, Two Photos: The De Golyer Foundation, Roland Collons; Above: Alfred W. Johnson.)*

RIDING THE NORTH WESTERN'S Omaha Line in 1902 sometimes provided excitement not listed on the operating timecard as when the Duluth Excursion was derailed on August 31 of that year. Salvaging their trunk from the wrecked baggage car while waiting for the town hack to pick them up was a lark for youths in the derby hats and knee pants of the then current fashion. Almost as much fun as a Methodist Church bake sale was the contretemps *(below)* on the Omaha Line near Belle Plaine, Minnesota, in December 1902. Even the Ladies' Aid meeting couldn't get the turnout occasioned by a nice train wreck. *(Two Photos: Wisconsin Historical Society, J. Foster Adams Collection.)*

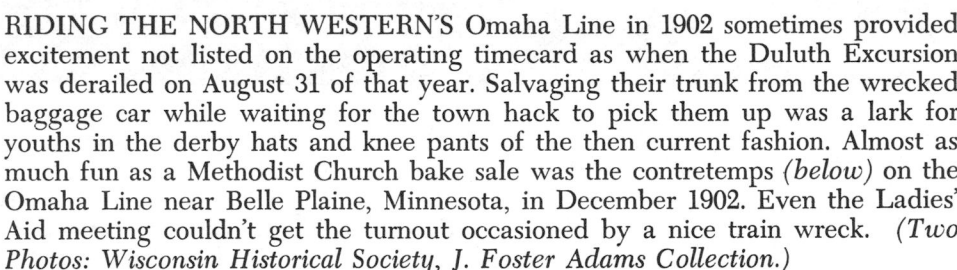

ANOTHER contretemps on
The Omaha Line saw
The North Western's ten
wheeler No. 326 appropriately
carrying the white markers
of a special when it was
assigned to unsnarl
the Duluth Excursion train
wreck of 1903. (*Wisconsin
Historical Society.*)

519

WISCONSIN dairy products in ample profusion were assured to patrons of The Soo Line who were prompt to the summons when the dinner chimes sounded through the cars. Three eggs for breakfast were available for the asking, and the butterfat content was high all down the menu. A carrier subject to the caprices of seasonal traffic The Soo overnight between Chicago and the Twin Cities *(below)* regularly double headed in summer months with as many as twenty Pullmans and coaches on the drawbar of the road engine. *(Right: Soo Line; Below: Leslie V. Suprey.)*

IN THE MID-1930s when these photographs were taken along the Minneapolis, St. Paul & Sault Ste. Marie Railway, more usually known as The Soo, its overnight trains between Chicago and the Twin Cities were not name trains and ran as numbers only. Bucking the competition of the North Western, the Burlington, and the Milwaukee, all of which ran crack name trains in this densely trafficked area, The Soo had a loyal following who rode its no-nonsense cars, coaches, Standard sleepers, and well-conducted lounges and diners on schedules devoid of urgency through the Wisconsin farmlands.

No. 1 is shown above double-heading out of Fond du Lac in classic pose by Leslie Suprey, The Soo's official jongleur and cameraman. The beaver insigne at the left rode the observation car *Fernie* via The Soo and the Canadian Pacific all the way to Vancouver in *The Soo-Dominion*.

The Metropolitan

Nos. 25 and 25-155—THE METROPOLITAN.
(Tables 4, 5, 6.)

Lounge Car....Pittsburgh to St. Louis—(10 S.). (Via Dayton.)
Sleeping Cars..New York to St. Louis—(12 S., D.R.) (Via Dayton.)
        Indianapolis to St. Louis—(12 S., D.R). (Open 8 00 p.m.)
        Pittsburgh to Louisville—(12 S., D R.). (Via Dayton.)
        (To No. 306 at Indianapolis.
        Pittsburgh to Detroit—(12 S., D.R.). (In No. 15-105
        from Pittsburgh.)
        Columbus to St. Louis—(12 S., D. R.). (Via Dayton.)
        (Open 10 00 p.m.)
Parlor Cars.....New York to Philadelphia—(Fountain Lounge).
        New York to Pittsburgh.
        Pittsburgh to Columbus—(Lounge Cafe).
        Pittsburgh to Cleveland (via Salem). (On No. 323.)
Parlor Coach,..Washington to Pittsburgh (in No. 15, arriving Pittsburgh
        6 05 p.m.).
Dining Cars ...New York to Pittsburgh.
        Terre Haute to St. Louis.
Cafe Coach ....Washington to Harrisburg
Coaches.......New York to Pittsburgh.
        Pittsburgh to St. Louis.

The Standard Railroad of The World

FOR UPWARDS of a century the Pennsylvania Railroad was rated by social historians as "the best gentleman's club in Philadelphia," a reference to the impeccable backgrounds, either acquired or inherited, of the long succession of magnificoes who served the carrier as president: Tom Scott, George Roberts and, most urbane and patrician of them all, the great Alexander Cassatt. All but forgotten in this refulgent tally were the founding fathers in the era of brass knuckles such as J. Edgar Thompson for whom the vast steel mills were named on the outskirts of Pittsburgh, and Andrew Carnegie, a one-time division superintendent whose destiny pointed elsewhere. As the best club in Philadelphia, it was only fitting that the Pennsylvania should occupy clubrooms suitable to its estate, and by and large the name trains of its passenger fleet in the great years of railroad travel served the purpose with distinction. No matter if a cynical commentator remarked of the Pennsy varnish: "When you've seen one, you've seen them all." The carrier spoke of itself as "The Standard Railroad of The World" and the superlative implied a degree of operational standardization over the vast network of high speed tracks that ranged from Montauk Point to St. Louis and from Louisville to the Straits of Mackinac. To the partisan of the Pennsylvania's special cachet of adequacy this uniform facade was no discouragement. It was a highballing organization. Its crack name trains to St. Louis and Chicago rolled double-headed across the countryside of Illinois and Indiana at speeds verging on a hundred miles an hour, and even when leaving the massive complex of Penn Station in Manhattan, the last car was a blur by the time it passed the end of the platform. Its most highly regarded name trains, *The Broadway Limited, The Liberty Limited* and *The Spirit of St. Louis,* each of them on a run explicitly in competition with rival carriers, had about it a character that was instantly perceptible to the seasoned traveler. Excepting on *The Broadway* its cuisine was seldom of an order to flutter pulses, at least within the memory of living men, although at the turn of the century there is evidence to suggest that its dining cars were conducted along more opulent lines. They had to be, if for no other reason than that a great deal of the road's traffic was in direct competition with the Baltimore & Ohio where the food was certifiably wonderful. When it came to passenger equipment, the Pennsylvania took a back seat to nobody and from the time of its primordial *Pennsylvania Limited* whose livery was so flamboyant it was known as "The Yellow Kid," down to the ultimate Tuscan red and cool beige interiors of its last *Broadway* the physical properties of its more regarded varnish runs were the envy of less affluent carriers. Where other carriers in the naming of their trains ran to regional history, folklore, mythology, zoology and horticulture, the Pennsy was patriotic: *The Liberty Limited, The Union, The Congressional, The General, The Admiral, The Jeffersonian, The Spirit of St. Louis, The American, The Senator* and *The Rainbow* (named for an Army division) all bearing witness to the road's essential patriotism. Now and then, as in the case of *The Red Bird, The Golden Arrow, The Gotham Limited* and *The Mercantile Express* it voided this generality, but mostly its lexicon was that of the national legend. It was a railroad steeped in protocol so that its stationmaster in New York, Big Bill Egan, like his English opposite numbers, as often as not appeared for duty in the silk top hat and morning attire of formal observance. And if the conductors of the Pennsylvania at one stage in the game enjoyed a widespread reputation for arrogance, were they not, after all, inheritors vicariously of the mantle of George Roberts and A. J. Cassatt, the symbol and operative authority of "The Standard Railroad of The World"?

523

HOLIDAY MENU.

BLUE POINTS ON HALF SHELL.

Terrapin Soup.

Kennebec Salmon with Green Peas.

Potatoes a la Parisienne.

Boiled Leg of Lamb, caper sauce.   Boiled Capon, cream sauce.

Ribs of Beef with brown potatoes.

Turkey, cranberry sauce   Tame Goose stuffed with apples

Roast Beef.

Sweetbreads larded with Mushrooms.

Salmi of Quail with Truffles.

Roast Partridge, bread sauce.

Chicken Salad.   Smoked Buffalo Tongue.   Paté of Snipe in Jelly

Celery.   Olives.

Baked Sweet Potatoes.   Pickled Beets.   Mashed Potatoes

French Peas.   Asparagus.   Marrow Squash.

Steamed Fruit Pudding, Cognac sauce.

Apple Pie.   Mince Pie.   Strawberry Ice Cream.   Roman Punch

Macaroons.   Confectionery   Assorted Cake.

Florida Oranges.   Apples.   Malaga Grapes.

Bent's Water Crackers.   Roquefort.   Edam.

Coffee.   Tea.

MEALS, ONE DOLLAR.

WHEN THE PERIOD which is the purview of the present volume opens, in general terms from 1890 to the 1941 war, although in some cases already established name trains have been followed beyond the latter terminal date, the Pennsylvania Railroad's crack *Pennsylvania Limited* on the New York-Chicago run was already seven years old. The menus from the company archives reproduced on the page opposite establish its existence at the Christmas season of 1883-84 and the same yellowing files indicate that it was not yet the candy train of matched Pullmans that it was shortly to become, but shared the miscellaneous passenger equipment then available to the *New York & Chicago Limited* and other overnight long run trains. By 1891, however, *The Pennsylvania Limited* was basking in the most benevolent regard of the frock coats and mutton chop whiskers that ordered the Pennsylvania's affairs from Broad Street, Philadelphia. Company literature for that year depicts *The Limited* in terms as glowing as the new electrical illuminating system which was one of its most advanced features. It was all-Pullman with a barber shop, bath and valet for gentlemen, lady's maid for feminine travelers, a superb wine list, while a young gentleman in cutaway coat and boutonniere is depicted seated at an L. C. Smith patent typewriter ready to take dictation from a gentleman in quilted smoking jacket and important cigar. By 1905, as suggested by the list of Chicago trains at the left, *The Pennsylvania Limited* had yielded the fast scheduling to *The Pennsylvania Special*. Below, opposite, *The Limited* at speed in 1890 from a rare photo in the files of Everett De Golyer, Jr. (*Other Photos: Pennsylvania Railroad.*)

PENNSYLVANIA RAILROAD.

SMOKING-ROOM CAR.

"NEW YORK & CHICAGO LIMITED."

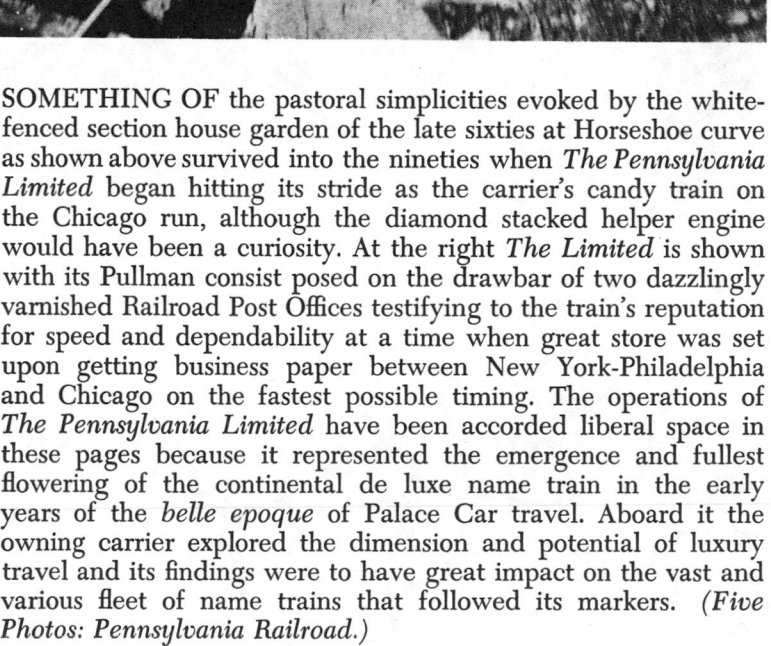

SOMETHING OF the pastoral simplicities evoked by the white-fenced section house garden of the late sixties at Horseshoe curve as shown above survived into the nineties when *The Pennsylvania Limited* began hitting its stride as the carrier's candy train on the Chicago run, although the diamond stacked helper engine would have been a curiosity. At the right *The Limited* is shown with its Pullman consist posed on the drawbar of two dazzlingly varnished Railroad Post Offices testifying to the train's reputation for speed and dependability at a time when great store was set upon getting business paper between New York-Philadelphia and Chicago on the fastest possible timing. The operations of *The Pennsylvania Limited* have been accorded liberal space in these pages because it represented the emergence and fullest flowering of the continental de luxe name train in the early years of the *belle epoque* of Palace Car travel. Aboard it the owning carrier explored the dimension and potential of luxury travel and its findings were to have great impact on the vast and various fleet of name trains that followed its markers. *(Five Photos: Pennsylvania Railroad.)*

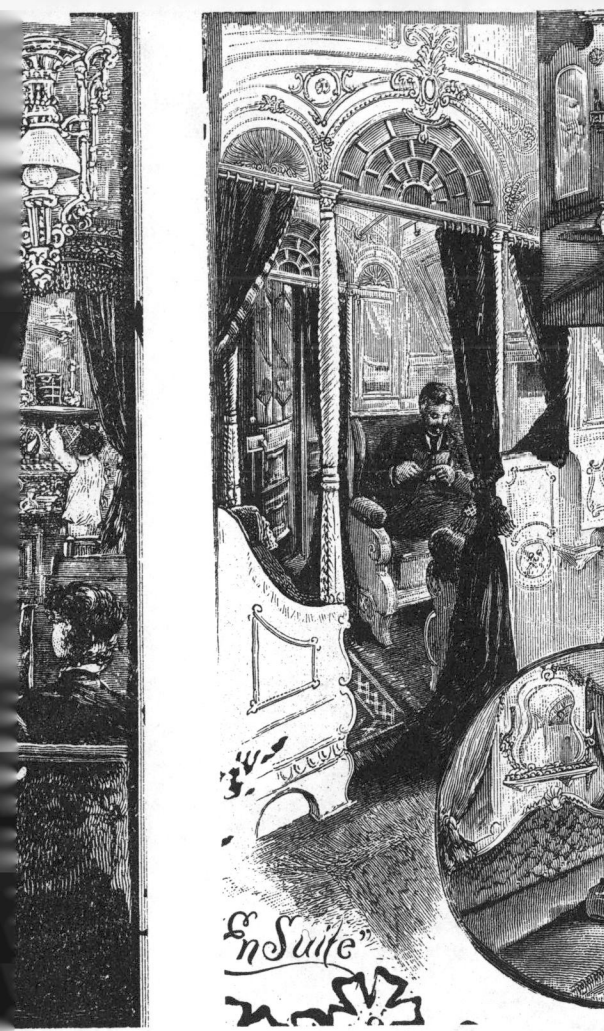

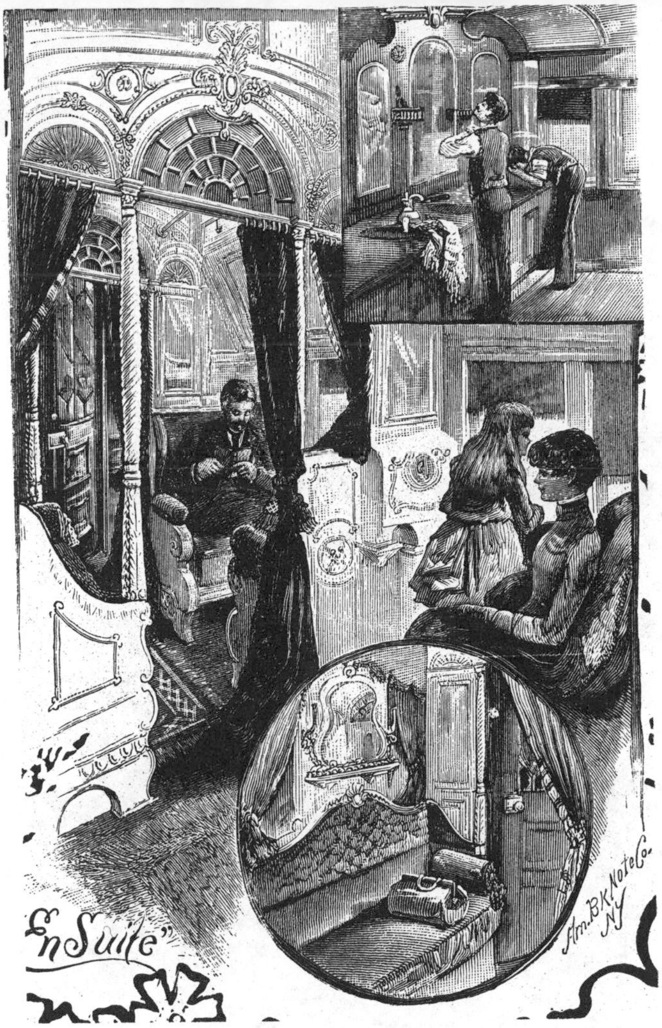

"En Suite"
Am. B.K. Note Co.
NY

Observation
Car.
Am. B.K. Note Co.
NY

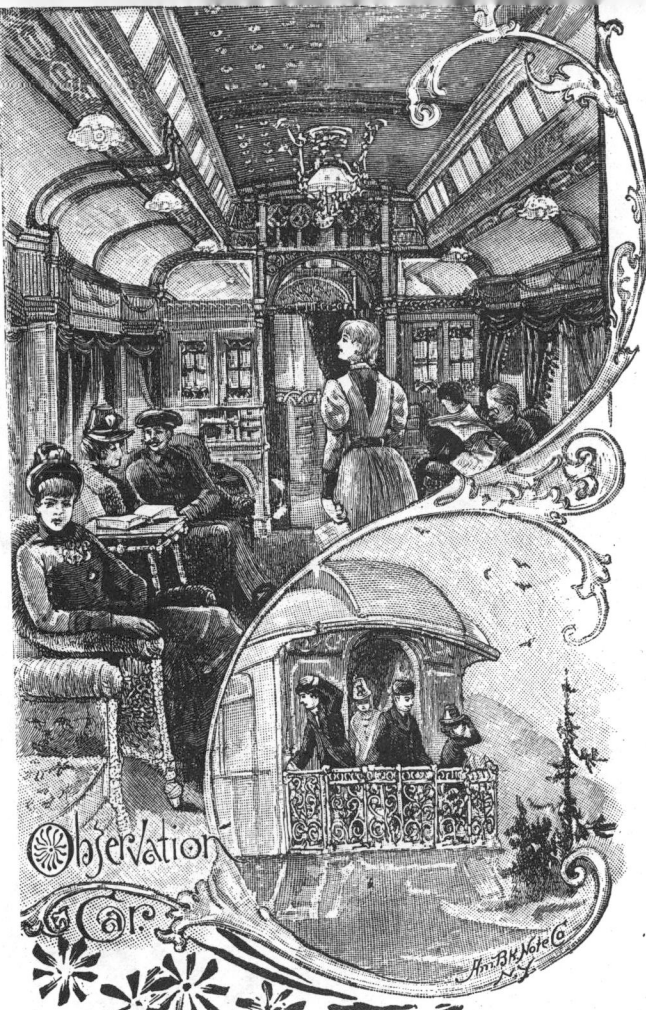

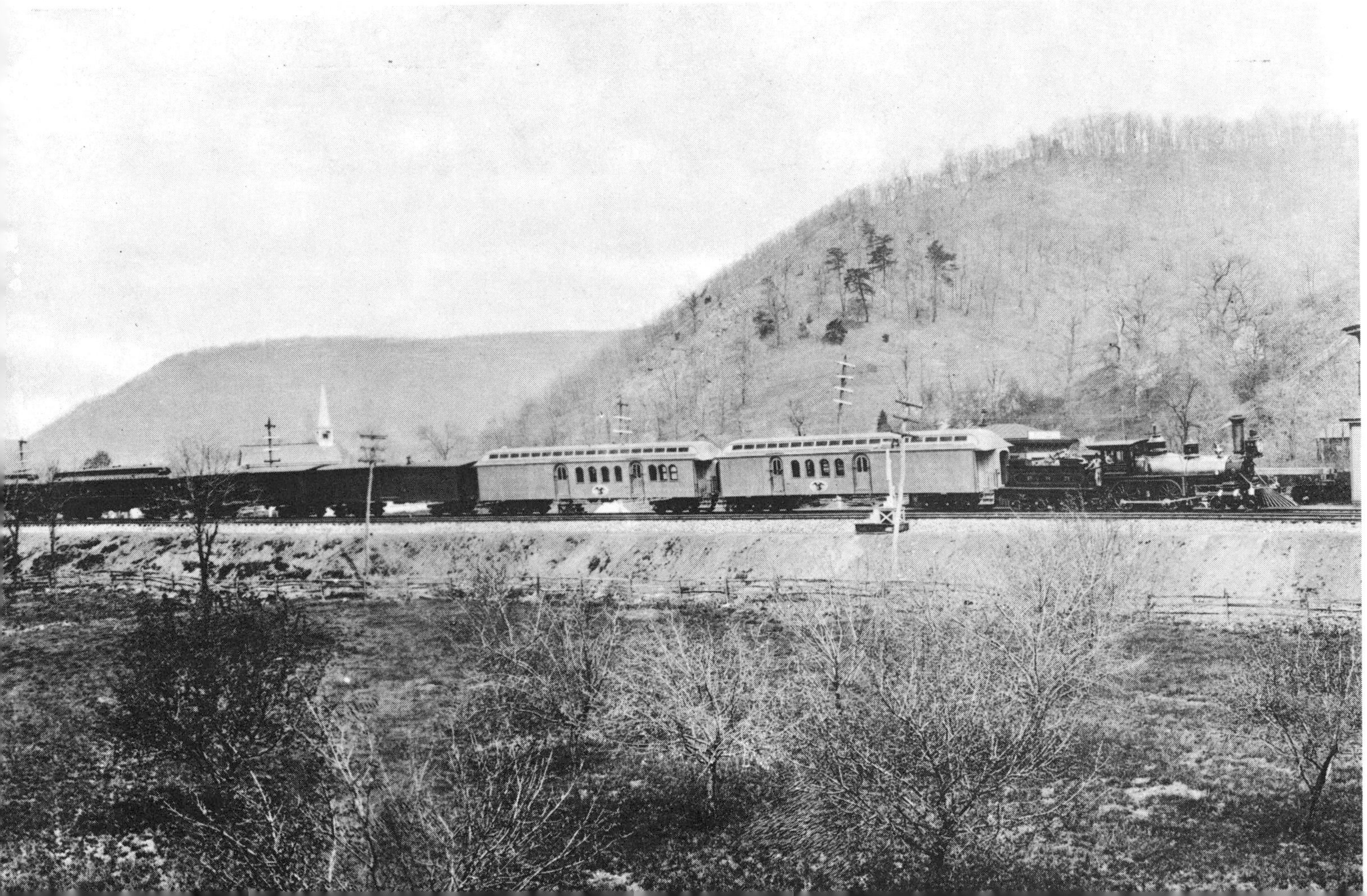

528

THE TRAFFIC situation in New York's West Street in 1890 as portrayed in the below drawing for *Harper's Weekly* that year would seem of a magnitude and complexity to equal anything evoked by the later and universal automobile. Here the Pennsylvania's passengers embarked aboard its considerable fleet of ferry boats, largely named for cities served by the railroad, *Washington, St. Louis, New Brunswick, Orange,* for the brief trip across the North River to the carrier's Jersey City terminal to board the cars. *Harper's* editorially applauded the construction of the covered footbridge across West Street, shown here, as well as the commodious double decked ferry boat *New Brunswick,* where horse drawn vehicles monopolized the lower deck and passengers rode the upper. On the opposite page a wintery photograph, to judge by the attire of its passengers, taken at a somewhat later date shows the Pennsylvania ferry *St. Louis,* the keystone emblem on its funnels, as it leaves the railroad's Jersey City terminal with its sister ship, *Washington* in the background. Notable in *St. Louis'* construction is the continuity of the Pullman theme, as exemplified in the photograph underneath, of the square window gothic of colored glass in both the varnish cars and ferry boats. The arched window gothic in the older vessel, *Washington* dates from a time when similarly curved window frames were in vogue in the car shops at Pullman, Illinois. *(Page Opposite, Above: The Mariner's Museum; Below: Alfred W. Johnson.)*

Double-deck Ferry-boat

Bridge across West St. N.Y.

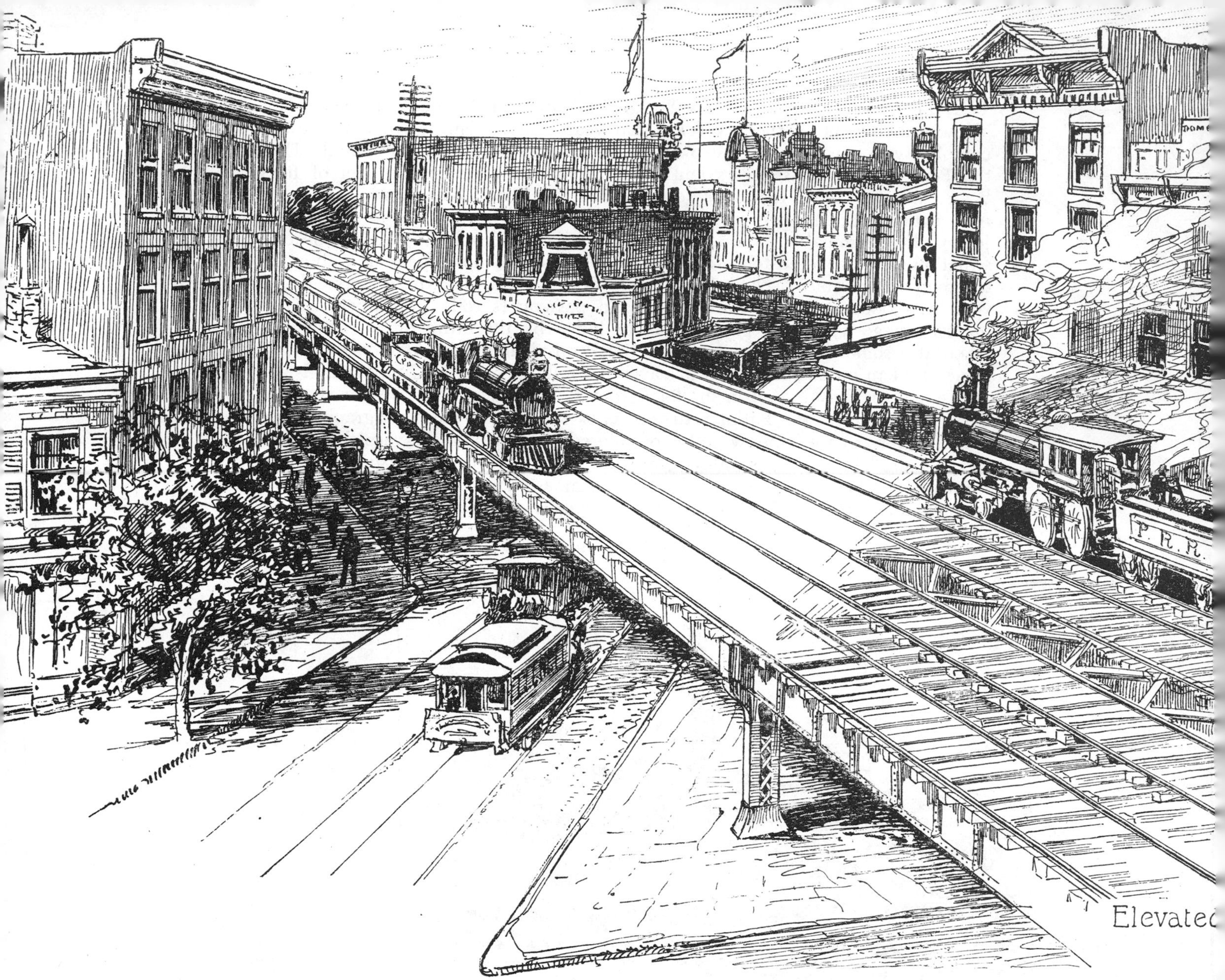

Elevated

TWENTY YEARS BEFORE the completion of Penn Station in Manhattan and its connecting tunnels under the East and North Rivers, patrons achieved the railroad's terminal in Jersey City by ferry from the West Street pier. In August 1890 *Harper's Weekly* commented that "The Pennsylvania Co., has notably moved in the right direction . . . the list of casualties at grade crossings about to be abolished is a long one." This referred to the construction at West Street of an overpass, shown on an adjacent page, and at Jersey City terminal the erection of "a four track iron structure 3/5 of a mile long, similar to but more substantial than the elevated roadways in New York City." The Jersey City viaduct is shown above. In 1890 the North and East River tunnels were unforeseen and speculation concerned a possible high bridge across the Hudson above Manhattan Island with connections to both New England and the Lower City. The woodcut at the right with its side-wheel tugboats dates from a much earlier period, perhaps 1875, but that the Pennsylvania already had a beachhead at Jersey City is indicated by the dock at the right of the engraving.

530

R. at Newark Ave., Jersey City.

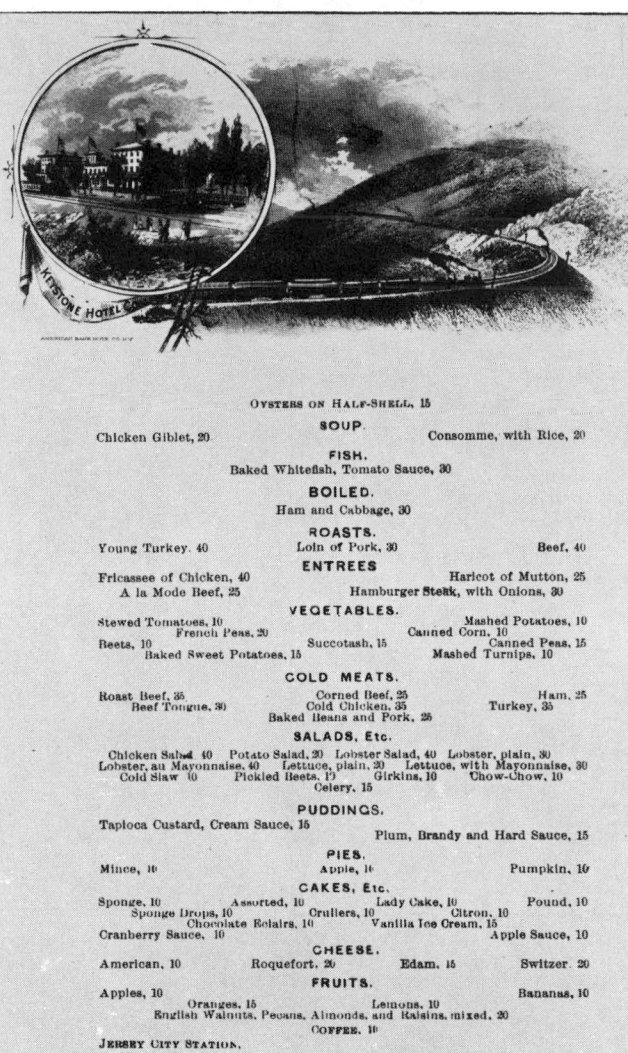

OYSTERS ON HALF-SHELL, 15

SOUP.

Chicken Giblet, 20.   Consomme, with Rice, 20

FISH.

Baked Whitefish, Tomato Sauce, 30

BOILED.

Ham and Cabbage, 30

ROASTS.

Young Turkey, 40   Loin of Pork, 30   Beef, 40

ENTREES

Fricassee of Chicken, 40   Haricot of Mutton, 25
A la Mode Beef, 25   Hamburger Steak, with Onions, 30

VEGETABLES.

Stewed Tomatoes, 10   Mashed Potatoes, 10
French Peas, 20   Canned Corn, 10
Beets, 10   Succotash, 15   Canned Peas, 15
Baked Sweet Potatoes, 15   Mashed Turnips, 10

COLD MEATS.

Roast Beef, 35   Corned Beef, 25   Ham, 25
Beef Tongue, 30   Cold Chicken, 35   Turkey, 35
Baked Beans and Pork, 25

SALADS, Etc.

Chicken Salad, 40   Potato Salad, 20   Lobster Salad, 40   Lobster, plain, 30
Lobster, au Mayonnaise, 40   Lettuce, plain, 20   Lettuce, with Mayonnaise, 30
Cold Slaw, 10   Pickled Beets, 10   Girkins, 10   Chow-Chow, 10
Celery, 15

PUDDINGS.

Tapioca Custard, Cream Sauce, 15
Plum, Brandy and Hard Sauce, 15

PIES.

Mince, 10   Apple, 10   Pumpkin, 10

CAKES, Etc.

Sponge, 10   Assorted, 10   Lady Cake, 10   Pound, 10
Sponge Drops, 10   Crullers, 10   Citron, 10
Chocolate Eclairs, 10   Vanilla Ice Cream, 15
Cranberry Sauce, 10   Apple Sauce, 10

CHEESE.

American, 10   Roquefort, 20   Edam, 15   Switzer, 20

FRUITS.

Apples, 10   Oranges, 15   Lemons, 10   Bananas, 10
English Walnuts, Pecans, Almonds, and Raisins, mixed, 20
COFFEE, 10

JERSEY CITY STATION,
Wednesday, December 28, 1887.

THE INTERIOR decor of the Pennsylvania's North River ferry boats as long as they lasted on the run was ornate in the extreme and enlisted the talents of many types of artisans in their building and furnishing. Rare woods in great abundance were employed by skilled joiners for the grand salon of *New Brunswick* (below) while its stained glass windows were fashioned by no less a firm than Tiffany in Fifth Avenue. Prices on the 1887 Jersey City depot restaurant menu are reassuring compared to the inflated prices of today. *(Pennsylvania RR.)*

PENNSYLVANIA RAILROAD DINING CARS.

Dinner.

LITTLE NECK CLAM CHOWDER CONSOMME

SLICED CUCUMBERS

BAKED WEAKFISH, SAUCE HOLLANDAISE
POTATOES DUCHESSE

JOWL, WITH SPINAGE

ROAST BEEF SPRING LAMB, MINT SAUCE
RIB ENDS OF BEEF, BROWNED POTATOES

BEEF A LA MODE, WITH MACARONI
FARINA CAKE, CREAM SAUCE

MASHED POTATOES POTATOES, CREAMED
SQUASH NEW BEETS ASPARAGUS

LETTUCE, FRENCH DRESSING

RICE CUSTARD

FRUIT

FRENCH ICE CREAM CAKE CANTON GINGER

PRESERVED FRUITS

ROQUEFORT AND EDAM CHEESE BENT'S WATER CRACKERS

CAFE NOIR

MEALS, ONE DOLLAR.

SUNDAY JUNE 3, 1894.

WINE LIST

Champagnes.

	Pts.	Qts.
Pommery Sec	$1 75	$3 50
G. H. Mumm's Extra Dry	1 75	3 50
Duminy Extra Sec	1 75	3 50
L. Roederer, Carte Blanche	1 75	3 50
Moet and Chandon White Seal	1 75	3 50

Claret and White Wines.

Imported expressly for the "New York & Chicago Limited" from the Houses of BRANDENBURG FRERES and JOURNU FRERES.

	Pts.	Qts.
Sauternes	$0 75	$1 25
Chateau Latour Blanche	1 50	2 50
Chateau Yquem	2 00	4 00
St. Julien	50	1 00
Chateau Belgrave	75	1 50
Pontet Canet	1 00	2 00
Chateau Leoville	1 00	2 00
Chateau Larose	1 75	3 50
Grand Vin Chateau Margaux, 1869, Brandenburg	2 25	4 00

Burgundy—R. Bruinghaus.

	Pts.	Qts.
Pommard	$1 00	$2 00
Chambertin	1 50	3 00

Hock Wines—C. Lauteren Sohn.

	Pts.	Qts.
Niersteiner	$0 75	1 50
Ruedesheimer	1 00	2 00

Wines, Liquors, &c.

	Pts.	
Ambassador Cognac, 1835		$6 00
Vieux, Old " 1842		4 00
Sour Mash Whiskey, 1867		2 50
Amontillado Sherry		2 00
Bass' Pale Ale and Guinness' Dublin Porter	$0 25	
Smith's Philadelphia Ale		20
Bass' Ale, White Label	30	
Belfast Ginger Ale	20	
Champagne Cider	25	
Milwaukee Lager Beer	15	
Ballantine & Co's Export Beer	15	
Everard's Canada Malt Lager Beer	15	
New York Lager Beer	10	
Club Soda	25	
Lemon Soda	10	
Sarsaparilla Soda	10	
Congress and Hathorn Water	25	
Apollinaris Water	20	
Sparkling Hygeia Water	20	
" " Ginger Ale	10	
" " Plain Soda	10	
	Glass.	
" " Seltzer	10	
" " Vichy	10	
Amontillado Sherry	15	
Old Sour Mash Whiskey	15	
Cognac, very old	Pony, 25	40
Old Holland Gin	15	
Old Tom Gin	15	

Cordials.

	Glass.
Absinthe	25
Vermouth	25
Chartreuse	25
Benedictine	25
Kirschwasser	25

Cigars—Imported and Domestic.
SPARKLING HYGEIA WATER A SPECIALTY.

A THIRD OF A CENTURY after the date of the menus on the page opposite, Henry L. Mencken was to write in *The Divine Afflatus* that, "No man within twenty-four hours after eating a meal aboard a Pennsylvania Railroad dining car could conceivably write anything worth reading." Such, however, was not the verdict of passengers aboard the railroad's dining cars in the nineties or patrons at the several on-line hotels and restaurants under the company's management, and some of the available reports on the cuisine of *The Pennsylvania Limited* verge on the ecstatic. Today's epicures may raise an eyebrow at "Jowl With Spinage" on the dollar dinner of 1894, but Louis Roederer's Carte Blanche Champagne and Mumm's Extra Dry at $2.50 each the full bottle will arouse gasps of envy. *The Limited* is shown opposite in 1897 at Ardmore, Pennsylvania. Above is one of its diners in the ornate Spanish style so much admired in the Pullman Palace Car Exhibit at the Chicago Fair of 1893. *(Opposite, Three Pictures: Pennsylvania Railroad; Above: Pullman Standard.)*

533

BY THE turn of the century, the curious old sheet iron sheathed beacons used as depot signals such as that at Sharpsburg on the Conemaugh branch had largely disappeared but whiskers survived and the derby hat was, of course, occupational headgear among railroaders. *The Chicago Special, (below)* double shotted out of Paoli behind two fine Atlantics comprised a period piece. *(Two Photos: Everett L. De Golyer Collection.)*

ALTHOUGH lacking the inferential grandeur of The Paoli Local or even the Wilmington run out of Broad Street, Philadelphia, locals, as shown opposite, out of the gloomy old trainshed at Pittsburgh did their share of sooting up the Golden Triangle along with Jones & Laughlin, Youngstown Sheet & Tube and the great J. Edgar Thompson works of U. S. Steel. *(John Barriger Collection.)*

THE PHOTOGRAPH reproduced below of *The Pennsylvania Limited* rounding Horseshoe Curve in 1910 is remarkable for its helper engine deriving from the stable of the Pittsburgh, Fort Wayne & Chicago whose runs usually came to an end at Pittsburgh. The road engine is a Class D American type 4-4-0 and more at home on the Altoona run. The Pullman drawing room suites on *The Limited* of the period show only vestigial traces of the ornate taste in decor which reached its zenith at the Chicago Fair of 1893. On the opposite page *The Limited* rounds Horseshoe Curve in its "Yellow Kid" livery of an earlier date while in the lower frame the self-exiled Duke of Windsor and his duchess suggest that even in the mid-thirties *The Limited* was still a train of enough éclat to lend itself to the occasions of royalty. (*Below and Top Opposite: Gerald Best Collection; Otherwise: Pennsylvania Railroad.*)

PENNSYLVANIA LIMITED

WITH THE ADVENT of the 1941 war, traffic between Chicago and the East achieved such dimensions that, as a companion train at least in name to *The General*, the Pennsylvania management added to its mainline schedules *The Admiral* which originated in Philadelphia. Leaving Thirtieth Street at nine in the evening, *The Admiral* arrived in Chicago just in time for lunch with through sleepers and a Washington sleeper it picked up at Harrisburg. *The Admiral* is shown below westbound at Valparaiso in 1942 when, even in wartime, it still carried an identifying nameplate on the smokebox of its scrupulously maintained K4s Pacific. As wartime and postwar traffic continued to tax the carrier's facilities and necessitated ever longer sleeping trains *The Admiral* was powered by assigned 4-4-4-4 duplexes identifiable as Raymond Loewy products by the sharknose profile and ornate portholes in their shrouding. The stately classic vistas of Chicago's Union Depot where *The Admiral's* passengers alighted were a fitting backdrop for the Pennsylvania's grand manner even in wartime. *(Opposite: Graham, Anderson, Probst & White, Inc.; Left: Pennsylvania Railroad; Below: Richard J. Cook.)*

WITH THE RISING sun of eight o'clock on its smokebox and side rods, Train No. 42, *The Rainbow* hastens on its eastbound occasions near Lewistown, Pennsylvania, under a flat trail of exhaust and with a liberal head-end tonnage to pay its way. *(John P. Ahrens.)*

ALTHOUGH its resplendent name closely approximated that of the Missouri-Pacific's *Rainbow Special* and it was accorded the panache of the carrier's keystone insigne on its observation railing, the Pennsylvania's New York-Chicago *Rainbow* wasn't especially notable for its character or distinction in the roster of Pennsy name trains. Christened in honor of the Rainbow Division of World War I celebrity, its almost only claim to attention was a handsome verandah observation car with its name in white against identifying red glass as it rolled on an unhurried carding. *(Right: Pennsylvania Railroad.)*

NEVER A TOTAL CASUALTY of technological progress, the car tonk found his duties measurably abated with the coming of high speed trucks and roller bearings. Once the sound of slamming journal boxes in the night at inspection points reassured uncounted Pullman passengers that their train was under the watchful eye of a benevolent management, and here a member of a venerable priesthood performs his ritual duties of inspection of the car *Tomhicken*. *(Pennsylvania Railroad.)*

541

THE STORY of the Pennsylvania's *Liberty Limited* on the Washington-Chicago run is remarkable because, in addition to being in its all-too-brief lifetime, a fine name train operation between major metropolitan terminals, it was brought into being at the apex of competition for passenger patronage between mainline carriers and because its final demise was encompassed through the agency of an intrigue that would have been suited to a ducal court in medieval Florence. Its legend has the dimension of a feud between Montagues and Capulets. For many years the cream of the Washington-Chicago traffic as well as that to Detroit, had been a near monopoly of the Baltimore & Ohio whose *Capitol Limited, Ambassador* and *Fort Pitt Limited* were celebrated for their cuisine, expeditious scheduling and courtly crews which combined to attract an enviable clientele of men of large affairs whose occasions took them between the Federal City, Pittsburgh and Lake Michigan. The management of the Pennsy viewed this traffic and the prestige accruing from it with unabashed envy. Its answer for many years was a Washington section of the *Broadway Limited* which in the beginning had been integrated to the New York section at Harrisburg and later, when traffic justified, ran as an extra section of the flagship of the Pennsylvania fleet. This was a successful operation, but failed to attract the anticipated business away from the B & O's name trains on the parallel run whose Chesapeake Bay seafood, Southern mammy type cooking and general urbanity caused it to be regarded by many regulars as a family institution. At length, in 1925 the Pennsylvania abolished the Washington section of *The Broadway*, largely because of the confusion arising from the similarity of names, and in its place inaugurated a new and entirely independent all-Pullman name train, *The Liberty*, leaving Washington in the late afternoon and arriving, as a well-conducted businessman's train should, shortly after breakfast at Chicago. *The Liberty Limited* remained all-Pullman until the late thirties, the peer in its amenities of long distance travel of other Pennsylvania headliners such as *The Spirit of St. Louis* and *The Broadway* itself. For two decades, until 1957, *The Liberty Limited* enjoyed an almost unquestioned supremacy on the Washington-Chicago run, deriving from its time advantage over the competing *Capitol Limited* which was sufficient to offset the B & O's hushpuppies and Jefferson Davis overtones of flawless service. In that year, however, *The Liberty Limited* was factually assassinated in an imbroglio that would have been acclaimed by members of the Borgia family. The Pittsburgh & Lake Erie, a subsidiary of the bitterly competitive New York Central, accorded trackage rights over its high speed right of way west of Pittsburgh to the Baltimore & Ohio, thus reversing the existing status of the two trains and giving the *Capitol Limited* a pronounced time advantage over *The Liberty Limited*. The combination of a faster schedule and a menu that included terrapin Maryland and Southern fried chicken recalled the B & O's vagrant patrons in droves and, in a matter of months, *The Liberty Limited* disappeared from the Pennsylvania timecards, its taking off as deliberately contrived a murder as any effected by the Medici. Opposite, in its splendid years, *The Liberty Limited* is portrayed in a spirited oil portrait double heading east of Harrisburg by Howard Fogg, dean of painters of the railroad scene.

BECAUSE of the scrupulously maintained competition of the Baltimore & Ohio trains on the Chicago-Washington run, *The Liberty Limited* received the best of everything at the hands of the Pennsylvania management. The handsome Fiesta type dining cars that were assigned to it late in the train's career, a profusion of cut flowers in public apartments and the top ranking personnel from the dining car pool all testified to the regard in which this classic long haul varnish was held by its owning carrier. Oceans of clean linen for its all-Pullman consist, as suggested by the servicing operation at Chicago depicted here were taken for granted. (*Two Photos: Pennsylvania Railroad.*)

THE GENERALITY to the effect that when you had seen one of the Pennsylvania name trains you had seen them all was possessed of a certain validity, but traces of identifying personality could be discerned, not only in the conduct of the carrier's pride and showpiece *The Broadway Limited* but in a number of other varnish runs where specially imprinted stationery, menus and other train literature, uniforms of the staff and the train name on the smokebox of assigned locomotives lent individuality and character to the operation. This was abundantly true in the case of *The Liberty Limited* as is suggested by this idealized official photograph of it at speed in the glory times of steam. (*Pennsylvania Railroad.*)

IN ITS SPLENDID years *The Liberty Limited* awaits a green light in Chicago's Union Station while a Burlington local lurks in the background. *(John Barriger Collection.)*

SOME SUGGESTION of the regard in which the Pennsylvania's management held *The Liberty Limited* in the years of its prideful going between Chicago and Washington may be implicit in the names assigned two of its built-to-order Pullman observation-lounges, *Thomas Alexander Scott* and *Alexander Johnston Cassatt*, two of the railroad's most swaggering presidents and architects of its destinies. After the advent of airflow design in the late thirties both rounded-end solariums and those with a squared-off bulkhead carried *The Liberty's* Keystone insigne as shown below in the car named for Tom Scott and in *Federal View*. (*Two Photos: Rail Photo Service, W. G. Fancher.*)

IN THE UNMISTAKABLY Chicago setting portrayed on the page above, *The Liberty Limited* and *The Golden Arrow* are shown eastbound as a single section behind two equally identifying and immaculately shopped K-4s Pacifics. The year is 1934 and the Depression suggested combining the two runs as far as Pittsburgh. Below the same train is shown in another view leaving Chicago with the conventional coach-smoker combine on the drawbar of the road engine. At the left *The Liberty Limited* is being christened in the presence of appropriate military brass and survivors of the nation's wars. To connoisseurs of Pennsy train launchings, none was authentic that didn't combine the best features of war and peace. There was always a military band in attendance and a ranking general, while Veterans of Foreign Wars rallied round The Flag and the champagne. (*Left and Opposite: Alfred W. Johnson; Above: Pennsylvania Railroad.*)

ON THE SEVENTEEN HOUR RUN between Chicago and New York, *The General,* shown at the top of the opposite page at speed through Valparaiso, Indiana, westbound and double headed with wartime traffic in 1942, was held in regard by the management second only to *The Broadway* on this important haul. House ads in company literature advertised it as "Every Inch a Leader" and it had its own menus and train stationery as long as these amenities of limited train status survived. The difficulties inherent in servicing the streamlined, articulated locomotives of experimental classes such as No. 6100 are also depicted as part of the routine of preparing the engine assigned to *The General* for its run between Chicago and Crestline. Running parts and essential lubrication points were so inaccessible that even before the demise of steam, streamlining was largely in the discard. *The New Yorker,* shown here eastbound at Valparaiso, with a single K-4s on the head end, was a full day and night haul between Manhattan and Lake Michigan and largely a train-of-all-work with a massive volume of mail and express. It was predominantly a daylight run to Pittsburgh eastbound with diner and parlor cars to that point and only a single Pullman sleeper regularly on the through assigned run to New York where it arrived before breakfast next morning. (*Above and Opposite: Richard J. Cook.*)

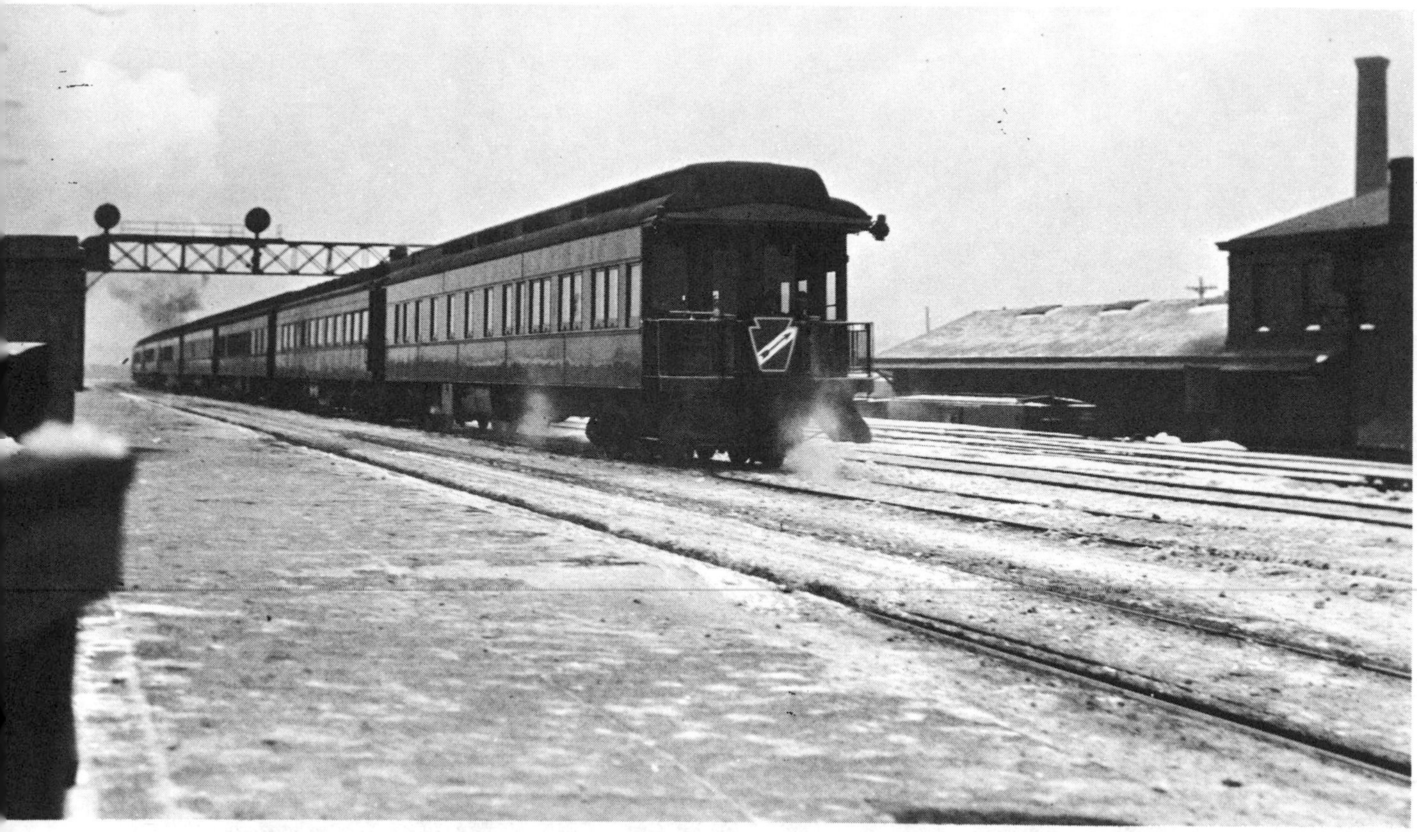

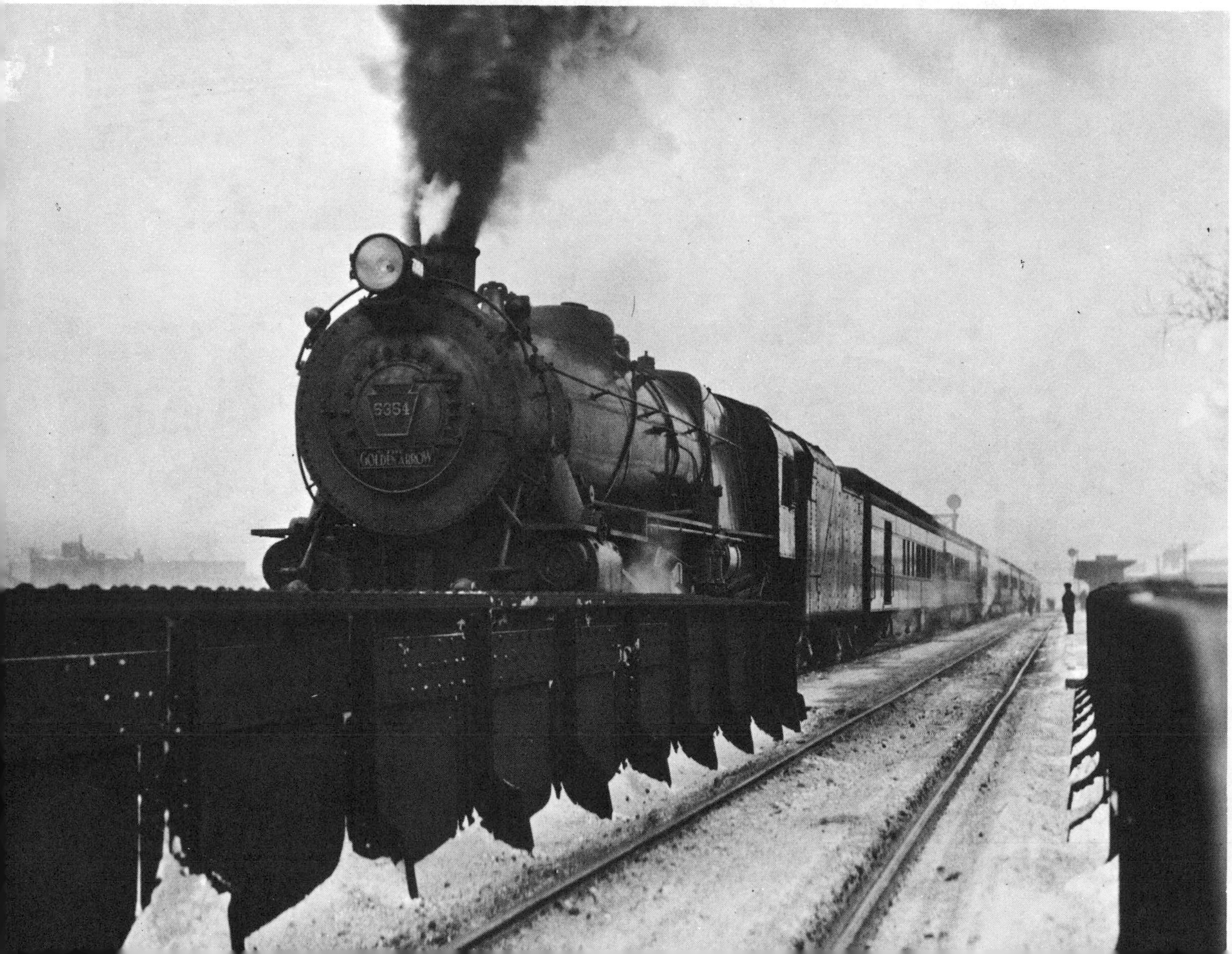
GOLDEN ARROW

ONLY A MATTER OF WEEKS before the stock market debacle of 1929 was to set off a long period of depression and economic stagnation, the Pennsylvania on September 29 added *The Golden Arrow* to its already impressive fleet of New York-Chicago varnish flyers on the then conventional twenty-hour running time. "I anticipate that this will be the first of several more fine trains on this run in the near future," said Vice President George Le Boutillier, somewhat mistakenly as the train was christened at the Pennsylvania Station before its maiden run. At the Chicago train bay in Union Station a casting agency Indian maiden posed with a bow and arrow symbolizing the train's swift passage over the Pennsy right of way. *The Golden Arrow*, at its inception as is suggested on the opposite page was a classic Pennsylvania varnish run with coaches, Pullmans, an open observation lounge car and the train's name on the steambox of a sleek, assigned K-42 between Chicago and Fort Wayne. *The Arrow* theme in train names was continued on the Pennsy timecards in the form of *The Detroit Arrow*, *The Red Arrow* and *The Florida Arrow*. (Page Opposite, Two Photos: Alfred W. Johnson; Left and Above: Pennsylvania Railroad.)

553

NOTORIOUS for the less than clement aspects of its winters, Chicago weather is at its most infamous when the northeast wind blows in from Lake Michigan with cold and snow from the vast reaches of arctic Canada. Below is shown Train No. 22, *The Manhattan Limited* eastbound train-of-all-work with head end, Pullmans and coaches on a relaxed schedule, paused in the clutches of Chaos and Old Night at the deserted platform at Englewood depot in suburban Chicago. At the right a yard worker undertakes to prevent the switches from freezing with a long snouted flame thrower. *(Two Photos: Owen Davies Collection.)*

HERE the archetypal eagle eye, god of the right hand cushions, the brave engineer of poetry and legend oils around the motive power for one of the Pennsylvania's vast fleet of name trains in the age of steam. The company caption says it is *The Duquesne,* but it might as well be *The Broadway, The Rainbow* or the *Red Bird.* The properties of his calling were identical to all. (*Pennsylvania Railroad.*)

TO ADD VARIETY to the already well represented points of the compass which were identified with the Boston & Maine's *East Wind*, the Louisville & Nashville-Seaboard Air Line's *Gulf Wind* on the overnight run between New Orleans and Jacksonville and the Burlington's several *Zephyrs* apostrophising the West Wind, the Pennsylvania added *The South Wind* as a seasonal coach train between Chicago and Florida. Designed to match the company's other bids for non-Pullman patronage represented by the *Trail Blazer* and *Jeffersonian*, *The South Wind* operated out of Nashville over the Louisville & Nashville and its construction and overall conduct couldn't have been further removed from such early attempts at attracting coach passengers as the New York Central's improvised *Pacemaker*. Smartly uniformed attendants staffed custom-built coaches. There was a conventional dining car of *moderne* decor and an eighty-five foot buffet-lounge-observation car with a completely appointed buffet kitchen from which light meals could be served in the late evening. Its shot-welded consist and specially assigned streamlined K-4s Pacific type engine made a brave showing on its maiden sailing from Chicago. *(Kaufmann & Fabry.)*

ALL THE ALLURE of tropic skies and fronded palms that had first been invoked when Steve Hannagan placed Florida on the map as a vacationland for the masses as Palm Beach had been created by Henry M. Flagler for the well-to-do, went into the promotion by its owning carrier of the *South Wind*. Diaphonously clad damsels swam in the lazy surf of idyllic lagoons in the pages of brochures that made the sybaritic resources of sea, sand and sun available to the thrift-conscious. Never were champagne tastes more dexterously reconciled to beer pocket-books. Beholders knew that forty-eight hours after passing the handsome train gate designation shown at the left in Chicago's Union Station, travelers would be sending home postcards inscribed: "Having wonderful time; wish you were here." *(Two Photos: Pennsylvania Railroad.)*

557

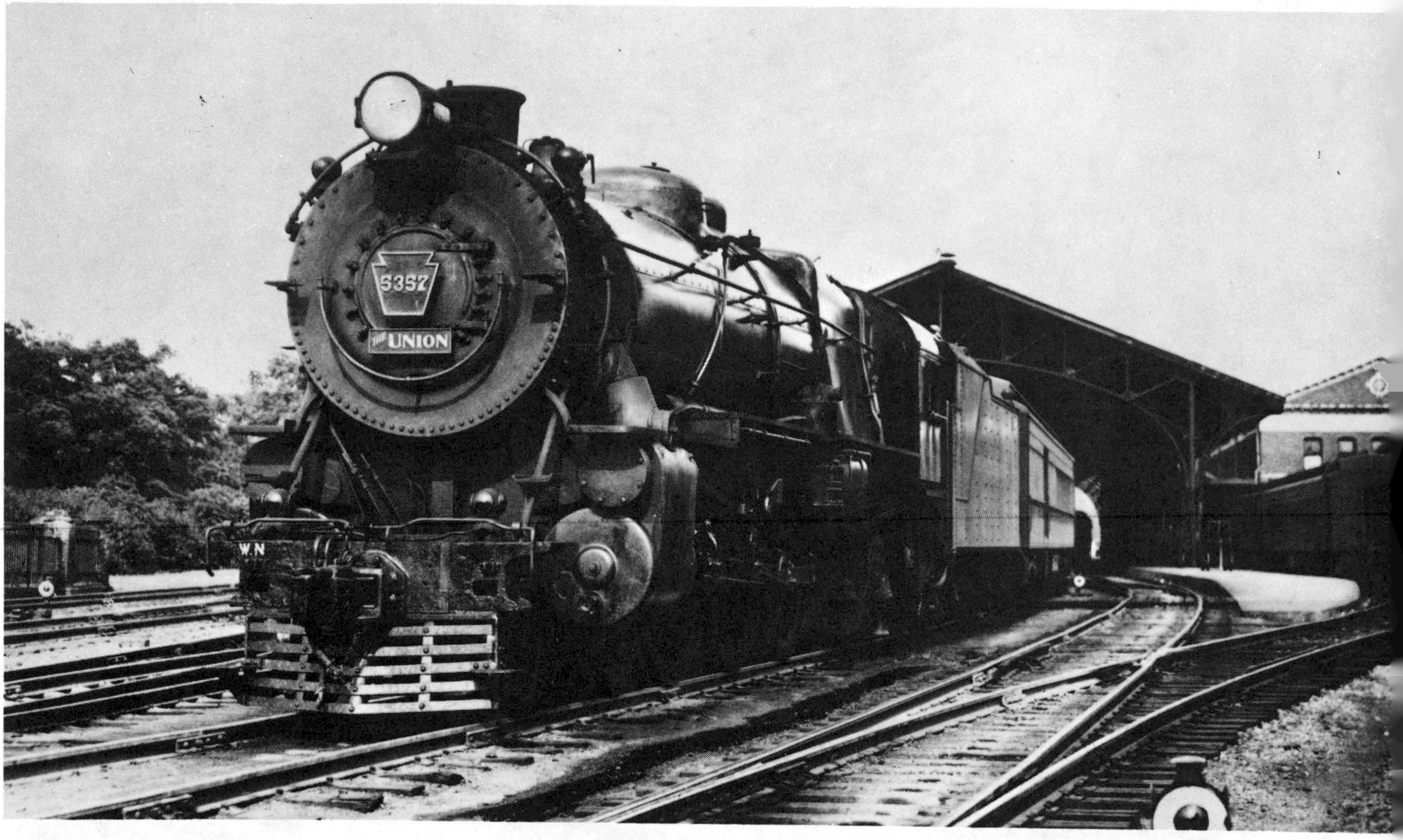
5357
THE UNION
W.N

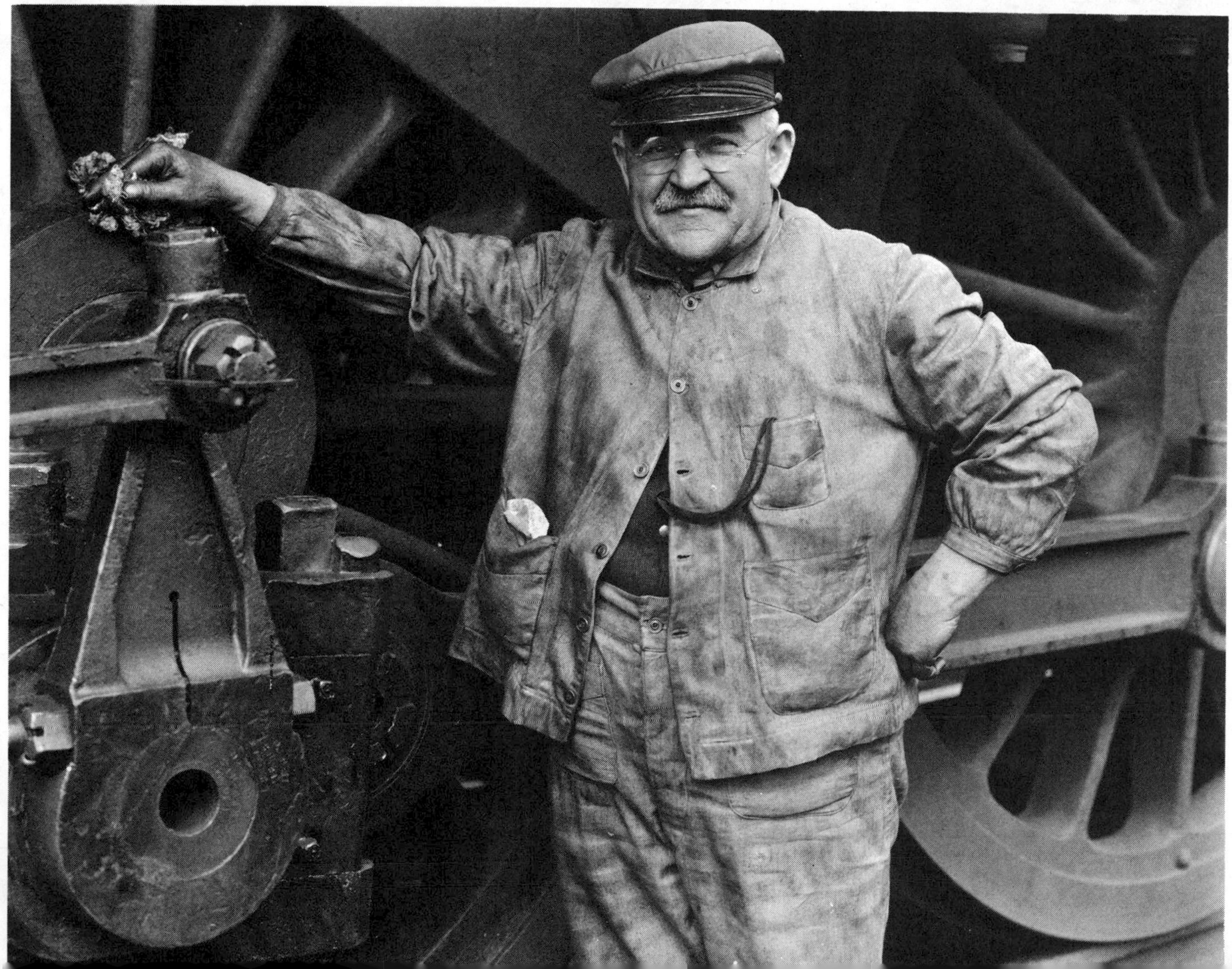

THE UNION, Train No. 72, was in effect the southbound section of Train No. 71, *The Red Bird* between Chicago and Norfolk, Virginia, with Pullmans set out and picked up at Cincinnati *en route*. On the page opposite, it is photographed behind a freshly shopped K-4s as it pauses at Richmond, Indiana, in 1938, while in the lower frame *The Union's* engineer keeps a rendezvous with celluloid immortality, resting his hand of authority on the rod assembly of his locomotive. On this page, in an officially approved photograph retouched to permit just sufficient stack exhaust to suggest, at the same time, speed and economical combustion, *The Union* races southward under a picturebook sky. (*Above, Opposite: Rail Photo Service, Glenn Grabille, Jr.; Two Photos: Pennsylvania Railroad.*)

AS LATE AS THE YEAR DEPICTED opposite a few veteran Pullman sleepers were still equipped with atmospheric Pintsch lamps as well as electricity. A decade later, *The Manhattan Limited* (below) in its train-of-all-work role with much head-end business pulls into Crestline, Ohio, behind two K-4s. (*Above: Pennsylvania Railroad; Below: Rail Photo Service.*)

IN KEEPING with his innate Republican conservatism which
rejected the extra-fare splendors of *The Broadway* for a candidate for
public office, Herbert Hoover in 1928 started his first tour of the
country as Presidential nominee by visiting Vice-President
Charles G. Dawes at the summer White House in Wisconsin aboard
the down-to-earth and no-nonsense *Manhattan Limited.*
Here in the double breasted suits of the financial great of the period
they pose with Mrs. Hoover on the iron-railed open observation
platform on the train's arrival at Chicago. Dawes, who was
an established regular on *The Twentieth Century Limited,* must have
felt the gesture was a sacrifice to political expediency.   *(Wide World.)*

JEFFERSONIAN patrons were served their Martinis and Daiquiris in a sunken cocktail lounge in the recreation car or in the full dress club car shown here amidst *moderne* lighting and quilted bulkheads that would have been approved on the *Île de France.* Unusually heavy consists sometimes required double-heading *The Jeffersonian,* as is suggested below with the westbound section doing eighty near Caseyville, Illinois, in July 1940. *(Right: Kaufmann & Fabry; Below: William Barham.)*

CUT FLOWERS, expensive carpets, solicitous attendants, all combined to give the patrons of *The Jeffersonian's* spacious observation lounge a taste of the good life advocated by the third President and endorsed by the management of the carrier. *(Pennsylvania Railroad.)*

TRAIN No. 25, *The Jeffersonian's* companion train on the St. Louis-New York run with conventional Pullman sleepers, *The St. Louisan* followed on a slower schedule, its coming heralded by volumes of smoke exhaust from one of the road's massive T-1 duplex locomotives that were unable to turn a wheel without Burning-of-Rome smoke effects. *(John P. Ahrens.)*

THE EGALITARIAN SPIRIT in which *The Jeffersonian* was conceived and named was completely betrayed by its haughty pose and aristocratic profile in this uncommonly stylish photograph taken on its maiden sailing between New York and St. Louis by Carl H. Bowers of the *Dayton* (Ohio) *Daily News*.

THE ALL-COACH STREAMLINER *The Jeffersonian* was inaugurated in the mid-thirties to provide low fare transport on a twenty-and-a-half hour schedule between New York-Philadelphia and St. Louis via Terre Haute, Richmond, Indianapolis, Dayton and Columbus. Company literature in a delightfully republican vein declared that "the name selected for the new train typified Thomas Jefferson's constant aim to see the desirable things of life become increasingly available among his countrymen." Adopting a sterner view and more patriotic stance, it went on to assert that "It also commemorates his greatest achievement as the nation's third President in the famed Louisiana Purchase, by which the entire Mississippi Valley became United States soil, and St. Louis, the new train's Western terminus, an American city." Three complete trains were required to maintain the fast daily two-way schedule; all seats were reserved, and west of Harrisburg specially assigned streamlined K-4s Pacific locomotives with the train name on the smokebox roared through the night en route to and from the Mississippi. Luncheon was .65¢ and dinner six bits in that now distant and, it seems, halcyon time, and there were pier glasses in all the washrooms. *(Three Photos: Pennsylvania Railroad.)*

What the third President of the United States would have thought of a recreation car furnished in chairs upholstered in black and white zebra fur may be left to conjecture. At least it brought luxury to the masses in a demonstrably tangible manner.

The maiden voyage of *The Jeffersonian* from its St. Louis terminal was accomplished through the agency of champagne and cut flowers in profusion and a reception to civic and business dignitaries with company police in attendance to discourage any but the invited.

UNTIL THE ADVENT of *The Spirit of St. Louis*, the candy
train on the St. Louis-New York run for many years was
The American, shown here eastbound the far side of Harrisburg
under a summer sky ominous with thunderclouds.
The American was a train of the sort that still retained its hold
on the affections of many regular patrons despite the de luxe
blandishments of *The Spirit*, and its personnel comprised
a number of veteran men of veteran status as company servants
of the Pennsylvania. One of them, Raymond Thomas,
pictured here in a study that might symbolize his honored
calling everywhere, had been on the St. Louis run
twenty-four years when the photograph was taken. *(Left: John
Barriger Collection; Above: Pennsylvania Railroad.)*

567

WHEN THE *Congressional Limited,* by then known simply as *The Congressional* rounded out its first half century on the Washington–New York run on December 7, 1935, it had covered 8,212,500 miles of service and carried better than 7,000,000 passengers, many of them the great, powerful and celebrated names of the world. Mere statistics, however, are a chill tally of the superlatives that attached to a train that had known every President of the United States and every figure of official distinction worth naming in the Federal City since its maiden run in 1885, had catered to the whims of cabinet ministers and had carried ambassadors and plenipotentiaries as the merest commonplace. When a head of state was carried on a ranking official mission, potted palms and an American flag at the train gate in Washington were the equivalent of *The Century's* red carpet at Grand Central. Here a business car attached to *The Congressional* carrying Prince and Princess Takamatsu of Japan en route to their official reception in Washington by President Hoover is being given godspeed from Penn Station, New York, by Stationmaster William II. Egan, a functionary in whose daily life a silk top hat and frock coat were working attire. Opposite, *The Congressional* is shown in two period poses, in each case powered by the high wheel Pennsy Atlantics which were the proudest motive power of 1912. The top view at speed is from the Smithsonian Institution while that paused at Germantown Junction, later North Philadelphia, is from the collection of Everett De Golyer. *(Above: Pennsylvania Railroad.)*

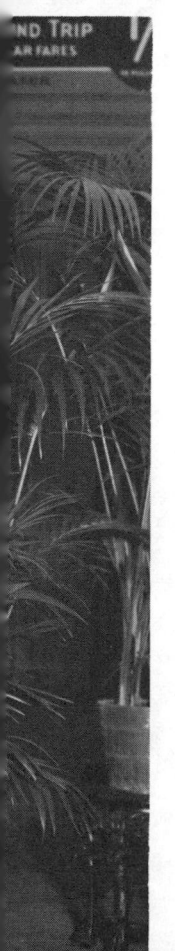

AS IS SUGGESTED by the appearance of *The Spirit of St. Louis* as depicted below, identification placques on the engine smokeboxes of name trains do not seem to have been operational practice east of Pittsburgh. Specially assigned locomotives out of St. Louis, Cincinnati and Chicago on the lines west alone appear in the photographic record as a panache of elegance, and positive identification of a name train had to await the passing of the observation end with its illuminated train herald in the form of the Pennsylvania keystone.

EAGER TO RIDE the wave of enthusiasm that greeted Lindbergh's epochal flight across the Atlantic, the Pennsylvania management hastily recruited the first *Spirit of St. Louis* from the available Standard equipment in its St. Louis division pool to come up with the train shown here rolling, double headed out of Harrisburg across the Rockville Bridge. In 1938 when streamlining was in vogue a Raymond Loewy sheathed K-4s was assigned to the run with the train name on its bullet nose. *(Above: John P. Ahrens; Right: Pennsylvania Railroad.)*

570

THE OBSERVATION car *Golden Hill* shortly made its appearance in the consist of *The Spirit of St. Louis* as *Colonel Lindbergh* where, for the maiden run of the new train, it attracted a peculiar type of patron seldom encountered elsewhere. The *Colonel Lindbergh* was not, as has been occasionally maintained, the only Pullman ever named for a still living celebrity. There was also *Amon G. Carter,* honoring the Fort Worth grandee-newspaper publisher, and the *Adolphus Busch* for the St. Louis beer baron, both of which were ridden by their namesakes in their lifetimes. *(Two Photos: Pennsylvania Railroad.)*

A MAJOR event of the railroad day at St. Louis Terminal was the departure, as depicted opposite, of the Pennsylvania's candy train on the New York run, *The Spirit of St. Louis.* The date of the photograph, by Elmer L. Onstott, was February 1940, and the identifying smokebox name plate was of a size more conventional than that shown in the photograph at the immediate left.

THE SPIRIT of St. Louis was well identified both fore and aft in its going. In the above frame on this page it leaves St. Louis terminal with an outsize name plate fixed to its automatic train control box. Below, some years later, the observation solarium crossed the diamond at St. Louis on its way East. *(Above: W. B. Cox; Below: Rail Photo Service.)*

573

EVEN THOUGH high speed streamlined runs
such as *The Senator* shown below might
streak over the Pennsy's main line east
of Washington and Diesels take over where the
electric catenaries ended west of Harrisburg,
here and there vestigial traces of an older order
of things along the high iron still survived
on branch lines such as the grass-grown
country depot somewhere along the Wilkes-
Barre-Philadelphia branch where a flag hung
out front called the cars to a halt.
Veteran, too, of another age was the grand old
man of the conductor's calling immortalized
opposite by a perceptive photographer as he
paused, orders in hand, at Ragan Tower
south of Wilmington while his train waited on
the dispatcher's caprice in the background.
(Three Photos: Pennsylvania Railroad.)

THE SOLARIUM-lounge of the streamlined *Senator* shown above and the parlor interior of the 1930 Pullman Standard *Senator* *(right)* illustrate the transition from the luxury tradition of rich upholstery and decor of repose to the easily cleaned decor that was one of the inevitable by-products of lightweight car construction. On the opposite page *The Senator* on its way to Boston is shown from the rear end as it passes Princeton Junction and behind a GG-1 electric motor from the lens of the master craftsman O. Winston Link. *(Above: Pennsylvania Railroad; Right: Pullman Standard; Opposite: Rail Photo Service, Wayne P. Ellis, and O. Winston Link.)*

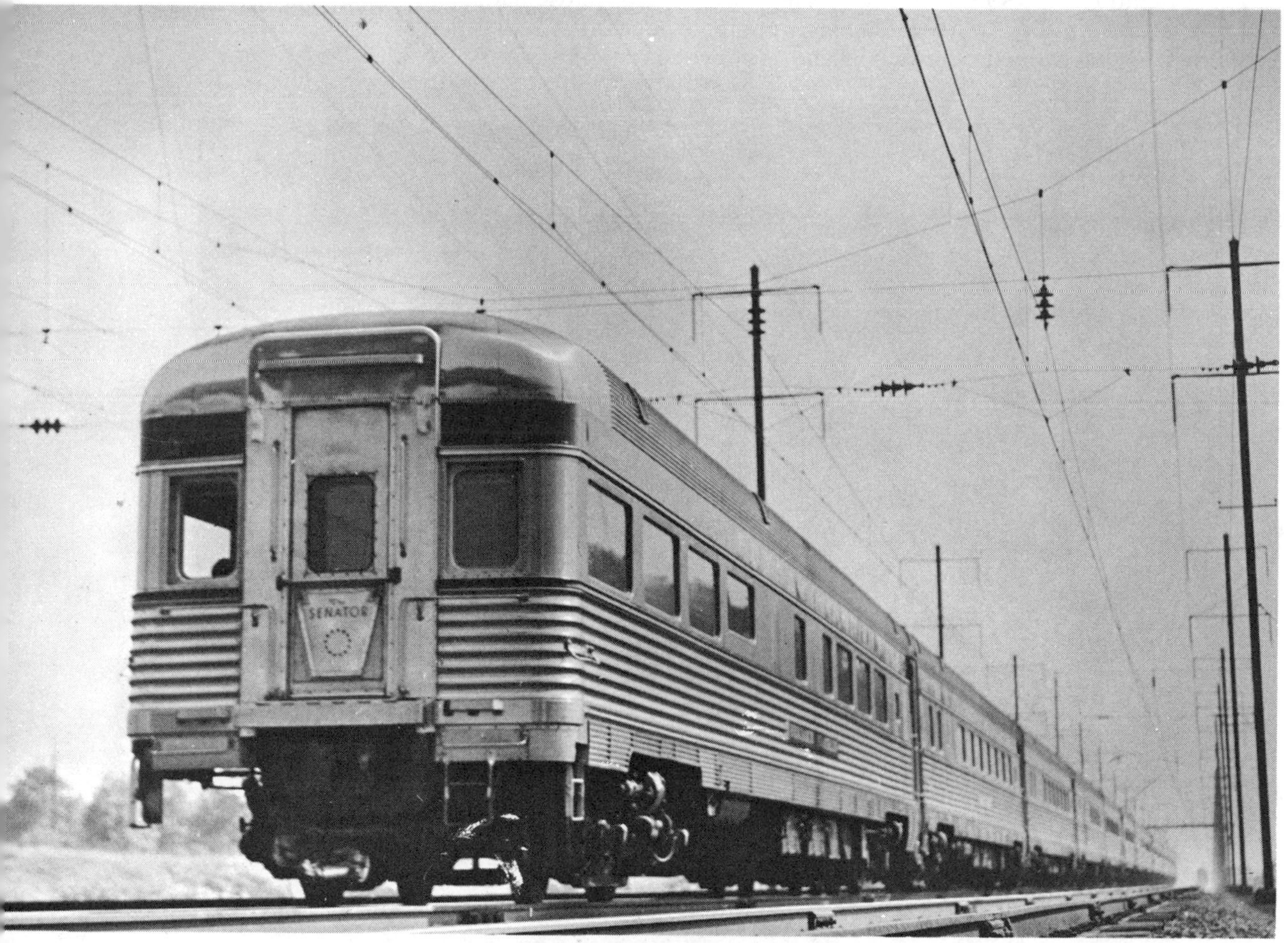
SENATOR

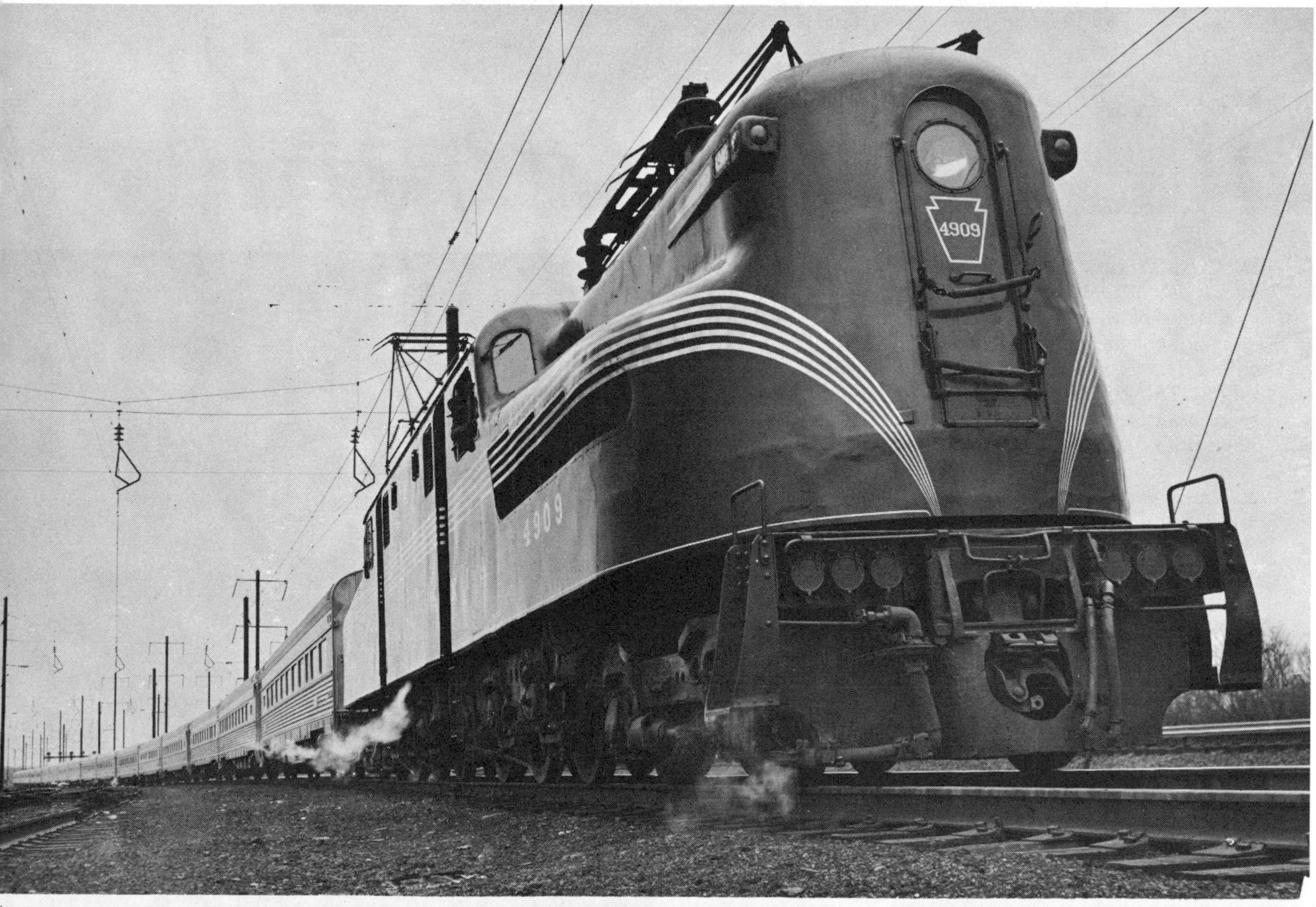
4909
4909

THE GAMUT of emotions was represented in the expressions of participants and bystanders alike at the *Trail Blazer's* christening, ranging from dismay, apprehension and mistrust to determined satisfaction and gratification.

WHEN, in the summer of 1939, the Pennsylvania management matched the all-Pullman, all-room sumptuousness of the new *Broadway Limited* with an all-new, all-coach run between Chicago and New York called *The Trail Blazer* many of its amenities approximated *The Broadway* itself. They included a seventeen hour schedule, airflow, lightweight equipment, flower-filled public apartments and a train company whose kitchen crew alone included fifteen cooks, two stewards and ten waiters. Attendants *(right)* as scrupulously uniformed as those on *The Congressional* showed passengers to their reserved space and *(opposite)* served meals in a two-car diner unit built in the company shops at Altoona with porthole type windows of polarized glass reminiscent of those on the *City of Los Angeles'* first observation lounge, *Copper King*. (Three Photos: Pennsylvania Railroad.)

RARE AS A company photograph because it actually shows smoke exhaust trailing from two K-4s Pacifics on the head end, is that reproduced below of *The Trail Blazer* eastbound at seventy miles an hour at Whiting, Indiana in the summer of 1941. Only infrequently have negatives been known to survive in company files unless clean engine stacks indicated the perfect combustion admired by the operating department. *(Pennsylvania Railroad.)*

THE TREND to de luxe accommodations for coach travelers before the 1941 war which was to find its ultimate expression in the Santa Fe's extra-fare all-day coach *El Capitan* operating on *Super Chief* schedules between Chicago and California had its inception in the *Trail Blazer* concept of low-cost speed and convenience. Many of the hallmarks of a status train hitherto reserved for such prestige runs as *The Broadway, The Liberty Limited* and *The Spirit of St. Louis* were incorporated in *The Trail Blazer's* equipment and conduct: specially assigned locomotives with name markers on the smokebox, the Pennsy Keystone insigne identifying it as a name train on the observation end, waiters, porters and lounge attendants in special train livery. It all added up to a not-so-poor man's second section of *The Broadway Limited* itself. *The Trail Blazer* insigne *(left)* showed in profile a backwoodsman in coonskin cap suggestive of the days when Fort Pitt had been a trading post in the Allegheny wilds. *(Left: Pennsylvania Railroad; Below: Lucius Beebe.)*

THE UNBRIDLED REVELRY depicted here was arranged for photographers from the Pennsylvania's publicity department, a liberally financed activity in the now distant year 1939, but there is no doubting that *The Trail Blazer's* commodious public apartments opened new vistas in the field of low cost travel. (*Two Photos: Pennsylvania Railroad.*)

THE PENNSYLVANIA'S candy train on the New York-Cincinnati overnight run, *The Cincinnati Limited*, had a pedigree old enough in the pages of the *Official Guide* to extend backward in time to the golden age of brass railed open platform observation cars such as is shown on the page opposite with passengers and train crew agog for the photographer's flash. The Keystone insigne rode through the Ohio night to place *The Limited* on a footing of equality with the other great name trains of the Pennsylvania peerage, *The Broadway, The Golden Arrow* and *The Spirit of St. Louis*. In the post-1941 war years when it was photographed being served *(below)* in Cincinnati yards, its solarium lounge *(right)* was identical with that of the streamlined *Broadway Limited.* (Below: TRAINS *Magazine, Wallace W. Abbey; Right and Top Opposite: Pennsylvania Railroad.)*

THE
CINCINNATI
LIMITED

PENNSYLVANIA
RAILROAD

RUNNING an hour off schedule in the summer months in the mid-thirties *The Cincinnati Limited* is shown here nearing its western terminal double headed in a typical Pennsylvania operation of a fast name train with perhaps sixteen cars on the drawbar of the road engine. *(John P. Ahrens.)*

BROAD STREET STATION, Philadelphia, as it was known to millions of Pennsylvania Railroad patrons over the decades of its long and useful existence was epitomized by many things. To some the massive facade of its exterior architecture symbolized the formidable presence of a great railroad of feudal and hierarchical dimensions. To some its undeniably cold and drafty precincts in winter represented a tenacious survival of nineteenth century discomforts into an age scornful of obsolescence and inconvenience. Almost nobody forgot the great sweep of staircase by which all passengers save the effete or invalid, who took a primordial sort of elevator, ascended to the train level from the grottos of Market Street. *(Pennsylvania Railroad: L. R. Brittingham.)*

IN THE eighties and in addition to the railroad's own fleet of carriages for public hire, public omnibus lines also converged on the Pennsylvania's focal landmark.

ALTHOUGH IT WASN'T EVEN on the railroad's main line and served out its years as a stub terminal with sixteen tracks at the height of its fortunes, the Pennsylvania's Broad Street Station in downtown Philadelphia achieved a world celebrity comparable to far larger and more magnificent depots such as Charing Cross in London, the Gare du Nord in Paris, Boston's South Station or New York's Grand Central. Broad Street had character of a sooty and raffish order comparable to other contemporary Pennsylvania stations such as those at Pittsburgh and Fort Wayne. It was drafty, unkempt and, except for some of its fine marble handrails and bronze ornamental trim, made no pretentions at grandeur. Yet by 1886, five years after it was opened to operation, Broad Street handled a million passengers a month and throughout its annals was celebrated not only for its traffic in cars and people but as the citadel of one of the most firmly entrenched hierarchies of wealth, power and dynastic inheritance in the world. As the stronghold of the Pennsylvania Railroad's administrative bureaucracy, the ten-story Gothic-Mooresque office building that rose behind its vaulted train shed symbolized not only the railroad but the character of Philadelphia itself, aloof, disdainfully possessive, hereditary, conservative and faintly arrogant. It was the first thing millions saw on arriving at Philadelphia and the last they saw on departing and it made a lasting impression. It suggested that it had been built in the era of silk-hatted railroad presidents with gold-headed walking sticks who ate luncheons of six courses including terrapin at the Philadelphia Club. It had.

Broad Street was planned and begun in the embattled era of Tom Scott in the Pennsylvania President's office. It was opened to traffic in 1881 when patrician George Roberts was at the helm and not completed until 1894. Its years of greatest glory were, of course, those in which the magnifico of all railroaders, the great Alexander Cassatt controlled its desti-

nies. Of all the railroads in the United States, the only one whose annals can appropriately be chronicled in terms of its presidents as English history is by the reigns of its monarchs is the Pennsylvania, and Broad Street was their palace and shabby-genteel seat of power. The power itself, of course, had nothing either shabby or genteel about it.

The Pennsylvania's main line ran nearly two miles to the west of Broad Street and to achieve the baronial brick castle next door to Philadelphia's City Hall which was the heart of the railroad system, there was built a massive stone causeway a city block wide that was known as "The Chinese Wall." Cross streets penetrated this gloomy barrier through tunnels under its tracks where water seeped at all seasons and froze solid on the cobbles and car tracks in winter. Over "The Chinese Wall" shuttle trains connected the stub tracks at Broad Street with through mainline trains at West Philadelphia and over it, too, ran the celebrated Clockers to New York and the Paoli Locals that became part of Philadelphia folk-legend.

A disastrous conflagration destroyed the vaulted train shed at Broad Street in 1925 and makeshift platform shelters protected passengers embarking on its trains after that. In 1952 Broad Street in its entirety was torn down and the last train departed amidst tears as the Philadelphia Symphony Orchestra played "Auld Lang Syne" but the glory had departed at an earlier date, both from the Pennsylvania's passenger operations and from the city they served. Christopher Morley, one of the Philadelphia Main Line's most distinguished men of letters, had immortalized Broad Street when he said that after his death the words "Paoli Local" would be found graven on his heart. It was an epitaph that might also have been written for the Pennsylvania's once spacious affluence when its presidents were selected from the ranks of Rittenhouse Square aristocrats and acted the part to the hilt.

WHATEVER MYSTIQUE may have elevated the Pennsylvania Railroad to a position of fantastic wealth, political power and well-bred Philadelphian arrogance had its source in the Moorish structure at Broad Street Station where the railroad's headquarters were located. The depot proper was opened in 1881, but its ten story corner tower and offices were not completed until 1894 so that, although implemented in the regime of Tom Scott, it was in fact a memorial to George Roberts. Here were plotted the great campaigns of territorial aggrandizement that were to make the Pennsylvania a massive power in state and national politics and the border warfare with the New York Central which was the major preoccupation of the successive dynasties of Scott, Roberts and Cassatt. One of the truly great railroad stations of the world, not because of either its architecture or volume of traffic, but because it personified the character of the carrier itself, Broad Street is shown about 1913 as the embodiment of solid conservatism, dynastic succession and a sense of corporate destiny. (Pennsylvania Railroad.)

THE ARTIST'S tracing shown here of the great Broad Street depot and its complex of offices shows the train shed as it looked in its final redaction before being destroyed by fire. In the view below the buildings of the Centennial Exposition of 1876 show beyond the bridge over the Schuylkill River. Broad Street then was only in the drawing board stage. (*Two Drawings: Pennsylvania Railroad.*)

SOMETHING OF the pastoral quality that characterized the Pennsylvania's
Main Line, both in its parochial or Philadelphia sense and further afield
where it signified "The Main Line of Public Works" between the East and
Pittsburgh, is latent in this fine engraving executed for the railroad's promotion
department in 1875. The station at Altoona was an important stop for a
variety of reasons including the railroad's ever enlarging machine shops
and erecting works there and the Logan House shown just across the platform
from the tracks, was a depot hotel of more than regional celebrity.
Here in an age before diners became universal the cars paused for the
conventional twenty minute meal stop and here drummers solicited the patronage
of railroad purchasing agents for all the vast inventory of hardware
incidental to a great railroad system. At the Logan House, so legend maintains,
Andrew Carnegie, fresh from England, convinced Tom Scott that steel rails
were the coming thing and would soon replace iron on all progressive
roads both for rails and bridges, thus laying the foundation for an immense
fortune. It was the age of Saratoga trunks, Dundreary whiskers and
skirted frock coats for travel as depicted above and also attested by the
photographic evidence seen on the opposite page.
The Logan House lasted until well after the turn of the century as a landmark
of the Pennsy, although with the inclusion of dining cars in almost
all trains, its function as a meal stop had long since become a memory.

BROAD STREET was conceived and its construction inaugurated in the brass-knuckles era when Tom Scott (*left*) was carving out its primal destinies in a period of ceaseless warfare with unions, Pennsylvania politicians and the embattled competition. As a result its architecture suggested a baronial stronghold from which the railroad's partisans might sally forth to give battle to the enemy, which was exactly what it was. A magnificent system map of the railroad, executed in bas-relief by the ubiquitous American Bank Note Company, was located in the main waiting room of the depot in a time when black kid gloves, bowler hats and well furled umbrellas were requisites for young men going places on the cars. (*Pennsylvania Railroad.*)

1. Eighteenth Street crossing.—2. Hansom cab system.—3. Fireplace in ladies' waiting room.—4. The station.—5 Baggage department.—6. Grand stairway.—7. Car house.—8. Main waiting room.

THE BROAD STREET PASSENGER STATION OF THE PENNSYLVANIA RAILROAD COMPANY AT PHILADELPHIA.

FROM the early eighties until shortly after the turn of the century when the auto-taxi made them obsolete, the Pennsylvania maintained a fleet of beautifully groomed horse cabs for its passengers and the company's officials, available at a favored cab rank and in competition with the somewhat less elegant public hackney coaches that roamed the Philadelphia streets. There were broughams, hansom carriages, as shown here, as well as victorias and even opera coaches, each painted in the company livery of maroon with a liveried driver on the box and the company name on the nameboards. No other carrier can be discovered at this remove affording such elegant service, the nearest being Parmelee Transfer in Chicago which served all the terminals in town. (*Pennsylvania Railroad.*)

IN THE YEAR 1883, two years after it had been opened for service, Broad Street Station was enough of a national institution to command the entire front page of *Scientific American*. The fact is significant because, while Philadelphians themselves considered Broad Street a parochial manifestation like Madeira at insurance company dinners, it was in actuality the front and facade Philadelphia showed to the outer world, a citadel of entrenched power and an abode of dynastic proprieties. In *Scientific American's* depiction of Broad Street Station in 1883 are many purely Gothic details of design which later and over the years became modified or disappeared altogether. Notable in this context are the grand stairway and main waiting room identified as panels No. 6 and 8, respectively, in the picture layout. Gothic, too, to a magnificent degree was the fireplace in the ladies' waiting room shown as panel 3 and the ornate baggage department in panel 5. The magazine's caption speaks of the train shed as "the car house" and specifically mentions hansom cab service to the exclusion of all other sorts of public conveyance. It is known from the company archives that the railroad's own cab ranks embraced a wide variety of other types of carriage.

Broad Street Was the Entrepot To Philadelphia's Innermost Being

IN 1895 and in what can only be described as an ill-advised if prophetic moment, management caused to be emplaced in the waiting room at Broad Street, a bas-relief by Karl Bittner entitled "The Progress of Transportation," as reproduced here. Along with symbolic likenesses of steam locomotives and ferry boats, the artist included his vision of a flying machine, an artifact which, in scarcely more than half a century, was to doom Broad Street itself and seriously menace the railroad business as a whole. When Broad Street was torn down and the ill-omened bas-relief reinstated at the main line depot at Thirtieth Street, its jinx was not felt to be abated. *(Three Photos: Pennsylvania Railroad.)*

THAT THE architects of Broad Street Station were obligated to allegory is explicit in the record of that Gothic pile. Its every vantage point bristled with classic figures representing, it may be presumed, carloadings, operating ratios and the on-time average of *The Broadway*. Details of the pediment shown on the opposite page depict the lion and the lamb in brownstone embrace, a scene whose symbolism was felt to open almost limitless vistas for its possible interpretation. Although the Market Street clock *(right)* was kept five minutes fast by the management, Clocker patrons traditionally arrived just as the guard slammed the train gates. It was a Philadelphia ritual.

593

NO SINGLE institution better typified Main Line Philadelphia than The Paoli Local whose train crew, in the days before the Main Line itself was electrified, are shown comparing watches. Leaving their reading glasses on The Paoli Local, according to Nathaniel Burt, to be reclaimed at the Broad Street lost and found was a hallmark of gentility in Merion, Ardmore and Haverford.

IT MAY BE DOUBTED that the personnel of Broad Street Depot felt themselves to be components and custodians of a *mystique* that was to become legendary in the annals of American travel, but the ticket taker at The Clocker gate, the brakeman taking down the markers from the arriving Paoli Local, and the train crew of The Paoli Local comparing watches, were all part of the essential personality that made Broad Street one of the great railroad terminals of the world with an individuality of its own. In the menacing grotto at the left, far beneath Market Street and dimly lit by naked bulbs, the baggage smashers of Broad Street posed for their portrait, too. The date was when the patent devisings of "innovation trunks" hadn't rendered their prudent cording for extra security obsolete. Anticipating by many years the proverbial genius of air lines for dispatching the bags of customers to the wrong continent, it may be pondered if George Baker's carefully identified possessions from Derbyshire, England, have yet arrived at their intended destination? *(Four Photos: Pennsylvania Railroad.)*

Graven on Christopher Morley's Heart Were the Words: "Paoli Local."

FEW TRAINS with such humble antecedents have become part of the regional body of regional folklore on a scale comparable to The Paoli Local, Philadelphia's Main Line suburban run that originated at Broad Street and ended at Paoli at the far edge of socially acceptable real estate. "The Paoli Local has been a source of pride, convenience and affection," wrote Nathaniel Burt in "The Perennial Philadelphians," while Christopher Morley, himself a Main Line resident, followed in the footsteps of Mary Tudor of England when she said that after her death, because she had lost it to the French, the word "Calais" would be found written on her heart. Morley asserted that after his death "Paoli Local" would be found on his. In a community which cherishes the continuity of established institutions, The Paoli Local gained access, not only to letters, but to the heart of Philadelphia itself, like passing the Madeira clockwise at Insurance Dinners and keeping money in the Girard Corn Exchange Bank. On the page opposite a Paoli Local conductor assumes his responsibilities not only as a trainman, but as custodian of an article of faith. At the right is Christopher Morley, minstrel of the commuter legend. *(Opposite and Below: Pennsylvania Railroad.)*

BRYN MAWR depot, shown in this engaging view in the mid-seventies, was named for a neighboring estate of one of the Main Line landed gentry and was a byproduct of George Roberts' penchant for Welsh atmosphere wherever it could be introduced into the railroad's scheme of things. In the years of the Paoli Local, Bryn Mawr was celebrated as being the point of origin for more lady commuters to town with a genius for leaving their eyeglasses on the cars than any other mainline stop. They were retrieved from lost and found at Broad Street as a matter of course.

597

THE ORIGINAL TRAIN SHED at Broad Street, shown at the top of the page opposite, in 1882 had three arched train bays and was flanked by the offices of the Adams Express Company, then one of the several great competing express companies of the East and South although it had withdrawn from California in defeat at the hands of Wells Fargo & Co. In the lower photograph is the same scene in 1890, a date which suggests itself because the original multiple arches of 1881 had been replaced by a single huge unit but the ten-story Moorish-Gothic corner tower of the main office building, completed in 1894, is not yet visible in the background. Clearly in view, however, is the turretted campanile of City Hall topped by a heroic statue of William Penn. The historic landmark, as the train shed had by this time become, was destroyed by fire in 1925 and passengers thereafter boarded the cars under makeshift shelters until the entire structure was demolished in 1952. *(Opposite, Two Photos: Everett De Golyer Collection; Above: The Philadelphia Record.)*

ALTHOUGH NOT DISTINGUISHED by the variety of noble and imposing names which identified the Pennsylvania's fleet of varnish trains on longer runs, the Clockers between Philadelphia and New York, so called because they departed their respective terminals on the hour throughout the day and well into the evening, were at one time among the most celebrated of all the railroad's multiplicity of services. Almost without exception the Clockers carried coaches, Pullman parlor cars, a diner and a club lounge car with parlor seats and two or four tables served by a self contained grill at one end. In the days of steam motive power when a change to and from electric engines was necessary at Manhattan Transfer the run between Broad Street and Penn Station in New York took an hour and fifty minutes. When electrification was completed it was ninety minutes. Here in the twenties behind a capped stack Pacific, a Clocker awaits its highball at Broad Street before setting out along "The Chinese Wall" to join the main line at North Philadelphia. *(Pennsylvania Railroad.)*

REGULARLY ASSIGNED to the Clockers were the "Club" series parlor-buffet cars such as *Banker's Club* whose solarium compartment is shown above and *Union League Club* (below). Admirers considered them among the handsomest lounge cars ever outshopped by Pullman and regulars aboard the run knew that the food from their miniature galleys, especially double English lamb chops, was remarkable. *(Two Photos: Pennsylvania Railroad.)*

Clocker leaving Broad
Street in electrified times
behind a GG1 type
motor. *(Everett De Golyer
Collection.)*

Clocker in Broad Street
Station waiting highball in
steam days behind a
K4s Pacific. *(Everett De
Golyer Collection.)*

TOM, DICK AND HARRY might and did ride aboard the crowded daycoaches of the Pennsy Clockers between Broad Street and Manhattan, "ninety miles in ninety minutes" as the company literature had it, but the clientele on the parlor cars was possessed of a social and professional *ton* comparable to that which rode the New Haven's extra fare trains out of Boston. Regular commuters found the hour and a half elapsed time between terminals useful for reading and took breakfast or tea aboard the early and late runs. Authors, editors and executives of Philadelphia publishing firms and names of distinction in science and the humanities perused learned periodicals in attitudes of fully attired decorum and there were no shirtsleeves allowed. The parlor compartment of *Engineers Club*, shown here, reflected the Clocker atmosphere of well-bred preoccupation with worldly matters of consequence.   (*Pennsylvania Railroad.*)

MANHATTAN TRANSFER, where the Pennsy trains changed from steam to electric power and patrons boarded the tube for downtown New York and Wall Street was so much an institution in the 1920s that it became the title of a novel by John Dos Passos, entering the national lexicon of belles lettres. Below, at about this time, a Clocker arrives at Manhattan Transfer to be taken over by steam for the ninety minute run over the ninety miles to Broad Street. The old-time courtesy characteristic of railroads in a less urgent age radiates from the venerable company servant at the right, whose memories when this photograph was taken reached back to the days of the by now almost godlike Alexander Cassatt. *(Three Photos: Pennsylvania Railroad.)*

THE FOLKLORE of the Pennsy Clockers between Broad Street and mid-town Manhattan is a body of legend comparable to that of Broad Street itself where they originated. Excepting possibly the New Haven's *Knickerbocker* and *Yankee Clipper* no trains in the record afforded such a density of names associated with journalism, belles lettres, advertising and communications generally. Christopher Morley, although his immortality in the Pennsylvania Railroad saga is associated with the Paoli Local, was a regular commuter to Manhattan for many years when he was columnist, successively for *The New York Post* and *The Saturday Review of Literature*. Stanley Walker, the most celebrated city editor of his time, tried it briefly but found the daily strain too much. Ted Patrick, editor of *Holiday,* maintained offices in both New York and Philadelphia and read his manuscripts between them. Because of Philadelphia's handy location many Broadway triumphs tried out there and the presence on the Clockers of such luminaries as Sir Laurence Olivier, Noel Coward, Cole Porter, Moss Hart or Alfred Lunt raised no eyebrows. One of the authors of this book, assigned in the thirties to a Broadway beat, frequently interviewed notables between Manhattan Transfer and North Philadelphia, taking another Clocker back to his office with a minimum of inconvenience. Under such circumstances and with the aid of highballs on *The Poor Richard Club* Lillian Hellman, John C. Wilson and George M. Cohan told him a prudent all for the Sunday editions. The midnight departure from Broad Street after an important opening was awash with mink and tailcoats. In the John Held Jr. short-skirted twenties, a Pennsy press agent undertook to suggest the emancipated atmosphere of the Clockers and tolerant attitude of the carrier generally by setting aside a special ladies' smoking room and the above publicity photo was the result. *(Pennsylvania Railroad.)*

605

EXPERIENCED COMMUTERS, boarding the seven or eight o'clock Clocker at Broad Street knew that if they could get a seat in the dining space of the *Poor Richard* or *Engineer's Club*, their breakfast eggs would be cooked to order and not from the steam table which was their origin on the formal diner in the middle of the train. Even in the years of the 1941 war, everything was better on the Clocker clubcars than elsewhere in the train. Since the year 1876, when the drawing at the right was made, Pennsylvania passengers crossing the Delaware River at Trenton, especially if it were winter, made mental note that they were following (approximately) in George Washington's footsteps. *(Everett De Golyer Collection.)*

606

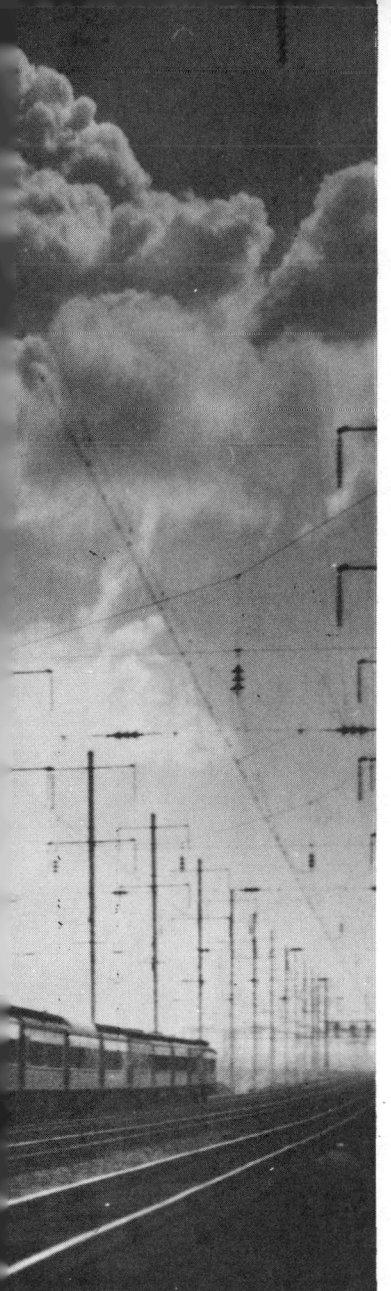

PENNSYLVANIA ticket clerks *(top)* crouched in the fastness of their grotto at Broad Street in attitudes of menace, as one critic remarked, daring anyone to attempt to negotiate a purchase. Making up the Clockers *(below)* at Broad Street was a casual chore with the better part of an hour at the disposal of switching crews and, in clement weather, as suggested here, could be a relaxed operation. *(Two Photos: Pennsylvania Railroad.)*

607

THERE HAD originally been sixteen stub tracks in the great vaulted train shed at Broad Street but one of them disappeared during the fire of the twenties. Throughout the latter years of Broad Street's life the New York Clockers for the most part left on Track 15 as is suggested opposite. Guards over the years became more or less accustomed to the ingrained habit of Clocker regulars of arriving with an irreducible margin of safety before traintime and getting through the half-closed gate by the skin of their teeth. The habit was probably entrenched in the comforting assurance that another Clocker would be along in sixty minutes and that there was a multiplicity of bars handy where one could spend the interval. Here a GG1 electric motor heads up a Clocker against the symbolic background of Philadelphia's City Hall with William Penn at its apex. The main stairway leading to the train level was much admired for its handsome marble trim and brass handrails, almost the only surviving traces of the era of George Roberts when they were conceived. (*Three Photos: L. B. Brittingham.*)

DURING THE BRIEF interregnum when the Pennsylvania's competition to the newly inaugurated *Twentieth Century Limited* was known as *The Twenty Hour Special* before it became, to everyone's confusion, *The Pennsylvania Special*, it was a train of enormous style as is suggested above and its consist, represented by the rich and massive buffet interior at the right, included the finest equipment its owning carrier could procure from Pullman. Not even *The Pennsylvania Limited* which was its contemporary in confused identity, was accorded more lavish favors in the way of luxury devisings and specially selected personnel. By the time *The Twenty Hour Special* appeared on the time cards, the Logan House, depicted twenty-five years earlier on the page opposite, was in decline as one of the notable railroad hotels of the continent. Its times of teem had been in the seventies and eighties before the universality of diners when it was celebrated as a meal stop on the Pittsburgh run as well as a legendary resort of drummers in the heyday of the traveling salesman. Here the knights of the sample case assembled in garments of voluptuous pattern and curly brimmed derby hats to exchange mendacities and cigars at the Logan Bar and buy uncounted smashes, slings and crustas for the proprietors of country stores who were their patrons. On its ample expanse of porch, as suggested here, they indulged the great American preoccupation of their time, watching the arrival and departure of the steamcars. *(Above: Everett De Golyer Collection; Opposite: Pennsylvania Railroad, Pullman Standard.)*

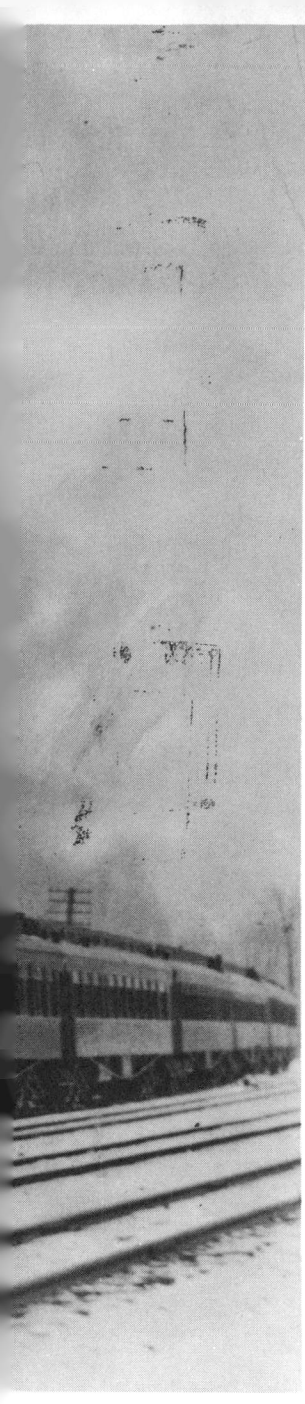

UNTIL THE YEAR 1902 the twenty-eight hour schedule of the *Pennsylvania Limited* and its opposite number the New York Central's *Lake Shore Limited* between New York and Chicago were considered adequate to the needs of the age. But in 1902 what the press was pleased to call "the great speed war" broke out between the two carriers when the Central inaugurated its epochal *Twentieth Century Limited* on a twenty hour schedule and the Pennsylvania, at the identical day and hour, countered with its equally fine and fast *Pennsylvania Special*. A great deal of confusion resulted from the similarity of names between the *Pennsylvania Special* and the long established *Limited,* but three years later *The Special* again made headlines when its schedule was reduced to eighteen hours and it was advertised as "The Fastest Long Distance Train in the World." As *The Pennsylvania Special* Trains 28 and 29 were operated until November 1912 when the confusion was resolved and the run renamed *The Broad Way Limited.* At the time of its emergence as an eighteen hour flyer *The Pennsylvania Special* was photographed arriving at Chicago with the four extra-fancy Pullman varnish cars specially assigned this favored run and the facing print was made from the original glass plate negative in the possession of The Chicago Historical Society. The eighteen hour train laid hold upon public imagination and immediately became the symbol of the fastest human travel in an age crazed with speed. Sheet music was composed in its honor and it is notable that Bandmaster Innes' two-step march was dedicated to the railroad's passenger agent, Samuel Moody, whose name appears in the company literature. *(Pennsylvania Railroad.)*

MOST ADVERTISED FEATURE of *The Pennsylvania Special* when it went into service on its eighteen hour schedule July 9, 1905 was the time it saved in transit and its extra fare was based on this advantage. But its equipment, if perhaps less ostentatious than that of *The Limited* of 1898, was the most sumptuous available as is suggested by these builder's interiors of the observation lounge. The chronologic chart *(below)* was part of the train literature given each passenger. *(Three Photos: Pennsylvania Railroad.)*

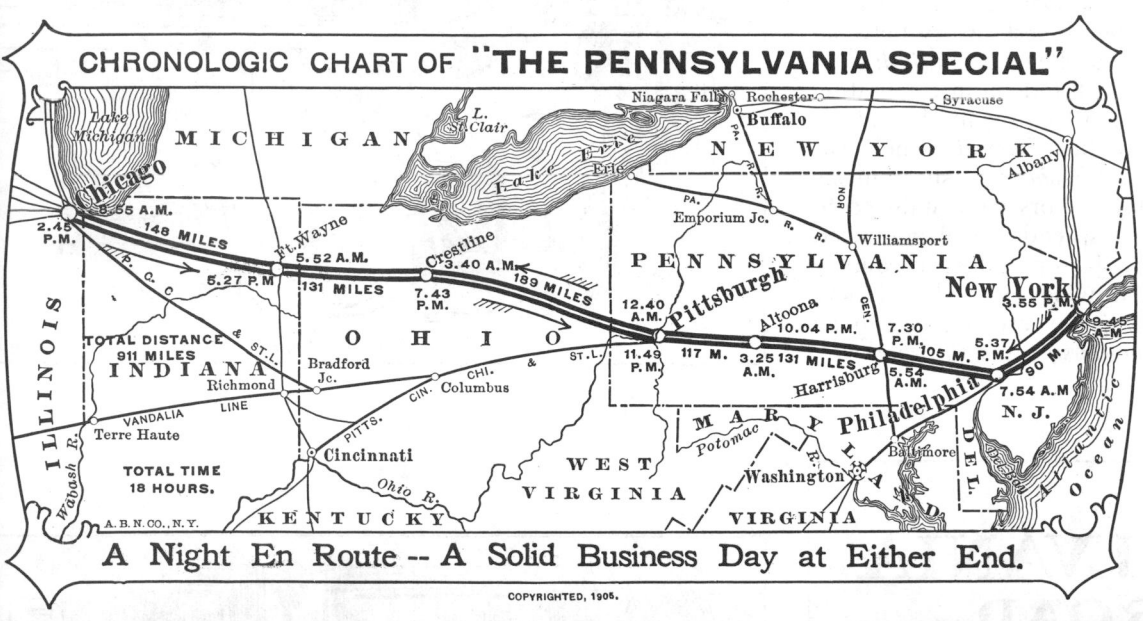

CHRONOLOGIC CHART OF "THE PENNSYLVANIA SPECIAL"

A Night En Route -- A Solid Business Day at Either End.

COPYRIGHTED, 1905.

ALTHOUGH IT LACKED the rival New York Central's transcendent genius of publicity and promotion, George Henry Daniels, the Pennsylvania in the years of the fiercest rivalry between *The Broadway Limited* and *The Twentieth Century Limited* did very well indeed in celebrating the train that was its most effulgent showpiece. To honor *The Pennsylvania Special*, which was soon to emerge as *The Broadway*, sheet music was composed, Sunday editors were induced to run formidable feature spreads, airplanes raced its progress across New Jersey (to lose of course). The delightful line drawings reproduced here together with the dust jacket are from company pamphlets of 1905. (*Pennsylvania Railroad.*)

PENNSYLVANIA
RAILROAD
THE
PENNSYLVANIA
SPECIAL

18 HOURS
BETWEEN
NEW YORK
AND
CHICAGO

ONLY A NIGHT EN ROUTE

THE FASTEST LONG DISTANCE TRAIN IN THE WORLD

W. W. ATTERBURY . . General Manager
J. R. WOOD . . Passenger Traffic Manager
GEO. W. BOYD . . General Passenger Agent

IN EFFECT JULY 9TH 1905

AMERICAN BANK NOTE CO., NEW YORK

"The Pennsylvania Special"

PIONEER 18-HOUR TRAIN

BETWEEN

Chicago = Miles 912 Miles = New York

SPEAKING GENERALLY, the original luxury equipment of *The Pennsylvania Special* when it was inaugurated in June 1902 was somewhat more elaborate in its decor and appointments than that of *The Century* which was hastily recruited from available car pools, some of it Wagner and some Pullman. Throughout its lifetime as a de luxe run *The Century* was to be more austere than its competition, even though after its first explosions of magnificence in the form of bevel edge mirrors and ball fringe curtains, *The Special* became more restrained as is suggested below. Here Pintsch illumination has been supplemented by Mazda bulbs, inlaid marquetry work by severe mahogany. The poster at the left includes in its economy the same photograph of *The Special's* stunning consist that is reproduced more faithfully on an adjacent page. (*Two Photos: Pennsylvania Railroad.*)

"CAB?" "KEB?" "COUPÉ?"

CHICAGO WAS ONLY a decade removed from The Great Fire and Mrs. O'Leary's legendary cow when the Union Station, shown opposite, was opened for occupancy in 1881. A stunning example of railroad architecture of its period with Mansard roof, Gothic windows and ornate wrought ironwork around its portes cochères and other entrances, it expressed the irrepressible optimism of the city that was even then becoming the railroad metropolis of the nation. Under its train shed arrived and departed the varnish runs of Pennsylvania, Alton, Burlington and Milwaukee as well as the Parmelee Transfer omnibuses shown ranked in their elaborately painted splendor in the photograph. The station was bounded by Canal and Adams Streets with a train shed 1,000 feet long and comprised, according to a contemporary account of "a handsome series of red brick pavilions with the larger one in the center." Telephone and telegraph wires traversed the streets in an age innocent of underground cables and gas lamps, of course, supplied illumination. It was beyond all compare a period piece. The new Union Station (above) which rose on the site of the old incorporated much of the Roman splendor of Caracalla that characterized Penn Station in New York and afforded stately vistas under lofty columns. The architects were Graham, Burham & Company and the engineer was William Braeger. (Two Photos: Pennsylvania Railroad.)

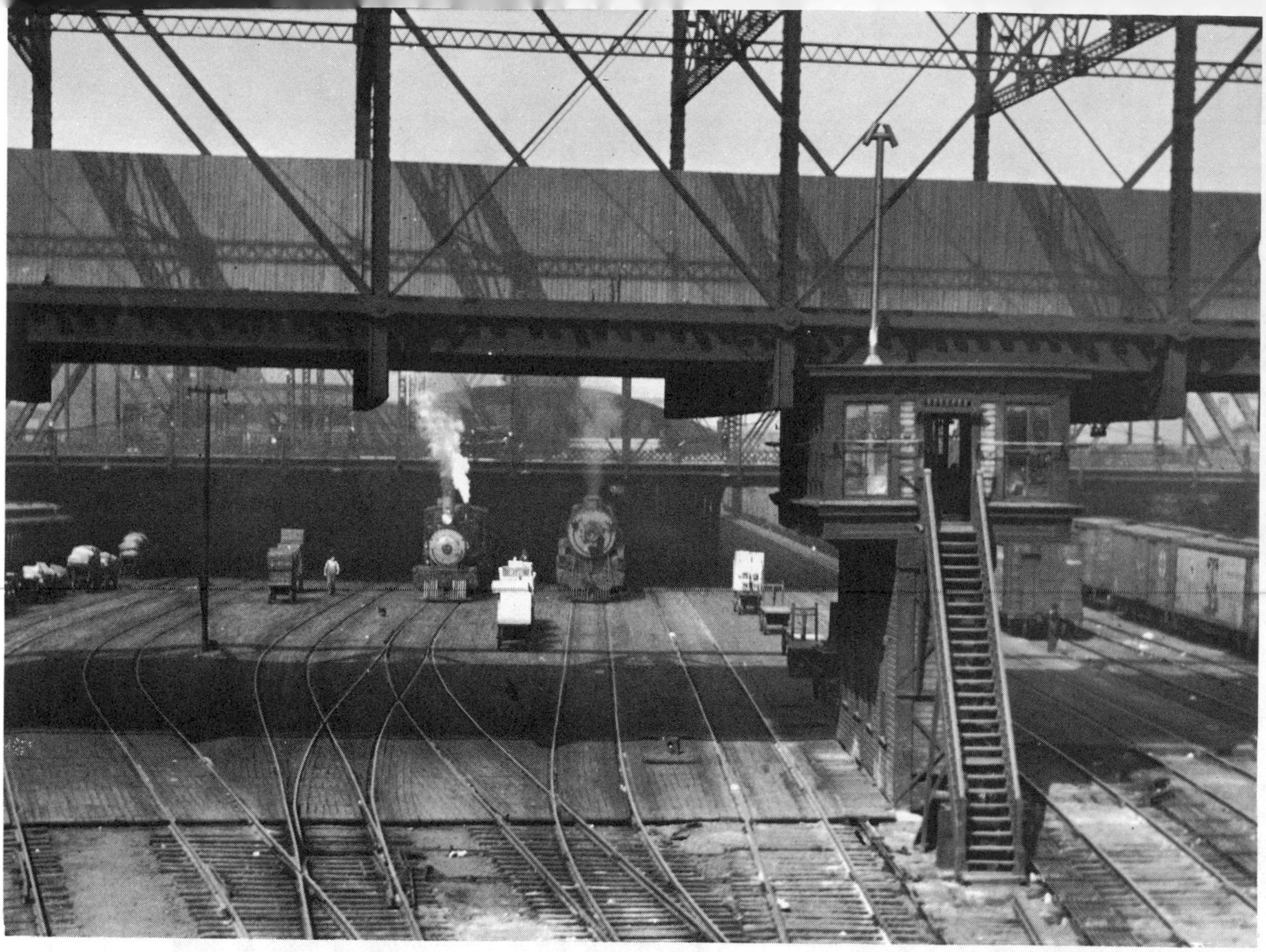

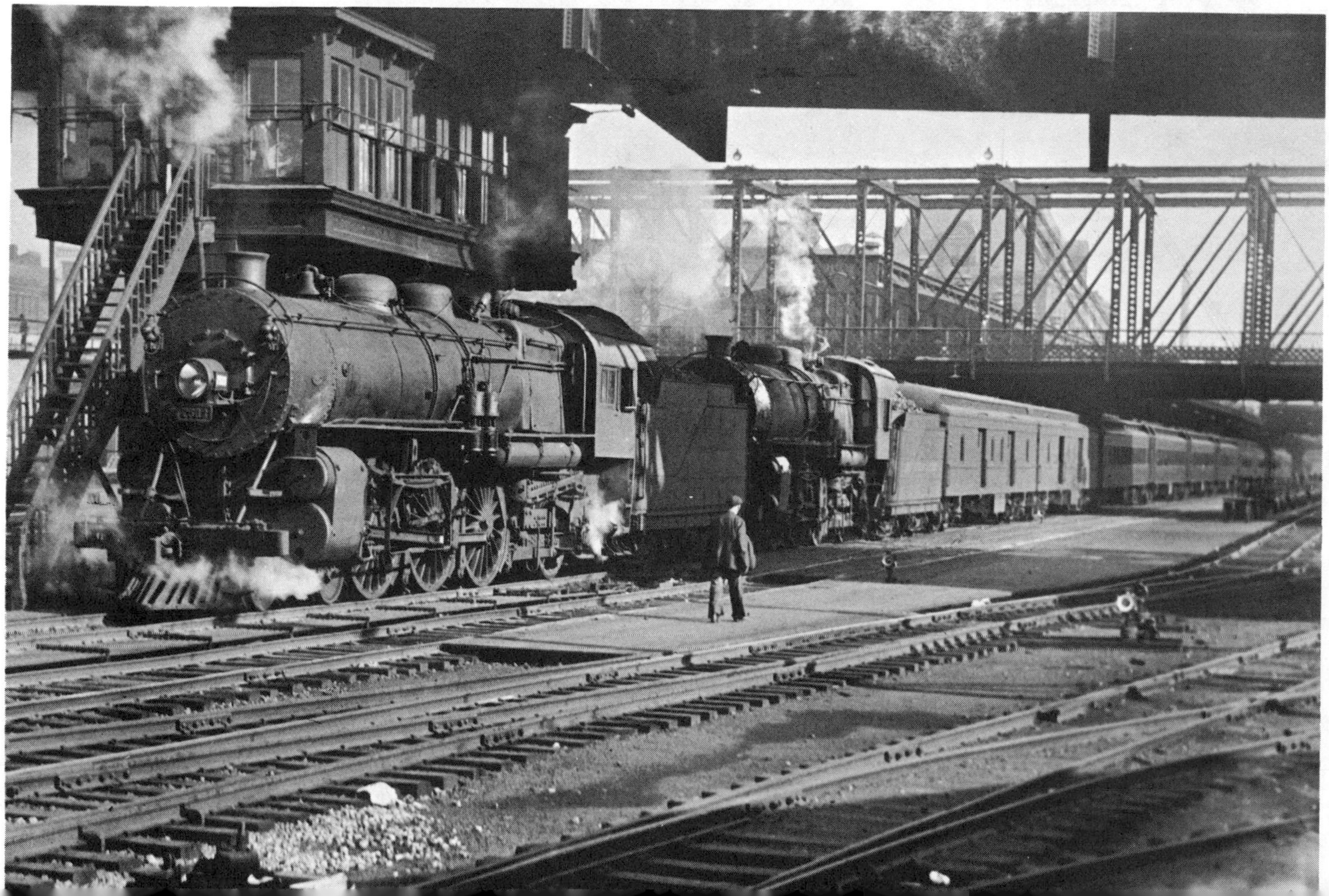

AS DETAILED and true to character as any Rembrandt portrait of a Flemish nobleman is this revealing camera study from the company files of a Pennsylvania engineer in the characteristic pose of his professional calling. The gantleted gloves, the stiff-billed cap, long snouted oil can and occupational watch chain are the hallmarks of the working stiff on the right hand cushions, while the narrowed eyes are adjusted to seeing far down the tangents of space and time in the face of the winds of hurry. On the opposite page the look and texture of Chicago's old Union Station are caught in two photographs from the recording camera of Alfred W. Johnson, venerable dean of railroad iconographers in the Chicago area. Above is a panoramic view of the great train shed with a Pennsy mainliner waiting its highball beside a Burlington suburban train. Below, *The Pennsylvania Limited* as of 1919 is ready to be off and running on the fast track to Fort Wayne behind two businesslike Pacifics.

DOUBLE HEADED with two K-4s Pacifics in tandem, the Pennsy's *New Yorker* emerges on a cold winter's day from the primordial catacombs of Union Station in Chicago with steam exhaust condensing for a magnificent urban portrait of double shotted steam power in varnish service. *(John Barriger Collection.)*

MANY of the phone numbers listed for the convenience of interested patrons on the Union Station blackboard which, in the 1920s, advertised the weekend excursion rates of the various carriers are the same as those assigned Chicago railroad offices forty years later. Below: business is only fair at the Union Depot arrival information desk where, in the early 1930s, the *Manhattan Limited* is announced as on time and later arrivals, *The Rainbow* and *The Union* are yet to be heard from. *(Left: John Barriger; Below: Pennsylvania Railroad.)*

Velvet Success Rode the Staterooms of The Broadway

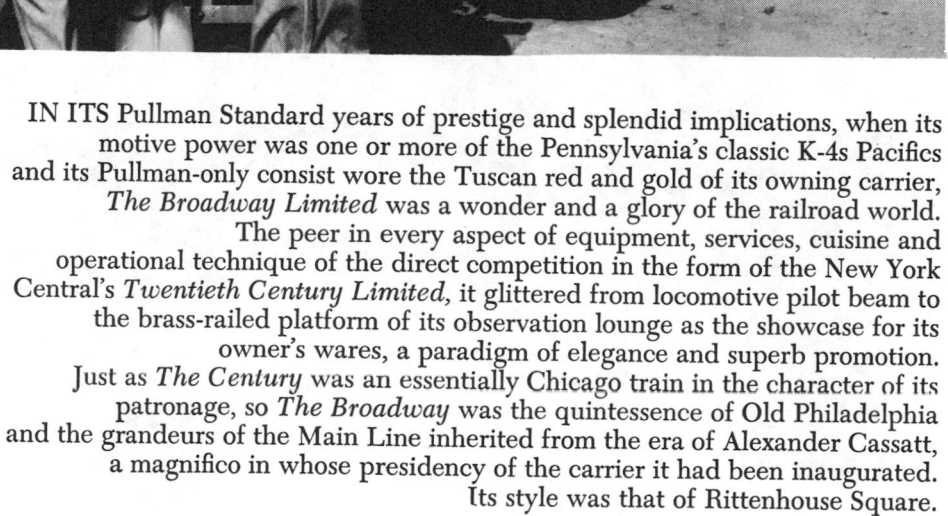

IN ITS Pullman Standard years of prestige and splendid implications, when its motive power was one or more of the Pennsylvania's classic K-4s Pacifics and its Pullman-only consist wore the Tuscan red and gold of its owning carrier, *The Broadway Limited* was a wonder and a glory of the railroad world.

The peer in every aspect of equipment, services, cuisine and operational technique of the direct competition in the form of the New York Central's *Twentieth Century Limited,* it glittered from locomotive pilot beam to the brass-railed platform of its observation lounge as the showcase for its owner's wares, a paradigm of elegance and superb promotion.

Just as *The Century* was an essentially Chicago train in the character of its patronage, so *The Broadway* was the quintessence of Old Philadelphia and the grandeurs of the Main Line inherited from the era of Alexander Cassatt, a magnifico in whose presidency of the carrier it had been inaugurated.

Its style was that of Rittenhouse Square.

Aboard it on their upholstered occasions in Chicago, rode Morrises, Biddles,
Reeves and Cadwaladers, Penroses and Lippincotts, and it was no error
in judgment on the part of the management that there was scrapple on the
breakfast menu and Chesapeake Bay oysters at dinner. If there was a smell of
money about *The Broadway* it was very old money, dating back to the
times of Stephen Girard and Nicholas Biddle's Bank of the United States.
Passengers who boarded it in Philadelphia or Paoli carried about
them the suggestion that they came directly from the Rittenhouse Club, much as
those on the New Haven's *Merchants Limited* suggested arrival from the
banking office of Kuhn Loeb & Co., via the bar at the Belmont Hotel.
Here *The Broadway* poses briefly on a summer afternoon at Englewood south
of Chicago for suburban passengers. Specially assigned K-4s Pacifics bore
the train's name on their smokebox and its conductors were aristocrats.
(A. W. Johnson; Pennsylvania Railroad.)

DRAMATIC CLIMAX of the working day at Chicago's Union Station was the afternoon sailing of *The Broadway Limited*, especially if it departed as shown here, in two or more sections. The train's partisans felt that it was the perfect expression of the *belle epoque* of surface travel and that its train services *(below)* embraced all the amenities a gentleman might require. *(Two Photos: Pennsylvania Railroad.)*

BROADWAY LIMITED

EASTWARD

Lv. CHICAGO......12.40 pm Central Time
Lv. ENGLEWOOD .12.56 pm Central Time
Ar. NEW YORK.... 9.40 am Eastern Time

WESTWARD

Lv. NEW YORK ... 2.45 pm Eastern Time
Ar. ENGLEWOOD. 9.22 am Central Time
Ar. CHICAGO...... 9.45 am Central Time

Solid train of all-steel vestibuled and electric-lighted Club Car, Drawing Room, Sleeping and Compartment-Observation Cars from Chicago through Pittsburgh to Pennsylvania Station— Only One Block from Broadway, New York City.

Also Sleeping Car arriving Washington 10.25 am, returning leaving Washington 3.10 pm.

Meals in Restaurant Car en route: Eastward—Luncheon and Dinner (a la carte) and Breakfast (a la carte). Westward—Dinner (a la carte) and Breakfast (a la carte).

ALL PASSENGERS have the freedom of the entire train. The following special features are at their command:

IN THE CLUB CAR
Shower Bath (hot and cold). Barber Shop. Writing Desk and Stationery. Magazines.

IN THE OBSERVATION CAR
Stenographer (letters and telegrams taken from dictation without charge and transmitted).
Library of Books and Magazines.
Writing Desk and Stationery.
Maid for ladies and children. Manicuring.
Valet will sponge and press gentlemen's garments over night for nominal charge.
Electric Lamps in all berths, convenient for reading after retiring.
Telephone connection in Observation Car while train is standing in Chicago Union Station and Pennsylvania Station, New York. (Calls within city free.)
Passengers may have Pullman reservations made for their return trip by applying to the Stenographer.
Passengers expecting letters or telegrams should notify the Sleeping Car Conductor.

CHARGES
Tonsorial Service

Hair Cut.......$0.50	Hair Singe.....$0.25
Shampoo....... .50	Trimming Beard .25
Facial Massage .50	Baths........... .75
Shave.......... .25	Manicure....... .75

Pressing of Clothes

Entire Suit.....$1.25	Overcoat.......$1.00
Coat...$0.75 Vest...$0.25	Trousers...$0.25

626

THERE WERE true believers to whom *The Broadway* behind a K-4s Pacific on the carrier's New Jersey speedway in Pullman Standard and Tuscan red was the noblest handiwork of God. In 1916, however, when it was photographed on a beautifully manicured main line by Charles B. Chaney it still was to sport the characteristic keystone emblem that would, in the 1920s, identify it as a train of pedigree. *(Rail Photo Service; The Smithsonian Institution.)*

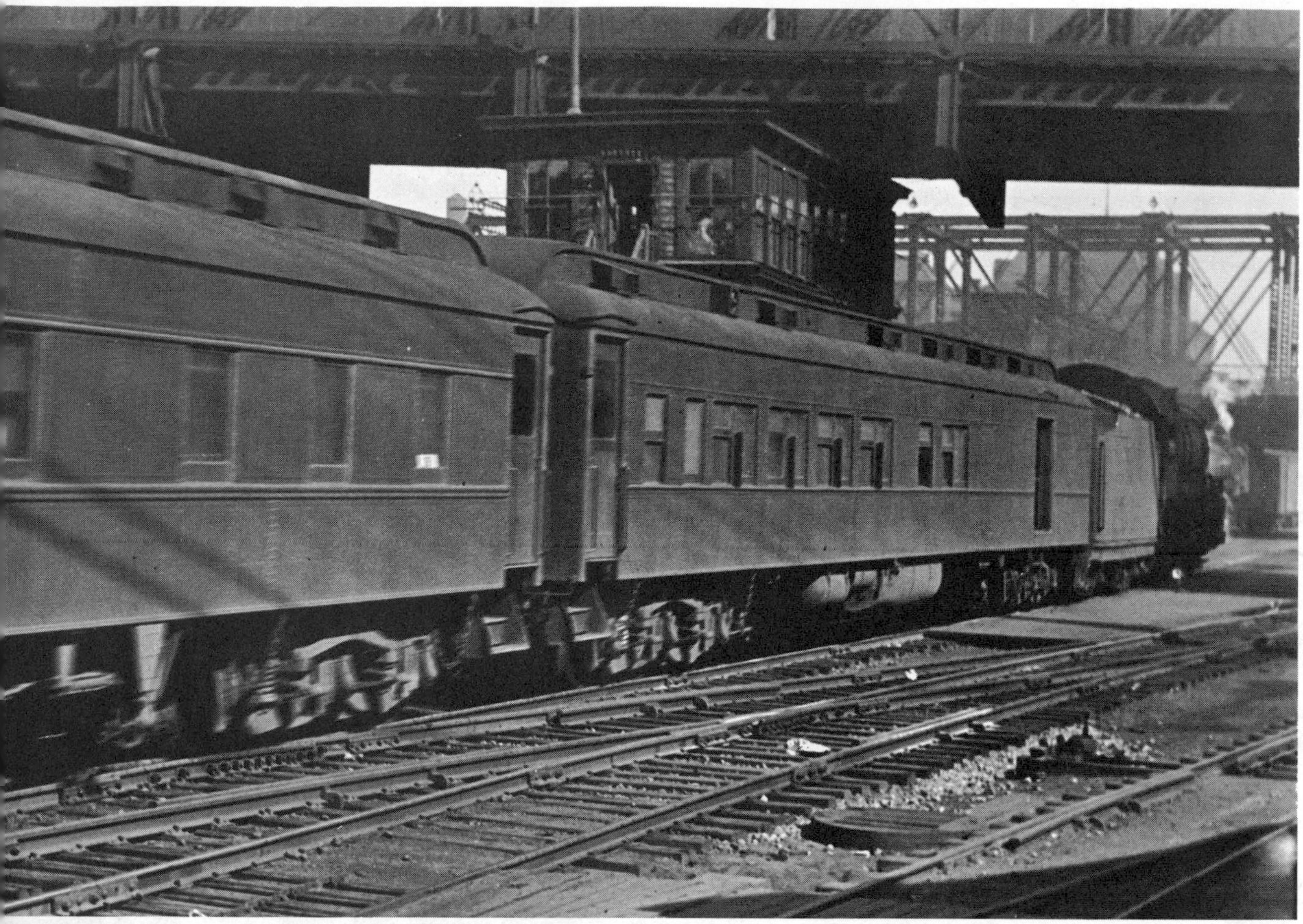

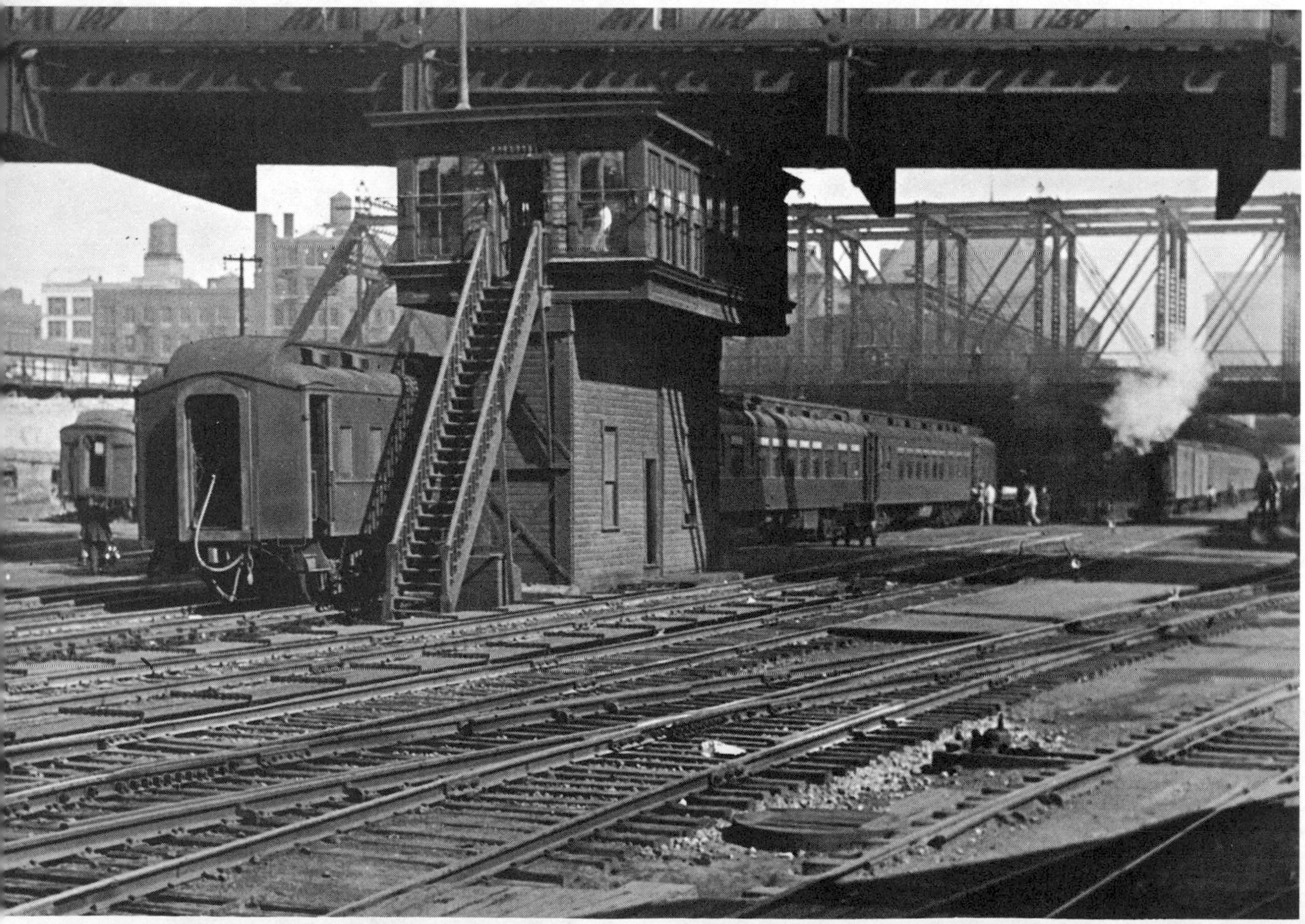

PICK OF the railroad's available personnel were regularly assigned to *The Broadway* whether they were members of the engine crew such as that shown above who changed en route or part of the train's company including waiters, porters and the train secretary. At the left the latter functionary takes dictation from a mogul of the world of finance impatient for his before-dinner Martinis. Opposite: all-Pullman and extra-fare though it was in 1919 when it is shown arriving at the old Union Station at Chicago in two atmospheric poses by Alfred W. Johnson, it didn't always end with the observation platfrom of certifiable elegance that later became mandatory in its consist. (*Left and Above: Pennsylvania Railroad.*)

629

SERVICING the club car of *The Broadway Limited* in the Chicago yards via a trap in the roof in the year 1945 differed little in its essentials from the same operation three quarters of a century earlier when, in 1870, a staff artist from *Leslie's Weekly* depicted the servicing of one of the primordial Pullmans of the Union Pacific. *(Pennsylvania Railroad.)*

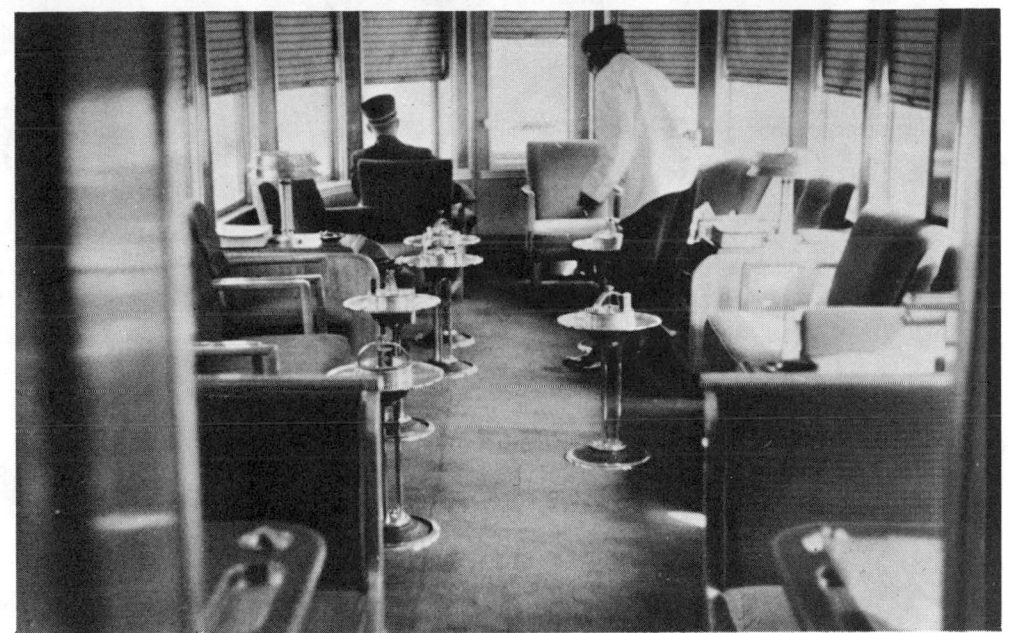

THE FINAL HOURS of *The Broadway's* run into its Chicago terminal find the scene of last evening's fraternal gathering over the Martinis deserted. In the observation end of the club car its only occupants are the rear brakeman working his train and the car attendant cleaning up. The center of population has shifted to the diner where Colonel Robert McCormick's opinionated *Chicago Tribune* is to be found at every place setting between the three minute eggs and the coffee. And finally, with the train berthed in its slip at Union Station and its passengers gone their several ways, the old time observation platform of *The Broadway* in Pullman Standard times is forlorn and abandoned until the switcher comes to take it away to the yards. (*Three Photos: John Barriger.*)

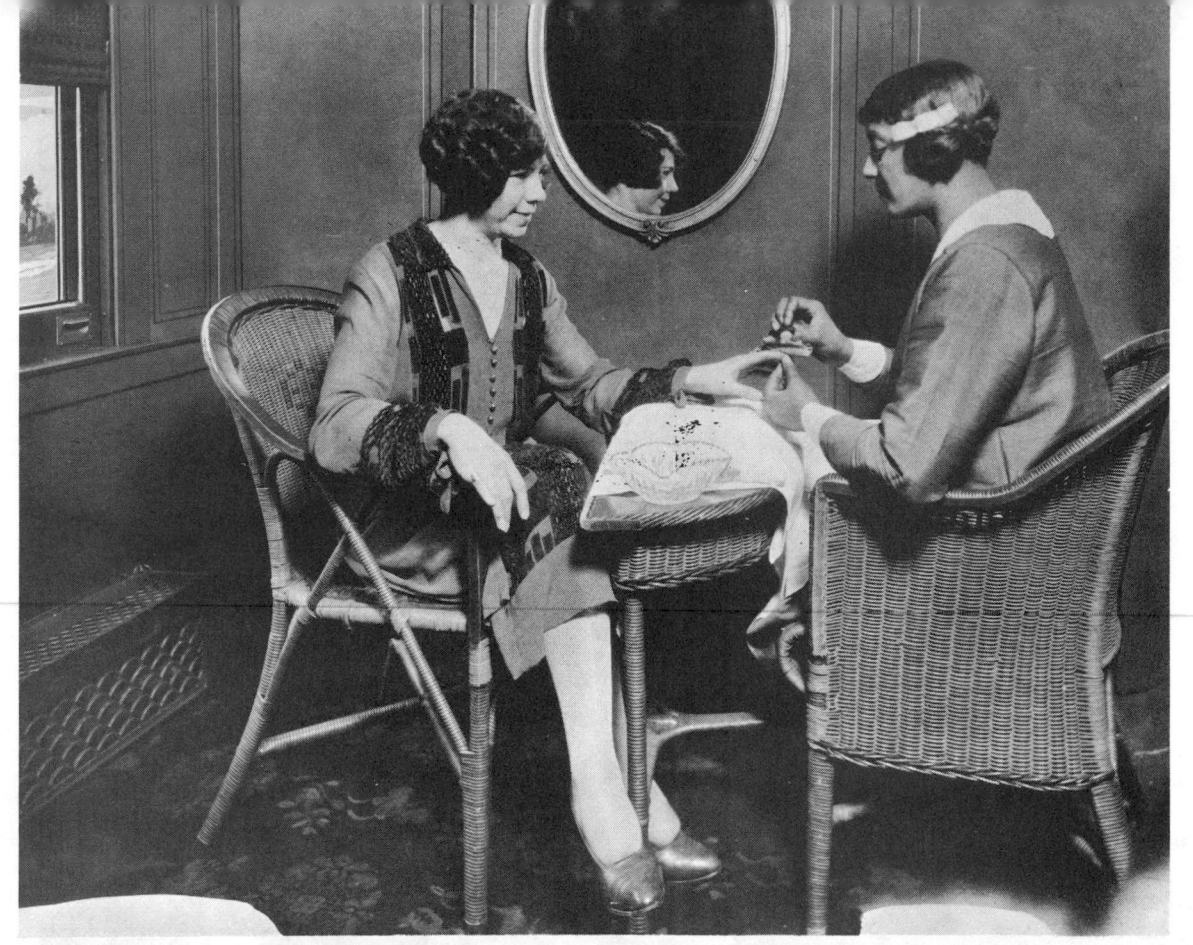

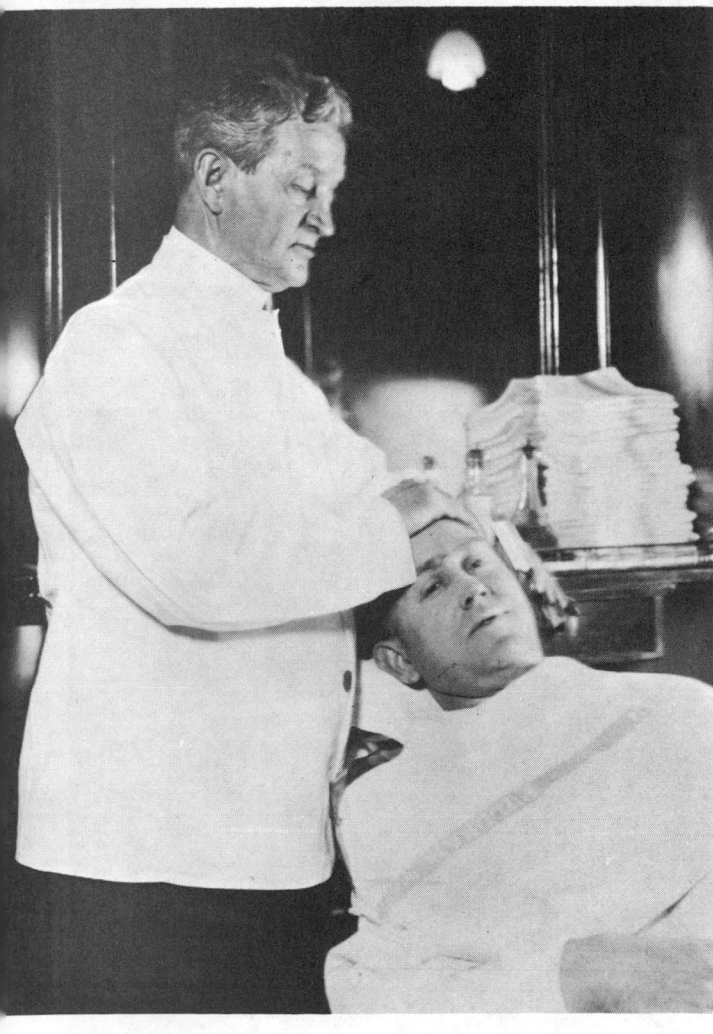

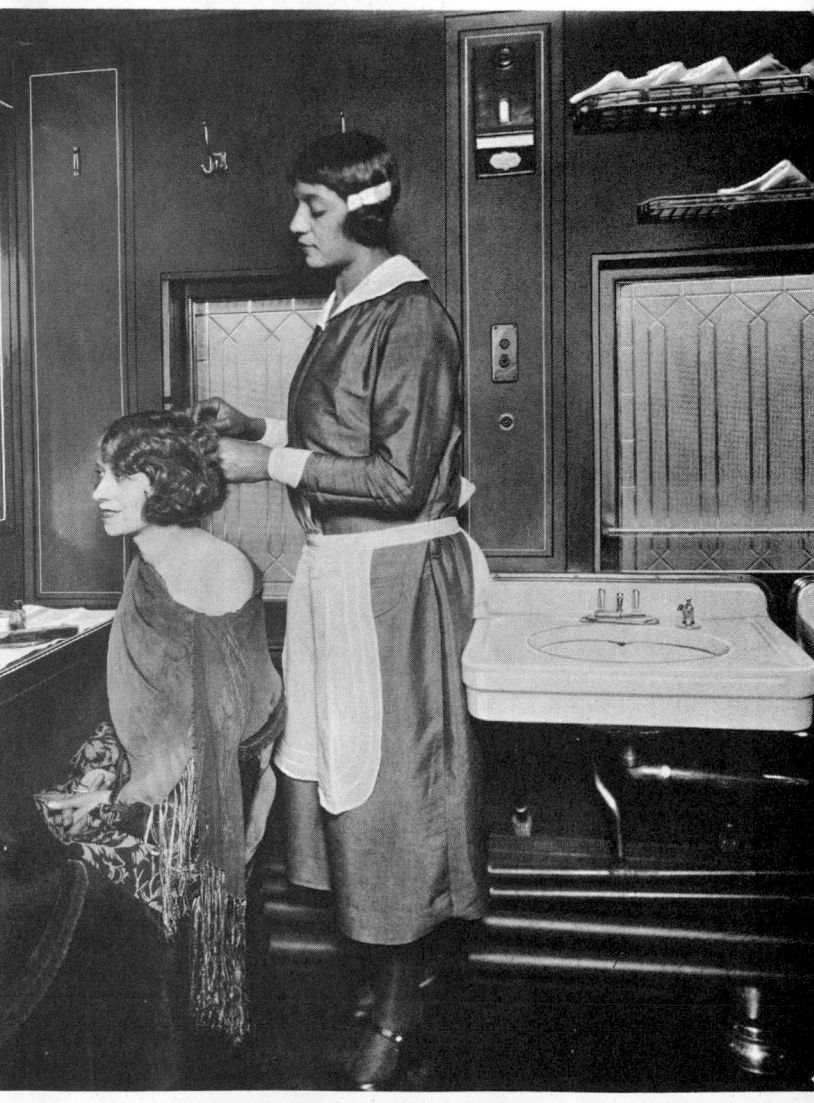

THE TRAIN BARBER on *The Broadway,* shown opposite at his professional stand, could if he wished trace his pedigree back to the ornate cars of *The Pennsylvania Limited* where, in 1898 when a singe and beard trim were in vogue, he was already an established member of the train's company. The services of a lady's maid and manicurist were also standard on the Pennsy's flagship as they were on consequential trains everywhere in the golden years of Pullman travel.

The sailing of *The Broadway* from Union Station in Chicago *(below)* while lacking the rich splendors of *The Century's* departure from Grand Central, was very much the event of the railroad day on the shores of Lake Michigan. Its tailgate insigne, visible through the grille, assured the ticket holder of a fast and very de luxe passage aboard one of the venerated name trains of the world.   *(Four Photos: Pennsylvania Railroad.)*

DEPARTURE OF *The Broadway* from Chicago's Union Station, while lacking the éclat of the sailing of the rival *Century* from New York with its panache of style and red carpet elegance, was still a major event in the railroad day as is suggested by the traingate photograph at the right and the authoritative pose of the conductor as he gives the head-end its highball. Sailing of No. 28 from Chicago was protected by "Drawbridge Rule" which provided for a flexible schedule of departure if drawbridges across the Chicago River delayed access to the West Side of town. (*Three Photos: Pennsylvania Railroad.*)

AS LONG as the passenger business continued to be a major
consideration in the operation of its enormous and powerful
system of transport, the Pennsylvania was aware of the
relentless competition of the New York Central and of the hot
breath of the heirs of Commodore Vanderbilt, breathing
quite literally on the back of its neck.

Every major metropolis to which its varnish ran, New York,
Chicago, St. Louis, Cincinnati, Toledo, Louisville, Detroit, only
excepting Baltimore, Philadelphia and Washington was
accessible also to the opposition. Even Pittsburgh, a citadel of
Pennsylvania power and authority, was at one time
achieved by through sleepers over the Central from New York
and Boston. Reversing this affront, the Pennsylvania, in the
form of *The Buffalonian,* penetrated into the very heart
of the Central domain in upper New York state.

When through cars came for the Pacific coast and via St. Louis
to the Southwest, they ran in competing trains of the two
giants of Eastern transportation. Never was the pressure relaxed,
the tension abated. Most dramatic symbols of the rivalry
that was once a legend of the railroad world were the
line's two crack trains, *The Broadway* and *The Twentieth
Century Limited,* shown here leaving Englewood on
parallel tracks and identical schedules. The year was 1952 and
there was no talk of mergers abroad in the land.
(Everett De Golyer Collection.)

635

IN THE YEARS before the antiseptic sterility of *moderne* decor, when railroad patrons expected from the carriers a more luxurious scheme of things than that represented by fluorescent lighting and the decorative warmth of an operating room, Pullman built for *The Broadway* such beautifully paneled mahogany diners as that shown opposite and rich fabrics were used in the upholstery. Stewards wore dinner jackets in the evening and striped morning trousers at breakfast and lunch and waiters on *The Broadway* wore distinctive tan mess jackets and wing collars. Dinner on the cars was an event and even the servicing of diners in the yards was not devoid of a certain degree of ceremony. (*Three Photos: Pennsylvania Railroad.*)

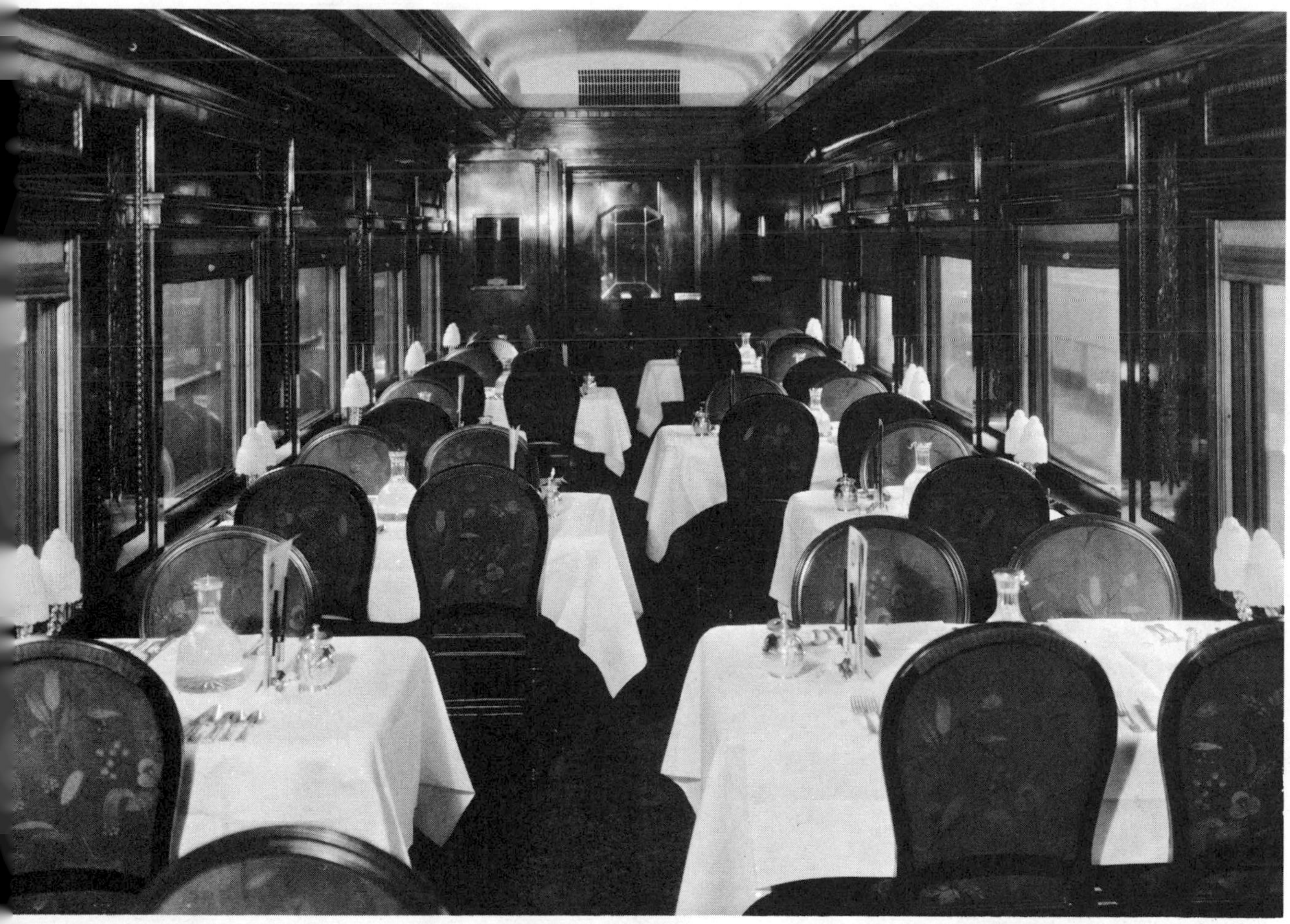

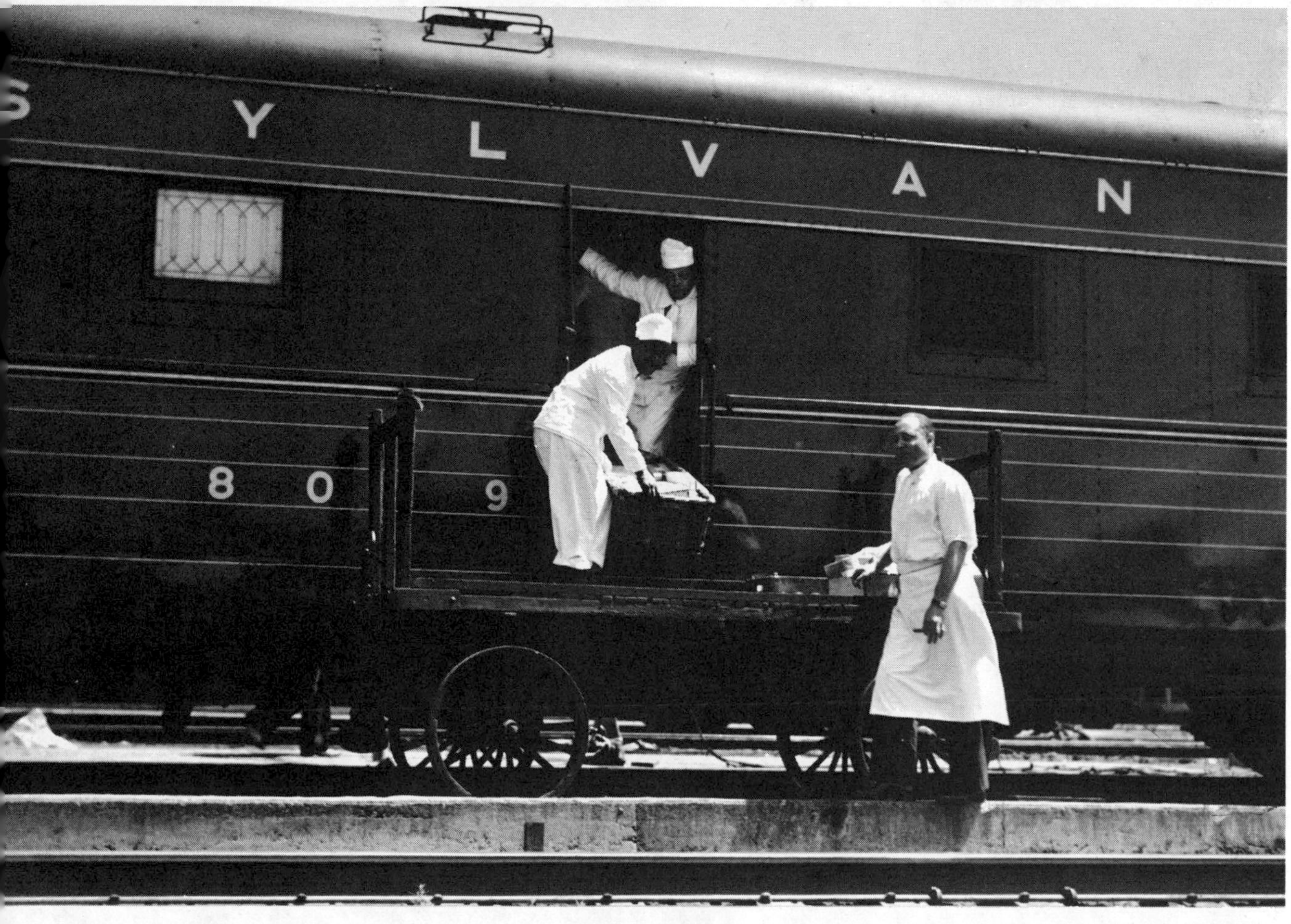
S Y L V A N
8 0 9

THICK AS autumn leaves on Vallombrosa stars of the theatrical and cinema worlds gathered aboard the lounge cars and diners of *The Broadway* in its spacious years, en route to luncheon with Ernie Byfield at The Pump Room before boarding *The Super Chief* for the ateliers of Hollywood.

On the opposite page in his years as one of the kingpins of the film world, Charlie Chaplin poses for a radiant portrait of fame still uncontaminated in a congenial setting of mobile opulence. Here *The Broadway* takes fuel on the fly at track pans just west of Paoli. At Chicago's Union Station in the apex days of railroad travel twenty-four information clerks answered 3,600 questions every day, 100,000 pouches of mail were cleared and patrons of the Harvey and other depot restaurants consumed 700 pies every twenty-four hours. *(Two Photos: Pennsylvania Railroad.)*

THE HANDSOME YOUTH and the pretty lady shown opposite, when they ordered *The Broadway* Dinner in 1925 paid no more than $1.75 for prime ribs with all the trimmings or perhaps a spendthrift $2.50 for Kansas City sirloin for two. In a time when the best food in America was being served on its dining cars, the carriers expected to lose money on meals and counted it money well spent. The rival *Twentieth Century Limited* expected to lose a dollar for every fifty cents it took in and *The Broadway* could hardly do less. At the top here, veteran steward C. F. Schmidt passes the Corona Corona puros, priced sixty cents and for the carriage trade only. Unlike the practice on *The Century* where no business car was ever carried until the regime of Al Perlman, *The Broadway* in 1921 if it were running in two sections might sometimes haul the varnish of high ranking brass in the second train. (*Top and Opposite: Pennsylvania Railroad; Below: Alfred W. Johnson.*)

641

AS FAR BACK as March 8, 1934 *The London Daily Mail* quoted the fast carding of *The Broadway Limited* in unfavorable comparison with accepted English service of the time which it claimed was lamentably slow. This was five years before the streamlined all-room, all-Pullman *Broadway* was inaugurated to give travel a dimension of luxury that would have startled Britons even more than its speed. It is shown below on its inaugural run for the press before entering service and without the buffet combine which shortly appeared in its consist in a photograph taken at Princeton by the senior author of this book.

Daily Mail

FOR KING AND EMPIRE

BROADCASTING PAG

LIGHTS UP 6.20 P.M.

"The Flying ————man" just under 7 hours from London ... faster than at present ...

In France "— ———— an av————

—— the "Côte d'Azur Pull———— Paris and Lyons, nearly 320

PERHAPS the most brilliant running in the world at present is made on the Pennsylvania Railroad.

"The Broadway Limited" is booked to run from Englewood to Fort Wayne, 141 miles, in 132 minutes. This schedule includes a very slow section at the start, so that to maintain the high inclusive speed of 64 miles an hour, the 116½ miles from Liverpool to Wayne Junction must be run in 101 minutes—an average speed of 69 miles an hour.

OVER THE YEARS and the decades the observation end of the *Broadway* and its antecedent *Pennsylvania Special* assumed many guises. For the first three decades of its life it ran with the brass railed open verandah which set the train of pedigree apart and indicated the regard in which it was held by the management. The keystone tailgate insigne was introduced in the 1920s, first as a ponderous illuminated steel herald affixed to the railing and plugged into the train electric line and finally as shown here built into the structural economy of the solarium end itself. The four track motif appeared with streamlining. *(Pennsylvania Railroad.)*

643

LACKING THE RED CARPET treatment which its owners accorded *The Century* at its sailings from Grand Central in New York and the later carnival departures from La Salle Depot in Chicago where floodlights, news photographers and interviews with celebrities over loudspeakers were for a time a daily practice, the departures of *The Broadway* from Union Depot, Chicago, were somewhat less than gala. The Pennsylvania, however, making a virtue of necessity, stressed the dignified and businesslike setting from which its crack train and showpiece departed and suggested, by inference, that *The Century* was ostentatious and vulgar. For many years in the field of prestige the two trains ran neck and neck until the great and shameful downgrading of *The Century* when daycoaches were for the first time included in its consist in 1957. After that, *The Broadway*, by default if nothing else, diverted most of the carriage trade to its Tuscan red, still all-Pullman cars. (*Pennsylvania Railroad.*)

644

IN 1938 the Pennsy's K-4s Pacific No. 3768, in a moment of exploratory whimsy and enthusiasm for the then universal vogue of streamlining, was given an "aerodynamic" cowl and briefly assigned to *The Broadway Limited.* The innovation lasted long enough to make the photographic record, but maintenance crews found it impossible to cope with and it went, unmourned, into oblivion. *(Left: Ivan Dimitri; Below: Pennsylvania Railroad.)*

THE SUSTAINED and bitter rivalry for supremacy on the New York-Chicago luxury run which had its beginnings when *The Twentieth Century Limited* and the first version of *The Broadway* inaugurated service on the same day and on identical schedules in June 1902 was a neck-and-neck race for fifty-five years until 1957 when the New York Central threw in the sponge and admitted defeat by carrying day coaches in what had always until then been an all-Pullman train. Largely the competition for prestige and patronage was confined to operational aspects and the amenities of luxury available to patrons, but in 1933 Ben Hecht and Charlie MacArthur wrote and George Abbott produced a sensational Broadway comedy called "Twentieth Century." Even in the depth of the depression the zany doings of Moffat Johnson, Eugenie Leontovich and Bill Frawley amongst the drawing rooms and public apartments of No. 26 eastbound were an instant hit and the play went on to become an equally successful Hollywood film. Maddened with jealousy of this more or less extra-curricular promotional coup, the Pennsylvania management negotiated with Hal Roach for participation in a screen comedy with the title "Broadway Limited." It was not a shattering success either as box office or promotion for the railroad. Shown below is Marjorie Woodworth in the starring role. Across the page, *The Broadway*, impervious to drama critics, rolls toward Manhattan near Princeton, New Jersey behind a classic GG1 electric motor in the Pullman Standard era. *(Right: Everett De Golyer Collection; Below: United Artists.)*

646

WHILE THE LOOPING catenaries and their furniture form a pleasing geometry of juice overhead, a streamlined, all-room car *Broadway Limited* heads into the last lap of its eastbound run over the Pennsylvania's main line at Monmouth Junction, New Jersey, reportedly at the period when this picture was taken, the busiest focus of railroad traffic in the world. Arriving on an earlier *Broadway* in Pullman Standard times, a genial notable was dapper and handsome Grover Whalen, official Major-Domo of New York City and greeter of celebrities in the reign of Mayor James J. Walker, shown here with morning trousers correctly hung and mustaches waxed despite the early hour. *(Left: Everett De Golyer Collection; Above: Pennsylvania Railroad.)*

"A Massive Affront To The Vanderbilts"

HALF A MILLION PEOPLE every day passed through the Pennsylvania Station in New York's Seventh Avenue, making it the busiest railroad terminal in the United States, and during the record year of 1945 when all the world was on the move a staggering 109,000,000 passengers were carried in and out of the station via its two tunnels under the North River and four under the East River to Long Island. Opened to service in 1910, Penn Station was designed by the great architectural firm of McKin, Mead & White as a *coup de maître* "its interior reflorescent of the Baths of Caracalla." Penn Station as well as providing a terminal for the Long Island Rail Road and a connection for the Pennsylvania and New Haven, sheltered a multiplicity of conveniences unknown to Caracalla, the fine Savarin Restaurant, luxury shops where everything imaginable might be purchased from an opera hat to rare first editions, communications centers of all sorts and a fully staffed emergency hospital. The graceful tracery of its glass domed concourse reminded travelers of London's Crystal Palace. So vast were the distances under its roof that Penn Station provided its own messengers to run errands and retrieve forgotten parcels as a sort of intra-mural Western Union. *(Two Photos: Pennsylvania Railroad.)*

650

A. J. CASSATT, patrician parent of
Pennsylvania Station, was the end
product of a long line of Philadelphia
grandees who had guided the
destinies of the carrier.
His spectacular affront to the
Vanderbilts, alas, was fated only by
a few decades to outlast the fortunes of the Vanderbilt family itself.

AN ABODE of Caracallan vistas, Penn Station abruptly reverted
to the twentieth century in its newsstands where, in 1910, no
fewer than eighteen competing New York newspapers were sold,
as well as *Leslie's, Judge, Everybody's* and many another periodi-
cal now remembered only by historians of journalism.

THE BUILDING of Penn Station in New York represented the determination of its aristocratic, horse racing, magnifico President Alexander J. Cassatt *(opposite)* to carry the railroad's brass knuckles warfare with the New York Central into the hereditary and hitherto sacrosanct domain of the Vanderbilts. As such, it had perforce to be conceived on a scale of grandeur and spaciousness comparable to the new Grand Central Terminal which was even then building on the other side of Manhattan Island. Pennsylvania Station had the moral effect of a mortal affront to the competition and the economic impact of diverting the riches of the West into the Port of New York, thereby reducing Philadelphia to the status of a secondary seaport and a third rate entrepot of continental commerce. "But the opening of the Penn Station in 1910 was still a glory for Philadelphia," wrote historian Nathaniel Burt, "a Trojan Horse right there on the island, a massive insult to the Vanderbilts." Until it was torn down in 1965 in the most barbarous act of vandalism in New York's long record of civic atrocities, Penn Station remained one of the glories of Manhattan, a landmark which gathered to itself its own body of legend and folklore as the prototype of the railroad station as the true cathedral of the American religion of movement. The Emperor Caracalla, after whose baths it was patterned, would have approved of it. *(Pennsylvania Railroad.)*

IN AN AGE innocent of loudspeakers and public address systems, approximately half the 850 trains that operated daily through the Pennsylvania Station were arrivals whose docking on their appropriate tracks was proclaimed by Stentor in company livery through a megaphone. The art of train calling was shortly to be relegated to the realm of folklore, one with the link and pin coupling and hand-fired locomotives, but it was an expertise much admired in its time and connoisseurs of train calling held strong opinions about the championship of the profession. Writing a good cursive hand was also a requirement as the bulletin board will suggest. On the page opposite, Penn Station when seen from above and illuminated for the night resembled a fairy palace. In the pre-electronic age, the sale and issuance of railroad tickets, like that of train calling, was contrived through human agency by expert functionaries arrayed in alpaca jackets crouching in grottos walled with racked tickets and rate books. Telephones were upright models and *The Official Guide* in the foreground was of a nobler dimension than it was to assume in the melancholy but unforeseen future. *(Three Photos: Pennsylvania Railroad.)*

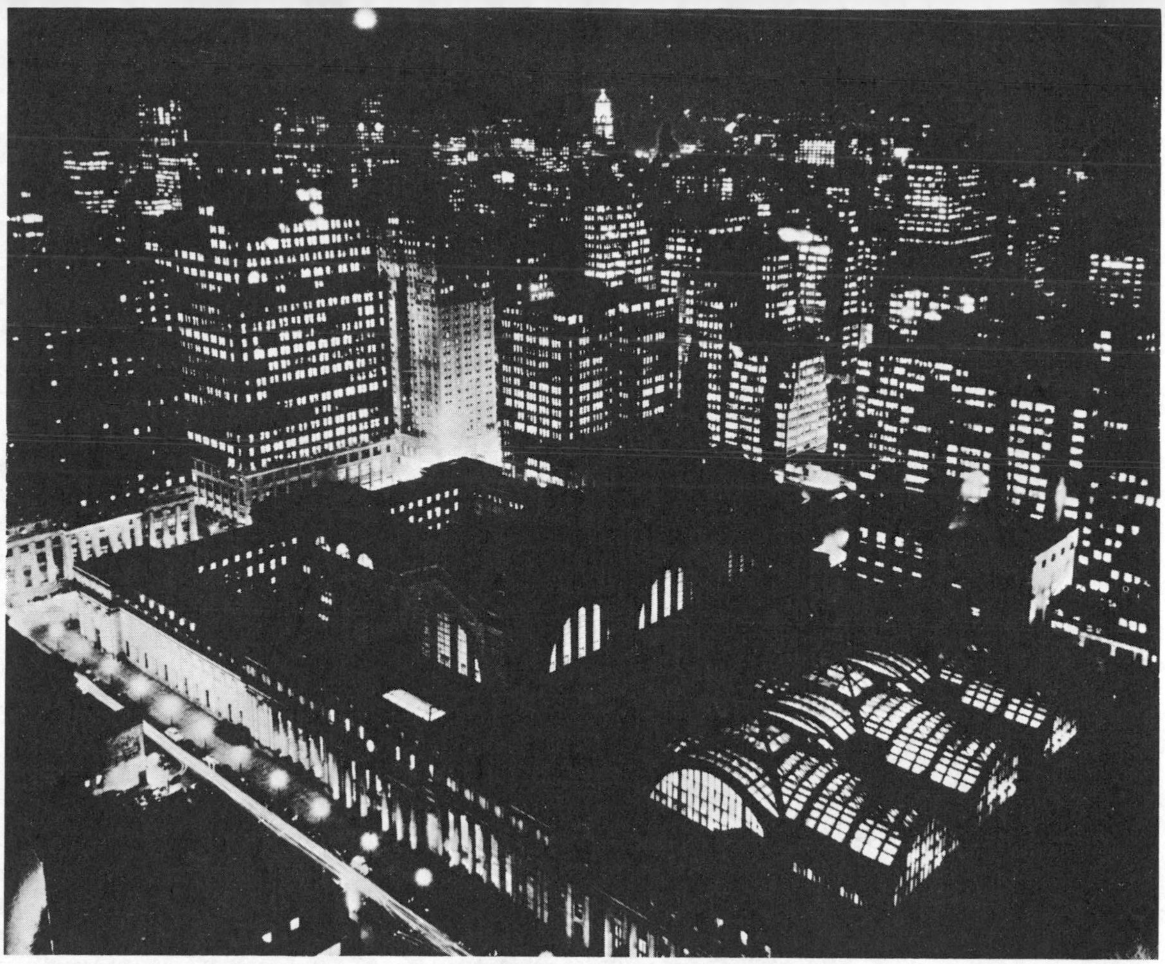

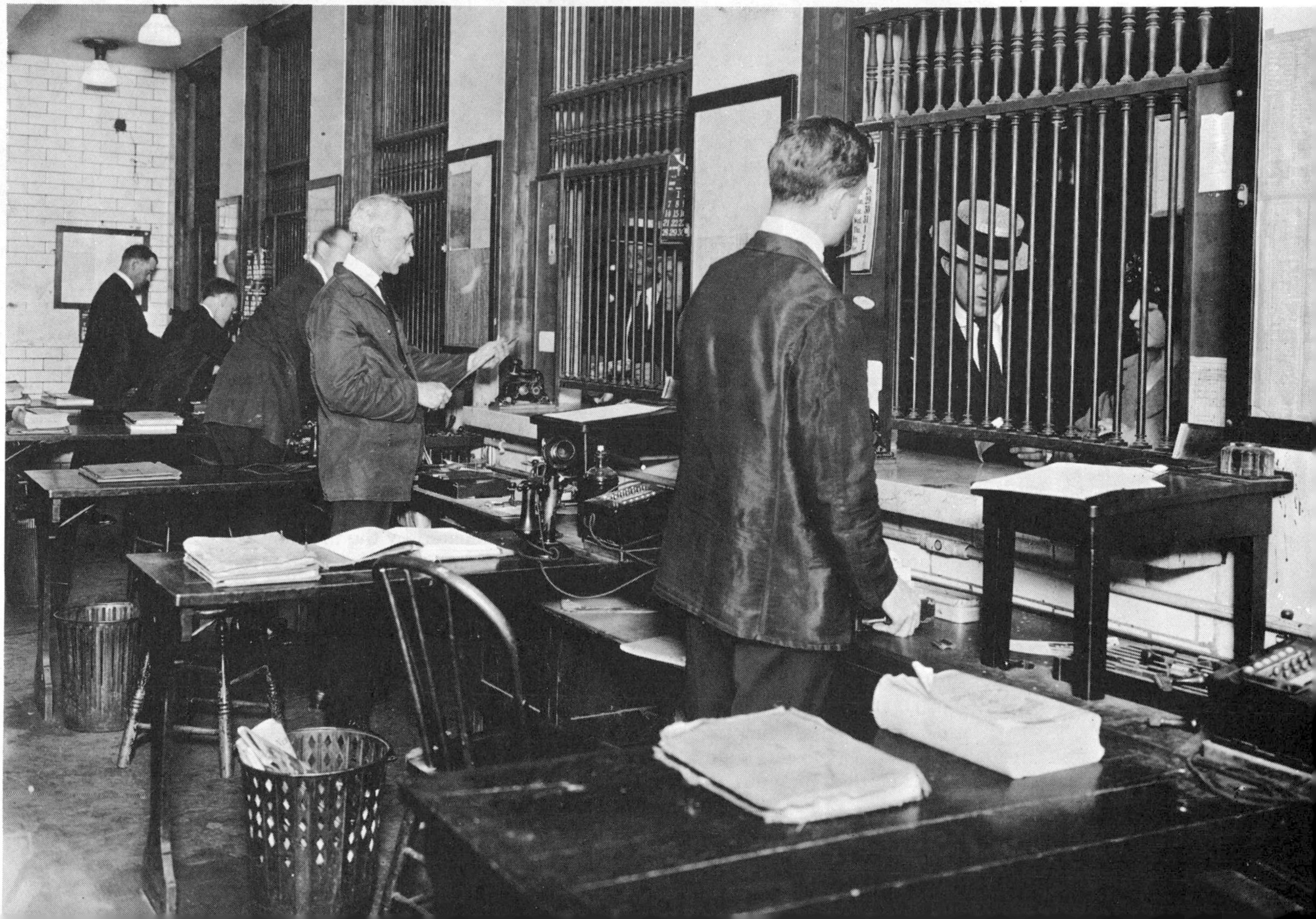

THE ENORMOUS VISTAS and majestic dimension of Penn Station as it
emerged from the drawing boards of McKim, Mead & White had a fantastic
impact on the imagination of travelers and even of blasé New Yorkers.
It amply endorsed the Pennsylvania's claim to being "The Standard Railroad of
The World." If the world of railroading was fascinated by the invasion it
represented with direct access to New England and Long Island by a hitherto
remote and perhaps parochial carrier, New Yorkers followed the construction of
the station's seven and a half acres of structural steel and stone as it had
never before followed an architectural project. No hint of the
impending assault upon the Vanderbilt citadel was contained in the news in
March 1900 of an increase in the Pennsylvania Railroad's capitalization
by $100,000,000.00. The plan to tunnel under two rivers, acquire the Long Island
and build the most majestic depot on the continent was only unveiled after
sufficient real estate between Seventh and Eighth Avenue had been
purchased, wiping out, incidentally, the very heart of New York's ancient
Tenderloin of vice. (Pennsylvania Railroad.)

656

BUILT AT A TIME when the automobile was obviously here to stay, Penn Station was enormously more accessible to motor traffic than Grand Central whose sole covered approach for departing patrons was through the narrow defile of Vanderbilt Avenue although an obscure grotto of the existence of which many New Yorkers never learned, was intended to accommodate arriving traffic under the Biltmore Hotel. Penn Station's distances were, however, seemingly greater and its several levels were eventually made available by escalators instead of the gentle ramps of Grand Central. Steep stairs from train gates such as that shown at the top of the page achieved all tracks in Penn Station and distances were so vast and problems of personal logistics so complex that a vast intercommunication system was maintained including a private uniformed messenger service. (*Two Photos: Pennsylvania Railroad.*)

657

IN ITS PASTORAL YEARS, before Long Island became one of New York City's ever multiplying bedrooms, its long beaches and wind-blown dunes were an extension of the South Shore of Cape Cod and its personality was predominantly that of New England. The trains of the Long Island Rail Road, although many of their operations were within sight of the skyscrapers of Manhattan on a clear day, were country trains and their concerns were with country things: garden truck from Mineola where now the inhabitants of a thousand apartment developments purchase their cabbages from a hundred market plazas, oysters from Blue Point and Great Peconic Bay that rode to town leaking brine from home-coopered casks, and only secondarily in heavy carloadings of any sort. Sea and sky met behind the tangents of the railroad that ran through places with seafaring names: Bellport, Brookhaven, Port Jefferson and Amagansett. The advancing trains, like the sea and sky, merged as in the photograph by O. Winston Link reproduced here. Until well after the century's turn the Long Island's station at West Islip was served by a single track precariously ballasted in sand, and, at the far end of the platform, there was an icehouse, as there was at every Long Island loading platform, to service the fresh seafood that rode toward Fulton Market night and day. (*Two Photos: Everett De Golyer Collection.*)

The
Long
Island
Was
A
Legend
of
Hard
Luck
and
Locust
Years

ONE DOES NOT instinctively think of the Long Island Rail Road, sometimes unwanted poor relation of the Pennsylvania and at length wholly rejected of its parent carrier, as the setting for great name trains associated with even the comparatively short-haul New Haven just the other side of Long Island Sound. The Long Island's longer of its two main lines between New York City and Montauk is a scant 117 miles, while its secondary main line to Greenport is but ninety-six. Its Port Jefferson run, the longest of its minor branches, is sixty miles in extent. Yet in the twenties, when the carrier's affairs were so chaotic that the parent Pennsylvania was resorting to financially evasive tactics that were to lead to complete eventual disinheritance, there were listed on its summer schedules a number of name trains with luxury equipment and at least one all-Pullman, extra fare varnish haul with club cars, diners and an open platform observation lounge that was the peer in pretentions of any daylight run name train elsewhere in the land. Some of the Long Island's name trains were merely timetable parodies of the grand manner, their equipment and scheduling of museum piece dimensions that became part of the fabric of local folklore, but they still staggered down the years trailing traces of seedy grandeur in losing competition with the massive network of parallel highways. In the mid-thirties there were scheduled over the Jamaica to Greenport run *The Banker, The Shelter Island Express, The Cannon Ball* and *The Peconic Bay Express.* To Montauk there were *The Hampton Express, The South Shore Express,* each with a parlor car, *The Cannon Ball* with a parlor buffet car, and the glory of the railroad, *The Sunrise Special* and *The Shinnecock Express,* each of which was all-Pullman, extra fare with dining cars, parlor lounges, and, in the case of *The Sunrise Special,* a barbershop and fine open platform observation-parlor car. When used by the

Long Island management the word "express" was almost invariably euphemistic. *The Wading River Express,* for example, made its first stop at Westbury, just eighteen minutes out of Jamaica, and thereafter all stops until it achieved its Wading River destination. Sleeping cars appear only infrequently in the Long Island record. At one time there was a through Pullman from Pittsburgh to accommodate a small but determined group of summer commuters to East Hampton. Another short lived venture involved Pullman sleepers carried between Boston and Brooklyn over the New York & New England connection in *The Long Island & Eastern States Express,* a *rara avis* among name trains today remembered almost exclusively by collectors of such matters. This car ferry run over the Old Air Line through Connecticut lasted only four months and was terminated after a disastrous wreck. Folklore and legend cluster thickly around the Long Island, not all of it flattering, so that in its locust years it became part of the national lexicon of humorous derogation like Brooklyn, Southern fried chicken and Texas millionaires. But good humor and happy times were associated with even its darkest years. Philip Dunne, writing of his famous father, Finley Peter Dunne, creator of the immortal Mr. Dooley, remarked that a sartorial panache of which the elder Dunne was particularly disdainful was the club hatband. "Men who were entitled to a somewhat doubtful privilege used to ameliorate the harsh and unlovely headgear known, in summer months, as a skimmer, with colorful hatbands. On Friday evenings when *The Cannon Ball* rolled in from New York, the Southampton Station bloomed like a garden with the colors of the Links, the Knickerbocker, the Racquet and other famous clubs. I could always pick out my father at a distance by his Spartan black hatband, the only one in sight."

SPEONK STATION in the Long Island's salad days was a vignette of pastoral dimensions with its quota of lobster crates drying beside the single track. In the lower frame in the year 1904 a Wading River summer-time only local pulls out of Huntington Station behind a typical Long Island American type 4-4-0 while a buckboard drawn by a white horse waits at the crossing. *(Top: Everett De Golyer Collection; Below: Ron Ziel Collection.)*

INCLUDING the Great Blizzard of 1888, the Long Island was repeatedly over the years tied up by blizzards of legendary ferocity which isolated remote townships for days on end. The snow blockade at the left was at an unidentified date but bears visual witness to the elemental winters combatted by the railroad. Below: the Long Island station at Centerport in 1878 was a country thing beside two tracks whose ballast and alignment might grieve an exacting roadmaster. (*Two Photos: Everett De Golyer Collection.*)

AT THE TURN of the century and as long as steam lasted on the Long Island, camelback motive power such as that at Jamaica shown above in 1903 kept the carrier in good standing in the Mother Hubbard Club along with Lackawanna, Erie, and other eastern coal haul roads. Not all the occupants of parlor car space aboard *The Cannon Ball* derived from the social Hamptons and the lordly summer homes of Quogue. Some, as is suggested opposite, were descendents of the oldest of all New England whaling families that had settled at Montauk and Gardiner's Island in Colonial times and viewed the Rolls-Royce set at East Hampton as the veriest parvenus. *The Sunrise Special*, shown opposite as it nears Jamaica, brought with it a cachet of big-time railroad operations in its all-Pullman consist and the glittering keystone emblem on the observation rail. *(Above: Ron Ziel Collection; Right: Everett De Golyer Collection; The Smithsonian Institution.)*

664

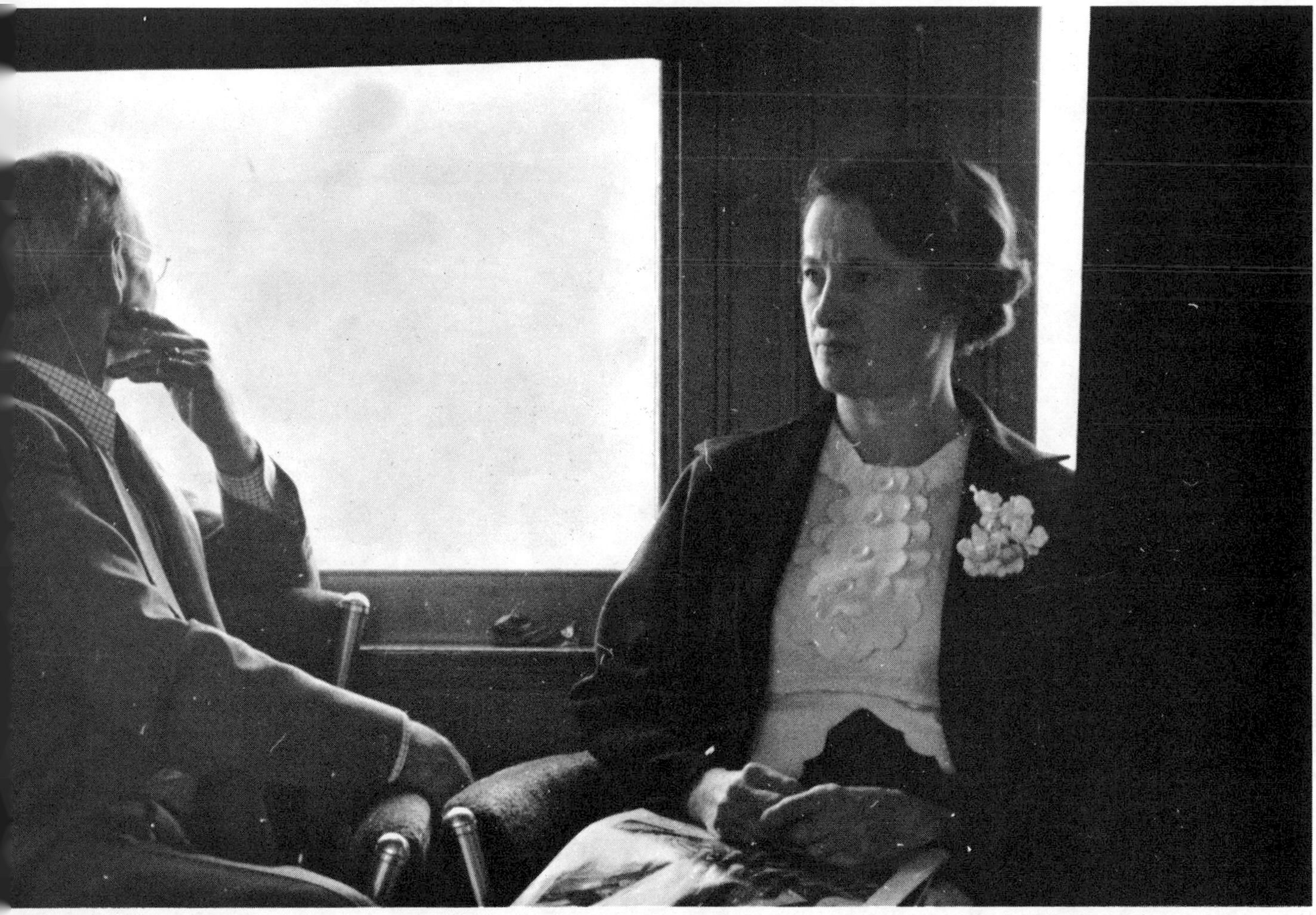

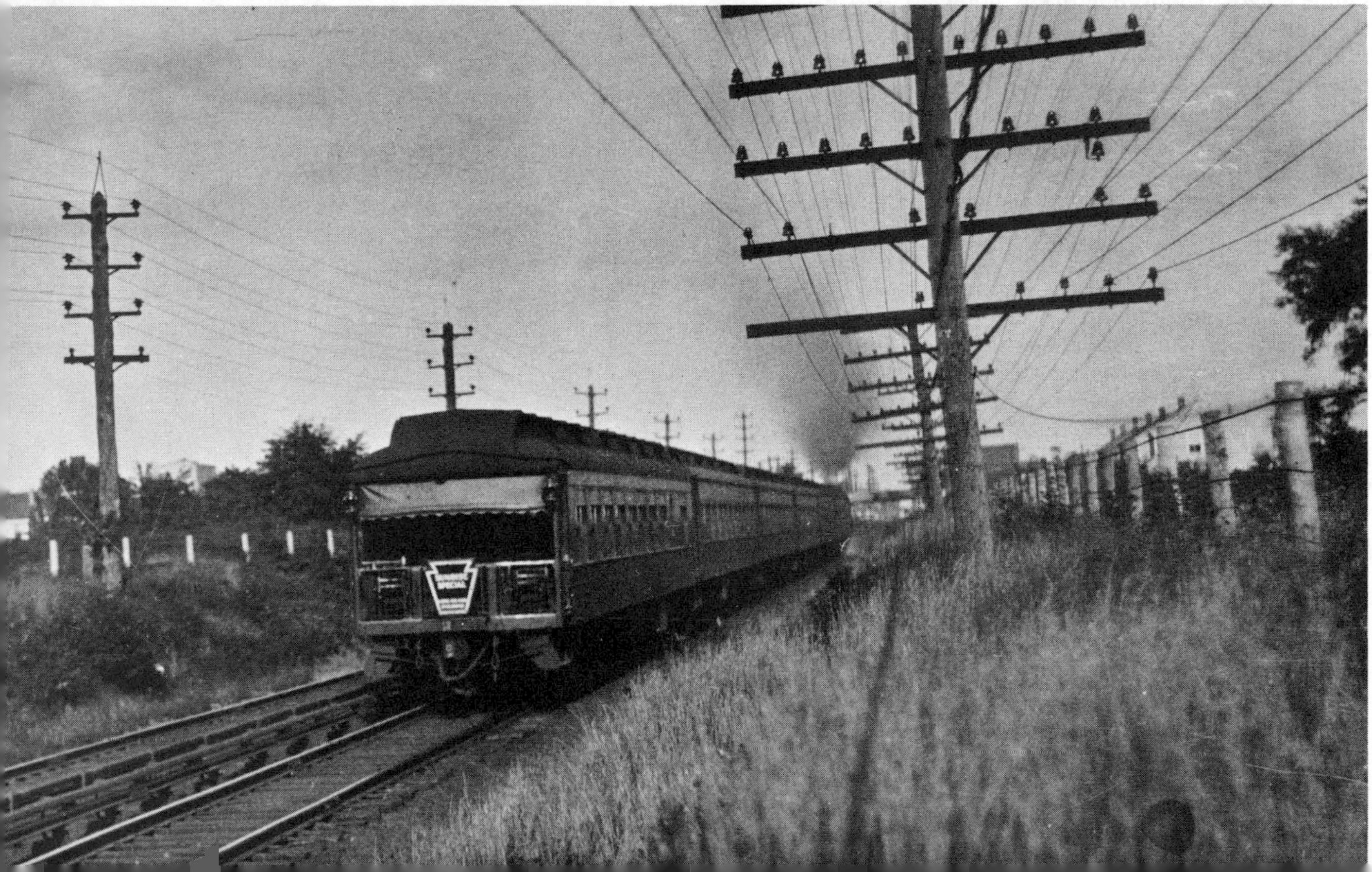

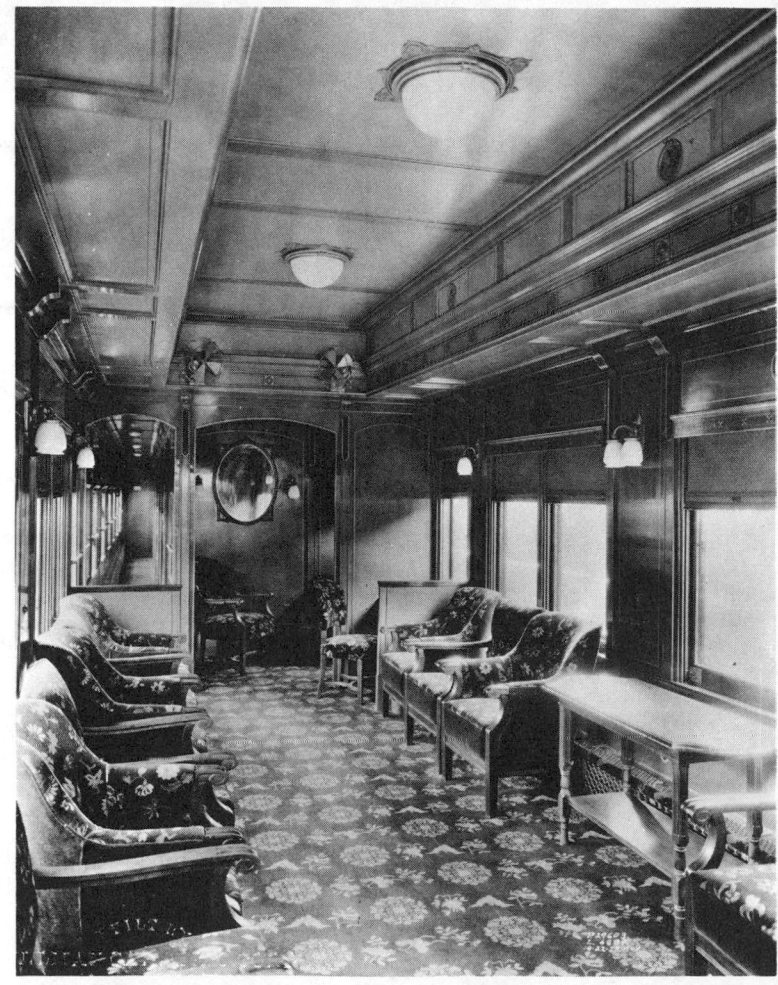

PULLMAN equipment on such runs as *The Sunrise Special* was, in the later years of the Long Island's faltering fortunes, hand-me-down Pennsylvania club cars and diners so that passengers had to look out the window to be sure they were not aboard *The Congressional* or a Philadelphia Clocker. *The Peconic Bay Express* (*above*) in the days when it ran behind a camelback ten wheeler carried its Pullman equipment on the head end, coaches at the rear, reversing this order in one direction to save turning the train at its terminals. The depot at Babylon and Fire Island is shown at a time when the only year-round inhabitants of Fire Island were the members of a Coast Guard Station at what was later to become celebrated as Cherry Grove. Wolcott Gibbs, for many years the *New Yorker's* drama critic and the singer and minstrel of Fire Island, at one time served an apprenticeship firing on the Long Island, experience which gave him a profound insight into the conduct of this whimsical and wayward carrier. (*Above: Smithsonian Institution; Right: Pullman Standard; Opposite: Everett De Golyer Collection.*)

666

DESPITE the evidence in the foreground that much of the traffic at the Long Island Rail Road's grade crossings was of a horse-drawn character, the year 1915 saw such a rise in automobile accidents, most of them due to optimism on the part of drivers in the matter of beating the cars to the crossing, that the railroad management undertook an extensive campaign of public education combined with a widespread replacement of crossing gatemen by really formidable barriers. Where an ancient with a lantern had been ineffectual to prevent motorists from contesting the right of way, boldly painted spars such as the one shown here soon cut the incidence of accidents in gratifying degree. (*John Barriger Collection.*)

SHOWN WEARING the straw boater hat with its plain
black ribbon which identified him in the club car of
The Cannon Ball, Finley Peter Dunne was one of the
Long Island's best friends and severest critics,
maintaining a literary relationship with the carrier that
was comparable to that of Philadelphia's
Christopher Morley with the Paoli Local. Once as the result
of tarrying at the bar of the Brook Club with his friend
Harry Payne Whitney, Dunne missed
The Cannon Ball when an arrogant attendant slammed
the train gate in his face. Dunne, who was in wine
at the time, demanded that the Long Island atone for the
affront with a special train to East Hampton, but
he was finally gentled by Big Bill Egan,
the Pennsy stationmaster, and sent on his way in a
company limousine.

DINING CARS on appropriate runs of *The Cannon Ball*, *Shinnecock Express* and *Sunrise Special* were, of course, hand-me-down Pennsylvania equipment and so infrequent even in the glory years of the twenties and thirties as to be an object of remark and subject of regional pride. The Long Island commissary was a subdivision of the Pennsylvania's dining car service and as such reflected Pennsylvania competence without any pretense at transcendental gastronomy. Although he was more of a regular on the Saturday afternoon *Cannon Ball*, Finley Peter Dunne occasionally rode the almost as elite *Hampton Express*, shown above pulling out of Bay Shore almost at the end of its run to Montauk. On the page opposite the creator of the immortal Mr. Dooley is shown in the skimmer with its solid black hatband which, Dunne claimed, made him a more distinguished figure of remark on the platform at East Hampton than the multicolored symbols of the Harvard, Racquet and Leash that surrounded him in the club car. (*Above: Everett De Golyer Collection; Opposite: Pennsylvania Railroad, Little Brown.*)

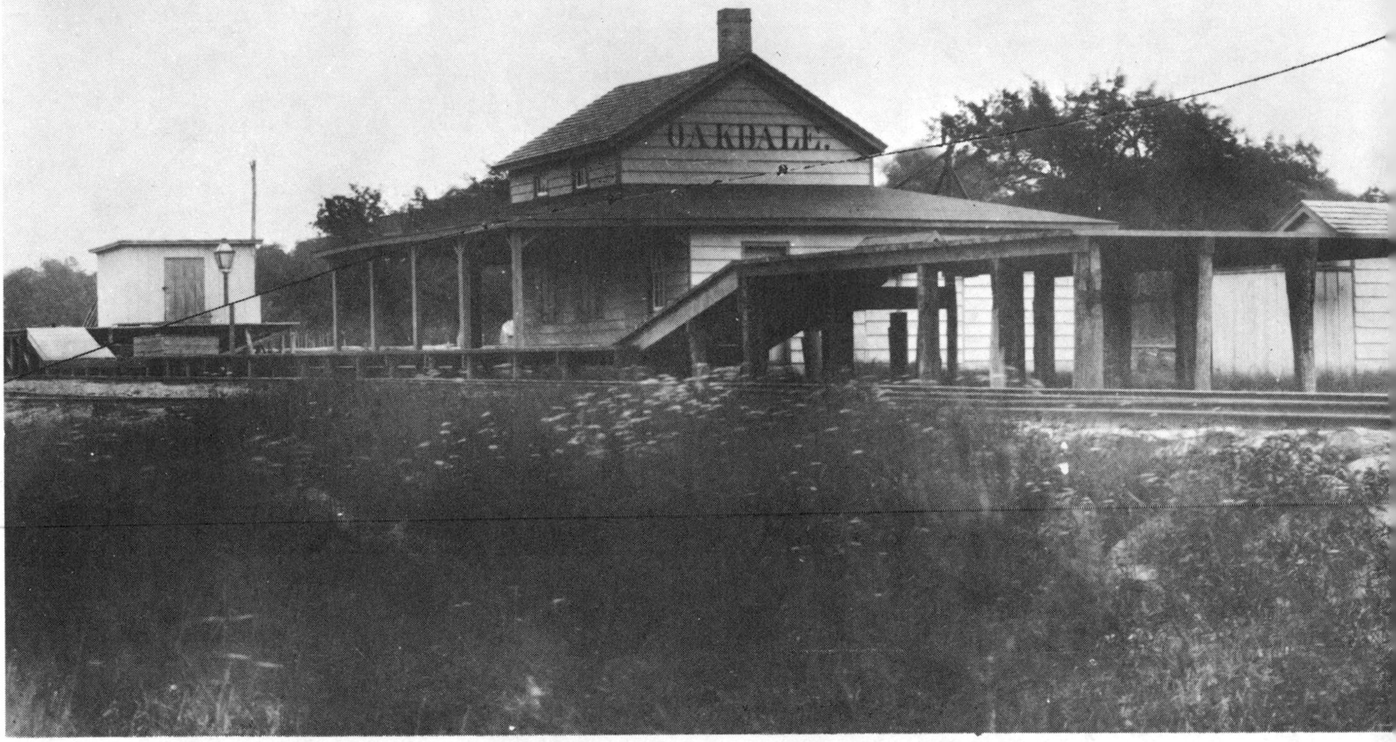
OAKDALE.

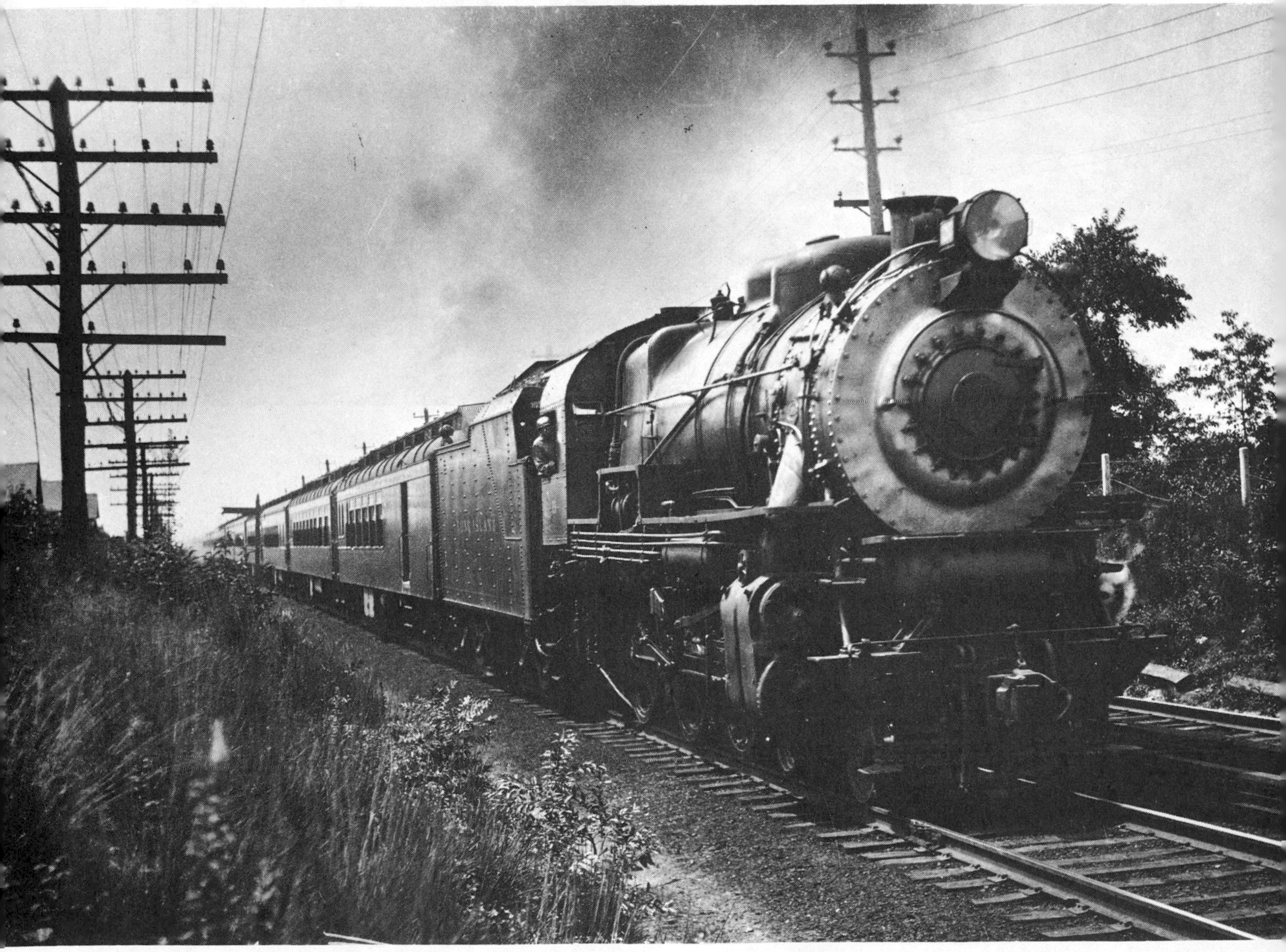

OAKDALE Station, on the Long Island's Montauk main line as it appeared in 1880 was only a memory by the time Charles B. Chaney took the fine action photograph of the *Sunrise Special* in 1927 at the left, but once it had been one of the more important structures along the railroad's rustic right of way. Few Long Island depots of the period boasted such architectural amenities as covered platforms, whitewashed outhouses or storey-and-a-half construction. At the platform end with its vault door was the characteristic ice house where seafood was chilled until shipment was possible to Fulton Market. *The Sunrise Special* ran in all-Pullman splendor with a barber and conventional dining car and was powered by specially assigned Class G-5 ten wheelers such as that depicted above. Their tender sides were engrossed with identifying heraldry incorporating the train's name amidst the rays of a symbolic rising sun. *(Above, Opposite: Everett De Golyer Collection; Three Photos: The Smithsonian Institution.)*

671

THE OPENING in 1910 of the Pennsylvania Station in New York City
with its connecting tunnels under the East and North Rivers
was part of the long-range strategy of the Pennsylvania Railroad for
control of Long Island traffic. In the early years of its control
from Broad Street the Long Island was beneficiary
of many improvements which included a vast electrification project
radiating out of Jamaica and, of course, the disappearance of the
ferry connection or bridge route between Manhattan Island
and the Long Island's western terminal. The impress of the
Pennsylvania on the Long Island's personality continued to manifest
itself long after the romance between the two carriers
had cooled and is apparent in the two magnificent action shots of
Long Island varnish on this and the opposite page by O. Winston Link.

THE KEYSTONE INSIGNE riding the observation platform tailgate of the *The Sunrise Special,* shown here awaiting its highball at Jamaica, was, like the train it identified, a rarely encountered symbol of the grand manner with its extra fare implications in the iconography of the Long Island. Years later, a reactivated *Cannonball* (with its name a single word) was also to carry a drumhead herald but its theme was one of parody lacking the august overtones of the chaste Pennsylvania keystone. On lesser Long Island varnish runs, the rear brakeman, as at the left, merely hung out his rear markers to show that his cut of cars had an engine and had been translated into a train; on the *Sunrise* he plugged in the cord and the illuminated keystone vanishing in splendor down the right of way ennobled the string of Pullmans to the status of *The Broadway Limited* or any other train you care to name of pedigree. (*Above:* W. J. Rugen; *Left:* Pennsylvania Railroad.)

THE IMMEMORIAL functions of a car tonk inspecting the journal boxes of one of the Pullman parlor cars of *The Sunrise Special* prior to its departure from Montauk on a summer's day reassured the carrier's often important passengers that the management had their best interests at heart. (*Lucius Beebe.*)

674

PENN STATION, Penn side, you told the cab driver if you wanted to be set down at the depot's pillared south portal where redcaps established liason between arriving mainline patrons and the train gates.
To achieve the Long Island trains you were set down at the north entry.
Time, ubiquitous, in Penn Station, was exact on all station clocks save only those in the Savarin Restaurant bar where, as a precaution, they ran five minutes ahead.

THE BLEAK winter speed shot, probably of *The Hampton Express*, by O. Winston Link reproduced at the top of the opposite page with its backdrop of industrial skyline provides a dramatic contrast to an earlier Long Island scheme of things represented by some of the railroad's rustic depots shown on the adjacent pages of this book. When the railroad came into being in the early decades of the nineteenth century it served a community that was almost altogether pastoral from Jamaica to Montauk. By 1950 the entire length of its right of way was industrialized and Long Island as a country residential community almost ceased to exist.

OTHER CARRIERS in the record might wheel their favored varnish runs behind museum piece motive power such as the Lackawanna's affection for camelback engines on even its well accredited *Lackawanna Limited* and the Pennsylvania's habit well into the 1920s of scheduling crack flyers behind the road's celebrated Atlantics, but few railroads of consequence maintained such extensive stables of archaism as the Long Island where all-Pullman consists were headed up by venerable camelbacks and express runs of pedigree rode behind ten wheelers. At the top of the opposite page *The Shinnecock Express,* one of the Long Island's more optimistically named varnish

hauls, is shown behind the road's ten wheeler No. 23 Below is reproduced the observation end of the special train which in 1924 was originated on the Long Island to convey the then Prince of Wales from the North Shore residence of oil millionaire Joshua Cosden to the White House to call on President Coolidge. Although not visible in this photograph taken as the special paused for change of motive power at Manhattan Transfer, it had started earlier in the day behind a Long Island 4-4-0 that had been in service since 1904. (*Above: O. Winston Link; Opposite Two Photos: The Smithsonian Institution.*)

676

RR 23-TR. 12   7-9-27   132

OPERATING OVER a complex interlocking network of
New Jersey carriers whose components were the Pennsylvania-
Reading Seashore Lines and the highly involved exchange
of services over the complex formed by the Reading-Central of
New Jersey-Baltimore & Ohio, there once sped on tight
schedules a not inconsiderable fleet of name trains
connecting metropolitan New York and Philadelphia with the
watering places of the New Jersey Coast.
The most celebrated single component of these services was the
Pennsylvania-Reading Seashore Lines over a
sixty-mile-an-hour speedway over almost flawless tangents
between Philadelphia-Camden and Atlantic City.
Name trains included *The Boardwalk Flyer, The Nellie Bly*
and *Quaker City Express.* Shown here in the tule marshes
of New Jersey is *The Atlantic City Express,* while action on the
Boardwalk for which *The Flyer* was named and where
countless newlyweds promenaded on their wedding
trips is suggested in the 1905 vignette captioned
"Dolly's Go-Cart" by its photographer.   *(Library of Congress.)*

679

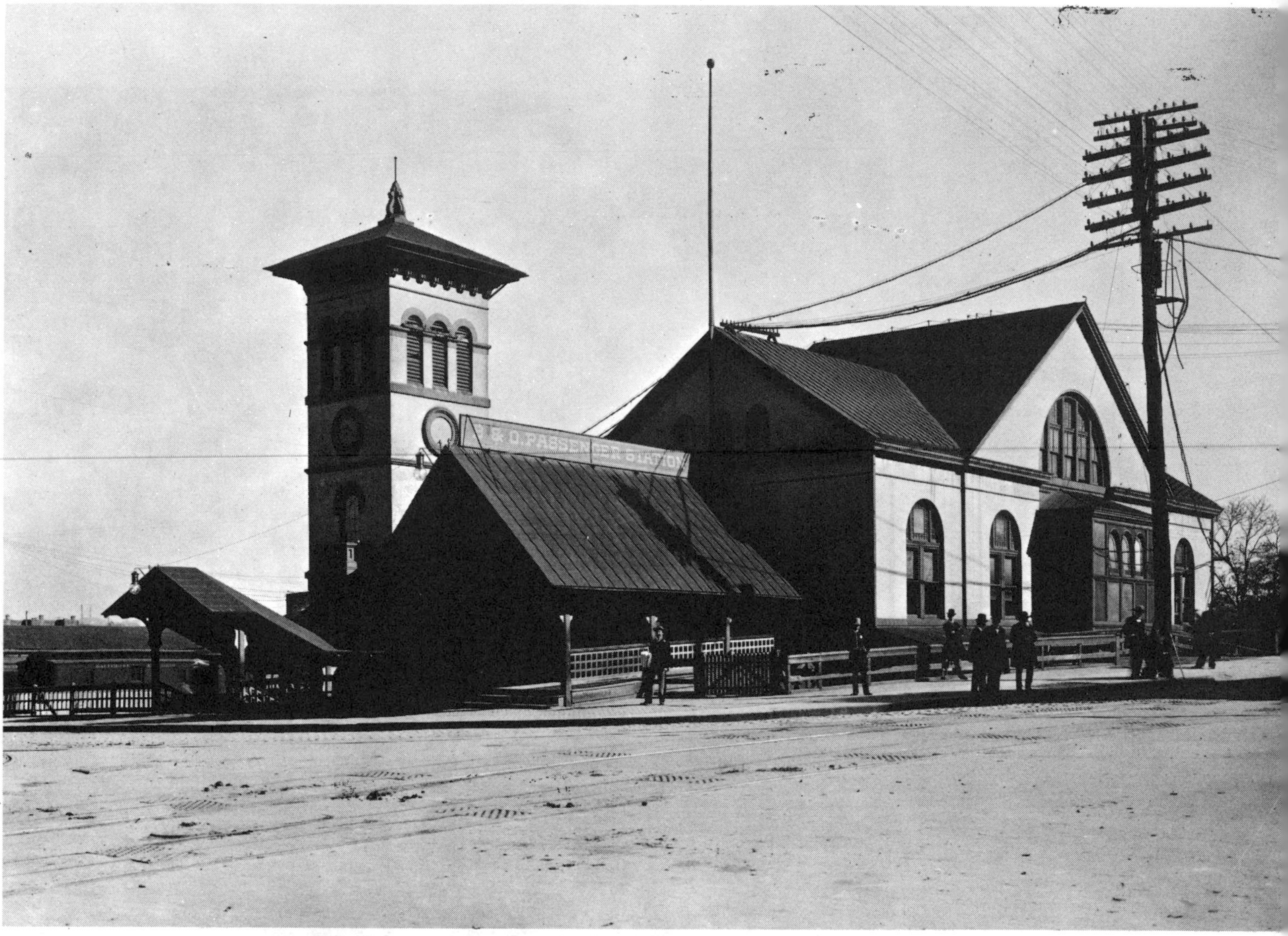
& O. PASSENGER STATION

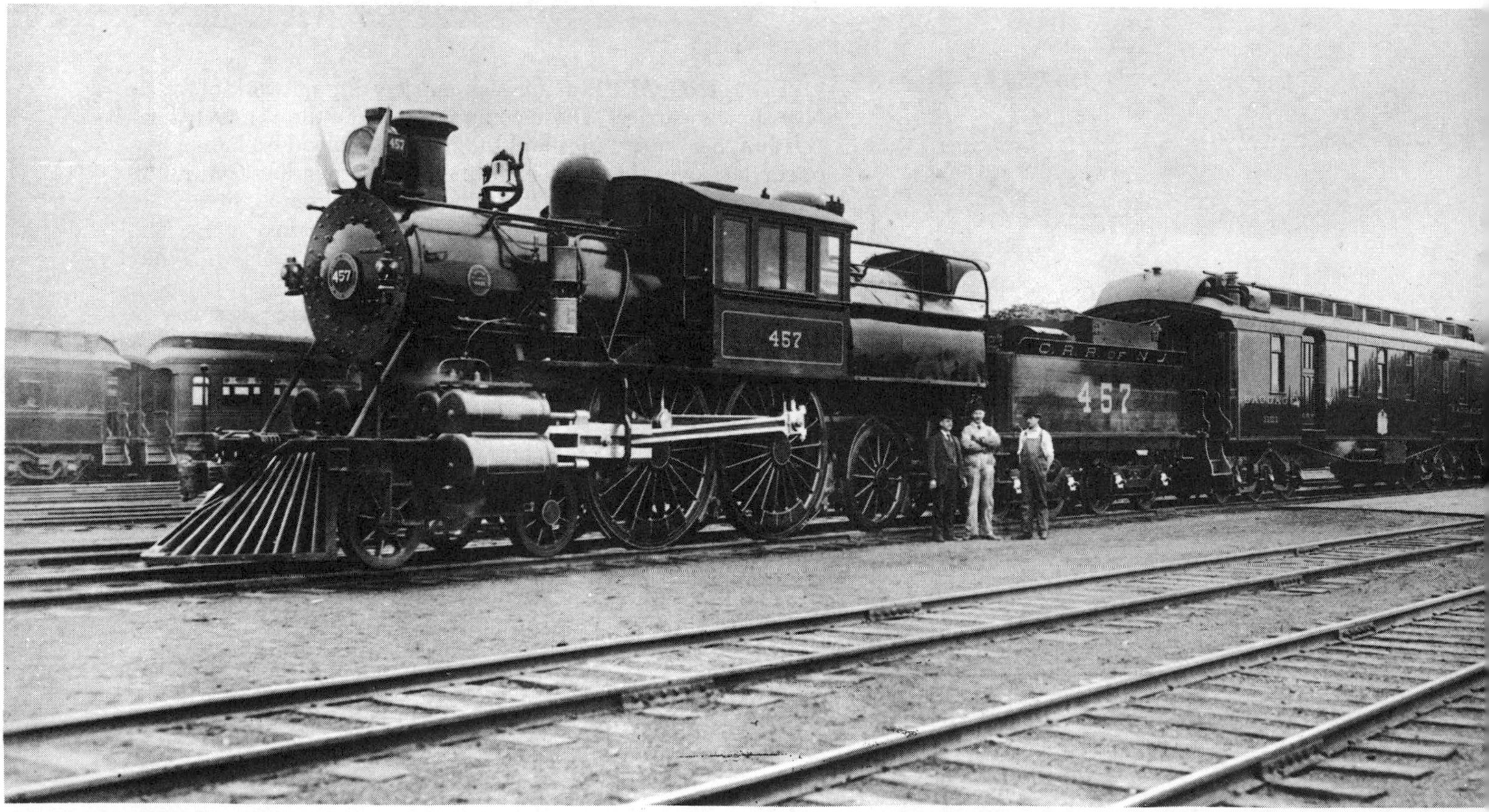
457
C.R.R. of N.J.
457

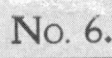

BOOK OF THE ROYAL BLUE

BALTIMORE & OHIO R.R.

SPECIAL NATIONAL EDUCATIONAL ASSOCIATION EDITION.

THE VENERABLE Baltimore & Ohio depot at Washington, shown on the page opposite, where Vice President Hobart would be set down at the end of the run of *The Royal Blue* was one of the old landmarks of Washington in a more tranquil time. The tall helmet of the policeman, the dignified news vendor and hard hatted loungers all bespoke an easy-going age in a semi-Southern capital city. *(Smithsonian Institution.)*

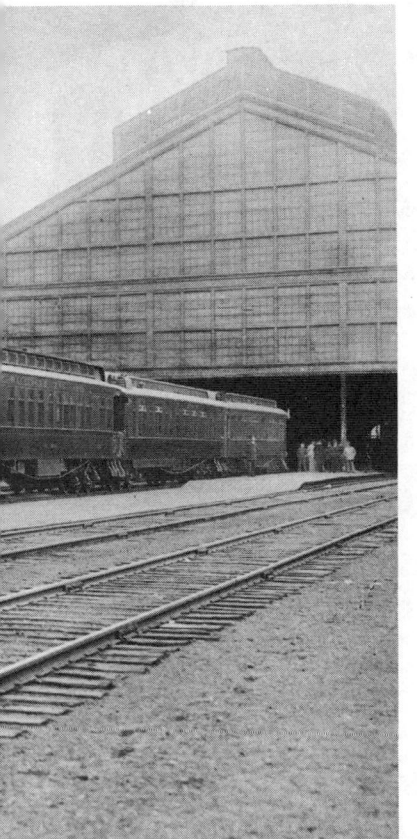

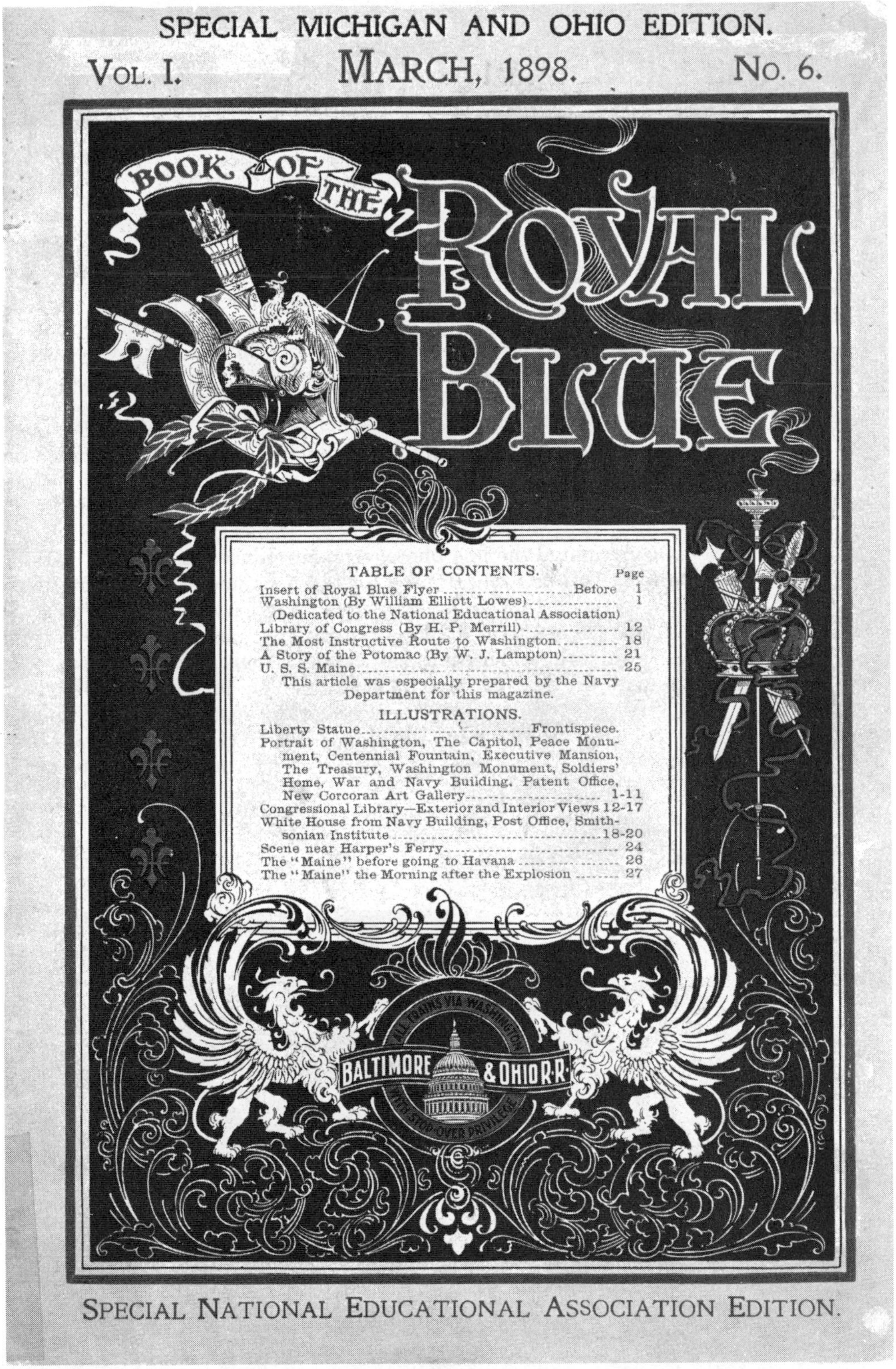

THE BEAUTIFUL all-Pullman consist pictured at the left at Jersey City on March 2, 1897, poised for a swift run to Washington, might well be taken as the paradigm of what a varnish train was felt to be at that now remote date, the most mature realization of the dreams of designers of effective motive power and the expertise of the Palace car builder. The photograph was taken by the ranking railroad photographer of the era with Central Railroad of New Jersey's proud camelback No. 457 on the head end and the train was specially assembled and run over the connecting lines of the Reading, C. of N.J. and Baltimore & Ohio for the accommodation of Vice President Hobart on what may be presumed to have been an occasion of urgency. The jacket design of the Baltimore & Ohio's house organ of the period suggests the pride of a rich and powerful carrier. *(Above: Fred Arone Collection; Left: Brown Bros.)*

THE MOST FAVORED of all American summer resorts in the mid-nineteenth
century and the summer capital of the nation in every Presidency
from that of Grant to Chester A. Arthur, Long Branch on the New Jersey
seacoast and its neighboring rival Cape May, for many decades reigned in
undisputed social supremacy as watering places until after the
Civil War when Newport achieved its ascendency. The Jersey seaside, later to be
reached aboard *The Blue Comet* and *The Nellie Bly* over the same
right of way, was originally the terminal of the old New York & Long Branch
Railroad at a time when summer cottage owners at Long Branch,
Spring Lake and Asbury Park didn't need to tip their hats in the direction of
Saratoga Springs, let alone Bar Harbor. In 1894 F. W. Blauvelt
copyrighted the fine photograph reproduced at the right with the caption
"The New York & Long Branch Express Scooping Water at 25 Miles an Hour."
The line drawing opposite shows the arrival, as depicted in
Leslie's Weekly, of the *Express* at Long Branch depot. Below on this page,
in a rite older even than calling signals with his fireman or comparing
watches with the train captain, a Central of New Jersey eagle eye oils around the
valve gear of his massive Atlantic type camelback.
Shall we say the date is 1914? *(Opposite: Brown Bros.; Below:
Everett De Golyer Collection.)*

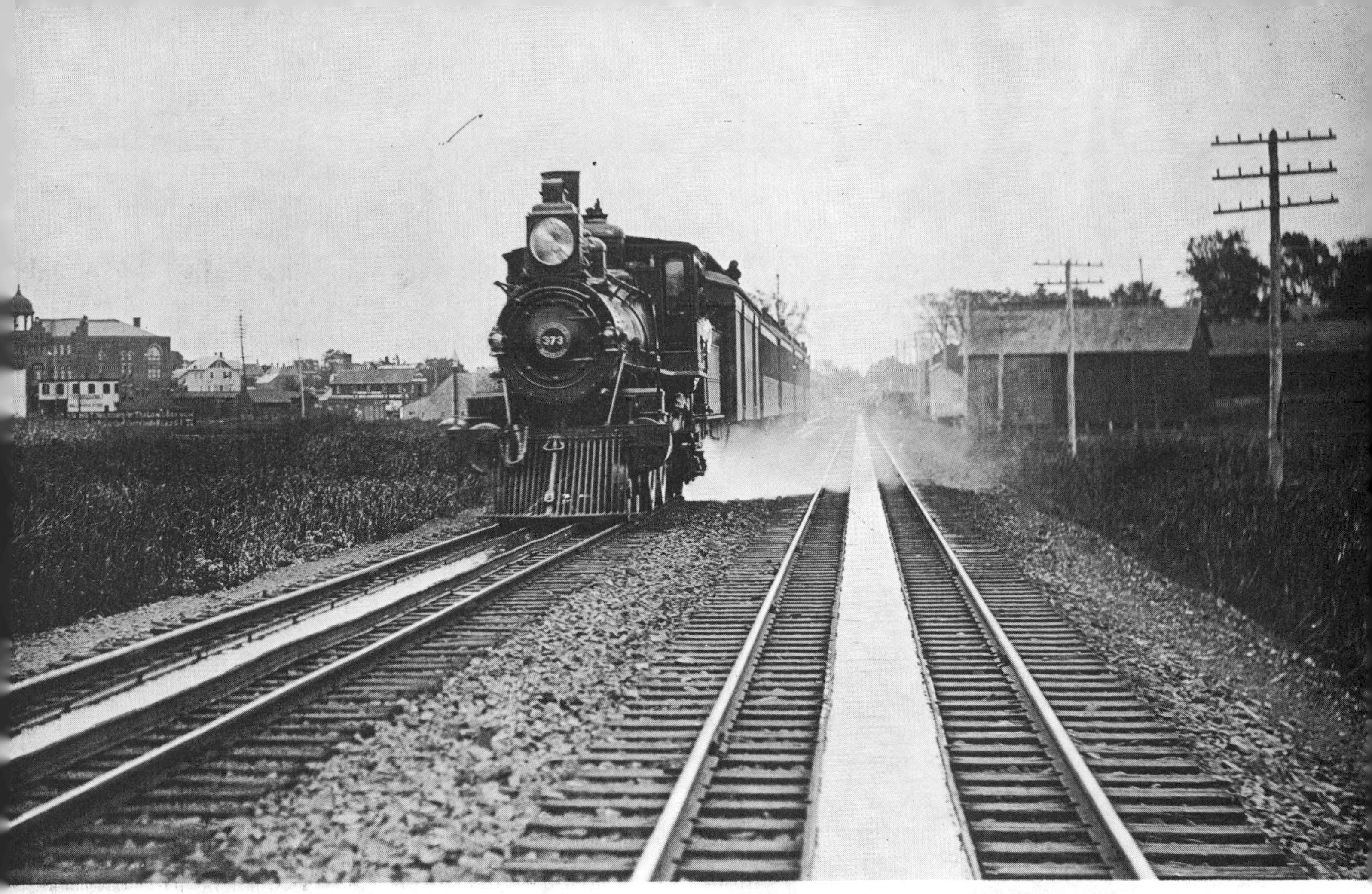
373

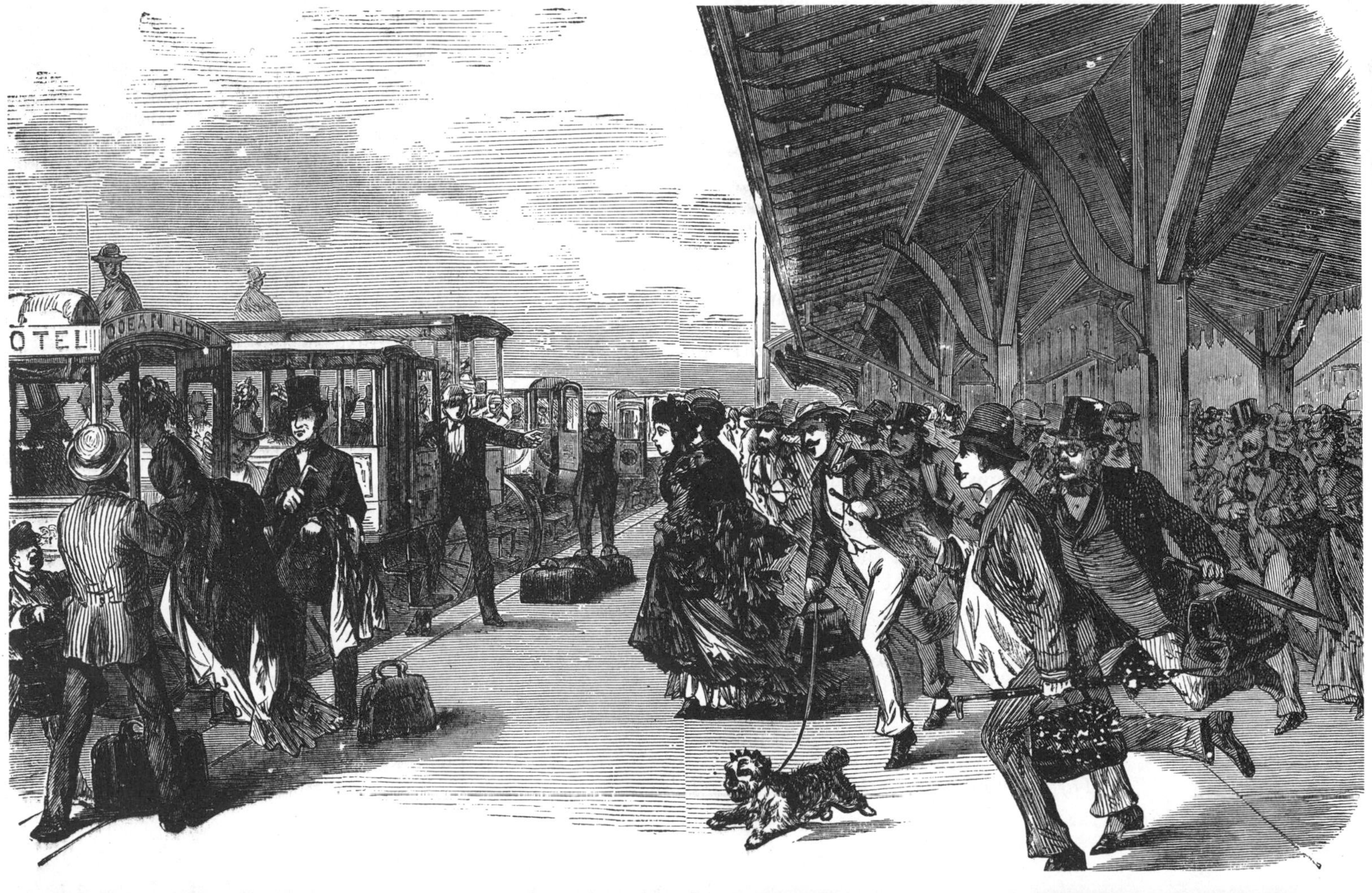
OTEL

ALTHOUGH as essentially "Old Philadelphia" in the social and moneyed implications of the phrase as the imperial Pennsylvania, the Reading Railway System, which is an integral part of the structural economy of the Reading Company, was at one time considered socially unthinkable, a sort of negative status symbol which, in the twenties and thirties, became curiously reversed into a hallmark of prestige and snobbism. "In the old days nice young Philadelphia girls were permitted to travel unescorted on Mr. Roberts' railroad (the Pennsy) but not the Reading," wrote Nathaniel Burt in "The Perennial Philadelphians." "But nowadays connoisseurs take the Reading to New York as being far more convenient and pleasant, to Wall Streeters at least. It has acquired the same detached superior, slightly intellectual prestige as Chestnut Hill itself, and partisans of the Reading regard the Pennsylvania as distinctly middle class." Another commentator noted that Philadelphians who ride the Reading "are more inclined to be readers of *The Philadelphia Public Ledger* than of *The Bulletin*," a subtle distinction which may be lost on outlanders but has vast validity in the precincts of Rittenhouse Square. The spirit of aloof superiority to time and change, not to mention rising real estate values, is suggested here by the depot at Hopewell, New Jersey, explicitly Victorian, mansarded and terraced with a manorial lawn on which peacocks might have paraded with complete propriety. The Reading's penchant for camelbacks is suggested by all three photographs on these pages. (*Three Photos: Everett De Golyer Collection.*)

AT THE TURN of the century, a multiplicity of ornate candlesticks on the pilot bar, usually fashioned from finely turned brass or bronze, characterized both Reading and Central of New Jersey motive power as is suggested in the two period photographs reproduced below. High speed compound Atlantic type camelbacks such as that on the commuter train at the bottom afforded a warm ride for the engineer, but opportunities for conversation with the fireman were few.

THE CONSERVATISM which retained bicycle type locomotives and camelbacks as suggested opposite, maintained fine fast Atlantic types such as No. 353 shown above long after Pacifics were fashionable. Typical, too, was the inclusion of Philadelphia scrapple on the breakfast menus of the Reading's diners and buffet meat breakfast menus *(right)*. The carrier's pedigree suggested Pennsylvania conservatism deriving from the company's founder, the aristocratic Moncure Robinson who was educated at William and Mary and married a cousin of Thomas Jefferson. The original survey of the road, eventually to the coal regions of Mt. Carbon, was a monument to his sagacity and Reading hard coal maintained ample dividends for more than a century. *(Above: Everett De Golyer Collection; Right: The Reading Co.)*

686

CEREALS—Cream or Milk (Hot or Cold) Served with all Cereals
Grape Nuts, Shredded Wheat, Oatmeal, Corn Flakes, Post Toasties, All Bran, Pep, Rice Flakes, Cream of Wheat, Wheaties, Puffed Rice or Wheat 30

FISH—Broiled or Fried Fresh Seasonable Fish with French Fried Potatoes 80
Filet of Kippered Herring 50   Creamed Finnan Haddie on Toast 60
Codfish Cakes (2) Tomato Sauce 50

EGGS & OMELETS—EGGS: Boiled, Fried, Shirred or Scrambled (2) 30; (1) 20;
Poached on Toast (2) 40; (1) 25
OMELETS: (3 Eggs) Ham, Tomato, Cheese, Jelly or Parsley 55   Plain 45
Spanish or Mushroom 65

MEATS—Single Rib Lamb Chop (1) 35; (2) 65   Small Sirloin Steak 90   Ham and Eggs 65
Bacon and Eggs 65   Breakfast Bacon (5) 50   Bacon Rasher (2) 20
Broiled or Fried Smoked Ham 60   Reduced Portion Ham or Bacon and One Egg 40
Corned Beef Hash with Poached Egg (1) 55   Creamed Dried Beef on Toast 50
Fried Sausage (4) 50   Calf's Liver with Bacon 65   Fried Philadelphia Scrapple 40

POTATOES—French Fried 20   Hashed Browned 20   Lyonnaise 25

BREAD, TOAST, ETC.—Dry or Buttered Toast 15   Rolls or Bran Bread 10
French Toast with Jelly, Syrup or Honey 35   Individual Boston Brown Bread 15
Milk Toast 30   Melba Toast 15   Griddle Cakes with Syrup or Honey 35

A BIG Pennsylvania blizzard in the winter of 1905 saw this Reading camelback halted in the depot at Lebanon with the bases of its multiple candlesticks buried deep in snow on the pilot beam. *(Harper's.)*

SO CONSERVATIVE was The Reading in the matter of motive power that exotic bicycle type wheel arrangements with a single pair of drivers survived on its light, fast runs long after they had vanished elsewhere in the land.

687

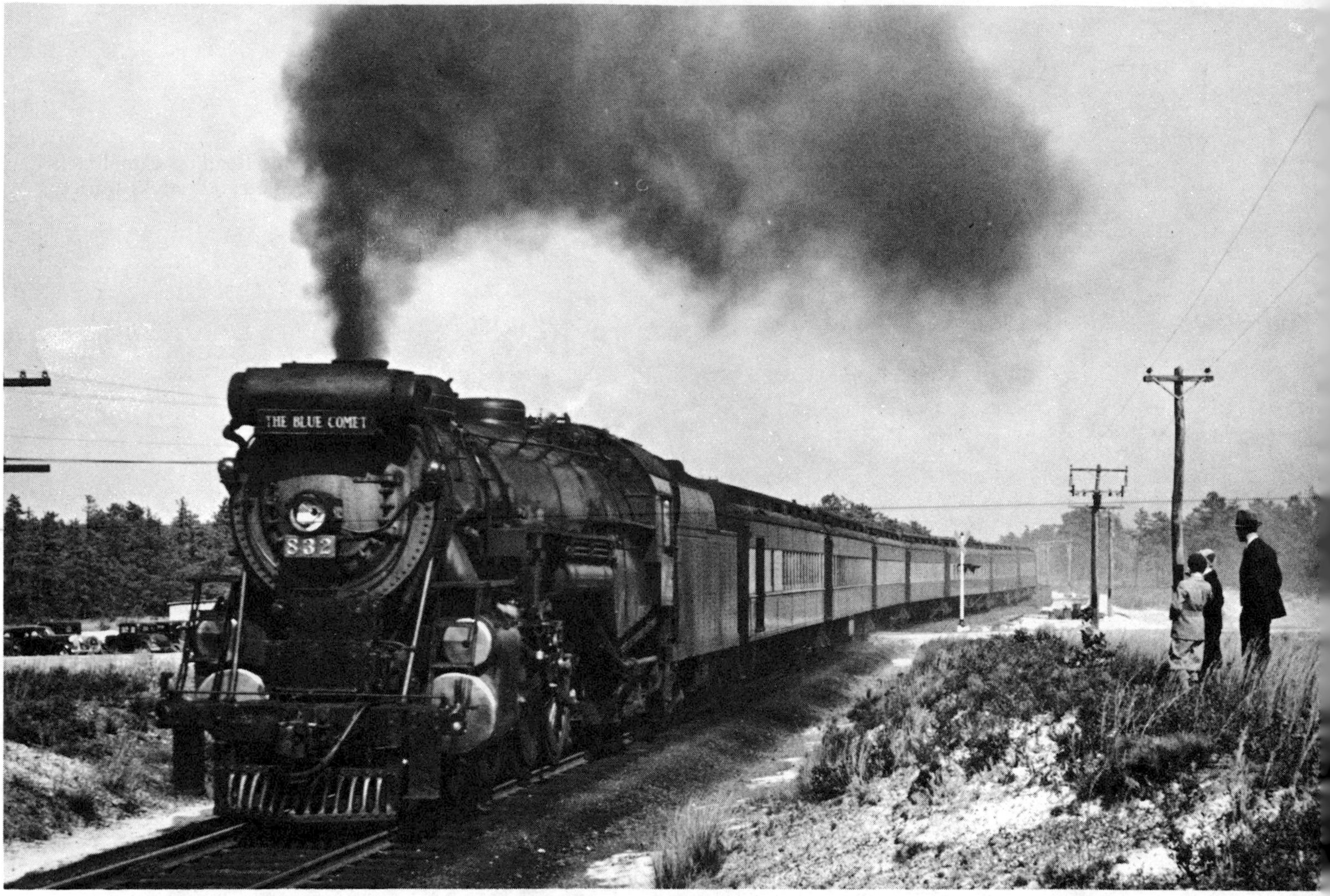

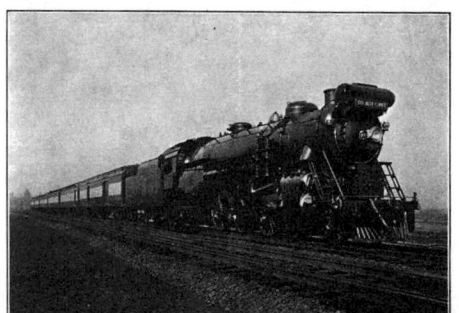

THE CENTRAL Railroad of New Jersey's *Blue Comet,* inaugurated in February of the fatal year 1929 on the New York City-Atlantic City run was the first de luxe all-coach train on a daylight routing designed to give passengers Pullman comfort and style at coach travel tariff. The brain child of the carrier's President R. B. White, *The Blue Comet's* consist included a number of C. of N.J. coaches and diners rebuilt and finished throughout in a striking cream white and royal blue decor with specially assigned Pacific type locomotives which carried the train's name on a bronze insigne under the feed water heater. Regularly assigned, too, was an open end-brass railed observation coach which later received a drumhead insigne. The train was sensationally handsome and residents turned out to watch its progress as shown above, along the C. of N.J.'s own right of way from Red Bank to Winslow, whence it ran to Atlantic City over the Pennsylvania-Reading Seashore Lines. Although a fatality of the depression years, *The Blue Comet* paved the way for all-coach trains on even longer hauls, *The Trail Blazer* and *Pacemaker* and *El Capitan* in years to come. *(Above: Everett De Golyer Collection.)*

The Seashore's Finest Train

THE BLUE COMET

Coach Train Deluxe: NEW YORK • ATLANTIC CITY

This blue streak is a gem of color, in and out—from nickel trimmed engine to illuminated emblem on the observation end. The color scheme of this train blends the restful blue of the sky and ocean with the cream-tinted warmness of the sand beach. The "Blue Comet" offers to the day traveler all the added comfort and pleasure of a "limited" train at the regular coach fare.

Observation Car—Comfortable Wicker chairs.
Individual seats—Assigned in advance.
Special lounge for ladies.
Smoking Car—blue leather individual seats.
Special train porter.
Every car named after a comet.
3 hours flat—no excess fare.
Quiet roller bearing smoothness.
Good Meals at moderate cost.

ALL *these features at the regular coach fare*

NEW JERSEY CENTRAL

SEE TABLE 4 FOR SCHEDULE

IF THE two splendid assigned Pacific locomotives with the train name riding proudly at the smokebox were in the shop, the Central of New Jersey reverted to a long standing motive power tradition and assigned a well maintained camelback to the run. (*Two Photos: Everett De Golyer Collection.*)

SMOKING SPLENDIDLY across the page in the frame above and sooting up the New Jersey landscape, a Pennsylvania Asbury Park-Seagirt local rolls down the iron of the New York & Long Branch's historic right of way at South Amboy, while on the page opposite No. 5412 with the headlight generator and solid steel pilot characteristic of the engines assigned to this run poses on the Atlantic City haul for a sunny portrait by Don Wood at Morgan, New Jersey in November 1955. Within the memory of living man some of the Pennsylvania-Reading Seashore Lines runs carried observation cars with open platforms where, in holiday mood, a family poses at the right in promotional attitudes. (*Pennsylvania Railroad.*)

THE SCENE AT THE LEFT is no
ordinary chore of oiling around
the valve gear, for the locomotive is
the Pennsy's immortal No. 460, the
great Atlantic type engine that,
on its day of glory, June 11, 1927,
averaged seventy-five miles
an hour between Washington terminal
and Manhattan Transfer with the
Lindbergh newsreel special.
No. 460 spent its final years on the
Atlantic City run.
(Philip R. Hastings.)

691

ALTHOUGH luxury equipment occupied but little track space in the Reading's passenger yards, over the years it ordered from Pullman a variety of restaurant cars and diners, of which Cafe Car No. 1197 was a handsome example of Pullman varnish style in the early years of the current century. In the 1930s Bound Brook tower *(right)* where traffic converged over the rails of the Lehigh Valley, the Central of New Jersey and the jointly operated tracks of the Reading and Baltimore & Ohio main line from Philadelphia was the counterpart, in its own purview, of Monmouth Junction on the Pennsylvania, long celebrated as the most densely trafficked trackage in the world. *(Right: Everett De Golyer Collection; Below: Pullman Standard.)*

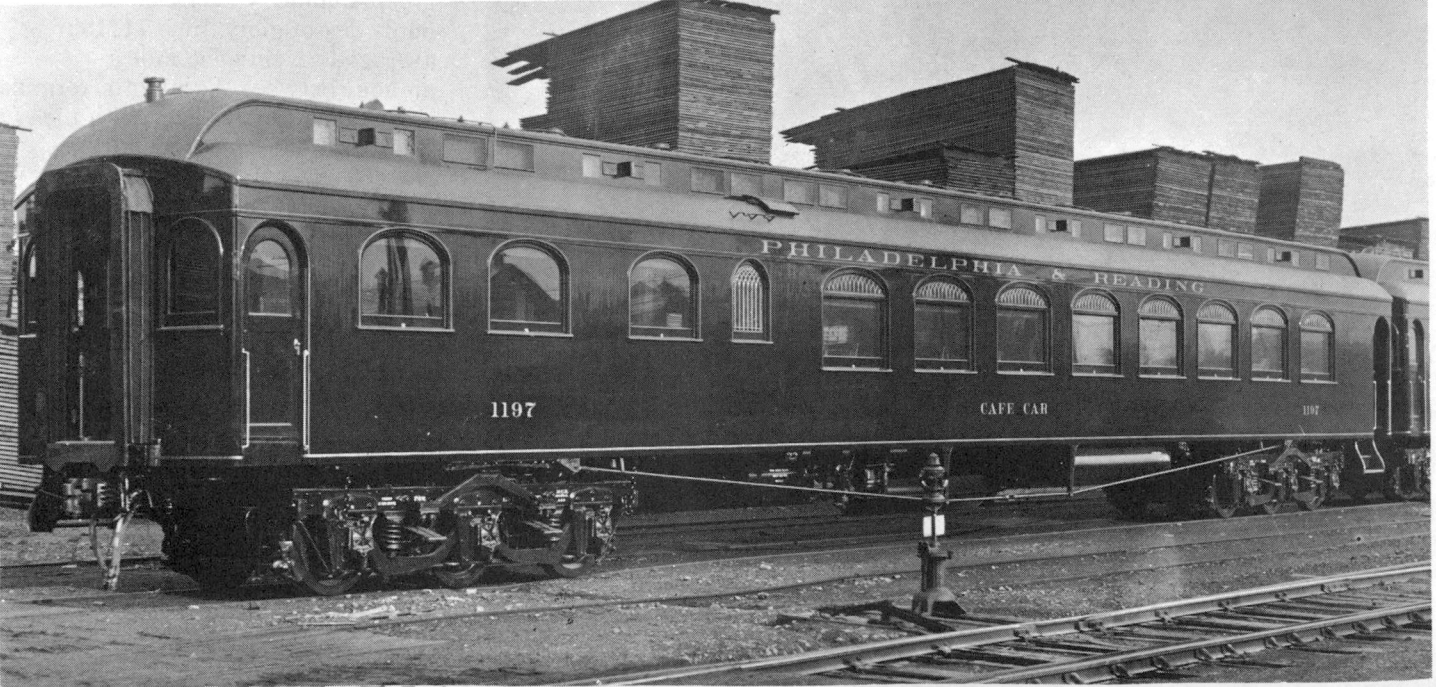

DINING CAR SERVICE

CLUB BREAKFAST SERVICE

Guests will please write on check each item desired, as our waiters are not permitted to accept oral orders. Please pay waiter only upon presentation of your check at conclusion of service.

The Price Opposite Each Selection Includes Choice of One Fruit, Fruit Juice or Cereal. Also Choice of Bread, Rolls or Toast and Beverage

FRUITS	FRUIT JUICES	HOT or DRY CEREALS	
Bartlett Pear Halves	Prune Juice	Cream of Wheat	Rice Krispies
Half Grapefruit	Tomato Juice	Corn Flakes	Bran Flakes
Jumbo Prunes	Grapefruit Juice	Oatmeal	Grape Nuts
Baked Apple	Fresh Orange Juice		
Kadota Figs			

SELECTIONS:

CREAMED CHIPPED BEEF ON TOAST—1.80

FRESH COUNTRY SAUSAGE, WHEAT CAKES, WITH SYRUP —1.90

GRILLED HAM OR FRESH COUNTRY SAUSAGE WITH EGGS, "AS DESIRED"—1.90

BROWNED CORNED BEEF HASH WITH POACHED EGG—1.80

PHILADELPHIA SCRAPPLE, FRIED EGG—1.50

SUGAR CURED BACON AND EGGS—1.80

DRY OR BUTTERED TOAST	ROLLS	HOT MUFFINS
APPLE BUTTER	JELLY	MARMALADE

Please Select from Jelly Tray Passed by Waiter

COFFEE	TEA	MILK	POSTUM	SANKA

For A LA CARTE Selections See Other Side

Four per cent sales tax applies in Commonwealth of Pennsylvania.

TWENTY YEARS after the photograph above showing The Reading's *Wall Streeter* speeding eastward down the long tangent into Elizabeth, New Jersey was taken, the breakfast menu on its successor, *The Wall Street* had kept abreast of the times. No longer could the hustling customer's man on his way to Dean Witter for a brisk day's scuffle with Minnesota Mining or General Dynamics do himself proud for six bits. Like the market itself, creamed chipped beef had soared from fifty cents to $1.80 and inflation had raised corned beef hash with poached egg in the same proportion. *(Above: Lucius Beebe; Left: Reading Railroad.)*

FOR NEARLY two decades the Reading Railroad, in direct competition on the New York-Philadelphia run with the Pennsylvania, maintained a train whose very name *The Seven O'Klocker* was an affront to the Pennsy's fleet of "Clockers" that ran every hour of the day between Broad Street and mid-town Manhattan. In 1937 *The Seven O'Klocker* was replaced by a steam powered, stainless steel streamlined luxury coach train named *The Crusader* because, as is suggested here, it was "Clad in Shining Armor." *The Crusader* served full course meat and potato breakfasts in the morning and enjoyed a brisk bar trade on its evening return to Philadelphia and twice a day gave the competing Pennsylvania a very stylish run for its money. A loyal following of conservative Philadelphia businessmen and brokers who considered the Pennsylvania trains undistinguished and lacking in exclusiveness transferred their loyalties to *The Crusader* when that streamliner was inaugurated. Usually powered by a specially assigned streamlined light Pacific, an equally well groomed locomotive in conventional livery took over when the assigned engine was being shopped. (*Lucius Beebe.*)

694

DEVOTIONAL reading aboard *The Crusader* was, of course, *The Wall Street Journal* and the Martinis on the Philadelphia-bound run late in the afternoon were of a dimension suitable to the demands of brokers who had spent a fatiguing day in the market place. (*Two Photos: The Reading Co.*)

Few But Choice Were the Name Varnish Runs on the Rock Island

POWERED by a stubby Pacific with solid steel pilot and the peculiar and characteristic Rock Island adaptation of a Vanderbilt tender, the *Rocky Mountain Limited* is shown above in a consist of four cars leaving Denver of a summer's noontime in 1939 with one of the season's inevitable thunder storms forming behind it. Although the practice varied with the years, the general operational procedure sent the full dimension dining car on with the stub section to The Springs while breakfast, arriving in Denver, and luncheon departing were served on the main section in the buffet. Rock Island cuisine, like that of the Burlington, ran to country style and was nothing to excite the raptures of *bon viveurs*, but what there was was good and plentiful. In lean years after the great passenger slump of the late fifties, economies attempted on the *Rocky Mountain Rocket* ran to paper plates, no table linen and prefabricated dinners, practices of infamy which the complaints of the patrons put a stop to in short order. (*Above: Richard H. Kindig; Right: Rock Island.*)

THE COLORADO SPRINGS section of *The Limited* is shown below arriving at Limon, Colorado, with a coach, diner and Pullman where it will be integrated to the main section out of Denver for the trip east. *(Everett De Golyer Collection.)*

IT MAY REASONABLY be presumed that it was hot on the July morning in Horton, Kansas, in 1914 when Eugene Bourquin, a dedicated photographer of the local scene, took these views down around the Rock Island depot when the Kansas City local, shown double headed in the picture below, pulled in. The women were in white shirtwaists and sensible skirts with summer parasols and the men in shirt sleeves with their jackets over their arms. The afternoon train, shown opposite, required but a single engine. The town hack and omnibus from the Horton House stood at the platform and a single vintage motor car, parked in the rear of the depot gave pastoral Horton a touch of worldliness. The Rock Island brakeman, at the bottom across the fold, wore white cotton gloves as much to protect his hands from the heat of switch stands and grabirons as against the dirt. With a jug of drinking water carried on the catwalk where it could catch the breeze, the Rock Island's one and only camelback locomotive and its crew were an irresistible subject for Bourquin's lens. Kansas and for that matter the whole middle west of that now distant year were filled with Hortons or their facsimiles, but only Horton, Brown County, Kansas boasted the presence of Eugene Bourquin to lend it celulloid immortality. *(Everett De Golyer Collection.)*

TIPPING the depot porter at Englewood just outside Chicago in the *Golden State's* streamlined days was a matter of financial import to both parties *(right)*. Below in 1940 when clouds upon its horizon were few, *The Golden State Limited* rolls in splendor out of Tucumcari, Chicago-bound with four head-end revenue cars and a long string of Pullmans trailing behind. *(Right: Fail Photo Service; Below: Richard H. Kindig.)*

THE STUB train out of
San Diego connecting with the
Golden State at Yuma over
the San Diego & Arizona
Eastern, left the Santa Fe depot
behind a Southern Pacific
ten wheeler with a single
through Pullman on the far end.
(Rail Photo Service.)

DESPITE the Fred Harvey cuisine and the Santa Fe legend of immaculately conducted transcontinentals, there were those who felt that in its days of Pullman Standard and even later when it was modestly streamlined, there was no way to achieve Southern California comparable to the *Golden State Limited*. It was a train of solid comforts, cut flowers in the public apart-ments, heavily embossed stationery in the lounges, fingerbowls with lemon water on the diner and an over-all sense of enormous well-being. A highball with a fellow traveler in the lounge as the New Mexican night rushed past the windows was a solace for human ills. *(Southern Pacific.)*

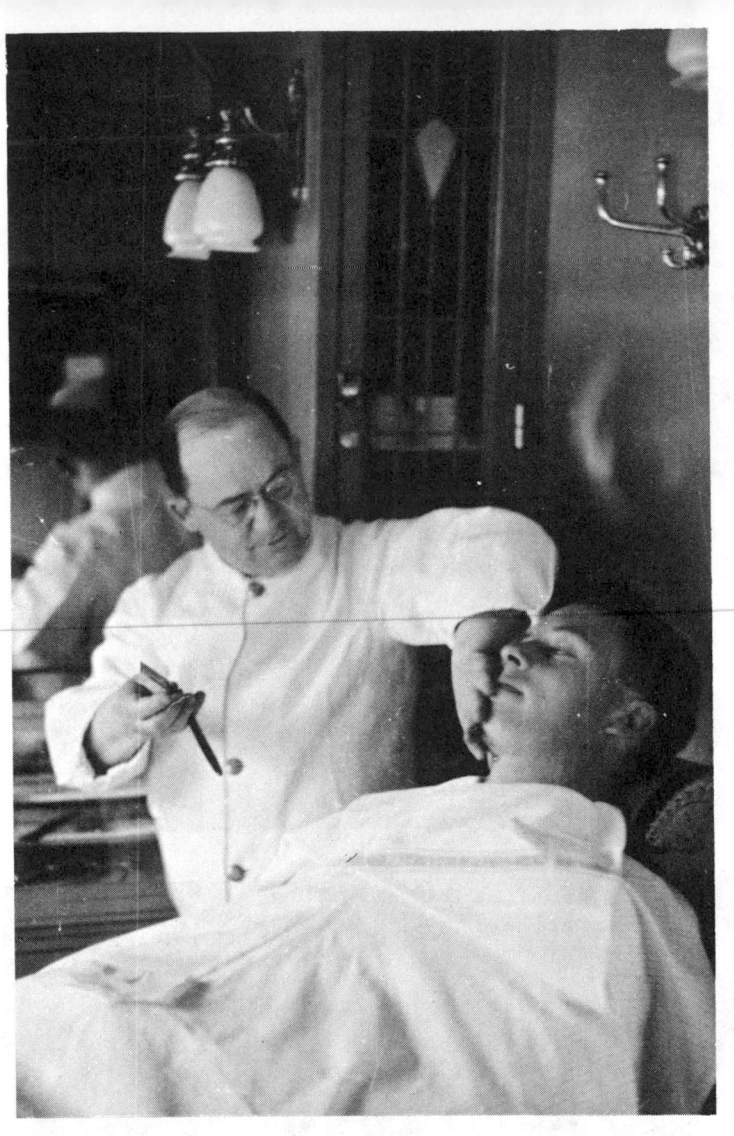

WHEN IT WENT into service on November 2, 1902 between Los Angeles and Chicago over the Southern Pacific-Rock Island connection as Trains No. 43-44, *The Golden State Limited*, even to its closely parallel name, was designed as direct competition with the Santa Fe's *California Limited* already an institution and well established in the travel habits of the Southwest. For the first five years of its life *The Golden State* was an all-Pullman consist though there is no record to show this other than a surcharge attached to its tickets. Curiously enough, because the Rock Island main line had not been consolidated to include this trackage, it ran between Kansas City and Joliet, Illinois, over the rails of the Chicago & Alton, then very much of the Kansas City-St. Louis-Chicago triangle competition. In its Pullman Standard days and in the era of later streamlining, *The Golden State* also faced the stiff competition of the Union Pacific's *Los Angeles Limited* over the Salt Lake line. Aboard it were available all the accustomed transcontinental amenities, barber and lady's maid, heavily embossed writing paper, fingerbowls and a de luxe *ambiance* generally. A noble train, it lived up to a noble name. (*Above: Richard H. Kindig; Opposite: Southern Pacific, Paul Stringham; Left: Arthur D. Dubin Collection.*)

703

JUST BEFORE accepting delivery from Pullman of the equipment which allowed it to place two entire new Standard trains on the run, the Rock Island's *Rocky Mountain Limited* is shown backing down to its appropriate train bay at La Salle Depot in Chicago in 1929. At the right its arrival eastbound is depicted at Englewood on a winter's day in 1930 when storm conditions have made its running in two sections prudent. The second section, snow encrusted from the Great Plains, included three head end revenue cars, a coach and two Pullmans. Company literature *(right)* suggested that a lower berth in a Standard Pullman sleeper was a snug place to be on a night when blizzards gripped the Rocky Mountain States, as indeed it was. *(Top, Two Photos: Alfred W. Johnson; Right: Rock Island.)*

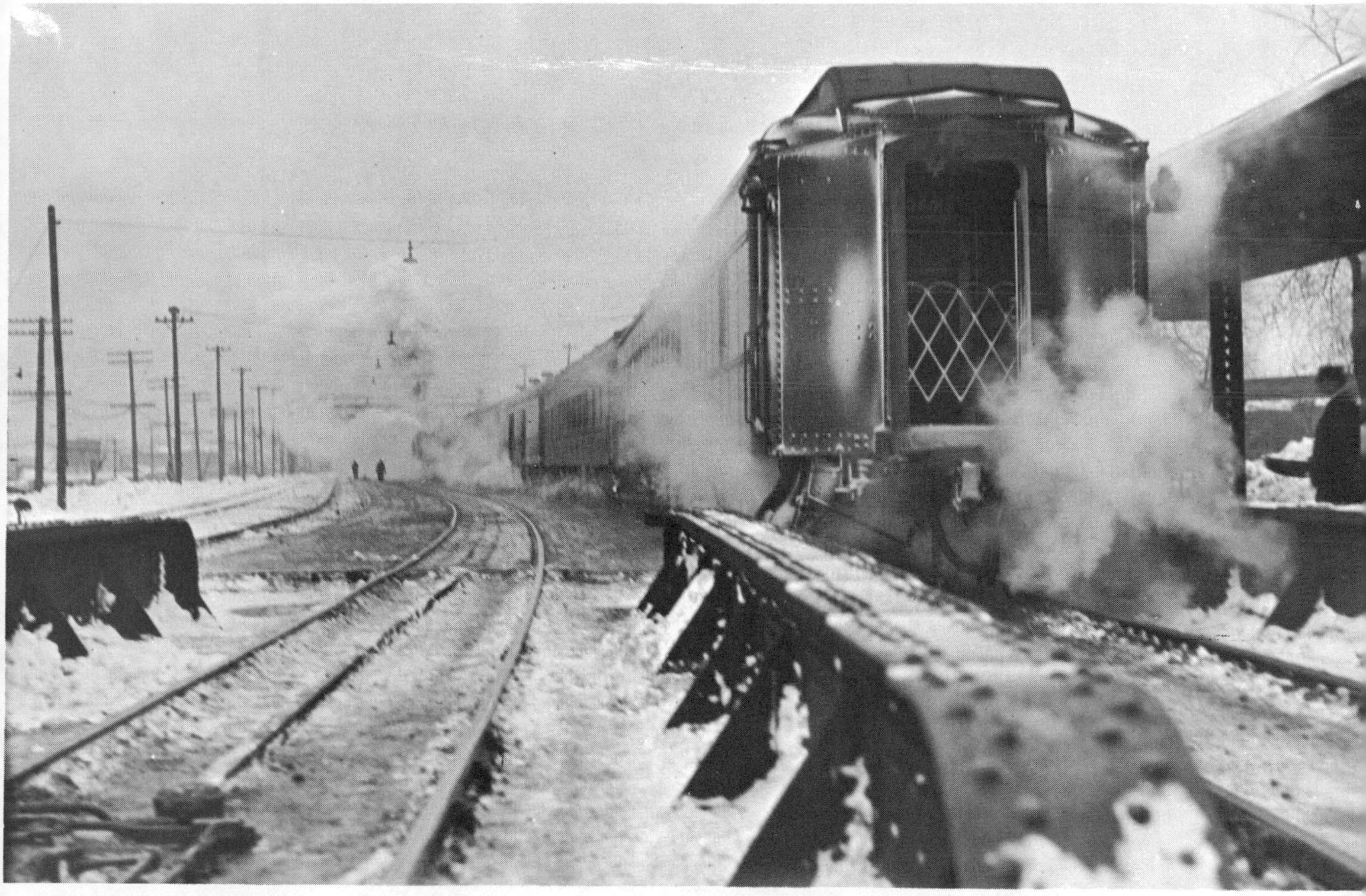

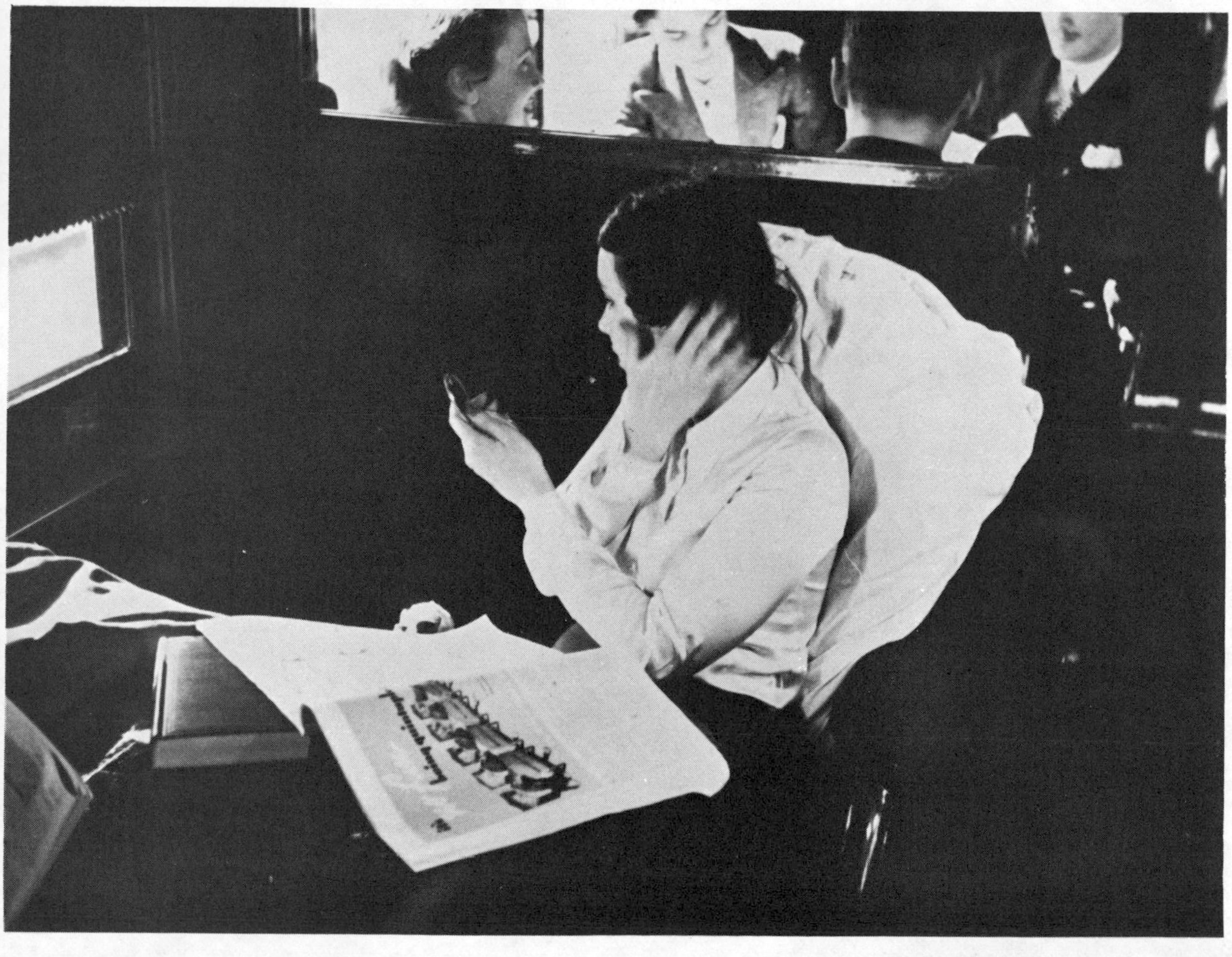

AT VARIOUS TIMES, the secondary run over the Golden State Route to Southern California via the Rock Island and the Southern Pacific connection at Tucumcari was known as *The Californian,* sometimes as *The Apache* as shown at the right. Always it was a sort of elegant second fiddle to the candy run, *The Golden State Limited,* shown below near Beaumont in San Timoteo Canyon. But if *The Apache* and *Californian* were both very highly regarded second fiddles, their culinary resources, although at reduced prices, had about them vestiges of the grander manner of *The Golden State* and they ended with the panache of an open platform observation car and the tailgate insigne that marked them trains of pedigree no matter what their scheduling or fares.

The occupants of Pullman space on *The Apache,* shown on the facing page, couldn't have been any more comfortable on an extra fare run.   (*Below: Donald Duke; Opposite: Two Photos Southern Pacific.*)

LEAVING DENVER in a prophetic mantle of
shrouded glory with the sunset behind it,
the *Rocky Mountain Limited (top opposite)*
made its last run on November 11, 1939 and was
photographed in its going by Otto Perry.
The next day saw the inaugural run in regular
service of *The Rocky Mountain Rocket*
and the age of streamlining was at hand.
The new and gleaming *Rockets* put the carrier
on competitive footing of equality with
the rival Burlington and Union Pacific which
already had streamliners on the Colorado
run, but there were those who lamented the
passing of Pullman Standard which had so long
been typified by the black leather
upholstered men's room, scene of pre-arrival
chaos in the morning and setting for the
whole long saga of traveling salesmen's tales
embracing the farmer's daughter and other
staples of masculine humor
dear to the student of American folkways.

BEFORE construction of the present La Salle Station in Chicago which it shares with the New York Central and the Nickel Plate, the old Van Buren Street Depot saw the departure of Rock Island trains "with California excursions daily, a choice of routes to Salt Lake, Ogden, Portland, Los Angeles and San Francisco." Chicago's Victorian terminals were atmospheric if not the quintessence of convenience. *(Chicago Historical Society.)*

A COMPANION train in the tourist brackets to the extra fare *Golden State* on the Rock Island-Southern Pacific run between Chicago and California was *The Californian* which its owning carriers hoped might be the answer to the Union Pacific's *Challengers* in the reduced fare brackets. The Espee, then very much in the passenger business, spent money in lavish quantities on the project, advertising the run in four-color brochures and stocking its diners with out-of-season viands usually reserved for the extra fare trade. Until the construction of its magnificent Union Station, Kansas City passengers on the Rock Island got down from the cars at the venerable depot depicted at the right. *The Californian* at the top of the page is from the Collons Collection at the De Golyer Foundation, Dallas.

A ROUND TRIP ticket to Los Angeles on *The Californian* was an unbelievable $74 and a lower berth $8.95 each way. Breakfast was two bits; dinner with chicken pie, 35¢. Nobody could figure how the carriers did it. An additional attraction was a standup bar where prices compared favorably with those on *The Golden State*. Willing as it was to take a loss on its 35¢ dinners, the management was disinclined to invite bankruptcy with bargain Martinis. *(Two Photos: Southern Pacific.)*

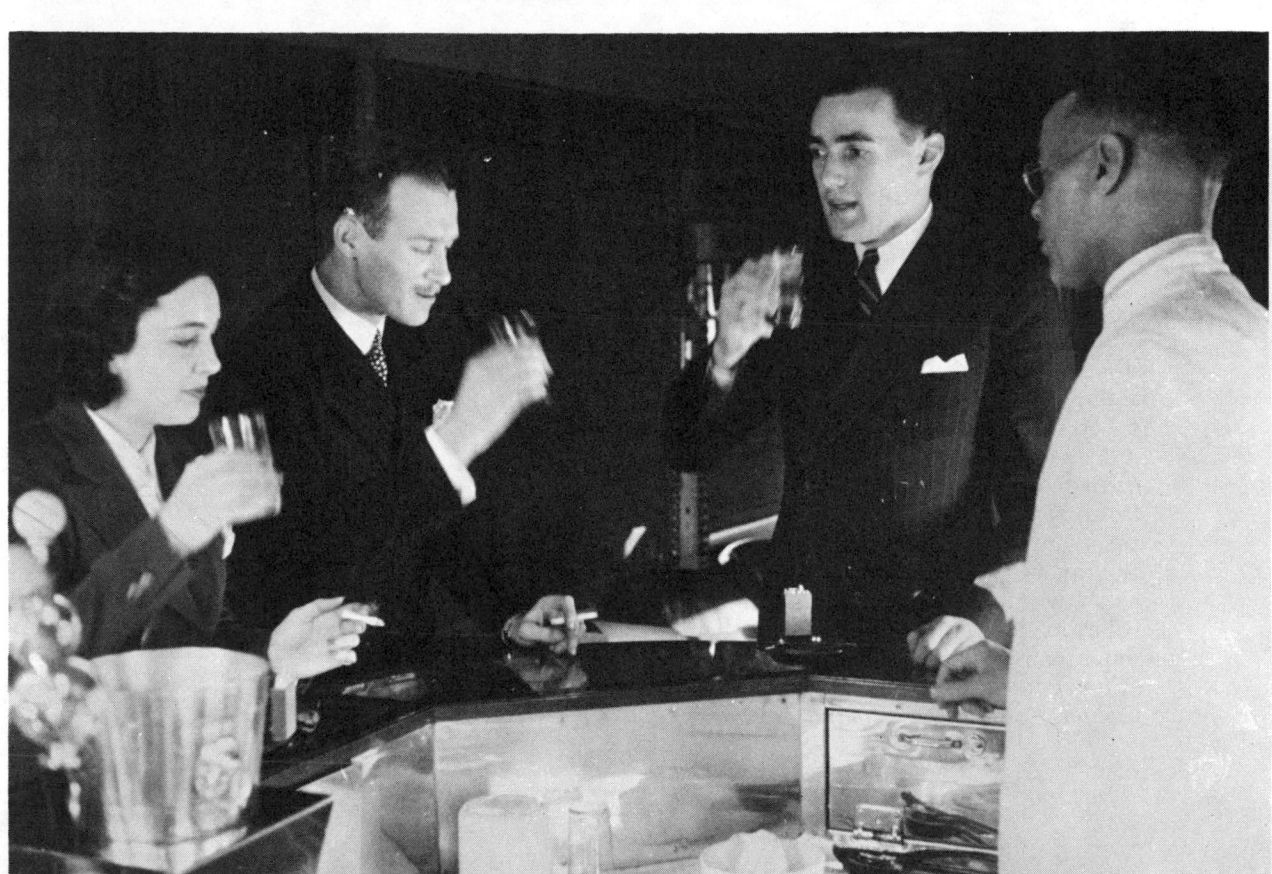

IN THE CLOSING years of the 1920s when the Union Pacific's *Columbine* and the Burlington's *Aristocrat* were reeling off the Chicago-Denver miles with the finest equipment and most luxurious amenities available to long distance travel, the Rock Island's entry in the Queen City sweepstakes was *The Rocky Mountain Limited* for which all new Pullman equipment was ordered in 1929 and is shown above at Bureau, Illinois, a decade later. Barber and valet service were taken for granted and a stub train, as was the Rock Island's practice, went on from Limon to Colorado Springs while the main section headed for Denver. In 1933, with air conditioning just around the corner, it ran, as shown at the right, with a non-a.c., solarium lounge in place of the then more conventional open observation. (*Top: Paul Stringham; Right: The De Golyer Foundation, Roland Collons.*)

712

CONFRONTED BY the fine new streamliners of the competition on the Chicago-Denver run, the Burlington's *Denver Zephyr (top)* and the Union Pacific's *City of Denver*, the Rock Island, although obviously not sure that either Diesel power or airflow design was here to stay, countered weakly with a lightweight *Rocket* of its own. Reminiscent of the Rio Grande's experimental *Pioneer* except that it had no sleeping accommodations at all, *The Rocket* went into service with coach space only on summer weekends in 1937 with a conspicuous lack of success. It was shortly replaced by the *Rocky Mountain Special*, a Diesel powered run with Standard sleeping equipment which in turn yielded place to the fully staffed, streamlined excellences of *The Rocky Mountain Rocket*. (*Two Photos: Richard H. Kindig.*)

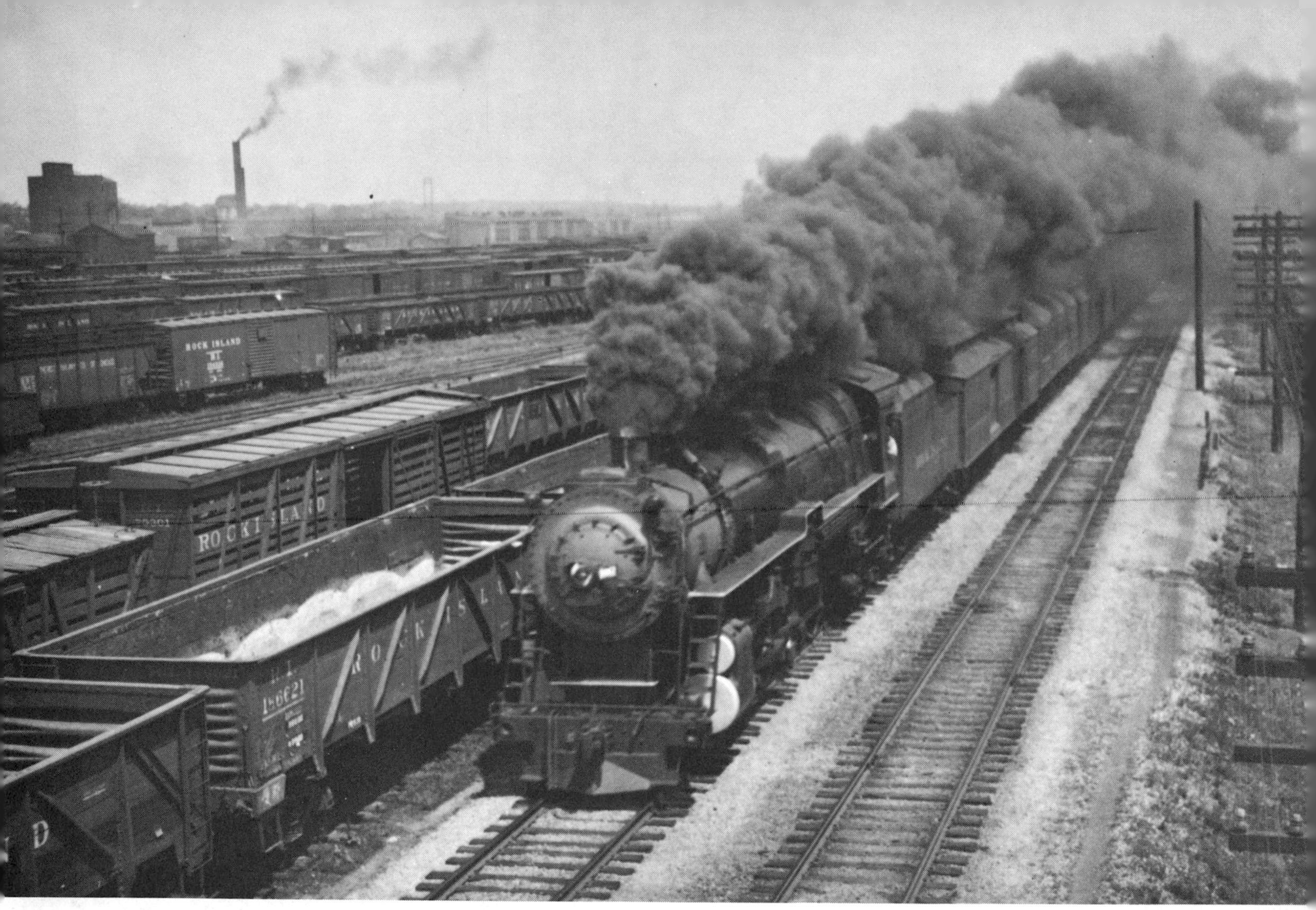
ROCK ISLAND
ROCK ISLAND

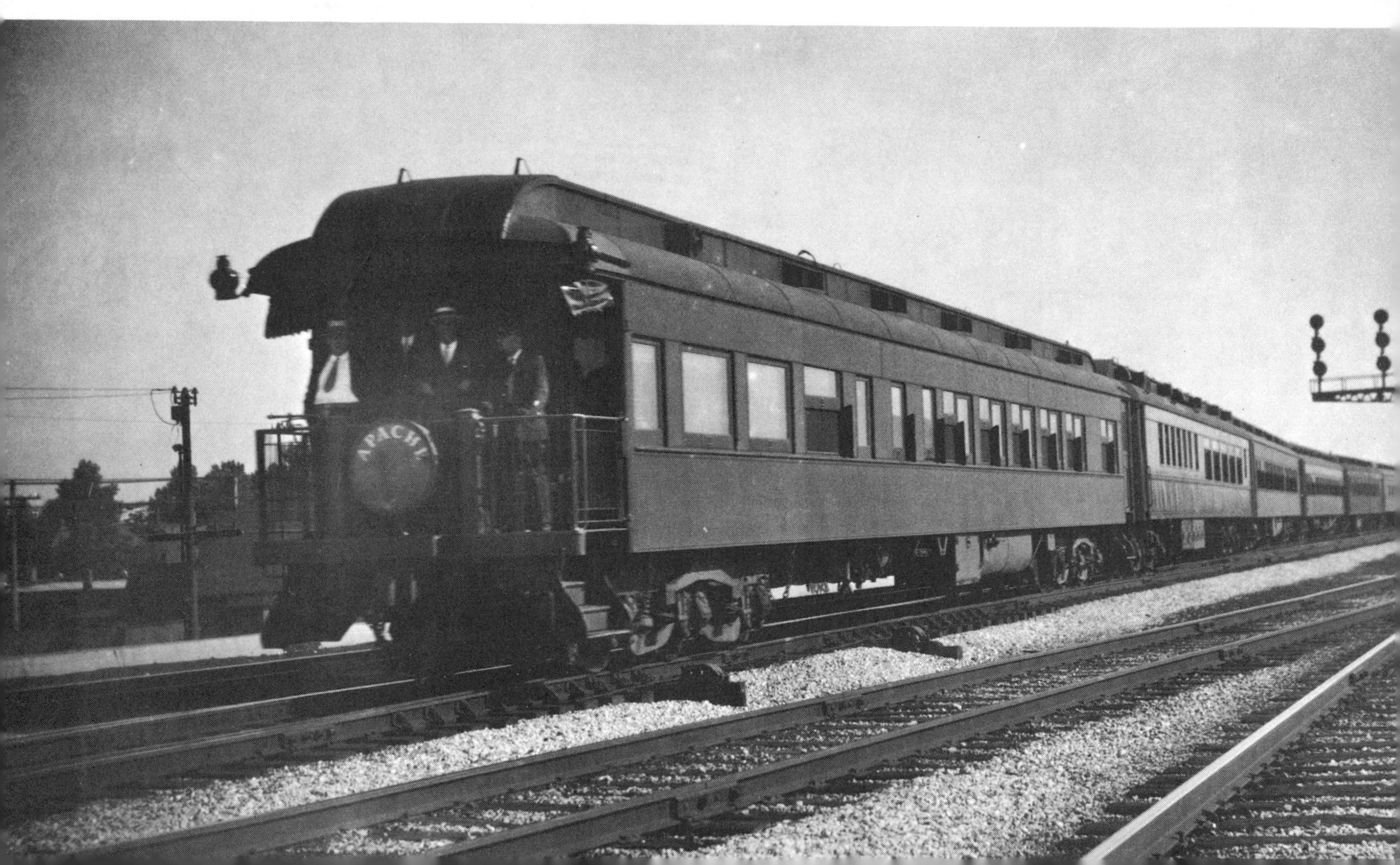
APACHE

PLACED IN SERVICE in 1926 soon after the cresting
of the wave of passenger traffic in the United States
which had reached its peacetime apogee in 1922,
The Apache was the secondary run to *The Golden State
Limited* on the Rock Island-Southern Pacific joint
operation between Chicago and Southern California.
Although it never knew an extra fare and its sailing daily
from La Salle Station in Chicago *(above)* had
about it none of the red carpet overtones of *The
Golden State, The Apache* carried its tourist
class patrons in something suggesting style as is
suggested by the open platform observation shown at
the left. In the above frame it smokes up the
Chicago skyline in 1936 in the very grand manner indeed
on its westbound way to a rendezvous with the
Southern Pacific at Tucumcari.
*(Two Photos: De Golyer
Foundation, Collons Collection; Above: William Rittase.)*

715

THE SHORT LIVED *Arizona Limited* was an extra fare de luxe varnish run over the Rock Island-Southern Pacific connection at Tucumcari for winter patrons of the Arizona vacation complex centering around Tucson-Phoenix but its star came into ascendancy in evil hour in 1940 when war was already inevitable and it perished, a victim of travel restrictions, after only two seasons in service. It cost a surcharge of $6 to ride *The Arizona Limited* and when it became only a memory on the yellowing trainsheets of time, there were those who remembered it for happy hours on a run once populous with name trains and operations of splendor. *(Above: Southern Pacific.)*

PERFECTION ON RAILS
THE ARIZONA LIMITED
BETWEEN CHICAGO—KANSAS CITY AND TUCSON—PHOENIX

THE ONLY THROUGH STREAMLINED TRAIN TO SOUTHERN ARIZONA

Styled in streamlined beauty, luxuriating in commodious comfort, the ARIZONA LIMITED is the *smart* means of travel to the resort and guest ranch country of sunny Southern Arizona.

It is an all-Pullman, all-private room accommodation train, with roomettes, double bedrooms, duplex single rooms, compartments and drawing rooms.

De luxe dining car service for all meals. Buffet Lounge-Observation Car.

Extra fare of $6.00 will apply in each direction between Chicago or Kansas City and Tucson or Phoenix. Proportionate extra fares between intermediate points.

ROCK ISLAND - SOUTHERN PACIFIC offers *the only main line through* service from Chicago to El Paso, Tucson, Phoenix and Palm Springs en route to Los Angeles.

GOLDEN STATE LIMITED—*for distinguished comfort*—daily between Chicago and Los Angeles. Standard Pullmans. Tourist Pullman westbound. Diner. De luxe Chair Cars. Club-Lounge Car.

Arizona Limited

No. 29		SCHEDULE		No. 30
8:45 pm	Lv.	Chicago	Ar.	9:30 am
8:56 pm	Lv.	Englewood	Ar.	9:16 am
7:30 am	Ar.	Kansas City	Lv.	11:25 pm
8:05 am	Lv.	Kansas City	Ar.	10:50 pm
1:15 am	Ar.	El Paso	Lv.	4:00 am
5:48 am	Ar.	Douglas	Lv.	11:27 pm
6:26 am	Ar.	Bisbee Jct.	Lv.	10:52 pm
8:44 am	Ar.	Tucson	Lv.	8:33 pm
10:40 am	Ar.	Chandler	Lv.	6:40 pm
11:25 am	Ar.	Phoenix	Lv.	6:00 pm

Departures every second day in each direction
(See Tables A and B)

CALIFORNIAN—*for luxurious economy*—daily between Chicago and Los Angeles. Club Lounge Car for Sleeping Car patrons. Tourist Pullmans and de luxe Chair Cars. Special Chair Car for women and children. Economy Meals in Dining Car. Tourist Pullman to and from San Diego.

Through service daily from St. Louis and Memphis. Connecting service from Twin Cities via Kansas City.

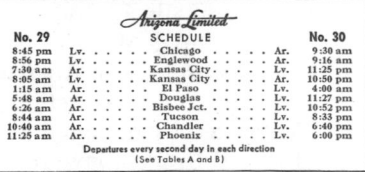

Rock Island THE DIRECT LOW ALTITUDE WAY

ALTHOUGH the distinction of being the last custom-tailored name train
to be placed in service before the 1941 war belongs to the
Empire State Express on the New York Central, which made its maiden
run within hours of Pearl Harbor, *The Arizona Limited* was in general terms
coeval with it and shares the nostalgic overtones of things born in the
shadow of great events and soon overwhelmed by them.
It was also one of the last extra fare trains to be commissioned before
the advent of an age which would see surcharges in almost
universal abatement, so that the comparatively small group of passengers
who experienced the satisfactions of this superb but short-lived
streamliner are members of an exclusive veterans club.   (*Southern Pacific.*)

The Grand Hotel Concept of Railroading Flourished Luxuriously on the Southern Pacific

OTHER RAILROADS might, and indeed did achieve an imperial dimension in the world of transport and finance, at least one of them, the Santa Fe in direct competition over continental distances with the Southern Pacific. None of them, not even the New York Central & Hudson River Railroad in the years of its Vanderbilt ownership or the Pennsylvania when its writ ran with feudal overtones from Broad Street to Lake Michigan and the far bank of the Mississippi, represented such a splendidly integrated pattern of passenger accommodations, not only aboard name trains of legendary luxury, but on much-loved ferry boats and aboard ocean-going steamships that were household words.* For a time, in its Central Pacific incarnation, the Southern Pacific owned the State of California almost outright and its word was law in state capitols at Carson City, Phoenix, Salem and Baton Rouge. On its name passenger trains for three generations the Southern Pacific lavished the rich gifts of an indulgent parent. Its corporate banner rode aboard *The Sunset Limited, The Shasta Daylight, Golden State* and *Californian,* and it showed the flag, metaphorically, from smokebox and tailgate of *The Apache, Owl, Overland* and *Cascade.* Unlike the Pennsylvania, it could never be said that having seen one Espee varnish run the beholder had seen them all. Custom staled not their infinite variety and no passenger aboard *The Forty-niner* of happy memory could for a moment imagine himself enjoying the resources of *The West Coast* or the brief-lived *Arizona Limited.*
While its politics and economic warfare were conducted on a scale of truculence and ferocity that would have frightened the warring barons of medieval Italy, the Southern Pacific's love affair with its passengers, as long as the management was so inclined, was on a positively idyllic scale. While it may not be possible, aboard even *The Golden State Limited,* to cite the $1,000 a month florist bills for the diners of *The Century,* the concept of a grand hotel was everywhere visible on the Espee in the form of watermarked stationery, silver fingerbowls, an encouraging assortment of fine whiskeys on the club cars, out-of-season strawberries, Eastern lobster and fresh brook trout on the menu and conductors who were very much the viceroys in an imperial scheme of things from Management at 65 Market Street, San Francisco. Marks of special favor abounded for notables on *The Overland* and *The Cascade* and no passenger who ever rode with Wild Bill Kurthy in the early days of *The City of San Francisco* forgot the gastronomic experience. In the number of its name trains, it is probable that the Southern Pacific must yield the palm to the Pennsylvania; in their amenities of comfort and expedition and the hold they exercised on the loyalties and imagination of the Western continent the Espee had few peers. On the opposite page in a day before tailgate insignes were universal, one of the Coast Route trains makes its way through flowering meadows against a backdrop of eucalyptus near Palo Alto. *(Southern Pacific.)*

---

*Amateurs of the Southern Pacific in search of a full scale pictorial and social history of this carrier are referred to "The Central Pacific & The Southern Pacific Railroads" by Lucius Beebe, with 121 photographs by Richard Steinheimer. Howell-North Books, 1963.

Departures of *The Sunset* from Third & Townsend were only a San Francisco memory by the time the fine snack bar shown at the right began running on a streamlined *Sunset Limited* but the picture record of the smiling porter and the two stylish women on the observation deck as it clears the yards testify to the glory it once knew. (*Three Photos: Southern Pacific.*)

NO LONGER a through train to the Golden Gate when this photograph of *The Sunset* was taken by Donald Duke in the mid-forties, it was still a many splendored thing as it surged, double headed, up San Timoteo Canyon at El Casco, California. The open platform shown at the left had by then been a casualty of the 1941 war but *The Sunset* was still a train in the grand manner with most of its amenities unimpaired. (*Left: Southern Pacific.*)

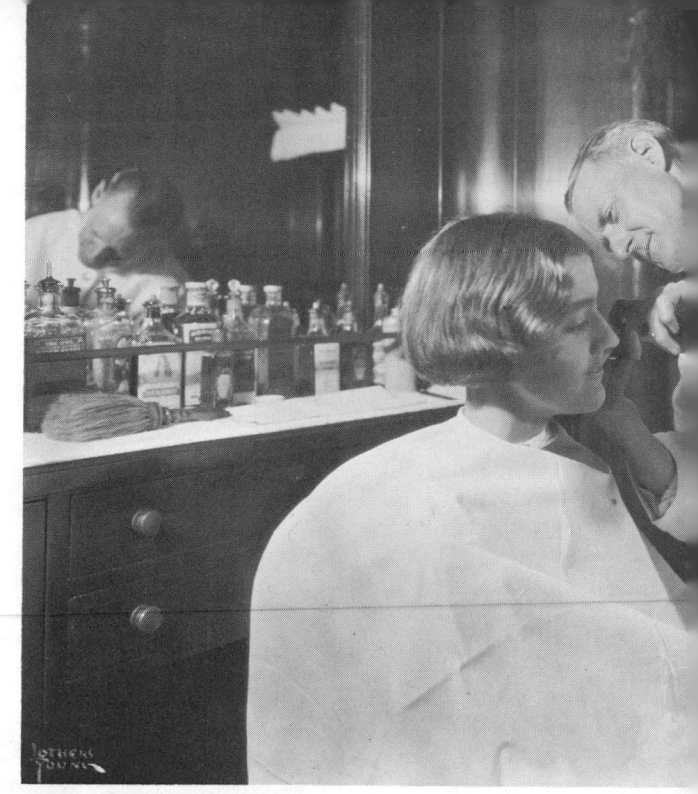

IN THE ERA of Pullman Standard when *The Sunset Limited* was flagship of the Southern Pacific's fleet of varnish trains, a barber was as requisite a part of its operation as the dining car or stock reports handed up at strategic points along the way. *(Southern Pacific.)*

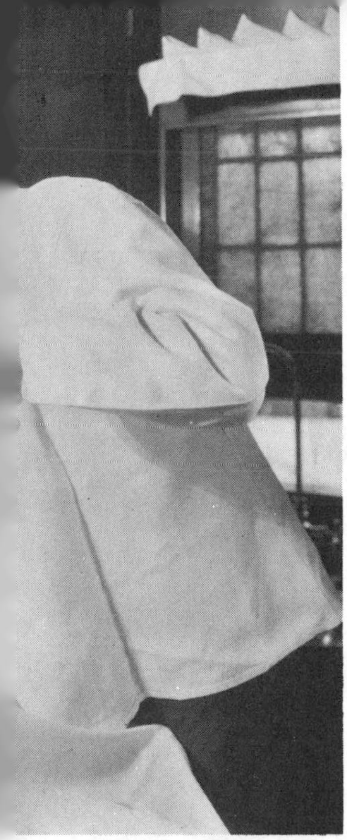

BOARDING *The Sunset Limited* east or west at San Antonio, Texas, in the
days when people of consequence went Pullman as a matter of course
and how you traveled was who you were, called up the most ample
resources of feminine wardrobes with the result that this patron of the
Espee's most choicely regarded flyer has donned her Nieman-Marcus
chinchilla and, in all probability, her Van Cleef & Arpel's emeralds for the
occasion. *The Sunset* itself, taken in its finest hour, might well be the
paradigm of all transcontinental luxury runs as it double-heads for the grade
in San Timoteo Canyon with fourteen cars on the drawbar of the road
engine in 1948.   *(Left: Donald Duke; Above: Southern Pacific.)*

IT WOULD SEEM unlikely that at any subsequent time in the history of overland travel in the United States, gentlemen aboard the cars ever even approximated the degree of sartorial elegance represented by pleated shirts, cummerbunds and curly-brimmed gray bowler hats depicted in this scene, identified as "a dinner stop in New Mexico" appearing on the center fold of *Harper's Weekly* supplement for February in 1891. *The Sunset Limited's* most sumptuous diners by Pullman were still four years in the future. Thirty-odd years later the Southern Pacific at its Fifth Avenue ticket office in New York *(opposite)* was suggesting that prospective patrons of *The Sunset* take through passage from the East aboard the *Piedmont Limited* or *The Crescent* over the Southern Railway-L. & N. connection at New Orleans for the 3839 miles to San Francisco. Along the way, as suggested below, the Sunset Route passed numerous reminders of mortality. The passengers paid them no mind. *(Three Photos: Southern Pacific.)*

Once
For a
Season
The
Sunset
Limited
Had
Covered
The
Longest
Continental
Run
Of All

726

4 4

6:45 P.M.
DAILY
TRAIN NO 78
SUNSET
LIMITED
FOR
SAN LUIS OBISP(
SANTA BARBARA
LOS ANGELES
SAN DIEGO
YUMA
EL PASO
SAN ANTONIO
HOUSTON
NEW ORLEANS
WASHINGTON
NEW YORK
AND
POINTS EAST

IN THE YEAR 1925 when the Southern Pacific through trains
ran all the way from San Francisco to New Orleans with
direct connections to the East, Los Angeles, instead of being a
terminal was an on-line division point and *The Sunset Limited*
eastbound on its way down the Peninsula passed the
landmark shown at the left known as Palo Alto Big Pine.
The Big Pine had been there, amidst a rural setting
almost unchanged until the photograph was taken, from the time
when the first iron of the San Francisco & San Jose Railroad
had been laid in its shadow. Great name trains rolled
under it for three quarters of a century until Palo Alto's once
casually fenced meadows were engulfed in a tide of commerce
and a last link vanished between the time when the Espee
had been a country carrier and the ever crescent industrial chaos
of the twentieth century. The trainboard at Third & Townsend
depot suggested *The Sunset* as a varnish run of truly
continental dimension.   (*Two Photos: Southern Pacific.*)

FOR TWO FULL decades previous to the coming of streamlining and through Pullmans between the East and West Coasts over a variety of routes, the Southern Pacific and the Southern Railway joined forces to stimulate and promote passenger traffic over the Sunset Route connecting at New Orleans with *The Crescent Limited* out of New York. *The Sunset Limited* and *The Argonaut* were the Espee beneficiaries of this arrangement; *The Crescent* and *The Azalean* east of the Mississippi. Schedules allowed liberal stopover time in New Orleans and passengers were encouraged to explore the culinary resources of ancestral Antoine's and the Absinthe House between trains. When the new streamlined, extra-fare *Sunset* went into service in 1950, the atmosphere of Creole New Orleans was conspicuous in its decor and a through Pullman between New York and Los Angeles was added, as is indicated at the right. Below *The Crescent* is shown leaving Atlanta in the age of the Southern Railway's splendor of green and gold motive power. *(Right: Southern Pacific; Below: Rail Photo Service.)*

Two of the nation's top streamliners...

THE SUNSET LIMITED

LOS ANGELES — NEW ORLEANS

and

THE CRESCENT

NEW ORLEANS — WASHINGTON, D. C.

now provide daily through Coast-to-Coast Pullman service between WASHINGTON, D.C. and LOS ANGELES via the OLD SOUTH and NEW ORLEANS, HOUSTON, SAN ANTONIO, EL PASO

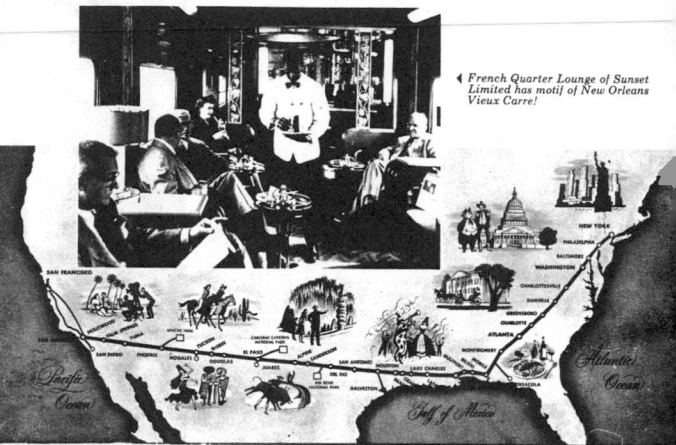

French Quarter Lounge of Sunset Limited has motif of New Orleans Vieux Carre!

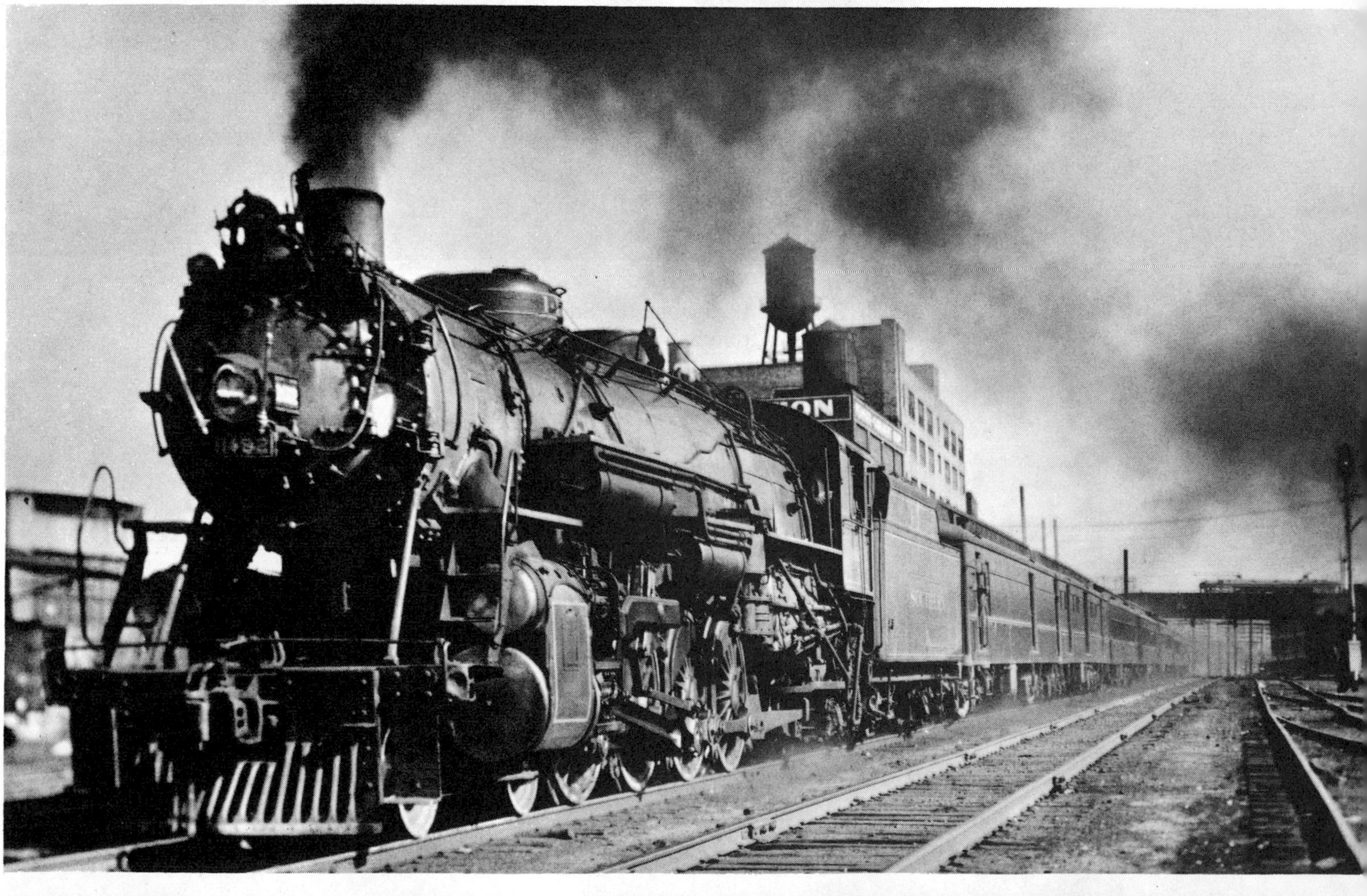

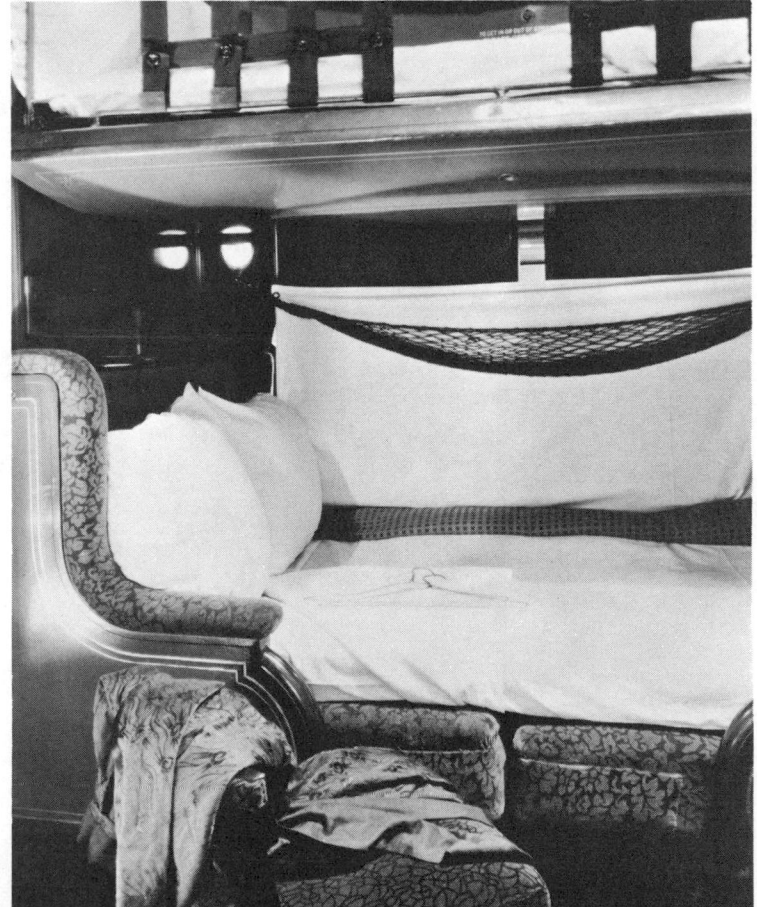

PRESUMING that the occupant of the Pullman Standard space shown here occupied a stateroom aboard both *The Crescent* and *The Sunset Limited* he would have occasion to don his Sulka watered silk bathrobe five full nights between New York and Los Angeles. Passengers aboard the *Mauretania* at this time occupied their staterooms for a similar period between New York and Southampton, but the voyage did not compare, in its duration at any rate, with that of the pre-1914 *Trans-Siberian Express* which took a full fortnight between terminals. Club cars on the Standard *Sunset (top)* showed few traces of the approach of *moderne* decor which was shortly to characterize public apartments in the name trains of the streamlined age. (*Two Photos: Southern Pacific.*)

IN SPACIOUS TIMES of rail travel between California and the Northwest when the Southern Pacific ran five regularly scheduled passenger trains in each direction, *The Cascade, Oregonian, Klamath, Shasta Limited* and *The West Coast, The Oregonian* shown above and at the right had taken over the fine Pullman equipment of the old *Cascade* which had been newly outfitted with all air-conditioned cars. *The Oregonian's* room observation lounge is depicted above and opposite; at the right the same train in a wintry setting at Dunsmuir when snow lies heavy on the rails. *(Two Photos: Southern Pacific.)*

SHOWN AT ODELL LAKE about 1930 *The Cascade* made it a summertime habit to include an open air observation car over the most spectacular portions of the Shasta route, a practice dating back to the first regular transcontinental trains on the Overland Route in 1871 when similar cars were attached at Truckee for the Sierra crossing. *The Oregonian's* observation presented a profile of enduring solidity in its conventional dimension.   *(Two Photos: Southern Pacific.)*

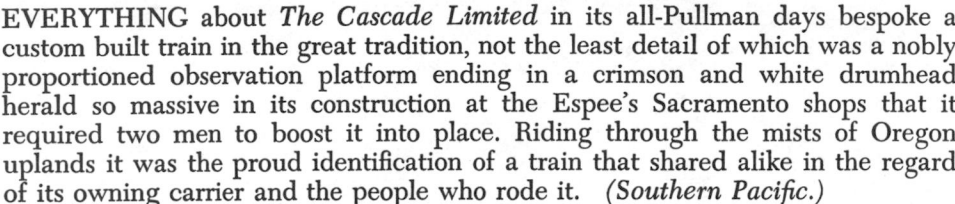

EVERYTHING about *The Cascade Limited* in its all-Pullman days bespoke a custom built train in the great tradition, not the least detail of which was a nobly proportioned observation platform ending in a crimson and white drumhead herald so massive in its construction at the Espee's Sacramento shops that it required two men to boost it into place. Riding through the mists of Oregon uplands it was the proud identification of a train that shared alike in the regard of its owning carrier and the people who rode it. *(Southern Pacific.)*

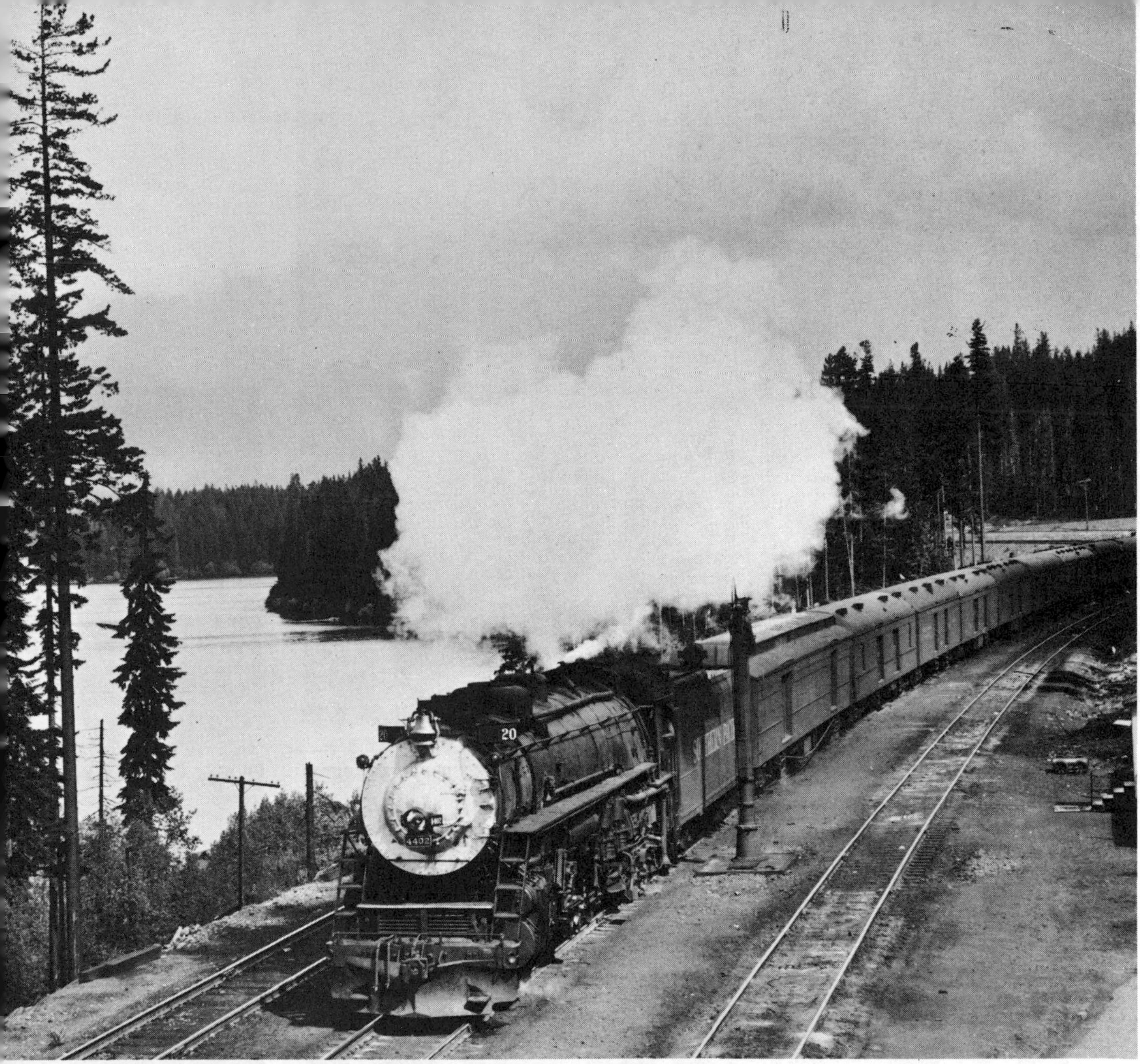

TO SAN FRANCISCO 536 7/10 M.
CASCADE SUMMIT
ELEVATION 4839 FEET.
TO PORTLAND

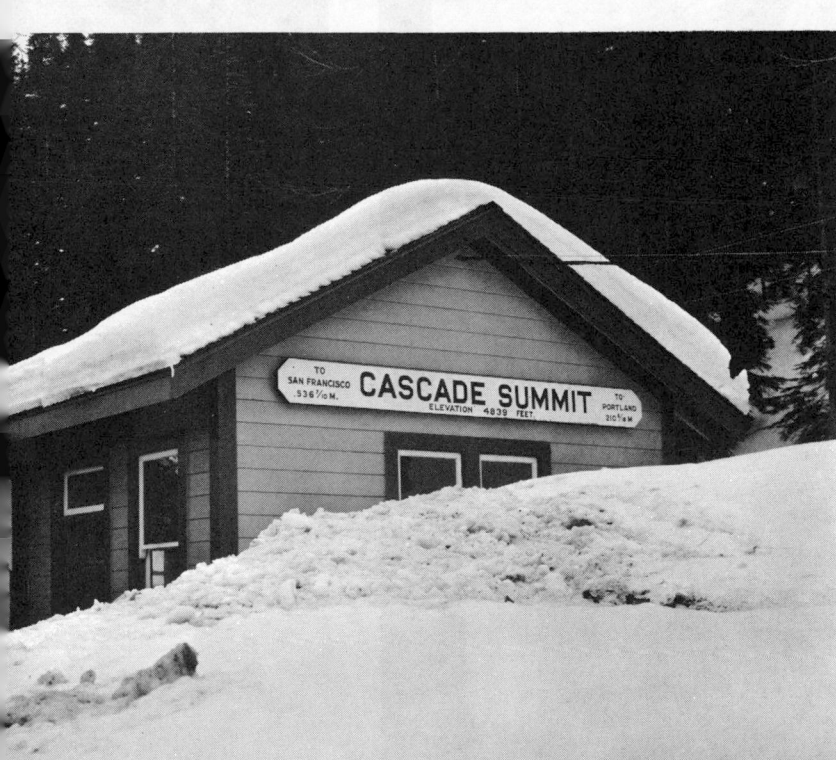

FOR THE LONG inland haul between Los Angeles and its northern terminal at Portland, the Southern Pacific maintained service aboard a train of all work called *The West Coast* which by-passed San Francisco and paid its way with vast quantities of head-end revenue. Never operated with pretentions to luxury, *The West Coast* was a service run with coaches, Pullman Standard sleepers, a diner and observation lounge whose open platform and illuminated train herald gave it its only trace of the grand manner. Below, *The West Coast* is shown against a pastoral background near Newhall, California, approaching its southern terminal. Opposite, a company photographer has invested an open section with an imaginative touch in the form of reading glasses and a copy of *Good Housekeeping*. (Below: Donald Duke; Opposite, Two Photos: Southern Pacific.)

THERE WAS PLENTY of time to catch up on one's reading or write letters on the lounge car of *The West Coast*, shown opposite on its long haul from Portland to Los Angeles over the inland route, while *The West Coast* itself *(below)* made a fine portrait of mainline passenger business as it passed through Saugus, California, doubleheaded in 1948. *(Above: Southern Pacific; Below: Donald Duke)*

SAILING TIME for *The Argonaut* on the secondary run to New Orleans coincided closely with departure time at the old Los Angeles Station of *The Golden State* and *The Californian* for Chicago, all of them names of consequence in the transcontinental passenger traffic of another age. The density of Southern Pacific name train travel out of Los Angeles barely lasted into the lifetime of the fine new Union Station where it shared facilities in spacious Spanish Mission surroundings with the Santa Fe and Union Pacific in the years of ever diminishing passenger revenue. *(Southern Pacific.)*

SEEN through the barbershop window with the end cars of the *City of San Francisco* and *The Cascade* spotted on their appropriate tracks, the dominant character of the train shed at Oakland was one of great age and gentle decline. Knowing that its years were numbered, the railroad ignored the inroads of time until departing from its confines was as from a museum of memories and a repository of sentimental souvenirs. For San Franciscans it was just that. (*Richard Steinheimer.*)

TRANQUILITY pervades the great train shed at Oakland Mole late in the evening in 1950 between arrivals and departures. The second section, an extra run between Fresno and Oakland, of the *San Joaquin Daylight* has discharged its passengers and will shortly back into the yards while on the farther track the Pullmans of *The Klamath* await loading for a late evening departure. One of San Francisco's now vanished pleasures was the approach to Oakland Mole aboard a Southern Pacific ferry *(opposite)* at the beginning of a train trip while uncounted thousands of travelers since 1875 when the first train shed was built there and the ferries began had caught their first glimpse of the Metropolis of The West from the same vantage point. Just as Broad Street set the mood for arriving in Philadelphia, everyone agreed the water passage was the only thinkable entrance to make to San Francisco. *(Two Photos: Richard Steinheimer.)*

AT VARIOUS TIMES in its checkered career *The Imperial* ran as a sleeper hop between Calexico and Los Angeles, as a Los Angeles-Chicago through train secondary to *The Golden State Limited* via the Imperial Valley and at length as a Chicago haul routed directly between Niland-Yuma instead of the Valley Route. Usually *The Imperial* in its Valley days as shown here in 1952 made its run both ways through the Imperial Valley in darkness, but when the camera of Richard Steinheimer caught it as shown opposite it was running twelve hours off schedule and hence as Extra 4436. A tropical morning sun shines on *The Imperial* amidst the irrigational properties of modern agriculture. At the left the conductor and head-end crew of *The Imperial* compare watches at Yuma. *(Southern Pacific.)*

AS LATE as the early 1950s when *The Imperial* was only a memory in the valley of its name, perhaps the last Southern Pacific passenger run to be powered in steam by a ten wheeler was the night passenger run from Calexico on the Mexican border to Los Angeles shown here at El Centro in the midnight hours. *(Richard Steinheimer)*

741

JUST TO SHOW the executive brass back at Fourth & Townsend that they were operating at concert pitch, the depot staff at Grants Pass, Oregon, in 1893 had itself photographed in this atmospheric group surrounded by every available property of the passenger agent's calling including an L. C. Smith writing machine, high speed telegrapher's bug, rate books and an alarm clock to show they were on their toes. It was an impressive documentary. *(Southern Pacific.)*

IN THE YEAR 1911 when this 2300 series 4-6-0 was photographed with *The Shasta Limited* near Woodburn, Oregon, by D. S. Warnock, the Oregon-Washington Railroad & Navigation Company observation car *(below)* carried the train name in a diminutive herald hung from the platform rail instead of the imposing drumhead of the years to come. *(Southern Pacific.)*

ALTHOUGH it was later to be shame-fully downgraded as a train of all work without a name, *The Klamath* in 1929 when it was inaugurated on the San Francisco-Portland run be-came the fifth daily train between the two terminals, a roster which included *The Cascade, The Shasta, The Beaver* and *The California-Oregon Express* and to which in a few years *The Shasta Daylight* was to be added. It is shown opposite, in a photograph by Herb H. Arey, paused at Ashland for the accustomed head-end business of a mainliner of long haul importance. At the top, opposite, its provisioning at the southern end of its run was ac-complished at the Espee's all-embrac-ing commissary at Oakland. Lounges *(left)* on long runs in those halcyon times were gentleman's clubs where a member of the Lambs or Players, far from home, could expect to find *Variety* in the reading rack along with the regional papers and *The Official Guide.*   *(Three Photos: South-ern Pacific.)*

CHECKING ROOM
SMOKING

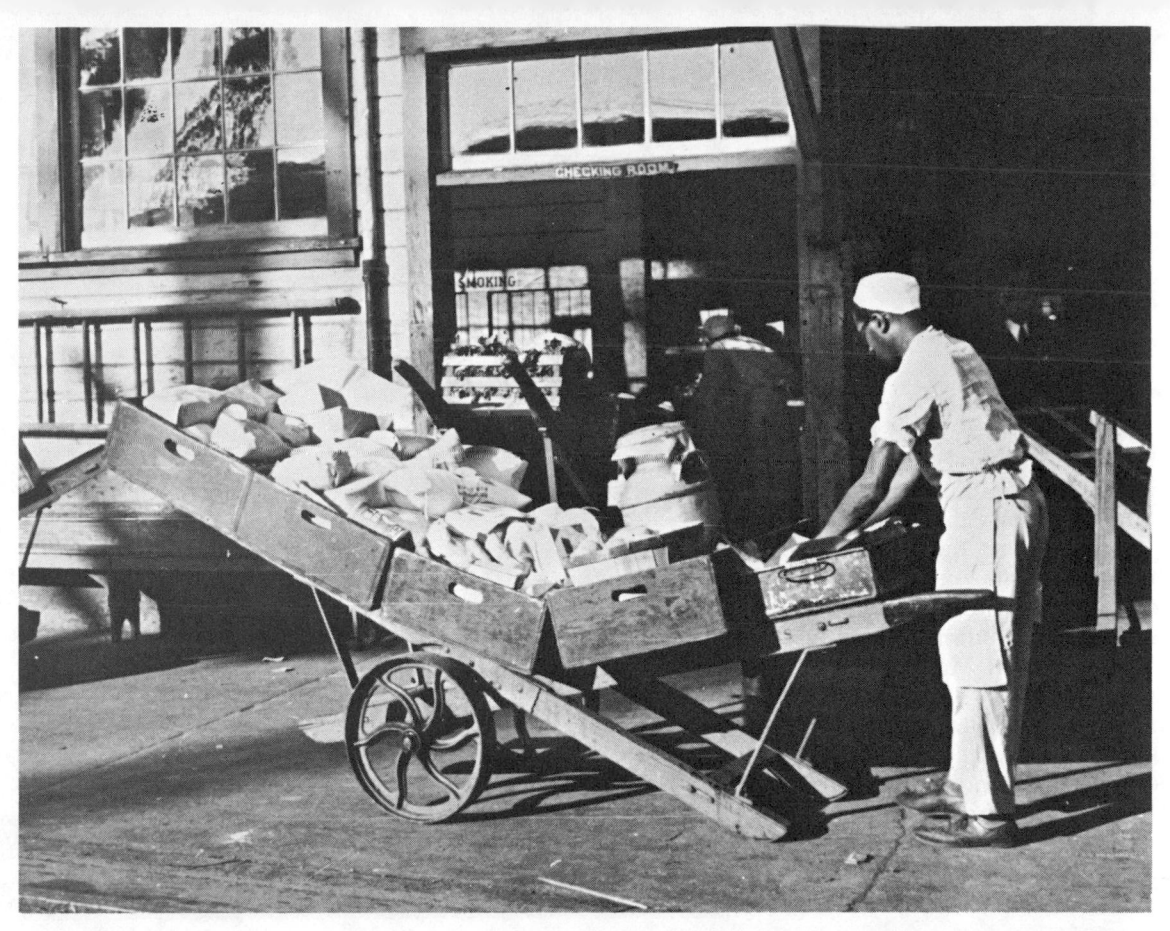

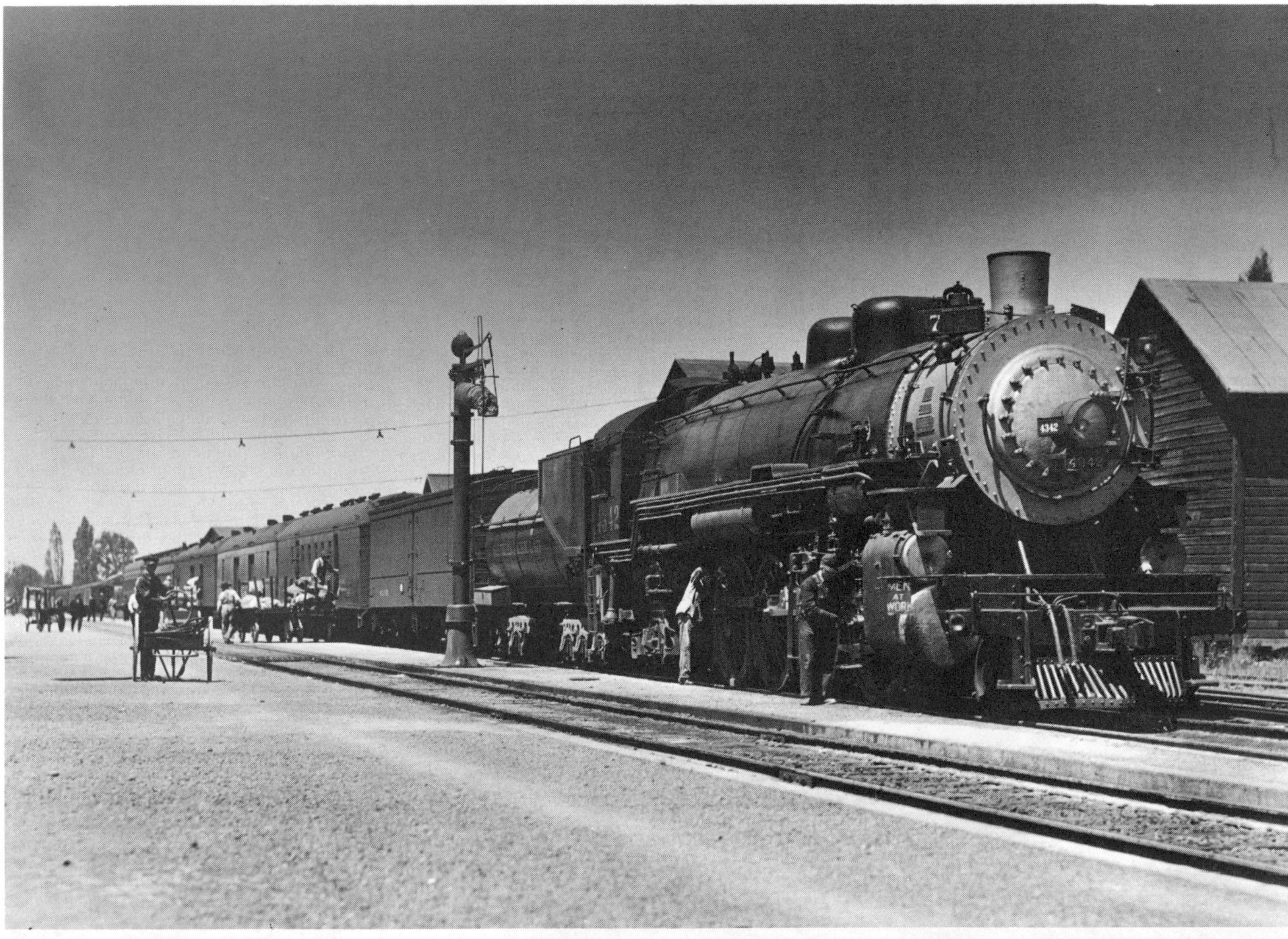
4342

IN A LESS DEMANDING age of railroad travel and before a more fastidious public became accustomed to all-room Pullmans, entire families traveled across the continent in open sections and in complete contentment. It was an age when staterooms and compartments were only for the aged and infirm or grandees of importance. Most of No. 10's passengers considered a lower berth to be luxurious. Below are depicted the celebrated snowsheds in the High Sierra at Cisco and the marvelous covered turntable where helper engines were turned for the return descent to Truckee. *(Right: Southern Pacific; Below: Fred Jukes.)*

THE SOUTHERN PACIFIC'S Train No. 10, *The San Francisco Limited* in 1915 was regularly scheduled out of Oakland Pier on a twenty-seven hour run to Ogden in two sections, the first with ten cars and an all-Standard Pullman consist through to Chicago including a ten-section observation sleeper, while the second section carried chair cars and tourist sleepers including one for St. Louis via Denver over the Rock Island. More exotic and a far heavier train was No. 6, *The Atlantic Express* which sailed five hours later with Standard sleepers for Truckee and Susanville, another for Minneapolis over the Chicago, St. Paul, Minneapolis & Omaha (North Western) and an observation car running only between Montello, Nevada, and Ogden. (*Fred Jukes.*)

IN THE YEAR 1915 when pioneer photographer Fred
Jukes, took this magnificent action shot at
Elko, Nevada, while snow was on the sagebrush
and steam exhaust condensed above the engine stack,
the Southern Pacific's Train No. 10 was
The San Francisco Limited running between
Oakland and Chicago via The Overland Route and
the connecting Union Pacific and North Western
railroads. Second in status to the all-Pullman
Overland Limited, No. 10 was still a train of style to
provide an immortal photographic vignette from
the camera of an old master in the iconography of an
as yet unspoiled West. Pullman equipment on
The San Francisco Limited included club cars in which
the smoking lounge was separated from the through
corridor by a partition with leaded glass windows.
(Above: Southern Pacific; Right: Fred Jukes.)

749

ELKO, Nevada, had changed but little since 1875 when the below sketch was made until 1916 when the photograph opposite of *The Pacific Limited* was made there. Until the coming of the motor car Nevada was still a frontier.

LIKE THE MORE STATELY likeness on an adjacent page, Train No. 20, *The Pacific Limited*, vignetted at the top of the page, was photographed coming out of Elko, Nevada, circa 1916 by Fred Jukes and was a favorite picture subject with the great pioneer photographer. It cleared Elko yards in the morning and hence achieved immortality in a number of Juke exposures. It is shown again below against the Nevada vastness of the Ruby Mountains in a panorama of desolation unchanged from that time until today. On the opposite page the lounge car of *The Limited* is comfortably filled with button boots and yawning young ladies while, to give a stateroom berth character a company photographer has spotted an orchid corsage on the Pullman sheets and a novel for the long jornada to Chicago. *(Opposite and Above: Southern Pacific; Top: Fred Jukes.)*

THREE VIGNETTES of traintime activity are characteristic of the depot at Ogden, Utah, where the Southern Pacific and Union Pacific interchanged at a period twenty years later than the portrait of No. 20 on the page opposite. *(Three Photos: Southern Pacific.)*

WHILE, IN THE NATURAL course of events the newest and finest equipment on the Ogden route to Chicago was assigned to the all-Pullman, extra fare *Overland Limited,* Trains No. 19 and 20, *The Pacific Limited* made up in fascinating variety of rolling stock what they lacked in de luxe panache of elegance. As of November 1915, the regularly assigned cars of the eastbound section of the *Pacific Limited* included a baggage car with a dynamo and complete electric plant for illuminating the train, two mail storage cars, two tourist sleepers for Chicago, one out of Omaha via the North Western and the other over the Milwaukee, a Standard diner, five Pullman Standard sleepers, one of them for Salt Lake over the Oregon Short Line out of Ogden and four for Chicago, one by way of Denver over the Rio Grande and Rock Island, one over the Rio Grande and Burlington, one through Omaha and the North Western and one via Omaha and the Milwaukee, and an observation sleeper via the U.P. to Omaha and the rest of the way by the Milwaukee. This complicated scheduling provided either tourist or first class accommodations from San Francisco to almost any imaginable point of importance in the trans-Mississippi West and divided its interchange with five mainline carriers. Even in a day of complex scheduling and involved interchange, *The Official Guide* could show few name trains of such diversification and versatility. No. 20 is shown here in a stylish action portrait taken at Elko, Nevada, in 1916 by Fred Jukes, the grand old man of Western railroad photography.

753

No.	TO	Will Leave
	AMERICAN CANYON ROUTE Via OGDEN	
24	Reno-Hazen-Mina-Tonopah-Goldfield via Stockton	1.50 A.M
2	"OVERLAND LIMITED" All Eastern Points.	11.30 " "
22	"ST. LOUIS EXPRESS" Ogden Kansas City & St Louis	1.30 P.M
20	"PACIFIC LIMITED" All Eastern Points.	6.32 " "
6	NEVADA EXPRESS Sacramento - Colfax - Reno - Goldfield - Susanville -	7.30 " "
10	ATLANTIC EXPRESS - Reno Ogden Salt Lake City Denver.	9.45 " "
	SHASTA ROUTE	
14	PORTLAND EXPRESS - Ashland Portland Tacoma Seattle.	8.50 A.M
12	"THE SHASTA" Portland Tacoma Seattle	4.27 P.M
16	OREGON EXPRESS - Klamath Falls Ashland Portland Tacoma Seattle.	8.55 " "
54	"OREGONIAN" Portland Tacoma Seattle & Puget Sound.	10.55 " "
	LOS ANGELES AND SAN JOAQUIN VALLEY	
36	Richmond. Martinez. Tracy. Newman. Los Banos. Kerman. Fresno.	6.30 A.M
32	"SACRAMENTO LOCAL" Sacramento via Niles - Stockton - Lodi - Galt - Ione.	7.50 " "
84	"VALLEY FLYER" Richmond Port Costa Martinez Tracy Modesto Turlock Merced Yosemite Madera Fresno	9.05 " "
82	Niles - Pleasanton - Livermore - Tracy - Newman - Los Banos - Patterson - Stockton - Oakdale - Sonora	9.05 " "
8	Richmond Pt. Costa Martinez Byron Hot Springs Tracy Modesto Fresno Bakersfield Los Angeles	11.07 " "
50	"TEHACHAPI" Fresno Bakersfield Los Angeles	4.30 P.M
26	"OWL" Fresno Bakersfield Los Angeles	6.27 " "
86	"Oil Fields Express" Martinez. via Yosemite Fresno. Visalia. Porterville. Tulare. Bakersfield. Los Angeles.	11.30 " "
	SACRAMENTO AND SACRAMENTO VALLEY	
24	Niles Tracy Stockton Lodi Galt Sacramento Colfax	1.50 A.M
28	Richmond Vallejo Pt. Costa Benicia Suisun-Fairfield Vacaville Davis Sacramento.	6.25 " "
32	"SACRAMENTO LOCAL" Sacramento via Niles Tracy Stockton Lodi	7.50 " "
18	"THE STATESMAN" Richmond Port Costa Benicia Suisun-Fairfield Davis Sacramento	8.05 " "
18	Red Bluff Redding Dunsmuir Via Woodland Williams Willows Corning	8.05 " "
14	Dunsmuir via Richmond Sacramento Marysville Red Bluff.	9.50 " "
22	"St. LOUIS EXPRESS" Truckee via Port Costa Benicia Sacramento Colfax.	1.30 P.M
22	Roseville Marysville Chico	1.30 " "
46	Richmond - Port Costa - Benicia - Suisun - Elmira - Dixon - Davis - Sacramento.	3.05 " "
38	Niles Pleasanton Livermore Tracy Lathrop Stockton Lodi Galt & Way to Sacramento.	4.24 " "
48	Richmond - Port Costa - Benicia - Suisun - Davis - Sacramento	5.25 " "
48	Gerber via Davis Williams Willows Orland Corning.	5.25 " "
80	"STOCKTON FLYER" Tracy Stockton Lodi	6.24 " "
20	"PACIFIC LIMITED" Colfax Grass Valley Truckee.	6.32 " "
6	Truckee Colfax via Benicia Davis Sacramento.	7.30 " "
16	Dunsmuir via Richmond Sacramento Marysville Red Bluff.	8.55 " "
	VIA VALLEJO OR MARTINEZ	
124	Ship Yard Train. (Daily except Sunday)	6.27 A.M
122	Richmond Oleum Selby Vallejo Jct. Crockett Port Costa (Daily except Sunday)	7.05 " "
42	Richmond Vallejo Napa St. Helena Calistoga Crockett Port Costa Martinez Concord San Ramon	8.27 " "
22	Vallejo - Port Costa.	1.30 P.M
50	Richmond Port Costa Martinez Pittsburg Brentwood Byron Hot Springs Tracy	4.30 " "
44	Richmond Pinole Vallejo Napa Santa Rosa Crockett Port Costa Martinez Bay Point	5.07 " "
130	Richmond Rodeo Oleum Pinole Crockett Martinez, Except Sunday	7.05 " "
132	Richmond Pinole Vallejo Crockett Port Costa Martinez, (Sunday Only)	8.05 " "
	LIVERMORE AND SAN JOSE VIA NILES OR NEWARK	
90	San Leandro Lorenzo Hayward Decoto Niles Irvington Warm Springs Milpitas San Jose.	7.05 A.M
32	Stockton via Niles Livermore.	7.50 " "
502	Way Stations to Santa Cruz & San Luis Obispo via Newark & San Jose.	8.10 " "
82	San Jose via Niles - Irvington - Warm Springs	9.05 " "
92	San Leandro Hayward Niles Irvington San Jose	12.05 P.M
902	Stonehurst Local	3.45 " "
96	San Leandro. Hayward Niles. Irvington. Milpitas. San Jose.	5.50 " "

A ROLL CALL of the names of the great departed which in the noontide of their going had been the good familiar things of California life made up the list of train departures from Oakland Mole in 1922, which as is suggested below, was the high water mark of passengers on American railroads. Here were rare birds in the lexicon of train amateurs: Train No. 24 for Tonopah and Goldfield a wistful souvenir of the time, more than a decade gone, when the Southern Mines of Nevada and the California border were the talk of every mining exchange in the world, the *St. Louis Express*, depicted opposite, and the old *Portland Express* which took the better part of two days time to achieve Multnomah. Oil was a new thing in Bakersfield and there was an *Oil Fields Express* on the inland run to Los Angeles. There was the *Tehachapi*, too, on the southland run, a name long since forgotten by all but aging students of the legend of Southern Pacific. Wonder, at this remove, rode them all and wonder, of course, rode in steam.

IN THE YEAR 1920 and for six years thereafter there were carried on the Southern Pacific trainsheets Trains No. 21-22, *The St. Louis Express,* an authentic *rara avis* to connoisseurs of such matters, almost as elusive in the pictorial record as the short lived *Arizona Limited* of 1940-41. *The St. Louis Express* ran to the Union Pacific connection at Ogden over the Espee, to Kansas City via the U.P. and into St. Louis by way of the Wabash. It carried a conventional consist of Pullmans, tourist sleepers and chair cars with an open platform observation lounge and tailgate insigne (*vide* "The Central Pacific & The Southern Pacific Railroads.") and its life span bracketed the all-time high in railroad passenger travel which is generally accepted as being reached in 1922. In 1926 it was merged with *The Pacific Limited* and a vestigial trace of this vanished run survives until now in the through St. Louis sleeper that leaves Oakland in *The City of San Francisco.* (Three Photos: Southern Pacific.)

OAKLAND PIER
Restaurant
PUBLIC TELEPHONE
WESTERN UNION

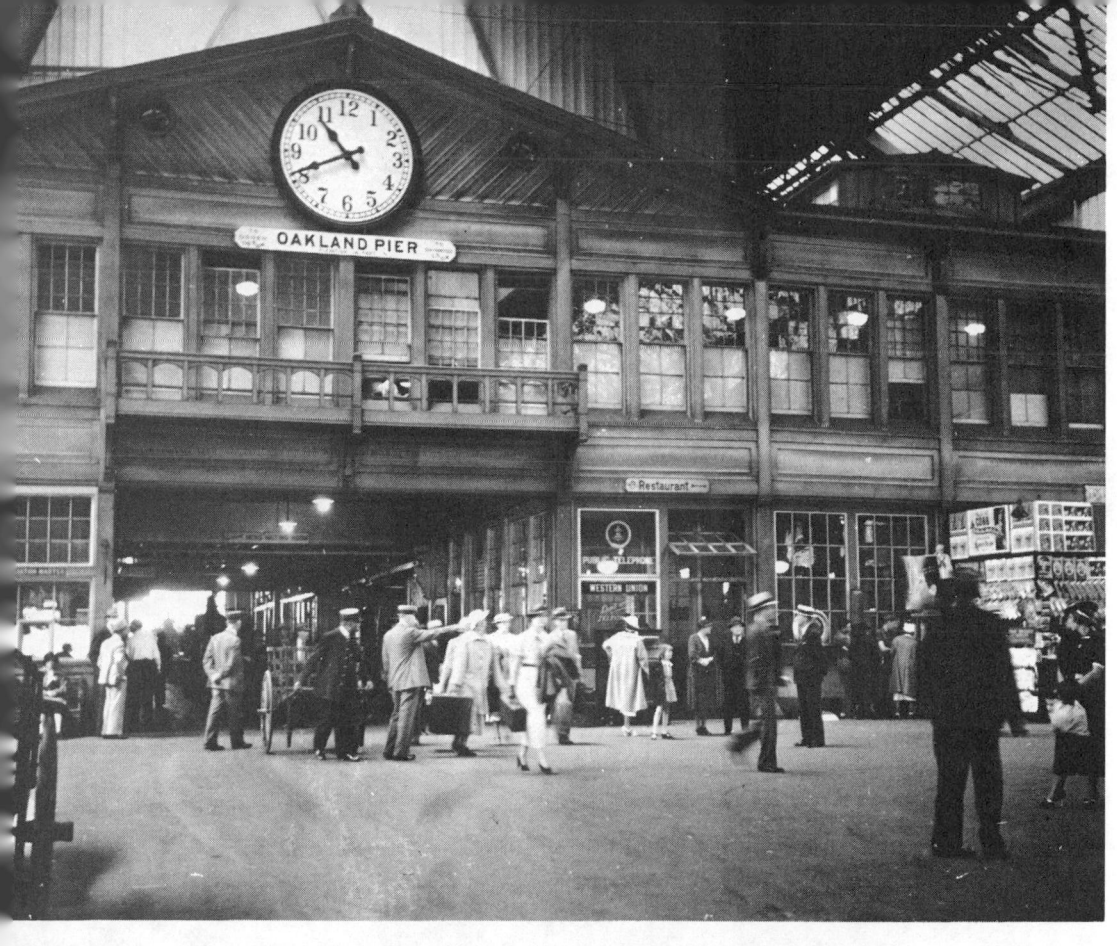

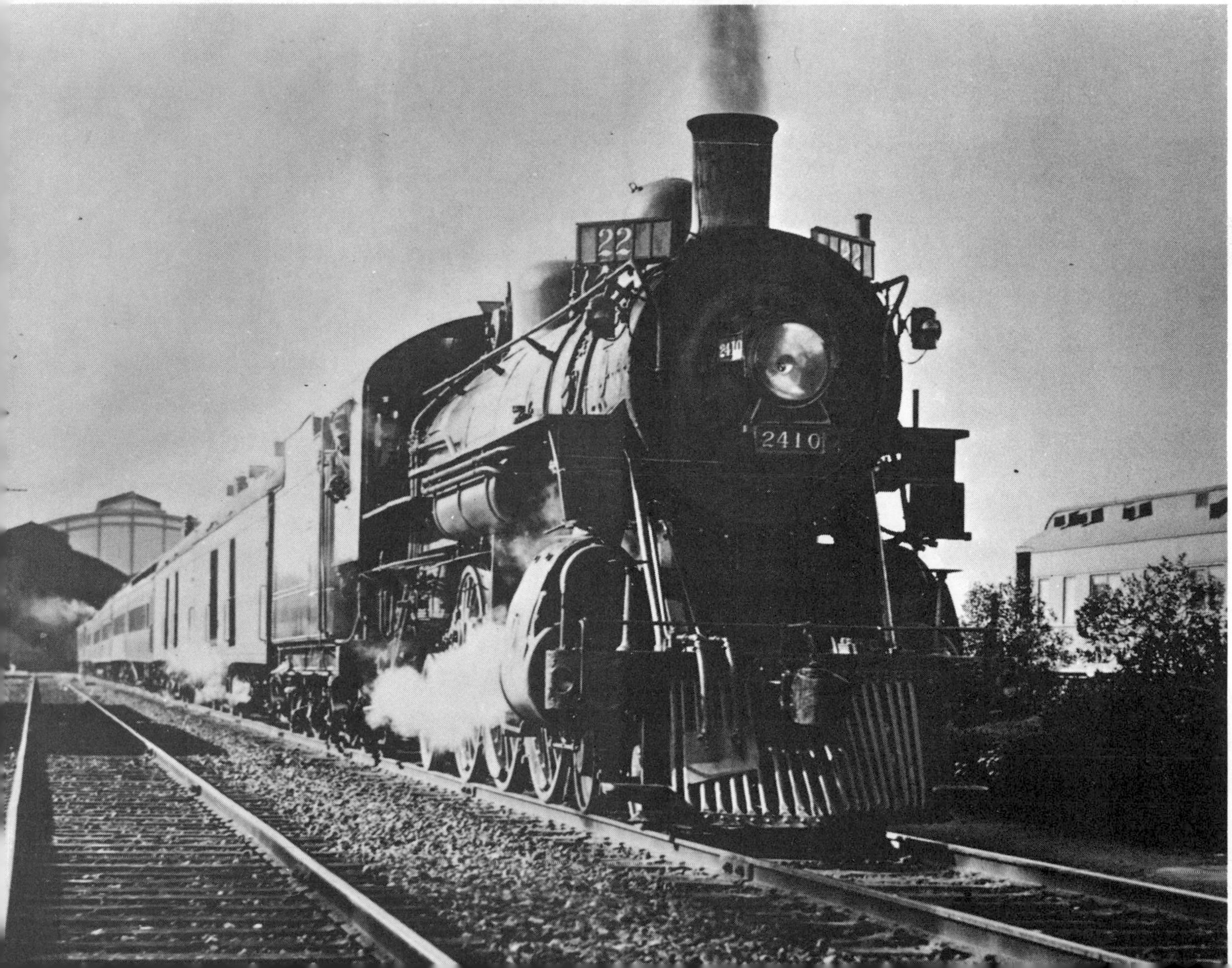
22
2410
2410

PERHAPS the noblest name in all the lexicon of Western railroading, *The Overland Limited* between San Francisco and Chicago for more than half a century set a standard of excellence widely imitated but seldom achieved on other transcontinental runs. Opposite in a magnificent portrait taken at Elko, Nevada, in the winter of 1916 by Fred Jukes, *The Overland* heads east through the snowy sage. Jukes, a celebrated pioneer action photographer believes this to be his best of many action views of *The Overland* and himself processed the print from which the reproduction was made. At the left is *The Overland* train gate at Oakland Mole in an atmospheric double exposure while below is its club car circa 1919 from the internal evidence of attire and manners. (*Opposite: Fred Jukes; Two Photos: Southern Pacific.*)

THE GOLDEN SPIKE Hotel at Promontory, Utah, a dodger or handbill for which, reproduced on the opposite page, was handed out aboard all Central Pacific trains without diners as late as 1905, was a relic of primeval times on the transcontinental run and dated from boom days at Promontory in 1869 when the rails were joined there. The inclusion of through diners on all first class runs and the completion of the Lucin cutoff across Great Salt Lake spelled the end for Promontory's foremost eating house as it did for the long haul around the north end of the Lake through the desolate Utah uplands. Above is shown *The Overland Limited* in the days when it was the most compelling name in Western travel taking off at sunset across the Lucin trestle that spelled the doom of Promontory. It is depicted from the head end in a portrait taken in 1916 at Elko, Nevada, by the pioneer railroad cameraman, Fred Jukes. *The Overland's* buffet *(right)*, in the days of hot filament Edison bulbs supplemented by Pintsch gas in case of power failure, was the finest thing on wheels west of Chicago. *(Opposite: Fred Jukes; Three Photos: Southern Pacific.)*

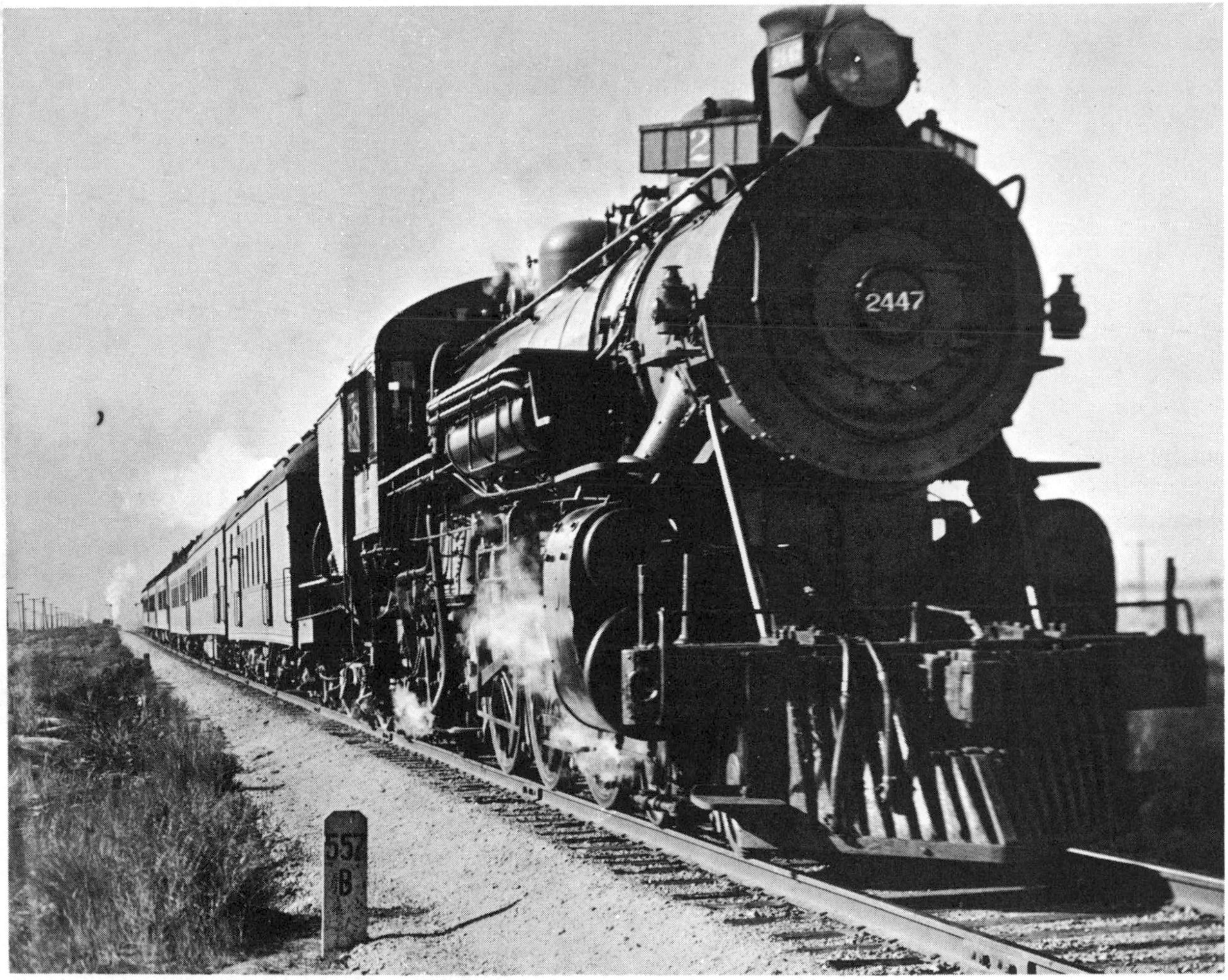

THIS TRAIN

STOPS

20 Minutes for Supper at the

Golden Hotel

PROMONTORY, UTAH.

FIRST-CLASS MEALS, 50 CENTS.

THE GOLDEN SPIKE

Completing the first Trans-continental Railroad was driven at this point May 10, 1869. Don't fail to treat yourself to a first class meal at this celebrated point.

T. G. BROWN, Prop.

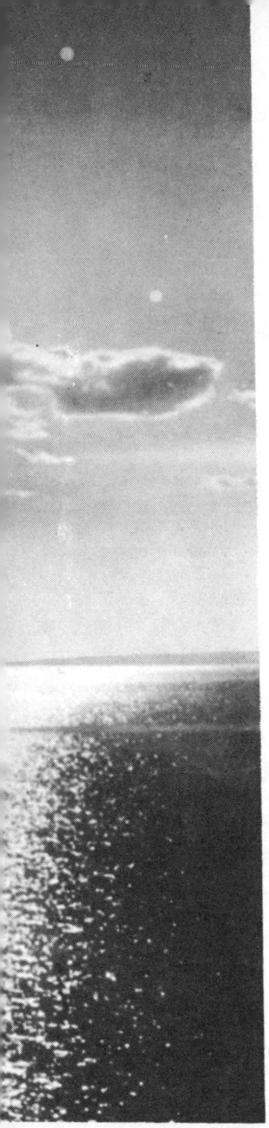

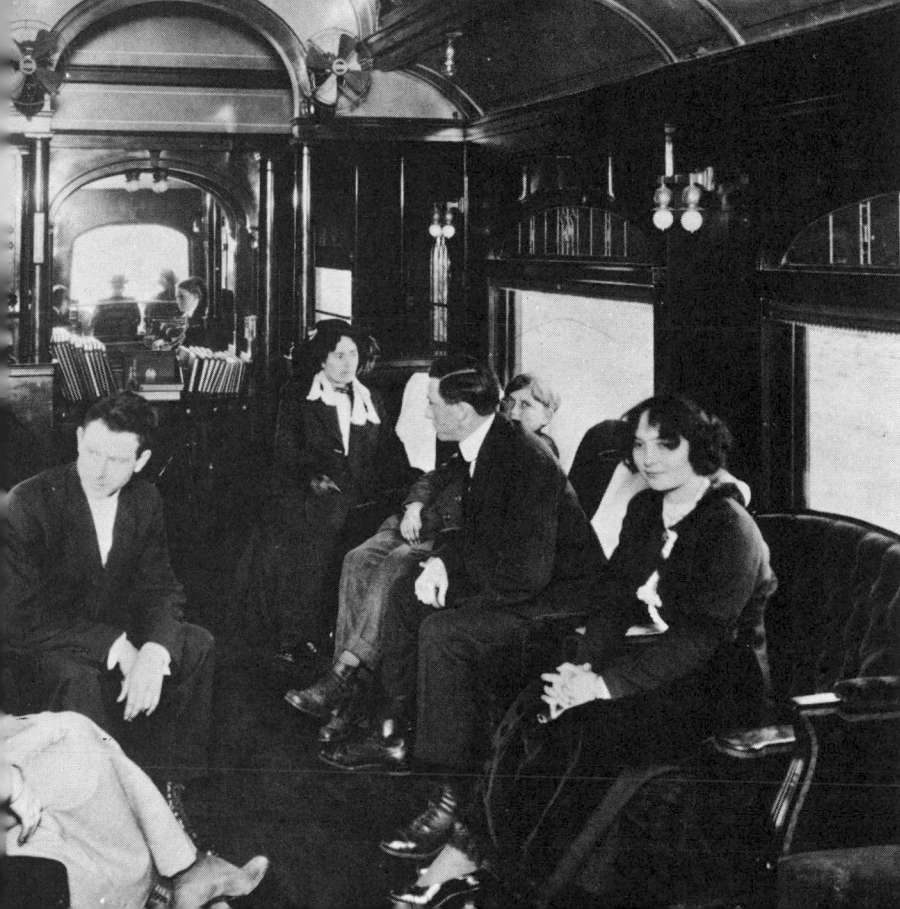

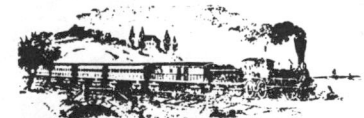

PEOPLE WROTE LETTERS and addressed postcards in the spacious days of
The Overland's supremacy between Chicago and San Francisco. Such pleasant
occupations were accomplished aboard the Southern Pacific's Pullman-Standard
lounge cars such as that shown here where abundant resources of heavily embossed stationery and company blotters were available and there was a handy
postbox which the car attendant emptied at Omaha, Cheyenne, Green River or
Ogden as might be required. It was all part of the pleasant way of travel.
(*Southern Pacific.*)

PRETENTIONS to transcendent gastronomy were, in the last years of *The Overland*, more or less abated, but steaks and chops were, until the shortages of the 1941 war, of splendid dimensions and breakfasts were always superb. The Southern Pacific Salad Bowl was institutional wherever the carrier's writ might run and not indigenous to *The Overland* but it was a favorite with passengers and so much in request that its formula was included on the menu. In summer months, as is suggested below, slip covers appeared on the diners and iced tea was in universal demand at meals. *(Two Photos: Southern Pacific.)*

AT WELLS, Nevada, in a series of sweeping curves mounting the only grades of importance between Truckee water and Great Salt Lake, *The Overland* eastbound as shown in the center of the page surged up the Ruby Mountains where to this day elk and antelope are a commonplace outside the car windows. Immediately above, in a view from about 1910, *The Overland* rides the Straits of Carquinez aboard the vast car ferry *Solano*.

At the cartop of the observation rides one of the first illuminated heralds proclaiming the train's name, predecessor of the later tailgate insignes that were the identification of trains of name and breeding everywhere. (*Above: Fred Jukes; Right: Southern Pacific.*)

FOR SIX full decades, *The Overland* breasted the
High Sierra, sometimes at dawn, other times at
dusk as a changed carding might indicate.
The abrupt ascent west of Truckee often demanded
helper engines, while double heading was less
frequent on the gentler approaches to the western
foothills out of Sacramento. But whatever
the scheduling or motive power a constant was the
forest solitude and the towering conifers of the
Sierra passes, muffled with snowfall in winter,
mysterious still in the clement seasons and, as is
suggested here a stately frame for the passing
of a great name train of an older West.
(Southern Pacific.)

WHEN THE second streamlined *City of San Francisco* on a bi-weekly schedule was the fastest thing on wheels between Chicago and the Golden Gate its Diesel units required a steam helper out of Roseville if its tight schedule was to be maintained over the Sierra, and it is shown so running as the shadows deepen on a summer's evening somewhere above Auburn. Its standup bar in the Pullman lounge did a land-office business at cocktail time and, during the war years, even its coach space *(opposite)* was sold out to travelers on urgent occasions who could have afforded better had it been available. *(Below: Jim Morley; Opposite, Two Photos: Southern Pacific.)*

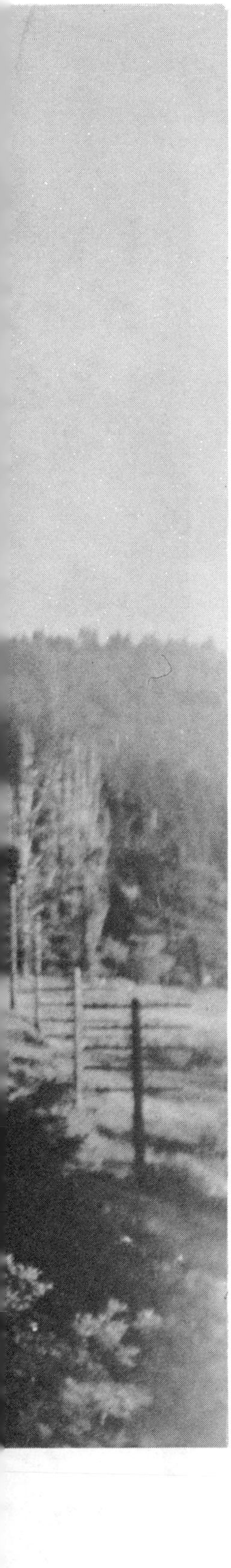

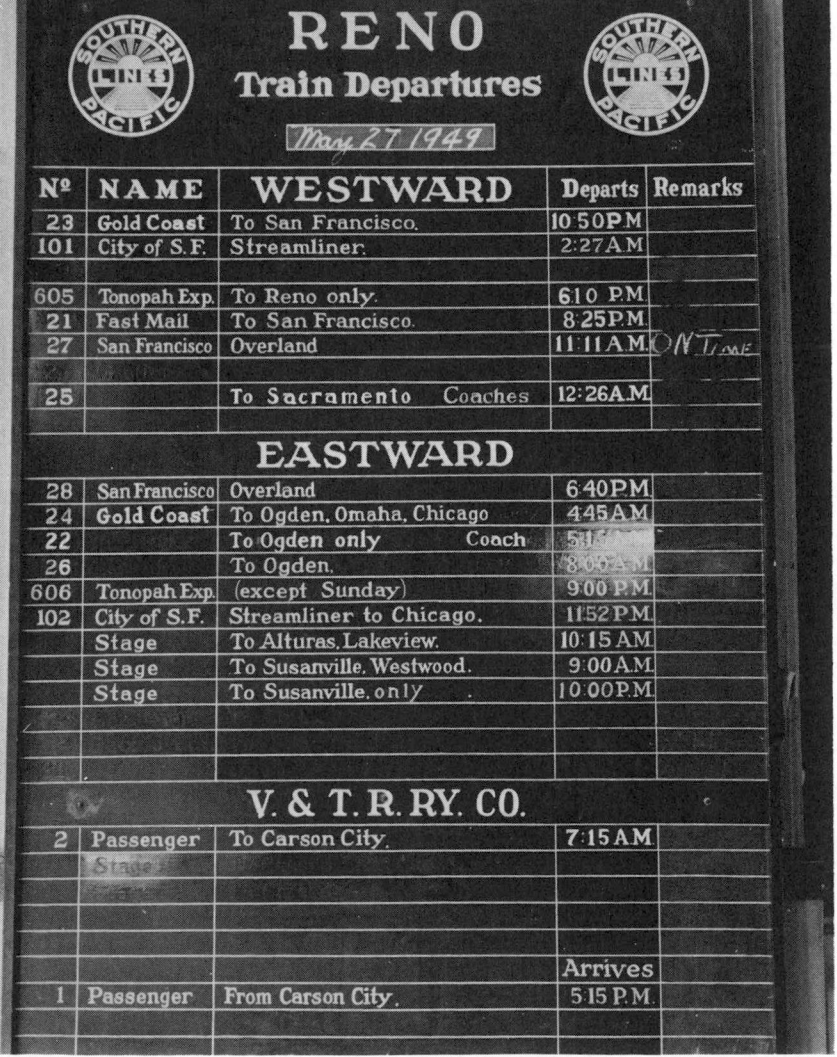

FOR EIGHTY full years the Virginia & Truckee cars met the mainline transcontinentals of the Southern Pacific at the depot they shared at Reno. The train board shown here was photographed in the last year of the long and useful partnership of two carriers with their roots in the legendary old West. (*Southern Pacific.*)

RENO Train Departures

SOUTHERN PACIFIC LINES

May 27 1949

Nº	NAME	WESTWARD	Departs	Remarks
23	Gold Coast	To San Francisco.	10:50 P.M.	
101	City of S.F.	Streamliner.	2:27 A.M.	
605	Tonopah Exp.	To Reno only.	6:10 P.M.	
21	Fast Mail	To San Francisco.	8:25 P.M.	
27	San Francisco	Overland	11:11 A.M.	ON Time
25		To Sacramento Coaches	12:26 A.M.	

EASTWARD

No	NAME		Departs	
28	San Francisco	Overland	6:40 P.M.	
24	Gold Coast	To Ogden, Omaha, Chicago	4:45 A.M.	
22		To Ogden only Coach	5:1?	
26		To Ogden,	8:02 A.M.	
606	Tonopah Exp.	(except Sunday)	9:00 P.M.	
102	City of S.F.	Streamliner to Chicago.	11:52 P.M.	
	Stage	To Alturas, Lakeview.	10:15 A.M.	
	Stage	To Susanville, Westwood.	9:00 A.M.	
	Stage	To Susanville, only	10:00 P.M.	

V. & T. R. RY. CO.

2	Passenger	To Carson City.	7:15 A.M.	
	Stage			
			Arrives	
1	Passenger	From Carson City.	5:15 P.M.	

OF ALL THE once populous and profitable short lines serving the Nevada bonanzas and connecting with the Central Pacific transcontinental main line in the nineteenth century, none was more celebrated or enjoyed as refulgent a longevity as the Virginia & Truckee built in 1870 to serve the Comstock Lode at Virginia City. Wealthy argosies of gold and silver rolled over the V & T's immaculately maintained operations as long as the bonanzas themselves lasted and the end only came in 1950 when the V & T had been an institution of the Old West for eighty glamorous years. In its final days it was a still functioning anachronism, its yellow wooden coaches and beautiful motive power reminders of a way of life that was gone forever. Below, the down train for Carson City rolls smokily through Washoe Canyon while opposite the wooden Kimball coaches appear against a background of the High Sierra near Washoe City. (*Two Photos: Lucius Beebe.*)

LONG A FAMILIAR PROPERTY of California travel, the *Lark* was placed in service on the Coast Route between Los Angeles and San Francisco in May 1910, traversing in the night hours the most spectacular seashore route in the world covered between breakfast and dinner on *The Daylight*. On the opposite page, the all-Pullman *Lark* approaches its Los Angeles terminal in a time when grade crossings were commonplace before construction of the present Union Station. Above, the breakfast time lounge of the *Lark*. *(Two Photos: Southern Pacific)*

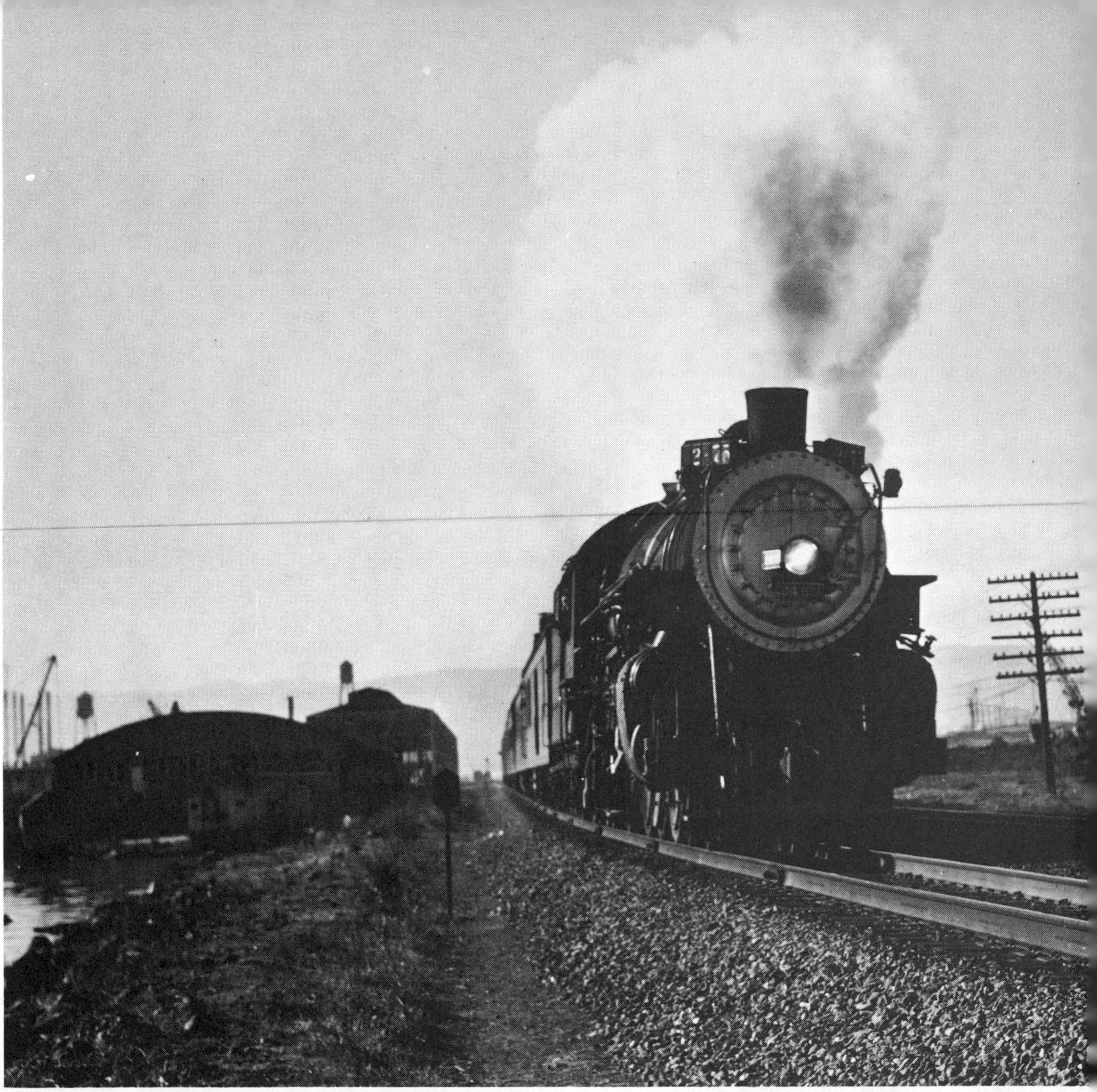

1011
1013
SOUTHERN PACIFIC COMPANY
SOUTHERN PACIFIC COMPANY

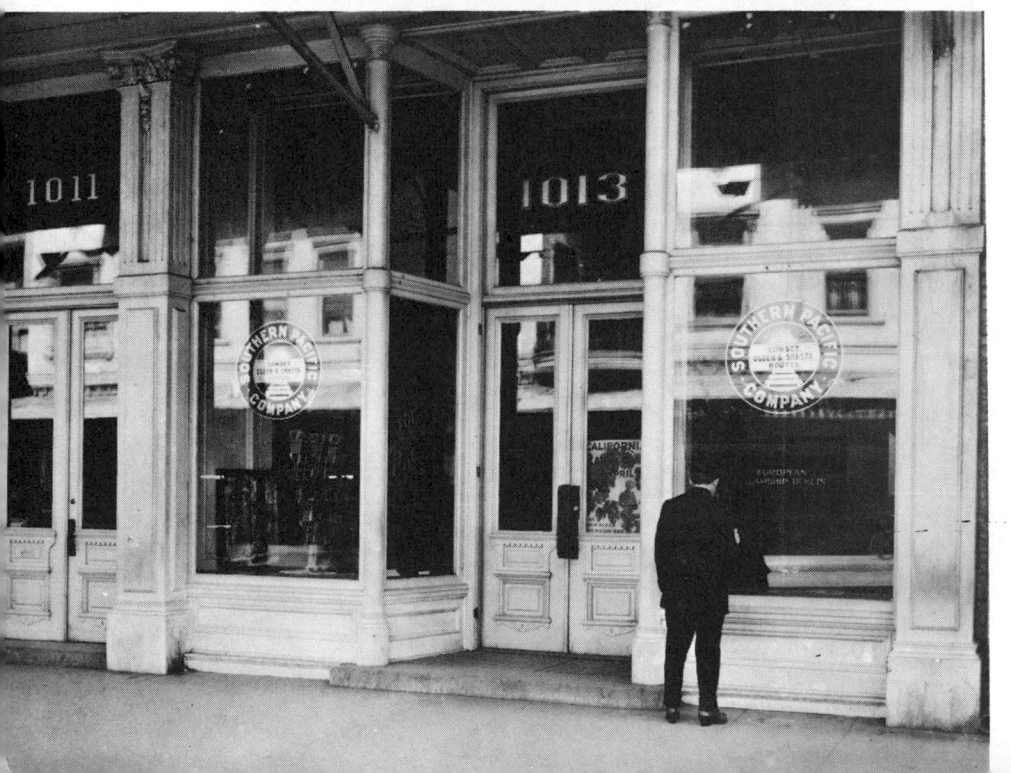

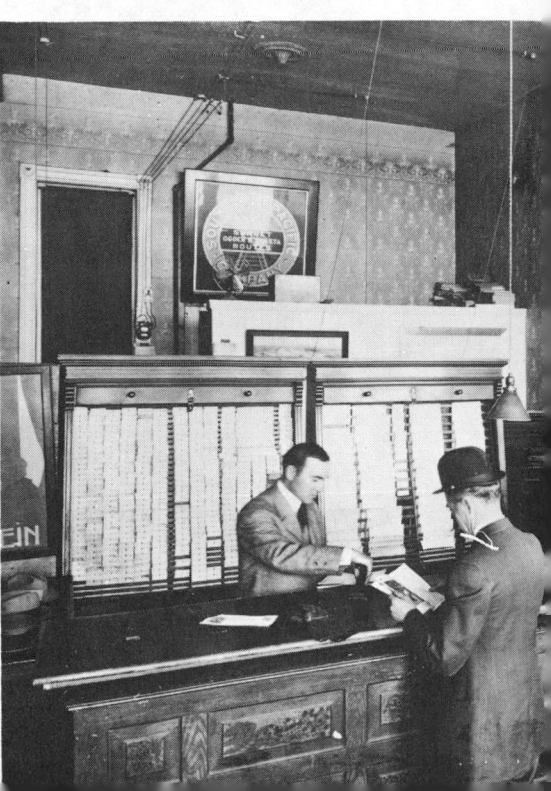

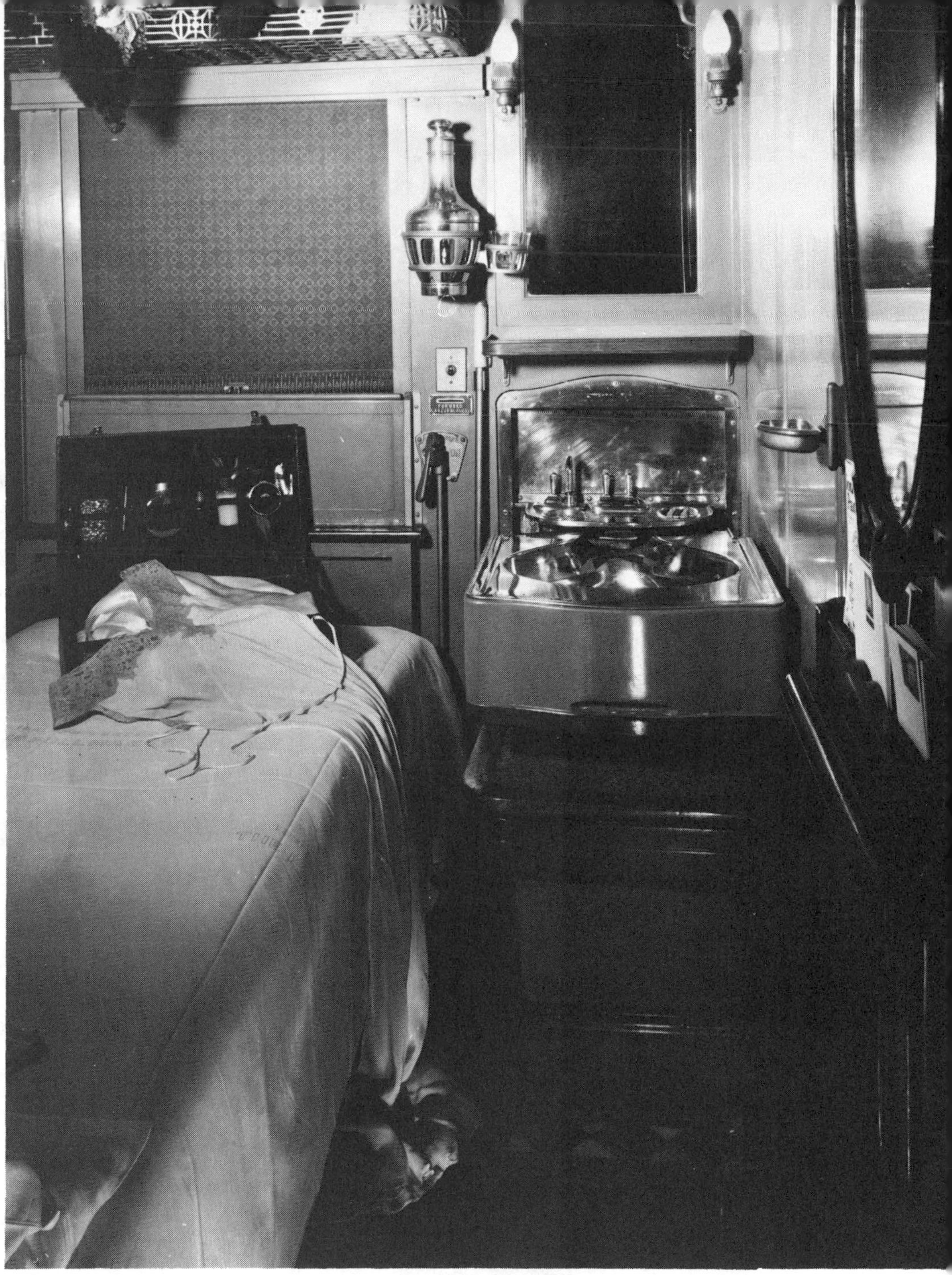

IN THE GREAT DAYS of passenger travel, the Southern Pacific maintained downtown ticket offices at strategic points in both San Francisco and Los Angeles, as shown on the page opposite, as well as in suburban Oakland and other population centers. There a derby hatted generation of travelers could book passage anywhere in the United States, much of it actually over company iron and, as an alternate, take space on the fine fleet of Espee steamers in service between California and New York. The northbound *Lark* is shown opposite passing through South San Francisco in a time when second sections were commonplace. Here the company photographer lent realism to a Pullman Standard single stateroom with a silk nightgown, silver-fitted dressing case and furs and orchids in the familiar Pullman rack above the window. *(Four Photos: Southern Pacific.)*

THE ESPEE station at Third and Townsend was one of the carrier's two entrepots in urban San Francisco, the other being the famed Ferry Building at the foot of Market Street where the ferries connected with Oakland Mole. Built in appropriate Spanish mission style, Third and Townsend was terminal for a large fleet of commute trains as well as Los Angeles and transcontinental runs in happier times. (*Southern Pacific.*)

SOMETIMES in its days of Pullman Standard equipment double-headed as
it appears on the opposite page, the *Lark* often ran in two sections
and is shown southbound at Glendale as it neared its southern terminus in
1935. The new streamlined equipment which was placed in service
after the 1941 war was actually liberally populated with the social
and worldly types depicted in the wash drawing shown here and the train
on its northbound run stopped not only at Palo Alto but also at
Burlingame to accommodate the convenience of San Francisco residents in
that exclusive suburb. *(Two Photos: Southern Pacific.)*

FEW NAME trains in the history of transport occasioned more elaborate promotional literature than the Espee's several *Daylights* when they were placed in service variously over the Coast Route between San Francisco and Los Angeles and the Valley Route between Sacramento-Oakland and Los Angeles. The card reproduced immediately below is evidence of the column of traffic the *Coast Daylight* enjoyed in its years as "The Most Beautiful Train in The World." *(Three Photos: Southern Pacific.)*

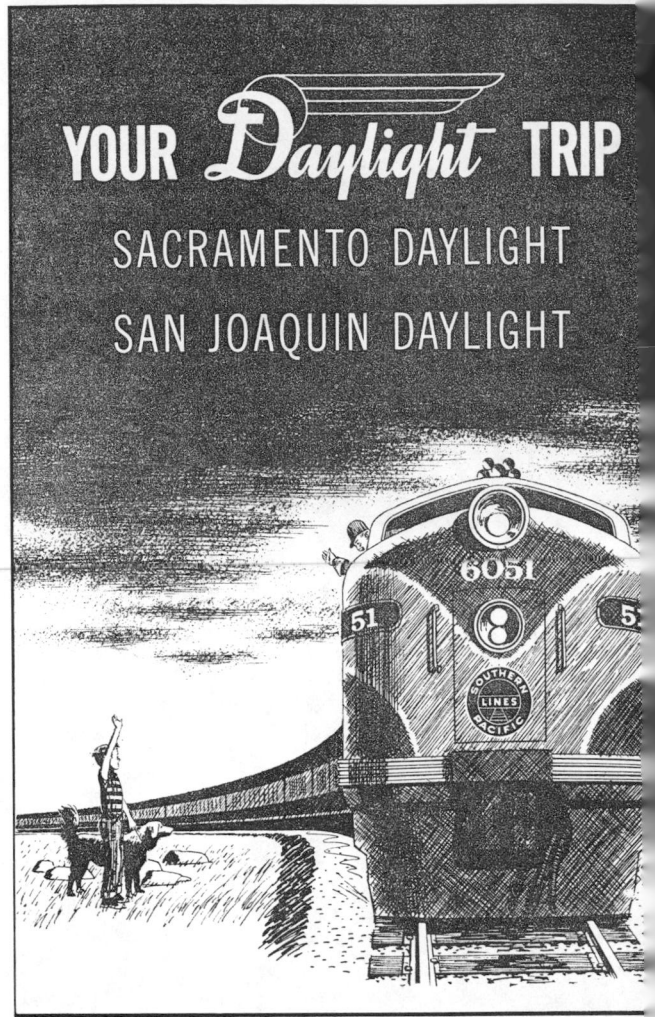

YOUR *Daylight* TRIP

SACRAMENTO DAYLIGHT

SAN JOAQUIN DAYLIGHT

To Our Patrons on the Second Section of the "Daylight":

Because all accommodations on the regular streamlined "Daylight" were sold out we are operating this second section. We regret that all could not be accommodated on the regular train but we are trying to do everything we can to make your trip on this section a pleasant one. On the other side of this card we give the schedule of the second section, believing you will want it for convenient reference, and call attention to the fact that the schedule is only 19 minutes slower than the first "Daylight" and is the fastest train schedule between Los Angeles and San Francisco with the exception of the "Daylight" itself. All available streamlined chair cars (like those on the "Daylight") are used on this train. When necessary other air-conditioned chair cars or coaches are used. In addition this train carries a diner, also a unique Tavern and Coffee Shop car which we feel sure you will be interested in seeing.

F. S. McGINNIS
Vice President, System Passenger Traffic.

LA

SOUTHERN PACIFIC COMPANY

BECAUSE OF its spectacular routing through the Tehachapi Mountains in the California southland, the *San Joaquin Daylight* at one time in its career was assigned a vista dome lounge car as an added attraction. *The Valley Daylight* itself is shown above, double-headed on its westbound run in Soledad Canyon in 1941 for a stately portrait of mountain railroading by Donald Duke.

775

TAKING A LEAF from the book of the Santa Fe's famous *de Luxe* (see Volume I) which boasted the only other luggage sticker of any name train in the American record, the Espee designed the cachet reproduced below with which passengers on *The Daylight* were urged to identify their bags and at the same time acquire a status symbol.

THE DEPARTURE of *The Daylight* from Third & Townsend Depot at San Francisco was the event of the day *(opposite)*. Well tended flowering shrubs blossomed at the track bumpers, station personnel stood at attention as one of the great name trains of the West made its departure in glory. *(Southern Pacific.)*

I'm just as good as *he* is!

It's terrible to have an older brother get all the breaks when he's really no better than you are. Take me. I'm just as good as the Morning Daylight - got baggage elevators, coffee shop, diner, tavern, foam rubber cushions, passenger agent and everything. But because the Morning Daylight was born first, all the boys are selling him instead of me. I'm doing fairly well, but I could do a lot better. Please don't forget me when people ask about the Daylight.

Thanks,

Your NOON DAYLIGHT

IN ITS Standard
equipment years, *The
Daylight* was still a
train of noble dimen-
sions and institutional
amidst the tropical
palms that lined the
Southern Pacific
right of way in the
vicinity of Santa Barbara.
The white faced
locomotives assigned
to the run even then
were semi-streamlined
with what was known
as a "skyline casing"
along their boiler tops.
(Donald Duke.)

778

ALTHOUGH in the years when it was advertised by the Southern Pacific as "The Most Beautiful Train in the World" the *Coast Daylight* in its red, orange and black streamlined livery was also perhaps the most photographed train in the world, its connecting stub run, *The Sacramento Daylight*, shown here at Lathrop with a rare Atlantic type locomotive, was one of the least frequently pictured. Although the magnificent equipment which ran in the *Daylight* when it was first placed in service was the most modern that could be had from any carbuilder, icing its cars through a trap in the roof differed but little from the same process which had been in vogue when the first Pullmans started rolling west after Promontory back in 1869. *(Left: Southern Pacific; Below: Donald Duke.)*

IN WINTER months during its glory years *The Daylight* arrived, as shown below, at its terminals by dusk or in total darkness. Here at Glendale in 1951 there still were train-watchers on hand for the arrival of "The Most Beautiful Train In The World" before it whistled off for the brief run to downtown Los Angeles. Its departure then *(right)* was a crowded hour for station personnel. *(Right: Southern Pacific; Below: Richard Steinheimer.)*

BORN UNDER ADVERSE stars despite its lovely name, *The Starlight,* a night companion coach train to *The Daylight* via the Coast Route between Los Angeles and San Francisco, was inaugurated just in time to be cut down by the ever crescent competition from highways and planes and lived a brief life. Here the northbound *Starlight* gets its highball out of Glendale station in the early fifties that will send it on its way through the perfumed California darkness over one of the most spectacular railroad routes in the world. *(Richard Steinheimer.)*

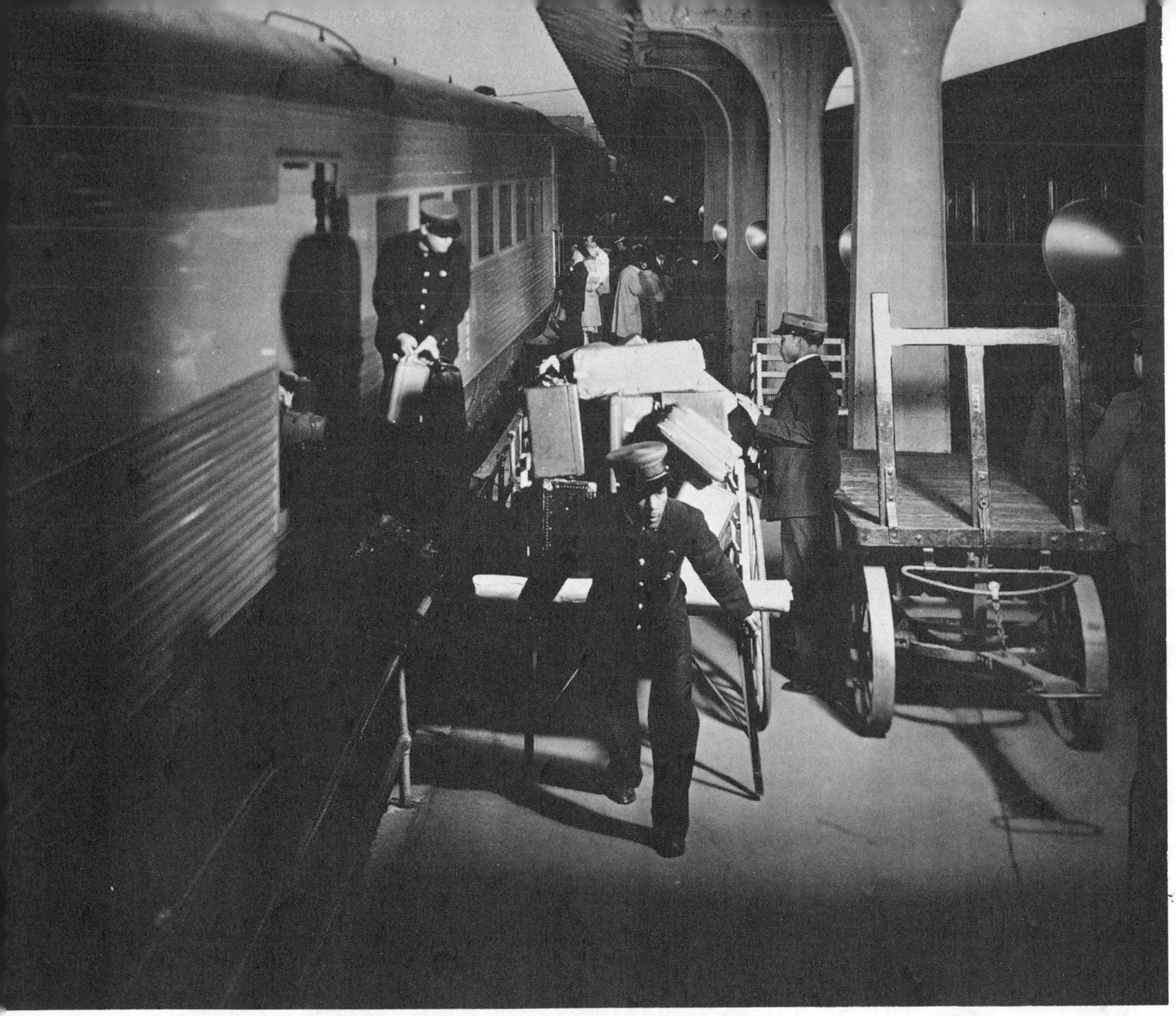

THE SAILING from Los Angeles of *The Daylight* in the years before the 1941 war was, as is suggested on these two pages, an event comparable in its own diminished way to the departure of *The Lurline* from the San Francisco Embarcadero or *The Queen Mary* in the North River. Often, in those happy times, the train was sold out and the management undertook to steer the overflow to *The Coast Passenger*, an accommodation run which left five minutes later. It was, however, a poor substitute for space aboard "The Most Beautiful Train in the World." *(Four Photos: Southern Pacific.)*

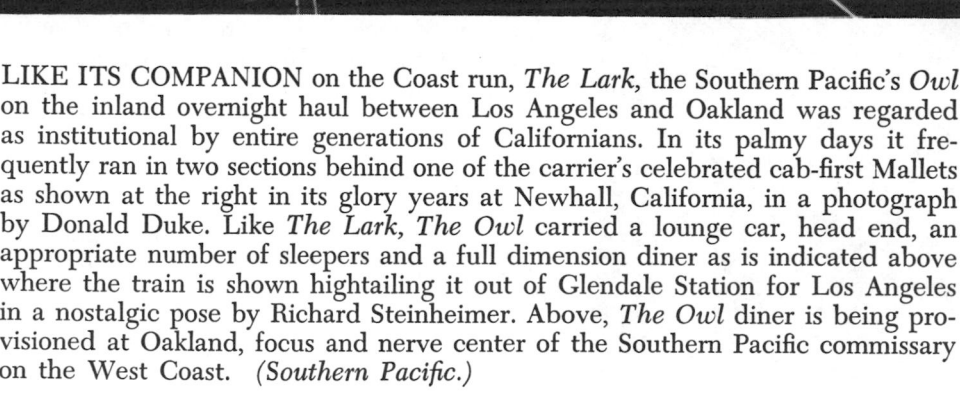

LIKE ITS COMPANION on the Coast run, *The Lark,* the Southern Pacific's *Owl* on the inland overnight haul between Los Angeles and Oakland was regarded as institutional by entire generations of Californians. In its palmy days it frequently ran in two sections behind one of the carrier's celebrated cab-first Mallets as shown at the right in its glory years at Newhall, California, in a photograph by Donald Duke. Like *The Lark, The Owl* carried a lounge car, head end, an appropriate number of sleepers and a full dimension diner as is indicated above where the train is shown hightailing it out of Glendale Station for Los Angeles in a nostalgic pose by Richard Steinheimer. Above, *The Owl* diner is being provisioned at Oakland, focus and nerve center of the Southern Pacific commissary on the West Coast.   (*Southern Pacific.*)

CELEBRATED AS perhaps the most convivial of all Southern Pacific name trains, *The Del Monte's* stand-up bar was a well recognized and approved rendezvous for thirsty patrons who found it inconvenient to wait for their first Martini of the evening in the butlered precincts of the Lodge at Pebble Beach or the stylishly maintained residences of Carmel. Here foregathered, often before the cars had cleared South San Francisco, entire generations of Tevises, Morses, Crockers and other feudal grandees of Monterey. The fashionable Stuyvesant Fish of Carmel was a regular and the two formidable brothers Lloyd and Gordon Tevis, descendents of the first president of Wells Fargo and swaggering magnificoes in their own right, laid down Tevis' Law to the effect that "Three House of Lords on the rocks before San Jose means straight to bed on arrival at Pacific Grove." Here a pair of less exalted patrons are cautiously sampling *The Del Monte's* liquid assets in a vignette by Richard Steinheimer.

NOT ALONE were the passenger accommodations on *The Del Monte* perfumed with privilege and an abode of the polite amenities. Up in the baggage car ahead rode elegant Towser in style to be delivered at Monterey to the chauffeured Bentley of his owner. Below, in the 1880s, *The Del Monte* was pictured in a pastoral setting of open meadows and rail fences at a time when its speed was as sensational as the exalted names on its passenger list. (*Left: Richard Steinheimer; Below: Southern Pacific.*)

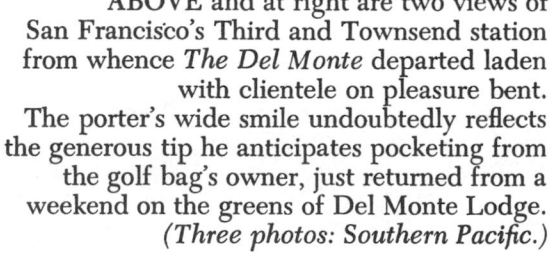

ABOVE and at right are two views of
San Francisco's Third and Townsend station
from whence *The Del Monte* departed laden
with clientele on pleasure bent.
The porter's wide smile undoubtedly reflects
the generous tip he anticipates pocketing from
the golf bag's owner, just returned from a
weekend on the greens of Del Monte Lodge.
(Three photos: Southern Pacific.)

LOCALLY KNOWN, in its
latter years as "The Rattler,"
The Del Monte as it neared its
southern terminal at
Pacific Grove traversed manicured vistas in a landscape
largely owned by
Samuel F. B. Morse, also locally
known as The Duke of
Del Monte.

Romance
Rode
The Mopac
Out Of
St. Louis
Into
The Old
Southwest

NO RAILROAD terminal in the American record ever saw the recurrent arrival and departure of such a rich multiplicity of eye-filling name trains under the corporate banners of so many carriers over so long a period of time as the Union Station in St. Louis. None ever will again. Built in 1894 in the mid-morning of railroad travel, St. Louis Terminal reached its apotheosis in the national folklore a decade later when the Louisiana Purchase Exposition brought hundreds of thousands through its train gates to "Meet Me at St. Louis, Louis, Meet Me at The Fair." No carrier was more entitled to think of the St. Louis Terminal as home than the Missouri Pacific, the greatest of the Gould railroads reaching south and west with connections for California and a purview that regarded the entire Southwest as its feudal domain. From its train bays there departed under the Mopac banner, *The Scenic Limited, The Kay-See Flyer, The Sunshine Special*, in many sections *The Southerner, The Missourian*, and *The Texan*. The last of these is shown here storming up from the river bottom toward St. Louis yards on a winter's day in the long ago of steam and Pullman Standard. *(Two Photos: Everett De Golyer Collection.)*

791

THE EARLY MORNING ARRIVAL (top) of The Sunshine Special from Texas
at the peak of the rush hour at St. Louis finds it waiting green from the
tower in company with overnight varnish of the Wabash, Illinois Central and
Gulf-Mobile & Ohio. Below is the interior of the stunning mission-style
observation-lounge car Xochimilco, one of the several similar public
luxury cars assigned The Sunshine which gave it luster in the highly competitive
traffic between St. Louis and East Texas. It was also a sample of
the carriers' passion for unpronounceable car names.
(Above: Rail Photo Service, Harold E. Williams; Below: Missouri Pacific.)

EAST TEXAS sections of *The Sunshine Special* running over the Texas & Pacific between Fort Worth-Dallas and Texarkana almost invariably rode behind specially assigned motive power with the train name and company heraldry on the smokebox or feedwater heater, and a sufficient pool of engines was maintained for second sections. Below, *The East Texas Sunshine* rolls out of Dallas in 1938 on its overnight run to St. Louis. *(Two Photos: Lucius Beebe.)*

LAST LANDMARKS outbound from the picture windows of *The Sunshine Special*, West Texas section, were the Texas & Pacific's turretted offices at Fort Worth and the vast water tank in the yards advertising the company's stock in trade of travel and transport. The beautiful Spanish Mission styled club-lounge-observation cars in use in the thirties on the El Paso run were numbered 10230-10237 and recapitulated the theme which dominated the public car decor of the St. Louis sections of *The Sunshine*. *(Right: Lucius Beebe; Below: Missouri Pacific.)*

THE WEST TEXAS section of *The Sunshine Special (opposite)* headed for the Great Plains in 1944 behind unmistakable Texas & Pacific motive power and often ran in fourteen car trains with heavy head end to pay the way on the long Lone Star haul to El Paso. *(Lucius Beebe.)*

ALTHOUGH, when the photograph at the right of *The Scenic Limited* was taken by Roland Collons, air conditioning and the general retreat from open observation platforms was still in the future, the Missouri Pacific provided an enclosed solarium observation car in the consist, a forerunner of a type of lounge that was to see far wider use once air conditioning became universal. Breakfast on *The Scenic's* diner and coffee over a copy of *The Post Dispatch* or *The Kansas City Star* could be an event of tranquil satisfactions. (*Above: Everett De Golyer Collection; Right: The De Golyer Foundation.*)

"I WASN'T fortunate enough to be on the initial run of *The Scenic Limited* (above) in the spring of 1915," wrote John Barriger of this important event, "but I stood on the platform at St. Louis in envy of a young schoolmate, Cecil Whitmarsh, who was a passenger. His father was a local lumber man who was a representative of the Business Man's League of St. Louis (as the Chamber of Commerce was then called) to the opening of the Panama Pacific Exposition at San Francisco. This picture, enlarged to a five or six foot dimension and done in sepia tones was widely distributed by the Missouri Pacific throughout the country and was for many years almost a company trademark." Mr. Barriger recalled the event a full half century after *The Scenic's* first run as a high point in the railroading of the period. (*Missouri Pacific.*)

THE DUST SCREEN portrayed below was neither a devising of Rube Goldberg nor a property of "Believe It Or Not," but a devising at least in operation long enough to take the photograph on which this drawing is based. "Patrons of the Missouri Pacific," read the caption in a house organ for the year 1930, "may now enjoy the pleasure of lounging on the observation platform of the modern new cars with a minimum of dust due to the placing of newly designed dust screens on the rear of that type of car. The screen is simplicity itself and its operation will contribute greatly to the comfort and convenience of passengers. It serves to prevent dust and dirt from being thrown in the air as the train speeds onward. At present these devices have been installed on many of the fast through trains and others will be installed in the immediate future." The lounge shown at the right rode in *The Scenic* at this time all the way to the coast via its Rio Grande connection out of Colorado. (*Right: Missouri Pacific; Below: Howard Fogg.*)

ROLLING THROUGH THE MISSOURI meadowlands behind a nicely maintained Pacific No. 1151, *The Scenic Limited* was a classic train in its true operational sense, with head-end revenue cars, coaches, diner, lounge and through Pullmans, all the components of a first class train just short of the limited of *grande luxe.* (Charles Clegg.)

THE SCENIC *Limited* after it left the rails of the originating Missouri Pacific at Pueblo became a Colorado institution as the brightest jewel in the diadem of the Denver & Rio Grande Western. Here it is shown pounding up the westbound grade toward Tennessee Pass with coaches and through Pullmans for the Western Pacific connection next day at Salt Lake. *(Richard H. Kindig.)*

THE BOMBAZINE lady crouching over the L. C. Smith Patent typewriter in the year 1907 is secretary to the Missouri Pacific's chief dispatcher at Pueblo. The chief dispatcher himself is the hard looking character in the foreground with the hard hat and hard jaw. The photograph was taken with a wide-angle lens by pioneer cameraman of the time, Fred Jukes.

AWASH with the handsome Gothic bay windows beloved of the period, the Missouri Pacific-Rio Grande uptown ticket office in Denver, also in 1907, was, in a manner, a crossroads of the Gould railroad empire midway between the Mopac and Texas Pacific to the east and the Rio Grande and Western Pacific to the west. *(Western Collection, Denver Public Library.)*

WHILE THE TRAFFIC of the other Nevada short lines, the Virginia & Truckee, Nevada Central and the Eureka & Palisade, connecting in each case to the north of their originating terminals with the Central Pacific main line, had been in precious metals, the commerce of the Nevada Northern which outlived them was in copper. When, in 1906, Mark Requa's Nevada Consolidated Copper Company, later to become the Kenecott Copper of today, brought the Nevada Northern Railroad into being, it was strictly a company carrier most of whose through or continental traffic derived from the Southern Pacific at Cobre and to a lesser degree from the Western Pacific at Shafter, where, at the left, one of its trains is shown silhouetted against the Ruby Mountains. First president of the Nevada Northern was incredibly rich Colonel Daniel C. Jackling, founder of Utah Copper and in its passenger carrying days it rode company officials in a rococo coach that met the *Overland* and other transcontinentals at Cobre. Half this car was a conventional coach, the other half was more elaborately decorated as a parlor-buffet for the benefit of the copper grandees who rode it in great numbers. The Western Pacific's exchange of passengers with the Nevada Northern, effected at Shafter, was largely in the time of the *Scenic Limited* and *The Exposition Flyer*, shown below double headed out of Salt Lake in war time. By the time of the *California Zephyr* it was negligible although the *Zephyr* still paused on demand at Shafter. No W.P. trains in recent years, however, stopped at nearby Tobar, a post office address which, in construction days had been indicated by a sign in the desert reading "To Bar." The name remained. *(Left: Robert Le Massena; Below: Lucius Beebe.)*

THE WESTERN PACIFIC's secondary run from Oakland to Salt Lake City, optimistically known as *The Feather River Express,* was very secondary indeed since it required just under twenty-nine hours to cover the 928 miles between its terminals. This was cut to a breathless twenty-four and a half hours when a railcar known as *The Zephyrette* replaced it but there was still time on its schedule to eat a full steak dinner at the Stockman's Hotel at Elko. Here *The Express* in its days of steam prepares to depart from Oakland Mole with a combine and coach which will lurch over the High Sierra and across the Nevada wastelands in a reasonable facsimile of second class travel in the Old West before the turn of the century. Only the conductor and a single fare share the venerable combine *(right)* as it sets out for Stockton and Marysville over the route followed long ago by the Wells Fargo stages. *(Two Photos: Richard Steinheimer.)*

ALL THE PANOPLY of a mainline sailing of *The City of San Francisco* was invoked in the ritual of departure for *The Feather River Express:* Mars light, air pressure gauges, full train crew and a meticulously lettered train gate board. There was no abridgment of protocol even for a milk run.   (*Richard Steinheimer.*)

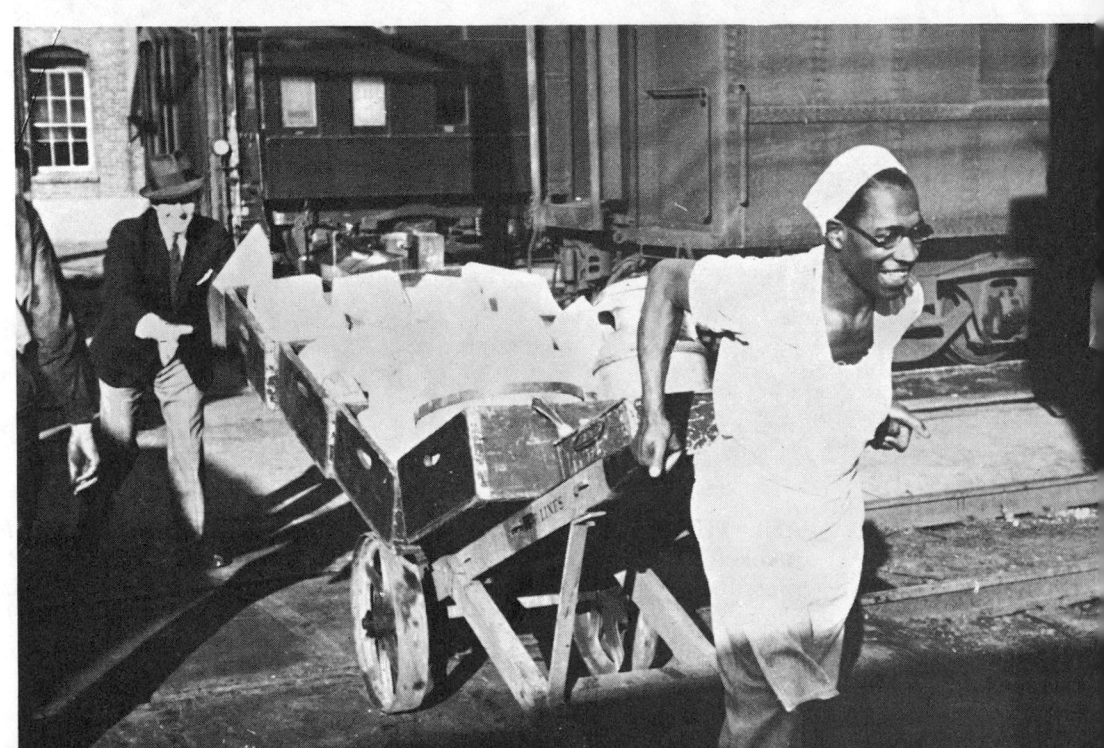

THE MISSOURI PACIFIC
was not, truth to tell, an
abode of transcendental
gastronomy. To be sure, its
diners in no way reflected the
dyspepsia that was one
of the several ills to afflict
Jay Gould, architect of
its original destinies; quite
the opposite; Mopac fare was
notoriously for heroes at
table and its plentitude
legendary, reflecting the outsize tastes of its Texas
clientele and the bounty of
the Ozarks through which it
ran. At the left a chef
aboard *The Kay-See Flyer*
prepares order of roast
Vermont turkey. Taken with
a bowl of the carrier's
navy bean soup this was
calculated to last a passenger
until he arrived. (*Two
Photos: Missouri Pacific.*)

806

THE GREYHOUND straining-at-the-leash look of the Missouri Pacific's massive No. 5339 shown below characterizes the carrier's *Texan* about to get its highball at St. Louis Terminal for its run westbound through the Ozark night. The unseen length of its consist may be imagined from the vast distance its motive power extends beyond the train shed. Below, the same train is shown from the rear end at Poplar Bluff, Missouri, in 1936, its seven head-end revenue cars suggesting the business it carried in mail and express as well as in passengers. *(Top: William Barham; Below: Everett De Golyer Collection, Roland Collons.)*

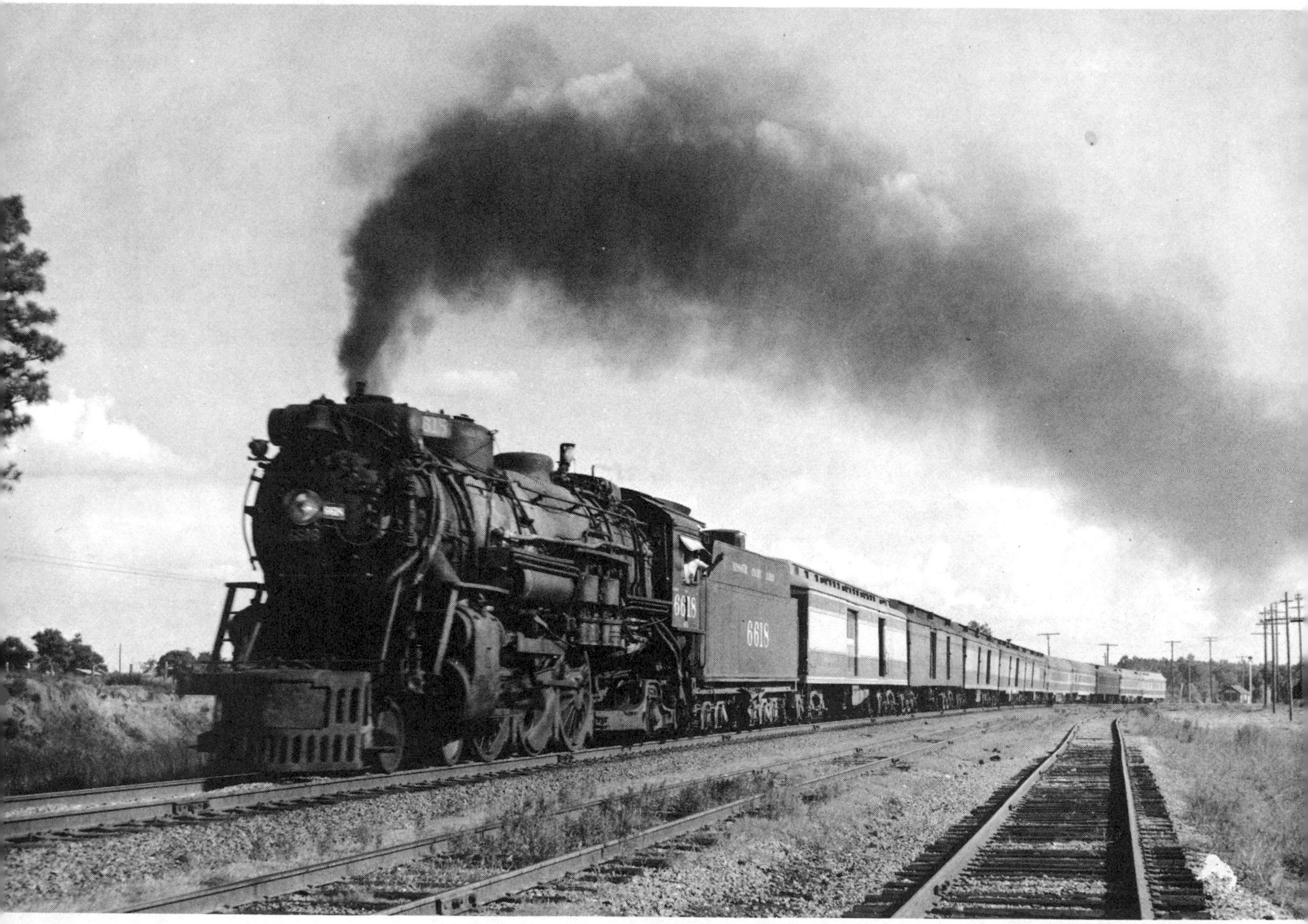

AS BEFITTED the most affluent of the great Gould network of carriers whose owning family was among the most conspicuous of the gold table service era, the Missouri Pacific's crack name trains were distinguished for the handsome service plates on their diners. The one of these reproduced at the far left bore the likeness of the *Sunshine Special* in steam, but by 1949 the management evidently felt that internal combustion was here to stay and replaced it by an image of *The Texas Eagle*. The plate at the immediate left, fabricated in 1951, was designed to be sold as a collector's item and was never placed in service. Dieselization was only months away when A. E. Brown took the spirited action shot of *The Louisiana Sunshine* on the page opposite epitomizing the ultimate of steam and Pullman Standard in the blue and white colors of *The Eagle. The Sunshine* is depicted at Tioga, Louisiana, en route from Lake Charles to Little Rock. The solarium-lounge was of the familiar *Puebla* and *Xochimilco* decor. *(Four Photos: Missouri Pacific.)*

ALTHOUGH DOUBLE HEADING on the Missouri Pacific's lines running through the steeply graded Ozarks was far more frequent than on the almost gradeless tangents of the connecting Texas & Pacific, it was rare enough to secure the interested attention of A. E. Brown of Shreveport when *The Fast Mail* came into view with tandem motive power out of Texarkana in 1944 as shown in the panoramic view above. The main signal tower *(right)* governing traffic in and out of St. Louis Terminal was burned on July 22, 1940 when traffic was mounting to an all-time peak on the eve of the 1941 war. A period of near chaos followed in which trains were guided in and out of their slips by lanterns and manual signals, and it was not until November of the same year that the first train was guided through the new interlocking by the senior collaborator in this book, acting in an honorary capacity and as the guest of the Terminal Association. *(Lucius Beebe.)*

810

EQUALLY as atmospheric as the Spanish Mission style lounge-buffet-observation cars on *The Sunshine* were the all-purpose cars listed by the management as dining-sunroom-lounges on such trains as *The Southerner* in whose consist it is listed on the page opposite. An exterior and interior of these versatile and opulent cars are shown below on this page. *(Two Photos: Missouri Pacific.)*

LITTLE ROCK
MEMPHIS
HOT SPRINGS

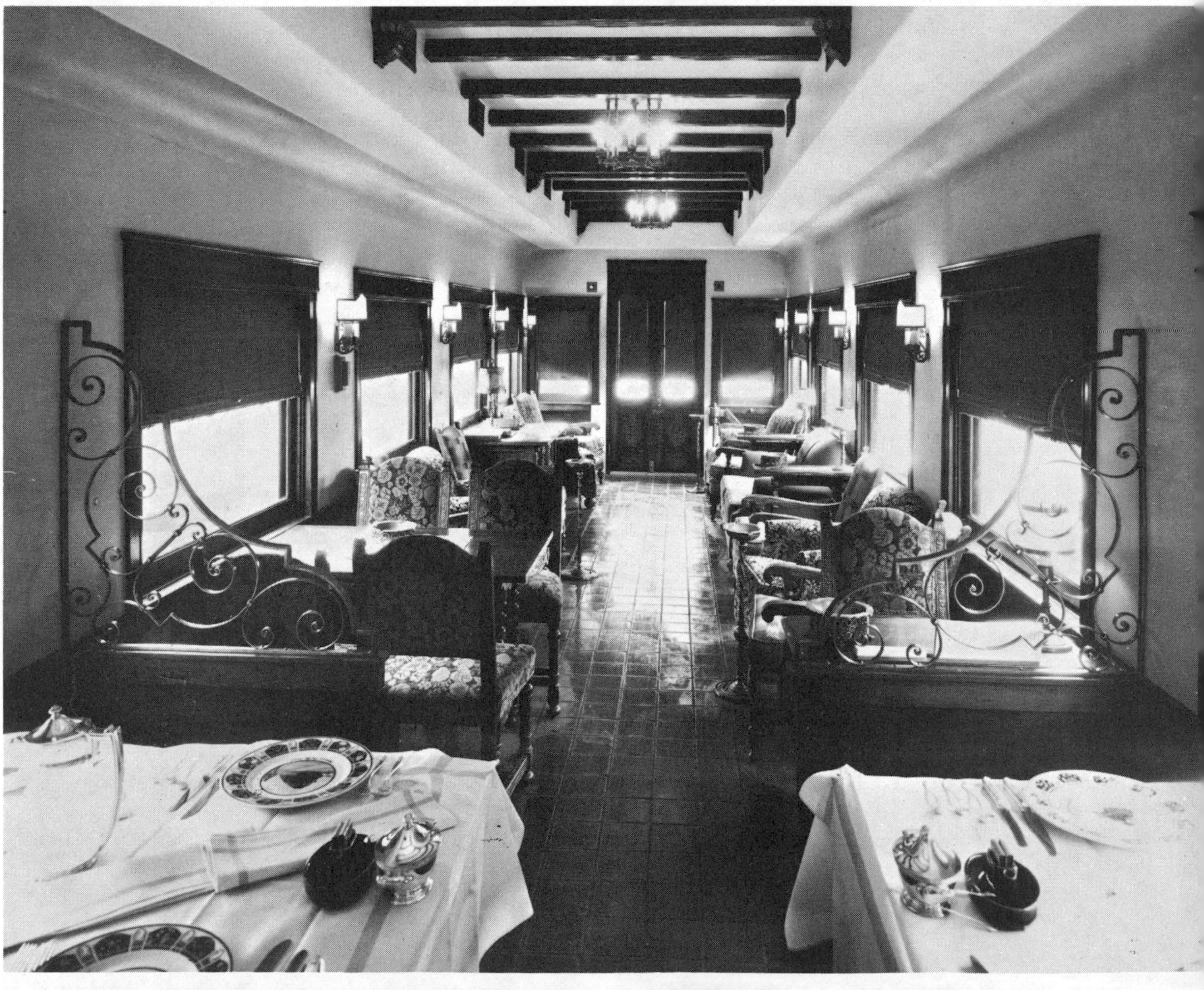

AS IS SUGGESTED by the full dress court portrait of *The Texan* in the opening layout of the Texas & Pacific-Missouri Pacific section of this book, the arrival of heavy Mopac varnish runs in St. Louis during the winter months was accomplished in a spectacular chaos of steam and smoke exhausts. The long grade up from the river bottoms to St. Louis yards was made with the engineer working steam to the limit of his engine's capacity and the effect is recorded here in *The Sunshine Special* with seventeen cars on the drawbar in the now distant year 1937. Carrying green to indicate an extra section, the big 4-8-2 puts on a show worthy of the varied assortment of cars it carries as recorded in the train's consist reproduced on the page opposite. (*Lucius Beebe.*)

813

ON ITS COMPARATIVELY gradeless runs, double heading was almost unknown on the Texas & Pacific in its years of steam save for the purpose of moving motive power to different points on the system without recourse to a caboose hop and special train movement. Here on the outskirts of Shreveport two 400 series ten wheelers hurry *The Louisiana Limited* in June 1939. The extra engine was in request at Marshall, Texas, for a football special and *The Limited* afforded the handiest way to get there.

On the page opposite is shown the maiden run over the Pennsylvania of a New York section of *The Sunshine Special* which was inaugurated in the first flush of passenger optimism that followed the 1941 war. The through Pullman sleeper for Mexico City made one of the longest through runs anywhere in the United States and informed travelers paused to look twice in Pennsylvania Station at a name made famous on the Missouri Pacific. *(Below: A. E. Brown.)*

MARY Hoegberg, a wartime train gate guard at Penn Station in New York charged with seeing *The Sunshine* off on its maiden run out of Manhattan, was so diminutive she had to look up to arriving patrons. *(Three Photos: Pennsylvania Railroad.)*

Union Pacific and The Old West
Were the Extension of One Another

The Pony Express, Adams, Colorado, 1939

MOTHER OF WESTERN MAIN LINES and a railroad whose name itself is forever part of the lexicon of the Old West, Union Pacific has been at various times the pioneer transcontinental, a synonym for political corruption, a component of the ambitious transport empire of Jay Gould, a gilt edge investment under Edward H. Harriman and at all times the strong bond and connecting link that joined America west of the Missouri River with The States in post-Civil War times. Like the Santa Fe and Burlington, one of the most influential architects of its maturity was a Boston Brahmin in the person of Charles Francis Adams, and in later years the Harriman heirs maintained continuity in its affairs to give Union Pacific the identity it still has with this powerful family. The first of the great luxury name trains to roll in the splendor of Palace Cars beyond the Mississippi, *The Golden Gate Special* between Omaha and San Francisco was a Union Pacific innovation. The romantic *Overland Limited* was a U.P. varnish run for ten full years before its name was recognized west of Ogden. Originally no more than an indispensible bridge carrier from Omaha to the edge of Great Salt Lake, the eventual absorption of Senator William Andrews Clark's Salt Lake Line to Los Angeles and The Oregon Short Line to Portland gave it access to Pacific entrepots and strategic continental importance. Perhaps because its long haul luxury trains shared trackage rights and prestige with its con-

nections east and west, Union Pacific in recent years originated few name trains of its own, among them the *Portland Rose, Los Angeles Limited, Columbine, Mountain Bluebird, Utah, Pony Express, Idahoan* and *Yellowstone Special*. But with the coming of the age of streamlined Diesel its *City* runs to Portland, Denver, San Francisco, Los Angeles and St. Louis became a hallmark of operational excellence. Its affairs on a truly imperial dimension have always been administered out of Omaha but the seat of executive authority and financial operation has been in downtown New York and in the shadow of Wall Street. For many years its connection with Chicago was divided between the Chicago & North Western and the Milwaukee, but in the fifties its entire passenger traffic was routed over the Milwaukee and the left hand operation over the North Western became a memory. Always there is the long continuity between today's Union Pacific and the heroic past where its roots are, one in the American awareness of a continental destiny with the Concord Coach, Wells Fargo and the Winchester repeater, with the Seventh Cavalry band playing "Garry Owen" and the days of the cattle trade on the Great Plains. It was no accident of chance that saw Buffalo Bill Cody as a professional hunter in construction days on the Kansas Pacific which was in the fullness of time to be the U.P. It has been a name at whose mention the American imagination has always stood at attention.

R. H. KINDIG

817

ONE OF THE HIGHLY REGARDED varnish runs over the iron of the Oregon Railway & Navigation Company before it was completely absorbed by the Union Pacific as a by-product of the Harriman regime was *The Chicago Express* shown below in a spirited action pose dating from 1902 from the collection of George Abdill, ranking Boswell of steam and steel in the Northwest. Like its opposite number, *The Oregon Express*, the eastbound train rolled out of Multnomah with coaches, Pullmans and a brass railed observation car. Denver and St. Louis cars were cut in and out at Cheyenne in a day before the Borie cutoff and may well be part of the photograph of Denver Union Depot at roughly the same period shown at the right. (*Below: George Abdill Collection; Right: Denver Public Library, Western Collection.*)

THE CLOTH traveling cap was de rigueur aboard the lounge cars of *The Chicago Express* soon after the turn of the century and the train's consist as it appeared on the Union Pacific main line near Rawlins is shown in the lower frame in a rare action pose by Fred Jukes and dated 1902 in his own handwriting. *(Library of Congress; Fred Jukes.)*

THE RAILROAD WEST of Fred Jukes, pioneer cameraman of 1906 along the Union Pacific, as depicted on these two pages was not too much removed from the original West of the U.P.'s contriving when it opened up the Great Plains and the route to California in 1869. True, coal had supplanted wood for locomotive fuel, block signals were universal and electric light had replaced the earlier coal oil, but the distances between towns was still immeasurably greater than they were to be in the motor car age, the elements were more hostile and population along the Overland Route was still minimal. Something of the Old West, vast, menacing and primordial, invests the photograph reproduced here of *The Pacific Limited* in 1906 westbound through the deep cut that marked the yard limit at Rawlins. Below, at the eastern approach to the same wide open town, Jukes captioned the lower action shot "A Cold Day at Rawlins, 1906." The above vignette of the Union Pacific's third depot structure at Julesburg, Colorado, conveys much of the flavor of the time and place, the vast coal oil storm lanterns, the shirt-sleeved loungers and the tarpaulin-covered baggage truck all bespeak the lonely Great Plains with the Denver cutoff unseen at the left. *(Western Collection, Denver Public Library.)*

820

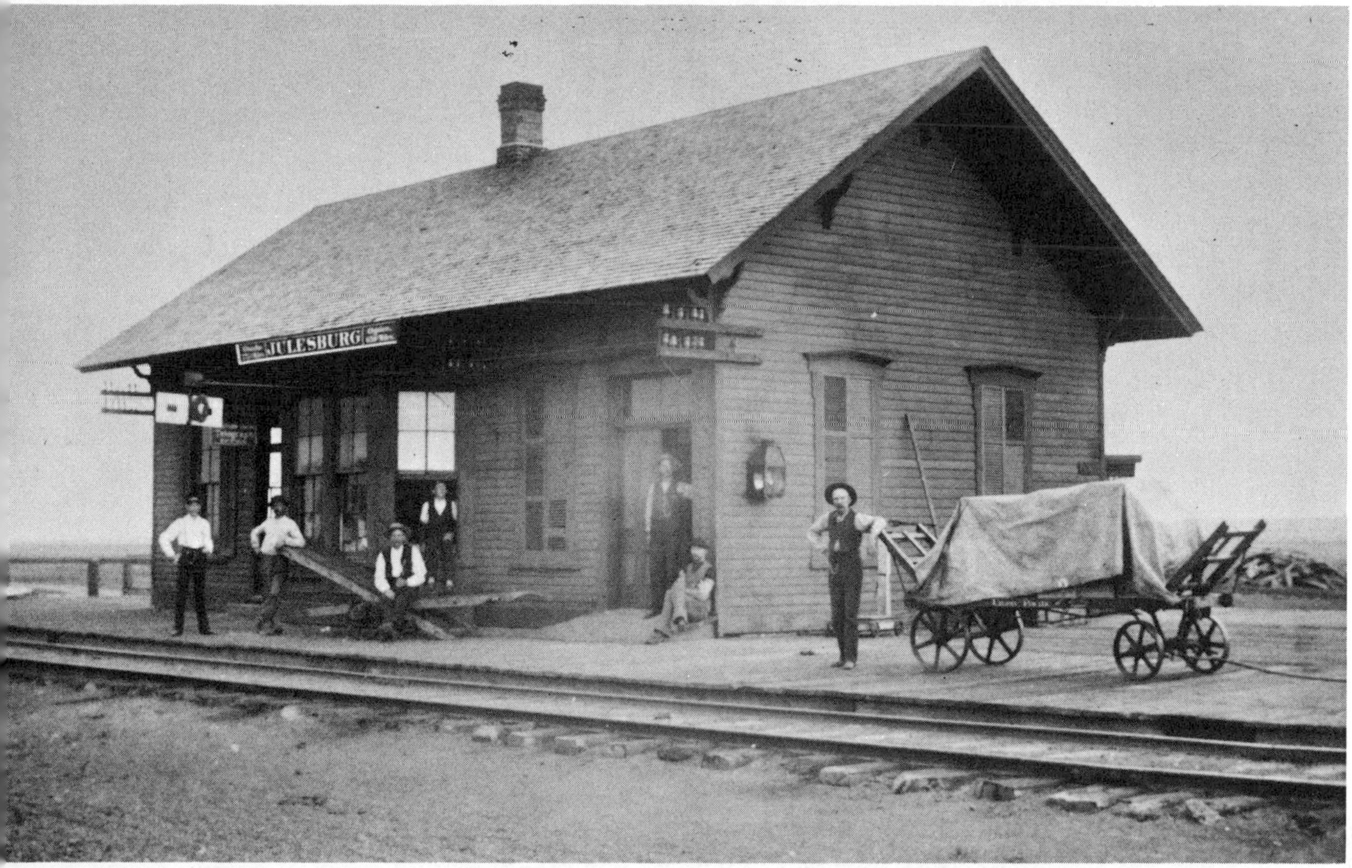
JULESBURG

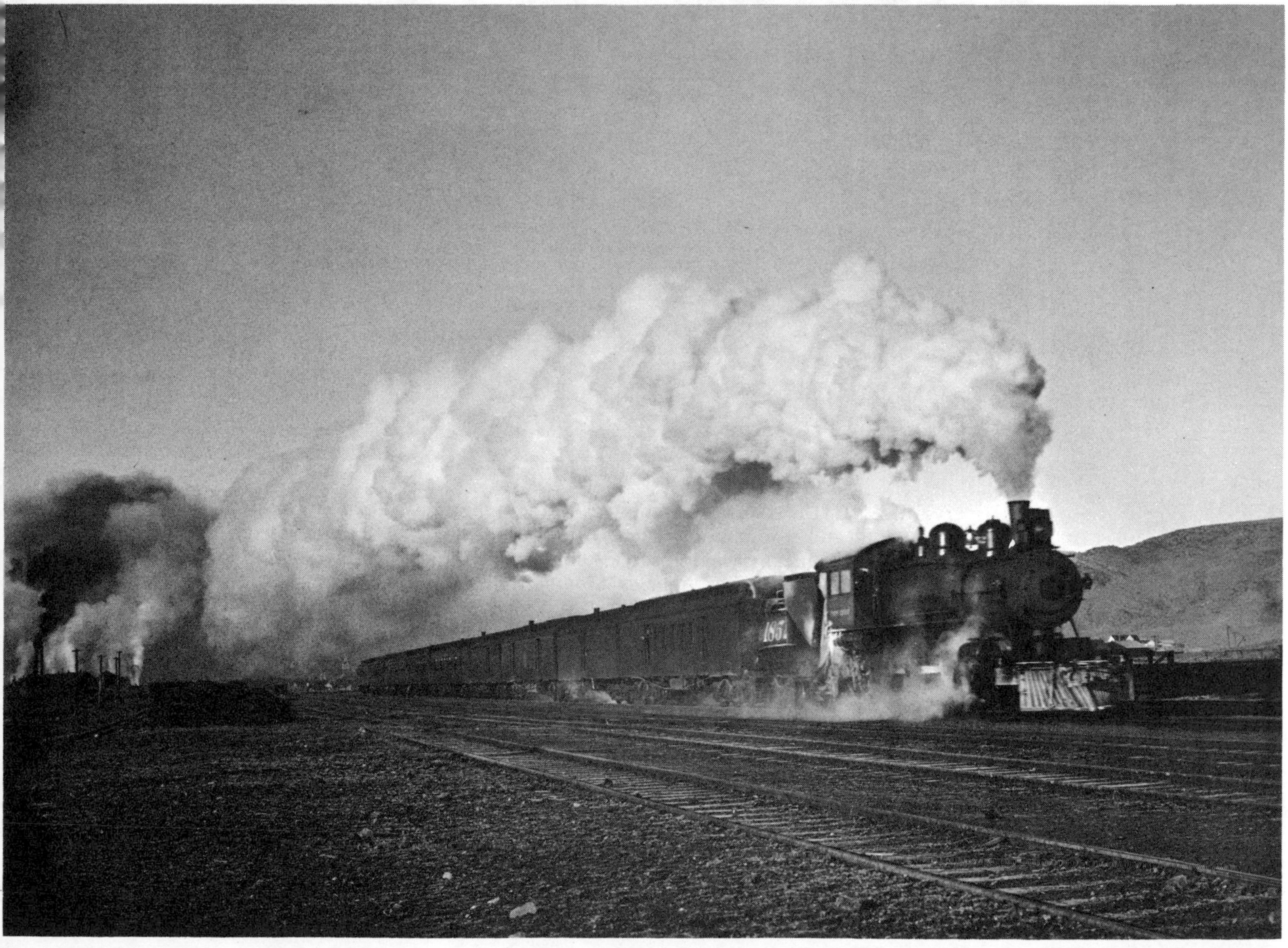

THE OVERLAND LIMITED operating as a through train to San Francisco was six years old and a resounding success from every angle in 1905 when the Union Pacific management placed in service an opposite number on the Southern California run named *The Los Angeles Limited*. The new train was fully as handsomely turned out as its transcontinental prototype with luxury equipment, such as the observation-lounge car shown opposite built to specifications by Pullman with the train's name on its nameboards and in a primeval illuminated insigne built into the observation platform roof. Here *The Los Angeles Limited* is shown westbound out of Rawlins from the camera of Fred Jukes. On the opposite page in a rare cracked glass plate from the Wyoming State Archives it is shown on its maiden run a few miles out of Ogden where it would commence the last leg of its routing over the rails of Senator William A. Clark's Los Angeles & Salt Lake Line. The crowded platform of the Union Pacific depot at Los Angeles represented a normal sailing of *The Los Angeles Limited* in the 1920s. *(Above: Fred Jukes; Opposite: Wyoming State Archives; Everett De Golyer Collection.)*

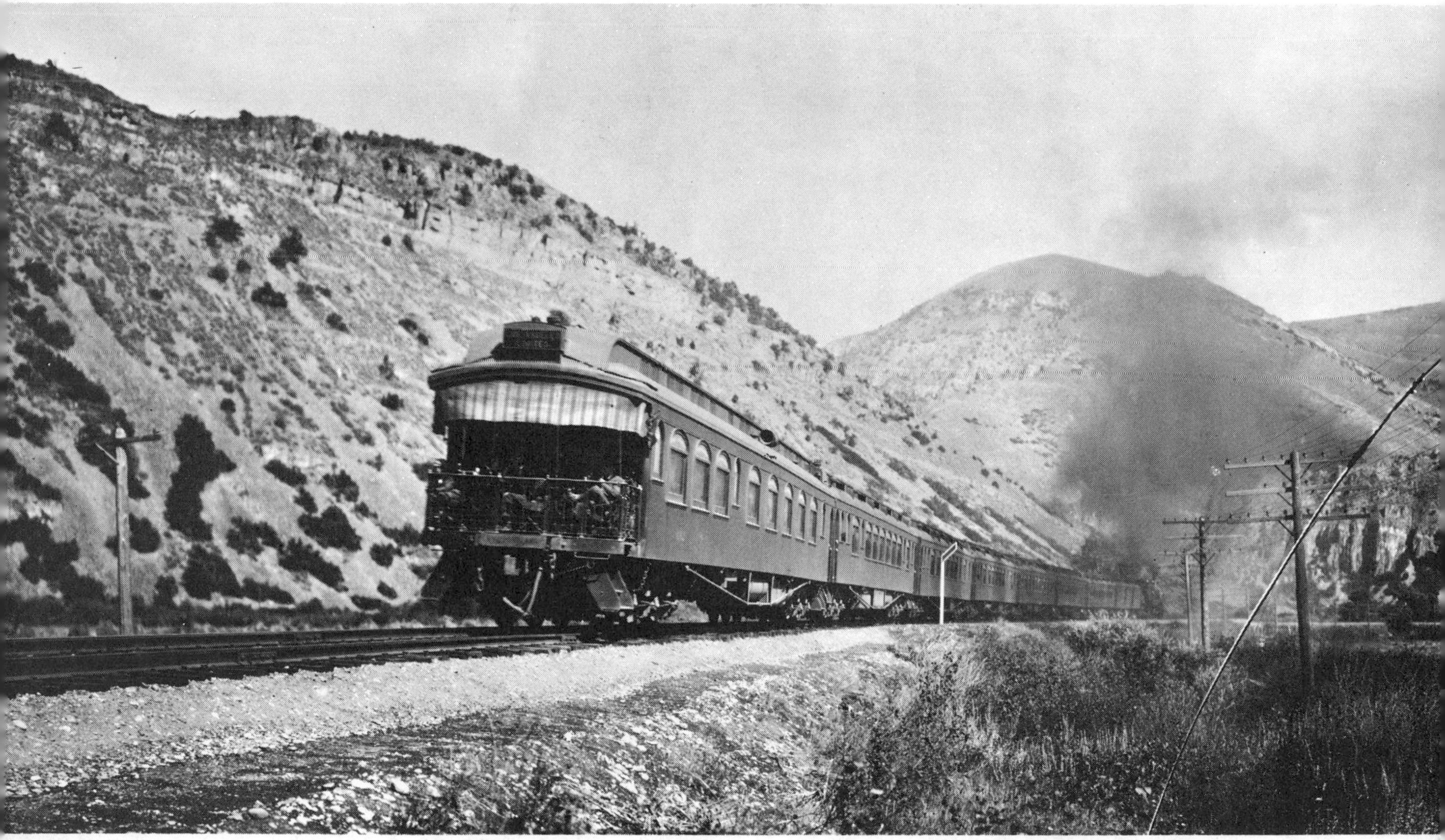

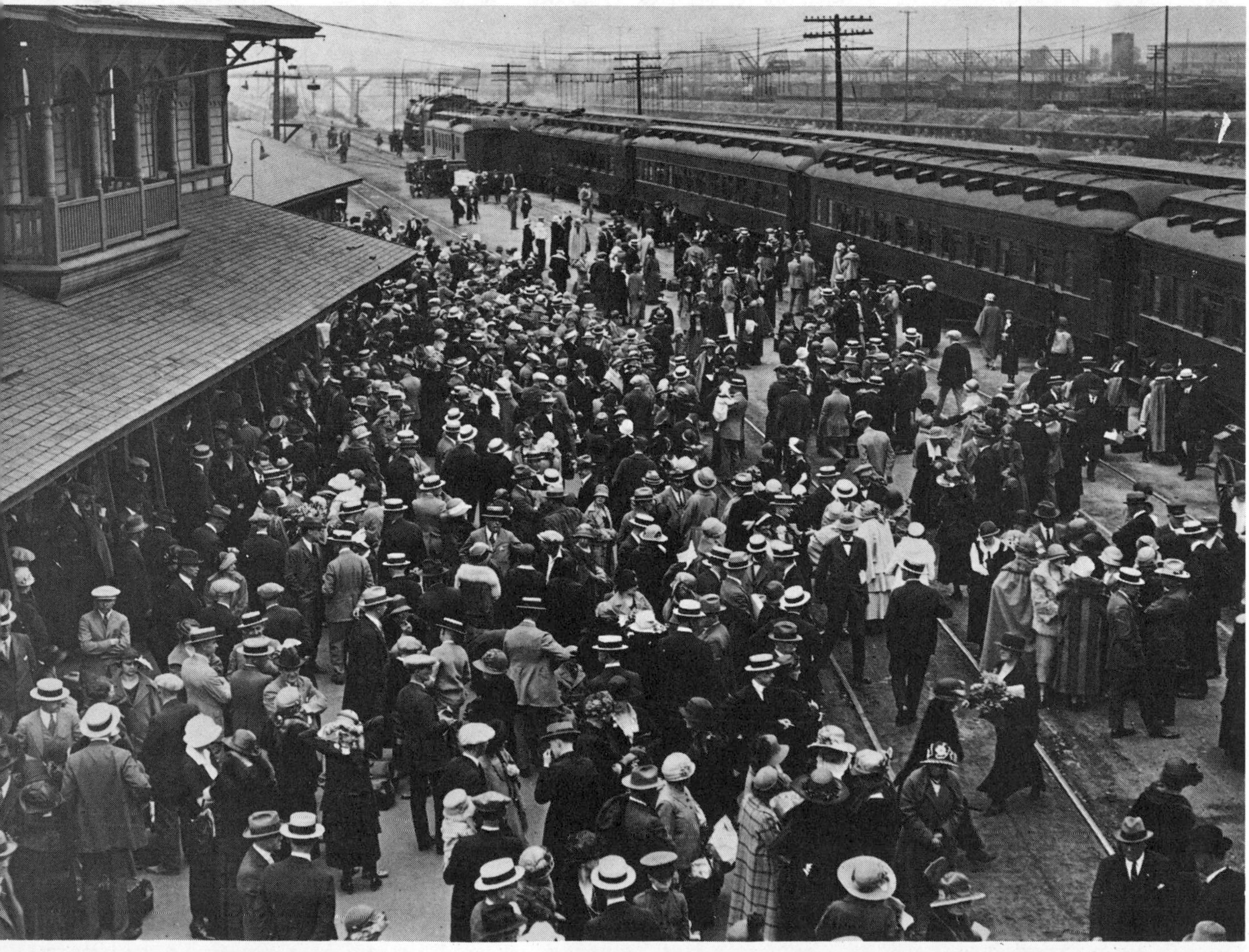

LIKE ITS INSPIRATION, *The Overland Limited,* running with fifteen or sixteen cars and often in two and three sections, *The Los Angeles Limited,* shown here in a massive consist in the thirties out of Ogden, Utah, en route to Salt Lake was a train of ample amenities if not actually de luxe dimensions. With the disappearance of open observation platforms and the introduction of the enclosed solarium lounge as shown opposite, something of the dusty charm of viewing the passing countryside disappeared from train travel. So, however, did painful cinders in the eye and the minstrel show appearance of determined platform riders who had spent protracted periods on the verandah riding over indifferently ballasted roadbeds. (*Above: Everett De Golyer Collection; Opposite, Top: Alfred W. Johnson; Below: Union Pacific.*)

A SPECTACULAR interlude in *The Limited*'s history was when, on October 17, 1917, it pulled into Laramie to find the depot burning briskly. Danger from falling walls halted the cars until the roof had fallen in. (*Wyoming State Historical Society.*)

THE INAUGURATION in 1906 of *The Los Angeles Limited* on the Overland Route west of Omaha and from Salt Lake to Southern California over Senator Clark's Salt Lake Line was a direct result of the success of *The Overland Limited* on the San Francisco run and the train itself was, in large measure, an opposite number to *The Overland* in conduct and equipment. It was scheduled in direct competition with the Santa Fe's long established *California Limited* and in a few years attracted to itself a following of loyal partisans who felt that Union Pacific was tops in transportation west of the Missouri River. Contrary to general belief and a legend which the Santa Fe was happy to help perpetuate, *The Los Angeles Limited,* not to mention the Rock Island's magnificent *Golden State Limited,* enjoyed a brisk trade in film celebrities of whom Alice Brady, photographed in 1916 at Chicago was one. Opposite, *The Limited* smokes up The Cajon for a portrait of double-headed action by Richard Kindig. Below, its observation end in pre-air-conditioned times was occupied by car No. 1551. *(Left: Chicago Historical Society; Below: The De Golyer Foundation.)*

A TRAIN OF GOLDEN memories in the Western continent, *The Overland Limited*, later known as *The San Francisco Overland* was as much a part of legend as the cable cars and Lotta's Fountain. Generations of San Franciscans took passage on *The Overland* with the same assurance of familiarity as Bostonians rode *The Merchants* on the New Haven and their grandchildren rode the same train when they in turn went east to St. Paul's or Groton and later to Yale or Harvard. Songs were written about *The Overland;* at least one full length book* was devoted to it and countless saloons, restaurants and hotels along its right of way from Nebraska to California bore its name and emplaced its likeness behind the back bar. Its life span lasted from a time when gentlemen took passage on the cars at Oakland Mole or Chicago's old Union Station in silk top hats carrying Gladstone valises until at long last the air age dimmed its marker lights forever. Here *The Overland* seventeen car consist is powered as it topped Sherman Summit double headed by a brace of what many amateurs considered the most beautiful of all locomotives, the Union Pacific's Northern type running under a flawless summer sky in 1953. Relaxed attitudes in open sections and in the diner made a trip from Chicago to the Pacific a lyric experience. *(Opposite: Richard H. Kindig; Two Photos: Southern Pacific.)*

*"*The Overland Limited*" by Lucius Beebe; Howell-North Books, 1963

THE CHRISTMAS season of 1963 found the Union Pacific depot at Boise, Idaho, a busy scene by night and by day. Above, an extra eastbound mail pauses in the midnight hours behind three Diesel units to set down its Yuletide mail and express matter. Below, Train No. 11 running three hours off schedule in below zero weather, is mostly mail and other head-end revenue but terminates its consist with a rider coach and single Pullman out of Salt Lake. *(Two Photos: Henry W. Griffiths, Jr.)*

OVER ITS trackage through the Blue Mountains of Oregon, the Union Pacific mainline to Portland and the Northwest traversed in the years of steam some of the last truly untamed wilderness areas of the continent, little changed in its essential components of the big sky and the big woods since it was first explored by Lewis and Clark a century and a half before. Here, double headed for the two and a half percent grade, the eastbound *Idahoan* passes a westbound freight that has taken siding for it at Kamola, Oregon, for a notable study of big motive power to match the landscape and the elements with which it contends. *(Henry W. Griffiths, Jr.)*

WHEN THE Union Pacific's rails during the seventies and eighties ran across the windy summit of Sherman Hill along the original survey, the transcontinental mainliners all paused to allow passengers to descend from the cars and admire the Ames Monument, a practice followed by other carriers in a generation that wanted to see all the sights: notably the Southern Pacific at Cape Horn in the Sierra and the Rio Grande in the Canyon of the Arkansas. The Ames Brothers, Oakes and Oliver of Boston had supplied most of the tools and earth moving machinery used in U.P. construction times when an Ames shovel was a standard of quality in its field comparable to jewels from Tiffany or dinner at Delmonico's. Subsequently the Ames Brothers figured in the Credit Mobilier revelations, a circumstance which in no way abated the esteem in which they were held either by the railroad or the general public. The Ames Monument, shown in a contemporary drawing at the right was at the highest point of Sherman Hill, 8,500 feet above sea level and was built of pink granite at a cost of $80,000. Likenesses of the Commonwealth Avenue nabobs adorned the faces of the pyramid. Successive relocations of the railroad right of way across Sherman Summit removed them from proximity to the monument and today it stands almost forgotten on a windy upland, a memorial at once to the men who helped build the railroad and to the odds against immortality in an unheedful generation.

AS LONG AS STEAM LASTED Sherman Hill on the Union Pacific's main line west of Cheyenne, Wyoming, was a continuous parade of noble motive power and great name trains, usually double headed westbound, and even after the advent of Diesel *The City of San Francisco*, *The City of Los Angeles* and *The Overland Limited* left Cheyenne depot, shown at the bottom of the page, with steam helpers to the top of the long grade. At the left, toward the end of its glory years, a second section of *The Overland* is running as an extra at the very summit of wind-swept Sherman. Below is depicted the rear end of the *City of Cheyenne*, the most abbreviated of all the U.P.'s *City* trains both in its consist and territory covered. It performed shuttle service between overland mainline trains at Cheyenne and Denver and passengers who made the short but fast two-hour ride aboard the all-aluminum Pullman lounge car *City of Cheyenne* complained bitterly of its rough riding qualities. *(Left and Below: Richard H. Kindig; Bottom: Western Collection, Denver Public Library.)*

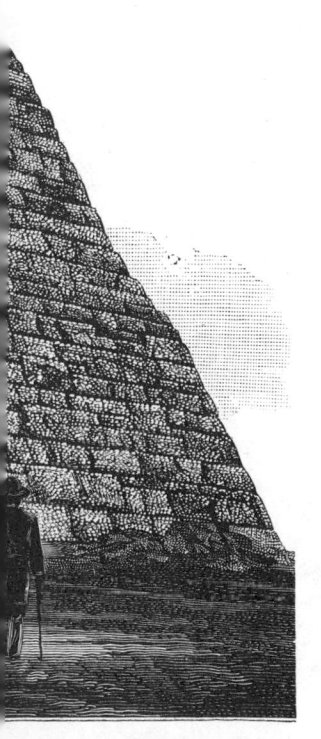

THE NAME OF the Union Pacific-Southern Pacific, all-Pullman, extra fare, super de luxe *Forty-niner* that ran from Chicago over the North Western connection to Oakland during the two summers of the San Francisco World's Fair of 1939-40 is marked with a star in the lexicon of Western railroading. Few trains were ever inaugurated with a happier objective, none was ever planned by its owning carriers on a more lavish scale of tangible and operational excellence. Painted grey with white finelining, it ran in steam all the way with specially assigned engines of its several carriers, terminating with a unique two-unit sleeping observation-lounge originally named *Advance* and *Progress* but, in the second year of its operation, more happily renamed *Bear Flag* and *California Republic*. *The Forty-niner* is shown below at Roseville in the Sierra foothills behind one of the Southern Pacific's legendary cab-first Mallets. *(Three photos: Southern Pacific.)*

NO FORMAL restaurant in New York or San Francisco boasted finer kitchen premises with more modern facilities for the service and preparation of luxury food than did *The Forty-niner* as is suggested by the view of its galley reproduced opposite. Every appointment of flowers, wine, cutlery, linen and personnel would have done credit to the Pump Room in Chicago or The Palace in San Francisco, whence many of its patrons derived at either end of its transcontinental run. *Forty-niner* staterooms actually afforded all the room suggested by its promotion photos, but its duplex singles were never intended for an occupant of more than modest size. They contained only token luggage space and use of their plumbing facilities taxed the ingenuity of tall men, but the train's public appointments were beyond reproach.

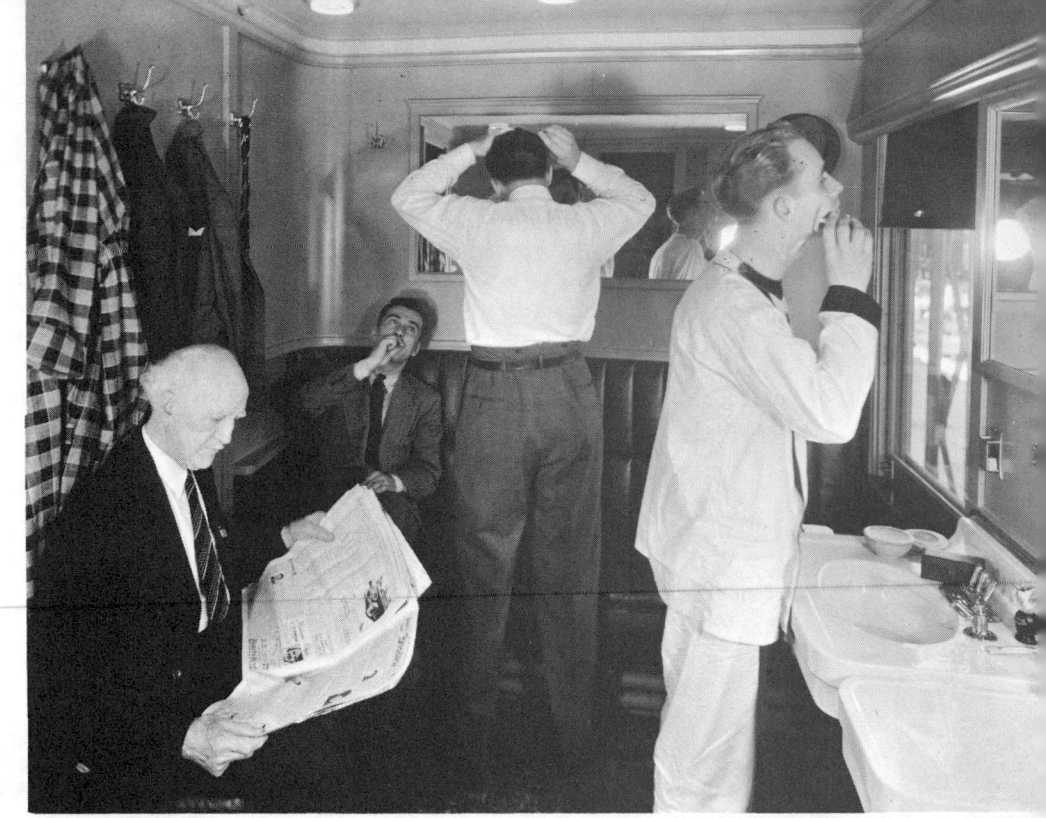

ROLLER BEARING trucks, then far from universal, mitigated the risks of shaving aboard *The Forty-niner* even though the hour when most passengers arose westbound found it on the looping curves of the Southern Pacific's high line above Donner Lake. *(Southern Pacific.)*

THE DINING CAR *Angel's Camp* on *The Forty niner* had originally been built to the specifications of a President of Mexico who had not survived to take delivery. Aboard it the Southern Pacific's legendary steward Wild Bill Kurthy plied his patrons with rare viands and suggested champagne for breakfast. *Angel's Camp* at cocktail time *(opposite)* had overtones of the Colony Restaurant in New York with a profusion of cut flowers, smartly uniformed attendants and a clientele of conservative affluence. The dinner hour *(left)* was an event that caused the train to linger in memory as one of the most beautiful and luxurious consists ever assigned to a continental run in the United States. *(Left and Opposite: Southern Pacific; Below: R. H. Kindig.)*

HIS NAME was George or Fred or Henry at the whim of the passenger and with only infrequent reference to the card in every car which proclaimed his proper given name, and he was an American institution. A man of infinite resource, limitless guile and the patience of Job, the Pullman porter has ridden a long way in the American legend. The first porter's name, according to Stewart Holbrook, an authority on such matters, was lost when the records of the Pullman Company were destroyed in the great Chicago fire of 1871, but his universal and generic name has to be George. All, that is except Daddy Joe, the bigger than life Pullman porter of folk-legend who is to the fraternity of Pullman attendants what Paul Bunyan is to woodsmen, a mythical character of incredible achievements. Often in critical moments he saved the day. Sometimes, when railroading was still an adventure, he lost his life doing it. This is not Daddy Joe, but Porter A. B. Jackson welcoming the occupant of Lower 6 to his car in Portland Union Station to ride all the way to Chicago on *The Portland-Chicago Special*. *(The Smithsonian Institution.)*

ONE OF THE FEW trains in *The Official Guide* to be named for a flower, *The Columbine, Bluebonnet, Mayflower* and *Azalean* are others—*The Portland Rose* replaced *The Chicago-Portland Special* and antedated *The City of Portland* as the Union Pacific's candy train on the prestige run between Multnomah and Lake Michigan. On it, in its *Portland Special* years, the finest devisings of Pullman craftsmen were lavished and luxury equipment, specially assigned to the run, carried its style in gold letters on the nameboards. At the left its Pullmans are being secured into train line at Portland Union Station in the era of wooden car construction. Above, No. 17 poses for an official photograph in a pose as richly regal as that of any train in the record. *(Two Photos: Everett De Golyer Collection.)*

839

IN 1913, the predecessor of *The Portland Rose* on the Oregon Short Line, *The Chicago-Portland Special* is shown at the right pounding up Sullivan's Gulch under the 12th Street Bridge at Portland. *(Herb H. Arey.)*

ALL THE AMENITIES of de luxe travel rode *The Portland Rose,* many of them aboard the company-built observation-club-buffet shown on the page opposite and including barber, valet service and soda fountain. With five head-end revenue cars as depicted here, it also carried set-out Pullmans from Salt Lake, Yellowstone, Denver and Green River as well as through cars from Puget Sound to Chicago. A charter member of the railroad horticultural club, along with *The Azalean* and *The Columbine, The Portland Rose* is shown here blooming smokily against the Idaho sky near Boise for its portrait by Henry W. Griffiths, Jr.

PERHAPS THE LAST of the long tally of name trains that rolled up to Denver
in the era of overstuffed sofas, lalique glass partitions and ornate radio consoles,
a list that must include the Burlington's *Aristocrat* and later the U.P.'s own *Denver
Limited, The Columbine* represented a final blaze of plush and ormolu before
the coming of *moderne* austerity in the decor of *The City of Denver* and, to a
lesser degree, in the first *Denver Zephyr. The Columbine's* lounge-observation-
buffet whose interior is vignetted above was outshopped in the U.P. car shops
at Omaha and furnished by company artisans in a voluptuousness suggestive
of the then vanished days of Pullman's Palace luxury. The exterior was painted
in royal blue and terminated with a bulkhead herald teeming with regional
symbolism. When *The Columbine* was retired in favor of the first *City of Denver*
the wonderful lounge cars were reassigned as shown at the right to *The Denver
Limited.* (*Union Pacific; Rail Photo Service.*)

842

FEW TRAINS, even on the Southern Pacific where identifying train numbers were shuffled in a complexity of change to baffle company historians, were so mutable in their train numbers as *The Columbine* which, at various stages in its life span, ran as No. 11-12, No. 19-20 and finally as No. 15-16. Here it is shown making an early morning arrival in Denver yards with six cars during the interlude when it was identified on company literature as No. 11. *(Richard H. Kindig.)*

843

The COLUMBINE
Flower of Travel Comfort to Colorado

You are viewing today what we have tried to make the finest train in America, a train built especially to typify and represent the state of Colorado. Its name is that of the state flower of Colorado; its beauty is inspired by the exquisite blue Columbine.

Notice the unusual features of the Columbine as you go through it today. Mark how well it typifies the beauty of Colorado. Its interior decorations are the Columbine motif throughout, combined with the state crest of Colorado. Even the china of the dining car is in Columbine design. Each of its new matched Pullmans is named for a flower or tree in the Colorado Rockies, each carries the picture of the flower or tree for which it is named. Dining car and observation car walls are hung with original paintings of Colorado scenes. While you are viewing the interior of the beautiful club observation, stop for a moment to try the luxurious easy chairs and divans in its lounge-rooms, and listen to its radio. Notice also the exterior of the observation car, painted in the colors of Colorado's state flag. Even the coaches are models of luxury, with deep-cushioned individual seats and porcelain-fitted smoking rooms, and decorated with Colorado pictures.

The Chicago & North Western-Union Pacific appreciate the interest you have shown in coming to view this new train, and hope that you will use this train on your trip to Colorado and will recommend it to your friends.

"Flower of Travel Comfort"

RIDE the Columbine this summer on a vacation to the cool Colorado Rockies. You can leave Chicago on the Columbine today and be in the shadow of Long's Peak tomorrow afternoon. It isn't far, and it costs no more than an ordinary vacation. For full information, call or write

H. G. VAN WINKLE   GEO. R. LEMMER
Chicago & North Western Ry.   Union Pacific System
148 South Clark St., Chicago   6 South La Salle St., Chicago

A RANKING member of the horticultural club which included such blooms as *The Azalean* and *Bluebonnet, The Columbine*, named for the state flower of Colorado, went into service between Denver and Chicago over the U.P.-North Western rails in 1927 to replace the older *Colorado Special*. Its twenty-eight and a half hour schedule would not have been breathless in comparison with *The City of Denver*, but in 1927 it was considered commendable. (*Top: Union Pacific; Below: Richard H. Kindig.*)

EVERYTHING about *The Columbine* bespoke the varnish run of pedigree basking in the regard of its owning carrier, nothing more than the limousine design, as the company's promotional literature was pleased to describe it, of the solarium lounge car *The Colorado Club* with its intricate blue and gold heraldry symbolic of The Centennial State. Although it antedated the age of air conditioning, the limousine lounge foreshadowed the time when the open observation platform with its aloof implications would be a casualty of air conditioning and vastly greater operational speeds than had hitherto characterized the timecards of even the fastest runs. *(Union Pacific.)*

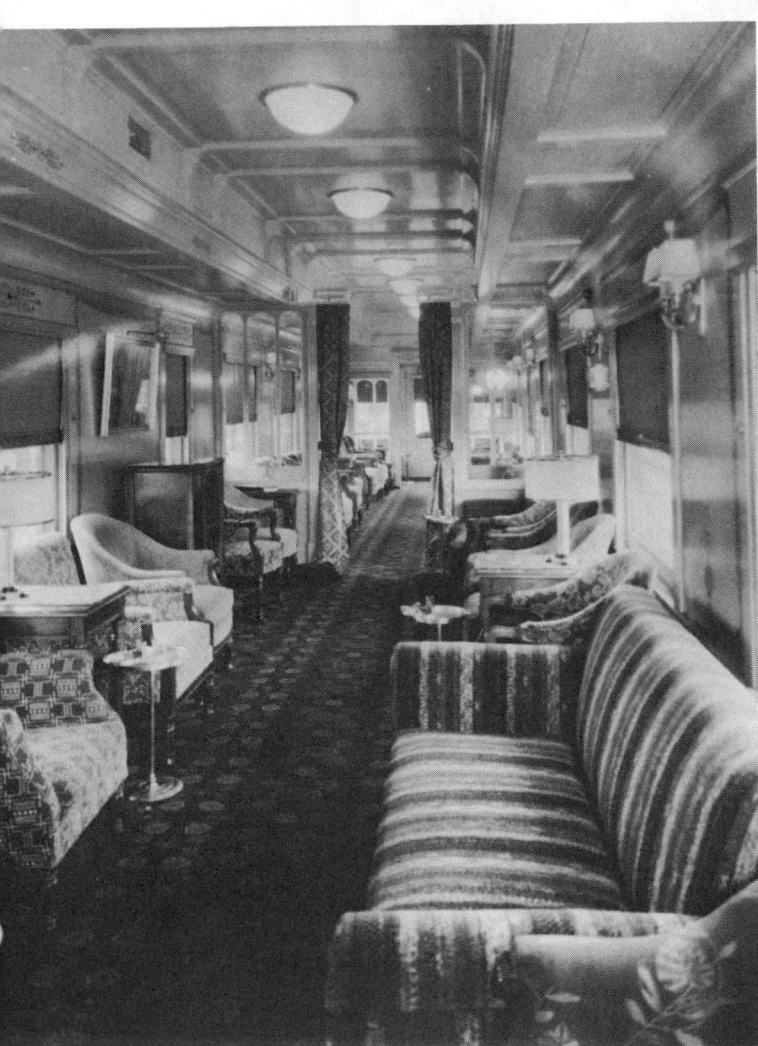

THE CONSIST of *The Columbine* which had been elaborately designed and built at the Union Pacific Omaha shops was on a scale of luxury to furnish explicit competition to the Burlington's *Denver Special* and later *The Aristocrat* (see Volume I of this book). Although antedating the actual advent of air conditioning, the lighter hues of its decor forecast a day when the abatement of soot in the cars would usher in a vogue for pastel shades and cheerier fabrics. *(Two Photos: Union Pacific.)*

845

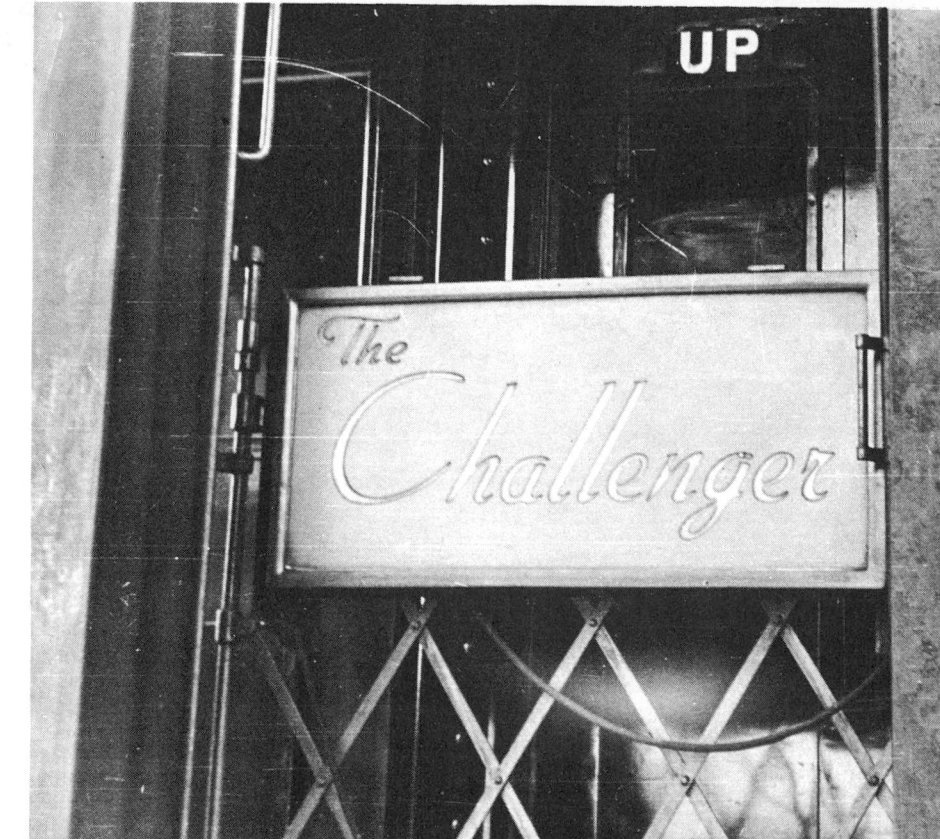

THE CHALLENGERS, which served both San Francisco and Los Angeles and ran during the 1941 war in as many as three sections to a train each way, were designed to carry coach passengers and tourist sleepers together with dining car service where breakfast was two bits and dinner an unbelievable thirty-five cents. *Challenger* coaches, as shown opposite, were outshopped specially for the run by Pullman. Sleepers were rebuilt Standard equipment lacking the drawing rooms of conventional usage. Above the *San Francisco Challenger* is shown at Archer, Wyoming, the week before Pearl Harbor. Lacking the panache of an observation, *The Challengers* carried their insigne on the tailgate of the last sleeping car. *(Above: R. H. Kindig; Right: Jim Ady.)*

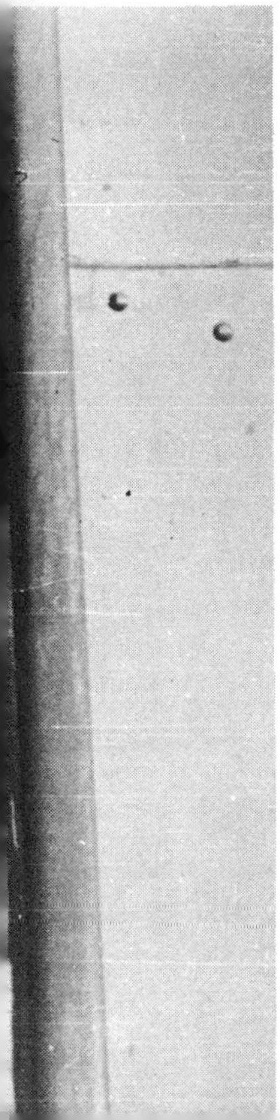

The Chicago & North Western's contribution to *The Challenger* pool was in the form of some of the handsomest and most luxurious streamlined coaches ever built by Pullman. In 1959 the Los Angeles section, as shown at the top of the page where it is being serviced at Cheyenne, carried a vista-dome coach No. 7010 which was cut out of the eastbound section at North Platte and cut into the next day's westbound when it came through. (*Above: Douglas Craig Wornom; Below: Pullman Standard.*)

847

RUNNING WITHOUT numbers on the Southern Pacific and as Nos. 47 and 48 on the U.P., *The Treasure Island Special* was the companion run on alternate dates to *The Forty-niner* between Chicago and the coast during the two summers of the World's Fair at Treasure Island in San Francisco. It was all-Pullman, extra fare, with the best of everything, lacking only the splendors of the diner *Angel's Camp* which made riding *The Forty-niner* an experience with Delmonico overtones. Here *The Special's* patrons are doing themselves proud in the steaks and chops department. At the right it pulls into Cheyenne in August 1939. (*Above: Southern Pacific; Right: Richard H. Kindig.*)

AT THE LEFT, President Leland Cutler of the 1938-1939 San Francisco Fair inspects the solarium lounge of *The Treasure Island Special* for the photographers. Company literature promoted *The Special's* fortunes in almost the degree *The Forty-niner* was advertised. *(Two Photos: Southern Pacific.)*

SUMPTER VALLEY
HOLSUM BREAD
LARGEST SALE IN THE WORLD

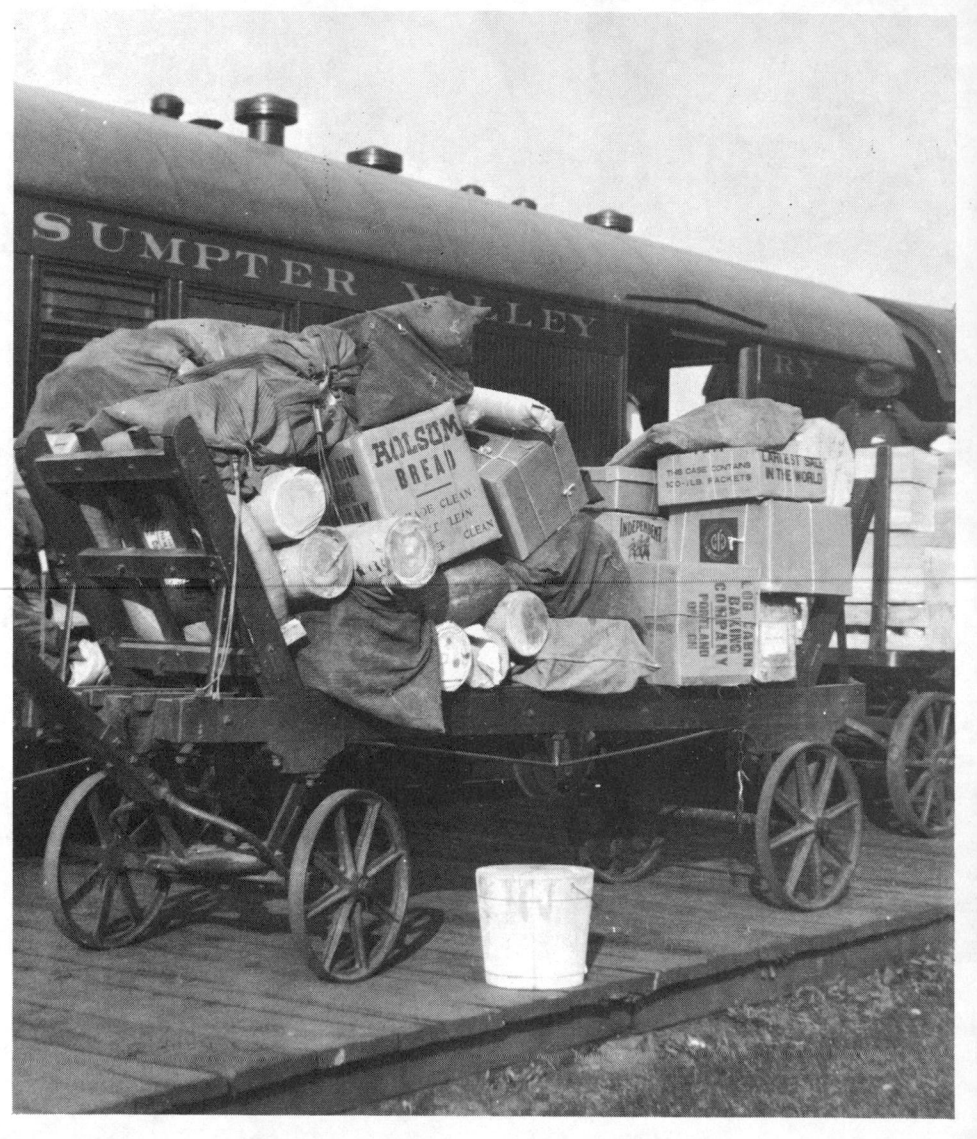

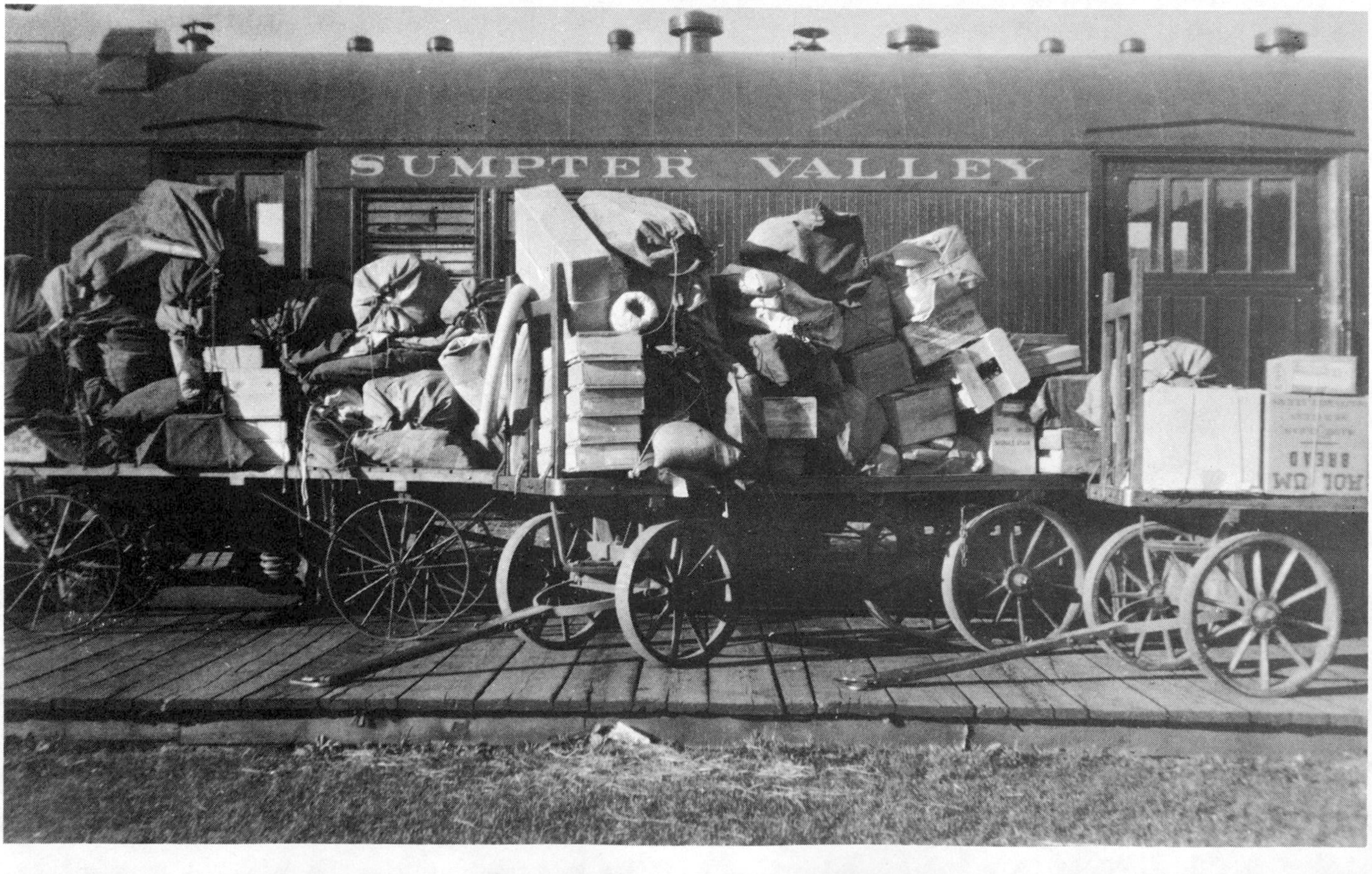
SUMPTER VALLEY

IN THE BELLE EPOQUE OF RAILROAD travel the fastest ride on many a railroad was not aboard the crack flyer or its most highly regarded varnish run but on *The Fast Mail* which carried the government's business and achieved higher speeds than the management would have cared to think about on the timecard of *The Limited. The Mail* always carried a rider coach for the accommodation of the crew where passengers who were in a hurry and could do without Pullman accommodations could ride for a first class fare. One of the great sights of riding the old *Chief* in the thirties was to watch the Santa Fe's pride take siding just west of Glorieta and see *The Fast Mail* roll up in thunder on the horizon behind it and pass in smoke and glory at a hundred miles an hour. Here is the Union Pacific's Train No. 26, *The Fast Mail & Express* in Snake River Canyon nearing Glenn's Ferry, Idaho. Opposite is the mail and merchandise it set down at Baker, Oregon, to be carried into the Blue Mountains by the narrow gauge Sumpter Valley Railway from its connection there. (*Above: Henry R. Griffiths, Jr.; Opposite: Owen Davies Collection.*)

A TRAIN OF ALL WORK with Standard Pullman sleepers from everywhere to everywhere from Kansas City to Puget Sound was the Union Pacific's *Pony Express*. As the *Pony Express* it existed in proper fact only between Denver and Salt Lake in competition to the more direct scenic route of the Denver & Rio Grande Western's several trains on the run, but it carried a through sleeper from Denver to Portland which was picked up by *The Portland Rose* at Green River, one from Denver to Los Angeles which went on from Salt Lake in No. 7, *The Los Angeles Limited* and another from St. Louis to San Francisco which joined *The Overland Limited* at Ogden. There was also a tourist sleeper from Kansas City to San Francisco which, together with a club-observation car, diner, chair cars and head end often made a twenty-car consist in and out of mile high Denver. To maintain its schedule on May 5, 1946, *The Pony Express* was assigned one of the U.P.'s fast, heavy duty Challenger type articulated engines shown passing Brighton, Colorado, at seventy miles an hour in the below photograph by Otto C. Perry.

AT BORIE TOWER where the Borie cutoff diverges from the Union Pacific main line to route traffic south to Denver and by-pass Cheyenne, the tower operator hands up orders to the rear brakeman of *The Pony Express* on the last Pullman. No. 38 will take the track to the left through Greeley on its way to the Queen City of the Plains. Like *The Pony Express* itself, Borie is now only a memory. (*Lucius Beebe.*)

THE ADVENT of the first primeval intimations of Diesel motive power in the West often found it integrated to established Pullman Standard steel name trains for which no lightweight equipment had yet been procured with two conspicuous results: the individuality of the consists so achieved made them acceptable as curiosities to die-hard enemies of internal combustion, and it resulted in frequent power failures and late trains because the Diesels couldn't handle the assigned tonnage. Here the Union Pacific's E-6 type Diesel-electric unit No. 8-M-2 rolls eastbound out of Denver in 1940 with seven Standard cars of the *Portland Rose-Pony Express* bound for Kansas City. Although its departure from the Queen City of the Plains was on schedule, nobody, least of all the management would make book on the hour of its arrival at Kansas City. (*Lucius Beebe.*)

CITY OF
LOS ANGELES

UNION PACIFIC
CITY OF LOS ANGELES
COPPER KING
CITY OF
LOS ANGELES

WHEN, in the late 1930s, the long established *Los Angeles Limited* was replaced by the streamlined, Diesel-powered *City of Los Angeles*, the equipment assigned to the run changed with such rapidity that confusion was excusable among the desert sourdoughs along the Utah and Nevada right of way of Senator Clark's original Los Angeles & Salt Lake Line. Within a decade no fewer than five different types of solarium-lounge cars terminated *The City's* consists, three of which are reproduced on these pages, together with a G.E. steam-electric experimental power unit. Most spectacular of the several innovations in car design was the portholed lounge car *Copper King* whose circular windows were individually adjustable to the desert sunlight. Other blind end cars, some with the train herald, others without identification for interchange with other trains, were sometimes assigned to the run. *(Opposite Two Photos: Everett de Golyer Collection; Below and Left: Union Pacific.)*

IT MAY BE difficult at this remove to imagine the impact on the general awareness of the new streamlined, Diesel-powered *City of Denver* when it was placed in service on the Chicago run in 1936. Diesel was something new and wonderful and not a threat to the entire structure and legend of conventional railroading. So were 100 miles an hour speeds as the veriest incidental to the carding of name trains, and so were the refinements of comfort which manifested themselves in air conditioning, rubber draft gear and unit trains. Nothing possessed greater customer appeal than The Frontier Shack bar car. Repeal was still a novelty and, for many, drinking was still a full time occupation and any departure from conventional decor and train appointments a source of delight. The vogue for Victorian atmosphere and the Old West was at its zenith and the Frontier Shack was so successful that imitations sprang up on every hand. Within the limitations of car construction, it was a decorator's dream and comprised all the atmospheric components that, elsewhere at *The City's* western terminal, could be encountered in the Victorian bar at the Cosmopolitan Hotel, the Teller House in Central City and, somewhat later, in the Strater Hotel at Durango. Here were "Wanted" posters from Wells Fargo, the bloodhounds on the ice from Civil War road companies of "Uncle Tom," the pugilistic profile of Jim Jeffries and the voluptuous likeness of Lillian Russell. Long forgotten race horses peered from ornate frames and playbills heralded the arrival nearly a century later, of Adah Isaacs Menken in "Mazeppa." There were crying towels at the bar and the barkeep wore roached hair and satin sleeve suspenders. The Frontier Shack had everything and, in time, the U.P. imitated its own success and emplaced a Little Nugget bar car on *The City of Los Angeles*. *(Three Photos: Union Pacific.)*

The Old West
Lived Once More
Aboard
The Frontier Shack

DINNER on the dining car has been, in the American awareness, possessed of a special significance as a sort of participation in a ritual or sacrament of travel. Its service on *The City of Denver*, where the tufted red leather upholstery was a hallmark of Union Pacific gastronomy, was an occasion at once for the lady passenger shown in silhouette as she lifts the first Martini of the evening and for the camera of Richard Steinheimer which was ready to hand for this moment. That *The City* afforded a variety of rear-end insignes is suggested below and opposite. (*Richard H. Kindig.*)

RAISING the window blinds of his midnight stateroom, the wakeful passenger on *The City of Denver* at Lincoln or Omaha beheld one of the ancient rituals of railroading, the icing of reefer cars laden with perishables from the rich farmlands of the West, some of which would almost certainly appear on the dining car breakfast table next morning. *(Above: Richard H. Kindig; Left: Richard Steinheimer.)*

859

THE VERITABLY Spartan
simplicity of decor that
characterized the public
apartments of *The City of
Denver* as shown on this page
was in dramatic contrast
to the wildly ornate
decorative scheme of the
train's Frontier Shack bar,
shown on an adjacent page
and to the profligate elegance
of The Little Nugget that
shortly appeared on
The City of Los Angeles.
With these splendid
exceptions, the era of plush
and ormolu had ended on
the Union Pacific.
The fact called attention to
the still modestly voluptuous
equipment of the
Burlington's *Denver Zephyr*
on the competing run
where matched woodwork
and rich appointments
still maintained continuity
with an older tradition
of railroad luxury. *(Three
Photos: Richard H. Kindig.)*

860

The Bird in The Gilded Cage Sang Again in The Little Nugget Bar

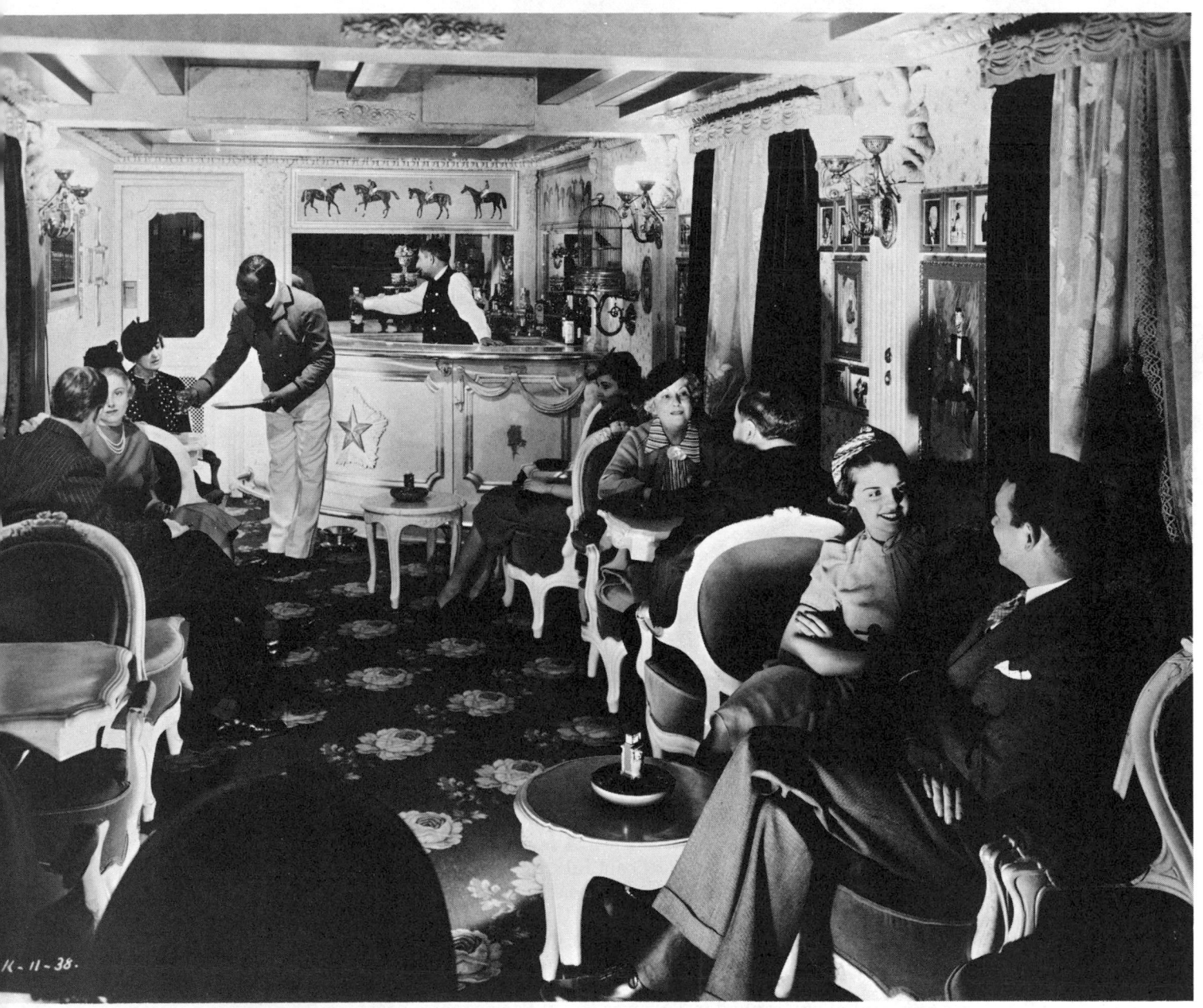

THE SHOW STOPPER of *The City of Los Angeles* was not so much the *Copper King* observation lounge with its $175 Polaroid lenses in porthole windows as it was The Little Nugget bar car which, if possible, transcended the atmospheric success of The Frontier Shack on *The City of Denver*. The Little Nugget was a decorator's dream of Victorian love seats, rich velvet portières, bevel-edged mirrors and gas lighting fixtures. The bartenders wore gay nineties attire with horseshoe tie pins and button boots, and late tarriers were sometimes moved to song which invariably turned out to be an approximation of "A Bicycle Built For Two." For a brief interlude before the advent of the 1941 war curtailed all non-revenue equipment, the Frontier Shack and Little Nugget were the sensations of Western railroading. *(Union Pacific.)*

THE NOW distant year of 1905 found Fred Jukes, boomer railroadman and the great pioneer of modern railroad photography, working the Union Pacific on its transcontinental main line between Cheyenne and Green River, a time and place where not all transport was aboard the steamcars as is suggested by the busy scene at Rawlins (right) as photographed by Jukes a decade later. The Saratoga & Encampment Valley Railroad, a U.P. feeder joining the main line at Walcott, Wyoming, had not yet been built and if you wanted to get to Encampment, a smelting town on the Wyoming-Colorado boundary, or fish the North Platte in the mountains to the south, you took the stage coach depicted above. "I was a passenger on that particular stage," recalled Jukes nearly six decades later, "having to take the train from Rawlins to Walcott which is a few miles east of the U.P. bridge across the North Platte River. It was beautiful country and the Saratoga & Encampment Valley line didn't then exist. The passengers on the stage when I took the picture were a couple of traveling men (salesmen) in hard derby hats, the others were ranchers for Saratoga, a small ranch town about two-thirds of the way to Encampment. The driver, a real old timer, wore engineer's goggles. It was something right out of the Old West you read about." Still another conveyance that Jukes rode and photographed in 1905 was Union Pacific motor coach No. 1 above and opposite. This experimental vehicle was assigned to local runs out of Rawlins where it is shown with C. M. Beard, its motorman, later U.P. Superintendent of Motive Power, and the car's mechanic, Floyd Schultz. These are vignettes of the legendary past when the century was young. (Three Photos: Fred Jukes.)

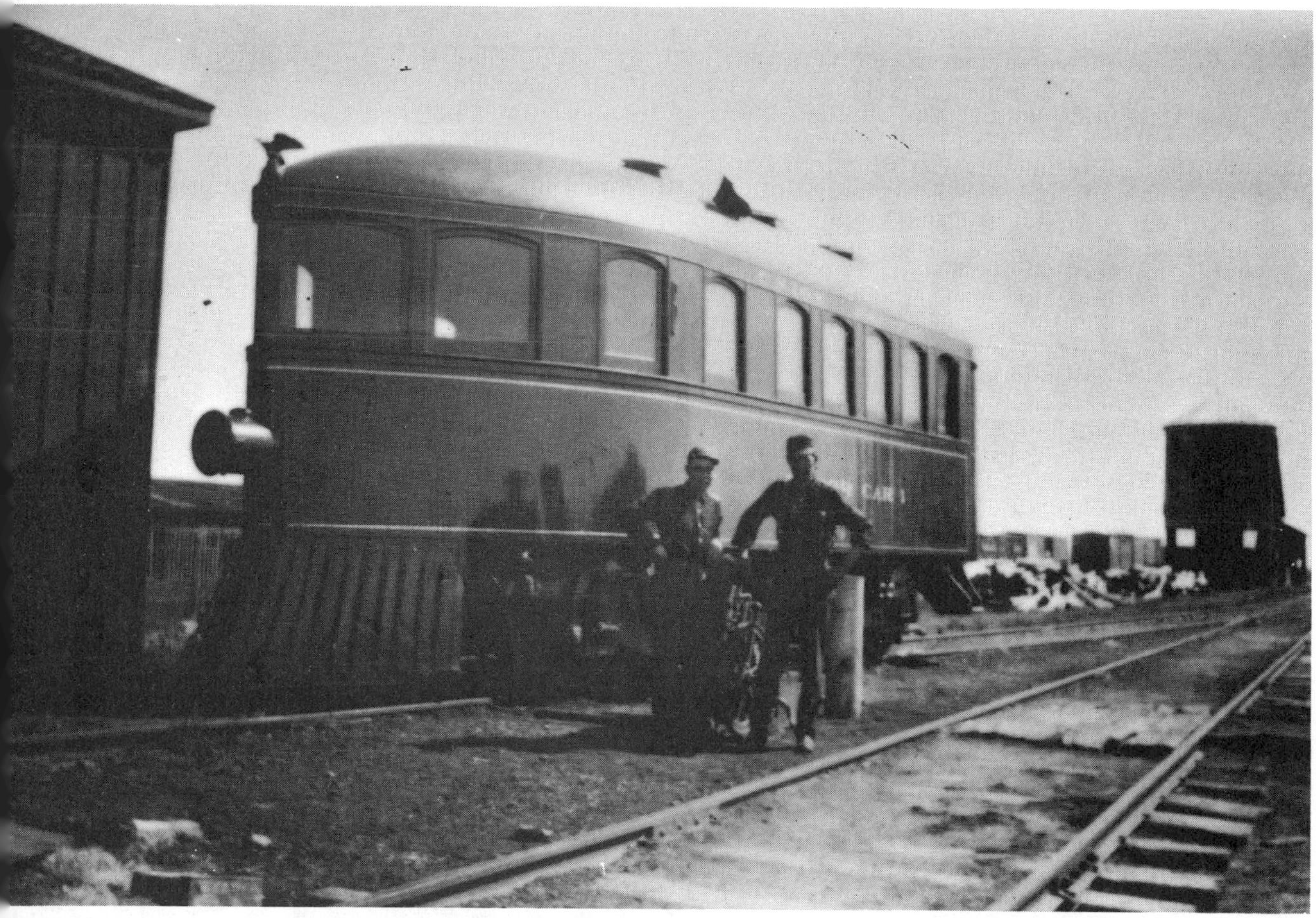

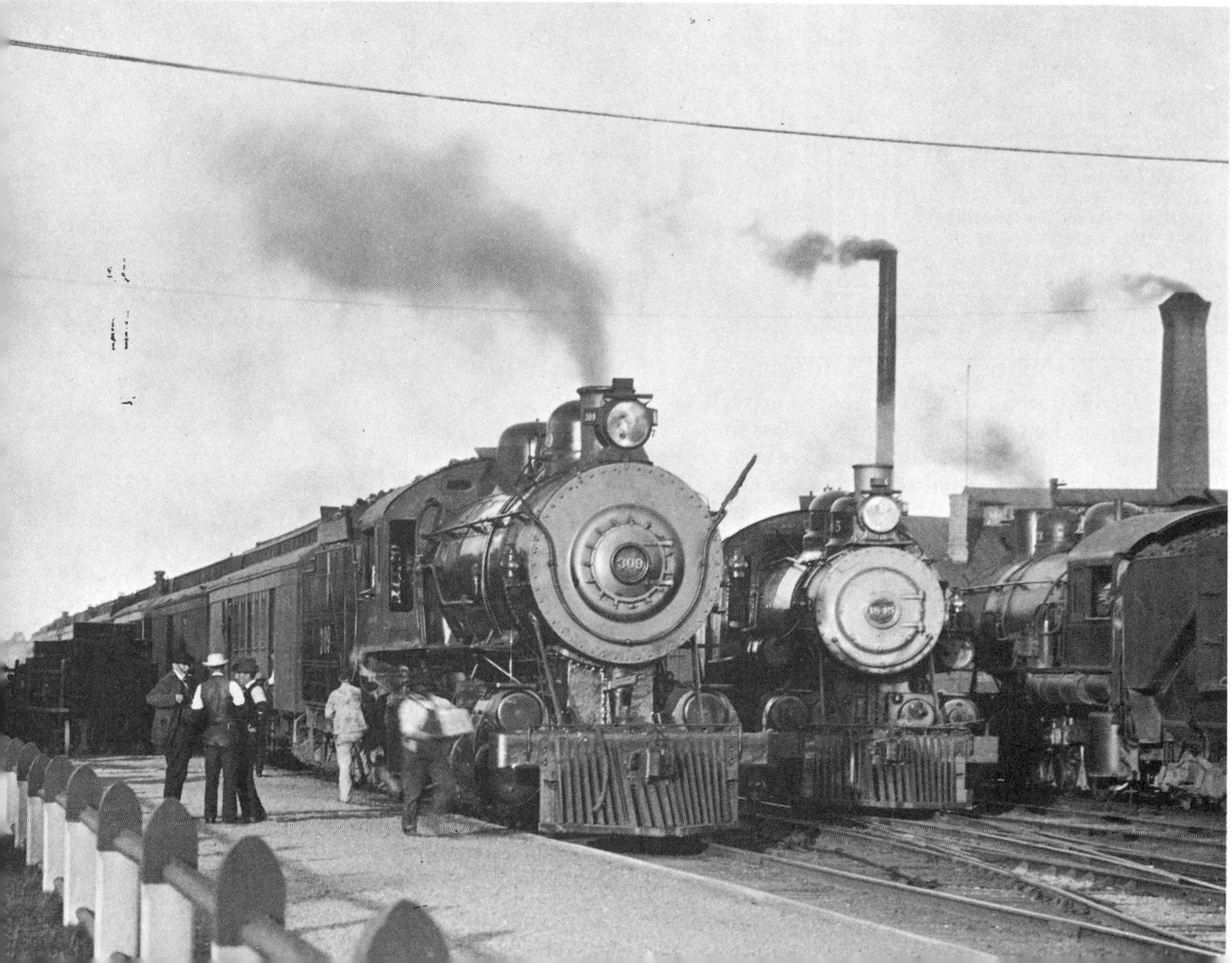

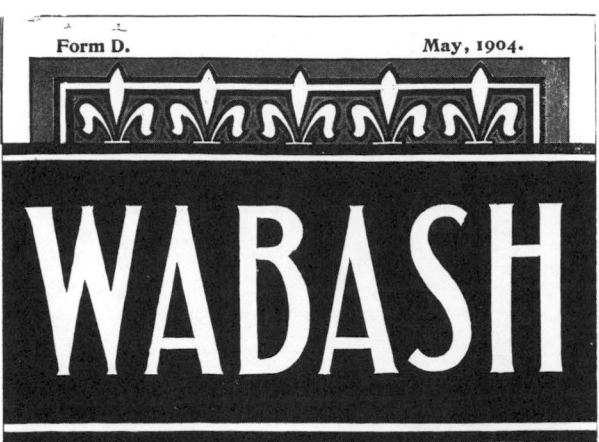

WABASH

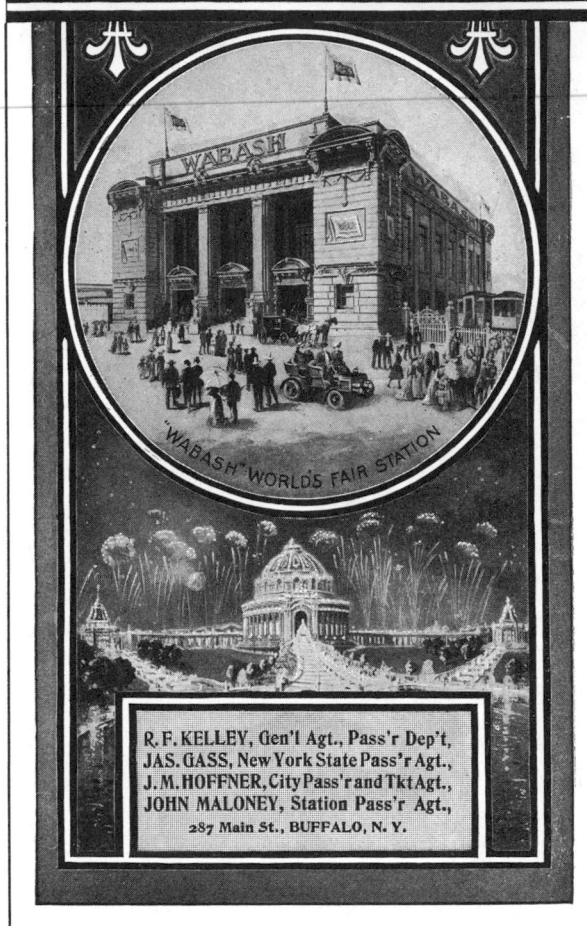

"WABASH" WORLD'S FAIR STATION

R. F. KELLEY, Gen'l Agt., Pass'r Dep't,
JAS. GASS, New York State Pass'r Agt.,
J. M. HOFFNER, City Pass'r and Tkt Agt.,
JOHN MALONEY, Station Pass'r Agt.,
287 Main St., BUFFALO, N. Y.

HEARTS and handkerchiefs fluttered as one to greet the arrival over the trestle of the great Eads Bridge across the Father of Waters at St. Louis of the Wabash's *Centennial Limited* with sleepers out of Boston over the Boston & Maine and from New York by the then flourishing West Shore Line, all concentered on Buffalo whence they achieved St. Louis itself over the Wabash's own iron. For it was the year of the great St. Louis Fair and all the world was telling Louis to meet it there. No motor car was visible beneath the deck of Eads Bridge where drays from the Levee were plentiful, but the Burlington Route, in competition with the Wabash west of The Gateway and for the Kansas City traffic flaunted its advertising in the background. The atmospheric photograph was taken in the now distant year of 1904 by Harry Boggs and is from the collection of Bernard Corbin.

A TRAIN which became a legend in commercial circles in its own lifetime, *The Detroit Arrow* maintained jointly by the Pennsylvania and the Wabash on the Detroit-Chicago run enjoyed such prestige as a businessman's train as almost to eclipse the rival New York Central *Twilight Limited* which was all-Pullman parlor car and provided a far more comfortable ride. "*The Detroit Arrow* of The Pennsylvania Railroad," said the company literature for 1938 rudely neglecting to mention the Wabash, "is the fastest train in America. It makes the run from Liverpool Tower (Gary, Indiana) to Junction (Fort Wayne) a distance of 116.4 miles in eighty-nine minutes—which is at a rate of 78.47 miles per hour." From Fort Wayne to Detroit over the rails of the Wabash no such spectacular carding was maintained, but sharing a pool of diners with the connecting carrier notably improved the Pennsy's indifferent cuisine. The Wabash cream chicken pie with dumplings was (and is) almost as celebrated a component of dining in motion as the lobster Newburg on *The Twentieth Century Limited*. Above, *The Detroit Arrow* with a K4s on the head end and a Wabash diner six cars back pulls out of Englewood depot in 1949. (*Rail Photo Service, Harold E. Williams.*)

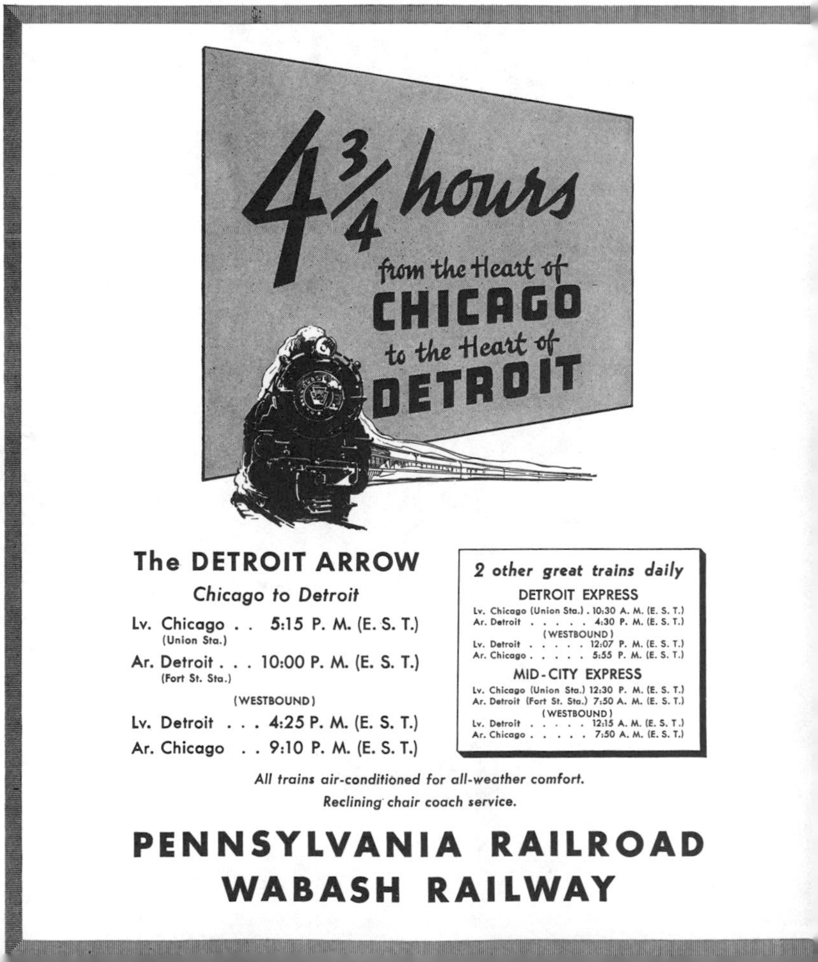

866

4¾ hours

from the Heart of **CHICAGO** to the Heart of **DETROIT**

The DETROIT ARROW

Chicago to Detroit

Lv. Chicago . . 5:15 P. M. (E. S. T.)
(Union Sta.)

Ar. Detroit . . . 10:00 P. M. (E. S. T.)
(Fort St. Sta.)

(WESTBOUND)

Lv. Detroit . . . 4:25 P. M. (E. S. T.)

Ar. Chicago . . 9:10 P. M. (E. S. T.)

2 other great trains daily

DETROIT EXPRESS
Lv. Chicago (Union Sta.) . 10:30 A. M. (E. S. T.)
Ar. Detroit . . . . . 4:30 P. M. (E. S. T.)
(WESTBOUND)
Lv. Detroit . . . . 12:07 P. M. (E. S. T.)
Ar. Chicago . . . . 5:55 P. M. (E. S. T.)

MID-CITY EXPRESS
Lv. Chicago (Union Sta.) 12:30 P. M. (E. S. T.)
Ar. Detroit (Fort St. Sta.) 7:50 A. M. (E. S. T.)
(WESTBOUND)
Lv. Detroit . . . . . 12:15 A. M. (E. S. T.)
Ar. Chicago . . . . . 7:50 A. M. (E. S. T.)

*All trains air-conditioned for all-weather comfort.
Reclining chair coach service.*

PENNSYLVANIA RAILROAD
WABASH RAILWAY

IN THE LONG AFTERNOON of Pullman Standard, *The Detroit Arrow* kept the faith with the open platform observation-parlor cars *Queen Anne* and *Queen Mary*, shown on an adjacent page, even though the train's speed made occupancy of the open platform a debatable pleasure. *The Arrow* was making tracks in the lower photograph behind K4s Pacific No. 5492 before it had cleared the shadow of Union Station in the Chicago background. (*Left: Rail Photo Service; Below: Pennsylvania Railroad.*)

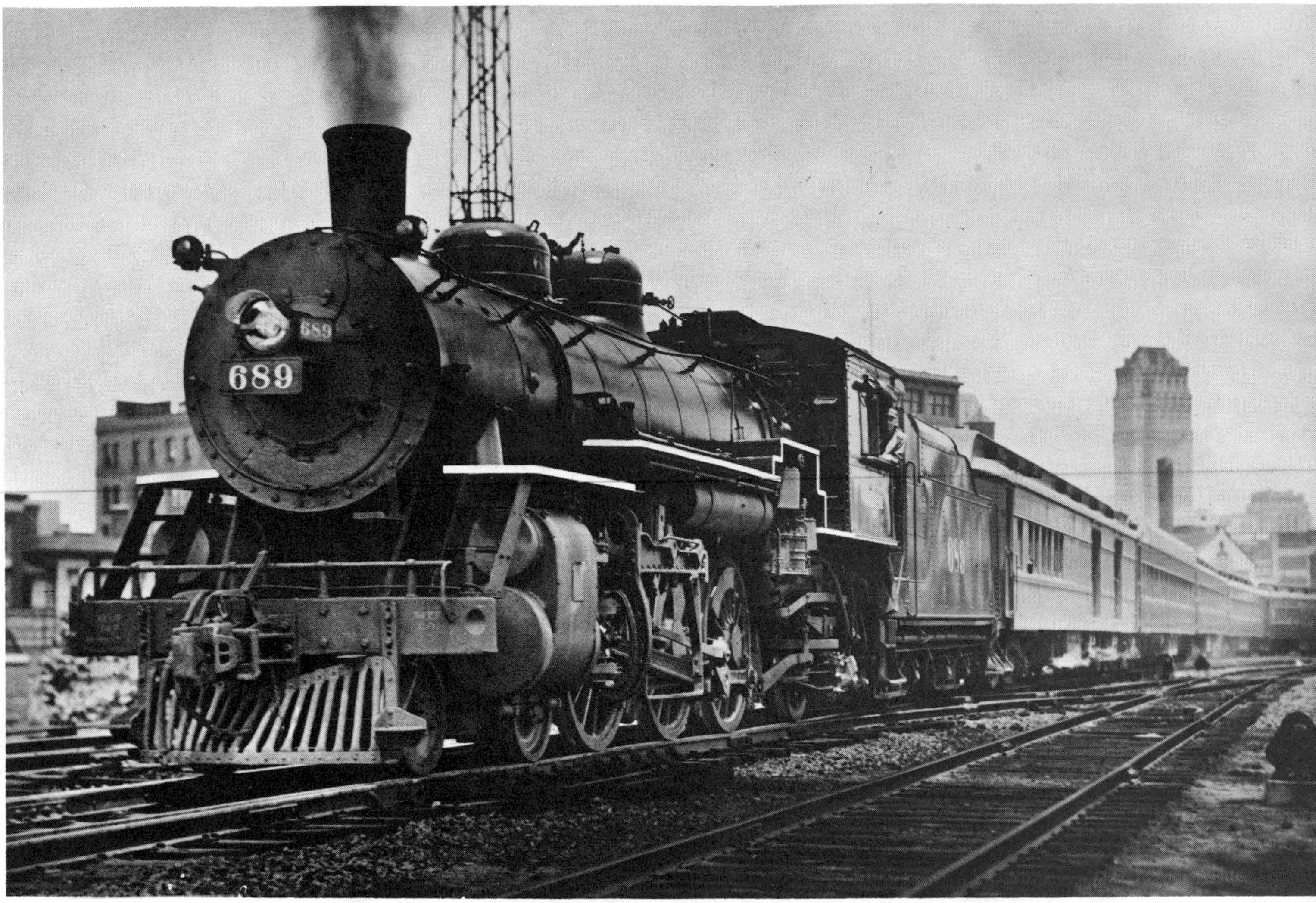

689

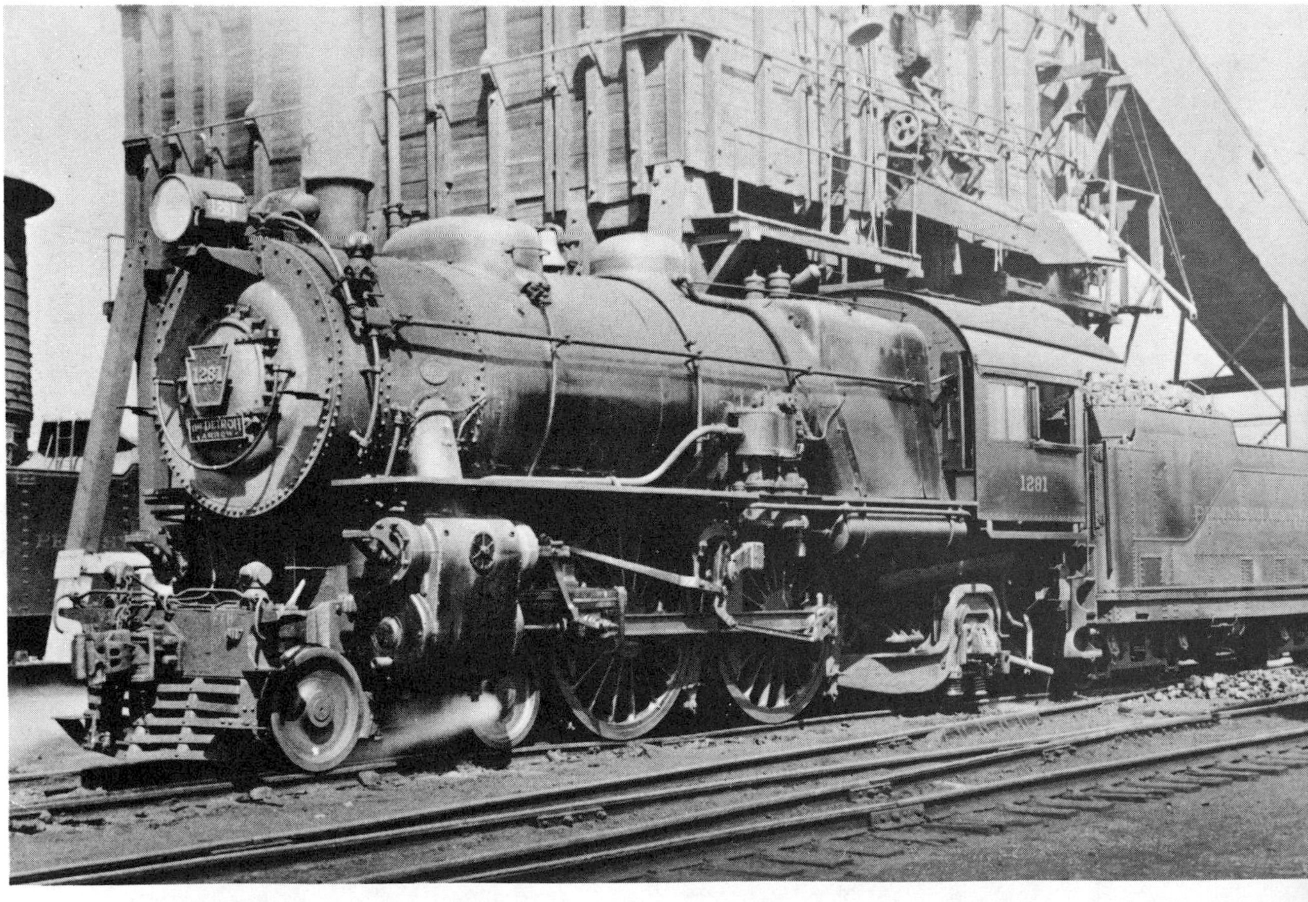

1281

AS STYLISH a daylight run as the most exacting perfectionist could ask, *The Detroit Arrow* on the page opposite rolls decorously out of Detroit yards behind Wabash Pacific No. 689 before hitting its full stride on the Wabash racetrack to Fort Wayne for its rendezvous with the Pennsylvania. The Pennsy's assigned engine for the run with the train name on its smokebox was a high-wheeled Atlantic entirely capable of hauling its valuable train on one of the tightest cardings on the timetable. On this page is reproduced an idealized view of *The Arrow* storming out of Chicago behind a K4s Pacific, while below in the carrier's familiar Tuscan red livery, the Pullman-built, parlor-observation car *Queen Mary* gleaming with gold finelining and brass was a tribute to the beloved English queen. At ninety miles an hour, however, admirers either of the monarchy or the scenery didn't care to use the open observation deck. *(Opposite, Two Photos: Rail Photo Service; Left: Pennsylvania Railroad; Below: Richard J. Cook.)*

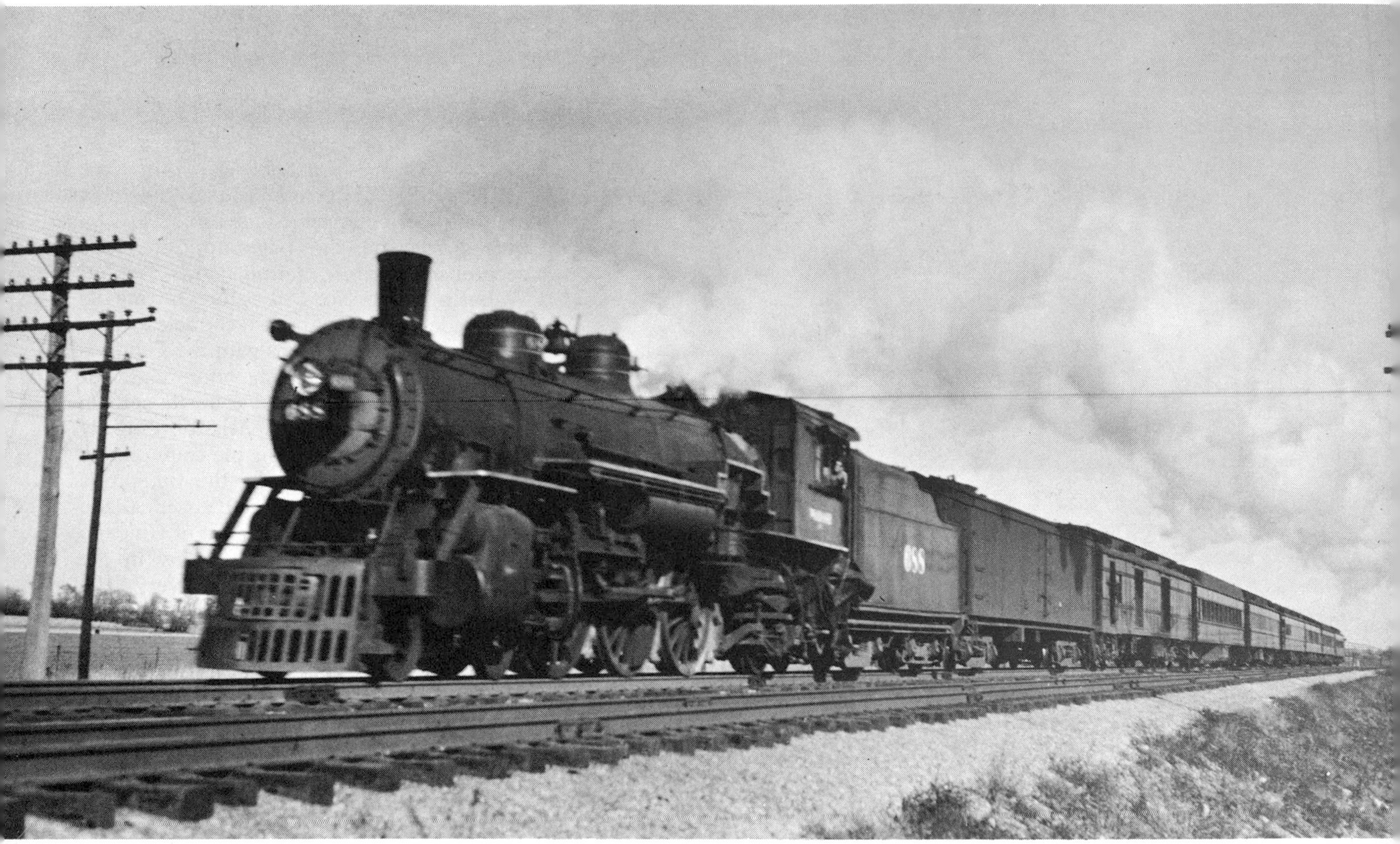
688

PULLMAN
DETROIT-ST LOUIS
WABASH
LIMITED

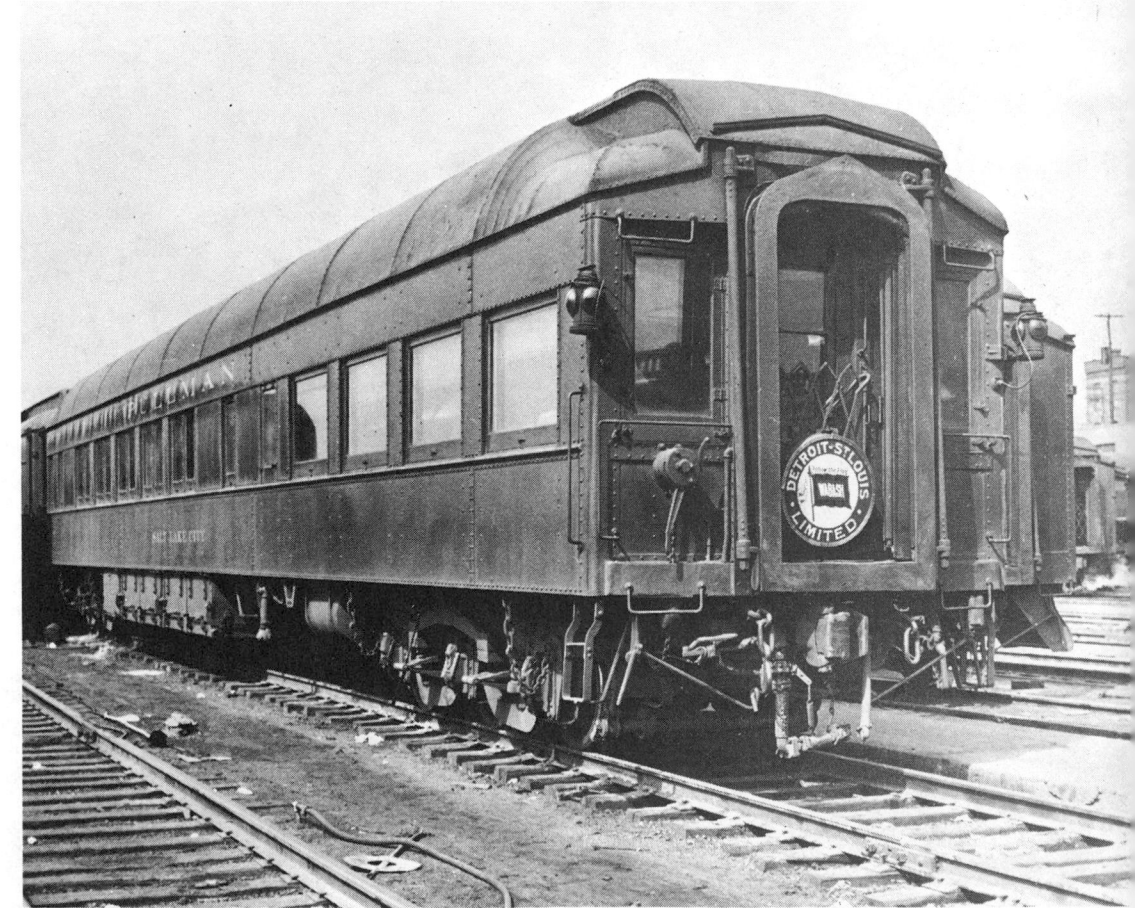

ROLLING OVER the 488 intervening miles between Detroit and St. Louis in the classic tradition of steam, the *Detroit-St. Louis Limited* was the overnight counterpart of *The Wabash Cannon Ball* on the daylight run. The Wabash delighted conservatives by retaining on both *The Cannon Ball* and *The Banner Blue* to Chicago the open platform observation car of tradition with its identifying train herald. Opposite, *The Limited* runs westbound through Sangamon, Illinois, in 1941 behind a characteristic light Pacific No. 688. The sleeper-lounge *Salt Lake City* is shown in detail at the bottom of the page and at the immediate left as it backs down past Perry Tower prior to leaving St. Louis. Below is the coach-buffet interior of *The City of Kansas City* built in 1947 by A.C.F. for the convenience of passengers desiring drinks and snacks. *(Opposite, Top: Paul Stringham, Rail Photo Service; Left: Rail Photo Service; Below: Wabash Railroad.)*

ON A COLD autumn morning in the mid-1930s when it was still a varnish run of pedigreed dimensions and the principal contender for daytime passenger traffic between St. Louis and Kansas City, The Mopac's *Kay-See Flyer* gives scant attention to grade crossings as it rolls through Webster Grove on the outskirts of St. Louis on its westbound run. For the carriage trade *The Flyer* carried a parlor car which brought up at the rear with a fine open observation platform. The carrier favored A.C.F. rather than Pullman with its patronage, a circumstance perhaps dictated by the presence of the former's shops within the St. Louis industrial complex. *(Right: Missouri Pacific; Below: Lucius Beebe.)*

AT Jefferson City, Missouri, *The Kay-See Flyer* pauses and car tonks give its journal boxes a hasty inspection to assure safety on its tight schedule. At the left it gets a wheel out of Kansas City while the Kansas City Southern's *Southern Belle* paces its departure with a business car on the track immediately to the right. *(Howard Fogg; Rail Photo Service.)*

873

ANCIENT, AMBLING and much loved, *The Carolina Special* came into being in 1911 as a Chicago-Charleston daily over the rails of The Big Four from Chicago to Cincinnati where it was taken over by the Southern Railway for an unhurried schedule through the cape jasmine (at appropriate seasons) to the ancient citadel of the Confederacy. Frequently operated in two sections with coaches, diner and Pullmans terminating in the brass-bound observation verandah of tradition, *The Special* was a name train of homely destinies and folksy ways. It made long stops to handle head end and seldom hurried between them. Five cars, as shown in this 1912 photograph meticulously copied from an original print by the master craftsman, Fred Jukes, were about as many as its motive power could haul and second sections, as shown on the page opposite, frequently carried additional coaches. The Southern's depot at Richmond in the year 1906 showed a conventional cab rank of victorias and growlers with a single high-backed touring car of unidentified make at the *porte cochere* to symbolize the dawning age of internal combustion. (*Cook Collection, Valentine Museum.*)

875

Competition For the Twin Cities Traffic
Was Conducted With Brass Knuckles

VERY MUCH OF a component in the Chicago-Twin Cities rivalry for passenger favor between the Big Three of the region was the Milwaukee's *Morning Hiawatha* shown here sooting up the skyline in a splendid display of ambitious firing as it clears the depot in downtown Milwaukee itself. Two other daytime *Hiawathas* not to mention the overnight pride of the line *The Pioneer Limited* with affable Dan Healy managing the diner were the road's entries in the sweepstakes whose other competitors were the North Western, the Burlington and, at one time, the Soo and Chicago Great Western. *(Lucius Beebe.)*

FULLY AS DETERMINED and almost as ruinous to the contestants as the competition for passenger traffic between Chicago and St. Louis in the great years of surface travel was the rivalry for the prestigious varnish business between Chicago and the Twin City terminals at St. Paul-Minneapolis. Here as many name trains cleared the Lake Michigan metropolis on competitive schedules at identical hours of day and night on the Big Three of the regional rivalry, the Milwaukee, the Chicago & North Western and the Burlington as cleared for the St. Louis Gateway on the Illinois Central, the Wabash, the Chicago & Alton, and the Chicago & Eastern Illinois. And on the North Woods run there was minor but still spirited competition from the Soo and the Chicago Great Western. The Burlington carried sleeper passengers west and parlor car patrons east in the Great Northern and Northern Pacific connecting runs for the *North Coast Limited* and *Empire Builder,* and in their own *New Black Hawk* and *Mississippi Riverview.* Patrons of the North Western by way of Milwaukee aboard *The North Western Limited, The Viking-Soo-Dominion, The Victory* and *The Duluth-Superior Limited* were offered an alternate routing via Madison on extra sections of the same trains with the addition of *The North Western Fast Mail, The*

Chicago Limited and *The World's Fair Special.* Partisans of the Chicago Great Western might take space, at various times, aboard *The Minnesotan, The Great Western Limited* and *The Legionnaire,* while perhaps the ranking name train of them all in Standard Pullman times was the Milwaukee's classic *Pioneer Limited,* flagship of the carrier's fleet of name trains made famous by the presence as dining car steward of venerable Dan Healy. There was also *The Day Express* and *The Olympian* which made St. Paul-Minneapolis as on-line stops on its through routing to Seattle. When the high speed runs with streamlining and airflow design arrived to stimulate competitive cardings, the North Western's *400* was briefly the wonder of the railroad world while the Milwaukee inaugurated an all-new streamlined *Pioneer Limited* and no fewer than three *Hiawathas* daily in each direction. The Burlington retained its old established *Black Hawk* and the conventional Great Northern-Northern Pacific connecting runs and laid on a *Morning Zephyr* and an *Afternoon Zephyr.* The Chicago-Twin Cities competition represented the last great brass-knuckles warfare for passenger patronage on parallel runs before the carriers began retrenching and ceased to care about revenues from their once proudly maintained varnish runs.

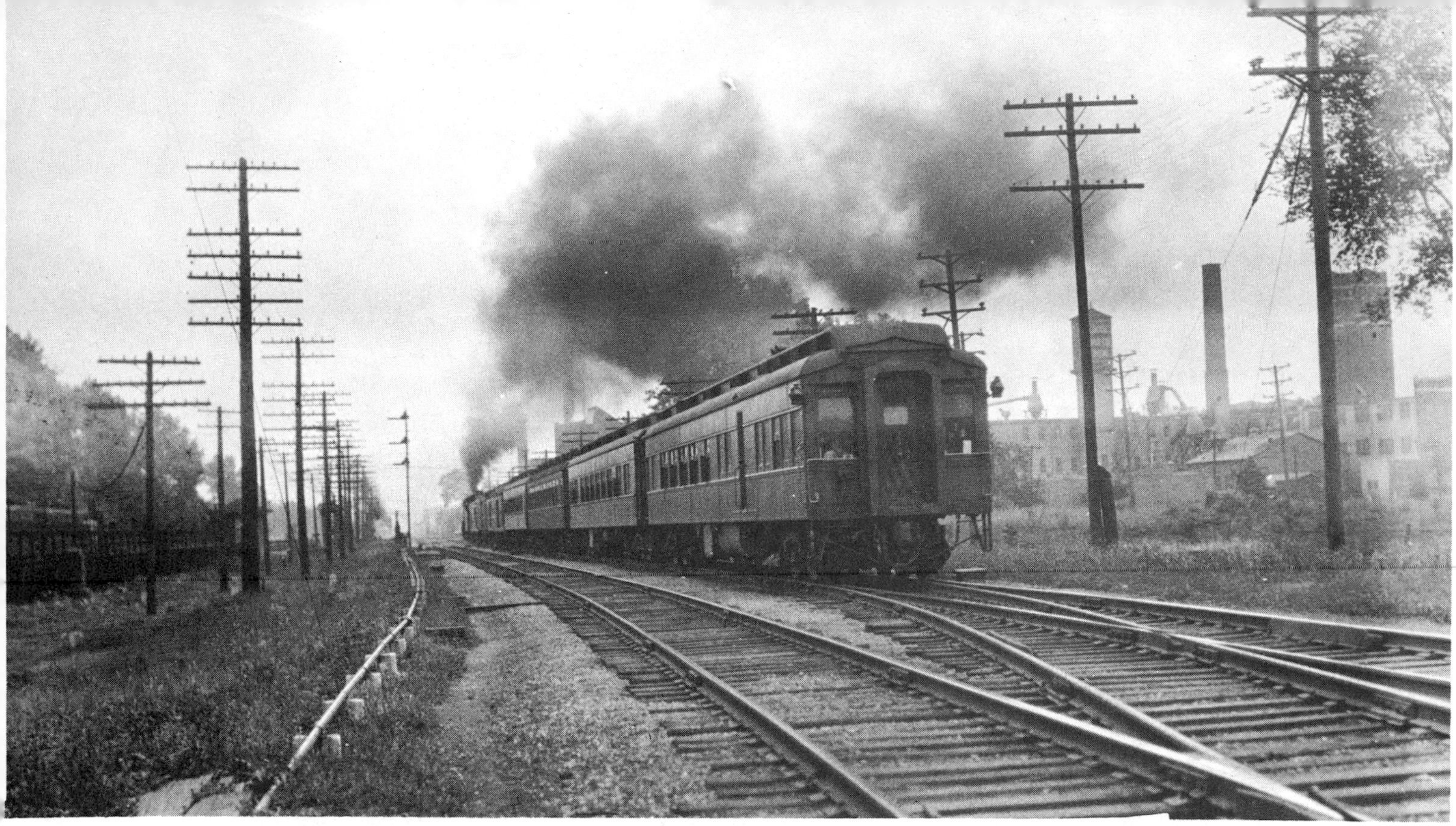

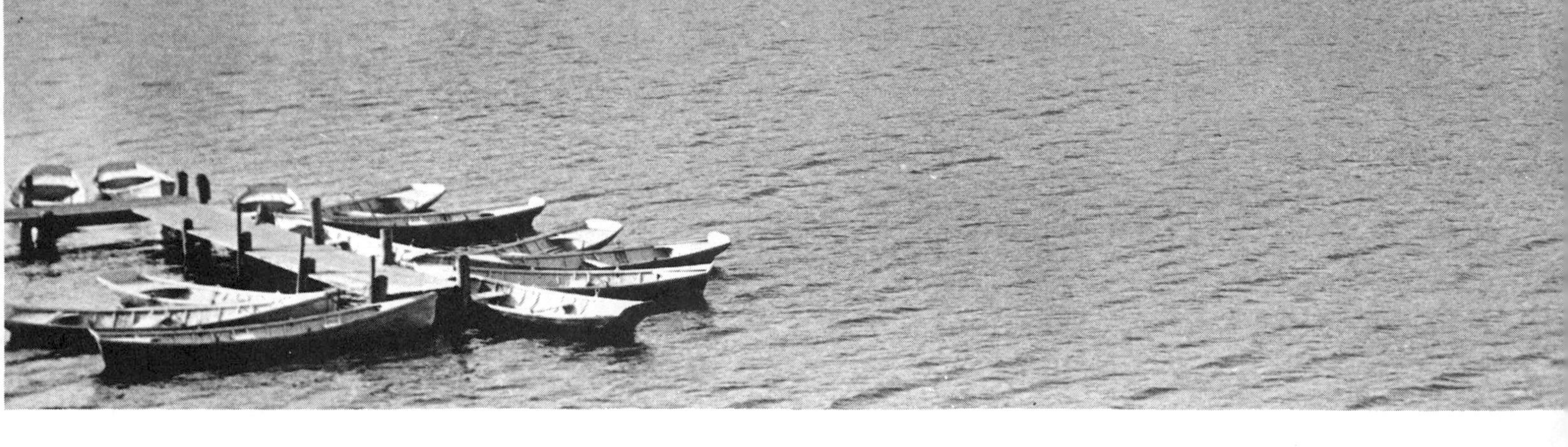

LEAST MENACING as a rival to the Big Three of the Chicago-Twin Cities passenger operations was the Chicago Great Western which in the flush times of the 1920s maintained *The Legionnaire* on the run with a full complement of coaches, Pullmans, diners and buffet-observation cars. *The Legionnaire* had displaced an earlier name train, *The Great Western Limited* and it in turn, when the depression of the 1930s came, was replaced by *The Minnesotan,* shown in various poses on these two pages. Aboard *The Minnesotan,* Pullman passengers rode in section-lounges such as that shown going away at the top of the page opposite, and the train made a brave showing with five cars as it rolled across Fox River at St. Charles, Illinois in 1934. A carrier with small request for full sized formal dining cars, the Great Western relied, in earlier days as well as later, on buffet-lounges from Pullman such as is shown here, some of which were elaborately fitted with mahogany paneling, velour drapes and crystal light fixtures. *(Opposite, Two Photos: Alfred W. Johnson; Above: Rail Photo Service, Pullman Standard.)*

Thru
Sleeping Car
between
Chicago
Milwaukee
and
Sault
Ste. Marie

Is operated daily by The Milwaukee Road via Pembine, thence the Soo Line. 12-Section, Drawing Room, Standard Sleeping Car.

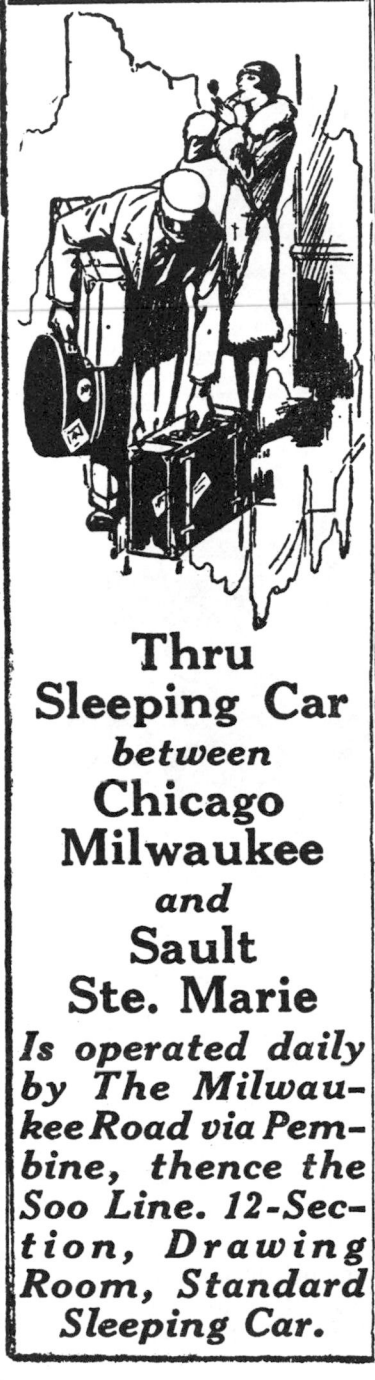

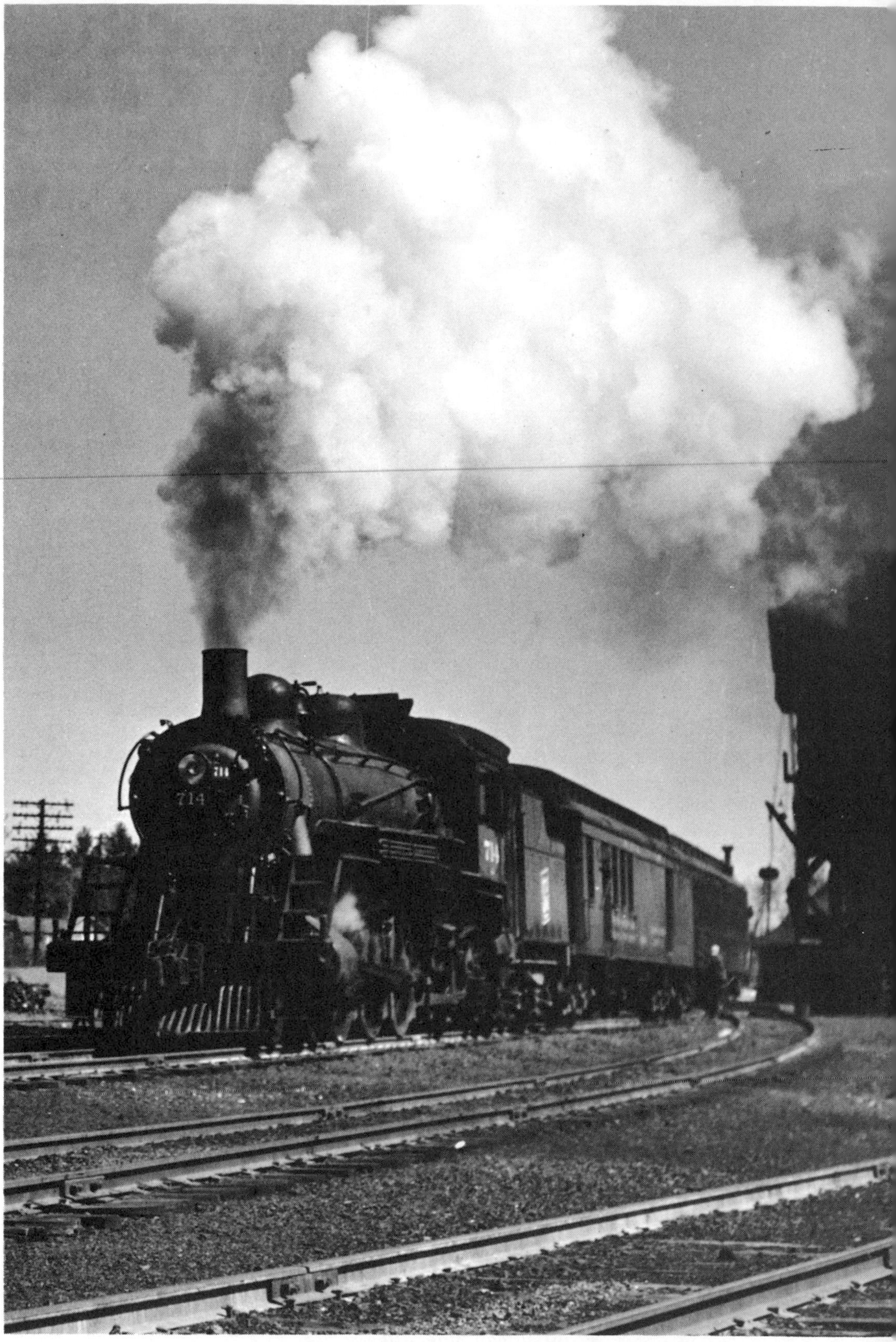

SOME CARRIERS were fortunate, before the end of steam came to abate their photogenic qualities, in having devoted photographic admirers who made a specialty of their regional pictorial record. The Southern Pacific had, among others, Richard Steinheimer, the Union Pacific gloried in Richard Kindig and Henry R. Griffiths, Jr., the Colorado narrow gauges had their pictorial minstrel in Otto Perry and the Chicago terminals achieved immortality through the camera of Alfred W. Johnson. The jongleur of the Soo was Leslie V. Suprey several of whose photographs are reproduced in this chronicle and who here presents a study of Train No. 65, the Moose Lake local as it clears the Moose Lake yards in 1948.

SEEN FROM Roosevelt Road overbridge at Chicago in 1949, *The Soo-Dominion*, freighted with intimations of a northern continent, races double headed into the yard on the overnight run from Minneapolis against an unmistakably Chicago backdrop of railroading. Lacking the panache of an observation car, the summer-time-only *Mountaineer* approaches its Chicago terminal with its train herald affixed to the tailgate of its final sleeper. *(Rail Photo Service, Robert H. Heurman; Alfred W. Johnson.)*

SO CLOSELY intertwined, in the case of *The Wabash Cannon Ball* are fact and folklore that it is difficult to establish where legend ends and the ascertainable record begins. As with the Lackawanna's *Phoebe Snow*, however, it seems likely that the myth antedated the actual train, since before the turn of the century there was a music hall ballad about "The Wabash Cannon Ball" although no such train appears in the company literature of the time. The song had little relationship with Wabash geography of fact since it depicted the carrier's tracks as reaching from the Atlantic to the Pacific and skirting the lakes of Minnesota. In 1946 the Wabash translated folk-legend into reality when it inaugurated *The Wabash Cannon Ball* on the daylight run between Detroit and St. Louis with new streamlined coaches, a company-owned diner-lounge and a parlor-observation car with a single drawing room. To power the train, as shown in Howard Fogg's painting, the carrier rebuilt several locomotives into truly beautiful 700 series 4-6-4s. Other *Cannon Balls* have run over the Long Island and the Texas & Pacific, the latter of which once figured in a spectacular head-on collision. Legend, too, ascribes immortality to Casey Jones while driving an Illinois Central "Cannon Ball" but no such train appears in the timetables of the period. When the Wabash's fine business car *City of Wabash* rode the end of *The Cannon Ball* its tailgate insigne was fixed to its observation rail as shown here. (*Above: Wabash Railroad; Right: Paul Stringham.*)

883

Way Down East

IN THE PEACEFUL WORLD that knew the summer of 1912, the Boston & Maine Railroad's *Montreal Express* out of Boston for the Canadian metropolis was photographed by Herbert Lincoln Arey as it stopped for water at Potter Place, New Hampshire. The fireboy pulled down the spout toward the tender of No. 1366, a couple of passengers descended from the cars to take the air, and an intelligent photographer recorded a scene that might have served as backdrop for the Broadway production, decades later, of "Ah, Wilderness!"

PASSENGER OPERATIONS north and west of Boston in the period which, in general terms confines the contents of this volume to between 1890 and 1950, might categorically be divided into runs originating and confined to Northern New England and those originating elsewhere and having New England terminals or vice versa. In the first group would fall, for example, *The Kennebec Limited, The Flying Yankee* and *The Pine Tree Limited* while the much larger classification would include *The Bar Harbor Express, The Minute Man, The Gull, The Ambassador, The State of Maine, The Alouette, Redwing* and *East Wind*. Obviously the greater number of luxury name trains were on the longer hauls, to Montreal, Philadelphia, Washington, Chicago, and in the more distant past, St. Louis, Pittsburgh and Cincinnati. Whether or not their destinations were within territorial New England or farther afield, the concern of the following pages is with trains of essentially Yankee character with part or all of their mileage through the New England heartland and the Way Down East that is the subconscious home of so many Americans even though they live in Wisconsin or Arizona. Their pictures are a nosegay of remembrance for the varnish that once ran over the Boston & Maine, the Maine Central, the Central Vermont, the Rutland and the immortal Fitchburg in their long ago country yesterdays. To those who loved them, if only at second remove and in the telling, their memory is an article of faith.

AT THE TOP of the page is a fine period view of the Causeway Street depots of the Eastern Railroad and, beyond it, the Lowell, when they were two of the components of Boston's "Railroad Row," the others being the Fitchburg and the Boston & Maine.

Gateway To The Yankee Heartland

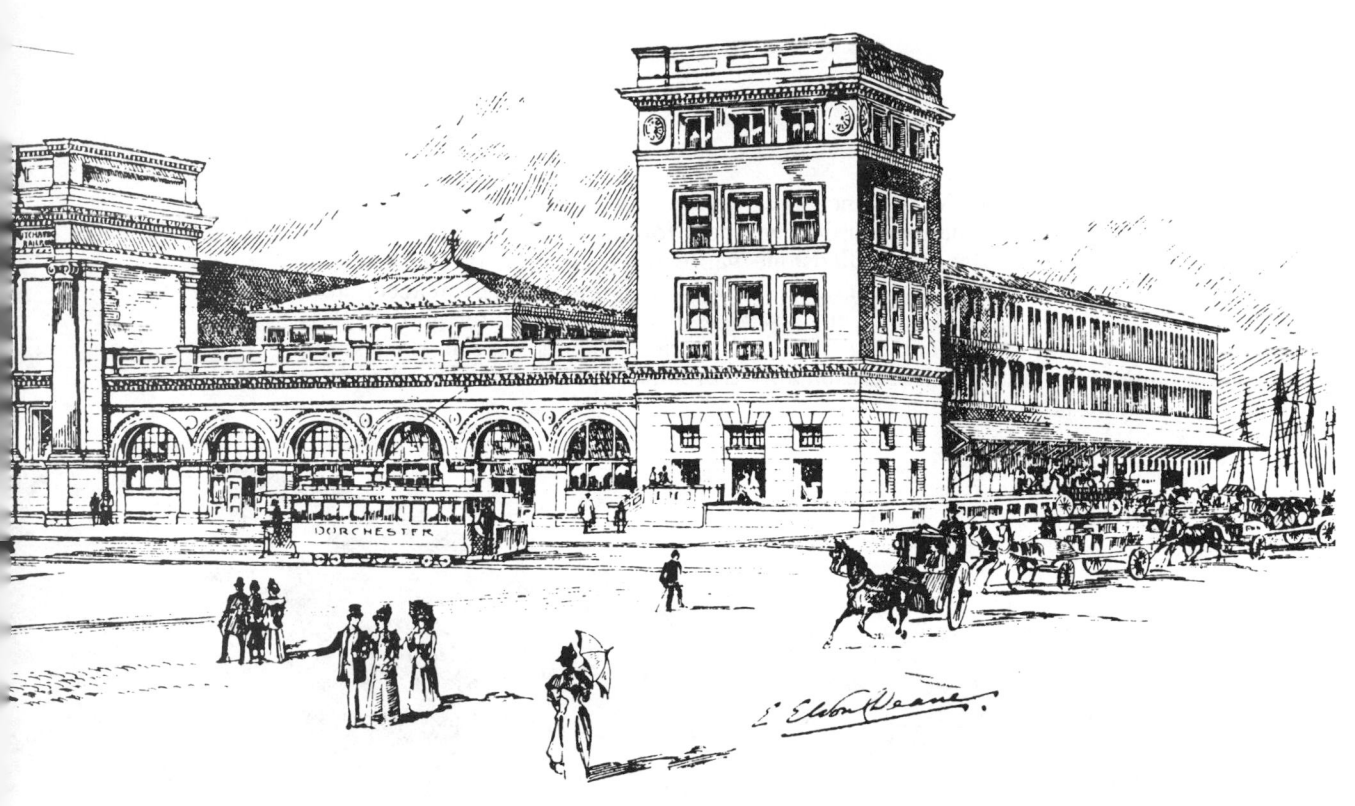

BOSTON'S UNION STATION, as it was formally known at the time of its construction in 1893, or more familiarly the North Station, was the terminal of the Boston & Maine-Maine Central complex of carriers which fanned out from its throat tracks across Charlestown Estuary to send varnish trains over the home iron as far west as Troy and by connecting carriers to Portland, Montreal and far-off St. John's, Newfoundland. Subsidiary roads, branches and short lines covered New England with a close-grained network of railroads, all of them terminating, like vines in a pot, in the train bays of North Station. No interchange existed between North Station and the New Haven-Boston & Albany terminal at South Station a mile and a half across town. Instead North Station routed its debouching passenger traffic to urban and suburban destinations over an equally complex network of public carriers via subway, elevated and surface trams and, of course, public hackney carriages and private conveyances. Few all-Pullman trains were ever scheduled out of North Station, the resoundingly named *Boston & Mt. Desert Limited Express* of 1897 being an exception to this generality, but there were sleeping cars and diners in rich profusion of vintages in the consists of *The Montreal Express, The Gull, The Ambassador, Minute Man, Flying Yankee, Kennebec Express* and *East Wind*. New England railroads had neither the resources nor the incentive of competition for updating equipment or motive power that animated carriers elsewhere and, as a result, the traffic that flowed north of Boston as long as steam and Pullman Standard lasted was an antiquarian's dream. Wooden underframe Pullmans, colored glass transoms, ornate wrought iron observation platforms rolled under summer suns and through the Down East winters in an animated facsimile of turn of the century operations that was perpetuated until the 1941 war. No all-room sleeping cars, no enclosed solarium lounges or chromium decor marred the facade of 1910. As long as passenger traffic lasted in New England it went fanwise north of Boston as it had done last year and year before that, and when at last it vanished into the coachyards of Acheron, it was beckoned to rest by a highball hoisted to a yard on rope halyards in the same manner the first varnish run had been given green more than a century before. New England railroading, to the end, kept faith with yesterday. *(Opposite: H. W. Pontin.)*

CUSTOMS INSPECTION at Vanceboro, Maine where the St. John & Maine Railroad crossed the Canadian border, was less formal in the year 1900 than it was to become at a later date. Gladstone valises and Saratoga trunks were inspected in the informal setting of a cow pasture, which may have been acceptable enough in summer months. What it must have been like in winter and the less clement seasons of spring and fall when sub-arctic elements were in possession, may be left to the imagination. Presumably travelers were a sterner breed of men in those days.   *(Brown Bros.)*

A FINE THING to see and very big time railroading in its place and era was the Boston & Maine's *Montreal Express* rolling downgrade at Gale, New Hampshire, in 1912 on its all-day *jornada* across New England. *(Herb L. Arey.)*

A PERIOD piece, the dispatchers' office at Boston's North Station in the year 1890 guided traffic over the Eastern and Western Division and the Fitchburg in a classic atmosphere of wing collars and propriety suitable to the conduct of one of New England's greatest enterprises. *(Bradlee Collection, Essex Institute.)*

THE REMARKABLE photographs on this and the opposite page represent the Boston & Maine depot at Lynn, Massachusetts, then the shoe and leather capital of the world, as it appeared in the fullest flower of daily traffic *(right)* in 1888 and *(below)* as seen from almost the identical spot after the Great Fire of November 26, 1889. In the before view a Boston-bound local is emerging from the arched train shed that spanned the tracks between the north and southbound waiting rooms. After the conflagration only structural elements have survived the flames and even the crossing tender's shanty has lost its windows while bowler-hatted commuters stand on the unsheltered platforms. *(Two Photos: Laurence Breed Walker Collection.)*

BEGINNING IN THE SIXTIES as the railroads eliminated the long rough journeys in stage coaches over usually execrable roads, the White Mountains of New Hampshire suddenly flowered with prosperity as vacation spots and idyllic retreats not only for the wealthy and leisured classes from Boston and New York but for the commonality much as the jet age a century in the future would see ribbon clerks vacationing in Hawaii and small tradesmen taking the grand tour of Europe in three weeks' time. "It was in those years," wrote Alvin Harlow in *Steelways of New England*, "that famous hotels had their heyday—the Profile House, the Crawford House, the Summit House on Mt. Washington, the Pemigewasset; Littleton, Bethlehem, North Woodstock, the Conways and other villages became tourist centers." The superb photograph reproduced here depicts the Boston & Maine's gleaming No. 775 with a varnish run paused at Franconia, New Hampshire, about 1900, Franconia Notch being the scene of some of the most rugged mountain vistas in New England. *(Everett De Golyer Collection.)*

WHEN THE White Mountains were first made available to the tourist trade on a large scale toward the end of the nineteenth century, it was through the agency of the railroads that first penetrated the primeval wilderness with trains originating from Boston and Portland. The Portland & Ogdensburg Railroad, a carrier enjoying an enviable summer trade, carried open observation cars such as that shown above on all through trains.

The same car is shown at the left traversing a roadbed only recently carved from the wilderness. *(Two Photos: New Hampshire Historical Society.)*

893

THE CONCORD & MONTREAL RAILROAD, whose two fine Palace Parlor Cars *Passaconaway* and *Lafayette* are shown at Boston's North Station in 1895, was a consolidation of the earlier Boston, Concord & Montreal which connected at Fitchburg, Massachusetts, with the Fitchburg Railroad out of Boston and achieved Wells River, Vermont, via Concord, New Hampshire, which gave it an entrepot to the rich White Mountain tourist trade in competition with the Boston & Maine, the Maine Central and the Portland & Ogdensburg. It connected for Canada over the Grand Trunk and was one of the richest railroad properties in New England until the time of its lease to the B.&M. for ninety-nine years the year these photographs were taken. Its proud title of Concord & Montreal was swallowed in the corporate entity of the Boston & Maine but its slogan, "The White Mountain Line," shown on the car nameboards was retained for many years. Over it *The Montreal Express* and the cars *Lafayette* and *Passaconaway* rolled on happy traffickings that provided the largest dividends of any New England carrier for several decades.

WHAT WILL attract students of railroad operations in this sketch of a Boston & Maine newspaper train from *Harper's Weekly* in 1890 is the inclusion, according to the specific testimony of the artist, of a Woodruff Parlor car as rider coach. More usual practice was the use for occupancy by the train crew of a downgraded day coach rather than a rare and exotic piece of luxury equipment. Not so exotic, perhaps, but still a rare item of varnish stock is the combination sleeper-parlor-observation car *Fernie* which for many years ran between Boston and Canada in the overnight *Red Wing*, a sleeper hop on the Boston & Maine and Canadian Pacific. *Fernie* had begun life when it was outshopped by Barney & Smith for the Soo's Chicago-Twin Cities service and rounded out its long and useful lifetime in the New England hills. (*Below: Arthur D. Dubin Collection.*)

HEAVILY patron-
ized in the summer
months, *Alouette* was
sometimes reduced
in winter to three
or four cars besides
head-end revenue.
Here, at Newport,
Vermont, in the
winter of 1947 the
management felt that
doubleheading was
indicated in the face
of a Yankee
blizzard and a 4-6-0
helper was taken
on ahead of a 4-6-2
road engine.

SHOWN below, *The
Alouette* is posed
beside a Concord
local under the
historic and ornate
Boston & Maine
train shed at Concord,
New Hampshire in
1946. *(Two Photos:
Philip Hastings.)*

IN THE TEEMING DAYS of railroad travel in New England, the Boston & Maine's day train, *The Alouette*, ran over its originating carrier from the North Station as far as Wells River, Vermont, where it was taken over by the Canadian Pacific for the remaining five hours' run to Canada. A train of leisured pace, it rolled all day through the lush New England countryside as shown above and passengers could get breakfast and lunch on the comfortable C.P. buffet-observation car, carrying one of the last brass-railed platforms with its identifying train herald north of Boston. It arrived at Montreal at 6:16 giving travelers plenty of time to check in at the Ritz or Mount Royal and tidy up for dinner. (*Two Photos: Rail Photo Service; Above: H. W. Pontin; Right: W. G. Fancher.*)

897

ALTHOUGH the terminal of the Boston & Maine's Gloucester Branch at Rockport was a scant thirty-five miles distant from North Station, the status of its patrons back in 1906 when the photograph at the bottom of the page was taken was so exalted that an all-parlor car train left Boston on Friday afternoon and returned Monday morning for the convenience of a clientele to whom coach travel would have been unthinkable. Patrons included Henry Cabot Lodge, Henry C. Frick and Searses, Lowells and Saltonstalls past all counting. When patrons of "The North Shore Dude" in a moment of hauteur changed the corporate name of their residence from Manchester to Manchester-by-the-Sea, Dr. Oliver Wendell Holmes subscribed his letters "Beverly-by-the-Boston & Maine." "The Dude" is shown below paused at East Somerville and arriving at Magnolia where it is being met by an ancestral Packard with a *Roi des Belges* tonneau. *(Rail Photo Service; Library of Congress.)*

THE LEGEND engrossed over its imposing main entrance ran for all to read "Union Station" but no Bostonian worth his salt codfish on Sunday morning knew it as anything but The North Station, to identify it from the South Station where the New Haven and Boston & Albany arrived on the other side of town. A vast preponderance of the North Station's traffic was in commuters bound for Melrose, Malden or Haverhill, Winchester or Woburn in the Boston & Maine's characteristic red and green upholstered, open platform day coaches impregnated from decades of service with a smell of valve oil and coal smoke that was all their own. The elite of these commuters, especially in the summer months, and many of them regulars on the "North Shore Dude" headed for Pride's Crossing, Beverly Farms, Magnolia and Nahant where servants were already preparing cooling drinks for them on the wide porches of massive Victorian mansions and the Eastern and Corinthian Yacht Clubs. Luxury equipment, except on a few through trains for Canada and the West was infrequent at North Station and such ostentations of splendor as private cars almost unknown. Carpet bags and chin whiskers and Yankee accents that could pronounce "cow" in four sylables, poke bonneted old ladies and shoebox lunches were a commonplace long after they had become the properties of comedy elsewhere in the land. (*Above: The Smithsonian Institution; Opposite: Rail Photos, The Library of Congress.*)

899

ALTHOUGH, in the Great Fire of 1872 which
flattened much of Boston's commercial district, the
Mansard roof had been much blamed as one
of the agencies in spreading the catastrophe, it
was still incorporated in the overall design
of the Boston & Maine North Station when it was
built, in part on the site of the old Eastern Railroad
depot, some twenty years later. Most prominent
feature of the truly noble brick, granite and
stone structure fronting on Causeway Street was a
massive colonnaded archway in classical style
seventy-five feet high "and said to be the largest
in the U.S." The public hack stand, which,
in order to abate the truly furious competition of
cabmen of the time, was a concession, was enclosed
against the elements, a fact noted with much
satisfaction by the Massachusetts Humane Society.
Two miles of track within the depot proper
terminated in twenty-three train gates under a
vast wire-glass canopy piped for steam
against the snows of winter. When this photograph
was taken in 1898 it is notable that the only
vehicles in sight not horse-drawn were two of the
open electric trolley cars immortalized in a
poem by Oliver Wendell Holmes as "broomstick
cars." The ark-like conveyance at the far left
was long a familiar sight in downtown Boston,
surviving well into the motor age and an era of
more sophisticated advertising. It was a
horse-drawn structure in the shape of a house
whose sides and roof were plastered with
advertising matter for Stewart's Cut Rate Railroad
Ticket Agency at 231 Washington Street.
Here frugal Bostonians were advised bargain
tickets to anywhere were sold, having been made
available by railroad patrons unable to use
transportation already purchased but unwilling to
abide the delay implicit in its redemption at
face value by the carrier. *(Library of Congress.)*

901

IN THE YEAR 1897 when the photograph immediately above was taken at the Fitchburg Railroad's imposing home depot at Fitchburg, Massachusetts, the *Green Mountain Flyer* on the Boston-Montreal daylight run was already a New England institution with a life expectancy of more than five decades ahead of it. Its classic 4-4-0 No. 47 had been built a few years before as Fitchburg No. 97 but renumbered in 1895 to take the *Green Mountain* through to its Rutland connection at Bellows Falls. The fine Fitchburg covered depot at Keene, New Hampshire, was also a classic of the covered shed station of the nineteenth century and the *Flyer* paused here too. The Asa Dunbar House with its handy railroad cafe at the left of the tracks had been the birthplace of the mother of Henry David Thoreau. *(Top: Essex Institute; Below: Herb H. Arey Collection.)*

IF THE FITCHBURG Railroad achieved immortality for nothing else (and it was in fact a major influence on Boston's highly solvent economy in the nineteenth century) it would have been famous for its massive Boston terminal shown here hard by the Boston & Maine's North Station in Causeway Street and for the circumstance that, running as it did past Walden Pond, it delighted Henry David Thoreau, patron and spirit of that enchanted mere. Quite unexpectedly in so anarchistic an individualist, he saw beauty in the approach of the locomotives at sunrise, marked the dedication of the track workers clearing snow in winter and discerned virtue in the flanged traffickings of commerce as readily as any Beacon Street shareholder. "What recommends commerce to me is its enterprise and bravery. . . . It seems as if the earth now had got a race worthy to inhabit it." Fitchburg Station in Boston, whence at one time through Pullmans departed via the West Shore, the Wabash and the Nickel Plate for Chicago, was in the best tradition of New England railroad architecture, which is to say it was designed to resemble something else. Built at a time when Italian villas, Egyptian temples, Roman baths and Islamic mosques enjoyed a widespread vogue, the Fitchburg took note of the already widely admired Boston & Maine station at nearby Salem and elected a Gothic castle as its paradigm. Like the structure at Salem it was built of massive masonry with crenelated and turreted towers. Unlike the Salem landmark which permitted trains to run right through it, the Fitchburg was a terminal depot ending in stub tracks. Shown at the right of the photograph are the horse cars to Charlestown where the carrier's first station had been before it moved in-town. (*Bostonian Society.*)

JUST three quarters of a century after the photograph reproduced below was taken in 1875 at the Boston & Maine-Rutland Railroad interchange at Bellows Falls, Vermont, the highball signal on its tall mast or a replacement thereof was still in place to govern the movements of the *Green Mountain Flyer* depicted on the opposite page with the Rutland's No. 92 on the business end. The train shown is No. 64, the southbound New York section of *The Flyer* and the River Street highball shows two globes to indicate a clear track into town. At the right the Rutland's No. 78 poses by the Bellows Falls coal dock waiting to take *The Flyer* north. *(Right and Opposite: Philip R. Hastings; Below: Everett De Golyer Collection.)*

SURROUNDED by racks of travel brochures, old fashioned letter presses, Cunard Line lithos and the other properties of his calling, William C. Hall was Boston & Maine ticket agent at Keene, New Hampshire, and for the Fitchburg before it. The photograph reproduced here was dated 1915 and the space on the *Green Mountain Flyer* sold by Mr. Hall could have been beyond all counting. *(David R. Roper Collection.)*

EVEN IN WHAT WERE DESTINED to be the declining years of its operations, the Rutland saw the smoke and heard the familiar sounds of railroading by day and by night in the Northern Vermont city of Burlington hard by the haunted shores of Lake Champlain. On the opposite page a series of photographs taken in the midnight hours in the year 1946 depict the pickup of the Burlington sleeper by the southbound *Mount Royal* with its early morning destination in New York City. At the top the southbound train arrives while the Pullman is still spotted on the far track while at the right a carman signals that it has been coupled into the train consist. Below, switcher No. 100 moves the darkened car with its occupants warm and secure in their berths into the trainline. *(Three Photos: Philip R. Hastings.)*

THE DAYLIGHT COUNTERPART of the midnight hours depicted opposite at the Rutland's station at Burlington, Vermont, was supplied by the arrival and departure in either direction of one of the oldest and most venerated names in New England railroading, *The Green Mountain Flyer* which had been running between Boston and Montreal since before the turn of the century. Here *The Flyer* heads west out of Burlington on its long tangent across the islands of Lake Champlain into a sun that is setting alike upon its coaches and parlor cars and on the fortunes of the railway itself. *(Philip R. Hastings.)*

IN 1923, the Montpelier
& Wells River Railroad in
Vermont had run six
daily passenger trains over
the thirty-eight miles
between the terminals of
its corporate name.
Twenty years later its
name had been changed
to the Montpelier & Barre
and its mileage had
shrunk to fourteen. In the
years between, however,
its daily mixed had regu-
larly picked up the
U. S. Mail at Boltonville
and set it down where
the postmistress is shown
here hanging it to the
mail arm and speeding its
way cityward in No. 4.

908

THE DEEP SOUTH and deepest New England alike were the last strongholds of the daily mixed, the train of all work that delivered the merchandise and picked up the milk, set out high cars on weed-grown sidings and carried the mails, and had modest accommodations for the train crew and occasional passengers, mostly intransigents too set in their ways to acknowledge the automobile. The daily mixed was strictly a country affair, its business was in remote inaccessible pockets of resistance to progress, and it ran from yesterday to yesterday without ever emerging altogether into the twentieth century or acknowledging the universal disaster of change. Here the Rutland's No. 7, at Mooers, New York, with five refrigerator cars of upstate milk, an express car and rider coach, rolls on its smoky occasions under a spectacular summer sky in 1949. Like the photographs on the opposite page, this study in pastoral tranquility is from the ubiquitous camera of Philip R. Hastings.

THE NEWS KIOSK at St. Johns Depot, Portland, about 1912, carried as its regular stock in trade *Judge, Leslie's, Everybody's Magazine, The World's Work* and, perhaps, Colonel William D'Alton Mann's scandalous *Town Topics* for the sophisticated social trade bound for Bar Harbor. For the young it stocked Tootsie Rolls, Crackerjack, Necco Wafers and a variety of sweets known only to antiquaries in a later generation. Below: in its daytime luxury consist of parlor cars, diners and de luxe coaches painted an eye-popping canary yellow and cream for its summer-only run between Maine seacoast resorts and New York and Washington, the Boston & Maine's *East Wind* gets a wheel from Pacific No. 3710 in September 1940 just twenty-five miles south of St. Johns Station, Portland. *(Gerald Best Collection.)*

PRECISELY on the site of the Eastern's depot in Causeway Street and half a century after its demolition there arose as shown below the many storied Manger Hotel as part of the structural complex that included the new North Station and a sports arena. Loading where the Eastern's platforms had been is *The Gull* headed for Way Down East and the Maritime Provinces. The straitened throat tracks leading from North Station across Charlestown Estuary were much in the same pattern as they had been in the Eastern's day. *(Two Photos: Railway & Locomotive Historical Society.)*

WHEN, in 1894, the wreckers demolished
the old Eastern Railroad depot in
Causeway Street where, together with the
Fitchburg and the Boston & Maine, it
had been part of "Railroad Row," to
make way for the new Union Depot, a
landmark disappeared and with it much of
the legend of early New England
railroading. Among its component
properties mourned by sentimentalists was
the station bell, recovered from an
ancient Spanish cathedral by one of the
road's early presidents which had tolled the
arrival and departure of trains.
Part of the Eastern's body of legend, when
it started business back in 1839 had
been a salute of welcome in the *Salem
Gazette* by Nathaniel Hawthorne, and the
long annals of its feuding and warfare
with the Boston & Maine were part of
Boston's financial geology. The end
was foreshadowed for the Eastern by the
great Revere disaster of August 1871
in which twenty-nine died and the
suits filed in consequence all but ruined
the carrier. Here Jehu in an Inverness
cape solicits business for his growler at the
Eastern's austere portal in an atmospheric
photograph from the archives of the
Railway & Locomotive Historical Society.

THE *Day White Mountain Express* shown on these pages, and its opposite number *The Night White Mountain Express* with Pullman sleepers instead of parlor cars was the Boston & Maine-New Haven connection via Springfield for the resorts of its title, Fabyan's, Bretton Woods and Whitefield with their terminal at Berlin. The day train carried a broiler-buffet and parlor cars to White River Junction and the night consist included sleepers to and from Bretton Woods. *The Day White Mountain* is shown immediately above emerging from a deep rock cut at Bradford, Vermont, while at the depot of that name a trainman emplaces a flag that will protect its departure for ten minutes. In the far frame, the lights are already on at Bradford as No. 77 loads mail and head end. *(Four Photos: Philip R. Hastings.)*

AT THE RIGHT, *The Day White Mountain Express* is shown near Randolph, New Hampshire in 1946 heading into a rare type of wooden covered bridge whose trusses are protected by wooden sheathing but lacks the protective roof and sidewalls of the more familiar covered bridges of tradition.

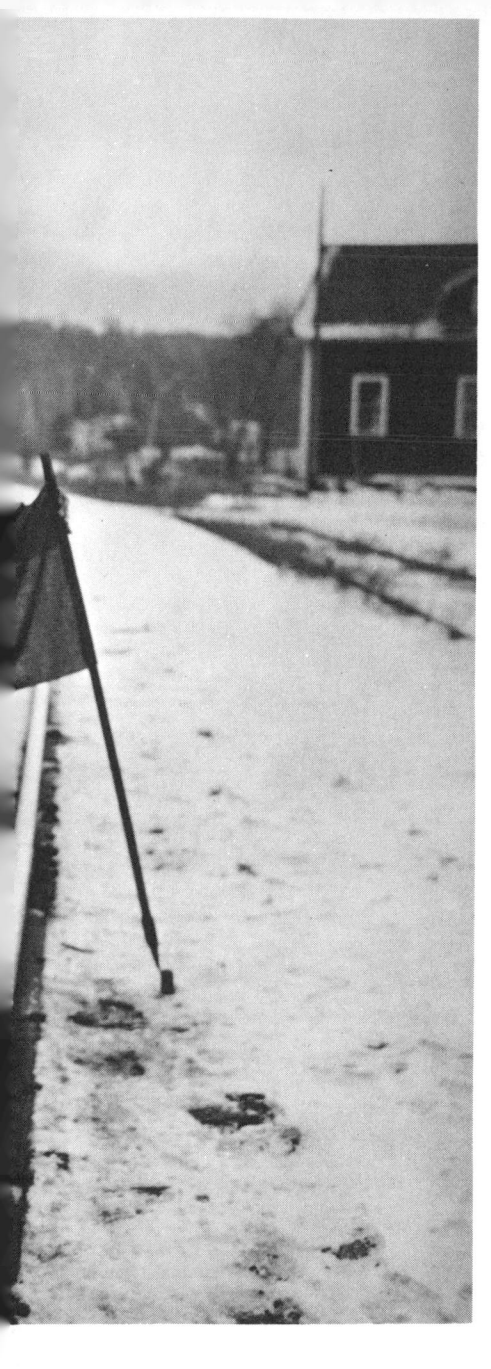

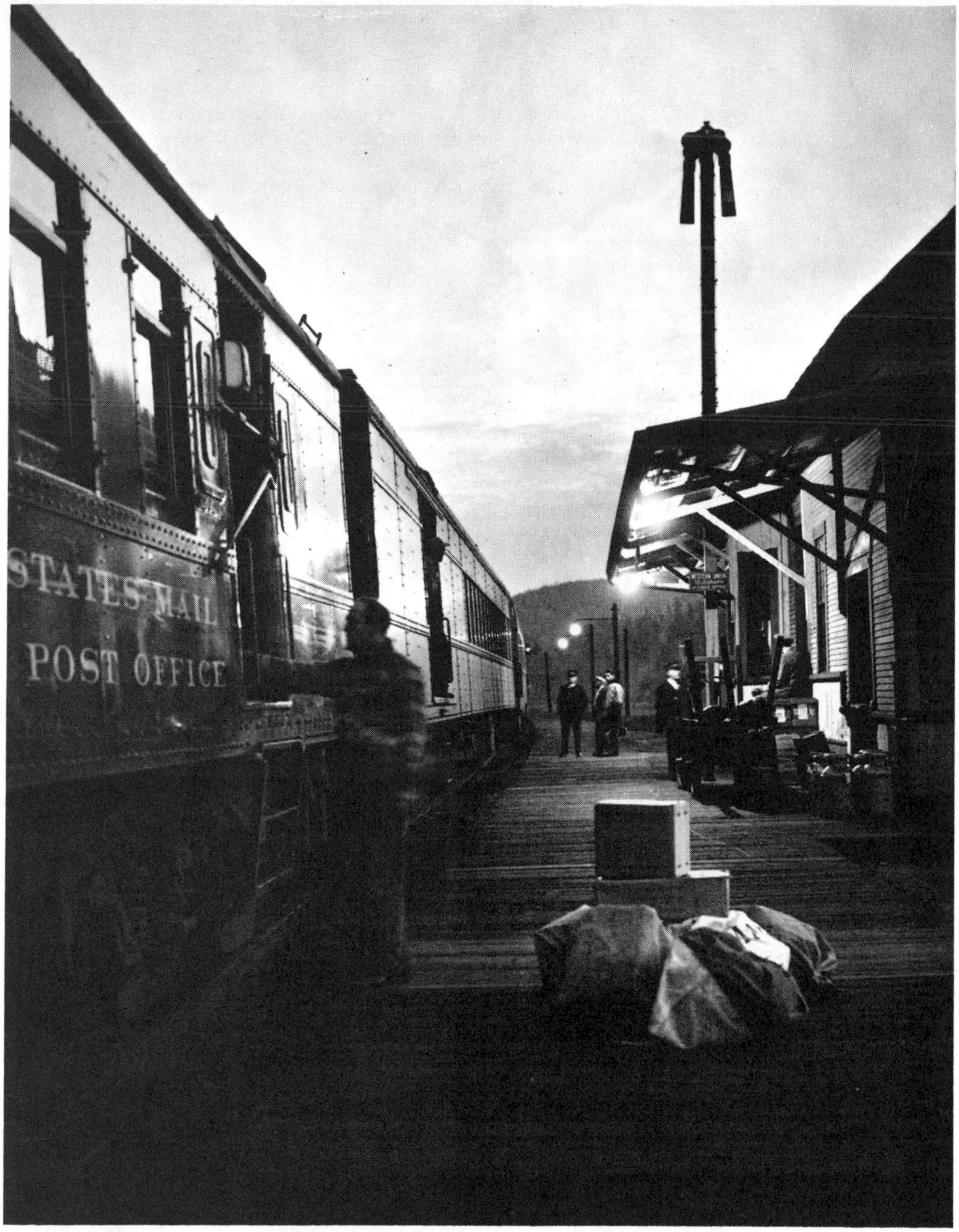
STATES MAIL
POST OFFICE

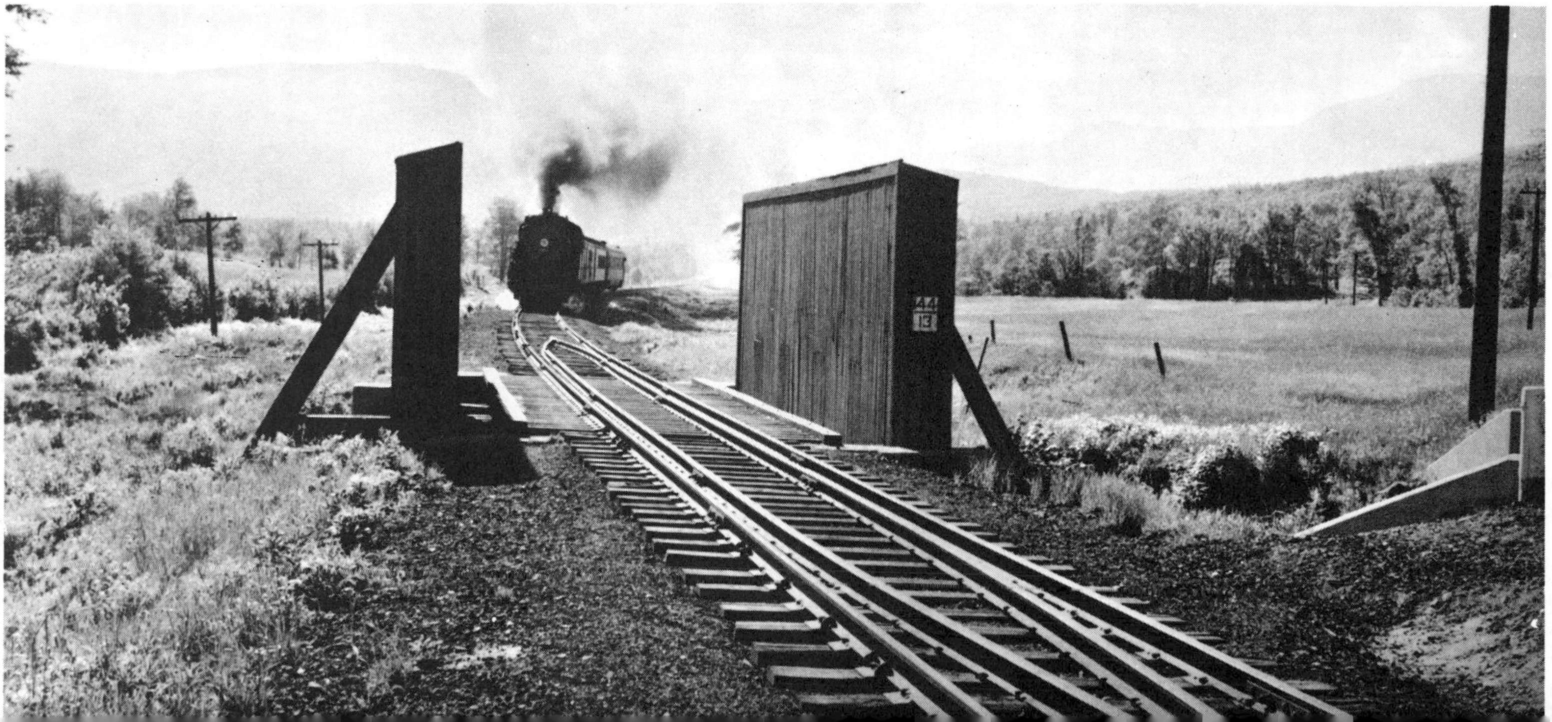
44
13

AT ROUSES POINT, New York, where they cross the River Richelieu, the gantleted rails of the Central Vermont, corporate entity of Canadian National in the United States, and the Rutland symbolized their interlocking yet divergent operations. *(Philip R. Hastings.)*

FROM EARLIEST TIMES the annals of railroading from New York-Boston to the several Canadian terminals of Montreal, Quebec and the Maritime Provinces were freighted with romance and partook of the flavor of foreign adventure. The Pullmans and their luxury consists took off over wildly improbable routings for storybook destinations, often in the teeth of formidable opposition from the elements and from the New England geology, so that through sleepers for the West once rolled out of Portland for Montreal via the wooden covered bridges of the St. Johnsbury & Lake Champlain and visionaries dreamed of Portland as the nation's principal entrepot from Europe. Prone as it was to flights of elfin whimsy, New England travel in the nineteenth century produced no more enchanting eccentricity than the rare and exotic Monarch Patent parlor-sleeping car *Queen Anne* shown opposite from the collection of Andrew Merrilees. A pure sport, in the biological sense of the word, *Queen Anne* went into service between Boston and Canada over the rails of the Quebec Central Railroad and its varnished exterior is shown posed with admirers around its open platform.

Immediately below, *The Red Wing* on the Boston & Maine-Canadian Pacific overnight run between Boston and Montreal establishes continuity with the nineteenth century as it passes under the spans of a venerable wooden covered bridge in upstate New Hampshire as it nears its northern terminal.   (*Two Photos: Philip R. Hastings.*)

THE MINUTE MAN, shown loading from North Station's ancient wooden low level platforms, was in reality a token luxury train rather than a veritable de luxe consist and carried but a single through Pullman for Chicago which was cut into the Central's all-Pullman *Lake Shore Limited* at Albany. It was, however, a conversation piece and a gesture of defiance in the direction of the Boston & Albany and its non-New England Vanderbilt management.

PINE TREE LIMITED

BOSTON
PORTLAND
BANGOR

SCHEDULE

WEEK-DAYS

EASTBOUND

Lv.	BOSTON	3.20 P.M.
"	Portsmouth	4.39 P.M.
Ar.	PORTLAND	6.00 P.M.
"	Augusta	7.51 P.M.
"	Waterville	8.20 P.M.
"	Bangor	9.45 P.M.

WESTBOUND

Lv.	WATERVILLE	5.35 A.M.
"	Augusta	6.04 A.M.
"	PORTLAND	8.00 A.M.
"	Portsmouth	9.18 A.M.
Ar.	BOSTON	10.40 A.M.

All Steel Coaches and Parlor Cars.
Dining Car serving evening meal.

BOSTON AND MAINE R.R.
in connection with
MAINE CENTRAL R.R.

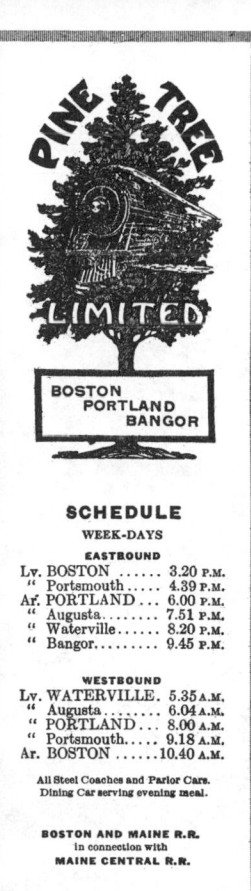

PULLMANS and parlor cars of uncertain vintage rolled on the mannered and leisurely occasions of the Boston & Maine's name trains through the New England countryside in modest numbers in the great years of rail travel, connecting with the outside world through such atmospheric runs as that of *The Minute Man* shown opposite, and *The Pine Tree Limited* depicted below in a full-dress portrait about to leave North Station for its Portland-Bangor terminals to the east. *The Minute Man* represented the B.&M.'s answer to the Boston & Albany's several daily trains for Chicago and afforded passage to the West without patronizing the B.&A. which many proper Bostonians regarded with suspicion as a property of the rascally Vanderbilts that had been forcibly ravished from its original Yankee ownership. The fact that *The Minute Man* connected via Troy and Albany with the New York Central, itself the Vanderbilt's most resounding property, was conveniently forgotten. *The Minute Man* had all the hallmarks of the grand manner, specially painted locomotives, PAUL REVERE and WILLIAM HENRY DAWES, full-length dining cars and an observation parlor car with red, white and blue awning and an illuminated train herald. *(Opposite: Rail Photo Service; Below: Everett De Golyer Collection.)*

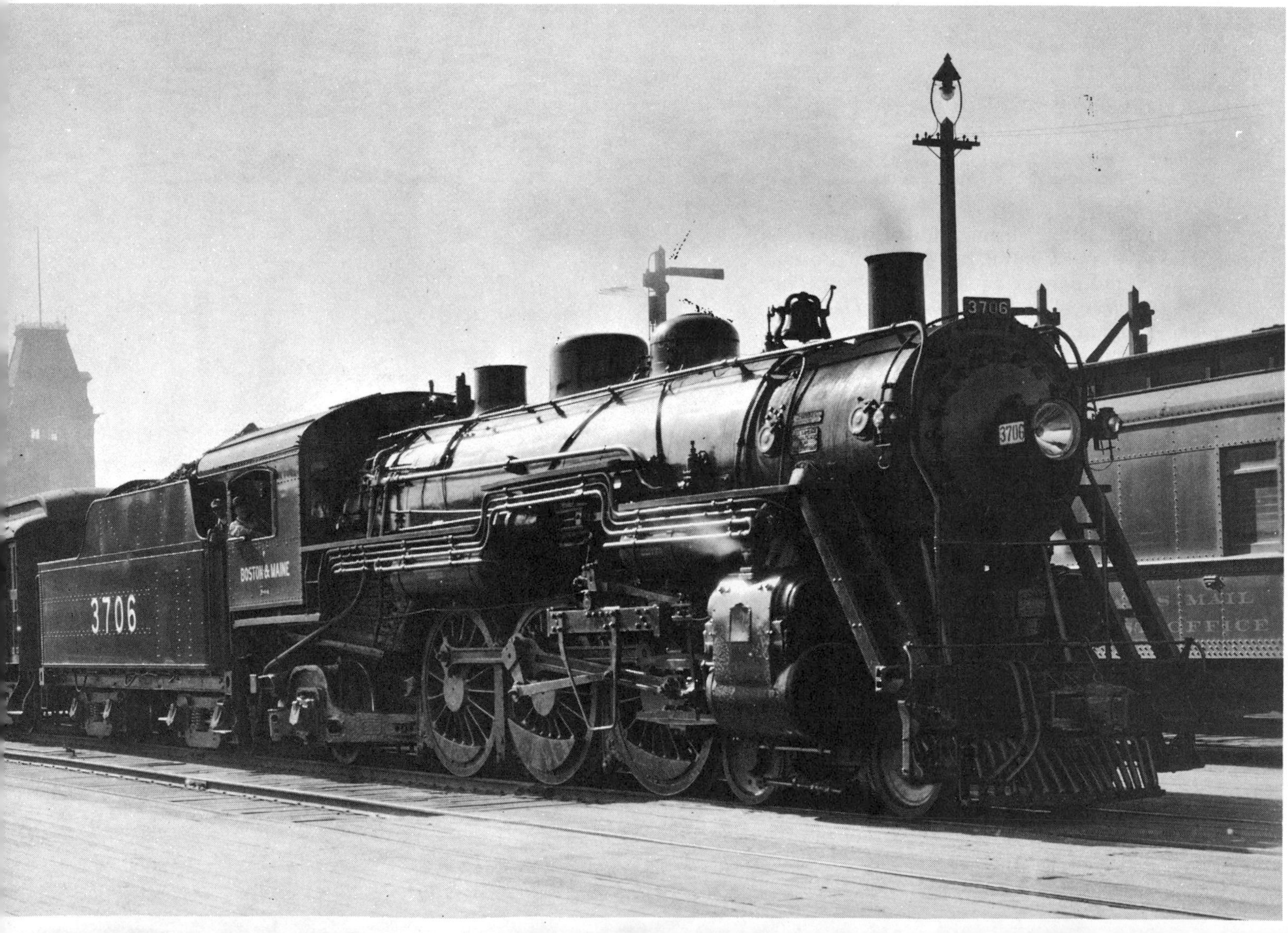

IN THE YEARS of steam, pride of the Boston & Maine-Maine Central run between Boston and Portland-Bangor by daylight were *The Flying Yankee, The Pine Tree* and *The Kennebec Limited*, all of them full dress name trains with coaches, head end, Pullman parlor cars and diners or, in slack seasons, observation cafes or buffet cars. As flagship of the fleet with a non-stop schedule of two and a quarter hours between Boston and Portland, *The Flying Yankee* rated an assigned locomotive with its name on the smokebox and, at the other end of its consist, a tailgate herald on the observation railing. On its tight schedule over the Western Division via Dover over which, approximately a century earlier, the engine *Antelope* with a car filled with newspaper reporters had achieved the world's first mile a minute speed, *The Flying Yankee* was a thing of splendor. Above it poses with a green and gold assigned engine at North Station; at the right, its bell gets a quick polish before hitting the road. (*Above: Laurence Breed Walker Collection; Right: Rail Photo Service.*)

ALTHOUGH *The Bar Harbor Express* ranked all other conveyances to Mount Desert in prestige and in the public awareness, it was not the only name train to converge from Boston and New York upon the vacation focus of the Maine summer resorts. There was also the Boston & Maine's Train No. 111, *The Yankee,* a sort of advance section of *The Flying Yankee,* which left Boston's North Station at breakfast time and delivered passengers on through cars which, until Labor Day, included a broiler-buffet-parlor, to the Ellsworth connection in time for tea in Bar Harbor itself via the bus which replaced the ferry in the 1930s. There was also a parlor observation car and de luxe coaches which added up to a very respectable name train indeed. At the left *The Yankee* is shown with an assigned engine carrying white flags as evidence of a second section and below on the Boston & Maine with a burnished Pacific and ample head-end revenue to pay its way. *(Left: Laurence Breed Walker Collection; Below: John P. Ahrens.)*

ALMOST as celebrated in the folklore of New England travel as Essex Junction, immortalized in doggerel poetry as a seat of transportational chaos, was White River Junction on the Vermont-New Hampshire border where two Boston & Maine main lines from Springfield and Boston-Concord, respectively, converged on the Central Vermont for interchange on the long haul to Canada. Here the *Red Wing* by night and *Alouette* by day paused to change crews, motive power and carriers. Here the *Day White Mountain Express* and *Night White Mountain Express* set out sleepers and picked up parlor cars on their far-flung occasions. *The Ambassador's* arrival and departure was an event and here *The Washingtonian* and *The Montrealer* changed engines and head-end revenue cars. All night and all day traffic converged upon White River Junction and retreated toward far horizons at the bidding of the dispatcher. For many years knowing travelers made a point of arranging their itineraries so that mealtimes found them available to the depot restaurant there. Celebrated for its New England dishes such as pork and beans, scrodded haddock on fish days and cakes with pure Vermont maple syrup for breakfast, Stewart Holbrook also remembered that in his Vermont youth a specialty of the house to rejoice juvenile voyagers was uncommonly powerful checkermint hard candies that came in miniature brakeman's lanterns with a choice of red or green globes. Not as famous a New England landmark, perhaps, as Deacon Shem Drowne's grasshopper weather vane at Faneuil Hall, but still a reassuring artifact was the locomotive that told where the wind blew atop the cupola of White River depot. In the lower frame the Boston & Maine's *Connecticut Yankee* heads south out of White River on a flawless summer day. *(Four Photos: Philip R. Hastings.)*

WHILE the mists of early morning still enshroud the Vermont countryside, and render the outline of White River depot hazy *(below)* the B.&M.'s No. 3653 awaits its highball to leave for Berlin while, at the left, Train No. 310 prepares to depart with Boston for its destination. At the left *The Ambassador,* southbound passes the venerable White River highball signal that established long continuity with the railroading past.

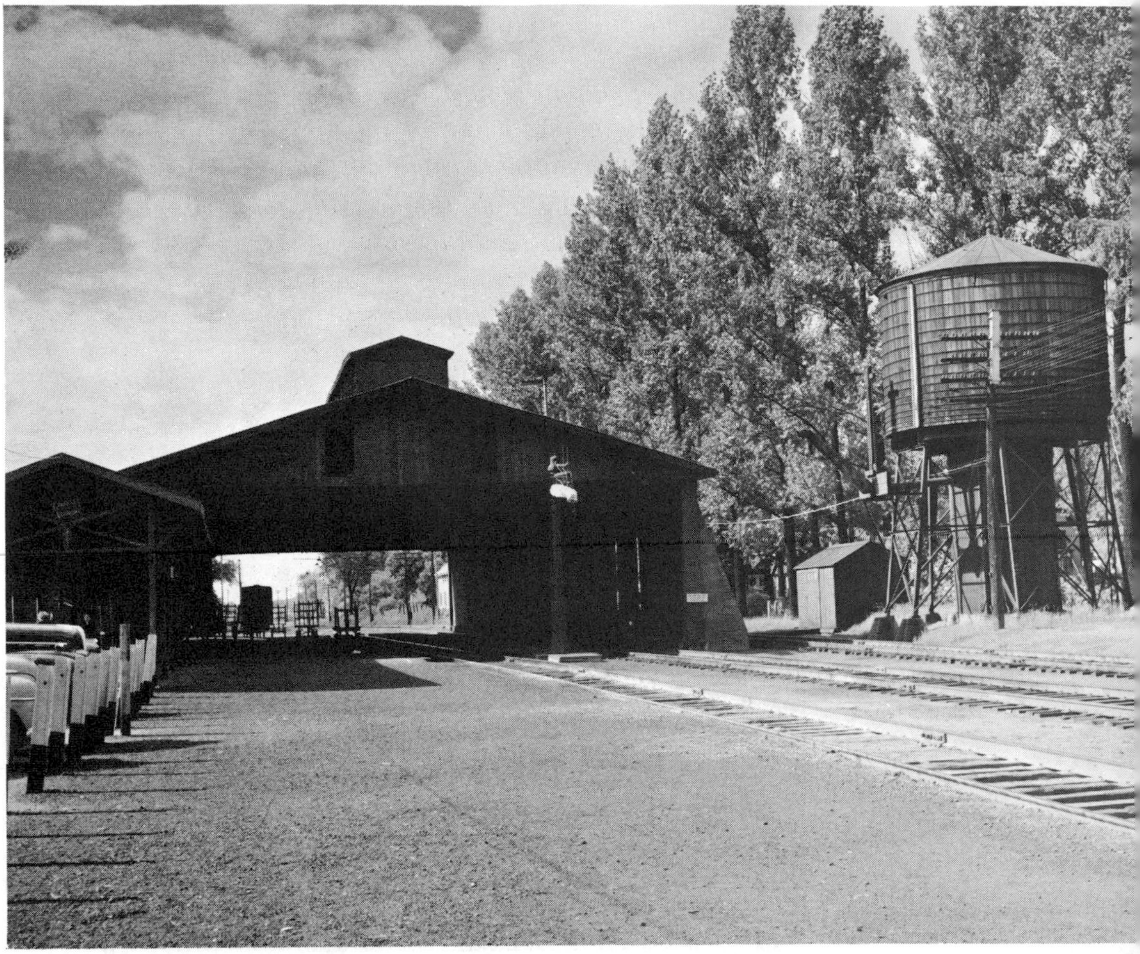

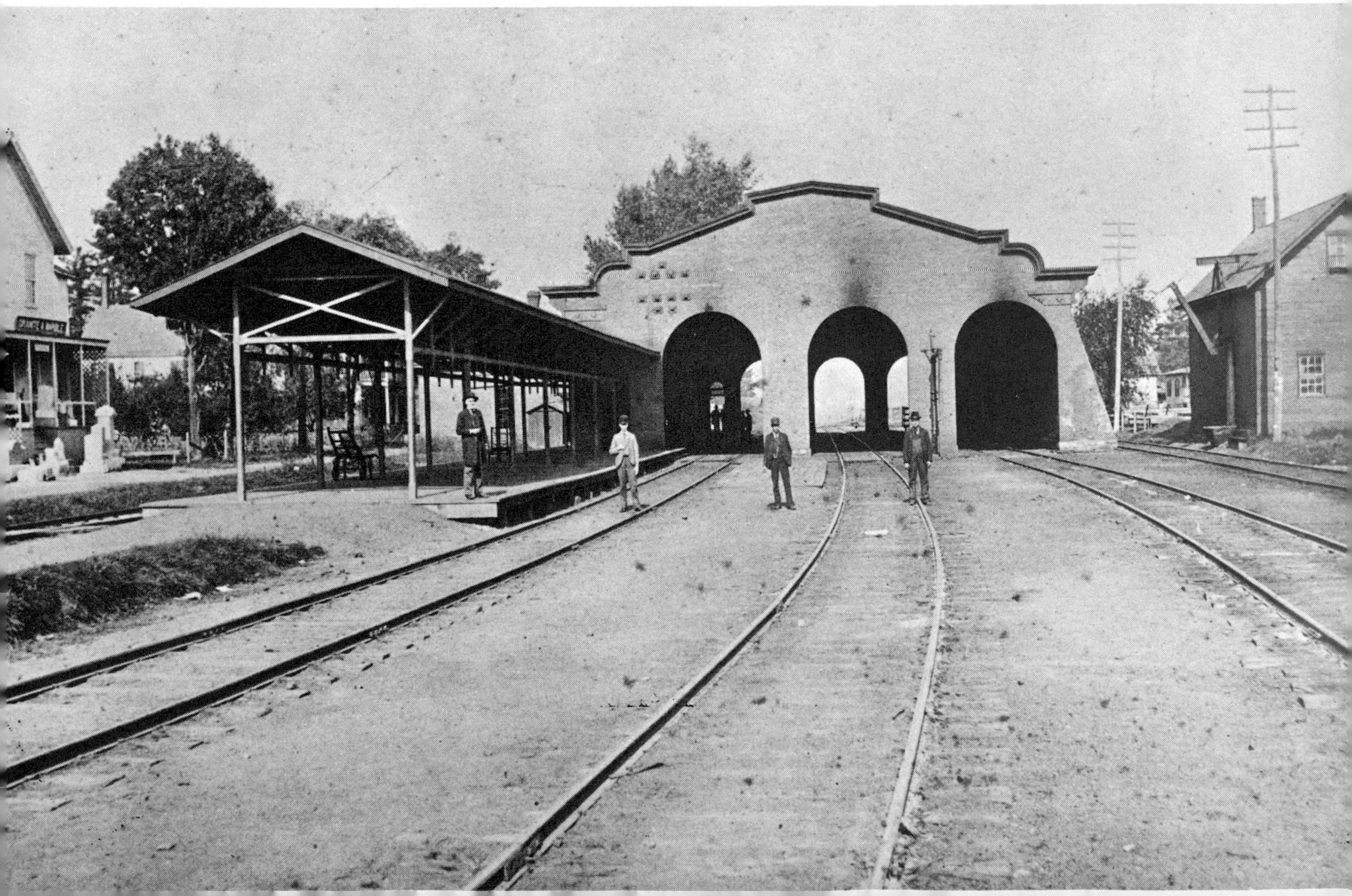

CELEBRATED in the doggerel verses that immortalized the baffled traveler who took the wrong train, Essex Junction and the Central Vermont's covered train shed there lasted a long time in the legend of New England railroading. Originally constructed, as is shown at the bottom of the opposite page with a red brick facade, the structure was rebuilt in 1890 and a wooden sheathing applied with through passage to accommodate the increased dimensions of motive power and equipment. It is shown at the top of the page after its face lifting. Here *The Ambassador* southbound pauses at Essex Junction with Central Vermont's fine No. 600 on the head end as a daylight train in the grand manner between Montreal and Boston-New York. At the left *The Washingtonian* on the night run to the Federal City brings animation to the ancient premises in the midnight hours. (*Below, Opposite: Jim Shaughnessy Collection; Three Photos: Jim Shaughnessy.*)

FAMED FOR THE NINETEENTH CENTURY DOGGEREL verses that brought it celebrity when a confused traveler who had taken the wrong connecting train made it part of the enduring folklore of New England, the Central Vermont depot at Essex Junction, Vermont, as late as the middle fifties was a scene of round-the-clock activity of transport. The identical wooden train shed dating from the time when the verses themselves had been written sheltered passengers who by daylight boarded the cars of the *Ambassador* on the Montreal-Boston run and by night *The Washingtonian* between Montreal and the Federal City. Here *The Washingtonian* is pictured ready to roll southward behind a huge Canadian National 4-8-4 No. 6173 which dwarfs its ancient train shed and strains the narrow clearances that resulted in 1890 when the original brick facade was removed to accommodate the even then larger equipment. On the opposite page *The Washingtonian* loads its head-end cars with mail and express for the Federal City while waiting a highball to move out into the gelid Vermont night. Sometime during the time exposure someone moved the baggage truck in the foreground, perhaps the ghostly hand of the long dead traveler whose saddened face and battered hat in the poem told of the black despair which possessed him at this very spot. *(Two Photos: Jim Shaughnessy.)*

926

IN the rugged climate of New England individualism and religious fervor, there survived later than elsewhere in the land oddball characters with a message. This prophet of doom and his wife met all trains at North Conway and distributed tracts pointing the way to salvation to the bemused arrivals. *(Herbert H. Harwood Collection.)*

THE LAST of the old and first of the new are represented here by the B.&M.'s summer-only *North Wind,* shown double-headed at Whitefield, New Hampshire, and the Diesel *Mountaineer* between Boston and Conway as it emerges from a primeval covered bridge to flush a barefoot country boy from the underbrush. The unit train started life as replacement for the conventional *Flying Yankee* but was found insufficient for the Boston-Portland traffic of the time. *(Philip R. Hastings; Wide World.)*

INCOMPARABLY the most celebrated of all New England railroad stations and one whose immutable Gothic architecture outranked in gloomy grandeur even the Fitchburg's Castle of Otranto premises in Boston, was the Boston & Maine's depot at Salem, Massachusetts. Its two polygonal towers of solid masonry had been reared in 1847 from the design of Gridley S. Bryant, an edifice contemporary with various Greek temples, Roman peristyles, Turkish mosques and Italianate villas that elsewhere afflicted the countryside. Salem was still a country village at the time of its construction and Nathaniel Hawthorne, its first man of letters and literary celebrity, admired the railroad inordinately. It was flanked by the town millpond and tall trees shaded its approaches where the tracks converged from north and south and passed directly through its train shed. A New England conversation piece for nearly a century, its merits of architecture were viewed by none with indifference and families were known to be divided pro and con. Esthetes, especially with the growing sophistication of the times, tended to deplore it; connoisseurs of gloom and students of Horace Walpole peopled it, in imagination, with noble ghosts from Carpathian castles of mystery. In time its adjacent waiting room and freight station were removed and the traffic of metropolis surged around its portals where trains proceeded at snail's pace through drays and trams accompanied by bells and whistles and agitated crossing tenders. Handy to its platforms, waiting rooms, lunch counters, ticket offices and baggage reception coexisted in a chaos of soot and sound which, to the fastidious, suggested a suburb of hell itself. When most of Salem was razed in a monster conflagration in 1915, excited partisans hurried from as far away as Boston on the report the depot was about to be dynamited, but it was spared at the last moment as thousands cheered. The only structure even comparable in its awful grandeur was the Fitchburg Station in Boston, but admirers until the very end hailed Salem Station, shown here in 1910, as the bravest of all monuments to vanished railroad times. *(Essex Institute.)*

SALEM Station as it was known to Nathaniel Hawthorne in the early 1860s was surrounded by the town as it had been in Colonial times with the town millpond visible in the distance and tree lined streets through which the railroad ran in an almost pastoral setting.
(Laurence Breed Walker Collection.)

ONE OF THE FEW varnish runs to be named for a tree—others were *The Palmetto* and *Royal Palm*, *The Pine Tree Limited* on the run between Boston and Portland carried, at various times, Pullman parlor cars, a diner or cafe car and a cafe-lounge in addition to coaches and head-end revenue. Here on the northern outskirts of suburban Boston, it rounds the long curve at Crystal Lake beside Wakefield Junction with a mile-long cloud of rolling soot to mark its going. (*Lucius Beebe.*)

WELL OVER a century after it had come into universal use to govern the movements of trains everywhere and to enter the American lexicon as a synonym for speed and clearance, the highball signal was still in active use throughout New England. The one shown here governed trains of three separate railroads, the Boston & Maine, Montpelier & Wells River and the Canadian Pacific at Wells River, Vermont. An even more sophisticated version *(opposite)* with night lanterns and warning bells is shown at White River Junction holding up *The Ambassador*, southbound behind Central Vermont's No. 460. Below on this page is an atmospheric view of the terminal of the Eastern Railroad at Portland when it was an autonomous operation and before the great Revere catastrophe had driven it into the hands of the waiting Boston and Maine. *(Opposite: Philip R. Hastings; Here, Two Photos: The Railway & Locomotive Historical Society.)*

INTRICATE wood and steel trusses of the Howe Patent that had been found culpable in so many of the fatal train wrecks of the nineteenth century when used for bridges and trestles, supported the depot roof at St. Albans and, when protected from the elements and not exposed to moving stresses, endured uncounted tons of snow in the structure's long lifetime. At the right the northbound *Ambassador* emerges from St. Albans train shed on its way to Montreal for a nighttime portrait by Jim Shaughnessy. (*Top: E. H. Royce.*)

932

LAST OF THE TRULY massive arching train sheds that were once part of the pattern of Victorian railroading everywhere in New England, the classic Central Vermont depot and adjoining offices at St. Albans, Vermont, never quite achieved its hundredth birthday. Built in 1866, it was found to have been so structurally weakened by age that it was demolished in 1964. Buttresses of red Vermont brick supported its 351-foot length and four arched train portals pierced its eighty-four foot bulkheads at the north and south. A venerable landmark that had withstood wintry gales of legendary ferocity, blown in from Lake Champlain, it was a monument to Yankee integrity to the end. It is shown below about 1910 without a motor car in sight and still boasting the minaret at its western extremity that disappeared in later years. At the left, snow falls gently on Train No. 332 awaiting its highball at the south portal while a setout sleeper from Boston steams quietly on an adjacent track. (Left: Jim Shaughnessy; Below: Railway & Locomotive Historical Society.)

AT TROY Union Station in the 1880s passengers changed cars for the last few miles to Saratoga.

A CARRIER OF limited passenger operations even though its right of way to Canada passed through some of the most spectacular scenery in the East, the Delaware & Hudson was a railroad of such pronounced character as to be felt eccentric in more conservative transportation circles. Its eccentricity derived largely from its most formidable President, Lenore Loree, himself a pronounced individualist from his name, which suggested a poem by Edgar Allan Poe, to his beard and scowl which suggested that much of the time he hated everybody, as indeed he may well have done. He was widely reputed to be an executive to whose ambitions no horizon existed, to whom fate had assigned a secondary role in life. Certainly not since Alexander Holmes of the Old Colony Railroad had, in a moment of purest Anglophilia, introduced compartment cars entered through individual doors from the side to the *Fall River Boat Train* had any American railroad assumed so English a look as did the D.&H. motive power in Loree's presidency. Here is Pacific No. 652 with the northbound *Laurentian* at Whitehall while the fireboy rakes the fuel nearer his footplate. (*Philip R. Hastings.*)

ALTHOUGH the last traces of its once unhurried
way of life were soon to disappear under the impact
of the ever more strident automotive age,
nineteenth century Saratoga, in the form of its most
resplendent hostelry, the United States Hotel,
lingered on until well into the time of
The Montreal Limited and *The Laurentian*.
Its endless verandahs and white and gold ballroom
no longer knew the tread of
Whitneys and Vanderbilts, but the horsey atmosphere
of August still maintained direct continuity
with another century. The Delaware & Hudson
yards at Saratoga were directly
under the windows of the United States Hotel
(below) and it was when awakened
by their nocturnal commotions that De Wolf Hopper
phoned the night clerk with his celebrated enquiry:
"Can you tell me what time this hotel
gets to Chicago?" At the left, in its years
of useful going, *The Montreal Limited* comes
to rest at Windsor Station at its northern terminal.
The time is eight o'clock and the knowing arrival
will have breakfast in the hotel of
the same name. *(Philip R. Hastings.)*

"THE CARS have rounded the last curve and speed on the home stretch for three miles, past The Geyser, whose crystal spray thrown up forty or fifty feet, glistens in the sunlight as though Undine and her troupe of fairies were showering out a welcome on the coming guests . . . and now come the streets and houses of Saratoga and from the car windows we read in succession, Clarendon, Grand Hotel, Grand Union, Congress Hall . . . There is an universal bustle, the whistle shrieks, the bell rings and the train slows up to the beautiful depot." Such was the lyric description of the scene depicted above when the Palace Cars of the Rensselaer & Saratoga (later the Deleware & Hudson) were the sole means of access to America's fastest and most moneyed summer resort, and the Mansard roofed station was indeed a thing of beauty. Indeed so fast and gamey was the reputation of Saratoga as an abode of Vanderbilts and high fashion that James Gordon Bennett, who wasn't asked to be present, termed it "a seraglio of the prurient aristocracy." If you rode the cars further upstate on the way to Montreal, you encountered the customs inspection at Rouses Point on the border and such was the bad celebrity of this inconvenience, especially on the sleeping cars, that *Leslie's Weekly* devoted a full front page to it in 1883 as shown at the right with the caption: "A Customs Officer at Rouse's Point Searching Baggage on the Night Train."

FRANK LESLIE'S ILLUSTRATED NEWSPAPER

Entered according to Act of Congress, in the year 1882, by Mrs. Frank Leslie, in the Office of the Librarian of Congress at Washington.— Entered at the Post Office, New York, N.Y., as Second Class Matter.

No. 1,429.—Vol. LV.] NEW YORK—FOR THE WEEK ENDING FEBRUARY 10, 1883. [Price, with Supplement, 10 Cents. $4.00 Yearly. 13 Weeks, $1.00

936

REPLACING *The Champlain* on
the daylight run between New York
and Montreal over the New York
Central-Delaware & Hudson connection
at Troy was the ten hour
Laurentian threading some of the
most spectacular scenery to be found
anywhere in the East. In ordinary
times it ran with a fine enclosed
solarium observation car on its
rear end as suggested here where the
photographer has surprised
David Morgan, editor of *Trains*
magazine in converse with the
parlor car porter at the pause
at Whitehall. In wartime, however,
The Laurentian ran bobtailed
without the glory of a tailgate
insigne through the upstate New York
heartland. *(Left: Philip Hastings;
Below: Charles Clegg.)*

WHAT *The Bar Harbor Express* was over the decades to the Down East resort areas of the Maine seacoast, the New York Central-Delaware & Hudson's *Laurentian* was to Saratoga Springs, a name train serving one of the last great American summer resorts with aristocratic character. Its nighttime counterpart *The Montreal Limited* set out sleepers at Saratoga and, as long as the age of railroad travel lasted, a ponderable part of the Delaware & Hudson's passenger traffic in summer was in the names that made news in the society columns of the world. Aboard its cars and that of its predecessor, the Rensselaer & Saratoga came the horsey set and racing enthusiasts bound for the vast verandahs of the Grand Union and United States Hotels where the great of fashion and finance assembled in August in the years celebrated by Edna Ferber in "The Saratoga Trunk." Here the north—and southbound sections of *The Laurentian* pass in the depot of Whitehall, New York, while opposite the same train pauses in the new Saratoga Springs depot that had replaced the Mansarded glories of an earlier structure shown on an adjacent page. *(Two Photos: Jim Shaughnessy.)*

938

MONTREAL
10 hours
quickest-shortest route...
Daily from Grand Central Terminal, New York City
Overnight Service from New York
The MONTREAL LIMITED
Montreal is just a good night's sleep away from Manhattan on this superbly appointed non-stop train. Through service to Ottawa and Quebec. All Pullman—Club Car—Drawing-room, Compartment and Open Section Sleeping Cars—All-steel Modern Equipment—No Extra Fare.
Lv. New York........... 9.45 P.M.
Ar. Montreal........... 7.50 A.M.
Ar. Ottawa (C.P.Ry.).......11.45 A.M.
Ar. Quebec (C.P.Ry.)....... 2.00 P.M.
Lv. Quebec (C.P.Ry.)....... 1.30 P.M.
Lv. Ottawa (C.P.Ry.) Except Sat. 5.00 P.M.
Lv. Ottawa (C.P.Ry.) Saturdays. 3.35 P.M.
Lv. Montreal........... 9.00 P.M.
Ar. New York........... 7.25 A.M.
Daily from Windsor Station, Montreal
New York to Montreal in 10 Hours
Daylight Service from New York
The LAURENTIAN
Delightful, comfortable ride along the Hudson, Lake Champlain, through the charming Adirondack region. Club Car—Parlor Cars—Coaches—Dining Car.
Lv. New York........... 9.45 A.M.
Ar. Montreal........... 7.45 P.M.
Lv. Montreal...........10.00 A.M.
Ar. New York........... 8.05 P.M.
"the D&H"
DELAWARE & HUDSON

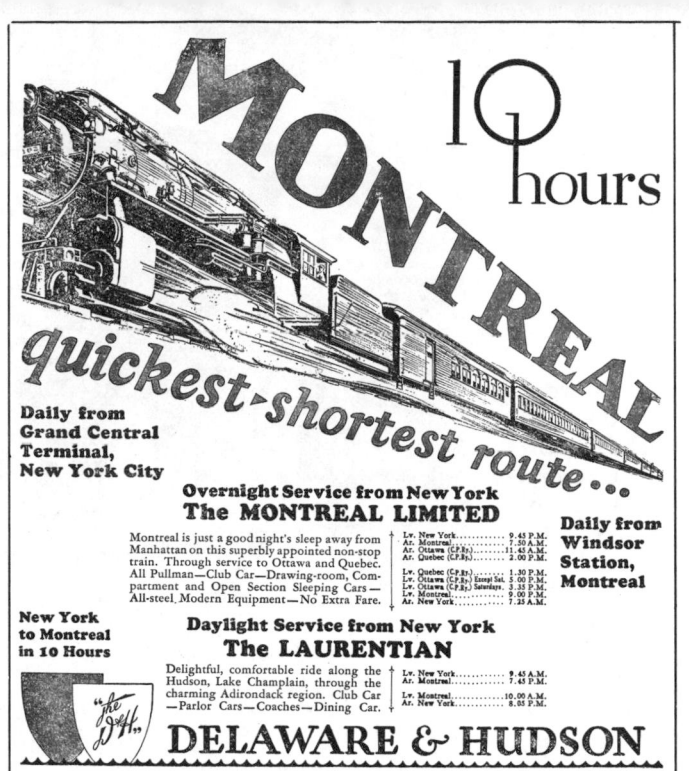

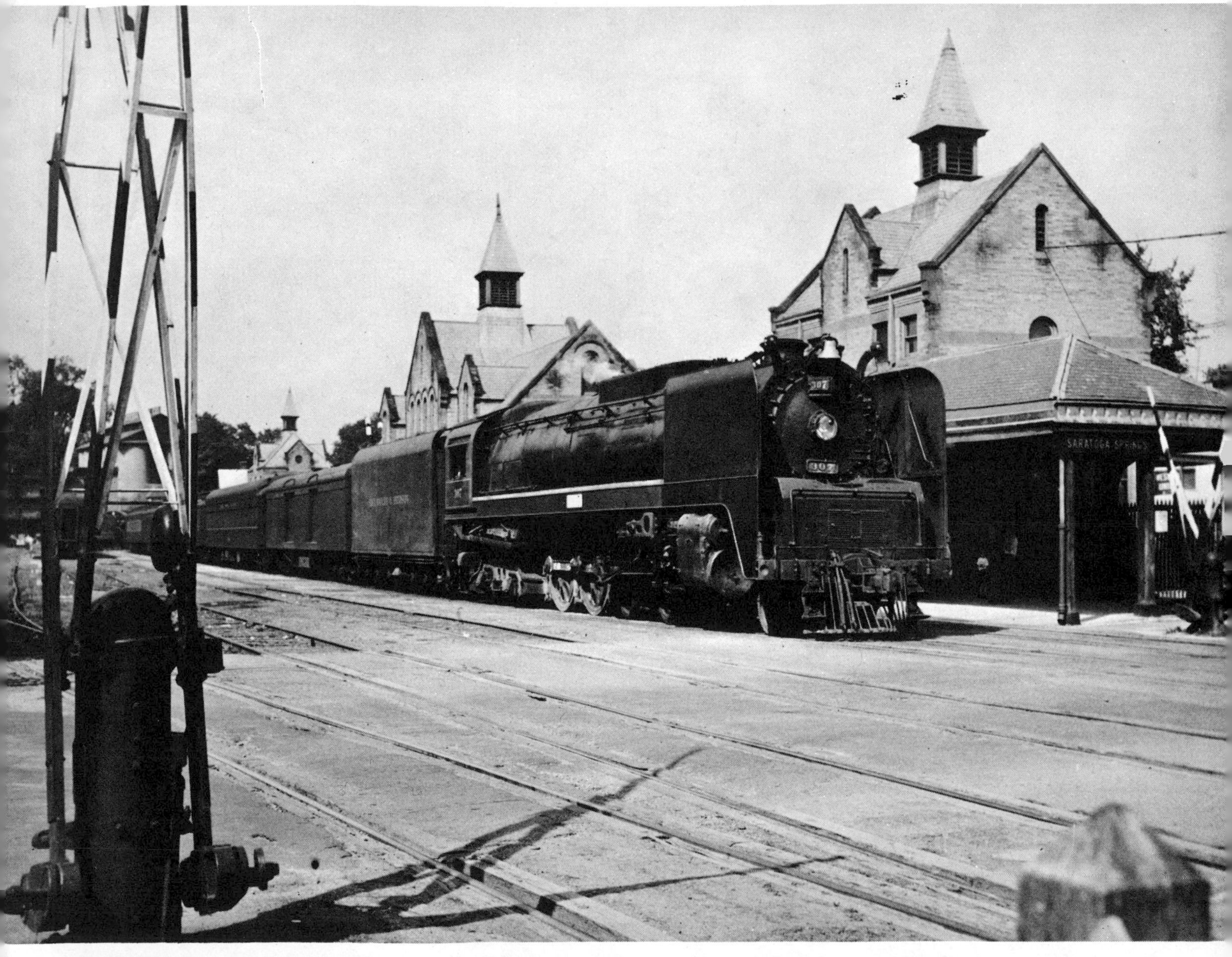

SARATOGA SPRINGS

TYPICALLY Bostonian is use of the word spa to denote a refreshment booth or counter so that one of The Hub's most famous businessmen's lunch resorts achieved world fame under the style of Thompson's Spa. It only followed that a North Station news and candy kiosk should be designated the Terminal Spa and the products available served to confirm its regional character: Brigham's buttermilk, Puroxia ginger ale and hot egg and milk against the winter chill of the train shed. *(Bostonian Society.)*

THE ALL-DAY RUN through the New England countryside between Boston and Montreal aboard *The Ambassador* could be a lyric experience in auspicious seasons of the year, but chill and without cheer in the inclement months. *The Ambassador* followed the Boston & Maine's own iron to White River Junction, Vermont, where it was taken over by Central Vermont motive power to enter Canada via the Canadian National. Above it is shown on a day of heavy traffic in the 1920s, double-headed with a matronly ten wheeler as helper engine. At the left *The Ambassador* enters the identifying arched train shed at St. Albans amidst wintry gloom. Opposite, it loads at an appropriate track in Boston's North Station sometime before the structure was rebuilt to include a sports arena and modern hotel. *(Opposite: Herb H. Arey; Above: Rail Photo Service; Left: Jim Shaughnessy.)*

941

THE Boston & Maine's North Conway station whose architecture was suggested by a ranking executive after an admiring visit to Russia survived into an age when no passengers arrived or departed from the shadow of its Slavic minarets. So highly regarded was it as a landmark that a local historical society undertook its preservation as a museum.   (*Railway & Locomotive Historical Society.*)

AS TWILIGHT gathered over the rails and enshrouded
the roundhouses of the New England countryside
where so much history had been made, nothing presaged
the coming night of railroad transport with more prophetic
gloom than the downgrading of once proud steam
motive power to make way for Diesel expediency. Fine
locomotives that had in happier times put a wheel to
the *Pine Tree Limited* and *Ambassador,* aye, had even
rolled the *Bar Harbor Express* to lordly destinations, ran out
their final mileage in commuter runs or in milk consists
such as those depicted on these pages.
Only the ghosts of Pullmans rode drawbars where once
the *Flying Yankee* or *The State of Maine* had glittered.
The men and the machines that had made legend in the
land were gone, with them Conductor Mike Downey
whose daily train out of Worcester up to Peterboro
and back had come to be known as "Mr. Downey's Train"
and who in fifty-two years of service on the Boston
& Maine had never failed to say thank you when he took
up a ticket. *(Left: Philip R. Hastings; Opposite & Below:
John P. Ahrens.)*

OVER THIS superbly ballasted speedway at Rollinsford, New Hampshire, their occasions governed, as they had been for the last 100 years, by primitive highball signals, rolled the Pullmans and other luxury properties of the Boston & Maine's name trains that were channeled through Dover on their way Down East: *The State of Maine, The Gull, The Yankee* and *The Flying Yankee*. None of them paused at Rollinsford, where a branch line connected for Somersworth and Rochester, but day and night the parade of varnish runs was reported O.S. by the operator in his bow window and Rollinsford saw the great world go by in steam and glory. The Maine Central's No. 701, shown here ready to leave Portland with *The State of Maine* was one of two fast and handsomely proportioned Hudsons specially designed for candy runs, most specifically *The Bar Harbor*. On a carrier not celebrated for modernity of its motive power, they were kings of the iron with an enviable record for on-time performance with as many as twenty Standard Pullmans on their drawbar. *(Right: Boston & Maine; Below: Laurence Breed Walker.)*

No. 82	STATE OF MAINE EXPRESS.	No. 81	
....			....
*8 00 P M	lve...**Portland**....(*B. & M.*) .arr.	*5 43 A M	....
8 36 P M	lve...**Biddeford** (Thornton St.)...arr.	5 13 A M	....
8 51 P M	lve.........**Kennebunk**.......arr.	4 58 A M	....
9 36 P M	lve.............**Dover**...........arr.	4 16 A M	....
10 00 P M	lve.............**Exeter**............arr.	d3 56 A M	....
10 26 P M	lve...........**Haverhill**...........arr.	h3 33 A M	....
10 59 P M	lve.........**Lawrence** ....arr.	*3 16 A M	....
*7 40 P M	lve...........**Concord**..........arr.	†7 40 A M	....
8 08 P M	lve........**Manchester**........arr.	7 05 A M	....
8 31 P M	arr..**Nashua** (*Union Sta.*)...arr.	6 28 A M	....
8 55 P M	arr...........**Lowell**..........lve.	†6 07 A M	....
11 17 P M	lve...........**Lowell**.........arr.	*2 38 A M	....
11 50 P M	lve.............**Ayer**............arr.	2 11 A M	....
12 40 A M	arr..........**Worcester**.......lve.	1 25 A M	....
4 25 A M	ar.**New Haven**(N.Y.N.H.&H.R.R.) lve.	8 55 P M	....
6 20 A M	arr.**New York** (*G. C. T.*) » lve.	*8 00 P M	....

Table 5b—PORTLAND, ME., AND NEW YORK.

LACKING the overtones of almost unearthly splendor of *The Bar Harbor Express* and terminating its run at Portland, whose St. Johns Station is shown below, *The State of Maine Express (left)* was still a long standing and institutional name train originating on the New Haven and, in summer season, not without consequential patronage, especially on weekends. There were setout sleepers for Concord, Rumford and Rockport and the cachets of the better yacht clubs and resort hotels identified the Louis Vuiton luggage in its drawing rooms and compartments. Here behind a Boston & Maine no-nonsense Pacific to give it a wheel, *The State of Maine* rolls down east as the long shadows of trackside grasses indicate the hour of sunrise. *(Left: Philip R. Hastings; Below: Everett De Golyer.)*

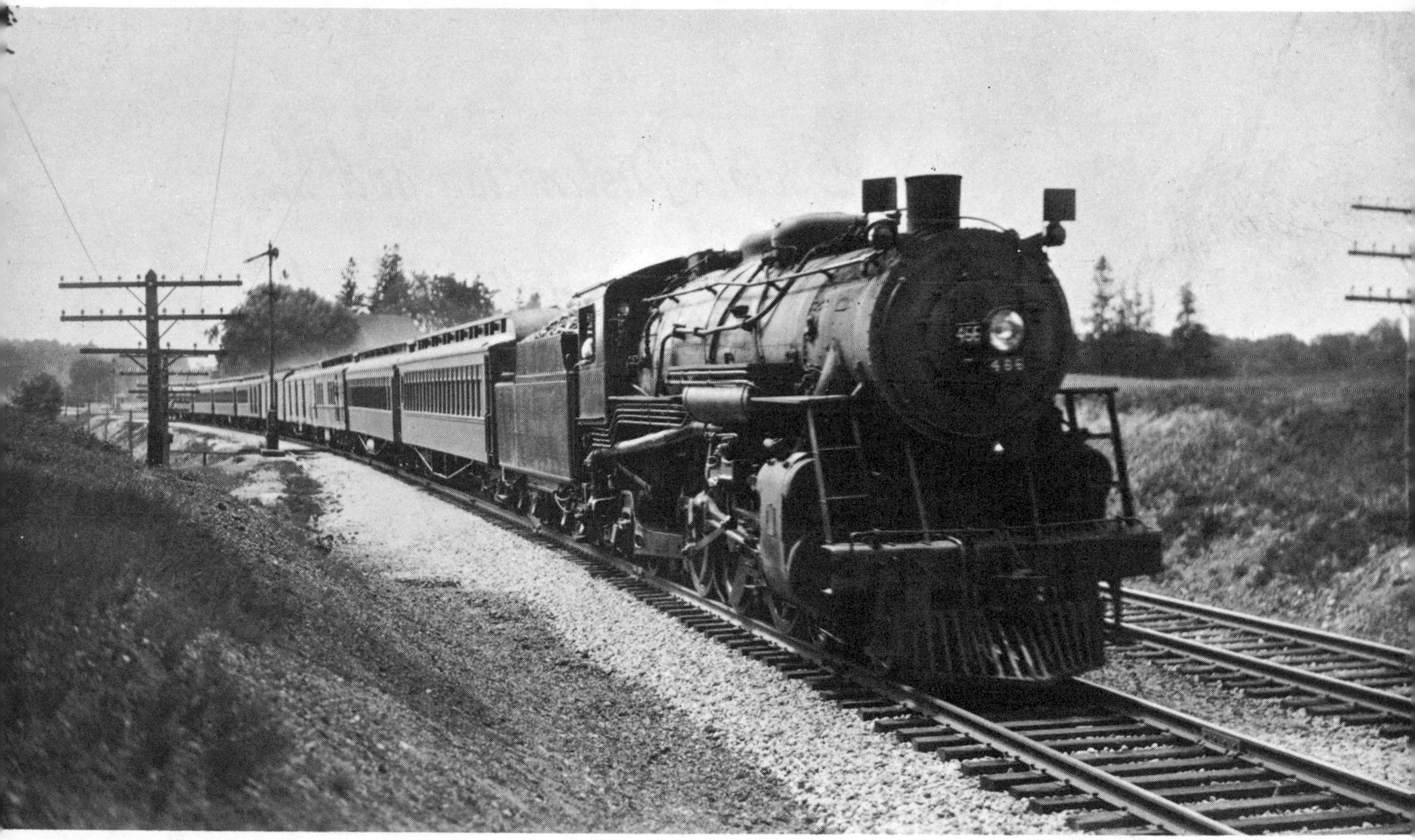

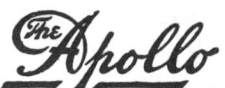

ON THE Down East run from Boston to the Maritime Provinces, the Boston & Maine-Maine Central's *Gull* represented the carriers' contribution to the railroad aviary elsewhere represented by various *Eagles, Larks, Hawks, Flamingos* and *Crows. The Gull,* depicted here on the Maine Central with the metal smokebox flags signifying a second section east of Portland and with heavy head-end revenue, was celebrated for the complexity of its passenger accommodations in the *Official Guide* where its seasonal variations, alternating diners and cafe cars and multiplicity of setout sleepers made it one of the most complicated of all name train listings. Passengers wishing to dine at Portsmouth, New Hampshire, an on-line stop for *The Gull,* were once assured in a handbill that they wouldn't be left behind by the unannounced departure of the cars. *(Below: Rail Photo Service.)*

THIS TRAIN STOPS AT

Portsmouth

for LUNCH

SANDWICHES, PASTRY, CAKE,
HOT SOUP, STEWS, CHICKEN PIES, Etc.

ALL READY **NO WAITING**

Ice Cream in Individual Boxes to take on the train

Popular Brands of Cigars Cigarettes and Tobacco

COLD DRINKS Etc.

The Apollo *"The Chocolates that are different"*

IN DISTINCTIVE PACKAGES

SOUVENIR CARDS, BOOKS, MAPS, GUIDES,
MAGAZINES, NEW YORK AND BOSTON PAPERS.

Passengers cannot get left as Train Conductor gives ample notice before Train leaves.

Social Distinction and the
Resources of Conservative Wealth
Rode The Bar Harbor Express
To the Least Accessible
Of All American Summer Resorts

WHAT *The Blue Train* was to traffic between Paris and Monte Carlo in the E. Phillips Oppenheim years of the Russian grand dukes, and what *The Florida Special* over the rails of the Florida East Coast was to Palm Beach before the coming of the planes, *The Bar Harbor Express* was to the Maine summer resort on a stern and rockbound coast that early in the game established itself as the seasonal capital of American social conservatism. Not as old in calendar years and the approval of the well-to-do as Saratoga Springs which dated from before the Civil War, but well enough ensconced as an enclave of wealth to regard Florida as the merest *arrivist*, Bar Harbor and, to a lesser degree, its neighboring Seal Harbor and Northeast emerged upon the general awareness in the early eighties when the Maine Central inaugurated the Mount Desert Ferry, a transfer alike of personalities and their chattels and retainers and of social destinies that was to survive until 1931 when a causeway to the mainland put an end to it forever. Fifteen years later and as though in protest against the island's availability to what its Old Guard regarded as a socially irresponsible element, Bar Harbor burned almost to the ground. It was widely regarded as an act of suttee, and when, in 1960, *The Bar Harbor Express* that had been its most celebrated agency of access ceased to run, Bar Harbor as a bastion of the aloof proprieties had itself long since ceased to exist. In the intervening three quarters of a century, however, Bar Harbor had been the most inaccessible of American resorts both in the field of logistics and in the more ephemeral realm of social acceptance. Some of the agencies which made Bar Harbor at least physically available if not an open city socially and which conveyed its devotees each summer from Beacon Street, Rittenhouse Square and Du Pont Circle are the subject matter of the pages immediately following.

946

Luxurious Bedroom Cars

WHEN it went into service in the summer of 1902,
The Bar Harbor Express originated on the New Haven and
its implications were solely those of a New York clientele.
In 1917, however, and in explicit recognition that
Bar Harbor was far more a summer suburb of Philadelphia
and Washington, it began its run on the Pennsylvania
with through Pullmans from those cities and it was on this
basis that it achieved its dimension as a convenience
of the social and economic *bon ton*. On its successive
carriers through the night, the Pennsy, the New Haven, the
Boston & Maine and finally the Maine Central its
progress was a choicely regarded jewel of their operational
crown, and its sometimes four and five sections moved
with the clockwork precision of sidereal time.
Here it is shown carrying white flags to indicate a following
section on the New Haven leg of its run at Auburn,
Massachusetts, in 1929. The photograph is
from the archives of The Smithsonian Institution.

FORERUNNER of such seasonal and celebrated resort trains as *The Bar Harbor Express* and *The State of Maine* was the Boston & Maine-Maine Central's first de luxe varnish run on a Down East schedule, the resoundingly named *Boston & Mount Desert Limited Express,* which went into service in the summer of 1887. Its all-Pullman consist included three superbly appointed parlor cars and a diner, all painted umber and boasting the new Sessions Patent enclosed vestibules. East of Portland, the Maine Central emplaced track pans at strategic points to facilitate a speedy run to Mount Desert Ferry where passengers embarked on successive generations of the company's steamers for the brief water passage to Bar Harbor. Here *The Limited* is depicted on the outskirts of Bangor, probably in its inaugural year in a rare photograph from the archives of the Railway & Locomotive Historical Society with Maine Central No. 14 on the drawbar.

948

WHEN *The Mount Desert Limited* went into service in 1887, all products of the Pullman Palace Car Company were hand crafted to the specifications of the purchasing carrier and no two cars were exactly alike. Even those built from identical floor plans differed in some detail of decor or design and the parlor cars outshopped for the Boston & Maine's first truly de luxe varnish were no exception. Pullmans on the Mount Desert Ferry run were as prestigeous as custom-built Rolls-Royces would be at a later date. Below, *The Boston & Mount Desert Limited Express* is shown in a full dress portrait behind the Boston & Maine's prideful locomotive Columbia at the time of the train's inaugural. Another likeness in full color has been painted for this book by the distinguished artist Howard Fogg and appears as its frontispiece. *(Left: Pullman Standard; Below: Railway & Locomotive Historical Society.)*

BAR HARBOR EXPRESS.
Tuesdays, Wednesdays, Thursdays and Fridays, September 4th to 21st, inclusive.

Club-Lounge...New York to Ellsworth.
Sleeping Cars..Philadelphia to Ellsworth—(10 S., 2 C., D. R.).
Philadelphia to Ellsworth—(6 C., 3 D. R.).
Washington to Rockland—(8 S., 2 C., D. R.).
Washington to Waterville—(10 S., 2 C., D. R.).
Philadelphia to Rockland—(8 S., 2 C., D. R.).
Washington to Plymouth—(12 S., D. R.). (Except Saturday, September 1st.)
Washington to Ellsworth—(10 S., 2 C., D. R.).
Washington to Portland—(10 S., 2 C., D. R.).
New York to Ellsworth—(10 S., 2 D. R.).
Washington to Oquossoc—(12 S., D. R.). (Fridays only until September 14th, inclusive.)
Dining Cars....Washington to New York.
Philadelphia to New Haven.
Portland to Ellsworth.
No Coaches New York to Ellsworth.
No baggage Philadelphia to New York.

BAR HARBOR EXPRESS.
Tuesdays and Fridays, September 25th to October 12th, incl.

Sleeping Cars..Philadelphia to Ellsworth—(10 S., 2 C., D. R.).
Washington to Portland—(10 S., 2 C., D.R.).
Washington to Ellsworth—(10 S., 2 C., D. R.).
New York to Ellsworth—(10 S., 2 C., D. R.).
Dining Cars....Washington to New York.
New York to New Haven.
Philadelphia to New York.   Portland to Ellsworth.
No Coaches New York to Ellsworth.
No baggage Philadelphia to New York.

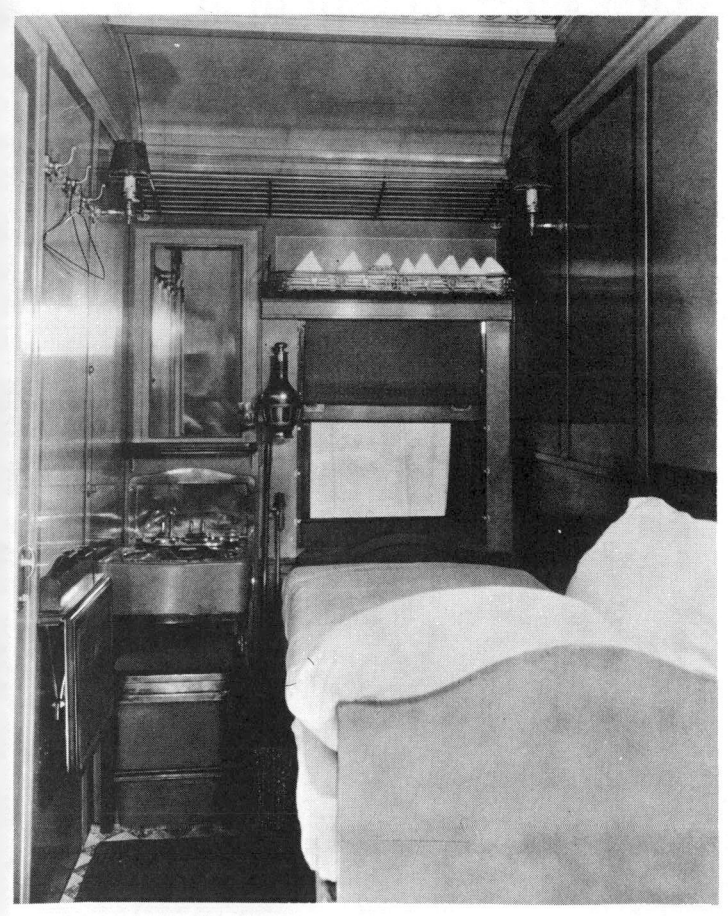

IN THE GLORY YEARS of *The Bar Harbor Express* as the most de luxe of all New England trains, some idea of the diversification of its through and setout Pullmans may be gathered from the excerpt opposite from the pages of *The Official Guide*. On the same page is depicted the Philadelphia section of "The Blue Train of America" as it was known to newspaper readers making up at Broad Street in the mid-1920s with the buffet lounge in evidence that will go all the way through to Ellsworth. Shown above at speed on the Pennsy's New York Division, *The Bar Harbor* is practically indistinguishable in its all-Pullman consist from *The Broadway Limited*. As a train of unassailable Rittenhouse Square character, it left Broad Street at three in the afternoon, an hour convenient for E. T. Stotesbury and A. Atwater Kent to finish luncheon at the Philadelphia Club and sign a few important papers before getting away from it all for the weekend. A diner ran as far as New Haven and a Maine Central diner was cut in for the breakfast trade east of Portland. One distinguishing identification of the pedigreed varnish train of its time it seems to have lacked in the form of an observation car terminating in a keystone herald with the train's name in lights. The frequent cuts and pulls to which its consist was available at New Haven, Portland and Ellsworth made this panache improbable and most of the time its confirmed patrons spent in their single bedrooms such as is shown here. (*Opposite, Two Photos: Pennsylvania Railroad; Above: Rail Photo Service; Left: Pullman Standard.*)

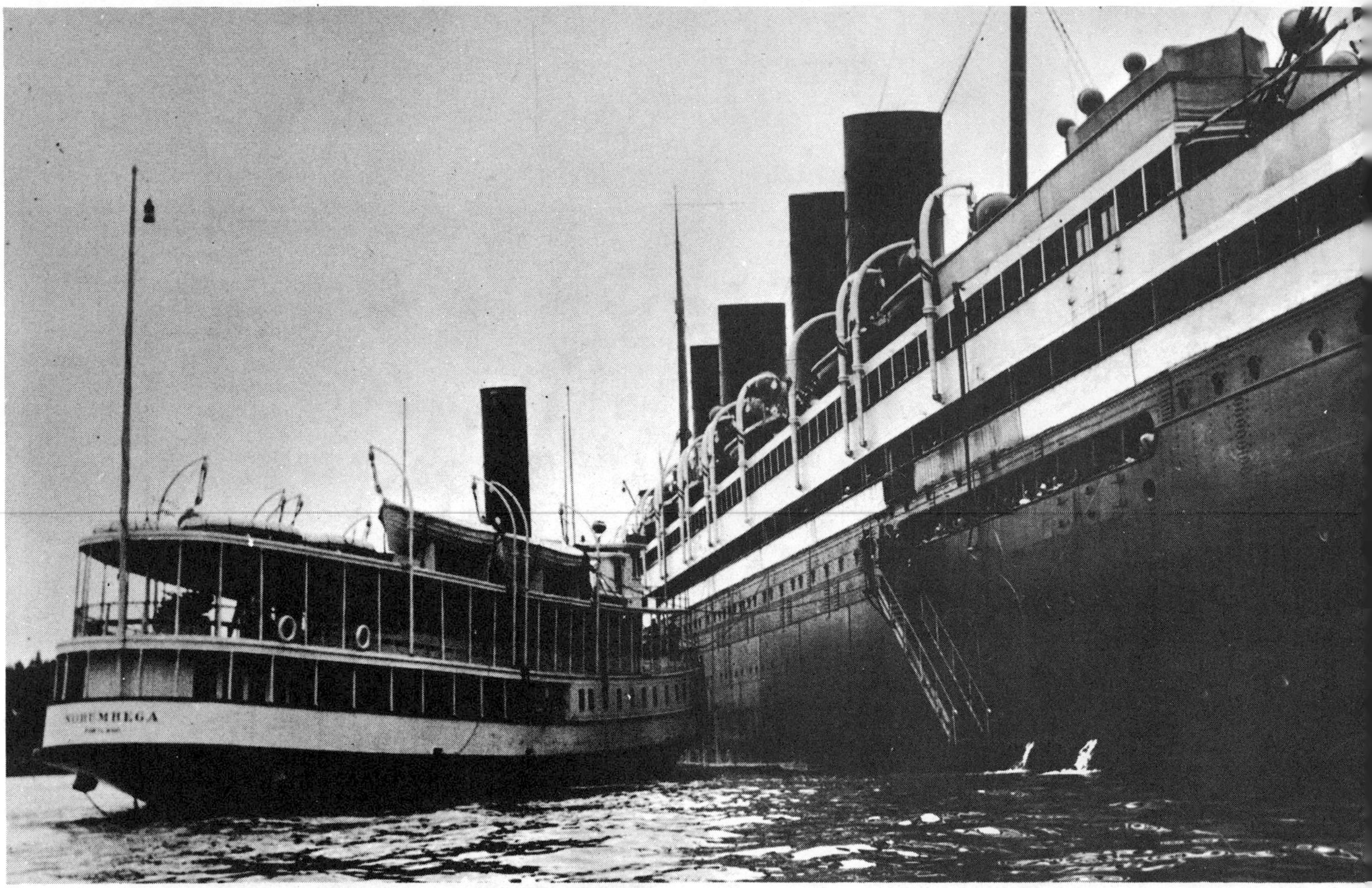

THE MOUNT Desert Ferry's hour of special glory arrived when, in August 1914, as the nations of Europe were flying to arms, the North German Lloyd liner *Kronprinzessin Cecilie*, at sea when England declared war on Germany and fearing seizure by the British Navy, sought refuge in the then neutral port of Bar Harbor. The town awoke one morning to find the sleek four stacker anchored in deep water at its front door, piloted there by an American yachtsman, Ledyard Blair. The eyes of the world turned briefly to the moment of drama before the vessel was interned. The Ferry shared in the limelight and here *Norumbega* is shown effecting the transfer of passengers to the mainland where special trains returned them to New York. Some idea of the density of passenger traffic to Mount Desert may be gathered from the Maine Central's summer schedule for 1911. (*Two Photos: Mariners Museum, Newport News.*)

MAINE CENTRAL RAILROAD

Bar Harbor and Bangor to Portland, Boston and New York

	Nos. of Trains	†110	†122	‡156	*114	*118	†120	§712	‡156	*114	*118	§718
		WEEK DAY TRAINS						**SUNDAY TRAINS**				
	STATIONS.	A.M.	A.M.	P.M.	P.M.	P.M.	P.M.	A.M.	P.M.	P.M.	P.M.	P.M.
	Manset......	......	†8 45	*1 20	†2 30	*7 20			*1 20		*7 20	
	Southwest Harbor.	......	†8 50	*1 30	†2 40	*7 30			*1 30		*7 30	
	Northeast Harbor.	......	†9 05	*1 40	†2 50	*7 40			*1 40		*7 40	
	Seal Harbor.....	......	†9 25	*2 00	†3 10	*8 00			*2 00		*8 00	
	Bar Harbor....... Steam'r lv	†6 10	†10 50	*3 00	†4 10	*9 00		§5 20	*3 00	▲4 15	*9 00	
	Sorrento........		†10 30		*4 00	†6 30				*4 00		
	Hancock Point....	†6 35	†10 40		†4 40	†6 40						
	Sullivan........		†11 05		*4 35					*4 35		
0	Mt. Desert Ferry......	†7 00	†11 45	‡3 40	*5 00	*9 50		§6 05	‡3 40	*5 00	*9 50	
3	Waukeag, Sullivan Ferry..	7 07	11 52	‡3 47	5 07	9 57		6 12	3 47	5 07	9 57	
4	Hancock......	7 15	f11 55		5 10			6 15		5 10		
8	Franklin Road.....	f7 22			5 19			6 23		5 19		
11	Washington Junction...	7 30	12 15		f5 28		†11 00	f6 32		f5 28		§10 0
14	Ellsworth.....	7 37	12 22	‡4 11	5 35	10 21	11 07	6 39	4 11	5 35	10 21	10 1
15	Ellsworth Falls....	7 42	f12 27		5 40	ᴇ10 25	11 12	6 47		5 40	ᴇ10 25	10 1
21	Nicolin......	f7 55	f12 40		6 00	ᴇ10 38	f11 25	f7 00		6 00	ᴇ10 38	f10 3
25	Green Lake.....	8 04	f12 49		6 08	ᴇ10 46	11 34	f7 08		6 08	ᴇ10 46	10 3
29	Phillips Lake.....	f8 11	f12 57		f6 16	ᴇ10 53	f11 41	f7 15		f6 16	ᴇ10 53	f10 4
32	Holden......	8 18	f1 05		6 24	ᴇ11 00	11 49	f7 21		6 24	ᴇ11 00	10 4
42	Brewer Junction....	8 38	1 24		6 44	ᴇ11 18	12 08	7 36		6 44	ᴇ11 18	11 0
43	Bangor........ [ ]ar	†8 45	†1 30	‡5 20	*6 50	*11 25	†12 15	§7 40	‡5 20	*6 50	*11 25	§11 1
	Bangor............ lv	†10 15	†1 50	‡5 30	*8 00	*11 35	¶12 40	§7 50	‡5 30	*8 00	*11 35	§11 3
	Portland............ ar	‡3 25	‡5 55	‡9 25	*12 50	*3 45	¶4 50	§12 20	‡9 25	*12 50	*3 45	§3 4
		P.M.	P.M.	P.M.	Night	A.M.	A.M.	Noon	P.M.	Night	A.M.	A.M.
182	Portland { via Dover.... [ ]lv	3 35	4 00				§5 10					
297	Boston { [ ]ar	6 45	9 00				§8 30	3 40				
	Portland { via Portsmouth lv		6 05		*1 05	*4 00		12 30		*1 05	*4 00	*4 0
	Boston { ar		9 05		*5 15	*7 00		3 40		*5 15	*7 00	*7 0
		P.M.	P.M.		A.M.	A.M.		P.M.		A.M.	A.M.	A.M.
	Portland............. lv	†7 20	†7 20	‡9 40		†8 35	†8 35		‡9 40		†8 35	
	Haverhill...........	‡9 43	‡9 43			†10 42	†10 42				†10 42	
	Lowell..............	†10 39	†10 39	‡12 28		†11 26	†11 26		‡12 28		†11 26	
	Worcester...........	‡12 17	‡12 17	†2 05		†12 50	†12 50		†2 05		†12 50	
	Springfield.........	‡2 00	‡2 00	†3 50		†2 10	†2 10		†3 50		†2 10	
	New Haven..........	‡3 35	‡3 35	†5 33		†3 39	†3 39		†5 33			
	New York...........	‡5 35	‡5 35	†7 40		†5 35	†5 35		†7 40		‡5 35	
		A.M.	A.M.	A.M.		P.M.	P.M.		A.M.		P.M.	

* Daily Sundays included.   [ ]Restaurant.   ¶ Except Monday.
f Stops on signal or on notice to conductor.
§ Sundays only.
ᴇ Stops only to leave passengers from east of Washington Junc. Sundays.
‡Daily except Saturday.
† Daily except Sunday.   ▲Sundays leave Bar Harbor 4.15 p. m.
Train 120 Sleeping Car Calais to Boston.   Train 122 Parlor Car Mt. Desert Ferry to Boston.
Train 156 Sleeping Car Mt. Desert Ferry to New York.   Dining Car Bangor to Portland and Cafe Car
    Bangor to New York for Pullman passengers only.
Train 114 Sleeping Car Mt. Desert Ferry to Boston.
Train 118 Sleeping Car Mt. Desert Ferry to Boston.

DINING aboard the cars North of Boston partook of the essential nature of the
New England through which they ran and its habit, therefore, was not one of
voluptuous attitudes or gastronomic debauch, but the diners and cafe cars built
in 1905 for the Maine Central and the Boston and Maine and assigned to *The
Bar Harbor Express* were perhaps the most beautiful of all Pullman products at
the high water mark of its artistry. In the last years of its run in steam, depicted
at the top of the page, *The Bar Harbor* often ran with streamlined head-end
equipment and lightweight sleepers from the equipment pool of the New Haven.
(Top: Philip R. Hastings; Below: Pullman Standard.)

COMPONENTS of the embracing panorama reproduced at the right are both of the rival means of transport through whose agency, until the construction of a causeway to the mainland and the surrender of the island to motorists, Bar Harbor was available to its once enviable residents. At the extreme right of the photograph is visible the pier and landing facilities of the Eastern Steamship Company aboard whose immortal *J. T. Morse* generations of Bar Harbor regulars arrived from Rockland where they had changed from the through steamers from Boston. In the immediate foreground with the ferry *Norumbega* in dock is the pier of the Maine Central Railroad where a long succession of much loved steamers, *Sebenoa, Sappho, Norumbega, Samoset, Moosehead* and *Rangeley* tied up between 1884 and 1931 when a causeway was built to the mainland. Of this noble succession, *Rangeley* alone is still operative at Bermuda where, as the oddly named *Chauncey M. Depew* it sees service as port tender at Hamilton. Immediately above is the lounge, crowded in inclement weather but otherwise little used, of *Sappho. Sebenoa,* shown opposite in a builder's photograph was constructed in 1880 as the legend suggests for the Eastern Steamboat Company at Bath for service on the Bath-Boothbay route and was sold four years later to the Maine Central for the Mount Desert run where, with variations of schedule, she remained, a summer season institution, until 1902 when she was replaced by *Norumbega.* In its golden years, Bar Harbor was very much a seaport.

(Three Photos: Mariners Museum, Newport News.)

954

Steamer Sebenoa,
OF THE EASTERN STEAMBOAT CO.

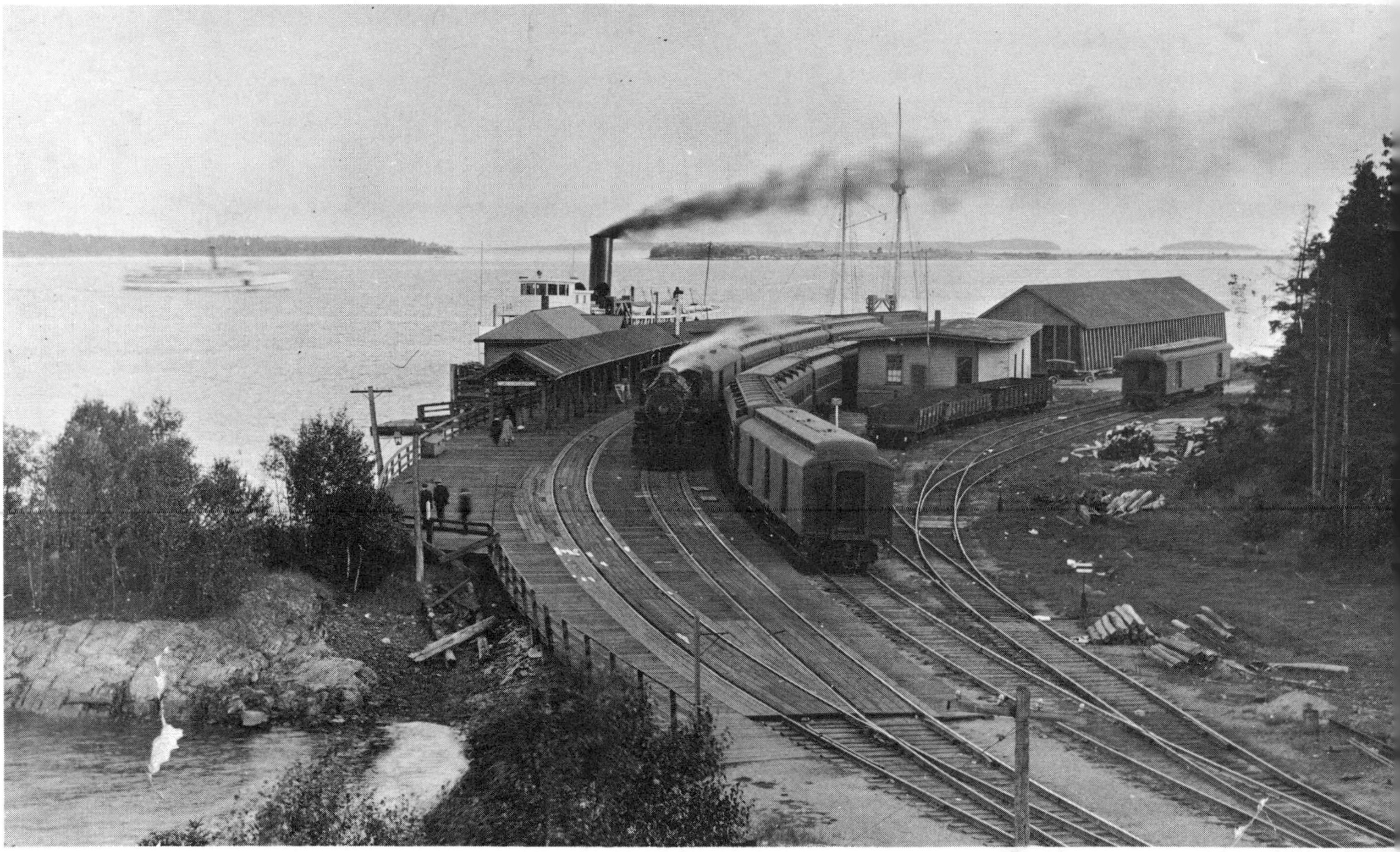

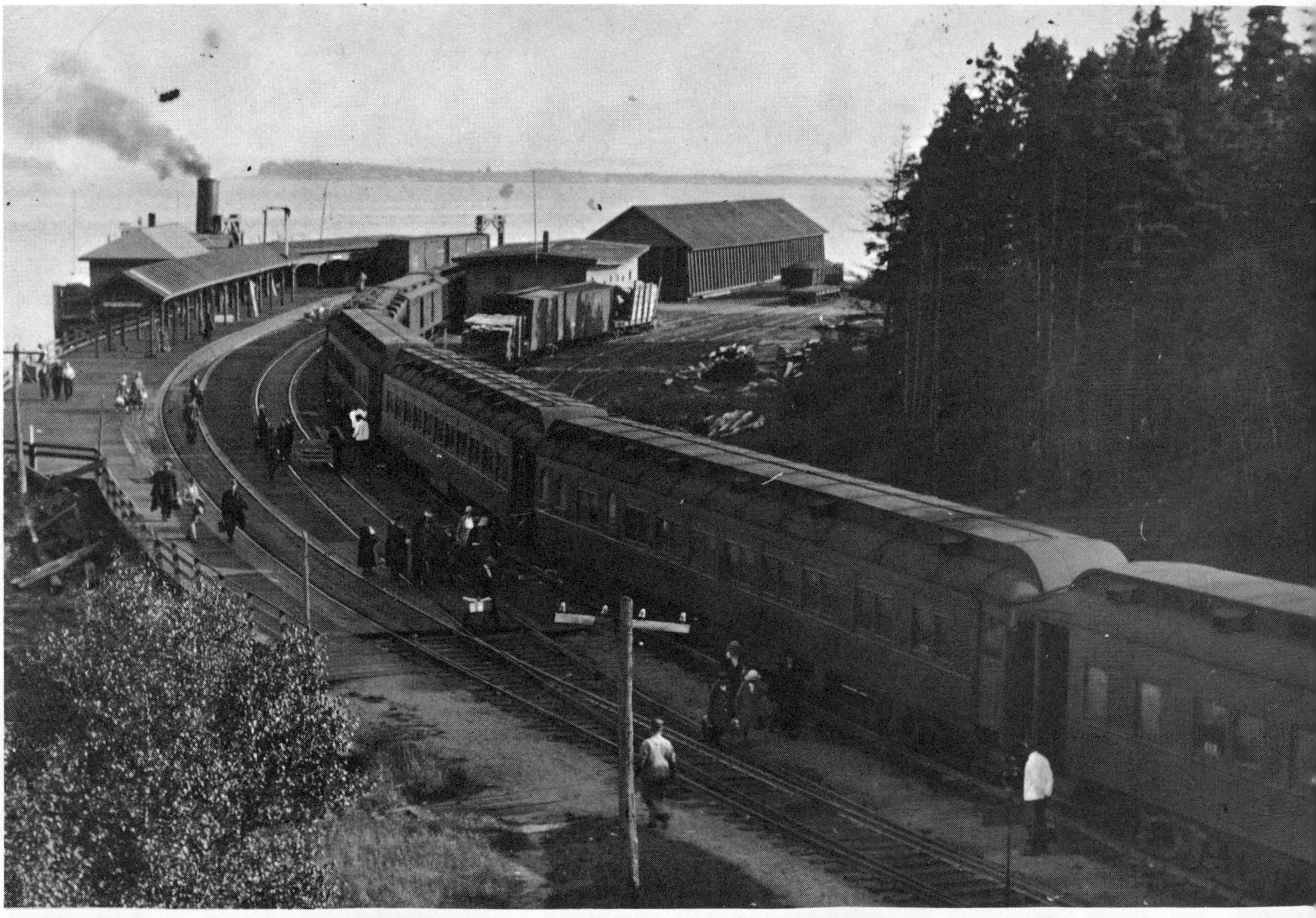

ABOARD the Maine Central's old-time favorite with the Bar Harbor regulars *Moosehead,* names of consequence were the veriest commonplace. In June eastbound for Bar, Seal or Northeast, or headed home when the season was over, its sailing list read more like that of the *Olympic* or *Mauretania* than of a fifty minute ferry operation to a summer resort whose seawater was so cold nobody ever swam in it. *(Maine Central.)*

IN 1884 the Maine Central's Waukeag Branch, running from the main line at Washington Junction to a rock-bound coastal point designated as Mount Desert Ferry, was completed and the ferry operation itself went into service in June of that year. It was destined to be one of the most celebrated, if shortest maritime operations in the record. Here, as shown in the two rare photographs on the page opposite, the well-placed of the world descended from the overnight Pullmans, variously, from New York, Philadelphia and Washington and boarded such famous ferry steamers as *Sebenoa* and *Sappho* for the brief water passage to Bar Harbor, Seal Harbor and Northeast. The agency of their arrival at the Ferry was, of course, the immortal *Bar Harbor Express* shown here toward the end of its long and exciting life in a photograph behind Maine Central motive power near Ellsworth by John P. Ahrens. *(Opposite, Two Photos: Carl E. Henry Collection, Courtesy Maine Central.)*

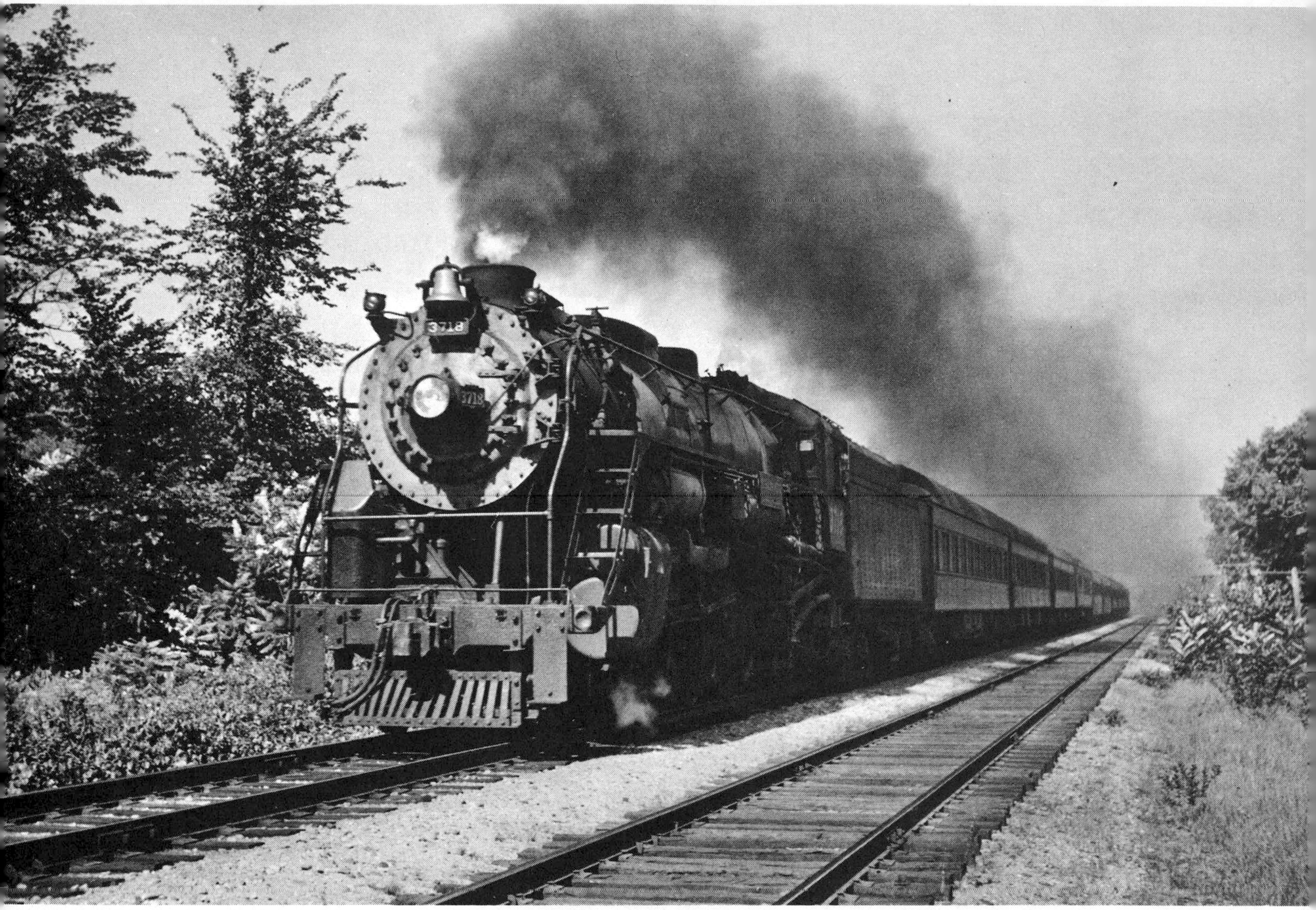

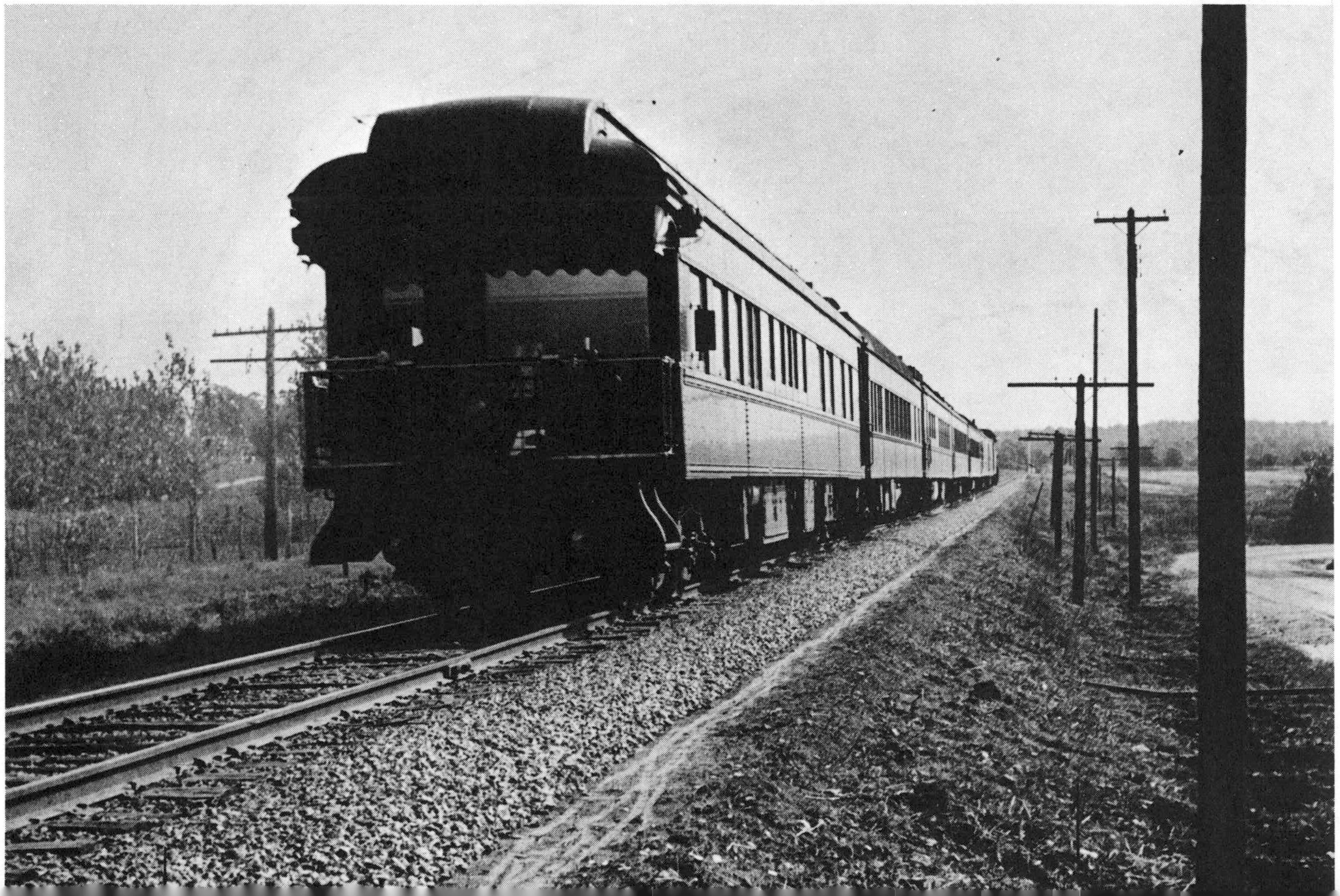

FEW NAME TRAINS in the record have about them the perfumed cachet of social aloofness associated with *The Bar Harbor Express* in the years when it ran with Pullmans only from June to September in sections from Washington, Philadelphia and New York, sometimes several from each. Originating on the Pennsylvania, it ran over the New Haven, the Boston & Maine and finally achieved the Mount Desert Ferry via the Maine Central and, almost to the exclusion of lesser mortals, its sailing lists teemed with the socially and financially elect whose conservative tastes inclined them to the old fashioned manners and measured pace of Bar Harbor, Dark Harbor, Seal Harbor and other long established Maine seacoast resorts rather than the more refulgent panache of Newport or East Hampton. Regulars aboard its all-

stateroom cars were lady novelist Mary Roberts Rinehart, gentleman novelist Arthur Train, physician novelist S. Weir Mitchell, clerical celebrities such as Bishop William Doane of Albany and secular celebrities such as Joseph Pulitzer, A. Atwater Kent and E. T. Stotesbury. One stateroom car on each trip was reserved exclusively for domestics and was known as "the butlers' car." On the page opposite, *The Bar Harbor Express* is shown in its all-Pullman splendor on the Boston & Maine. In the rare photograph below *The Bar Harbor Express* in 1920 is spotted at the Mount Desert Ferry while the Maine Central's fine steamer *Rangeley* strains at its moorings at the pierside. *(Opposite: Everett De Golyer Collection; Below: Carl E. Henry Collection.)*

WITH THE EXCEPTION of such notable rendezvous of members of the private car club as Palm Beach and Louisville at the time of the Kentucky Derby, no resort witnessed a greater concentration of privately owned varnish often augmented by the business cars of ranking railroaders than did the Bar Harbor run in its last fine flowering in the 1920s. On one celebrated occasion *The Bar Harbor Express* running in three sections brought in no fewer than twenty-one private cars in a single day. On the opposite page an extra section of *The Bar Harbor Express* is depicted near Brunswick, Maine, with the business car of a railroad bigwig to judge from the track lamps, perhaps General Atterbury of the Pennsy who was a notable Bar Harbor resorter in its golden age.

LEGEND AND FOLKLORE clustered in a rich aura of seacoast mythology around the Eastern Steamship Company's Rockland connection for Bar Harbor in the form of service by *The J. T. Morse* which constituted direct and unequivocal competition with the Maine Central's Mount Desert Ferry. "One of the handsomest of all Eastern Steamship vessels," according to Professor George Hilton, a ranking authority in the field, *The Morse* was a venerable sidewheeler freighted to the waterline with the social history of America's most inaccessible summer resort. It met the Boston boats, *City of Rockland* and *City of Bangor* at Rockland at the unearthly hour of four in the morning and required two hours in the cold Maine darkness for the transfer of passengers and merchandise before sailing for a crossing that could on occasion be as rough as the English Channel. *The Morse* was also celebrated for the presence of Stewardess Maggie Higgins who, for decades on end, ruled crew and passengers alike with the heavy hand of a practiced despot. "All true resorters rode *The Morse*," wrote Cleveland Amory in his definitive history of Bar Harbor, "and her passenger list included everybody from Lord Bryce to Hetty Green, while her social pitch reached that of her whistle." Like all steamships of pronounced personal character, *The Morse* had her shortcomings, one of which was a propensity for grounding if shoal water was even remotely available. One Bar Harbor cave dweller of ancestral occupancy of the Island, when she found herself stranded in Penobscot Bay after a three day rainfall, took her grievance to the captain. "I don't see how the water can be low," she proclaimed, "especially after all the rain we've had." In the below photograph *The Morse* is shown at her Bar Harbor mooring across the bonnet of a symbolic motor car whose presence was at length to relegate to the discard both the railroads and the ferry and the Boston steamers too. Eventually it was to doom the character of Bar Harbor itself. (*Four Photos: Mariners Museum, Newport News.*)

A DIRECT CONFRONTATION with the competition was afforded from the deck of *The Morse* at its Bar Harbor mooring in the form of the equally handy and even more frequently used landing of the Maine Central which was a scant fifty yards distant.

ALTHOUGH in 1911, the Maine Central scheduled four other daily through trains connecting with the Mount Desert Ferry, the big event of the day was the arrival of *The Bar Harbor Express* with its cargo of social notables that attracted the most attention. In the above photograph the arriving train has just pulled in while the ferry *Norumbega*, awaiting the transfer of its passengers, is barely visible beyond the train shed at the right. By the period represented above the eye-popping luxury of parlor cars from the original *Mount Desert Express*, shown at the left, had become more subdued, but the train's equipment represented the finest available at any given time. *(Above: Mariners Museum; Left: Railway & Locomotive Historical Society.)*

NOT ALL sections of *The Bar Harbor Express* which, by the mid-1930s had been shortened in general usage to the *Bar Harbor,* rolled in all-Pullman glory, perhaps with "the butlers' car" in their consist. When traffic was heavy, third and fourth sections brought up in the rear of the parade with head-end revenue cars, section sleepers and extra Pullmans added to accommodate unforeseen traffic at the last moment. On one famous night in 1923 the Maine Central turned over no fewer than 102 cars running in five sections of the *Bar Harbor* for interchange with the Boston & Maine at Portland. Above, a third section nears Ellsworth on a fine July morning in 1940, its leading refrigerator car perhaps filled with perishables for the fittingly named Bar Harbor Society Market. At the left one of the Ellsworth Pullmans, appropriately the *Cosmopolitan,* drowses through the Maine night. *(Top: John P. Ahrens; Left: Philip R. Hastings.)*

Venice (Fla.), 199
Vestibuled Limited, 514
Veterans of Foreign Wars, 549*
Victor (Colo.), 81*
Victory, The, 517, 877
Vietor, Dr. John A., 222
Vietwood (Pullman), 222
Vieux Carré, 264
Viking, The, 517
Viking-Soo-Dominion, 877
Villard, Henry, 479
Vineyard Gazette, 328
Vining (Ga.), 203
Vinton, Louis, 911
Violet (Pullman), 307
Virginia & Truckee, 106, 766*, 803
Virginia City (Nev.), 767
Virginia City (Pullman), 222*, 230*
"Virginian, The," 151
Vuiton, Louis, 73, 298

– W –

Wabash (R.R.), 15, 25-33, 36-41, 89, 208, 219, 459, 754, 792, 864-871, 877, 882, 903
Wabash Cannon Ball, 871, 882*
Waco (Texas), 292
Wading River (N.Y.), 660, 662
Wading River Express, 660
Wagner, Webster, 150*, 368, 373*, 376*, 514
Wakefield Junction (Mass.), 930
Wakeman, Frederick, 57
Walcott (Wyo.), 862*
Walden Pond, 903
Waldorf Astoria Hotel, 12
Walker, Mayor J. J., 407*, 649
Walker, Stanley, 605
Wall Street, The, 24, 693*
Wall Street Journal, 298, 344, 348, 361, 695
Wall Streeter, The, 693*
Wallace (Kans.), 83*
Walpole, Horace, 929

Wareham (Mass.), 326
Warnock, D. S., 743*
Warrior River, 204
Washington (ferry), 528*
Washington, George, 606
Washington Junction (Maine), 957
Washingtonian, The, 925*-927*
Washington *Times Herald*, 193
Washoe Canyon, 767*
Washoe City (Nev.), 766*
Water Level Route, 434, 494
Waukeag Branch (Me.C.), 957*
Wayne Junction (Ind.), 642
Wayne Junction (N.J.), 113
Webb, Clifton, 57
Webb, William S., 373, 419
Webster, Daniel, 318
Webster Groves (Mo.), 872*
Weehawken (ferry), 446*, 448
Weehawken (N.J.), 443, 446*, 448*
Wellesley College (Mass.), 401
Wells Fargo Express, 174*, 599, 786, 804, 817, 856
Wells (Nev.), 762*
Wells River (Vt.), 894, 897, 931*
Wenatchee (Wash.), 246*, 481
West Coast, The, 719, 730, 734*-737*
West Islip (N.Y.), 659*
West Palm Beach (Fla.), 11, 191-195*, 199, 222*
West Philadelphia (Pa.), 585
West Shore Express, 446*
West Shore (R.R.), 864, 903
West Shore Route, 443-448
Westbury (N.Y.), 660
Western Pacific, 158, 800-805*
Western Special, 485, 497
Western Star, The, 244, 251*
Western Union, 233, 392, 650

Westfield (N.Y.), 384*
Westport (Conn.), 348*
Wetzel, 233
Whalen, Grover, 649*
White Diamond (Pullman), 282*
White Mountains, 892*-894, 914
"White Mountain Line," 894
White, R. B., 688
White River Junction (Vt.), 922*, 931*, 941
White Sulphur Springs (W.Va.), 500-505*
White Train, 307, 330*-333
Whitefield (N.H.), 914, 928*
Whitefish (Mont.), 242*
Whitehall (N.Y.), 934*-938*
Whitelight Limited, 485
Whitemarsh, Cecil, 797
Whiting (Ind.), 579*
Whitney family, 935
Whitney, Harry Payne, 298, 668
Whitney, John Hay, 502
"Wickford Point," 346
Widener, George D., 222
Widener, Joe, 222
Wilberton (Ill.), 63*
Wilkes-Barre (Pa.), 284, 574
Willard, Daniel, 223*
Willard's Hotel, 105, 114
William & Mary College, 686
William Henry Dawes (locomotive), 919
Williams, James H., 429
Williams, Mrs. Harrison, 193
Williamson, F. E., 407*
Willimantic (Conn.), 331*
Wilmington (Del.), 574
Wilson, John C., 605
Wilson, President Woodrow, 474
Winchester (Mass.), 899
Windsor, Duke, Duchess, 502*, 537*
Windsor Hotel (Denver), 167*
Windsor Station, Montreal, 935*
Winslow (N.J.), 688

Woburn (Mass.), 899
Wolfhurst (Colo.), 164*
Wolverine, The, 177, 368, 439, 450*, 485
Wood, Don, 690
Woodburn (Ore.), 743*
Woodridge (N.Y.), 280*
Woodruff Parlor Car, 895*
Woods Hole (Mass.), 326
Woodworth, Marjorie, 646*
Wootton (Colo.), 84*
Worcester (Mass.), 394*-397*, 943
World Almanac, 233
World's Columbian Exposition (Chicago, 1893), 15, 113, 368, 512, 533, 536
World's Fair Special, 877
World's Work (magazine), 149, 910
Wright, Fred, 342
Wyoming State Archives, 823*
Wyoming Valley Express, 283

– X –

Xochimilco (Pullman), 792*, 809

– Y –

Yakima (Wash.), 466
Yakima River, 481*
Yale Club, 429, 432
Yale University, 297-298, 829
Yankee Clipper, The, 12, 15, 177, 298, 325, 348, 355, 358*-367*, 429, 605
Yankee, The, 921*, 945
Yardley (Wash.), 248*
"Yellow Kid," 523, 537*
Yellowstone (National Park), 474
Yellowstone Comet, 479*
Yellowstone Special, 817, 841
Young, Robert R., 439, 502*
Young's Hotel, 307
Yuma (Ariz.), 701, 741*

– Z –

Zephyrette, The, 804